CASSESE'S INTERNATIONAL CRIMINAL LAW

CASSESE'S INTERNATIONAL CRIMINAL LAW

Third Edition

REVISED BY

ANTONIO CASSESE

PAOLA GAETA

LAUREL BAIG

MARY FAN

CHRISTOPHER GOSNELL

AND

ALEX WHITING

OXFORD
UNIVERSITY PRESS

OXFORD
UNIVERSITY PRESS

Great Clarendon Street, Oxford, OX2 6DP,
United Kingdom

Oxford University Press is a department of the University of Oxford.
It furthers the University's objective of excellence in research, scholarship,
and education by publishing worldwide. Oxford is a registered trade mark of
Oxford University Press in the UK and in certain other countries

British Library Cataloguing in Publication Data

Data available

ISBN 978-0-19-969492-1

Printed in Great Britain by
Bell & Bain Ltd, Glasgow

Links to third party websites are provided by Oxford in good faith and
for information only. Oxford disclaims any responsibility for the materials
contained in any third party website referenced in this work.

CONTENTS

PART II SUBSTANTIVE CRIMINAL LAW

SECTION I INTERNATIONAL CRIMES

SECTION II MODES OF CRIMINAL LIABILITY

SECTION III CIRCUMSTANCES EXCLUDING CRIMINAL LIABILITY

PART III PROSECUTION AND PUNISHMENT

SECTION I INTERNATIONAL AND NATIONAL CRIMINAL JURISDICTION

SECTION II INTERNATIONAL CRIMINAL TRIALS

PREFACE TO THE THIRD EDITION

Antonio Cassese passed away on 22 October 2011, while the third edition of *International Criminal Law* was in the final stages of preparation. In order to assist him with the new edition, he had approached several friends and colleagues, including myself, to revise and update specific chapters. I agreed to help coordinate the respective submissions, to revise and update some existing chapters myself, and to write a new chapter on the repression of international crimes in national jurisdictions. More generally, I also agreed to assist with the final revision of the entire book. Such was Antonio Cassese's generosity that he insisted that our names appear on the cover.

When he passed away, he had completed the updating and revision of his own chapters and revised those of the other contributors. The book had now to be edited and revised as whole. It took some time before I felt ready to carry out this task alone. I wish therefore to thank all at OUP, and in particular Helen Davis, for their understanding. I also wish to express my gratitude to Laurel Baig, Mary Fan, Christopher Gosnell, and Alex Whiting for being so patient with me and for conducting a further update to their chapters at a time when I felt ready to work on the book and when the book was ready to go to press. Above all, I am indebted to Sylvia Cassese, who allowed me to accomplish this task and to honour my promise to Antonio Cassese.

This new edition largely maintains the structure of the previous one, although a few changes have been inserted: former Chapter 21 on 'The Specificity of International Trials' has been removed, and some of its content integrated into other chapters of the book (see, in particular, current Chapter 14); former Chapter 2 on 'The General Principles of International Criminal Law' has been replaced by a chapter entirely devoted to 'The Principle of Legality'; the pleas of having acted in obedience with superior orders and in an official capacity now form a separate chapter in the section devoted to excuses and defences (Chapter 13); two new chapters have been included, one on the domestic prosecution of international crimes (Chapter 15) and the other (which had already appeared in the first edition) on legal impediments to the exercise of criminal jurisdiction over international crimes (Chapter 17). The content of all chapters has been entirely revised, in light of both recent practice and case law, in particular that of the ICC, and the doctrinal debate on some of the more controversial issues. Some chapters have also been shortened to ensure a more concise and accessible presentation of the various topics and relevant institutions.

The book continues to be characterized by its reference to the facts and the law concerning an impressive number and variety of cases on which Antonio Cassese had already reported in previous editions, keen as he was to illustrate not only the legal issues involved, but also their historical and human dimension. As he explained in the preface to both the first and second edition: 'Law, it is well known, filters and rarefies the halo of horror and suffering surrounding crimes. As a consequence, when one reads a law book or a judgment, one is led almost to forget the violent and cruel origin of criminal law prescriptions. One ought not to become oblivious to it. To recall it may serve as a reminder of the true historical source of criminal law. This branch of law, more than any other, is about human folly, human wickedness, and human aggressiveness. It deals with the darkest side of our nature. It also deals with how society confronts violence and viciousness and seeks to stem them as far as possible so as "to make gentle the life on this world".'

The contribution Antonio Cassese gave both as a judge and as an academic to the development and clarification of international criminal law is immense. He was, however, fully aware that international criminal law was still in its adolescence, still in need of refinement and adjustment. This book is essential to our understanding of just how much has been achieved since the first attempts to establish a system of international criminal justice. It is also an indispensable reference for those who do not content themselves with the existing law, but aim for changes and improvement.

This edition of the book is dedicated to all those who share the simple secret that the fennec fox revealed to the Little Prince while saying goodbye: 'It is only with the heart that one can see rightly. What is essential is invisible to the eye.' (*Adieu, dit le renard. Voici mon secret. Il est très simple: on ne voit bien qu'avec le cœur. L'essentiel est invisible pour les yeux.*)

Paola Gaeta
Geneva, 1 September 2012

PREFACE TO THE SECOND EDITION

In this book I have tried succinctly to expound the fundamentals of both substantive and procedural international criminal law. In so doing, I have made an effort to conceptualize as much as possible; that is, give what I hope is a coherent theoretical framework to the patchwork of disparate rules, principles, concepts, and legal constructs that at present make up international criminal law.

I would be content if this book could serve as a general introduction, for both students and practitioners, to this fascinating branch of law and as a stimulus to other scholars or practitioners to delve deeper into the basic notions of international criminal law.

All the national or international cases that seemed relevant to a particular matter under discussion have been cited. The purpose of my mentioning cases (mostly in footnotes, in order to make the text smoother) is not only to support a specific proposition by reference to the jurisprudence relating thereto, or to show how courts have applied a rule of law, or what interpretation they have placed on it. My aim is also to point to the historical and human dimension of cases. For this purpose, I have as far as possible recounted the facts behind the courts' legal findings. For one should never forget that this body of law, more than any other, results from a myriad of smaller or greater tragedies. Each crime is a tragedy, for the victims and their relatives, the witnesses, the community to which they belong, and even the perpetrator who, when brought to trial, will endure the ordeal of criminal proceedings and, if found guilty, may suffer greatly, in the form of deprivation of life, at worst, or of personal liberty, at best. Law, it is well known, filters and rarefies the halo of horror and suffering surrounding crimes. As a consequence, when one reads a law book or a judgment, one may tend to forget the violent origin of criminal law prescriptions. That origin, however, remains the underpinning of those prescriptions. To recall it may serve as a reminder of the true historical source of criminal law. This branch of law is about human folly, wickedness, and aggressiveness. It deals with the darkest side of our nature. It also deals with how society confronts vicious violence and seeks to stem it as far as possible so as 'to make gentle the life on this world'.

To provide the English-speaking reader with details of cases in other languages, I have relied extensively upon relevant judgments in Dutch, French, German, Italian, and Spanish, besides the most significant cases in English. Translations are mine, unless indicated to the contrary.

The reader interested in consulting the treaties and other documents cited in this book, as well as the relevant legal literature in English, may use the Oxford University Press companion website: www.oxfordtextbooks.co.uk/orc/casseseicl3e/

I am grateful to Laura Magi for skilfully helping me to revise, update, and enrich this text.

In this second edition I have restructured the book, revised and updated all the chapters, and expunged some sections that have now appeared to me to be less relevant.

I am much beholden to Paola Gaeta for kindly reading and making insightful comments on some chapters. Of course, the responsibility for any misapprehension that may remain rests solely with me.

Judge Antonio Cassese, 2008

AUTHOR BIOGRAPHIES

The late **Judge Antonio Cassese** was President of the Special Tribunal for Lebanon. He was formerly a Professor of International Law at Florence University and member of the Institut de Droit International. He was also President of the International Criminal Tribunal for the former Yugoslavia (ICTY).

Paola Gaeta is a Professor at the Law Faculty of the University of Geneva and Adjunct Professor at the Graduate Institute of International Development Studies. She is also Director of the Geneva Academy of International Humanitarian Law and Human Rights and a member of the Editorial Board of the Journal of International Criminal Law.

Laurel Baig is an appeals counsel in the Office of the Prosecutor of the ICTY. She has also worked in a Trial Chamber of the ICTR and in the Appeals Chambers of the ICTR, ICTY, and SCSL. Previously, she was in private practice in Toronto, Canada and served as a law clerk to Justice Bastarache of the Supreme Court of Canada. She holds law degrees from Oxford and LSE.

Mary Fan is an Associate Professor at the University of Washington School of Law. She specializes in U.S. and international criminal law and procedure. She is an elected member of the American Law Institute and an Advisor to the Model Penal Code Sexual Assault and Related Offenses project. She was previously a federal prosecutor in the Southern District of California and an Associate Legal Officer at the UN ICTY.

Christopher Gosnell is a private practitioner who has represented defendants before the ICTY and the ICTR. He has also represented victims before the ICC and the STL. He was a judicial clerk to Judge Erik Møse, former president of the ICTR, and Justice Michel Bastarache of the Supreme Court of Canada. He holds law degrees from Oxford, McGill, and Columbia, and is a lecturer at the Geneva Academy of International Humanitarian Law and Human Rights.

Alex Whiting is currently Prosecution Coordinator of the Office of the Prosecutor at the International Criminal Court. He has worked as a Senior Trial Attorney for the Office of the Prosecutor at the ICTY and was a federal prosecutor in the United States for ten years. He has also taught at Harvard Law School.

The views expressed herein are those of the authors alone and do not necessarily reflect the views of the ICTY, the ICC, or the United Nations.

ABBREVIATIONS

2004 UK *Manual*	UK Ministry of Defence, *The Manual of the Law of Armed Conflict* (Oxford: Oxford University Press, 2004)
AC	Appeals Chamber
AFDI	*Annuaire français de droit international*
AFP	Air Force Pamphlet
AILC	American International Law Cases
AJCL	*American Journal of Comparative Law*
AJIL	*American Journal of International Law*
AP	Additional Protocol
Ashworth, *Principles*	A. Ashworth, *Principles of Criminal Law*, 5th edn (Oxford: Oxford University Press, 2006)
BILC	British International Law Cases
British Military Manual	The War Office, *The Law of War on Land* (being Part III of the Manual of Military Law) (London: War Office, 1958)
Bull. Crim.	*Bulletin des arrêts de la Cour de Cassation*, Chambre Criminelle (Paris)
BYIL	*British Yearbook of International Law*
Cassese, Gaeta, and Jones, *ICC Commentary*	A. Cassese, P. Gaeta, and J. R. W. D. Jones (eds), *The Rome Statute of the International Criminal Court: A Commentary* (Oxford: Oxford University Press, 2002)
Cassese's Companion	A. Cassese, *The Oxford Companion to International Criminal Justice* (Oxford: Oxford University Press, 2009)
CLForum	*Criminal Law Forum*
CLR	*Columbia Law Review*
CrimLR	*Criminal Law Review*
CSCE	Conference on Security and Cooperation in Europe
CSJN	Corte Supreme de Justicia de la Nación
Delmas-Marty and Spencer, *European Criminal Procedures*	M. Delmas-Marty and J. A. Spencer (eds), *European Criminal Procedures* (Cambridge: Cambridge University Press, 2002)
ECCC	Extraordinary Chambers in the Courts of Cambodia
EJIL	*European Journal of International Law*
Entscheidungen	*Entscheidungen des Obersten Gerichtshofes für die Britische Zone: Entscheidungen in Strafsachen*, 3 vols (Berlin and Hamburg: Walter de Gruyter, 1949–51)

Fischer, Kress, Lüder, *International and National Prosecution*	H. Fischer, C. Kress, and S. R. Lüder (eds), *International and National Prosecution of Crimes under International Law: Current Developments* (Berlin: Berlin Verlag Arno Spitz, 2001)
Fletcher, *Basic Concepts*	G. P. Fletcher, *Basic Concepts of Criminal Law* (New York and Oxford: Oxford University Press, 1998)
Fletcher, *Rethinking*	G. P. Fletcher, *Rethinking Criminal Law* (Boston and Toronto: Little, Brown & Co., 1974)
Friedman	L. Friedman, *The Law of War: A Documentary History*, 2 vols (New York: Random House, 1972)
FRUS	Papers relating to the Foreign Relations of the United States
FRY	Federal Republic of Yugoslavia (Serbia and Montenegro)
FYROM	Former Yugoslav Republic of Macedonia
GA	General Assembly of the United Nations
GC	Geneva Convention
Glaser, *Culpabilité*	S. Glaser, 'Culpabilité en droit international pénal', 99 HR (1960–I), 473–591
Glaser, *Introduction*	S. Glaser, *Introduction à l'étude du droit international pénal* (Bruxelles, Paris: Bruylant-Recueil Sirey, 1954)
GP	*Giustizia penale*
HILJ	*Harvard International Law Journal*
HLR	*Harvard Law Review*
HR	*Recueil des Cours de l'Académie de droit international de La Haye*
HRL	Human Rights Law
IA	Interlocutory Appeal
IACHR	Inter-American Commission of Human Rights
ICC	International Criminal Court
ICJ	International Court of Justice
ICL	International Criminal Law
ICLQ	*International and Comparative Law Quarterly*
ICTR	International Criminal Tribunal for Rwanda
ICTY	International Criminal Tribunal for the former Yugoslavia
IHL	international humanitarian law
ILC	International Law Commission
ILR	*International Law Reports*
IMT Tokyo	R. J. Pritchard and S. Magbanua Zaide (eds), *The Tokyo War Crimes Trial* (The Complete Transcripts of the Proceedings of the International Military Tribunal for the Far East) (New York and London: Garland Publishing House, 1981)
International Conference on Military Trials	*Report of Robert H. Jackson, United States Representative to the International Conference on Military Trials, London 1945* (Washington, DC: Department of State, 1949)

IRRC	*International Review of the Red Cross*
IYHR	*Israeli Yearbook on Human Rights*
IYIL	*Italian Yearbook of International Law*
JAIL	*Japanese Annual of International Law*
JCE	Joint Criminal Enterprise
JCP	*Journal of International Criminal Justice*
Jescheck, *Lehrbuch*	H. H. Jescheck, *Lehrbuch des Strafrechts, Allgemeiner Teil*, ed. T. Weigend (Berlin: Duncker und Humblot, 1996)
JICJ	*Juris-classeur périodique (la semaine juridique)*, France
Justiz und NS-Verbrechen	*Justiz und NS-Verbrechen, Sammlung Deutscher Strafurteile wegen Nationalsozialistischer Tötungsverbrechen 1945–1966*, 22 vols (Amsterdam: University Press Amsterdam, 1968–75), also available on CD-ROM
Kelsen, *Principles*	H. Kelsen, *Principles of International Law* (New York: Rinehart & Co., 1952)
LJIL	*Leiden Journal of International Law*
LRTWC	*Law Reports of Trials of War Criminals*, 15 vols (London: UN War Crimes Commission, 1949)
Mettraux, *Landmark Decisions*	Mettraux G. (ed.), *International Criminal Law before National Courts: A Collection of Landmark Decisions* (Oxford: Oxford University Press, 200)
NAM	Non-Aligned Movement
NederJ	*Nederlandse Jurisprudentie*
NILR	*Netherlands International Law Review*
NLA	Albanian National Liberation Army
NSDAP	German National Socialist (Nazi) party
NSKK	German National Socialist (Nazi) commandos
Nuremberg Tribunal	International Military Tribunal for the Major War Criminals, Nuremberg
OTP	Office of the Prosecutor
PIL	Public International Law
PCIJ	Permanent Court of International Justice
Pradel	J. Pradel, *Droit pénal comparé* (Paris: Dalloz, 1995)
PrepCom	Preparatory Committee on the Establishment of an International Criminal Court
PTC	Pre-Trial Chamber
RDMDG	*Revue de droit militaire et de droit de la guerre*
RDPC	*Revue de droit pénal et de criminologie*
RGDIP	*Revue générale de droit international public*
Röling, *The Law of War*	B. V. A. Röling, 'The Law of War and the National Jurisdiction since 1945', 100 HR (1960–II), 329–453

RPE	Rules of Procedure and Evidence
RSK	Republic of Serbian Krajina
SA	Sturm Abteilung (Nazi paramilitary force)
SAO	Serbian Autonomous District
Sassòli and Bouvier	M. Sassòli, A. Bouvier, and A. Quintin (eds), *How Does Law Protect in War? Cases, Documents and Teaching Materials*, 3rd edn (Geneva: ICRC, 2011)
SC	UN Security Council
SCSL	Special Court for Sierra Leone
SG	UN Secretary-General
Smith and Hogan	Smith and Hogan, *Criminal Law*, 9th edn (London: Butterworths, 1999)
SPSC	Special Panels for Serious Crimes
SS	Schutz Staffel (Nazi elite corps)
STL	Special Tribunal for Lebanon
TC	Trial Chamber
Tokyo Tribunal	International Military Tribunal for the Far East, Tokyo
Trial of the Major War Criminals	*Trial of the Major War Criminals before the International Military Tribunal, Nuremberg 14 November 1945–1 October 1946*, 42 vols (Nuremberg, 1947)
Triffterer, *ICC Commentary*	O. Triffterer (ed.), *Commentary on the Rome Statute of the International Criminal Court*, 2nd edn (Munchen/Oxford/Baden-Baden: Verlag/Hart/Nomos, 2008)
TWC	*Trials of War Criminals before the Nürnberg Military Tribunals under Control Council Law no. 10*, 12 vols (Washington, DC: US Govt Printing Office, 1950)
UNMIK	United Nations Interim Administration in Kosovo
UNTAET	United Nations Transitional Administration in East Timor
Verhandlungen	*Verhandlungen des Reichstags I. Wahlperiode 1920*, Band 368, *Anlagen zu den Stenographischen Berichten Nr 2254 bis 2628* (Berlin: Julius Sittenfeld, 1924): contains the original text of the cases tried by the German Supreme Court at Leipzig
WCC	War Crimes Chamber
YIHL	*Yearbook of International Humanitarian Law*
YILC	*Yearbook of the International Law Commission*

TABLE OF CASES

TABLE OF TREATIES
AND CONVENTIONS

TABLE OF NATIONAL LEGISLATION

TABLE OF INTERNATIONAL INSTRUMENTS

TABLE OF STATUTES OF INTERNATIONAL TRIBUNALS

PART I

INTRODUCTION

1

FUNDAMENTALS OF INTERNATIONAL CRIMINAL LAW

International criminal law (ICL) is a body of international rules designed both to proscribe certain categories of conduct (war crimes, crimes against humanity, genocide, torture, aggression, international terrorism) and to make those persons who engage in such conduct criminally liable. These rules consequently either authorize states, or impose upon them the obligation, to prosecute and punish such criminal conducts. ICL also regulates international proceedings before international criminal courts, for prosecuting and trying persons accused of such crimes.

The first limb of this body makes up *substantive* law. This is the set of rules indicating what acts are prohibited, with the consequence that their authors are criminally accountable for their commission; these rules also set out the subjective elements required for such acts to be regarded as criminalized, the possible circumstances under which persons accused of such crimes may nevertheless not be held criminally liable, and also the conditions on which states may or must, under international rules, prosecute or bring to trial persons accused of one of those crimes. This whole corpus of rules is premised on the general notion that international legal prescriptions are capable of imposing obligations directly on individuals, without the intermediary of the state wielding authority over such individuals. As the International Military Tribunal at Nuremberg (hereinafter 'Nuremberg Tribunal'; see 14.2) stated in 1946, 'the essence of the [Tribunal's] Charter [i.e. the international treaty establishing the Tribunal and regulating its powers] is that individuals have international duties which transcend the national obligations of obedience imposed by the individual state (*Göring and others*, at 223; for a comment, see *Cassese's Companion*, at 696). An Indonesian court echoed this dictum in 2002 by saying that 'each individual must comply with international obligations beyond the laws of its nation (*Soares*, at 87; for a comment, see *Cassese's Companion*, at 927).

The set of rules regulating international proceedings before international criminal courts and tribunals—that is, *procedural* criminal law—governs the action by prosecuting authorities and the various stages of international criminal trials.

1.1 THE MAIN FEATURES OF ICL

ICL is a branch of public international law (PIL). The rules making up this body of law emanate from sources of international law (treaties, customary international law, etc.).[1]

---

[1] For a succinct survey of these sources, see A. Cassese, *International Law*, 2nd edn (Oxford: Oxford University Press, 2005), 153–237.

Hence, they are subject, among other things, to the principles of interpretation and application proper to that law. However, one should not be unmindful of some unique features of ICL that are worth brief examination.

1.1.1 A RELATIVELY NEW BRANCH OF INTERNATIONAL LAW

The list of international crimes regulated by ICL, namely the list of types of conduct for whose accomplishment international law makes the authors criminally responsible, has come into being by gradual accretion. Initially, in the late nineteenth century, and for a long time after, only war crimes were punishable. It is only since the Second World War that new categories of crime have developed, while that of war crimes has been restated. In 1945 and 1946, the Statutes of the Nuremberg and the International Military Tribunal for the Far East (hereinafter 'Tokyo Tribunal'; see 14.2), respectively, were adopted, laying down new classes of international criminality: crimes against humanity and crimes against peace (chiefly wars of aggression). This was followed in 1948 by genocide, and then in the 1980s, by torture as a discrete crime. The assertion can be made that recently also international terrorism has been criminalized, subject to certain conditions.

As for rules on international criminal proceedings, they were first laid down in the Statutes of the Nuremberg and Tokyo Tribunals, then in those of the International Criminal Tribunal for the former Yugoslavia (ICTY) and the International Criminal Tribunal for Rwanda (ICTR), and more recently in the Rome Statute of the International Criminal Court (ICC), the Statute of the Special Court for Sierra Leone (SCSL), the Rules of the Extraordinary Courts for Cambodia (ECCC), as well as the Statute of the Special Tribunal for Lebanon (STL) (on all these courts and tribunals see Chapter 14). Nonetheless they are still scant and, what is even more important, they only pertain to the specific criminal court for which they have been adopted; that is, they have no general scope. A fully fledged corpus of generally applicable international procedural rules is only gradually evolving.

1.1.2 A RUDIMENTARY BRANCH OF LAW

Another distinguishing trait of ICL is that the broadening of both substantive and procedural international rules has been a slow and complex process.

As for the substantive rules, when a new class of crime has emerged, its constituent elements (the objective and subjective conditions of the crime, or, in other words, actus reus and mens rea; see Chapter 3) have not been immediately clear, nor has any scale of penalties been laid down in international rules. This process can be easily explained.

First, for a long time, either treaties or (more seldom) customary rules of international law, in particular the rules of warfare (the so-called *ius in bello*) have confined themselves to *prohibiting* certain conduct (for instance, killing prisoners of war or attacking civilians). These prohibitions were, however, addressed to states as *belligerent parties*, not directly to *individuals*: it followed that, if any such conduct was carried out by an individual whose acts or omissions were attributable to the state under international law, it was the state that was internationally responsible, not the individual. Gradually, by bringing to trial before their courts enemy servicemen who had breached international rules of warfare, states made individuals directly and personally accountable and arguably they believed that individual criminal accountability was provided for international law. In other words, the notion that violations of international rules of warfare could also give rise to the criminal responsibility of the individual under international law gradually asserted itself. However, the process of criminalization of individual conduct was insufficient and inadequate: indeed international rules did not specify with sufficient clarity the objective and subjective requirements for individual criminal responsibility to arise. In addition, they did not clarify the different forms of individual criminal responsibility, the possible defences available, and the penalty to be attached to the crimes.

Second, and as a consequence of the situation just described, international law left to *national courts* the task of prosecuting and punishing the alleged perpetrators of those acts. When they sat in judgment over these crimes, national courts therefore applied their national procedural rules and rules on 'the general part' of substantive criminal law; that is, on the definition and character of the objective and subjective elements of crimes, on defences, etc. Among other things, very often national courts, faced with the *indeterminacy* of most international criminal rules, found it necessary to flesh them out and give them legal precision by drawing upon their own criminal law. They thus refined notions initially left rather loose by international rules.[2]

Finally, when international criminal courts were set up (first in 1945–7, then in 1993–4, and more recently in 1998 and 2002–7; see Chapter 14), they did indeed lay down in their constitutive instruments the various classes of crime to be punished; however, these classes were couched merely as offences over which each court had jurisdiction. In other words, the crimes were not enumerated as in a criminal code, but simply as a specification of the jurisdictional authority of the relevant court. The value and scope of those enumerations was therefore only germane to the court's jurisdiction and did not purport to have a general reach.

Given these characteristics of the evolution of ICL, it should not be surprising that even the recent addition of the sets of written rules referred to above has not proved sufficient to build a coherent legal system, as is shown by the heavy reliance by the newly created international criminal courts upon rules of customary international law or general principles.

As for *procedural* rules, some of them were scantily delineated in the Statutes of the Nuremberg and Tokyo Tribunals. Only recently have they been fortified, when various international criminal courts have been set up, as noted above. Nonetheless, even international criminal procedural law remains at a rather underdeveloped stage and in any case has no general purport (in that each international criminal court has its own rules of procedure).

1.1.3 THE INTERPLAY WITH OTHER BRANCHES OF LAW

ICL also presents the unique characteristic that, more than any other segment of PIL, it simultaneously *derives its origin from* and continuously draws upon both *international humanitarian law* and *human rights law*, as well as *national criminal law*.

International humanitarian law (IHL) embraces principles and rules designed to regulate warfare both by restraining belligerents in the conduct of armed hostilities and by protecting those persons who do not take part, or no longer take part in combat (having been wounded or having fallen into the hands of the enemy). ICL, at its origin, was chiefly concerned with offences committed during armed hostilities in time of war (war crimes; see Chapter 4): as mentioned above, violations of the rules of international law of warfare,

---

[2] Still very recently a national court, the Hague Court of Appeal in the *van Anraat* case, faced with the problem of determining the mental element of aiding and abetting (or complicity), discussed whether to apply Dutch criminal law rather than ICL, in view of the unclear status of ICL on the matter (§ 7). The Court in the event applied Dutch law (§§ 11.9–11.19 and 12.4). The Court, however, concluded: 'From an international criminal law perspective, these requirements [set out in Dutch criminal law] for the contribution of the so-called "aider or abettor" are not essentially more severe'.

which normally only generated *state* responsibility, gradually came to be considered as breaches of law also entailing *individual* criminal liability. For instance, previously the indiscriminate bombing of civilians was only considered a wrongful act attributable to the relevant belligerent state and entailed the international responsibility of that state vis-à-vis the enemy belligerent. Gradually the same act also came to be regarded as a war crime for which those ordering and executing the indiscriminate attack had to bear individual criminal liability. The description of the prohibited conduct that thus came to be criminalized was to be found in rules of IHL; consequently those applying ICL had perforce to refer to that body of law to establish which particular conduct IHL rules enjoined belligerents to refrain from, hence which conduct, if taken, amounted to a crime of the individuals concerned.

Human rights law (HRL) essentially consists of rules of treaty and customary international law granting fundamental rights to individuals by simultaneously restricting the authority yielded by states over such individuals. It also includes the copious case law of international bodies such as the European Court of Human Rights (ECHR), the Inter-American Court of Human Rights (IACHR), and the UN Human Rights Committee (HRC). This corpus of legal provisions and decisions has contributed to the development of ICL in many respects. It has expanded or strengthened, or created greater sensitivity to, the values (human dignity, the need to safeguard life and limb as far as possible, etc.) to be protected through the prohibition of attacks on such values. Furthermore, HRL lays down the fundamental rights of suspects and accused persons, of victims and witnesses; it also sets out the basic safeguards of fair trial. In short, this increasingly important segment of law has impregnated the whole area of ICL.

In addition, most rules of ICL of a customary international law nature have primarily evolved from *municipal case law* relating to international crimes (chiefly war crimes). This element, as well as the paucity of treaty rules on the matter, explains why ICL to a great extent results from the gradual *transposition* on to the international level of rules and legal constructs proper to national criminal law or to national trial proceedings.

The grafting of municipal law notions and rules on to international law has not, however, been a smooth process. National legal orders do not contain a uniform regulation of criminal law. On the contrary, they are split into many different systems, from among which two principal ones emerge: that prevailing in common law countries (the UK, the USA, Australia, Canada, many African and Asian countries), and that obtaining in civil law countries, chiefly based on a legal system of Romano-Germanic origin (they include states of continental Europe, such as France, Germany, Belgium, the countries of Northern Europe such as Norway, Sweden, Denmark, as well as Latin American countries, many Arab countries, and Asian states including, for instance, China). The heterogeneous and composite origin of many international rules of both substantive and procedural criminal law, a real patchwork of normative standards, complicates matters, as we shall see.[3]

---

[3] As has already been noted, this applies in particular to the so-called 'general part of criminal law'; that is the set of rules regulating the subjective elements of crimes, the various forms or categories of criminal liability (for instance, joint responsibility for common criminal purpose, aiding and abetting, and so on), conditions excluding criminal liability, etc. It was only natural for each national court pronouncing on war crimes or crimes against humanity to apply the general notions of criminal law prevailing in that country. As a result, one is confronted with hundreds of national cases where judges have relied upon different conceptions of, or approaches to, the 'general part', or have even resorted to the national definition of some subjective or objective elements of the relevant international crime. For instance, in *Fröhlich*, a British Court of Appeal (established in Germany under Control Council Law no. 10), to satisfy itself that the offence of the accused (a German charged with, and convicted by a court of first instance of killing four Russian prisoners of war) amounted to a war crime consisting of murder, applied the German notion of 'murder' (280–2). For a comment on the case, see *Cassese's Companion*, at 681.

It follows that ICL is an essentially *hybrid branch of law*: it is PIL impregnated with notions, principles, and legal constructs derived from national criminal law, IHL as well as HRL. However, the recent establishment of international criminal courts, and in particular of the ICC, has given a stupendous impulse to the evolution of a corpus of international criminal rules proper. It can therefore be safely maintained that we are now heading for the formation of a fully fledged body of law in this area.

1.1.4 THE RELATIONSHIP BETWEEN ICL AND PIL

A further major feature of ICL, in particular of its substantive rules, closely bound up with the feature to which it has just been drawn attention, ought to be emphasized. This law has a *twofold relationship* with the general body of PIL.

The first relationship is one of *mutual subsidiarity or support*. Strikingly, most of the offences that ICL proscribes and for the perpetration of which it endeavours to punish the individuals that allegedly committed them, are also regarded by international law as wrongful acts by states; to the extent that they are large-scale and systematic, they are international wrongs entailing the 'aggravated responsibility' of the state on whose behalf the perpetrators may have acted.[4] (This holds true not only for genocide and crimes against humanity, but also for systematic torture, large-scale terrorism, and massive war crimes.) Thus, when one of these crimes is committed by an individual whose conduct is attributable to a state under international law, a dual responsibility may follow: criminal liability of the individual, falling under ICL, and state responsibility, regulated by international rules on this matter.[5] Admittedly, there is at present a tendency in the international community to give pride of place to the former category of responsibility whilst playing down the latter. Political motivations underpin this trend, chiefly the inclination of states to avoid invoking the aggravated responsibility of other states except when they are prompted to do so out of self-interest or on strong political grounds. It is nevertheless a fact that, theoretically, both legal avenues remain open and may be utilized, as is shown by the proceedings for genocide instituted by some states before the International Court of Justice (ICJ)[6] while at the same time genocide trials were taking and had taken place before the ICTY.[7]

The second relationship between PIL and ICL is more complex. Two somewhat *conflicting philosophies* underlie each area of law. ICL primarily addresses the conduct of *individuals* and aims at protecting society against the most harmful transgressions of legal standards perpetrated by such individuals (whether they be state agents or persons acting in a private capacity). It therefore aims to punish the authors of those transgressions,

---

[4] On the notion of 'aggravated State responsibility', see Cassese, *International Law*, cit. n. 1, at 262–75.

[5] It is notable that the four Geneva Conventions of 1949, while they institute a special legal regime for the criminal repression of a specific category of war crimes (the so-called grave breaches; see 4.3.2), at the same time provide for the 'state responsibility' of contracting parties for the case of commission of such 'grave breaches'. See, for instance, Articles 129–30 of the Third Convention (on Prisoners of War), concerning the penal sanctions for 'grave breaches' and Article 131 on state responsibility. (Under the latter provision, 'No High Contracting Party shall be allowed to absolve itself or any other High Contracting Party of any liability incurred by itself or by another High Contracting Party in respect of breaches referred to in the preceding Article.')

[6] See the cases brought by Bosnia and Herzegovina and by Croatia against the then Federal Republic of Yugoslavia (*Application of the Convention on the Prevention and Punishment of Genocide, Bosnia and Herzegovina* v. *Serbia and Montenegro*, and *Croatia* v. *Serbia*).

[7] See, for instance, the judgment in *Krstić* (TC) as well as the amended indictment against *Milošević Slobodan* (of 22 November 2002, concerning Bosnia and Herzegovina), and the amended indictment against *Karadžić* of 28 April 2000.

while however safeguarding the rights of suspects or accused persons from any arbitrary prosecution and punishment. It follows among other things that one of the mainstays of ICL, and of criminal law in general, is compliance with the principle of legality (see Chapter 2), which requires that criminal prohibitions be as clear, detailed, and specific as possible. This is required by a basic demand of modern legal civilization: anybody, before engaging in a particular conduct, is entitled to be aware of whether such conduct is criminally prohibited or instead allowed. Another, closely linked, fundamental requirement is that no one should be punished for conduct that was not considered as criminal at the time when it was taken. In short, any person suspected or accused of a crime is entitled to a set of significant rights protecting him from possible *abuse* by the prosecuting authorities.

PIL, on the other hand, primarily regulates the behaviour of *states*. It pursues, in essence, the purpose of reconciling as much as possible the conflicting interests of sovereign entities (although in modern times somehow it also takes into account the concerns and exigencies of individuals and non-state entities). True, part of PIL is concerned with the violations by states of the rules protecting the most fundamental values of the international community as a whole and the ensuing state responsibility. This area of PIL is, however, relatively less conspicuous than the corresponding segment of ICL. In fact, the thrust of PIL is legally to regulate and facilitate a minimum of peaceful intercourse between states, much more than calling to account states for their breaches of law. To put it differently, the *normative* role of law is more important and effective than its *repressive* function.

What is even more important from our present viewpoint is that, in order to take account of the conflicting interests and preoccupations of states, the law-making process is often actuated by dint of gradual evolution of sweeping and often loose rules through custom or even so-called 'soft law' (that is, standards and guidelines devoid of legally binding force). Often even treaties lay down ambiguous, or at any rate not well-determined provisions; this happens whenever the need to harmonize conflicting state interests makes it necessary to agree upon vague formulas. In short, the need for detailed, clear, and unambiguous legal regulation is less strong in the general area of PIL than in the specific area of ICL, where this need becomes of crucial relevance, given that the fundamental rights of suspects, accused persons, and victims are at stake.

The inherent requirements underlying ICL (not less than any national body of criminal law) may therefore collide with the traditional characteristics of PIL. The tension between the different philosophy and approach underlying each of these two bodies of law (PIL and ICL) explains the unease with which national criminal lawyers look upon ICL. In particular, those criminal lawyers that are conversant with the Romano-Germanic tradition and live in civil law countries take issue with the loose character of many provisions of ICL. Notably, they assail the fact that ICL relies to a large extent upon customary international law.

Be that as it may, what counts on the practical side is that, as a result of the contrast between the relative indeterminacy and 'malleability' of international criminal rules (mainly due to their largely customary international law origin), and the imperative requirement that criminal rules be clear and specific, the *role of national or international criminal courts* has become conspicuously crucial. It falls to them to try to cast light on, and give legal precision to, rules of customary international law, whenever their content and purport is still surrounded by uncertainty, as well as to spell out and elaborate upon the frequently terse content of treaty provisions. In particular, criminal courts play an indispensable role in: *i*) ascertaining the existence and contents of customary international law rules; *ii*) interpreting and clarifying treaty provisions; and *iii*) elaborating, based on general principles and rules, legal constructs indispensable for the application of international criminal rules. It is mainly due to judicial decisions that ICL is progressing so rapidly.[8]

In addition, one must observe that more than other branches of PIL, but like those legal areas where rapid changes in technology impose speedy normative updating (for instance, international environmental law or international trade law), ICL is changing very quickly. This is because unfortunately, in the world society there is a staggering increase in atrocities, whether or not linked to armed conflict. There is, therefore, a widely felt need to respond to them by, among other things, criminal repression. However, what is even more striking in this branch of law is that legal change goes hand in hand with increasing sophistication of the legal system (we are now moving from a rudimentary jumble of rules and principles to a fairly consistent body of law). In addition it is accompanied by a gradual shift in its philosophical underpinning: in particular, a shift from the doctrine of substantive justice (whereby the need to protect society requires the punishment of harmful actions even if such actions had not been previously criminalized) to that of strict legality (whereby the need to protect individuals' human rights, in particular to safeguard individuals from arbitrary action of the executive or judicial powers, requires that no one may be punished for any action not considered criminal when performed). (On this matter see Chapter 2).

1.2 SOURCES OF ICL

Since ICL is but a branch of PIL, the sources of law from which one may derive the relevant rules are those proper to international law; in addition, they must be resorted to in the hierarchical order dictated by international law.

Hence, one may draw upon *primary* sources (treaties, customary international law), *secondary* sources (law-making processes envisaged by customary international law rules or treaty provisions, such as binding resolutions of the UN Security Council), general principles of international law, or in the final analysis such *subsidiary* sources as general principles of law common to national legal systems.

The order in which one may use such sources can be derived from the structure and hierarchy of the sources of international law. One should first of all look for treaty rules or secondary rules, if applicable. When such rules are lacking or contain gaps, one should resort to customary international law. When even this set of rules is of no avail, one should apply general principles of international law, particularly those related to the relevant branches of international law (ICL, HRL, and IHL). These principles can be inferred, by a process of induction and generalization, from treaty provisions or rules of customary international law. If one still does not find the applicable rule or, more often, if the rule contains a gap or is at any rate insufficient, one may have resort to general principles common to national jurisdiction, in particular those related to criminal matters (such as the

---

[8] These characteristic features of this body of law have in some respects a negative connotation, while other features may prove advantageous. The drawback is that the rights of the accused risk being jeopardized by the *normative flux* that still characterizes this branch of international law. It is chiefly for courts to endeavour as far as possible to safeguard the rights of the accused from any unwarranted deviation from the fundamental principles of criminal law and human rights law. The advantage of the unique nature of ICL is that change and adaptation to evolving historical circumstances occur more easily and smoothly than in legal systems based on codes and other forms of written law. In this respect, courts may become instrumental in reconciling the demands for change with the requirement of respect for the rights of the accused.

ban on denial of justice, the doctrine of *res judicata*, i.e. of the binding force of a judicial decision, and so on.)

It is important to clarify that these sources create international rules that must be applied also by *national* courts, although some legal constraints might exist. In many respects each national legal system provides for its own mechanism for the implementation of international rules. However, even in cases where a monistic approach is adopted, and international rules can be directly applied in the domestic legal systems, the principle of *strict legality* in criminal matters (see 2.1) might hamper the direct application of international criminal rules. In such instances, in order for national courts to be authorized to refer to and apply those rules, it is necessary for the legislature to have passed appropriate legislation, for instance: *i*) defining the crimes; *ii*) providing for the relevant penalties; and *iii*) providing for the exercise of criminal jurisdiction by the national courts over those crimes. Thus, the system of sources utilized by national courts for the purpose of trying persons accused of international crimes is to a large extent bound up with the general manner in which the national system puts international rules into effect at the domestic level and the way the principle of legality in criminal matters is implemented and applied at the domestic level.

It is also important to note that many criminal lawyers, particularly in countries of Romano-Germanic tradition, being used to interpreting and applying criminal rules laid down in written criminal codes, tend to believe that the major source of ICL can be found in the Statute of the ICC, or at least that such Statute is a sort of 'code of international criminal law'. This is a wrong assumption, although admittedly that Statute is the only international written instrument laying down international rules on both the 'general part' of ICL and a fairly comprehensive definition of international crimes. The truth of the matter is, however, that the ICC Statute embraces a set of rules only applicable by the ICC itself: the Statute does not apply to other international criminal courts (the ICTY, the ICTR, the SCSL, the STL, and so on), each of which is regulated by, and must apply, above all, its own Statute. It is the ICC that must comply with the provisions defining the various crimes under the Court's jurisdiction and also apply the Statute's provisions on mens rea, defences, etc. In other words, the ICC Statute, far from constituting an 'international criminal code', only lays down the rules that the Court must apply when it exercises its jurisdiction over the crimes it is called upon to adjudicate. This conclusion does not of course detract from the importance of the ICC Statute as a set of rules which clarify many points in ICL and therefore may, in this respect, also prove useful to consider by other international criminal courts. Thus, some provisions of the ICC Statute may be held to codify customary international law; others may be deemed to lay down a rule that clearly chooses between two conflicting interpretations previously offered in international case law; others instead go beyond what is prescribed by customary international law. Furthermore, it should not be ruled out that, particularly after the ICC engages in its judicial activity more intensely, some of the Statute's provisions may gradually turn into customary international law as a result of other international criminal courts broadly accepting and applying these provisions as encapsulating the world society's *opinio juris* on the matter.

Unlike the Statutes of other international criminal courts, the ICC Statute expressly indicates the sources to which the Court must refer. In accordance with Article 21(1), the Court shall first of all apply: *i*) the Statute, the Elements of Crimes and the Rules of Procedure and Evidence (the 'Rules'); *ii*) 'where appropriate', applicable treaties, and the principles and rules of international law (including the established principles of international law of armed conflict; 'failing that', general principles of law derived from national legal systems, including (where appropriate) those of states that would normally exercise jurisdiction and provided that they are not inconsistent with the Statute or with international law. The ICC has clarified in which cases it will have to refer to the sources mentioned above under *ii*) and *iii*), namely when 'there is a lacuna in the written law contained in the Statute, the Elements of Crimes and the Rules, and such lacuna cannot be filled by the application of the criteria provided for in Articles 31 and 32 of the Vienna Convention on the Law of the Treaties and article 21(3) of the Statute'.[9]

As is well known, Articles 31 and 32 of the 1969 Vienna Convention codify the rules of interpretation of treaty provisions. Article 21(3) of the ICC Statute provides that 'the application and interpretation of law' pursuant to Article 21 'must be consistent with internationally recognized human rights, and be without any adverse distinction founded on grounds such as gender ..., age, race, colour, language, religion or belief, political or other opinion, national, ethnic or social origin, wealth, birth or other status'. This provision requires the ICC not only to interpret the Statute and all the other rules created by the sources mentioned in Article 21 in conformity with international human rights, but also to refuse to apply the Statute and the other rules where inconsistent with international human rights.[10] Article 21(3) establishes therefore a hierarchy between internationally recognized human rights and the sources referred to in Article 21(1), providing that the former must prevail in case of contradiction. It will be now for the ICC to define the contours of the notion 'internationally recognized human rights'.

1.2.1 THE STATUTES AND THE RULES OF INTERNATIONAL CRIMINAL COURTS

Like every other international body or organization, international criminal courts are set up to perform specific tasks and are therefore governed by the 'principle of speciality', that is—as the ICJ put it with respect to international organizations in general—'they are invested by the States which create them with powers, the limits of which are a function of the common interests whose promotion those States entrust to them' (ICJ, Advisory Opinion on *Legality of the Use of Force by a State of Nuclear Weapons in Armed Conflict*, § 25). It is therefore clear that international criminal courts must first and foremost apply their Statutes, and that this is the case also for those tribunals—such as the ICTY and the ICTR—that were established through 'secondary legislation', namely by virtue of a binding decision of the UN Security Council. Therefore, while the Statutes of the international criminal courts established by treaties are binding only upon the contracting parties, the ICTY and ICTR Statutes are binding upon all UN member states pursuant to Article 25 of the UN Charter.

Chief among Statutes of international criminal courts are the London Agreement of 8 August 1945, setting out the substantive and procedural law of the IMT, and the 1998 Statute of the ICC, a long and elaborate instrument that lays down both a list of crimes subject to the jurisdiction of the ICC and some general principles of ICL, and in addition sets forth the main rules on the proceedings before the ICC. Of considerable importance are also the Statutes of the SCSL, laid down in an Annex to the Agreement between the UN and Sierra Leone of 16 January 2002, and of the STL, enshrined in an Agreement between the UN and Lebanon of 10 June 2007 whose provisions have entered into force by virtue of the UN Security Council's resolution 1757 (2007). Other international instruments endowed with legally binding force and regulating the activity of international criminal courts are

---

[9] See e.g. *Al-Bashir* (*Decision on the Prosecutor's Application for a Warrant of Arrest*), § 44.

[10] See D. Akande, 'Sources of International Criminal Law', in *Cassese's Companion*, at 47 (also for the authors taking a different view).

the resolutions passed in 1993 and 1994, respectively by the UN Security Council under Chapter VII of the Charter to adopt the Statutes of the ICTY and the ICTR.

The Statutes of international criminal courts establish, among other things, the scope of their jurisdiction *ratione materiae*, i.e. they set forth the crimes over which the relevant court or tribunal may sit in judgment. Usually those Statutes do not spell out in detail all the legal ingredients of the crimes, something which has obliged the relevant court to turn to customary rules or to applicable treaties to identify or clarify those elements. Things are different for the ICC Statute, which contains a fairly detailed list and elucidation of the crimes under the jurisdiction of the Court. In addition, the ICC is assisted by the so-called 'Elements of Crimes', containing additional clarification as regards the objective and subjective elements of each crime mentioned in the Statute, and that guide the Court in the application and interpretation of the relevant provisions of the Statute (Article 9(1)). The Court has clarified that it shall not refer to the Elements of Crimes in a discretionary manner, but that it will apply them unless it finds 'an irreconcilable contradiction' between them and the Statute.[11]

Proceedings before international criminal courts are normally governed by Rules of procedure and evidence (the 'Rules'). These Rules may be adopted by the international criminal court itself, by virtue of a provision contained in the relevant Statute, as in the case of the ICTY and the ICTR. For the ICTY and ICTR, the adoption of such Rules is thus provided for in an international instrument (the Statute) adopted on the strength and by virtue of an international treaty (the UN Charter). It follows that the passing of such Rules amounts to 'tertiary legislation'. In the case of the ICC, under Article 51(1) and (2) it is the Assembly of States Parties that adopts the Rules by a two-thirds majority. However, under Article 51(3), 'in urgent cases where the Rules do not provide for a specific situation before the Court, the judges may, by a two-thirds majority, draw up provisional Rules to be applied until adopted, amended, or rejected at the next ordinary or special session of the Assembly of the States Parties'.

The Rules must not conflict either with the Statute of the relevant court governing the same matter or with rules and principles laid down in customary law. In case of inconsistency, a court should refrain from applying the relevant Rule, or else it must construe and apply them in such a manner that they prove consonant with the overriding rules.[12]

1.2.2 APPLICABLE TREATIES

Often provisions of the Statutes of international criminal courts refer, if only implicitly, to specific international treaties. For instance, Article 2 of the ICTY Statute, conferring on the Tribunal jurisdiction over grave breaches of the Geneva Conventions of 1949 (a specific class of war crimes, see 4.3.2), explicitly refers to these Geneva Conventions with regard to the notion of 'protected persons' and 'protected property'. Article 4 of the ICTR Statute, granting jurisdiction over violations of Article 3 common to the four 1949 Geneva Conventions and the Second Additional Protocol (which constitute war crimes in non-international armed conflict, see 4.3.2), admittedly incorporates in terms only the main provisions of common Article 3 and the Second Additional Protocol; nevertheless,

---

[11] *Al-Bashir* (*Decision on the Prosecutor's Application for a Warrant of Arrest*), §§ 128–32.

[12] In *Blaškić* (*Subpoena*) the ICTY Appeals Chamber asked itself whether the term 'subpoena' used in Rule 54 of the Rules should be understood 'to mean an injunction accompanied by a threat of penalty in case of non-compliance', or instead should be taken to designate a binding order not necessarily implying the assertion of a power to imprison or fine. The Chamber held that, since under customary international law tribunals were not empowered to issue to states subpoenas capable of being enforced by a penalty, the term was to be given a narrow interpretation: it was to be construed as indicating compulsory orders, which, only when addressed to individuals acting in their private capacity, could imply the possible imposition of a penalty (§§ 21, 24–5, and 38).

for its interpretation the Tribunal may need to look at all the others provisions of the Conventions or the Protocol.

Treaties may come into play from another viewpoint. By definition treaties are only binding upon the contracting states and any international body they may establish. Nonetheless, they may also be taken into account, whenever this is legally admissible, as evidence of the crystallization of customary international law rules.

Treaties relevant to our subject matter are those laying down substantive rules of IHL (for instance, the Regulations annexed to the Fourth Hague Convention of 1907, the four Geneva Conventions of 1949, the two Geneva Additional Protocols of 1977, various recent treaties prohibiting the use of certain specific weapons,[13] and so on); that is, rules the serious violation of which may amount to war crimes (or, in the case of the Geneva Conventions and the First Additional Protocol, to 'grave breaches' of these Conventions or Protocol). Other treaties refer to other international crimes: for instance, the 1948 Convention on the Prevention and Suppression of the Crime of Genocide ('Genocide Convention') (the most important provisions of which have subsequently turned into customary international law); the 1984 Convention against Torture and Other Cruel, Inhuman or Degrading Treatment or Punishment ('Convention against Torture'), various international treaties on terrorism, etc.

1.2.3 CUSTOMARY INTERNATIONAL LAW

Written rules on ICL are not numerous. Hence, resort to rules of customary international law may prove necessary to clarify the content of written provisions or to fill gaps in these provisions. Resort to customary international law may also prove necessary for the purpose of pinpointing general principles of criminal law, whenever the application of such principles becomes necessary (see 1.2.4).

On this score ICL bears a strong resemblance to the criminal law of such common law countries as England, where next to statutory offences there exist many common law offences, developed through judicial precedents. However, the deficiency deriving from the unwritten nature of customary law is less conspicuous in England than in ICL. The existence of a huge wealth of judicial precedents built up over centuries, the hierarchical structure of the judiciary coupled with the doctrine of 'judicial precedent' (whereby courts are bound by the decisions of higher courts) tend to meet the exigencies of legal certainty and foreseeability proper to any system of criminal law. In contrast, ICL is still in its infancy, or at least adolescence: consequently, many of its rules still suffer from their loose content, contrary to the principle of specificity proper to criminal law (see 2.3.1). As noted in 1.1.4, the role of international, as well as national, courts thus becomes crucial for the building of a less rudimentary corpus of legal rules.

As noted, customary international rules may normally be drawn or inferred from judicial decisions, which to a very large extent have been handed down, chiefly in the past, by *national* criminal courts (whereas by now there exists a conspicuous number of judgments delivered by international criminal courts). As each state court tends to apply the general notions of national criminal law even when adjudicating international crimes, it often proves arduous to find views and concepts that are so uniform and consistent as to evidence the formation of a rule of customary international law.

---

[13] See e.g. the 1925 Geneva Protocol for the Prohibition of the Use in War of Asphyxiating, Poisonous or Other Gases, and of Bacteriological Methods of Warfare, or the 1980 UN Convention on Prohibitions on Restrictions on the Use of Certain Conventional Weapons which may be deemed to be excessively injurious or to have Indiscriminate Effects, or the 1997 Ottawa Convention on the Prohibition of the Use, Stockpiling, Production and Transfer of Anti-personnel Mines and their Destruction.

In addition, differences originating from *varying legal approaches* may influence the appraisal by an international criminal judge of the significance of case law. Judges trained in common law systems naturally tend to attach great importance to cases as 'precedents' and are inclined to apply such 'precedents' without asking themselves whether they evince the formation of, or crystallize, a rule of customary international law, or instead testify to the proper interpretation of a treaty or customary rule offered by another court. In contrast, judges from civil law countries, where judicial precedents have less weight and criminal codes enjoy a decisive legal status, tend to play down judicial decisions, or at least to first ask themselves, before relying upon such decisions, what legal status should be attached to them in international proceedings. This difference in cultural background and legal training of international judges often leads to different legal decisions.

Many examples can be cited of instances where national or international criminal courts have taken into consideration national case law (plus, if need be, treaties and other international instruments) to establish whether a rule of customary international law had evolved on a specific matter. For instance, in *Furundžija* (TC) the ICTY held that a rule on the definition of rape had come into being at the customary international law level (§§ 168–9). In a case decided in 1950 a Brussels Court Martial had already ruled that torture in time of armed conflict was prohibited by a customary international law rule.[14]

In many cases courts have resorted to customary international law to determine the content and scope of an international rule that made a crime punishable without, however, properly defining the prohibited conduct. (For instance, in *Kupreškić and others* the ICTY Trial Chamber had carefully to consider treaties and case law to establish what was meant by *persecution* as a crime against humanity (§§ 567–626); on persecution see 5.4.2). In some cases courts reached the conclusion that, contrary to the submissions of one of the parties, a specific matter was not governed by customary international rules. Thus, for instance, in *Tadić* (AC) the ICTY Appeals Chamber held that 'customary international law, as it results from the gradual development of international instruments and national case law into general rules, does not presuppose a discriminatory or persecutory intent for all crimes against humanity' (§§ 288–92).

Conversely, as pointed out above, in some cases international or national courts, following an approach akin to that of common law courts, did not take into consideration case law for the purpose of determining whether it had brought about the crystallization of a rule of customary international law. Rather, they viewed and used case law as a set of precedents that could be of assistance in establishing the applicable law. (One should note, however, that on a typical common law approach, precedents are *binding*, not merely of assistance. *Obiter dicta* are of assistance, but by definition they are not precedents.)[15]

---

[14] In *K.W.* German officers had been accused of ill-treating civilians in occupied Belgium. After noting that Article 46 of the Hague Regulations imposed upon the Occupant to respect the life of individuals but did not expressly forbid acts of violence or cruelty, the Court Martial held that a customary rule had evolved on the matter. To this effect it relied upon the celebrated Martens Clause as well as Article 5 of the Universal Declaration of Human Rights, concluding that 'hanging a human being by his hands tied behind his back from a pulley specially rigged for the purpose' was torture, whereas 'blows to the face, delivered so repeatedly and violently that they caused it to swell up and, in several cases, broke some teeth' amounted to cruel treatment (at 566). See also *Auditeur v. K.* (at 654).

[15] For instance, in *Kvočka and others*, the ICTY Trial Chamber, when discussing the issue of how to distinguish co-perpetrators from aiders and abettors in the case of participation by a number of persons in a joint criminal enterprise, merely relied upon case law as such ('A number of cases assist the Trial Chamber in its assessment of the level of participation required to incur criminal responsibility as either a co-perpetrator or an aider and abettor in a criminal endeavour in which several participants are involved': § 290; and see §§ 291–312). Perhaps, the Chamber was trying to discover the content of customary international law but did not say in so many words that that was what it was doing.

1.2.4 GENERAL PRINCIPLES OF ICL AND GENERAL PRINCIPLES OF PIL

General principles of ICL include principles specific to this branch of international law, such as the principles of legality, of specificity, the presumption of innocence, the principle of equality of arms, the principle of command responsibility, a corollary in ICL of the principle of responsible command existing in IHL,[16] and so on. The application of these principles at the international level normally results from their gradual transposition over time from national legal systems on to the international order. They are now firmly embedded in ICL.

General principles of international law consist of principles inherent in the international legal system. Hence, their identification does not require an in-depth comparative survey of all the major legal systems of the world, but can be carried out by way of generalization and induction from the main features of the international legal order. The principle of PIL that is more germane to ICL is that of respect for human rights (or 'respect for human dignity', as held by the *Furundžija* Trial Chamber (§ 183)).

Resort to general principles of ICL may be had when the rules contained in the applicable Statute or in treaty or customary international rules are unclear or incomplete. If even these principles prove of no avail, one can then draw upon general principles of PIL, if any.

1.2.5 GENERAL PRINCIPLES OF CRIMINAL LAW RECOGNIZED IN DOMESTIC LEGAL SYSTEMS

While the general principles just mentioned may be inferred from the whole system of ICL or of PIL, the principles we will now discuss may be drawn from a *comparative survey* of the principal legal systems of the world. Their articulation is therefore grounded not merely on interpretation and generalization, but rather on a comparative law approach. With respect to criminal law, these principles are expressly referred to in such human rights treaties as the UN Covenant on Civil and Political Rights (Article 15(2)) and the European Convention on Human Rights (Article 7 (2)). These treaties, while laying down the principle of legality (*nullum crimen sine lege*) and the consequent principle of non-retroactivity of criminal law, add however that individuals may be tried and punished (by national courts) for acts or omissions which, at the time when they were committed, were criminal 'according to the general principles of law common to the community of nations'.

This source is subsidiary in nature; hence, recourse to it can only be made if reliance upon the other sources discussed above (Statutes of the relevant international tribunals, applicable treaties, rules of customary international law, general principles of ICL, general principle of PIL) has turned out to be of no avail. It is at this stage that the search for general principles shared by the major legal systems of the community of nations may be initiated. This is precisely the approach taken in Article 21(1)(c) of the ICC Statute.[17] A compelling approach to principles was taken by the ICTY in *Kupreškić and others*.[18]

---

[16] On these principles see ICTY, *Hadzihasanović and others (Decision on Interlocutory Appeal Challenging Jurisdiction in Relation to Command Responsibility)*, AC, §§ 14–18.

[17] 'Failing that [i.e. an applicable rule of the ICC Statute, of the Elements of Crimes and the ICC Rules of Procedure and Evidence, as well as of applicable treaties and the "principles and rules of international [customary] law"] [the Court shall apply] general principles of law derived by the Court from national laws of legal systems of the world including, as appropriate, the national laws of States that would normally exercise jurisdiction over the crime, provided that those principles are not inconsistent with this Statute and with international law and internationally recognized norms and standards.'

[18] In that case Trial Chamber II held that: '[A]ny time the Statute [of the ICTY] does not regulate a specific matter, and the *Report of the Secretary-General* [submitted to the SC and endorsed by it as a document

Clearly, a principle of criminal law may belong to this class only if a court finds that it is shared by common law and civil law systems as well as other legal systems such as those of the Islamic world, some Asian countries such as China and Japan, and the African continent. (It is more and more frequently pointed out in the legal literature that limiting comparative legal analysis to civil law and common law systems alone is too restrictive.)[19]

International criminal courts have sounded a note of warning about resorting to general principles. They have emphasized that one ought not to transpose legal constructs typical of national legal systems into international law, whenever these constructs do not harmonize with the specific features of the international legal system. The ICTY has taken this approach. In 1998, the *Furundžija* Trial Chamber set out an articulate delineation of the limitations inherent in resorting to general principles.[20]

International criminal courts have often relied upon these principles. For instance, the ICTY has had the opportunity to discuss this subsidiary source of law fairly often. In some cases the ICTY found that there existed general principles common to the major legal systems of the world, and accordingly applied them. For instance, in *Furundžija*, the Trial Chamber had to find a definition of one of the categories of war crimes and crimes against humanity, namely rape. After going through international treaties and having

accompanying the resolution establishing the Tribunal] does not prove to be of any assistance in the interpretation of the Statute, it falls to the International Tribunal to draw upon (i) rules of customary international law or (ii) general principles of ICL; or, lacking such principles, (iii) general principles of criminal law common to the major legal systems of the world; or, lacking such principles, (iv) general principles of law consonant with the basic requirements of international justice' (§ 591).

[19] This distinction (still to a large extent upheld in such standard works as R. David and C. Juaffret Spinosi, *Les Grands Systèmes de droit contemporains*, 10th edn (Paris, 1992)—as is well known, David divided the legal world into four families: common law, civil law, socialist law, other conceptions of law) is held to be on the wane by such writers as, for instance, J. Gordley, 'Common Law and Civil Law: eine überholte Unterscheidung', 3 *Zeitschrift für Europäisches Privatrecht* (1993), 498; H. P. Glenn, 'La Civilization de la common law', 45 *Revue internationale de droit comparé* (1993), 599; B. S. Markesinis (ed.), *The Gradual Convergence: Foreign Ideas, Foreign Influences, and English Law on the Eve of the 21st Century* (Oxford: Clarendon Press, 1994). See also H. P. Glenn, *Legal Traditions of the World* (Oxford: Oxford University Press, 2000).

A distinguished author (U. Mattei, 'Three Patterns of Law: Taxonomy and Change in the World's Legal Systems', 45 *American J. of Comparative Law* (1997), 5–44) has suggested a tripartite scheme: in his view there exist three patterns of law, according to the relative prevalence of 'the rule of professional law', 'the rule of political law', and 'the rule of traditional law'. The 'rule of professional law', which predominates in the Western world (North America, western Europe, South Africa, and Oceania) can be subdivided, in his opinion, into three subsystems: common law, civil law, and mixed systems (such as Scotland, Louisiana, Quebec, South Africa) including the Scandinavian countries (41–2).

[20] After mentioning the need to look for 'principles of criminal law common to the major legal systems of the world' (§ 177), the Trial Chamber went on to specify the following: 'Whenever international criminal rules do not define a notion of criminal law, reliance upon national legislation is justified, subject to the following conditions: (i) unless indicated by an international rule, reference should not be made to one national legal system only, say that of common-law or that of civil-law States. Rather, international courts must draw upon the general concepts and legal institutions common to all the major legal systems of the world. This presupposes a process of identification of the common denominators in these legal systems so as to pinpoint the basic notions they share; (ii) since 'international trials exhibit a number of features that differentiate them from national criminal proceedings' [reference is made here to Judge Cassese's Separate and Dissenting Opinion in *Erdemović*, AC, 1997], account must be taken of the specificity of international criminal proceedings when utilising national law notions. In this way a mechanical importation or transposition from national law into international criminal proceedings is avoided, as well as the attendant distortions of the unique traits of such proceedings' (§ 178). The same Trial Chamber conclusively set out this notion in *Kupreškić and others* (§ 677 and see also § 539). It would seem that the ICTR Appeals Chamber mechanically transposed onto ICL the notion of 'abuse of process doctrine' upheld in common law countries but unknown to most countries of Romano-Germanic tradition, in *Barayagwisa* (*Decision on Defence Counsel Motion to Withdraw*, AC), §§ 73–101.

considered the relevant case law for the purpose of establishing whether it evinced the formation of a customary rule on the matter, the Chamber stated that no elements other than the few resulting from such examination could be

> drawn from international treaty or customary law, nor is resort to general principles of ICL or to general principles of international law of any avail. The Trial Chamber therefore considers that, to arrive at an accurate definition of rape based on the criminal law principle of specificity [. . .] it is necessary to look for principles of criminal law common to the major legal systems of the world (§ 177).

After undertaking this examination, the Chamber reached the conclusion that in spite of inevitable discrepancies, most legal systems in the common and civil law worlds consider rape to be the forcible sexual penetration of the human body by the penis or the forcible insertion of any other object into either the vagina or the anus (§ 181).[21]

Far more numerous are, however, the cases where the ICTY has ruled out the existence of a general principle of law recognized by all nations.[22]

As for the principles of interpretation, once again they should be those upheld in international law and codified in the 1969 Vienna Convention on the Law of Treaties: see to

---

[21] However, on one point, namely whether forced oral penetration could be defined as rape or sexual assault, the Court found that there was no uniformity in national legislation. In *Kupreškić and others*, the Trial Chamber took into consideration the question of general principles on a number of occasions. Thus it considered whether there were 'principles of criminal law common to the major systems of the world' outlining the 'criteria for deciding whether there has been a violation of one or more provisions' when the same conduct can be regarded as breaching more than one provision of criminal law (the question of *cumulation of offences*), and concluded that such criteria did exist (§§ 680–95). In *Blaškić*, the Trial Chamber held that the principle on the various forms of individual criminal responsibility laid down in Art. 7(1) of the ICTY Statute was consonant 'with the general principles of criminal law' as well as international customary law (§ 264). Subsequently, in appraising the various elements to be considered for the determination of the appropriate penalty, the Chamber held that the 'principle of proportionality' [of the penalty to the gravity of the crime] is a 'general principle of criminal law' (§ 796).

[22] Thus, in *Tadić (Opinion and Judgment)*, the Trial Chamber rightly excluded a principle whereby *unus testis nullus testis* (one witness is no witness), i.e. a principle requiring corroboration of evidence. It found that this principle was not even universally upheld in civil law systems (§§ 256, 535–9). In *Erdemović* (AC, 1997), Judges McDonald and Vohrah in their Joint Separate Opinion, as well as Judge Li in his Separate and Dissenting Opinion, held that there was no general principle on the question of whether duress can serve as a defence to the killing of innocent civilians (§§ 46–58 and 4, respectively). Judge Cassese, in his Dissenting Opinion, contended, on the basis of the international case law, that no *special* rule excluding duress as a defence in a case of *murder* had evolved in ICL and that, in the absence of such a special rule, the Tribunal had to apply the general rule, which was to recognize duress as a defence without specifying to which crimes it applied and to which crimes it did not. Consequently, and subject to the strict requirements enumerated in his dissent, duress could be admitted as a complete defence even to the crime of killing innocent persons: see §§ 11–49). Similarly, in *Tadić* (AC) the Appeals Chamber held that the criminal doctrine of acting in pursuance of a common purpose, although rooted in the national law of many states, did not amount to a general principle common to the major legal systems of the world (§§ 224–5). In *Kupreškić and others* (TC), the Trial Chamber looked for general principles common to the major systems of the world on the question of how a *double conviction* for a single action must be reflected in sentencing, and concluded that no such principles could be discerned (§§ 713–16). It reached the same negative conclusion in another area: the specific question of 'how a Trial Chamber should proceed when certain legal ingredients of a charge [made by the prosecutor] have not been proved but the evidence shows that, if the facts were differently characterised, an international crime under the jurisdiction of the Tribunal would nevertheless have been perpetrated' (§§ 728–38). The Court therefore held that, lacking a general principle common to the major legal systems of the world, it fell to it 'to endeavour to look for a general principle of law consonant with the fundamental features and the basic requirements of international criminal justice' (§ 738). It is also notable that in *Aleksovski* (AC), the Appeals Chamber pointed out that the principle of *stare decisis*, or binding precedent, tended to underpin the general trend of both common and civil law. However, the Chamber rightly held that in the event the issue was to be settled in light not of a general principle common to the systems of the world, but of international law (§ 98).

this effect the judgment of the ICTY Appeals Chamber in *Jelisić*, where the judges rightly relied upon the Vienna Convention to construe Rule 98 *bis* (B) (§ 35).

1.2.6 THE ROLE OF JUDICIAL DECISIONS AND THE OPINION OF SCHOLARS

As stated above, judicial decisions—even of the same court—do not constitute per se a source of ICL. Formally speaking they may only amount to a 'subsidiary means' for the determination of international rules of law (see Article 38(1)(d) of the ICJ Statute, which can be deemed to reflect customary international law). This is true also for the ICC, since Article 21(2) of the Statute provides the Court 'may apply principles and rules of law as interpreted in its previous decisions', therefore expressly rejecting the so-called doctrine of *stare decisis* (or binding precedent).

Nevertheless, given the characteristics of ICL one should set great store by national or international judicial decisions. They may prove of crucial importance, not only for ascertaining whether a rule of customary international law has evolved, but also as a means to establish the most appropriate interpretation to be placed on a treaty rule.

In *Aleksovski*, the ICTY Appeals Chamber held that it could depart from a previous decision by the same Chamber if it had cogent reasons for so doing (§§ 92–111). One may wonder whether the Chamber purported to establish a form of precedent at the Tribunal. The objection is possible that this would be trying to pull oneself up by one's own bootstraps: one cannot establish a doctrine of precedent *by precedent*, for it would be tautological. In any event, it could be contended that this decision was not really precedent. Besides, according to the traditional and strict doctrine of precedent, one court has to follow another court's decision, if the prior decision dealt with the same issue, whether or not it has cogent reasons for departing from it. It would therefore seem that the *Aleksovski* approach should be construed to the effect that one Appeals Chamber's decision may only be *persuasive authority* for a following one. However, a decision by an Appeals Chamber *in the very same case* (e.g. the Appeals Chamber directing a Trial Chamber to do *x* or *y*) is binding on the Trial Chamber. That, however, is not really a matter of precedent but rather of the hierarchy of power between the appellate and trial levels: the Appeals Chamber has the power to 'order' the Trial Chamber to act in a certain way as a matter of the division of labour between them and their respective powers.

Legal literature, although it carries less weight than case law, may significantly contribute to the elucidation of international rules.

1.3 THE NOTION OF INTERNATIONAL CRIMES

At the international level, the criminalization of individual conducts is a recent phenomenon that mainly occurred around the early 1990s.[23] Until that time, international law was principally instrumental in allowing states to better organize the joint repression of certain criminal offences, more specifically those that damaged their collective interests and had a strong transnational dimension. In other words, international law was merely a tool used by states to achieve stronger cooperation in judicial matters to oppose transnational criminality. During the first decades of the twentieth century, treaties for the repression of crimes such as counterfeiting, slavery, and the traffic in women and children began

---

[23] This section reproduces partially P. Gaeta, 'International Criminalization of Prohibited Conduct', in *Cassese's Companion*, 63.

to emerge and continued to be concluded throughout the century up until the present day, for example to fight 'terrorist' crimes, money laundering, corruption, and so on. All these treaties follow the same pattern: they contain an agreed definition of the prohibited conduct, oblige contracting states to criminalize that conduct within their legal systems (i.e. to adopt the necessary national criminal legislation to repress the conduct), provide for certain heads of criminal jurisdiction, and ensure the mutual extradition of alleged offenders.

One clear example of the instrumental role international law plays in repressing such crimes is piracy. Due to a well-established rule of customary international law, each state is authorized to seize and capture pirates on the high seas and bring them to trial, regardless of whether the pirates had attacked one of their ships. This age-old customary rule does not itself prohibit or criminalize piracy: it merely provides that acts of violence on the high seas amounting to piracy can be repressed by *any* state that has captured their perpetrators on the high seas. Here again, international law helps states to realize a more effective criminal repression of a crime which puts in jeopardy safety at high sea.

Interestingly, it is this approach that inspired states to tackle a different form of criminality, namely 'state criminality'; that is, crimes perpetrated by state officials in their official capacity or backed by the apparatus of the state, or within the context of widespread and collective violence (such as wars and armed conflicts in general). With the exception of the Nuremberg and Tokyo Tribunals, which were created to experiment with an innovative approach to the repression of these unique forms of criminality, states applied traditional methods. While debating the establishment of a permanent international criminal court, they drafted treaties or treaty provisions for the prosecution and punishment of crimes such as genocide, grave breaches of the 1949 Geneva Conventions, torture, apartheid; these treaties 'simply' enjoined contracting states: *i*) to criminalize those conducts within their own legal orders; and *ii*) to punish the responsible persons (or, in the case of grave breaches and torture, to extradite them to another contracting state). In other words, also with regard to crimes perpetrated within the context of state criminality or state violence, the international community reacted by resorting to the traditional institutional framework of specific treaties or treaty rules aimed at imposing on states a duty to criminalize the prohibited conducts, and organizing judicial cooperation for their repression.

Unfortunately, this traditional institutional framework was not well suited to the job at hand, and consequently was seldom employed by contracting states: some of them even failed to pass the necessary implementing criminal legislation; or, when they did possess all the necessary legal requirements for the exercise of their criminal jurisdiction, they simply failed to make use of it. For a long time the scheme under which it was up to national criminal jurisdictions to deal with forms of state criminality, committed either 'at home' or abroad, simply proved unworkable (and to some extent still it is today). This should come as no surprise. The method was originally conceived of to react to forms of 'private' transnational criminality that states, moved by selfish but shared interests, wanted to repress by enhancing their judicial cooperation. Things are radically different concerning crimes committed by state officials on behalf of, or with the support of, their state. Hence, when those crimes are committed abroad, a 'negative' comity of nations comes into play: it forces states not to interfere with the internal or external affairs of other states, although—faced with mass-scale crimes—international law allows (and in some cases even obliges) them to act. When crimes are committed 'at home', various reasons can stand in the way of prosecution: if the crimes are perpetrated under an authoritarian regime, prosecutors and judges have to wait for its toppling; however, when this occurs, amnesty laws are normally passed 'for the sake of' national reconciliation, or immunities or the statute of limitation are urged by the culprits, or other political and legal hurdles are relied upon.

The establishment of the ICTY and the ICTR by the UN Security Council opened a new era: for the first time in history truly international criminal tribunals were set up to prosecute and punish genocide, crimes against humanity, and war crimes, i.e. the so-called 'core-crimes'. Their creation paved the way to the establishment of the ICC (in 1998) and of a group of mixed criminal tribunals, some of them with a strong international component, as is the case with the SCSL. All these international or mixed criminal courts exercise their jurisdiction over individuals who may be indicted on account of criminal rules of *a truly international nature*. Those rules are provided for in their constitutive instruments: they describe the prohibited conducts and indicate what criteria must be applied for sentencing; in addition, they are normally supplemented by other international rules, chiefly customary rules, and by general principles of law common to national legal orders. These international and mixed criminal tribunals, in particular the ICTY and ICTR, have spawned a copious case law, thus contributing to the emergence of new international customary rules supplementing those which already existed. Finally, and more importantly, their functioning, although not flawless, has contributed to disseminating the idea that there are criminal conducts that may not go unpunished, and that individuals responsible for them must be brought to justice. Therefore it can be submitted that there now exists a branch of international law comprising a truly *international* criminal law for the repression and punishment of international crimes proper.

International crimes proper therefore result from the cumulative presence of the following elements. First, they consist of violations of rules of customary international law as well as treaty provisions (but if such provisions do not codify or spell out customary law, only with respect to conduct carried out in the territory or by the nationals of contracting parties). Second, such rules are intended to protect values of the whole international community as such and consequently bind all states and individuals. The values at issue are not propounded by scholars or thought up by starry-eyed philosophers. Rather, they are laid down in a string of international instruments, which, however, do not necessarily spell them out in so many words.[24] Third, there exists a universal interest in repressing these crimes. Subject to certain conditions, under international law their alleged authors may in principle be prosecuted and punished *by any state*, regardless of any territorial or nationality link with the perpetrator or the victim, at the moment of the commission of the crime (see Chapter 15). Finally, if the perpetrator has acted in an official capacity, i.e. as a *de jure* or *de facto* state official, the state on whose behalf he has performed the prohibited act is *barred* from claiming the immunity from the civil or criminal jurisdiction of foreign states accruing under customary international law to state officials acting in the exercise of their functions (although, if the state official belongs to one of these categories, namely head of state of government, foreign minister, or diplomatic agent, and is still

---

[24] They include the 1945 UN Charter, the 1948 Universal Declaration of Human Rights, the 1950 European Convention on Human Rights, the two 1966 UN Covenants on Human Rights, the 1969 American Convention on Human Rights, the UN Declaration on Friendly Relations of 1970, and the 1981 African Charter on Human and Peoples' Rights. Other treaties also enshrine those values, although from another perspective: they do not proclaim the values directly, but prohibit conduct that infringes them: for instance, the 1948 Convention on Genocide, the 1949 Conventions on the protection of victims of armed conflict, and the two Additional Protocols of 1977, the 1984 Convention against Torture, and the various treaties providing for the prosecution and repression of specific forms of terrorism.

serving, then he enjoys complete *personal* immunity as long as he or she is in office: see *Pinochet*,[25] *Fidel Castro* (Legal Grounds 1–4), and the *Congo* v. *Belgium* case, §§ 57–61; on immunities, see 13.2 and 17.4).

Under this definition international crimes include war crimes, crimes against humanity, genocide, torture (as distinct from torture as one of the categories of war crimes or crimes against humanity), aggression, and international terrorism. By contrast, and for the reasons explained above, the notion at issue does not embrace other classes of criminal offences, such as piracy, or other illegal conduct such illicit traffic in narcotic drugs and psychotropic substances; unlawful arms trade; the smuggling of nuclear and other potentially deadly materials; money laundering; slave trade; traffic in persons, or exploitation of prostitution.

It is the category of international crimes proper mentioned above that this book considers.

---

[25] *Pinochet* (UK), speeches of Lord Browne-Wilkinson (at 112–15), Lord Hope of Craighead (at 145–52), Lord Saville of Newdigate (at 169–70), Lord Millet (171–91), and of Lord Phillips of Worth Matravers (at 181–90).

2

THE PRINCIPLE OF LEGALITY

To grasp fully the significance of the principle of legality (which is usually described by using the Latin maxim *nullum crimen nulla poena sine lege*), a few words of introduction are necessary.

National legal systems tend to embrace, and ground their criminal law on either the doctrine of *substantive justice* or that of *strict legality*. Under the former doctrine the legal order must primarily aim at prohibiting and punishing any conduct that is socially harmful or causes danger to society, whether or not that conduct has already been legally criminalized at the moment it is taken. The paramount interest is defending society against any deviant behaviour likely to cause damage or jeopardize the social and legal system. Hence this doctrine favours society over the individual (*favor societatis*). Extreme and reprehensible applications of this doctrine can be found in the Soviet legal system (1918– 58) or in the Nazi criminal law (1933–45). However, one can also find some variations of this doctrine in modern democratic Germany, where the principles of 'objective justice' (*materielle Gerechtigkeit*) have been upheld as a reaction to oppressive governments trampling upon fundamental human rights, and courts have had recourse to the celebrated 'Radbruch's formula'. Radbruch, the distinguished German professor of jurisprudence, created this 'formula' in 1946. In terms subsequently taken up in some German cases,[1] he propounded the notion that positive law must be regarded as contrary to justice and not applied where the inconsistency between statute law and justice is so intolerable that the former must give way to the latter. This 'formula' has been widely accepted in the legal literature.[2]

In contrast, the doctrine of strict legality postulates that a person may only be held criminally liable and punished if at the moment when he performed a certain act this act was regarded as a criminal offence under the applicable law. Historically, this doctrine stems from the opposition of the baronial and knightly class to the arbitrary power of monarchs, and found expression in Article 39 of *Magna Charta libertatum* of 1215

---

[1] The German Federal Constitutional Court referred to that 'formula' in its judgment of 24 October 1996 in *Streletz and Kessler*. The question at issue was whether the accused, former senior officials of the former German Democratic Republic (GDR) charged with incitement to commit intentional homicide for their responsibility in ordering the shooting and killing by border guards of persons trying to flee from the GDR, could invoke as a ground of justification the fact that their actions were legal under the law applicable in the GDR at the material time, which did not make them liable to criminal prosecution. The defendants submitted that holding them criminally liable would run contrary to the ban on the retroactive application of criminal law and Art. 103(2) of the German Constitution laying down the *nullum crimen* principle. The Court dismissed the defendants' submissions. Among other things, it noted that the prohibition on retroactive law derived its justification from the special trust reposed in criminal statutes enacted by a democratic legislature respecting fundamental rights.

[2] Of course, the notion propounded by Radbruch could simply be termed the Natural Justice view that an unjust law is no law and must be disregarded. As such, it might be susceptible to the criticism of positivists that it makes the law subjective, since the sense of justice varies from person to person.

(so-called 'Magna Carta').[3] One must, however, wait for the principal thinkers of the Enlightenment to find its proper philosophical and political underpinning. Montesquieu and then the great American proclamations of 1774 and of the French revolution (1789) conceived of the doctrine as a way of restraining the power of the rulers and safeguarding the prerogatives of the legislature and the judiciary. As the distinguished German criminal lawyer Franz von Liszt wrote in 1893, the *nullum crimen sine lege* and *nulla poena sine lege* principles 'are the bulwark of the citizen against the state's omnipotence; they protect the individual against the ruthless power of the majority, against the Leviathan. However paradoxical it may sound, the Criminal Code is the criminal's *magna charta*. It guarantees his right to be punished only in accordance with the requirements set out by the law and only within the limits laid down in the law.'[4]

2.1 THE PRINCIPLE OF LEGALITY IN CIVIL LAW AND IN COMMON LAW COUNTRIES

At present, most democratic civil law countries tend to uphold the doctrine of strict legality as an overarching principle. In these countries the doctrine is normally held to articulate four basic notions.

First, criminal offences may only be provided for in written law, namely legislation enacted by Parliament, and not in customary rules (less certain and definite than statutes) or in secondary legislation (which emanates from the government and not from the parliamentary body expressing popular will); this principle is referred to by the maxim *nullum crimen sine lege scripta* (criminal offences must be provided for in written legislation).

Second, criminal legislation must abide by the principle of specificity, whereby rules criminalizing human conduct must be as specific and clear as possible, so as to guide the behaviour of citizens; this is expressed by the Latin tag *nullum crimen sine lege stricta* (criminal offences must be provided for through specific legislation).

Third, criminal rules may not be retroactive; that is, a person may only be punished for behaviour that was considered criminal at the time the conduct was undertaken; therefore he may not be punished on the strength of a law passed subsequently. The maxim referred to in this case is *nullum crimen sine proevia lege* (criminal offences must be provided for in a prior law).[5]

---

[3] 'It is only through the legal judgment by his peers and on the strength of the law of the land that a freeman may be apprehended or imprisoned or disseized or outlawed or exiled or in any other manner destroyed, nor may we go upon him or send upon him.'

[4] F. von Liszt, 'Die deterministischen Gegner der Zweckstrafe', 13 *Zeitschrift für die gesamte Strafrechtswissenschaft* (1893), 325–70, at 357 (an English translation of some excerpts from this paper has been published in 5 JICJ (2007), 1009–13). The Latin tag *nullum crimen* had been coined by another German criminal lawyer, P. J. A. Feuerbach, *Lehrbuch des gemeinen in Deutschland gültigen peinlichen Rechts*, 11th edn (Geissen: Heyer, 1832), at 12–19 (English trans. in 5 JICJ (2007), at 1005–8).

[5] The German Federal Constitutional Court set out the principle in admirable terms in its aforementioned decision of 24 October 1996 in *Streletz and Kessler*. In illustrating the scope of Art. 103(2) of the German Constitution, laying down the principle at issue, it stated the following: '(1.a) Article 103 § 2 of the Basic Law protects against retroactive modification of the assessment of the wrongfulness of an act to the offender's detriment [...] Accordingly, it also requires that a statutory ground of justification which could be relied on at the time when an act was committed should continue to be applied even where, by the time criminal proceedings begin, it has been abolished. However, where justifications are concerned, in contrast to the definition of offences and penalties, the strict reservation of Parliament's law-making prerogative does not apply. In the sphere of the criminal law grounds of justification may also be derived from customary law or case-law.'

Fourth, resort to analogy in applying criminal rules is prohibited (analogy would allow to punish, at the whim of courts, conduct similar or approximate to that already prohibited, thereby unduly extending the scope of existing criminal provisions).

Plainly, as stated above, the purpose of these principles is to safeguard citizens as far as possible against both the arbitrary power of government and possibly excessive judicial discretion. In short, the basic underpinning of the doctrine of strict legality lies in the postulate of *favor rei* (in favour of the accused) (as opposed to *favor societatis*, or in favour of society).

However, in common law countries, where judge-made law prevails, or is at least firmly embedded in the legal system, there is a tendency to adopt a qualified approach to these principles. For one thing, common law offences (as opposed to statutory offences) result from judge-made law and therefore may lack those requirements of rigidity and certainty proper to written legislation. For another, common law offences are not strictly subject to the principle of non-retroactivity, as is shown by recent English cases contemplating new offences, or at any rate the removal of traditional defences (see, for instance, *R. v. R.* (1992), where a court held that the fact of marriage was no longer a common law defence to a husband's rape of his wife).[6] It is notable that the European Court of Human Rights did not regard such cases as questionable or at any rate contrary, to the fundamental provisions of the European Convention (see *S. W. and C. R. v. United Kingdom*, 1995).

2.2 THE PRINCIPLE OF LEGALITY IN ICL

As seen above, the principle of legality in criminal law is not uniformly applied in common law and civil law countries. Let us now see which of the two aforementioned doctrines is applied in ICL.

One could note that ICL, being also based on customary processes, is more akin to English law than to French, German, Argentinean, or Chinese law. However, this would not be sufficient. The main problem is that for a long period, and until recently, the doctrine of *substantive justice* was prevailing in ICL; it is only in recent years that it has been gradually replaced with the doctrine of *strict legality*, albeit with some important qualifications.

2.2.1 THE INITIAL ADOPTION OF THE DOCTRINE OF SUBSTANTIVE JUSTICE

That in ICL the former doctrine has long been applied is not to be attributed to a totalitarian or authoritarian streak in the international society. Rather, the rationale for that attitude was that states were not prepared to enter into treaties laying down criminal rules, nor had customary international rules evolved covering this area. In practice, there only existed customary international rules prohibiting and punishing war crimes, although in a rather rudimentary or unsophisticated manner (see 1.1.2). Hence the need for the international community to

---

[6] It would seem that the English law used to be that a man could not rape his wife because, by agreeing to marry, she had implicitly consented to sexual intercourse for all time. This was obviously a somewhat medieval approach. The defence existed only as a matter of common law—it was not in any statute. The judge in *R. v. R.* rightly held that societal attitudes had changed and that it was no longer acceptable to hold that a husband could in law never be held guilty of raping his wife; hence he did not allow the old common law defence. In fairness, it was not the introduction of a *new offence*—rape had always been an offence. It was a question of disallowing a (retrograde) common law defence.

rely upon substantive justice when new and extremely serious forms of criminality (crimes against peace, crimes against humanity) suddenly appeared on the international scene.

The Nuremberg Tribunal clearly enunciated this doctrine in *Göring and others*. From the outset the Tribunal had to face the powerful objections of German defence counsel that the Tribunal was not allowed to apply *ex post facto* law (the objections were raised in relation to crime against peace, concerning the planning and waging of a war of aggression). These objections were grounded in the principle of legality in criminal law embedded in civil law countries, and also upheld in German law before and after the Nazi period. The French Judge H. Donnedieu de Vabres, coming from a country where the principle of strict legality is deeply ingrained, also showed himself to be extremely sensitive to the objections grounded upon alleged violations of the principle. As a consequence, when dealing with the crimes against peace of which the defendants stood accused, the Tribunal followed a reasoning which is worth careful consideration.

First of all, the Tribunal considered that it was bound by its Statute (the Charter, annexed to the London Agreement of 8 August 1945). It found that this Statute was not 'an arbitrary exercise of power by the victorious nations' but that it was 'the expression of international law existing at the time of its creation; and to that extent [was] itself a contribution to international law'. Consequently the Tribunal considered that, since the Charter made 'the planning or waging of a war of aggression or a war in violation of international treaties a crime', it was not 'strictly necessary to consider whether and to what extent aggressive war was a crime before the execution of the London Agreement [containing the Charter of the Tribunal]'.

This stand, which gives priority to the Charter of the Tribunal over pre-existing international law, would have sufficed to reject the objections raised by the defendants. Nonetheless, because of 'the great importance of the questions of law involved', the Tribunal decided 'to express its view' on the matter. After examining international practice, it found that crimes against peace were in fact already prohibited at the time when they were perpetrated (at 219–23). This finding seems highly questionable, since it was grounded more in elements of international practice relating to the war of aggression as entailing international state responsibility than in elements demonstrating that it was a crime giving rise to individual liability. In addition, however, the Tribunal noted that in any case it was not contrary to justice to punish those crimes even if the relevant conduct was not criminalized at the time of their commission. As the Tribunal put it:

> In the first place, it is to be observed that the maxim *nullum crimen sine lege* is not a limitation of sovereignty, but is in general a principle of justice. To assert that it is unjust to punish those who in defiance of treaties and assurances have attacked neighbouring states without warning is obviously untrue, for in such circumstances the attacker must know that he is doing wrong, and so far from it being unjust to punish him, *it would be unjust if his wrong were allowed to go unpunished*. (219; emphasis added)

In other words, the Tribunal considered that substantive justice punishes acts that harm society deeply and are regarded as abhorrent by all members of society, even if these acts were not prohibited as criminal when they were performed.

Interestingly, in his Dissenting Opinion in the Tokyo trial (*Araki and others*), Judge B. V. A. Röling spelled out the same principle, again with regard to crimes against peace. He noted that in national legal systems the *nullum crimen* principle 'is not a principle of justice but a rule of policy'; this rule was

> valid only if expressly adopted, so as to protect citizens against arbitrariness of courts [. . .] as well as arbitrariness of legislators [. . .] the prohibition of *ex post facto* law is an

expression of political wisdom, not necessarily applicable in present international relations. This maxim of liberty may, if circumstances necessitate it, be disregarded even by powers victorious in a war fought for freedom. (1059)

Judge Röling then delineated two classes of criminal offence:

Crime in international law is applied to concepts with different meanings. Apart from those indicated above [war crimes], it can also indicate acts comparable to political crimes in domestic law, where the decisive element is the danger rather than the guilt, where the criminal is considered an enemy rather than a villain and where the punishment emphasizes the political measure rather than the judicial retribution. (1060)

Judge Röling applied these concepts to crimes against peace and concluded that such crimes were to be punished because of the dangerous character of the individuals who committed them, hence on security considerations. In his view, however, given the novel nature of these crimes, it followed that persons found guilty of them could not be punished by a death sentence (at 1060).

The doctrine of substantive justice was upheld in a number of other cases, among which one may cite *Peleus*,[7] *Burgholz (No. 2)*,[8] and later on *Eichmann* (Supreme Court of Israel, at 281).[9]

2.2.2 THE SHIFT TOWARDS THE DOCTRINE OF STRICT LEGALITY

After the Second World War, the doctrine of substantive justice was gradually replaced by that of strict legality. Two factors brought about this change.

First, states agreed upon and ratified a number of important human rights treaties which laid down the *nullum crimen* principle as legal standard for national courts.[10] The same principle was also set out in such important treaties as the Third and Fourth Geneva Conventions of 1949, respectively, on Prisoners of War and on Civilians.[11] The expansive force and striking influence of these treaties could not but impact on international criminal proceedings, leading to the acceptance of the notion that also in such proceedings the

---

[7] In *Peleus*, the prosecutor, in his closing speech, maintained that maxim of *nullum crimen sine lege, nulla poena sine lege*, was 'only applicable to municipal and state law, and could never be applicable to International Law'. In his summing up the Judge Advocate stated: 'You have heard a suggestion made that this Court has no right to adjudicate upon this case because it is said you cannot create an offence by a law which operates retrospectively so as to expose someone to punishment for acts which at the time he did them were not punishable as crimes. That is the substance of the Latin maxim [*nullum crimen sine lege, nulla poena sine lege*] that has been used so much in this Court. My advice to you is that the maxim and the principle [of legality] that it expresses has nothing whatever to do with this case. It has reference only to municipal or domestic law of a particular State, and you need not be embarrassed by it in your consideration of the problems that you have to deal with here' (at 12). It should be noted that the defendants had been accused of killing survivors of a sunken merchant vessel, the Greek steamship *Peleus*; they had raised the pleas of 'operational necessity' and superior orders. For a comment on the case, see *Cassese's Companion*, at 872.

[8] After noting that the Allies had set up tribunals in Germany and Japan 'with the object of bringing to justice certain persons who have outraged the basic principles of decency and humanity', the British Judge Advocate pointed out: 'It may well be that no particular concrete law can be pointed to as having been broken, and you remember what Defence Counsel Dr. Meyer-Labastille said yesterday on the principle of "no punishment without pre-existing law". That principle I agree with but to this extent, that I do not regard it as limiting punishment of persons who have outraged human decency in their conduct' (at 79).

[9] For a comment on the *Eichmann* case, see *Cassese's Companion*, at 653.

[10] See e.g. Art. 15 of the UN Covenant on Civil and Political Rights, Art. 7 of the European Convention on Human Rights, or Art. 9 of the American Convention on Human Rights.

[11] See Art. 99(1) of the Third Convention and Art. 67 of the Fourth Convention. See also Art. 75(4)(c) of the First Additional Protocol of 1977.

nullum crimen principle must be respected as a fundamental part of a set of basic human rights of individuals. In other words, the principle came to be seen from the viewpoint of the human rights of the accused, and no longer as essentially encapsulating policy guidelines dictating the penal strategy of states at the international level.

The second factor is that gradually the network of ICL expanded both through a number of treaties criminalizing conduct of individuals (for instance, the 1948 Convention on Genocide, the 1949 Geneva Conventions, the 1984 Convention on Torture, and the various treaties on terrorism) and by dint of the accumulation of case law. In particular, case law contributed to either the crystallization of customary international rules of criminal law (for instance, on the mental element of crimes against humanity) or to clarifying or specifying elements of crimes, defences, and other important segments of ICL. As a consequence, the principle of strict legality was laid down, albeit implicitly, in the Statutes of the ICTY and ICTR,[12] which referred to it in their case law.[13]

The principle of legality seems to be set forth explicitly in the ICC Statute, Article 22(1) of which provides that 'A person shall not be criminally responsible under this Statute unless the conduct in question constitutes, at the time it takes place, a crime within the jurisdiction of the Court.' However, the reference in this provision is to the rules of the ICC Statute itself and not to general international criminal law. In the ICC Statute's list of crimes, there might be conduct that was not criminalized by general international criminal law either at the moment of the entry into force of the Statute or subsequently, at the moment when the conduct took place. This means that, when the Court exercises its jurisdiction over acts committed by nationals or in the territory of non-member states (such as in the case of a Security Council referral, see 20.1.1), the question of the respect for the principle of legality could arise. The same is true in cases when a non-member state decides to accept retrospectively the jurisdiction of the Court by an ad hoc declaration, in accordance with Article 12(3). In such cases, charges might be brought before the Court against individuals who were not in a position to know that their conduct was criminal at the time it was carried out, since the Statute was not in force in the territory where the conduct was performed or with respect to their state of nationality. It remains to be seen what stand the Court will take if facing such an issue.

Be that as it may, the conclusion seems to be warranted that nowadays the principle of legality must be complied with also at the international level, albeit subject to a number of significant qualifications, which we shall presently consider.

2.3 ARTICULATIONS OF THE PRINCIPLE OF LEGALITY

2.3.1 SPECIFICITY

Under this corollary of the principle of strict legality criminal rules must be as detailed as possible, so as to clearly indicate to their addressees the conduct prohibited, namely,

---

[12] See, for instance, Arts 1–8 of the ICTY Statute, as well as § 29 of the UN Secretary-General's Report to the Security Council for the establishment of the Tribunal (S/25704) ('It should be pointed out that, in assigning to the International Tribunal the task of prosecuting persons responsible for serious violations of international humanitarian law, the Security Council would not be creating or purporting to "legislate" that law. Rather, the International Tribunal would have the task of applying existing international humanitarian law.')

[13] On this principle see, among other decisions by the ICTY *Tadić* (*Interlocutory Appeal*), AC, § 92; *Delalić and others*, TC, §§ 402–7; *Jelisić*, TC, § 61; *Hadzihasanović and others* (*Interlocutory Appeal Challenging Jurisdiction in Relation to Command Responsibility*), AC, §§ 32–6.

both the objective elements of the crime and the requisite mens rea. Specificity is aimed at ensuring that all those who may fall under the prohibitions of the law know in advance which specific behaviour is allowed or proscribed. They may thus foresee the consequences of their action and freely choose either to comply with, or instead breach, legal standards of behaviour. Clearly, the more accurate and specific a criminal rule, the greater is the protection accorded to the agent from arbitrary action of either enforcement officials or courts of law.

The requirement of specificity of criminal rules is still far from being fully applicable in ICL, which still includes many rules that are loose in their scope and purport. In this regard, suffice it to mention, as an extreme and conspicuous instance, the provision first enshrined in the London Charter of 1945 establishing the Nuremberg Tribunal and then restated in many international instruments (Control Council Law no. 10, the Statutes of the Tokyo Tribunal, the ICTY, the ICTR, and the SCSL), whereby crimes against humanity encompass 'other inhumane acts'.[14] Similarly, the provisions of the four 1949 Geneva Conventions on grave breaches among other things enumerate, as 'grave breaches', 'inhuman treatment'. In addition, many rules contain notions that are not clearly defined, such as 'rape', 'torture', 'persecution', 'enslavement', etc. Furthermore, most international rules proscribing conduct as criminal do not specify the subjective element of the crime. Nor are customary rules on defences crystal clear: they do not indicate the relevant excuses or justifications in unquestionable terms.

Given this indeterminacy and the consequent legal uncertainty for the possible address-ees of international criminal rules, the contribution of courts to giving precision to law, not infrequent even in civil law systems, and quite normal in common law countries, becomes of crucial importance at the international level, as has already been pointed out above. Both national and international criminal courts play an immensely important role in gradually clarifying notions, or spelling out the objective and subjective ingredients of crimes, or better outlining such general legal concepts as excuses, justifications, etc. (see 1.1.4).

Thus, for instance, the District Court of Tel Aviv, in *Tarnek* spelled out, by way of construction, the notion of 'other inhumane acts' in a manner that seems acceptable (at 540, and § 7).[15] Similarly, in defining the concept of 'rape' the ICTY Trial Chamber in

---

[14] The ICC Statute fleshes the notion out, by providing that crimes against humanity may include 'other inhumane acts of a similar character [to the other, specifically enumerated, classes of such crimes] intentionally causing great suffering, or serious injury to body or to mental or physical health' (Art. 7(1)(k)).

[15] For a comment on the case, see *Cassese's Companion*, at 950. The Court stated that: 'The defence counsel argue, secondly, that the words "other inhumane acts" which appear in the definition of "crimes against humanity" should be interpreted subject to the principle of *ejusdem generis*. That is, that an "other inhumane act" should be of the type of the specific action mentioned before it, in the same definition, which are "murder, extermination, enslavement, starvation and deportation" [...] We believe that there is truth in the defence counsel's second claim. The punishment determined in Article 1 of the [Israeli] Law [of 1950 on the Doing of Justice to Nazis and their Collaborators] for "crimes against humanity" is death (subject to extenuating circumstances pursuant to Article 11(b) of the Law), and it can be assumed that the legislator intended to inflict the most extreme punishment known to the penal code only for those inhumane actions which resemble in their type and severity "murder, extermination, enslavement, starvation and deportation of a civilian population". If we measure by this yardstick the actions proven against the defendant [beating with bare hands other detainees and making detainees kneel, in the Concentration camp of Auschwitz-Birkenau, where the defendant herself was an inmate, with the role of custodian of Block 7] we shall find that even if some of these actions could be considered inhumane from known aspects, they do not, under the circumstances, reach the severity of the actions which the legislator intended to include in the definition of "crimes against humanity" in Article 1 of the Law' (§ 7).

Furundžija had recourse to general principles of ICL as well as general principles common to the major legal systems of the world, and general principles of law.[16]

One should not underestimate, however, another drawback of ICL: the lack of a central criminal court endowed with the authority to clarify for the whole international society the numerous hazy or unclear criminal rules. To put it differently: the contribution of courts to the gradual specification and precision of legal rules, emphasized above, suffers from the major shortcoming that such judicial refinement is 'decentralized' and fragmentary. In addition, when such process is effected by national criminal courts, it suffers from the another flaw: each court tends to apply the general notions proper to the legal system within which such court operates. Hence, the possibility frequently arises of a contradictory or 'cacophonic' interpretation or application of international criminal rules.

Fortunately, the draftsmen of the ICC Statute made a significant contribution when they endeavoured to define as precisely as possible the various categories of crimes. (However, as the Statute is not intended to codify customary international law, one ought always to take it with a pinch of salt, for in some cases it may go beyond current law, whereas in other instances it is narrower in scope than rules of customary international law. Furthermore, formally speaking that Statute is only binding on the ICC.)

For the time being, international criminal rules still make up a body of law in need of legal precision and some major refinement at the level of definitions and general principles. To take account of these features and at the same time safeguard the right of the accused, currently some notions play a role that is far greater than in most national systems: the defence of mistake of fact (see 12.2.2), the principle of strict interpretation (barring extensive or broad constructions of criminal rules; see 2.3.3), the principle of *favor rei* (imposing that in case of doubt a rule should be interpreted in such a manner as to favour the accused; see 2.3.4). These notions act as countervailing factors aimed at compensating for the present flaws and lacunae of ICL.

2.3.2 NON-RETROACTIVITY

A. General

Another logical and necessary corollary of the doctrine of strict legality is that criminal rules may not cover acts performed prior to their enactment, unless such rules are more favourable to the accused. Otherwise the executive power, the judiciary, or even the legislature could arbitrarily punish persons for actions that were allowed when they were carried out.

In contrast, the ineluctable corollary of the doctrine of substantive justice is that, for the purpose of defending society against new and unexpected forms of criminality, one may go so far as to prosecute and punish conduct that was legal when taken. These two approaches lead to contrary conclusions. The question is: which approach has been adopted in ICL?

---

[16] It is worth citing the relevant passage, for that Trial Chamber proved alert to the principle of specificity. It stated the following: 'This Trial Chamber notes that no elements [for defining rape] other than those emphasised may be drawn from international treaty or customary law, nor is resort to general principles of international criminal law or to general principles of international law of any avail. The Trial Chamber therefore considers that, to arrive at an accurate definition of rape based on the criminal law principle of specificity (*Bestimmtheitgrundsatz*, also referred to by the maxim "*nullum crimen sine lege stricta*"), it is necessary to look for principles of criminal law common to the major legal systems of the world. These principles may be derived, with all due caution, from national laws' (*Furundžija*, TC, § 177). For a comment on the case, see *Cassese's Companion*, at 683.

It seems indisputable that the London Agreement of 1945 establishing the Nuremberg Tribunal provided for two categories of crime that were new: crimes against peace and crimes against humanity. The Nuremberg Tribunal did act upon the Charter provisions dealing with both categories. In so doing, it applied *ex post facto* law; in other words, it applied international law retroactively, as the defence counsel at Nuremberg rightly stressed (at least with regard to crimes against peace; see 2.2.1).[17]

Many tribunals sitting in judgment over Germans in the aftermath of the Second World War,[18] as well as the German Supreme Court in the British Occupied Zone,[19] endorsed the legal approach taken by the Nuremberg Tribunal, for all its deficiencies. This stand, while having scant persuasive force with regard to the past, nonetheless contributed to the slow consolidation of the principle of non-retroactivity in ICL.

Subsequently, as a logical consequence of the emergence of the *nullum crimen sine lege* principle a general rule prohibiting the retroactive application of criminal law gradually evolved in international society. Thus, the principle of non-retroactivity of criminal rules is *now* solidly embedded in ICL. It follows that courts may only apply substantive criminal rules that existed at the time of commission of the alleged crime. This, of course, does not entail that courts are barred from refining and elaborating upon, by way of legal construction, *existing* rules. The ICTY Appeals Chamber clearly set out this notion in *Aleksovski*.[20]

B. Expansive adaptation of some legal ingredients of crimes laid down in international rules to new social conditions

One should duly take account of the nature of ICL, to a large extent made up of customary rules that are often identified, clarified or spelled out, or given legal determinacy by courts. In short, that body of law to a large extent consists of judge-made law (with no doctrine of precedent). Consequently, one should reconcile the principle of non-retroactivity with these inherent characteristics of ICL. In this respect some important rulings of the European Court of Human Rights may prove of great assistance. In particular, in the already mentioned decision in *C. R.* v. *United Kingdom*[21] the Court held that the European

---

[17] See the Motion adopted by all defence counsel on 19 November 1945, in *Trial of the Major War Criminals*, vol. I, at 168–9.

[18] See in particular the *Justice* case (at 974–85), *Einsatzgruppen* (at 458–9), *Flick and others* (at 1189), *Krauch and others* (*I. G. Farben* case) (at 1097–8, 1125), *Krupp* (at 1331), *High Command* (at 487), *Hostages* (at 1238–42). For a comment on all these cases, see the relevant entries of *Cassese's Companion*.

[19] See the *Bl.* Case, at 5; for a comment, see *Cassese's Companion*, at 607; the *B. and A.* case, at 297; the *H.* case, at 232–3; for a comment, *Cassese's Companion*, at 708; the *N.* case (at 335), and *Angeklagter H.* (at 135).

[20] After commenting on the significance and legal purport of the *nullum crimen* principle, the Appeals Chamber added that this principle 'does not prevent a court, either at the national or international level, from determining an issue through a process of interpretation and clarification as to the elements of a particular crime; nor does it prevent a court from relying on previous decisions which reflect an interpretation as to the meaning to be ascribed to particular ingredients of a crime' (*Aleksovski*, AC, § 127). For a comment on the case, see *Cassese's Companion*, at 580.

[21] In 1989 a British national went back to see his estranged wife, who had been living for some time with her parents, and attempted to have sexual intercourse with her against her will; he also assaulted her, squeezing her neck with both hands. He was charged with attempted rape and assault occasioning actual bodily harm, and convicted. Before the European Court he repeated the claim already advanced before British courts, that at the time when the facts occurred, marital rape was not prohibited in the UK. Indeed, at that time a British Statute only prohibited as rape sexual intercourse with a woman who did not consent to it if such intercourse was 'unlawful' (see section 1(1) of the Sexual Offences (Amendment) Act 1976); hence the question turned on determining whether forced marital intercourse was 'unlawful'. Various English courts had ruled, until 1990, that a husband could not be convicted of raping his wife, for the status of marriage involved that the woman had given her consent to her husband having intercourse with her during the

Convention could not be read 'as outlawing the gradual clarification of the rules of criminal liability through judicial interpretation from case to case, provided that the resulting development is consistent with the essence of the offence and could reasonably be foreseen' (§ 34).[22] In a subsequent case, *Cantoni* v. *France*, the Court insisted on the notion that, in order for criminal law (that is, a statutory provision or a judge-made rule) to be in keeping with the *nullum crimen* principle, it is necessary for the law to meet the requirements of accessibility and foreseeability. It added two important points. First, a criminal rule may be couched in vague terms. When this happens, there may exist 'grey areas at the fringe of the definition':

> This penumbra of doubt in relation to borderline facts does not in itself make a provision incompatible with Article 7 [of the European Convention on Human Rights, laying down the *nullum crimen* principle], provided that it proves to be sufficiently clear in the large majority of cases. The role of adjudication vested in the courts is precisely to dissipate such interpretational doubts as remain, taking into account the changes in everyday practice. (§ 33)

The second point related to the notion of foreseeability. The Court noted that the scope of this notion

> depends to a considerable degree on the content of the text in issue, the field it is designed to cover, and the number and status of those to whom it is addressed [. . .] A law may still satisfy the requirement of foreseeability even if the person concerned has to take appropriate legal advice to assess, to a degree that is reasonable in the circumstances, the consequences which a given action may entail [. . .] This is particularly true in relation to persons carrying on a professional activity, who are used to having to proceed with a high degree of caution when pursuing their occupation. They can on this account be expected to take special care in assessing the risk that such activity entails. (§ 35)[23]

It would seem that the following legal propositions could be inferred from the Court's reasoning. First, while interpretation and clarification of existing rules is always admissible, adaptation is only compatible with legal principles subject to stringent requirements. Second, such requirements are that the evolutive adaptation, by courts of law, of criminal prohibitions, namely the extension of such legal ingredients of an offence as actus reus, in order to cover conduct previously not clearly considered as criminal must: *i*) be in keeping with the criminal rules relating to the subject matter, more specifically with the rules defining 'the essence of the offence'; *ii*) conform with, and indeed implement fundamental principles of ICL or at least general principles of law; and *iii*) be reasonably

---

subsistence of the marriage and could not unilaterally withdraw such consent. In contrast, Scottish courts had first held that that view did not apply where the parties to a marriage were no longer cohabiting, and then ruled, in 1989, that the wife's *implied* consent was a legal fiction, the real question being whether as a matter of fact the wife consented to the acts complained of. The word 'unlawful' in the Act referred to above was deleted in 1994 by the Criminal Justice and Public Order Act. This being the legal situation in the UK, before the European Court the applicant argued that the British courts had gone beyond a reasonable interpretation of the existing law and indeed extended the definition of rape in such a way as to include facts that until then had not constituted a criminal offence.

Both the European Commission and the European Court held instead that the British courts had not breached Article 7(1) of the European Convention on Human Rights ('No one shall be held guilty of any criminal offence on account of any act or omission which did not constitute a criminal offence under national or international law at the time when it was committed').

[22] See also *S. W.* v. *United Kingdom*, §§ 37–47.

[23] In the case at issue the applicant was the owner of a supermarket, convicted of unlawfully selling pharmaceutical products in breach of the Public Health Code. In his application he had contended that the definition of medicinal product contained in the relevant provision of that Code was very imprecise and left a wide discretion to the courts.

foreseeable by the addressees. In other words the extension, although formally speaking it may turn out to be detrimental of the accused, could have been reasonably anticipated by him, as consonant with general principles of criminal law.[24]

To put it differently, courts *may not create* a new criminal offence, with new legal ingredients (a new actus reus or a new mens rea). They *can only adapt* provisions envisaging criminal offences to changing social conditions (for instance, by broadening the actus reus or, possibly, lowering the threshold of the subjective element, i.e. from intent to recklessness, or from recklessness to culpable negligence) as long as this adjustment is consonant with, or even required by, general principles.

This process, particularly if it proves to be disadvantageous to the accused (which is normally the case) must presuppose the existence of a broad criminal prohibition (for instance, the proscription of rape) and no clear-cut and explicit enumeration, in law, of the acts embraced by this definition. It is in the penumbra left by law around this definition that the adaptation may be carried out. Admittedly, the frontier between such adaptation process and the analogical process, which is instead banned (see below), is rather thin and porous. It falls to courts to proceed with great caution and determine on a case-by-case basis whether the 'adaptation' under discussion is legally warranted and consonant with general principles, and in addition does not unduly prejudice the rights of the accused.

An instance of this process of 'adaptation' of existing law can be seen in the judgment delivered by the ICTY in *Tadić* (*Interlocutory Appeal*), where the Appeals Chamber unanimously held that some customary rules of international law criminalized certain categories of conduct in non-international armed conflict (see §§ 94–137).[25] It is well known that until that decision many commentators, states as well as the ICRC, had held the view that violations of the humanitarian law of internal armed conflict did not amount to war crimes proper, for such crimes could only be perpetrated within the context of an international armed conflict. The ICTY Appeals Chamber authoritatively held that the contrary was true and clearly identified a set of international customary rules prohibiting as criminal certain classes of conduct. Since then this view has been generally accepted.

Similarly, contrary to the submission made by defence counsel in *Hadzihasanović and others*,[26] an 'adaptation' of existing rules (corroborated by a logical construction) warrants the contention that persons may be held accountable under the notion of command responsibility even in non-international armed conflicts. Two arguments support this proposition. First, generally speaking the notion is widely accepted in international humanitarian law that each army or military unit engaging in fighting either in an

---

[24] The notions of foreseeability and accessibility were taken up by the ICTY Appeals Chamber in *Hadzihasanović and others* (*Interlocutory Appeal Challenging Jurisdiction in Relation to Command Responsibility*), AC, at § 34.

[25] Before pointing to practice and *opinio juris* supporting the view that some customary rules had evolved in the international community criminalizing conduct in internal armed conflict, the Appeals Chamber emphasized the rationale behind this evolution, as follows: 'A State-sovereignty-oriented approach has been gradually supplanted by a human-being-oriented approach. Gradually the maxim of Roman law *hominum causa omne jus constitutum est* (all law is created for the benefit of human beings) has gained a firm foothold in the international community as well. It follows that in the area of armed conflict the distinction between interstate wars and civil wars is losing its value as far as human beings are concerned. Why protect civilians from belligerent violence, or ban rape, torture or the wanton destruction of hospitals, churches, museums or private property, as well as proscribe weapons causing unnecessary suffering when two sovereign States are engaged in war, and yet refrain from enacting the same bans or providing the same protection when armed violence has erupted "only" within the territory of a sovereign State? If international law, while of course safeguarding the legitimate interests of States, must gradually turn to the protection of human beings, it is only natural that the aforementioned dichotomy should gradually lose its weight' (§ 97).

[26] See ICTY, *Hadzihasanović, Alagić and Kubura* (*Joint Challenge to Jurisdiction*), TC, §§ 15–39.

international or in an non-international armed conflict must have a commander charged with holding discipline, ensuring compliance with the law, and executing the orders from above (with the consequence that whenever the commander culpably fails to ensure such compliance, he may be called to account). The notion at issue is crucial to the existence and enforcement of the whole body of IHL, because without a chain of command and a person in control of each military unit, anarchy and chaos would ensue and no one could ensure compliance with law and order. Second, and with specific regard to the Statute of the ICTY, Article 7(3) of this Statute is couched in sweeping terms and clearly refers to the commission by subordinates of any crime falling under the jurisdiction of the Tribunal: any time such a crime has been perpetrated involving the responsibility of a superior, this superior may be held accountable for criminal omission (of course, if he is proved to have the requisite mens rea: see 10.2.2). If this is so, it is sufficient to show that crimes perpetrated in non-international armed conflicts fall under the Tribunal's jurisdiction, as held by the ICTY Appeals Chamber in 1995 in *Tadić* (*Interlocutory Appeal*), for inferring that as a consequence the Tribunal has jurisdiction over a commander who failed to prevent or punish such crimes.[27]

2.3.3 THE BAN ON ANALOGY AND ON EXTENSIVE INTERPRETATION

The principle of strict legality usually implies that national criminal courts (particularly in civil law countries) do not extend the scope and purport of a criminal rule to a matter that is unregulated by law (*analogia legis*). The same principle applies in ICL and is prohibited with regard to both treaty and customary rules. Such rules (for instance, norms proscribing certain specific crimes against humanity) may not be applied by analogy to classes of acts that are unregulated by law. Article 22(2) of the ICC Statute thus codifies existing customary law where it provides that 'The definition of a crime shall be strictly construed and shall not be extended by analogy. In case of ambiguity, the definition shall be interpreted in favour of the persons being investigated, prosecuted or convicted.'

In addition, as this provision makes clear, a prohibition closely bound up with that of analogy is the ban on broad or extensive interpretation of international criminal rules, and the consequent duty for states, courts, and other relevant officials and individuals to resort to strict interpretation. This principle entails that one is not allowed to broaden surreptitiously, by way of interpretation, the scope of criminal rules, so as to make them applicable to instances not specifically envisaged by those rules.

An example of strict construction can be found in some post-Second World War cases relating to the notion of crimes against humanity. In *Altstötter and others* a US Military Tribunal sitting at Nuremberg held that that notion, as laid down in Control Council Law no. 10,

> must be strictly construed to exclude isolated cases of atrocity or persecution whether committed by private individuals or by governmental authorities. As we construe it, that section [of the aforementioned Law] provides for the punishment of crimes committed against German nationals only where there is proof of conscious participation in systematic governmentally organized or approved procedures, amounting to atrocities and offences of that kind specified in the act and committed against populations or amounting to persecution on political, racial or religious grounds. (284–5)

---

[27] The notions set out in the text are to a large extent coincident with the rulings in *Hadzihasanović and others* made in 2001 by the ICTY TC (*Joint Challenge to Jurisdiction*), TC, at §§ 150–79, and later, in 2003, by the Appeals Chamber (*Interlocutory Appeal Challenging Jurisdiction in Relation to Command Responsibility*), at §§ 10–36.

The finding was cited with approval in *Flick and others*, handed down by another US Military Tribunal sitting at Nuremberg (at 1216), where the Tribunal also held that under a strict interpretation of the same notion, crimes against humanity do not encompass offences against property, but only those against persons (at 1215).[28]

Three qualifications must, however, be set out restricting the ban on analogy. First, ICL only prohibits the so-called *analogia legis* (that is, the extension of a rule so as to cover a matter that is formally unregulated by law). It does not bar the regulation of a matter not covered by a specific provision or rule, by resorting to general principles of ICL, or to general principles of criminal justice, or to principles common to the major legal systems of the world (so-called *analogia juris*). National and international criminal courts have repeatedly affirmed that it is permissible to rely upon such principles for establishing whether an international rule covers a specific matter in dispute. To be sure, the question has always been framed as one of interpretation, rather than analogical application. Nevertheless, whatever the terminology employed, the fact remains that gaps or lacunae have been filled by resort to those principles. It should, however, be clear that drawing upon general principles should never be used to criminalize conduct that was previously not prohibited by a criminal rule. It may only serve to spell out and clarify, or give a clear legal contour to, prohibitions that have already been laid down in either customary law or treaties. In other words, this approach may only be resorted to for the interpretation of existing rules, not for the creation of new classes of criminal conduct. To hold the contrary would mean to admit serious departures from the *nullum crimen* principle, contrary to the whole thrust of current ICL.

Second, in quite a few cases international rules themselves invite or request analogy, through the *ejusdem generis* canon of statutory construction (whereby when in a legal rule a general clause follows the enumeration of a particular class of persons or things, the general clause must be construed as applying to persons or things of the same kind or class as those enumerated). For instance, the customary and treaty rules prohibiting and penalizing as crimes against humanity 'other inhumane acts', as well as the provisions of the 1949 Geneva Conventions criminalizing as 'grave breaches' of the Convention 'inhuman acts' in addition to torture, impose upon the interpreter the need to look at acts and conduct similar in gravity to those prohibited. This indeed was the reasoning of the Tel Aviv District Court in *Tarnek* (see n. 15). The draftsmen of the ICC Statute took the same approach when they criminalized in Article 7(1)(k) 'other inhumane acts *of a similar character* intentionally causing great suffering, or serious injury to body or to mental or physical health' (emphasis added).

Thirdly, in some cases ICL allows a logical approach that at first glance runs foul of the ban on analogy, but is in fact permissible because it applies to general principles. An example will clarify this proposition. In the case of a new weapon that does not fall under any specific prohibition precisely because of its novel features, analogical extension of an existing treaty ban is not allowed, as pointed out above. Nevertheless, one is authorized to enquire whether the new weapon is at variance with the general principle proscribing weapons that are inherently indiscriminate or cause unnecessary suffering. For this purpose, one may justifiably look at those weapons that have been prohibited by treaty because they are either indiscriminate or cause superfluous sufferings. The object of this enquiry will not be the application of these treaty prohibitions by analogy, but rather

---

[28] Subsequently the Dutch Special Court of Cassation took up in *Ahlbrecht*, at 397–8 (for a comment on the case see *Cassese's Companion*, at 576); and in *Bellmer*, at 543 (for a comment see *Cassese's Companion*, at 603), as well as in *Haase*, at 432 (for a comment, *Cassese's Companion*, at 709), the same strict interpretation advanced in *Altstötter and others* (the so-called *Justice Trial*).

to better ascertain whether the characteristics of the new weapon are such as to make them contrary to the general principle. It would seem that the District Court of Tokyo in *Shimoda and others* took precisely this approach (although it had been requested to pronounce on a question of civil liability, not of criminal law).[29]

2.3.4 THE PRINCIPLE *FAVOR REI* (FAVOURING THE ACCUSED)

Another principle is closely intertwined with the ban on analogy, and is designed to invigorate it. This is the principle imposing, when faced with conflicting interpretations of a rule, the construction that favours the accused (*favor rei*): see also ICC Statute, Article 22(2). The ICTR *Akayesu* Trial Chamber upheld this principle with regard to the interpretation of the word 'killing' in the Genocide Convention and the Statute of the ICTR.[30] An ICTY Trial Chamber reaffirmed the principle in *Krstić*. The question was how to interpret the notion of 'extermination' as a crime against humanity. The Chamber pointed out that the ICC Statute provides that extermination may embrace acts 'calculated to bring about the destruction of *part* of the population', namely only a limited number of victims; it stressed that under customary international law extermination generally involves a large number of victims. It went on to hold as follows:

> this definition [that is, that contained in the ICC Statute] was adopted after the time the offences in this case were committed. In accordance with the principle that where there is a plausible difference of interpretation or application, the position which most favours the accused should be adopted, the Chamber determines that, for the purpose of this case, the definition should be read as meaning the destruction of a numerically significant part of the population concerned. (§ 502)

It should be noted that the principle of construction in favour of the accused has also been conceived of as a standard governing the appraisal of evidence: in this case the principle is known as *in dubio pro reo* (in case of doubt, one should hold for the accused). For instance, in *Flick and others*, a US Military Tribunal sitting at Nuremberg held that it must be guided among other things by the standard whereby 'If from credible evidence

---

[29] For a comment on the case, see *Cassese's Companion*, at 919. After noting that the use of an atomic bomb was 'believed to be contrary to the principle of international law prohibiting means of injuring the enemy which cause unnecessary suffering or superfluous injury are inhuman', the District Court of Tokyo noted that the bomb was a new weapon. It then pointed out that the employment of asphyxiating, poisonous, and other gases and bacteriological methods of warfare was prohibited, noting that it could 'safely be concluded that besides poisons, poisonous gases and bacteria, the use of means of injuring the enemy which cause injury at least as great as or greater than these prohibited materials is prohibited by international law'. The Court concluded that 'it is not too much to say that the sufferings brought about by the atomic bomb are greater than those caused by poisons and poisonous gases; indeed the act of dropping this bomb may be regarded as contrary to the fundamental principle of the law of war which prohibits the causing of unnecessary suffering' (at 1694–5).

[30] With regard to the word '*meurtre*' (in French) and 'killing' in English, contained in the phrase 'killing members of the group' (as a category of genocide), the Trial Chamber noted the following: 'The Trial Chamber is of the opinion that the term "killing" used in the English version is too general, since it could very well include both intentional and unintentional homicides, whereas the term "*meurtre*", used in the French version, is more precise. It is accepted that there is murder when death has been caused with the intention to do so, as provided for, incidentally, in the Penal Code of Rwanda, which stipulates in its Article 311 that "Homicide committed with intent to cause death shall be treated as murder". Given the presumption of innocence of the accused, and pursuant to the general principles of criminal law, the Chamber holds that the version more favourable to the accused should be upheld and finds that Article 2(2)(a) of the Statute must be interpreted in accordance with the definition of murder given in the Penal Code of Rwanda, according to which "*meurtre*" (killing) is homicide committed with the intent to cause death' (§§ 500–1).

two reasonable inferences may be drawn, one of guilt and the other of innocence, the latter must be taken' (at 1189).[31] The notion was also upheld in *Stakić*.[32]

2.4 THE PRINCIPLE OF LEGALITY OF PENALTIES

It is common knowledge that in many states, particularly in those of Romano-Germanic tradition, it is considered necessary to lay down in law a tariff relating to sentences for each crime, so as: *i*) to ensure the uniform application of criminal law by all courts of the state; and *ii*) to make the addressees cognizant of the possible punishment that may be meted out if they transgress a particular criminal provision.

This principle is not applicable at the international level, where these tariffs do not exist. Indeed, states have not yet agreed upon a scale of penalties, due to widely differing views about the gravity of the various crimes, the seriousness of guilt for each criminal offence, and the consequent harshness of punishment. It follows that courts enjoy much greater judicial discretion in punishing persons found guilty of international crimes. However, some Statutes of international criminal courts set forth limitations on the absolute discretion of judges. Thus, for instance, Article 24(1) of the ICTY Statute provides, first, that penalties will be limited to imprisonment (thus ruling out the death sentence), and, second, that 'In determining the terms of imprisonment, the Trial Chambers shall have recourse to the general practice regarding prison sentences in the courts of the former Yugoslavia.' This last provision was applied in various cases,[33] although it was generally not held mandatory. Article 23 of the ICTR Statute is identical, but it refers, of course, to the general practice regarding prison sentences in the courts of Rwanda.

As for the Statute of the ICC, Article 23 provides that 'A person convicted by the Court may be punished only in accordance with this Statute' and Article 77 confines itself to envisaging imprisonment for a maximum of 30 years, while at the same time admitting life imprisonment 'when justified by the extreme gravity of the crime and the individual circumstances of the convicted person'. It thus implicitly rules out the death penalty, but does not establish a scale of sentences, nor does it suggest that the Court should take into account the scale of penalties of the relevant territorial or national state. The Court is thus left with a very broad margin of appreciation.

---

[31] Another US Military Tribunal sitting at Nuremberg upheld the principle in *Krauch and others* (*I. G. Farben* case) (at 1108). For a comment on the case, see *Cassese's Companion*, at 771.

[32] 'The TC explicitly distances itself from the Defence submission that the principle *in dubio pro reo* should apply as a principle for the interpretation of the substantive criminal law of the Statute. As this principle is applicable to findings of fact and not of law, the TC has not taken it into account in its interpretation of the law' (TC, § 416).

[33] See e.g. in *Tadić* (*Sentencing Judgment 1997*), §§ 7–10, *Tadić* (*Sentencing Judgment 1999*), §§ 10–13; *Delalić and others*, TC, §§ 1193–212); and *Kupreškić and others*, TC, §§ 839–47.

3

THE ELEMENTS OF INTERNATIONAL CRIMES, IN PARTICULAR THE MENTAL ELEMENT

Two main features characterize international crimes proper (see 1.3).[1] First, they consist of conduct undertaken or acts performed by either *i*) state officials (for instance, servicemen engaged in war, or political leaders planning or ordering genocide, etc.); or *ii*) private individuals. What is notable is that this conduct is either connected to an international or non-international armed conflict or, absent of such a conflict, has a political or ideological dimension, or is somehow linked with (instigated, influenced, tolerated, or acquiesced in) the behaviour of state authorities or organized non-state groups or entities. Thus, it is characteristic of such crimes that, when perpetrated by private individuals, they are somehow connected with a state policy or at any rate with 'system criminality'[2] or with a context of armed violence (as in the case of an armed conflict). On this score international crimes are thus different from criminal offences committed for personal purposes (private gain, satisfaction of personal greed, desire for revenge, etc.), as is the case with ordinary criminal offences such as theft, robbery, assault, kidnapping for extorting a ransom, etc., or such other crimes that have a transnational dimension but pursue private goals, such as piracy, slave trade, trade in women or children, counterfeiting currency, drug dealing, etc. The fundamental hallmark of international crimes is also called 'the international element' of such crimes.

The second notable feature of these crimes, inextricably intertwined with the one I have just emphasized, is that they normally possess a twofold dimension or are *double-layered*. They constitute criminal offences in domestic legal systems: serious bodily harm, murder, rape, sexual assault, torture, etc., in that they infringe municipal rules of criminal law. In addition, they have an international dimension, in that they breach values recognized as universal in the world society and enshrined in international customary rules and treaties. It follows that normally these crimes consist of an 'underlying offence' (for example, murder or torture) with the requisite objective and subjective elements of such offence, plus an additional objective and/or mental element required by the international rules that

---

[1] See more extensively on this matter P. Gaeta, 'International Criminalization of Prohibited Conduct', in *Cassese's Companion*, at 63.

[2] The notion of system criminality as opposed to individual criminality was set out by the great Dutch scholar and judge B. V. A. Röling, 'The Law of War and the National Jurisdiction Since 1945', 100 *Hague Recueil*, 1960-II, 335; see also 'The Significance of the Laws of War', in A. Cassese (ed.), *Current Problems of International Law* (Milano: Giuffré, 1975), 137–9.

contemplate the crime at issue. For instance, we will see that murder as a crime against humanity requires: *i*) the objective element of murder (causing the death of another person) as well as a mental element (intent to bring about by one's action the death of another person); plus *ii*) a broader objective context (the existence of a widespread or systematic attack on the civilian population, whether in time of armed conflict or in time of peace) and an additional mental element, namely the awareness of the existence of such broader context.

These features relate to the vast majority of cases. There are, however, also crimes that do not possess this double dimension, in that they do not encompass an underlying criminal offence. For instance, the use of prohibited weapons in time of war or the indiscriminate attack of civilians in an internal armed conflict is per se an international crime (i.e. a war crime), without necessarily having a 'domestic' underpinning (see 4.3.2). It follows that what is required for the crime to be perpetrated is an illegal conduct defined in international rules (for example, using a weapon that is proscribed by international law) as well as a mental element (the intent to use the weapon). The same holds true for a sub-category of crimes against humanity, namely persecution (see 5.4.2).

3.1 THE OBJECTIVE STRUCTURE

As is normally the case in domestic legal systems with all criminal offences, international crimes can also be split into *i*) conduct; *ii*) consequences; and *iii*) circumstances, from the point of view of their objective structure.[3]

The *conduct* is described by the international rule that criminalizes a certain behaviour (for instance, the prohibition of torture of a protected person in an international armed conflict as a war crime, or prohibition of murder as a crime against humanity, and so on and so forth).

Consequences are the effects caused by one's conduct. Between conduct and consequences there is, of course, a causation nexus: for instance, I fire a missile at a hospital and thus bring about the destruction of the building and the death of dozens of civilians and wounded persons. Consequences of a crime are the effects of criminal conduct. From this point of view crimes may be held to belong to two different categories: crimes of conduct and crimes of result. The former category comprises offences consisting in the breach of an international rule that imposes a specific behaviour; there, it is irrelevant whether or not this breach brings about any harm or injury to prospective victims. (Think, for instance, of the rule that obliges belligerents to refrain from declaring that no quarter will be given—that is, that in combat operations enemies will not be captured but will be killed, even if they surrender; the same holds true for the rule prohibiting the use of a certain means of warfare, for instance dum dum bullets or chemical or bacteriological weapons; the use of these weapons constitutes a breach of IHL and a war crime, even if in a specific case no damage to the adversary is in fact caused by such use.) Crimes of result embrace instead violations of rules that confine themselves to imposing the achievement of a certain end, regardless of the modalities for the realization of that end; for instance, causing disproportionate casualties among civilians when attacking a military objective, or starving prisoners of war.

---

[3] See A. Eser, 'Mental Element—Mistake of Fact and Mistake of Law', in Cassese, Gaeta, and Jones, *ICC Commentary*, vol. I, 911–20.

Most international criminal rules concern crimes of result, i.e. they focus on the harm caused by human behaviour and proscribe conduct that is such as to bring about such harm: for instance, they criminalize the killing of civilians, the wounding of prisoners of war, the rape of women. The rationale behind this emphasis is that the primary goal of international criminal law is to prevent and punish behaviour that injures protected persons. On this score 'consequences' are particularly relevant with regard to this category of international crimes.

Circumstances are 'any objective or subjective facts, qualities or motives with regard to the subject of the crime (such as the perpetrator and any accomplices), the object of the crime (such as the victim or other impaired interests) or any other modalities of the crime (such as means or time and place of commission)'.[4] Thus, for instance, in the rule imposing on military commanders and, more generally, on superior authorities to prevent and repress crimes by their subordinates, one of the circumstances of the crime is that a person is a military commander or a civilian superior. Similarly, in the rule banning as a crime against humanity the 'forcible transfer of population', the use of force in bringing about the movement of a multitude of civilians from one place to another is a 'circumstance' required by the rule.

3.2 THE MENTAL ELEMENT

In any legal system, including in ICL, criminal liability arises when the person carries out the prohibited conduct with a given *state of mind*; that is, a psychological element required by the legal order for the conduct to be blameworthy and consequently punishable (also called culpable frame of mind or mens rea).

It is not easy to identify the various forms and shades of the mental element in ICL. Two problems arise.

First, substantive rules concerning crimes often do not specify the subjective element required for each specific offence. An exception may be found in the various substantive provisions of the ICC Statute: Articles 6 (on genocide), 7 (on crimes against humanity), and 8 (on war crimes), and the accompanying 'Elements of Crime' elaborated pursuant to Article 9. Most of the time these provisions set out the subjective element required for each class of crime. However, in this respect the provisions of the Statute are, as I have already pointed out, hedged about with two major limitations. They are only designed to set out the categories of crime over which the ICC may exercise jurisdiction; in other words they are not couched as provisions of a 'criminal code' proper. Furthermore, they are not intended to codify, or restate, or contribute to the development of customary international law. Their legal value is therefore limited (although, of course, they may gradually have a bearing on, and bring about a change in, existing law).

Second, there is no customary rule setting out a general definition of the various categories of mens rea (such as intent, recklessness, or negligence). In this respect the only exception is Article 30 of the ICC Statute, on 'mental element'. However, it is doubtful that it reflects customary international law. In addition, as we shall see, even at the level of treaty law, it is not certain that it encompasses all the various possible subjective elements of international crimes.

This difficult condition is compounded by the failure of national case law to cast light on the matter. It is state courts that have handed down the bulk of judicial decisions dealing

---

[4] Eser, cit. n. 3, at 919.

with this matter, and each court has applied the general rules of criminal law proper to its own domestic system. Depending on the legal tradition to which it belonged, each court has placed its own interpretation on the notion of intent, fault, or negligence.

Consequently, to tackle the first of the two problems outlined above (the frequent failure of international criminal rules to themselves point to the subjective elements of the crime), one should first identify those international substantive provisions which lay down, if only implicitly, the subjective element required for their violation to amount to an international crime. One ought also to draw upon the case law of international criminal tribunals, to the extent that they have pronounced on the matter. To come to grips with the second problem, one must start from the assumption that here, as in other fields of ICL, what matters is to identify the possible existence of general rules of international law or, in the absence of such rules, principles common to the major legal systems of the world. To pinpoint such rules, one may chiefly rely on: *i*) the case law of courts, with special attention being paid to the judicial decisions of international criminal courts, in particular the ICTY and the ICTR (these decisions have in fact proved to be of crucial importance in the gradual elaboration of the various mental elements of each category of international crime); and *ii*) the existence of some basic notions common to all major legal systems of the world, as evidence of a convergence of these systems and confirmation that parallel principles have also taken shape at the international level.

I shall briefly mention some instances of how the first of the two problems is sometimes solved. I shall then concentrate on the second problem (the general definitions of the various categories of subjective element that one may deduce from a perusal of international rules and the relevant case law).

3.2.1 SUBSTANTIVE RULES SETTING OUT THE MENTAL ELEMENT REQUIRED FOR CRIMES

With regard to such substantive rules, one may recall, as major illustrations, a set of important treaty provisions. The first is Article II of the 1948 Genocide Convention (now turned into a rule of customary international law), whereby genocide as an international crime requires that there be 'the intent to destroy, in whole or in part, a national, ethnical, racial or religious group, as such'.

Similarly, Article 1 of the 1984 Convention on Torture prohibits torture when it is, among other things, 'intentionally inflicted'. By the same token, various paragraphs of Article 8 of the ICC Statute, relating to war crimes, require intentionality ('intentionally directing attacks' against the civilian population or civilian objects: Article 8(2)(b), iv). Also, Article 7(1)(k) classifies as crimes against humanity 'other inhumane acts' of a character similar to that of the crimes against humanity the same provision enumerates before, if they 'intentionally' cause great suffering or serious injury to body or to mental or physical health. Plainly, all these provisions require intentional conduct, thereby automatically excluding any other subjective frame of mind such as recklessness, negligence, etc.

Furthermore, Article 85(3) and (4) of the First Additional Protocol of 1977 makes punishable a host of violations of the Protocol so long as they are committed 'wilfully'. Under the interpretation of this adverb authoritatively suggested in the ICRC Commentary, the word 'wilful' implies that

> the accused must have acted consciously and with intent, i.e. with his mind on the act and its consequences, and willing them ('criminal intent' or 'malice aforethought'); [this] encompasses the concepts of 'wrongful intent' or 'recklessness', viz., the attitude of an agent who, without being certain of a particular result, accepts the possibility of it happening. (§ 3474, at 995)

In other words, under this interpretation those violations of the Protocol may entail the criminal liability of the perpetrator if they are committed either intentionally or with recklessness: on this notion, see 3.5).

3.2.2 GENERAL NOTIONS OF MENS REA COMMON TO MOST DOMESTIC LEGAL SYSTEMS

By way of introduction, it may prove fitting to undertake a brief comparative survey of the attitude taken towards the definition of the major facets of mens rea by the major legal systems of the world. It is apparent that, in spite of broad differences in terminology, most legal systems tend to take the same basic approach to the specific regulation of each aspect of mens rea and its implications. They tend to require one of the following frames of mind, for conduct to be considered criminally punishable (these are listed in decreasing order of culpability).

First, intention, namely awareness that a certain conduct will bring about a certain result in the ordinary course of events, and will to attain that objective: for example, I use a gun to shoot at a person because I want to cause his death and anticipate that as a consequence of my shooting he will die. This class of mens rea is normally called *intent* (*dol direct, Vorsatz, dolus directus*).[5]

Second, awareness that undertaking a course of conduct carries with it an unreasonable or unjustifiable risk of producing harmful consequences, and the decision nevertheless to go on to take that risk. For instance, I perceive the risk that using a certain weapon may entail killing dozens or even hundreds of innocent civilians, and nevertheless willingly ignore this risk. This class is normally called *recklessness* (*dolus eventualis*).[6]

---

[5] For instance Section 15 of the 1998 German Criminal Code provides: 'Only intentional conduct is punishable, unless the law expressly provides punishment for negligent conduct.' Art. 40 of the Norwegian Criminal Code (of 1902, as amended up to 2005) provides: 'The penal provisions of this code are not applicable to any person who has acted unintentionally unless it is expressly provided or unambiguously implied that a negligent act is also punishable.' Under Art. 12(2) of the Swiss Criminal Code: 'Agit intentionnellement quiconque commet un crime ou un délit avec conscience et volonté. L'auteur agit déjà intentionnellement lorsqu'il tient pour possible la réalisation de l'infraction et l'accepte au cas où celle-ci se produirait.'

[6] Under Art. 2(2)(c) of the US Model Penal Code, 'A person acts recklessly with respect to a material element of an offense when he *consciously disregards a substantial and unjustifiable risk* that the material element exists or will result from his conduct. The risk must be of such a nature and degree that, considering the nature and purpose of the actor's conduct and the circumstances known to him, its disregard involves a gross deviation from the standard of conduct that a law-abiding person would observe in the actor's situation' (emphasis added). Art. 43 of the Norwegian Criminal Code provides: 'When the law provides for an increased penalty in cases in which a criminal act entails some unforeseen consequence, such penalty shall only be applicable when the perpetrator could have foreseen the possibility of such a consequence, or if he has failed to prevent it to the best of his ability after he has become aware of the risk.'

Under Art. 121-3 (3) of the French Criminal Code: 'A misdemeanour also exists, where the law so provides, in cases of recklessness, negligence, or failure to observe an obligation of due care or precaution imposed by any statute or regulation, where it is established that the offender has failed to show normal diligence, taking into consideration where appropriate the nature of his role or functions, of his capacities and powers and of the means then available to him.'

In the case as referred to in the above paragraph, natural persons who have not directly contributed to causing the damage, but who have created or contributed to create the situation which allowed the damage to happen who failed to take steps enabling it to be avoided, are criminally liable where it is shown that they have broken a duty of care or precaution laid down by statute or regulation in a manifestly deliberate manner, or have committed a specified piece of misconduct which exposed another person to a particularly serious risk of which they must have been aware.

Under Art. 189 of the Criminal Code of Lebanon (1983), 'L'infraction est réputée intentionnelle encore bien que l'effet délictueux de l'action ou de l'omission ait dépassée l'intention de l'auteur si celui-ci en avait prévue l'éventualité et accepté le risque.'

Third, failure to pay sufficient attention to or to comply with certain generally accepted standards of conduct thereby causing harm to another person when the actor believes that the harmful consequences of his action will not come about, thanks to the measures he has taken or is about to take. For instance, an attendant at a mental hospital causes the death of a patient by releasing a flow of boiling water into the bath; one of two persons playing with a loaded gun points it at the other and pulls the trigger believing that it will not fire because neither bullet is opposite the barrel; however, as the gun is a revolver, it does fire, killing the other person.[7] This class is normally referred to as *advertent* or *culpable negligence* (*négligence consciente, bewusste Fahrlässigkeit*) where the agent's conduct seriously or blatantly fails to meet the standards of the reasonable man test.[8]

Fourth, failure to respect generally accepted standards of conduct without, however, being aware of or anticipating the risk that such failure may bring about harmful effects. To prevent road accidents, some countries envisage this state of mind for drivers who act negligently (for instance, cause the death of a pedestrian by not stopping at the stop sign, or by driving at excessive speed or in a state of intoxication). This class is normally termed *inadvertent negligence* (*négligence inconsciente, unbewusste Fahrlässigkeit*).

These are, of course, only general trends of national criminal law. The courts of some states often do not draw such a fine distinction between the aforementioned shades on the scale of criminal culpability.[9] Similarly, national laws or military

---

A similar regulation can be found in Art. 25 of the 1996 Russian Criminal Code stipulating: '1. An act committed with express intent or extreme recklessness shall be recognized as a crime committed intentionally. 2. An act shall be deemed to be committed with clear intent, if the person was conscious of the social danger of his action or inaction, foresaw the possibility of the inevitability of the onset of dangerous social consequences, and willed such consequences to ensue. 3. A crime shall be deemed to be committed with indirect intent, if the person realized the social danger of his actions (inaction), foresaw the possibility of the onset of socially dangerous consequences, did not wish, but consciously allowed these consequences or treated them with indifference.'

On *dolus eventualis*, see in particular G. Fletcher, *Rethinking Criminal Law*, 1978 reprint (Oxford: Oxford University Press, 2000), 445–9.

[7] See A. Ashworth, *Principles* at 191–5. See also A. P. Simester and G. R. Sullivan, *Criminal Law—Theory and Doctrine* (Oxford: Hart, 2002), 139–40. According to D. L. Hart ('Negligence, Mens Rea and Criminal Responsibility', in *Punishment and Responsibility*, Oxford: Oxford University Press, 1968, at 149), 'Negligence is gross if the precautions to be taken against harm are very simple, such as persons who are but poorly endowed with physical and mental capacities can easily take.' Simester and Sullivan (at 140) provide a telling example: 'It may be negligent to drive around a particular bend at 50 mph; if so, it is grossly negligent to do so at 80 mph. It will also be gross negligence if the risk created by the defendant is very obvious.'

[8] Under Art. 2(2)(d) of the US Model Penal Code, 'A person acts negligently with respect to a material element of an offense when *he should be aware of a substantial and unjustifiable risk* that the material element exists or will result from his conduct. The risk must be of such a nature and degree that the actor's failure to perceive it, considering the nature and purpose of his conduct and the circumstances known to him, involves a gross deviation from the standard of care that a reasonable person would observe in the actor's situation' (emphasis added).

Pursuant to Art. 26 of the 1996 Russian Criminal Code: '1. A criminal deed committed thoughtlessly or due to negligence shall be recognized as a crime committed by negligence. 2. A crime shall be deemed to be committed thoughtlessly, if the person has foreseen the possibility of the onset of socially dangerous consequences of his actions or inaction, but expected without valid reasons that these consequences would be prevented. 3. A crime shall be deemed to be committed due to negligence if the person has not foreseen the possibility of the onset of socially dangerous consequences of his actions or inaction, although he could and should have reasonably foreseen these consequences.'

[9] For instance, in 1975 in *Robert Strong* the Court of Appeals of New York held that, from the point of view of the mental state of the defendant at the time the crime was committed, the essential distinction between the crime of 'manslaughter in the second degree' (that is, recklessly causing the death of a person, or intentionally causing or aiding a person to commit suicide, or committing upon a female an abortion

manuals may set out notions that do not necessarily fit in the above enumeration of forms of mens rea.[10]

Depending on the category of crime and the degree of responsibility, rules of customary international law (resulting from *opinio juris seu necessitatis*, i.e. the conviction that a certain behaviour is necessary or is dictated by a legal rule, and international practice, as evidenced by case law, treaty provisions if any, the views of state officials, and the convergence of the major legal systems of the world) envisage various modalities of mental element. As mentioned above, the ICC Statute includes a provision, Article 30, that specifically deals with this matter (see 3.8). However, this provision has a limited purport, for it only applies to the crimes falling under ICC jurisdiction and in addition does not necessarily reflect or codify a rule of customary international law. It therefore may not apply to other international criminal courts or tribunals, which are bound either by their own Statute or, if such Statutes do not regulate the matter (which is indeed the case), by customary international law.

3.3 INTENT

As mentioned above, by intent or intention (*dolus directus*) is meant: *i*) awareness that by engaging in a certain action or by omitting to act I shall bring about a certain result (such as, for example, the death of a civilian); coupled with *ii*) the will to cause such result. For instance: I want to kill a civilian. So I shoot him and he dies as a result of my act. I must therefore answer for this crime. Or else, I think he is dead but in fact he has not died; he only dies later of exposure because he is left in the cold. It does not matter that my conduct did not kill him—I am guilty of murder because I intended him to die (mens rea); and he died as a result of my acts (because he would never have been lying exposed were it not for my acts). As a rule, my intent only has to be linked to a certain result (the death of the victim).

International rules require intent for most international crimes, although, as we shall see, under certain circumstances other states of mind are admissible.

As an illustration of intent, *Enigster* may be mentioned. The accused, a Jewish internee in a Nazi concentration camp having the rank of *Schieber* or group leader, had been charged with crimes against humanity, in particular, grievous injuries, against his fellow inmates. In examining the alleged grievous attack on another inmate, named Schweizer,

---

causing her death), and 'criminally negligent homicide' (that is, causing the death of a person with criminal negligence) is that in the former class of crime 'the actor perceives the risk but consciously disregards it', whereas in the latter the actor 'negligently fails to perceive the risk'. In the case at issue the accused, a leader of a Muslim sect with a sizeable following, purportedly exercising his powers of 'mind over matter' used to perform ceremonies such as walking though fire, performing surgical operations without anesthesia, or stopping a follower's heartbeat and breathing while he plunged knives into his chest without any injury to the person. Although he had performed this last-mentioned ceremony countless times without once causing an injury, in the case brought before the Court the follower had died as a result of the wounds. The jury found that the defendant was guilty of manslaughter in the second degree, as charged, without considering whether he could have been guilty of the lesser crime of criminally negligent homicide. The Court of Appeals held that in this case the jury could have found that the defendant 'failed to perceive the risk inherent in his actions […] The defendant's conduct and claimed lack of perception, together with the belief of the victims and the defendant's followers, if accepted by the jury, would justify a verdict of criminally negligent homicide' rather than manslaughter in the second degree (568–9).

[10] Thus, for example, according to the Australian Defence Force Discipline Manual, 'A person can be said to have acted *recklessly* when he is aware that certain harmful consequences are likely to flow from a particular act but he performs the act despite the risk. A person acts *negligently* when he performs an act without consideration of the probably harmful consequences which will flow from it but where those harmful consequences would be foreseeable by a reasonable man' (§ 533).

the District Court of Tel Aviv had to establish whether all the necessary elements were present; it therefore asked itself, among other things, whether the requisite intent also existed. It noted that in this respect no special testimony had been brought to the Court; it nonetheless had to determine whether the accused had that intent. The Court noted the following:

> As to 'intent', it is a well known rule that any person in his right mind is held to intend the natural consequences of his actions. As it appears from the severe results of the blows struck by the defendant, the blows were landed with some significant force, and for this reason, and barring any proof that the defendant landed the blows other than from his own free will, it must be concluded of his mind, that he intended to cause Schweizer grievous damage.[11]

Premeditation, which is normally not required for international criminal responsibility, occurs when the intent to engage in unlawful conduct is formed before the conduct is actually embarked upon. As the Turin Military Tribunal pointed out in *Sävecke* in 1999 (at 14) and repeated in *Engel* in 2000 (at 13), premeditation necessarily requires two elements: one of a temporal nature, namely that some time must pass between the formation of the criminal intent and its being carried out; the other of a psychological nature, namely that the criminal intent must persist from the moment of its formation until the perpetration of the crime.[12]

In some instances premeditation may coincide with, or overlap, *planning* the criminal action. However, while planning has an autonomous scope and legal significance, premeditation has not. In ICL premeditation can only be material to sentencing, for it may amount to an aggravating circumstance.[13]

3.4 SPECIAL INTENT (*DOLUS SPECIALIS*)

International rules may require a special intent (*dolus specialis*) for particular classes of crime. Such rules, in addition to providing for the intent to bring about a certain result by undertaking certain conduct (for example, death by killing), may also require that the agent pursue a *specific* goal that goes beyond the result of his conduct.

---

[11] For a comment on the case, see *Cassese's Companion*, at 658. The Court went on to say that 'In regard to this it must be remembered that the defendant denied the entire action and did not give any explanation that could have shown another intent or arouse doubts as to his evil intent. In addition, it is clear from the testimony that no Germans were present while the blows were being landed, and it was not proven, as mentioned above, that the defendant was bound by the orders of the Germans, to do the deed he did in general, and in the way he did it, in particular' (§ 14). See also *Götzfrid*, at 22–3, 62.

On the notion of 'deliberate' (attack on a civilian population) in crimes against humanity, see some Indonesian cases: *Herman Sedyono and others* (at 69); *Asep Kuswani* (at 47–8); and *Yayat Sudrajat* (at 8).

[12] In 1971 a US military judge took a similar stand in *Calley*, although less accurately spelled out, when he issued instructions to the Court Martial. He pointed out that premeditated murder (which under US law is a distinct category from, and not an aggravating circumstance for, unpremeditated murder) is a murder where the actor had 'a premeditated design to kill'; this expression means 'formation of a specific intent to kill and consideration of the act [...] or the acts intended to bring about death [...] prior to doing them. It is not necessary that the "premeditated design to kill" shall have been entertained for any particular or considerable length of time, but it must precede the killing.' In contrast, in the case of unpremeditated murder, only 'intent to kill' is required (whereas in the case of voluntary manslaughter the person entertains 'an intent to kill but kills in the heat of sudden passion caused by adequate provocation') (at 1708–10). For a comment on the case, see *Cassese's Companion*, at 629. See also *Manuel Goncalves Leto Bere* (at 10).

[13] In the two cases quoted above, the Turin Military Tribunal held that premeditation had been proved and consequently considered it an aggravating circumstance: see *Sävecke*, at 14–15, and *Engel* at 13. Comments on both cases can be found in *Cassese's Companion*, at 902 and 657, respectively.

International rules require a special intent for genocide: the agent must possess 'the intent to destroy, in whole or in part, a national, ethnical, racial or religious group'. Thus, it is not sufficient for the person to intend to kill, or cause serious mental or bodily harm, or deliberately inflict on a group seriously adverse and discriminatory conditions of life, or forcibly transfer children from one group to another, etc. It also must be proved that he did all this with the (further and dominant) intention of destroying a group. For, as the German Federal Court of Justice (*Bundesgerichtshof*) stated in *Jorgić* on 30 April 1999, in the crime of genocide a single person is the object of an attack 'not as an individual but rather in his capacity as a member of a group whose social existence the perpetrator intends to destroy [...] the particular inhumanity that characterizes genocide as distinct from murder lies in that the perpetrator or perpetrators do not see the victim as a human being but only as a member of a persecuted group' (at 401).[14]

Similarly, a special intent is required in some categories of crimes against humanity, for instance persecution. Here, in addition to the intent necessary for the commission of the underlying offence (murder, rape, serious bodily assault, expulsion from a village, an area or a country, etc.) a discriminatory intent is called for, namely the will to discriminate against members of a particular national, ethnic, religious, racial, or other group. As an ICTY Trial Chamber put it in *Kupreškić and others* (§ 634) (and another Trial Chamber restated it in *Kordić and Čerkez* (§§ 214 and 220)), the acts of the accused must have been 'aimed at singling out and attacking certain individuals on discriminatory grounds', for the purpose of 'removal of those persons from the society in which they live alongside the perpetrator, or eventually from humanity itself'. In *Blaškić*, another Trial Chamber worded that intent as follows: 'the specific intent to cause injury to a human being because he belongs to a particular community or group' (§ 235).

Under the ICC Statute special intent is also required for the crime of forced pregnancy as a crime against humanity. Pursuant to Article 7(2)(f),

> Forced pregnancy means the unlawful confinement of a woman forcibly made pregnant, with the intent of affecting the ethnic composition of any population or carrying out other grave violations of international law. [...]

The rule criminalizing terrorism requires a special intent: that of spreading terror in the population by killing, hijacking, blowing up buildings, etc. (see 8.3.2). Arguably, also the rule criminalizing aggression requires special intent (see 7.2.2).

In all these cases pursuance of a special goal is essential, while its full attainment is not necessary for the crime to be consummated. Clearly, the murder of dozens of Muslims, Kurds, or Jews may be termed genocide if the required special intent is present, regardless of whether the general purpose of destroying the group as such is achieved. The same holds true for terrorist attacks, which may amount to international crimes even if in fact a specific attack does not achieve the purpose of terrorizing the population. Similarly, the forcible expulsion of a number of Muslims from their homes amounts to persecution even if not all Muslims are in fact driven out of the area.

3.5 RECKLESSNESS OR INDIRECT INTENT

Recklessness is a state of mind where a person foresees that his or her action is likely to produce its prohibited consequences, and nevertheless willingly takes the risk of so

---

[14] That a specific or special intent is required for genocide has also been stressed in *Akayesu*, TC, § 498; *Musema*, TC, §§ 164–7; *Jelisić*, AC, §§ 45–6; *Krstić*, TC, §§ 569–99; AC, §§ 24–38.

acting. In this case the degree of culpability is less than in intent. There, the actor anticipates and pursues a certain result and in addition knows that he will achieve it by his
action; here instead he only envisages that result as *possible* or *likely* and deliberately takes
the risk; however, he does not necessarily will or desire the result. Recklessness, thus, is
made up of foresight and a volitional act (deliberately taking the risk).[15]

Instances of recklessness are clearly envisaged in some international criminal rules.
Thus, for instance, the rule on superiors' responsibility provides that the superior is criminally liable for the crimes of his subordinates if 'he consciously disregarded information
which clearly indicated' that his subordinates were about to commit, or were committing, international crimes (see 10.2.2). In this case the superior is liable to punishment for
consciously having taken the risk, knowing that his subordinates were likely to commit
or were committing crimes.

Furthermore, in the case of responsibility for crimes perpetrated by a multitude of
persons pursuant to a common design, or joint criminal enterprise (see 9.1), as the ICTY
Appeals Chamber held in *Tadić* (*Appeals Judgment*), what is required is that, under the
circumstances of the case, *i*) a member of a group engaging in a joint criminal action foresaw the possibility that a crime previously non-concerted or agreed upon by the group
might be perpetrated by another member; and *ii*) he consciously and deliberately took
that risk (§§ 227–8).

The notion of recklessness was also applied in many cases brought before German
courts after the Second World War. These courts, which administered criminal justice
under Control Council Law no. 10, were seized with crimes against humanity committed
by Germans against other Germans. Most cases concerned denunciations to the Gestapo,
with all the ensuing inhuman consequences. Frequently those courts held that, for the
denunciation to amount to a crime against humanity, it was not necessary for the author
of the denunciation to foresee and will all the nefarious consequences of his act; it was
sufficient that he be aware of the authoritarian and arbitrary system of Nazi violence then
prevailing in Germany and of the consequent risk that the victim would be subjected to
persecution and great suffering. In this connection the German Supreme Court in the
British Occupied Zone employed the German equivalent of the notion of recklessness,
namely *Eventualvorsatz* (or *bedingter Vorsatz*).[16]

---

[15] According to the ICTY Trial Chamber in *Stakić*, 'The technical definition of *dolus eventualis* is the following: if the actor engages in life-endangering behaviour, his killing becomes intentional if he "reconciles
himself" or "makes peace" with the likelihood of death. Thus, if the killing is committed with "manifest
indifference to the value of human life", even conduct of minimal risk can qualify as intentional homicide.
Large-scale killings that would be classified as reckless murder in the United States would meet the continental criteria of *dolus eventualis*. The Trial Chamber emphasises that the concept of *dolus eventualis* does not
include a standard of negligence or gross negligence' (*Stakić*, TC, § 587). In *Blaškić* the ICTY Trial Chamber
defined recklessness as the situation where 'the outcome is foreseen by the perpetrator as only a probable or
possible consequence' of his conduct; according to the TC the agent takes 'a deliberate risk in the hope that the
risk does not cause injury' (*Blaškić*, TC, § 254).

A good definition of this notion—as set out in the criminal law of the State of New York—can be found
in Rule 15.5(3) of the New York Penal Code, whereby 'A person acts recklessly with respect to a result or to
a circumstance described by a statute defining an offence when he is aware of and consciously disregards
a substantial and unjustifiable risk that such result will occur or that such circumstance exists. The risk
must be of such nature and degree that disregard thereof constitutes a gross deviation from the standard of
conduct that a reasonable person would observe in the situation.' See also Art. 2(2)(c) of the US Model Penal
Code, reported n. 6.

[16] For instance, one can mention *K. and M.*, decided by the Offenburg Tribunal (*Landgericht*) on 4 June
1946 (for a comment on the case, see *Cassese's Companion*, at 741). In January 1944, K., the principal accused,
a member of the Nazi party, over a dinner with friends and acquaintances had a discussion with Könninger,
a soldier who was on home leave. Already tipsy, Könninger inveighed against the German leadership, noting

The Supreme Court in the British Occupied Zone also required recklessness in other cases not dealing with denunciations. For instance, in *L. and others* (the so-called *Pig-cart parade* case) the events had occurred on 5 May 1933. In a parade by SA (assault troopers) through the main streets of a small German town a prominent socialist senator and a Jewish inhabitant were publicly humiliated and subjected to inhuman treatment (they were led along in a pig cart, with demeaning inscriptions hung around their necks and were vilified in various ways). The defendants took part in the parade. The Court held that, as far as the involvement of three accused went, 'it was inconceivable' that they, who were old officials of the Nazi party, 'did not at least think it possible and consider that in the case at issue, through their participation, persons were being assaulted by a system of

among other things that the war was about to be lost. A few weeks later K. reported Könninger's tirade to various persons, including some dignitaries attending a party meeting at a restaurant. As a result, the Gestapo arrested Könninger and brought him to trial. In July 1944 he was sentenced to death for defeatism and executed. Before the Offenburg Court K. submitted that he had not intended to have the victim prosecuted and punished for his utterances. The Court held, however, that when he reported his statements to the party meeting, 'he must expect that his words would have adverse consequences for Könninger. The accused caused proceedings against Könninger to be instituted, witnesses to be heard, and the victim eventually to be sentenced. It is entirely credible that the accused K. did not intend all that. However, he was to expect that this would be the result of his talk at the restaurant. He must foresee this result. He tacitly approved it. There was therefore recklessness on his part' (67). The Court found K. guilty of a crime against humanity (persecution on political grounds) under Article II(1)(c) of Control Council Law no. 10.

A very similar case is *W.*, brought before the Tribunal of Waldshut (judgment of 16 February 1949, at 147). For a comment, see *Cassese's Companion*, at 970.

K., decided on 27 July 1948 by the German Supreme Court in the British Occupied Zone, is also interesting. In February 1942 the accused, a member of the Waffen SS working at the headquarters of the Gestapo in D., had denounced at his headquarters a Jewish businessman (M.) because the latter had gone to the apartment of a non-Jew. The denunciation led to the Jew being taken into preventative custody for three weeks. The accused was found guilty of a crime against humanity. On appeal the Supreme Court confirmed the judgment. It held that under the relevant rules the accused had engaged in 'offensive conduct that was conscious and deliberate'; he must be aware that he was 'handing over the victim directly or indirectly to forces which [would], on account of the facts in the denunciation, treat him solely according to their purposes and ideas without being bound by considerations of justice or legal certainty'. According to the Court the accused 'was aware that the denunciation could have entailed the most grave consequences for M., as the accused knew of the criminal and arbitrary manner in which the Gestapo abused its power at the time'. This mental element was sufficient: it was not required for the perpetrator to have acted with 'an inhumane cast of mind', nor was 'approval of the result' required (50–1). For a comment on the case, see *Cassese's Companion*, at 741.

R. was heard by the Supreme Court in the British Occupied Zone, and decided on 27 July 1948. In March 1944, in Hamburg, the accused, a member of the Nazi party, had an argument with a soldier in uniform, who had insulted the political leaders while drunk. Later on he reported him to the police, and as a result the victim was arrested on the Eastern front, brought back to Germany in September 1944, charged with undermining military morale and brought to trial. He was sentenced first to five years' imprisonment and then a death sentence was sought, but not imposed due to the Russian occupation. The Court held that for the denunciation to be a crime against humanity, it was necessary that 'the offensive behaviour of the perpetrator be conscious and intentional (or at least the perpetrator took the risk), that it actually occurred and the perpetrator, through his act, willed that the victim be handed over to powers that did not obey the rule of law, or at least, that he took this possibility into account'. The Court insisted that the mental element of the crime was met if the perpetrator had intended 'to deliver the victim to the uncontrollable power machinery of the power and the State or at the very least he had taken the risk that he would be treated arbitrarily'. And the Court added that 'negligence' (*Fahrlässigkeit*) was not sufficient (at 47).

The Supreme Court took the same position in *O.* (judgment of 19 October 1948; for a comment, see *Cassese's Companion*, at 861) (at 106–7), and in *Th.* (judgment on the same date), where it restated that, for the accused's denunciation of another person to the police to be characterized as a crime against humanity, it was necessary that a mental element be present, namely that she 'at least was cognizant of and took into account the possibility that the victim, as a consequence of her denunciation, would be treated in an arbitrary manner' (at 115–16). The same judgment was restated in other cases of denunciation: *J. and R.* (at 170), *S.* (at 260–1), and *F.* (at 367); for a comment on these cases, see the relevant entries of *Cassese's Companion*.

violence and injustice; more is not required for the mental element' (at 232). In contrast, in the case of another defendant, who had simply followed the procession among the onlookers and in civilian clothes, the Court held that he was not guilty because he 'had not participated in causing the offence nor had he at least entertained *dolus eventualis* in taking part in the causation of the offence' (at 234).[17] It would thus seem that, according to the Court, some of the defendants took an unjustified risk of the victims being assaulted.

As for the case law of international criminal courts, it bears mentioning *Blaškić* (where the ICTY Appeals Chamber held that to establish liability under Article 7(1) of the ICTY Statute for ordering the commission of a crime, it is required that a person 'orders an act or omission with the awareness of a substantial likelihood that a crime will be committed in the execution of that order', because 'ordering with such awareness has to be regarded as accepting the crime', at § 42) and *Stakić* (where the ICTY Trial Chamber held that recklessness or *dolus eventualis* could suffice for the crime of murder as a war crime and for extermination as a crime against humanity, at §§ 587 and 642).[18]

It must be noted, however, that what in this book is defined as recklessness or *dolus eventualis* in the case law of the ICTY is often referred to as 'indirect intent' (as opposed to 'direct' intent).[19] In particular, a clear distinction between 'direct' and 'indirect' intent was drawn by the Trial Chamber in *Strugar*, when it stated:

> It is now settled that [in murder cases] the *mens rea* is not confined to cases where the accused has a direct intent to kill or to cause serious bodily harm, but also extends to cases where the accused has what is often referred to as an indirect intent. While the precise expression of the appropriate indirect intent has varied between decisions, it has been confirmed by the Appeals Chamber that the awareness of a mere possibility that a crime will occur is not sufficient in the context of ordering under Article 7(1) of the Statute. The

[17] Another significant case is *P. and others* (for a comment, see *Cassese's Companion*, at 868). On the night after Germany's partial capitulation (5 May 1945) four young German marines had tried to escape from Denmark back to Germany. The next day they were caught by Danes and delivered to the German troops, who court-martialled and sentenced three of them to death for desertion; on the very day of the general capitulation of Germany, i.e. 10 May 1945, the three were executed. The German Supreme Court found that some of the participants in the trial before the Court Martial were guilty of complicity in a crime against humanity. According to the Supreme Court, the glaring discrepancy between the offence and the punishment proved that the execution of the three marines had constituted a clear manifestation of the Nazis' brutal and intimidatory justice. The acts performed by the defendants involved a crime against humanity. As for the mental element of the crime, the Court held that intent (indisputably present in the case of the judges who had sentenced the marines to death and of the military commander who had confirmed the sentence and ordered the execution) was not necessarily required; recklessness, for instance in the case of the prosecutor, was sufficient: 'it is sufficient for the defendant concerned to have taken into account the possibility and have consented to the fact that his conduct would contribute to cause the resulting killing' (224).

In *Eschner*, the accused, an SS officer who had held an important position in the concentration camp of Gross-Rosen between 1941 and 1945, was accused, among other things, of having requested Kapo V., a criminal by profession, to 'get rid of' a camp inmate who had tried to escape; the inmate had probably died. The Würzburg Tribunal held that the accused knew the violent behaviour of Kapo and 'approvingly took into account that the inmate might suffer death as a result of the intended ill-treatment. Thus he willed recklessly the death of a man contrary to law.' However, in view of the fact that the inmate's death was not certain, the Court found the accused guilty of 'attempted murder' by recklessness (253). For a comment, see *Cassese's Companion*, at 663.

[18] As for the ICTR, see for instance *Musema*, TC, § 215 and *Kayishema and Ruzindana*, TC, § 146.

[19] See *Blaškić*, TC, § 254, where the Trial Chamber referred to 'direct or indirect malicious intent or recklessness'. In the same case, before the Appeals Chamber the prosecution submitted that 'recent decisions of the International Tribunal have shown that *dolus eventualis* or indirect intent could be an acceptable standard' (*Blaškić*, AC, § 30). The Appeals Chamber however, confined itself to acknowledging liability for being aware of the substantial likelihood that a crime be committed, without further classifying the class of mens rea. It held that 'a person who orders an act or omission with the awareness of the substantial likelihood that

knowledge of a higher degree of risk is required. In some cases the description of an indirect intent as *dolus eventualis* may have obscured the issue as this could suggest that *dolus eventualis* as understood and applied in a particular legal system had been adopted as the standard in this Tribunal (§ 235).

The Trial Chamber then added an important qualification:

it should be stressed that knowledge by the accused that his act or omission might *possibly* cause death is not sufficient to establish the necessary *mens rea*. The necessary mental state exists when the accused knows that it is *probable* that his act or omission will cause death. (§ 236)

In *Delić Rasim*, the Trial Chamber, building on other precedents,[20] held:

The mens rea for murder includes both direct and an indirect intent. Direct intent is a state of mind in which the perpetrator desired the death of a victim to be the result of his act or omission, whereas indirect intent comprises knowledge that the death of a victim was a 'probable' or 'likely' consequence of such act or omission. Negligence and gross negligence do not form part of indirect intent. (§ 48)

In this book the notion of recklessness or *dolus eventualis* is preferred as more appropriate, although sometimes reference will also be made to 'indirect intent' to cover the same notion.

3.6 KNOWLEDGE

'Knowledge' is not a notion familiar to civil law countries, where it is not regarded as an autonomous category of mens rea, being absorbed either by intent or by recklessness. In contrast, the notion as a distinct class of mental attitude in criminal behaviour is widespread in some common law countries, particularly the United States, where one can find a clear-cut definition in the Model Penal Code. There it is stated at section 2.02 that

A person acts knowingly with respect to a material element of an offence when:

(i)   if the element involves the nature of his conduct or the attendant circumstances, he is aware that his conduct is of that nature or that such circumstances exist; and

(ii) if the element involves a result of his conduct, he is aware that it is practically certain that his conduct will cause such a result.[21]

a crime will be committed in the execution of that order, has the requisite *mens rea* for establishing liability under Article 7(1) pursuant to ordering. Ordering with such awareness has to be regarded as accepting that crime (*Blaškić*, AC, § 42; see also § 166).

The Appeals Chamber took a substantially similar stand in *Kordić and Čerkez* where, however, it held that in addition to 'direct intent' a lower form of mens rea (again, what is here defined as recklessness or *dolus eventualis*) could also entail the responsibility of the accused: '[T]he Appeals Chamber has held that a standard of *mens rea* that is lower than direct intent may apply in relation to ordering under Article 7(1) of the Statute. The Appeals Chamber held that a person who orders an act or omission with the awareness of the substantial likelihood that a crime will be committed in the execution of that order, has the requisite *mens rea* for establishing responsibility under Article 7(1) of the Statute pursuant to ordering. Ordering with such awareness has to be regarded as accepting that crime'(AC, § 30).

[20] *Limaj et al.*, TC, § 241; *Martić*, TC, § 60 ('The *mens rea* of murder is the intent to kill, including indirect intent, that is the knowledge that the death of the victim was a probable consequence of the act or omission'). See also Stakić, TC, § 587; Brđanin, TC, § 386; Orić, TC, § 348.

[21] See *Model Penal Code and Commentaries (Official Draft and Revised Comments)*, Part I, vol. I (Philadelphia, Pa.: The American Law Institute, 1985), 225–6. The Model Penal Code then specifies that 'when knowledge of the existence of a particular fact is an element of an offence, such knowledge is established if a person is aware of a high probability of its existence, unless he actually believes that it does not exist' (at 227).

In such countries as the UK, some distinguished commentators consider knowledge as having the same value and intensity as intent, with the difference that intent 'relates to the consequences specified in the definition of the crime' (for instance, death as a result of killing, in the case of voluntary murder), whereas knowledge 'relates to circumstances forming part of the definition of the crime'[22] (for instance, the circumstance that property belongs to another person, in the case of criminal damage to property).

In short, it would seem that in some common law countries, knowledge denotes two different forms of mental attitude, depending on the contents of the substantive criminal rule at stake: *i*) if the substantive penal rule prescribes the existence of a particular fact or circumstance for the crime to materialize, knowledge means awareness of the existence of this fact or circumstance; *ii*) if instead the substantive criminal rule focuses on the result of one's conduct, then knowledge means (a) awareness that one's action is most likely to bring about that harmful result, and nevertheless (b) taking the high risk of causing that result. Plainly, in category *i*) knowledge is part of intent (which involves not only the will to accomplish a certain action and thereby attain a certain result, but also awareness of the factual circumstances implicated in the action). Instead, in category *ii*) knowledge substantially coincides with recklessness, as defined above (see 3.5). Probably under the influence of US negotiators, Article 30(2) of the ICC Statute incorporates both versions of knowledge, in that it stipulates that knowledge 'means awareness that a circumstance exists or a consequence will occur in the ordinary course of events'.

In addition, some international rules also rely upon or require a third notion of knowledge, i.e. as the mere fact of being apprised of a certain fact. Here, knowledge is disconnected from intent or recklessness; it is not part of, nor is it closely connected to intent or recklessness (in contrast to the murder of a civilian, where there is intent to cause the death of a human being and awareness of his status as a civilian; or the bombing of a military objective situated in a densely populated area, where there is intent to bring about the destruction of the military objective and the deliberate taking of the risk of killing civilians in the knowledge that those living around that objective have the status of civilians). In the third category under discussion, knowledge constitutes an element per se of mens rea, an element that is normally required in addition to another, distinct, mental element. For example, such is the case with crimes against humanity; there, in addition to the intent required for the underlying offence (such as murder, rape, torture, or extermination) the substantive criminal rules also require that the agent have knowledge of a factual circumstance, namely that those offences were part of a widespread or systematic attack directed against a civilian population (see e.g. Article 7(1) of the ICC Statute).

Let us see instances of the three notions of knowledge.

i) *Knowledge as part of intent* can be found, for example, in Article 85(3)(e) of the 1977 First Additional Protocol of the 1949 Geneva Conventions. It enumerates among the grave breaches of the Protocol (which must be 'committed wilfully' and cause 'death or serious injury to body or health') the fact of 'making a person the object of attack in the knowledge that he is *hors de combat*'. Here, knowledge means awareness of the requisite circumstances, namely that the person is *hors de combat*.

As another example of knowledge as awareness of facts, hence as part of intent, one can mention that, to be held responsible for complicity in planning or waging an aggressive war, it must be proved either that an accused participated in the preparation or execution of these plans (and in this case the criminal intent may be inferred from such participation), or that the accused was *apprised* of the plans, in addition to taking some sort of

---

[22] See Ashworth, *Principles*, at 191–7. In contrast, the notion is discussed only in passing by Smith and Hogan (see at 103 and 117).

action furthering their implementation. In *Göring and others*, in considering the charges of crimes against peace made against Schacht (President of the Reichsbank and Minister without Portfolio until 1943), the Nuremberg Tribunal noted that he was responsible for rearmament of Germany, but this as such was not a crime; for it to become a crime it must be shown that he carried out rearmament as part of the Nazi plans to wage aggressive wars. However, the Tribunal found that while organizing rearmament, Schacht did not know of the Nazi aggressive plans; hence it acquitted him (at 307–10). A US Military Tribunal at Nuremberg took the same position and came to the same conclusion in *Krauch and others* (*I. G. Farben* case), where it also held that the defendants' lack of knowledge of Hitler's aggressive plans proved that they lacked the requisite criminal intent (at 1115–17).

Another important instance where knowledge is required by international criminal rules is *aiding and abetting an international crime* (for example, a war crime such as killing a prisoner of war or an enemy civilian). Here criminal responsibility arises if the aider and abettor *knows* that his action will assist the commission of a specific crime by the principal. Various courts have taken this position.[23] As the ICTY Trial Chamber put it in *Furundžija*, the accomplice need not share the mens rea of the principal: 'mere knowledge that his actions assist the perpetrator in the commission of the crime is sufficient to constitute mens rea in aiding and abetting the crime' (§ 236).[24]

As will be shown (see 10.2.2), knowledge is also required in most cases of *command responsibility*.[25] Thus, international rules on command responsibility require knowledge of circumstances, in the event of a commander who knows that his subordinates have committed crimes, and yet fails to take any action to repress those crimes. He is criminally liable if, in addition to knowledge, he culpably fails to take any action for the prosecution and punishment of the culprits (intentional omission to take the prescribed action). Here, awareness of the fact that troops under the control or authority of the commander have committed international crimes is a mental element constituting the preliminary sine qua non condition of intent, and is part and parcel of intent.

---

[23] For instance, a US Military Tribunal sitting at Nuremberg, in *Einsatzgruppen* (at 568–73), two British courts respectively in *Schonfeld* (at 64) and *Zyklon B* (at 93), the German Supreme Court in the British Occupied Zone in the *Synagogue* case (at 229), and the Appeals Chamber in *Tadić* (*Appeal*), § 229. In *Veit Harlan* the Court of Assizes of Hamburg held in 1950 that in the case at issue there existed the requisite subjective element of the offence of complicity in a crime against humanity (persecution of Jews), in that the accused, a film director who had produced a strong anti-Semitic film at the behest of Goebbels, 'knew the intention of Goebbels, namely to justify through the film, beyond the usual propaganda, the persecutory measures against Jews that had been taken and planned' (at 66), and in addition 'had taken into account the possible materializing of the [adverse] consequences of the film, such consequences having been described [in general terms] by the Supreme Court [in the British Occupied Zone]' (at 66). For comments on all these cases, see the relevant entries of *Cassese's Companion*.

[24] In this case the accused interrogated the victim while she was being subjected to rape and serious sexual assaults by another person; the Trial Chamber found that the accused's presence and continued interrogation of the victim while she was being subjected to violence amounted to aiding and abetting the crime, for accused provided assistance, encouragement, or moral support to the sexual offender, and knew that these acts assisted the commission of the rape and sexual assault.

[25] The issue was well put by the US Judge Advocate in his instructions to a US Court Martial in *Medina* '[A] commander is [...] responsible if he has *actual* knowledge that troops or other persons subject to his control are in the process of committing or are about to commit a war crime and he wrongfully fails to take the necessary and reasonable steps to insure compliance with the law of war. You will observe that these legal requirements placed upon a commander require actual knowledge plus a wrongful failure to act. Thus mere presence at the scene without knowledge will not suffice. That is, the commander–subordinate relationship alone will not allow an inference of knowledge. While it is not necessary that a commander actually see an atrocity being committed, it is essential that he know that his subordinates are in the process of committing atrocities or are about to commit atrocities' (at 1732). For a comment on the case, see *Cassese's Companion*, at 805.

ii) Some international criminal rules focus on *result*, and hence substantially consider knowledge as amounting or equivalent to recklessness. Thus, Article 85(3)(b) of the First Additional Protocol considers as a grave breach 'launching an indiscriminate attack affecting the civilian population or civilian objects in the knowledge that such attack will cause excessive loss of life, injury to civilians or damage to civilian objects'. A fairly similar definition is laid down in Article 8(2)(b)(iv) of the ICC Statute. In the cases considered above, knowledge is not an autonomous criminal state of mind, but only a means of entertaining criminal intent or recklessness.

iii) In contrast (and we thus move on to the third category), in some instances knowledge cannot be reduced to either of those classes of mental state, and it remains *indispensable as a subjective element on its own*. One example has already been given above. It refers to crimes against humanity: the accused must know of a widespread or systematic attack against a civilian population. It is not that he intends the civilian population to be subject to the attack, nor that he knows that there is a risk of them being subjected to an attack—both of which are beside the point. What is crucial is simply that he knew of the attack. In these instances knowledge is irreducible to other mental elements and exists per se (see ICTR, TC, *Kayishema*, §§ 133–4; and ICTY, TC, *Kupreškić and others*, § 556).

Finally, let it be emphasized that in ICL knowledge as awareness of circumstances does not mean awareness of the *legal appraisal* of those circumstances. It only denotes cognizance of the factual circumstances envisaged in a particular international rule. International law, like most national systems, does not require awareness of the illegality of an act for the act to be regarded as an international crime. It starts from the assumption that everybody must know the law; it therefore makes culpable even acts that were performed without the author being fully aware of their unlawfulness (as long as the required intent, recklessness, knowledge, etc. are there).[26] ICL only takes into account knowledge, or lack of knowledge, of the law when the defence of mistake of law can be regarded as admissible, for the law on a particular matter is uncertain or unclear (see 12.2.2). In other words, international rules do not attach importance to the subjective mental attitude of the perpetrator with regard to law, unless this subjective attitude coincides with the objective condition of the law, namely its uncertainty.

3.7 CULPABLE OR GROSS NEGLIGENCE

Generally speaking, negligence entails that the person *i)* is expected or required to abide by certain standards of conduct or take certain specific precautions with which any reasonable person should comply; *ii)* acts in disregard of these standards or precautions; and *iii)* either (a) does not advert at all to the risk of harm to another person involved in his conduct, which falls short of the standards or precautions (simple negligence), or (b) is aware of that risk but believes that it will not occur, and in addition takes a conduct that is blatantly at odds with the prescribed standards (gross negligence). Mere negligence is

---

[26] In *Burgholz (No. 2)*, the British Judge Advocate, in delineating to the Military Court the scope of mens rea in international crimes, stated: '[Y]ou might think it difficult to say that any man could have a guilty mind in respect of his conduct if he is not aware that his conduct is in breach of any law, or if there is no formalized law to fit his participatory conduct and to involve the breach thereof. But *Mens Rea* goes a little further than that. If a man ought to have known that he was doing wrong, then the law presumes a guilty mind, and the requirements of the doctrine of *Mens Rea* are fulfilled if you find the accused either knew that they were doing wrong or ought to have known: the fact that they may have had no conscious thought of wrongdoing will not protect them from conviction if a breach of law has been committed' (84–5).

the least degree of culpability. Normally it is not sufficient for individual criminal liability to arise.

It would seem that, given the intrinsic nature of international crimes (which always amount to serious attacks on fundamental values) in ICL negligence operates as a standard of liability only when it reaches the threshold of gross or culpable negligence (*culpa gravis*). Because of the nature of international crimes, the mental element under discussion only becomes relevant when there exist some specific conditions relating to the objective elements of the crime; that is, the values attacked are fundamental and the harm caused is serious.[27]

That national legal systems may penalize a mental state that is less grave than the one criminalized at the international level should not be surprising. Given the consequences following from, and the stigma inherent in, international crimes, it is only natural that international criminal rules should be more exacting, with regard to subjective conditions of the offence, than some national criminal legislation.[28]

Gross negligence is clearly required by the customary rules on superiors' responsibility, whereby a superior is responsible for the crimes of his subordinates if he did not know but 'should have known' that they were about to commit, or were committing, or had committed crimes (see 10.2.2). In this case, the superior is required to become cognizant of, and verify, all the information necessary to monitor the activities and the conduct of his

---

[27] This definition of culpable negligence is in some respects at variance with that upheld in some common law and civil law countries. For instance, under the New York Penal Code, Rule 1505(4): 'A person acts with criminal negligence with respect to a result or to a circumstance described by a statute defining an offence when he fails to perceive a substantial and unjustifiable risk that such result will occur or that such circumstance exists. The risk must be of such nature and degree that the failure to perceive it constitutes a gross deviation from the standard of care that a reasonable person would observe in the situation.' Clearly, this definition corresponds to what we termed above 'inadvertent negligence', or *culpa levis*.

[28] Case law bears out the above international notion. *John G. Schultz*, a case brought before a US Court of Military Appeals in 1952, deserves mention (for a comment on the case, see *Cassese's Companion*, at 906). Schultz, driving a car, had struck and killed two Japanese pedestrians in 1950 in Japan (although Japan was still under US military occupation this, of course, was not a war crime). The US Court stated the following: 'A careful perusal of the penal codes of most civilized nations leads us to the conclusion that homicide involving less than culpable negligence is not universally recognized as an offense. Even in those American jurisdictions—still relatively few in number—which have given statutory recognition to either negligent homicide or vehicular homicide, the degree of negligence required is often held to be 'culpable' or 'gross'— the same as that required for involuntary manslaughter. Imposing criminal liability for less than culpable negligence is a relatively new concept in criminal law and has not, as yet, been given universal acceptance by civilized nations' (115–16).

A definition of negligence as a possible subjective element in international crimes can be found in the instructions given by the Judge Advocate to a Canadian Court Martial in *Major Seward A. G.* The defendant had, among other thing, been charged with negligently performing his military duty while in Somalia in 1993. The particulars of his negligence were stated to be that 'by issuing an instruction to his subordinates that prisoners could be abused, [he] failed to properly exercise command over his subordinates, as it was his duty to do'. As a result of his instructions, some of his subordinates had beaten up and killed a Somali civilian. In instructing the Court Martial on the notion of negligence, the Judge Advocate stated: '[A]s a matter of law the alleged negligence must go beyond mere error in judgment. Mere error in judgment does not constitute negligence. The alleged negligence must be either accompanied by a lack of zeal in the performance of the military duty imposed, or it must amount to a measure of indifference or a want of care by Major Seward in the matter at hand, or to an intentional failure on his part to take appropriate precautionary measures' (at 1081). The Court Martial found the defendant guilty on this count. In commenting on this finding by the Court Martial, the Court Martial Appeal Court of Canada stated that the Court Martial 'must be taken to have concluded that the respondent did issue an "abuse" order and that his doing so was no mere error in judgment. He himself confirmed that he was taking a "calculated risk" in doing so and that nothing in his training or in Canadian doctrine would permit the use of that word during the giving of orders' (at 1081). Arguably, recklessness more than negligence was at issue in this case.

subordinates. If he disregards these standards of conduct, he acts with gross negligence and is consequently liable for dereliction of duty, if all the other conditions are fulfilled.[29] It may suffice to cite in this respect the *Krnojelac* case, where the ICTY Trial Chamber noted that

> the question for the Trial Chamber was not whether what was reported to Krnojelac was in fact true but whether the information he received from the detainees was enough to constitute 'alarming information' requiring him, as superior, to launch an investigation or make inquiries. (§ 59)

Culpable negligence has also been considered sufficient in other circumstances. A case where a court held negligence to be the mental element of a war crime is *Stenger and Crusius*, decided in 1921 by the Leipzig Supreme Court.[30] Another court also took into account negligence, this time with regard to crimes against humanity: *Hinselmann and others*, decided by the British Court of Appeal in the British Zone of Control in Germany, in 1947.[31] A Trial Court had convicted a group of German doctors and police officers of crimes against humanity, under Control Council Law no. 10 (Article I(c)). It had found that they were concerned with carrying out, in 1944–45, sterilization operations 'on a number of persons of gypsy blood, to prevent the increase of the race' (three doctors had performed the operations and two police officers had induced persons to sign consent to the operations by threats). Counsel for one of the doctors, Günther (a gynaecological specialist), argued that there was no evidence that he knew that the gypsies were being sterilized on account of their race. In counsel's view, the case against Günther could only be one of negligence; however, negligence was not sufficient to constitute an offence under Control Council Law no. 10, which required *extremely gross negligence*. Hence, Günther, if he were to be convicted at all, could only be convicted under section 230 of the German Criminal Code.[32] The prosecutor countered that Günther must have known

---

[29] Among the cases that may be cited to support the applicability of gross negligence in cases of superior responsibility, *Schmitt* stands out (for a comment on the case, see *Cassese's Companion*, 904). This case, concerning the commander of a concentration camp in Breendonck, was brought before the Brussels Military Tribunal, which held in 1950 that 'although it is true that generally speaking jurisprudence does not consider that, in case of murder, simple lack of action or negligence are punishable, this however does no longer apply when a person's failure to act amounts to the non-fulfilment of a duty [...] in this case failure to take action amounts to material conduct sufficient for the realisation of criminal intent' (at 936–7).

[30] For a comment on the case, see *Cassese's Companion*, at 935. In the battle near Saarburg in Loraine between the French and the German Army, on 21 August 1914 the accused, Crusius, a captain of the German army, thought that Major-General Stenger had verbally ordered the killing of all French wounded. Acting under this erroneous assumption, he passed on this alleged order to his company. The Court concluded that Crusius was guilty of causing 'death through culpable negligence' (*fahrlässige Tötung*) and sentenced him to two years' imprisonment. The Court held that: 'the act of will which in the further course of events caused the objectively illegal outcome [...] included an act of carelessness which ran contrary to his duty, and neglect of the consideration required in the situation at hand which was perfectly reasonable to expect from the accused. Had he applied the care required of him, he would not have failed to notice what many of his men realized immediately, namely that the indiscriminate killing of all wounded represented an outrageous and by no means justifiable war manoeuvre [...] Captain Crusius was certainly familiar with the provisions of the field operating procedures which require a written order as the basis for troop command by the higher troop leaders, as well as the drill manual which makes the written order a rule, especially concerning orders for brigades and higher. This circumstance is also not entirely without significance, particularly in view of the personality of the accused who was described as a diligent, zealous and benevolent officer. In view of the accused's background and personality, he should have anticipated the illegal outcome which was easily demonstrated even if his mental and emotional states at the time were to be fully taken into consideration' (at 2567–8).

[31] For a comment on the case, see *Cassese's Companion*, at 725.

[32] Under this provision, 'Whoever through negligence causes bodily harm to another is punished by a pecuniary penalty or imprisonment up to three years' (see A. Schönke, *Strafgesetzbuch für das*

the correct procedure in the case of sterilization, but made no enquiries, and saw no legal documents.[33] The Court of Appeals found that the appellant's frame of mind amounted to negligence: a German law of 1933, as amended in 1935, made it clear that sterilization operations were illegal unless: *i*) they were performed to avert a serious threat to the life and health of the person operated upon, and with the consent of that person; or *ii*) they were carried out in pursuance of an order of the Eugenics Court. The Court of Appeals noted that in the case at issue neither of these conditions was fulfilled.[34] The crucial point was, however, whether negligence (*Fahrlässigkeit*) could suffice for the requisite mens rea in the case of a crime against humanity. The Court of Appeals held that in the case at issue there was 'no suggestion that the operations were cruelly performed, and the evidence was inadequate to establish a degree of negligence which could have amounted in any event to a Crime against Humanity'. It consequently reduced the sentence of two years' imprisonment to six months.[35]

It may be clearly inferred from this finding that, for the Court of Appeals, crimes against humanity may result from negligence, provided, however, that negligence is gross.

Finally, it should be pointed out that there are also cases where culpable negligence has been so conceived of as to border on recklessness.[36]

Deutsche Reich—Kommentar, 2nd edn (Munich and Berlin: Beck, 1944), at 484; and see 172–3 for the notion of negligence).

[33] In addition, in his view there was no difference 'in the degree of negligence required to constitute an offence under Section 230 and that required to constitute an offence under [Control Council] Law 10'.

[34] 'The operations were of so special a nature, and the limits within which they could be legally performed so narrow, that Günther was put upon his enquiry before he operated. His failure to make the necessary enquiry was negligence. Although "negligence" as used by British lawyers [in English law there is negligence when the conduct of a person fails to measure up to an objective standard and the person ought to have fore-seen the risk involved in his conduct; see, for instance, Smith and Hogan, 90–6] and "*Fahrlässigkeit*" as used by German lawyers are not co-extensive terms [in German law there is negligence when a person, acting in breach of a duty of precaution brings about a certain result he has not willed, and this result occurs either because the person is not cognizant of the breach of duty, or else is aware that the breach may occur, but trusts that the result will not materialize; see, for instance, Jescheck, *Lehrbuch*, at 563] there was undoubt-edly *Fahrlässigkeit* on Günther's part; and the sterilization of the persons operated upon was a bodily injury' (68–60).

[35] As mentioned above, counsel for the appellant had argued that negligence, if any, on the part of Günther was not serious enough to constitute an offence under Control Council Law no. 10; German law was therefore applicable. However, under this law, unless the rule under which a person was charged expressly stated that negligence was sufficient, the person could not be convicted of a criminal offence if the act consti-tuting it was merely negligent and not intentional. The Court dismissed this argument. The Court of Appeal stated as follows: 'We do not accept the proposition that this is necessarily so [namely that negligence may not amount to the requisite subjective element unless this is explicitly provided for in the relevant law] where a charge under [Control Council] Law 10 is tried in a Control Commission Court; but, in the present case, there is no suggestion that the operations were cruelly performed, and the evidence was inadequate to establish a degree of negligence which could have amounted in any event to a Crime against Humanity.' The Court consequently set aside Günther's conviction under Control Council Law no. 10 and substituted it with a finding that he was guilty of an offence under section 230 of the German Criminal Code (at 60).

[36] Thus in *Medina*, in 1971 a US military judge issued to the Court Martial instructions with regard to command responsibility arising in a case where the commander allegedly had actual knowledge that troops or other persons subject to his control were in the process of committing war crimes (killing of innocent civilians in the Vietnamese village of My Lai), and wrongfully failed to take the necessary and reasonable steps to ensure compliance with the laws of war. The military judge pointed out that the legal requirements of international law 'placed upon a commander require actual knowledge plus a wrongful failure to act'. He then stated that the omission to exercise control must constitute culpable negligence and then pointed out that 'culpable negligence is a degree of carelessness greater than simple negligence. For purposes of making the distinction between the two, you are advised that simple negligence is the absence of due care, that is an omission by a person who is under a duty to exercise due care, which exhibits a lack of that degree of care for

3.8 THE MENTAL ELEMENT IN
THE ICC STATUTE

As stated above, the ICC Statute contains the only international provision setting out a general definition of the subjective element of international crimes: Article 30. This provision envisages intent and knowledge as the only mental elements of those crimes (as set forth in Articles 6–8 of the ICC Statute). Article 30(1) provides

> Unless otherwise provided, a person shall be criminally responsible and liable for punishment for a crime within the jurisdiction of the Court only if the material elements are committed with intent and knowledge.

Paragraph 2 then defines those two notions.[37]

Article 30 raises two problems. First, it does not refer expressly to recklessness or culpable negligence, although recklessness may be held to be encompassed by the definition of intent laid down in paragraph 2. Second, it always requires *both* intent and knowledge, whereas there may be cases where only intent, as defined in the provision, is sufficient, and other cases where instead only knowledge (which, according to the definition given in the provision, may be regarded as equivalent to recklessness) would be sufficient.

To solve the first problem one may focus on the initial proviso of the rule ('Unless otherwise provided'): whenever a provision of the Statute or a rule of customary international law requires a different mental element, this will be considered sufficient by the Court. For instance, Article 28(a)(i) provides for the responsibility of superiors where the 'military commander or person [...] owing to the circumstances at the time, should have known that the forces [under his effective command, control or authority] were committing or about to commit [...] crimes'. Plainly, this provision envisages culpable negligence. This case would be covered by the proviso just referred to. This also holds true for the war crime provided for in Article 8(2) (xxvi), on conscripting or enlisting children under the age of 15, where clearly the perpetrator 'should have known' that they were minors.

Nonetheless, when a specific substantive provision of the Statute does *not* specify the mental element required, one may deduce from Article 30 that one must take that substantive provision to require intent and knowledge. In this manner the Statute may eventually require a mental element *higher* than that set down in customary law. Indeed, differences may arise between customary international law and treaty law whenever a customary rule concerning a specific crime considers as a sufficient requirement for that crime a subjective element other than intent (for instance, culpable negligence).

---

the safety of others which a reasonable, prudent commander would have exercised under the same or similar circumstances. Culpable negligence, on the other hand, is a higher degree of negligent omission, one that is accompanied by a gross, reckless, deliberate, or wanton disregard for the foreseeable consequences to others of that omission; it is an omission showing a disregard of human safety. It is higher in magnitude than simple inadvertence, but falls short of intentional wrong. The essence of wanton or reckless conduct is intentional conduct by way of omission where there is a duty to act, which conduct involves a high degree of likelihood that substantial harm will result to others' (at 1732–4). For a comment on the case, see *Cassese's Companion*, at 805. See also the *Major Seward A. G.* case (reported in n. 28).

[37] Para. 2 provides that: 'For the purposes of this article, a person has intent where (a) in relation to conduct, that person means to engage in the conduct; (b) in relation to a consequence, that person means to cause that consequence or is aware that it will occur in the ordinary course of events.'

Para. 3 provides that: 'For the purposes of this article, "knowledge" means awareness that a circumstance exists or a consequence will occur in the ordinary course of events. "Know" and "knowingly" shall be construed accordingly.'

As for the second problem (the use of the conjunctive 'and'), one ought to note that in international law there is a rule of construction whereby a purely grammatical construction must yield to a logical interpretation whenever this is dictated by the principle of effectiveness (*ut res magis valeat quam pereat*) and is consonant with the object and purpose of the rule. It is therefore admissible to construe the word 'and' as also including the word 'or' when this is logically required.[38]

3.9 JUDICIAL DETERMINATION OF THE MENTAL ELEMENT

As in national criminal law, in ICL a culpable state of mind is normally proved in court by circumstantial evidence. In other words, one may infer from the facts of the case whether or not the accused, when acting in a certain way, willed, or was aware, that his conduct would bring about a certain result. To put it differently, one may normally deduce from factual circumstances whether the action contrary to ICL was accompanied by a mental attitude denoting some degree of fault.

This is the position taken by national and international criminal courts. For instance, one can refer to the statement made by the Judge Advocate addressing a Canadian Military Court in *Johann Neitz*. The question at issue was whether the accused, who had shot at a member of the Royal Canadian Air Force taken prisoner by Germans, wounding the prisoner without killing him, had intended to cause his death. The Judge Advocate put the issue to the Military Court as follows:

Intention is not capable of positive proof, and, accordingly, it is inferred from the overt acts. Evidence of concrete acts is frequently much better evidence than the evidence of an individual for, after all, an individual alone honestly knows what he is thinking. The Court cannot look into the mind to see what is going on there. The individual may protest vehemently what his intentions were, but such evidence is subject to human frailty and human perfidy. Accordingly, intention is presumed from the overt act. It is a simple application of the principle that actions speak louder than words, and, I add, often more truthfully. It is also a well-established maxim of law that a man is presumed to have intended the natural consequences of his acts. If one man deliberately strikes another over the head with an axe, the law presumes he intended to kill the other. Similarly so, if one man deliberately shoots a gun at another, an intent to kill will be presumed [...] If a man points a gun at another and deliberately fires, it is presumed that he intends to kill the other. However, this is a presumption of fact, but it may be rebutted. (209)

The Court found the accused had committed a war crime with intent to kill and sentenced him to life imprisonment.[39]

---

[38] An application of this rule of construction was made by the ICTY Trial Chamber in *Tadić*, TC, §§ 712–13.

[39] For a comment on the case, see *Cassese's Companion*, at 841.

A court of Bosnia and Herzegovina took the same approach in *Tepež* with regard to intent. In setting out the mental element of the crimes of torture and murder of civilians, the Sarajevo Cantonal Court stated that: 'The accused perpetrated the crime deliberately; he was aware that together with others from Rajko Kuj's group he was taking part in torture, beatings and killing of prisoners. Since the accused repeated these actions many times, he definitely wished to do that and was aware that repeated beatings of prisoners with hard objects, fists and boots in vital parts of their bodies can certainly result in their death. By repeating these actions it is evident that the accused wanted these people killed' (at 7).

With regard to the subjective element of command responsibility, the ICTY *Delalić and others* Trial Chamber pointed out that it could be established 'by way of circumstantial evidence'. The Trial Chamber

Interestingly, in *Jelisić* an ICTY Trial Chamber, in order to establish whether the accused had entertained the special intent required for genocide, examined various statements he had made to the effect that he wished to exterminate Muslims, for he hated them and wanted to kill them all (§§ 102–4). The Chamber concluded, however, that these utterances revealed a disturbed personality and consequently, for lack of the requisite special intent, the acts of the accused were not 'the physical expression of an affirmed resolve to destroy in whole or in part a group as such' (§ 107). The Appeal Chamber, while holding that the Trial Chamber had erred in acquitting the defendant of genocide (*Jelisić*, AC, §§ 53–72), surprisingly did not uphold the Appellant's request that the case be remitted to a Trial Chamber for retrial (§§ 73–7). It held that such remittal was 'not in the interests of justice' (§ 77).

pointed out that 'in the absence of direct evidence of the superior's knowledge of the offences committed by his subordinates, such knowledge cannot be presumed, but must be established by way of circumstantial evidence' (*Delalić and others*, TC, § 386).

Again, with regard to 'knowledge' that the subordinates were committing or had committed crimes in the case of command responsibility, the ICTY *Kordić and Čerkez* Trial Chamber stated: 'Depending on the position of authority held by a superior, whether military or civilian, *de jure* or *de facto*, and his level of responsibility in the chain of command, the evidence required to demonstrate actual knowledge may be different. For instance, the actual knowledge of a military commander may be easier to prove considering the fact that he will presumably be part of an organized structure with established reporting and monitoring systems. In the case of *de facto* commanders of more informal military structure, or of civilian leaders holding *de facto* positions of authority, the standard of proof will be higher' (*Kordić and Čerkez*, TC, § 428).

PART II
SUBSTANTIVE CRIMINAL LAW

SECTION I

INTERNATIONAL CRIMES

4

WAR CRIMES

The notion of war crimes gradually emerged in the second half of the nineteenth century. Together with piracy (which, however, is a much older category), it constituted the first exception to the concept of 'collective responsibility' prevailing in the international community. (Under this notion only states as such could be held responsible for acts performed by state officials or by individuals, when state officials had wrongly failed to prevent them from committing internationally unlawful acts, or had failed to punish them. Hence the whole state community 'paid' for the wrongful act, if the state was then to grant reparation to the aggrieved state.)

Two factors gave great impulse to the emergence of the class of war crimes. The first was the codification of the customary law of warfare, as it was then called, at both private or semi-private level and at state level. At the private level, there emerged the famous Lieber Code, in 1863[1] (which, issued by Army order no. 100 of President Lincoln, as 'Instructions for the Government of the United States in the Field', was applied during the American Civil War, 1861–5). Also notable was the adoption by the Institut de Droit International of the important Oxford Manual, in 1880.[2] At the state level, a remarkable impulse was given by the Hague codification (1899–1907). Second, some important trials were held at the end of the American Civil War (which in fact amounted to an international armed conflict, from the viewpoint of law), notably *Henry Wirz* (a case of serious ill-treatment of prisoners of war), heard by a US Military Commission (1865). Later on, many cases were brought in 1902 before US Courts Martial at the end of the armed conflict (1899–1901) of the USA against insurgents in the Philippines (which Spain had ceded by treaty to the USA in 1898).[3]

Traditionally such crimes were defined as violations of the laws of warfare committed by combatants in international armed conflicts. War crimes entailed two things. First, enemy belligerents acting as state officials (chiefly low-ranking servicemen) could be brought to trial and punished for alleged violations of the laws of warfare. The exceptional character of war (a pathological occurrence in international dealings, leading to utterly inhuman behaviour) warranted this deviation from traditional law (which granted to any

---

[1] Text in Friedman, I, 158–86.

[2] See *Les Lois de la guerre sur terre, Manuel publié par l'Institut de Droit International* (Brussels and Leipzig: C. Muquardt, 1880).

[3] One should mention in particular *General Jacob H. Smith* (about a superior order to deny quarter), the case of *Major Edwin F. Glenn* (concerning an order to torture a detained enemy), that of *Lieutenant Preston Brown* (about the killing of an unarmed prisoner of war), and *Augustine de La Pena* (again, a case of torture of an enemy detained person).

US courts held many other trials in relation to crimes committed in armed conflict. See the numerous cases cited in W. Winthrop, *Military Law and Precedents*, 2nd edn (Buffalo, NY: William S. Helm & Co., 1920), 839–62.

individual in an official capacity immunity from prosecution by foreign states).[4] Second, individuals could be punished, not only by the enemy state but also by their own state.

In actual fact for many years war crimes were chiefly prosecuted and punished by the culprits' own national authorities after the end of the hostilities.[5] This holds true for the numerous war crimes trials held in 1902 by US Courts Martial for offences committed by Americans in the armed conflict in the Philippines, as well as for the trials conducted in 1921 by the German Supreme Court against alleged German perpetrators (although in this case Germany had been compelled by the Allies to hold such trials). In some instances, however, it was a belligerent that brought to trial an enemy serviceman during the armed conflict: see two cases brought before Austrian Military Courts during the First World War (the case of the *Russian prisoner of war J. K.* (1915) (at 17–20), and *Stanislaus Bednarek* (1916) (at 1–2)). The *Henry Wirz* case, referred to above, was decided by enemy courts after the end of the war.

The creation of the Nuremberg Tribunal and the subsequent trial at Nuremberg of the major German criminals (followed in 1946 by the Tokyo Trial), marked a crucial turning point. As noticed above (see 2.2.1), two new categories of crime were envisaged: crimes against peace and crimes against humanity. In addition, until that time (with the exception of the provisions of the 1919 Treaty of Versailles relating to the German Emperor, which, however, remained a dead letter), senior state officials had never been held personally responsible for their wrongdoings. Until that time states alone could be called to account by other states, plus servicemen (normally low-ranking people) accused of misconduct during international wars. In 1945, for the first time in history, the principle was laid down—and carried through, in contrast to what had happened in 1919—that other state agents (high-ranking officers, politicians, men in charge of official state propaganda, prominent administrators or financiers, and even private individuals who had engaged in vicious propaganda against an ethnic or religious group, instigating the destruction of the group) could also be made answerable for gross misconduct in time of armed conflict. Those men were no longer protected by state sovereignty; they could be brought to trial

---

[4] The contrary view of A. Verdross, *Völkerrecht* (Berlin: Springer Verlag, 1937) at 298 was (and is) wrong. (According to the distinguished Austrian international lawyer, 'punishment [of authors of war crimes] must be ruled out when the action was not performed on one's own impulse, but must be exclusively attributed to the state of which the person is a national'). H. Kelsen (*Peace through Law* (Chapel Hill: University of North Carolina Press, 1944, at 97) shared Verdross's view.

Characteristically, the 1912 British *Manual on Land Warfare* stipulated that 'war crimes is the technical expression for such an act of enemy soldiers and enemy civilians as may be visited by punishment on capture of the offenders' (§ 441).

[5] According to the authoritative *History of the United Nations War Crimes Commission and the Development of the Laws of War*, compiled by the 'United Nations War Crimes Commission' (London: His Majesty's Stationery Office, 1948, at 29), 'The right of the belligerent to punish as war criminals persons who violate the laws or customs of war is a well-recognized principle of international law. It is the right of which a belligerent may effectively avail himself during the war in cases when such offenders fall into his hands, or after he has occupied all or part of enemy territory and is thus in the position to seize war criminals who happen to be there. [...] And although the Treaty of Peace brings to an end the right to prosecute war criminals, no rule of international law prevents the victorious belligerent from imposing upon the defeated state the obligation, as one of the provisions of the armistice or of the Peace Treaty, to surrender for trial persons accused of war crimes.'

This view, also shared by H. Kelsen (*Peace through Law*, cit. n. 4, at 108–10) does not seem, however, to reflect the status of traditional international law. As was conclusively demonstrated by A. Mérignhac ('De la sanction des infractions au droit des gens commises, au cours de la guerre européenne, par les empires du centre', 24 RGDIP (1917), 28–56) and L. Renault ('De l'application du droit pénal aux faits de la guerre', 25 RGDIP (1918), 5–29), state practice shows that belligerents are entitled to prosecute and punish their *servicemen* as well as *enemy military* both *during* the armed conflict and *after* the end of hostilities.

before courts—representative if not of the whole international society, at least of the large group of the allied victors—and punished by foreign states.[6] For the first time the basic principle was proclaimed that, faced with the alternative of complying with either national legal commands or international standards, state officials and individuals must opt for the latter. As the Nuremberg Tribunal forcefully stated, 'the very essence of the Charter [instituting the Tribunal] is that individuals have international duties which transcend the national obligations of obedience imposed by the individual State' (at 223).

After the Second World War the prosecution of war crimes was normally effected by the victor state, as well as by one of its allies, on the basis either of the principle of territoriality (the crime had been committed on its territory), or of passive nationality (but it was sufficient for the victim to have the nationality of an allied country). Although various national legislations also made provision for punishment on the basis of the principle of 'active nationality' (the law-breaker had the nationality of the prosecuting state), in practice scant use was made of this principle, for obvious reasons. (One notable exception is the trials conducted by German courts against Germans during 1946–51, under a set of provisions jointly passed by the four Allies, the Control Council Law no. 10.)

The adoption in 1949 Geneva Conventions marked a great advance as regards the extension both of substantive law (new categories of war crimes were added: they were termed 'grave breaches of the Geneva Conventions': see 4.3) and of the law for the enforcement of substantive prohibitions. With regard to this last issue, the relevant provisions represented a momentous departure from customary law, since the Conventions laid down the principle of universal jurisdiction (a contracting state could bring to trial a person held in its custody and accused of a 'grave breach', regardless of his nationality, of the nationality of the victim, and of the place where the alleged offence had been committed). It is probable that the exceedingly bold character of this regulation contributed to its remaining ineffective for many years. The Geneva Conventions were followed by the two Additional Protocols in 1977, with the First Additional Protocol expanding the list of grave breaches.

Later on, as the ICTY Appeals Chamber authoritatively held in *Tadić (Interlocutory Appeal)* (§§ 94–137), the notion of war crimes was gradually extended to serious violations of IHL governing non-international armed conflict (see 4.2).

4.1 THE NOTION

War crimes are *serious violations* of customary or treaty rules belonging to international humanitarian law (IHL), also called international law of armed conflict. As the Appeals Chamber of the ICTY stated in *Tadić (Interlocutory Appeal)*, war crimes *i*) must consist of 'a serious infringement' of an international rule, that is to say 'must constitute a breach of a rule protecting important values, and the breach must involve grave consequences for the victim'; *ii*) the rule violated must either belong to the corpus of customary law or be part of an applicable treaty; and *iii*) 'the violation must entail, under customary or conventional law, the individual criminal responsibility of the person breaching the rule' (§ 94); in other words, the conduct constituting a serious breach of international law, in

---

[6] The idea propounded by such distinguished international lawyers as the American Hyde (C. C. Hyde, 'Punishment of War Criminals', *Proceedings of the ASIL* (1943), at 43–4) and the Austrian Kelsen (H. Kelsen, *Peace through Law*, cit. n. 4, at 111–16) that the international court should consist of neutral nationals was not upheld, clearly for political reasons; that is, because the victors wished to be and remain in control of the trials.

addition to being an interstate violation involving the responsibility of the state to which the serviceman belongs, must be criminalized.

In the same decision the Appeals Chamber gave the following example of a non-serious violation: 'the fact of a combatant simply appropriating a loaf of bread in an occupied village' would not amount to such a breach, 'although it may be regarded as falling foul of the basic principle laid down in Article 46(1) of the [1907] Hague Regulations [on Land Warfare] (and the corresponding rule of customary international law) whereby "private property must be respected" by any army occupying an enemy territory' (§ 94).

War crimes may be perpetrated in the course of either international or non-international armed conflicts (the latter being mainly civil wars or large-scale and protracted armed clashes breaking out within a sovereign state). Traditionally, war crimes were held to embrace only violations of international rules regulating war proper; that is, international armed conflicts and not civil wars. After the already mentioned ICTY Appeals Chamber decision in *Tadić* (*Interlocutory Appeal*), it is now widely accepted that serious infringements of international humanitarian law of non-international armed conflicts may also be regarded as amounting to war crimes proper, if the relevant conduct has been criminalized. As evidence of this new trend, suffice it to mention Article 8(2)(c–f) of the ICC Statute.

What is meant by 'armed conflict'? The question was correctly settled in 2010 by the ICTY Appeals Chamber in *Boškoski and Tarčulovski*. The Chamber confirmed the finding of the Trial Chamber that an armed conflict existed at the relevant time in the Former Yugoslav Republic of Macedonia (FYROM) between the FYROM security forces and the ethnic Albanian National Liberation Army (NLA) (§§ 21 and 24). It held that the Trial Chamber had correctly set out the relevant legal test that 'an armed conflict exists whenever there is a resort to armed force between States or protracted armed violence between governmental authorities and organised armed groups or between such groups within a State'(§ 21). Furthermore, the Appeals Chamber upheld the Trial Chamber's view that in order to distinguish an armed conflict from 'banditry, unorganized and short-lived insurrections or terrorist activities', two closely related criteria, namely *i*) the intensity of the conflict; and *ii*) the level of organization of the parties to the conflict must be applied on a case-by-case basis in light of the particular evidence (§ 21). Also, the Appeals Chamber found no error in the Trial Chamber's analysis of factors relevant to the assessment of the intensity of the conflict (§ 22) and the level of organization of the NLA (§ 23). The Appeals Chamber also upheld the Trial Chamber's conclusion based on these factors, whereby, despite the relatively limited number of casualties and damaged houses, the intensity of the conflict in the FYROM at the relevant time and the characteristics of the NLA as an organized armed group met the criteria for armed conflict (§§ 21 and 24).

Armed conflicts are governed by IHL, which is a vast body of substantive rules comprising what are traditionally called 'the law of the Hague' and 'the law of Geneva'. The former set of rules includes some Hague Conventions of 1899 or 1907 on international warfare. These rules, in addition to providing for the various categories of lawful combatants, primarily regulate combat actions (means and methods of warfare) and the treatment of persons who no longer take part in armed hostilities (prisoners of war). The so-called 'law of Geneva' comprises the various Geneva Conventions (at present the four Conventions of 1949 plus the two Additional Protocols of 1977), and is essentially designed to regulate the treatment of persons who do not, or no longer, take part in armed conflict (civilians, the wounded, the sick and shipwrecked, as well as prisoners of war). Furthermore, Article 3, common to the four Geneva Conventions and the Second Additional Protocol, regulates non-international armed conflict. The Third Geneva Convention of 1949 also regulates the various classes of lawful combatants, thereby updating the Hague rules. In addition, the First Additional Protocol of 1977 to some extent updates those rules of the Hague law which deal with means and methods of combat, for the sake of sparing civilians as far as possible from armed hostilities. It is thus clear that the traditional distinction between the two sets of rules is fading away; even assuming it has not become obsolete, its purpose now is largely descriptive.

War crimes may be perpetrated *by combatants* or *by civilians* of a party to the conflict against *combatants* or *civilians or non-other military targets* (for instance, private property) of the other party to the conflict. Conversely, crimes committed by combatants of one party to the conflict against members of their own armed forces do not constitute war crimes.[7] Such offences may nonetheless fall within the ambit of the military or domestic criminal law of the relevant belligerent.

4.2 THE CRIMINALIZATION OF THE SERIOUS VIOLATION OF A RULE OF IHL

In order for an individual to be held criminally responsible for a war crime, first of all it is necessary that he seriously infringed a rule of IHL. However, the rules belonging to this body of law normally ban given behaviours of states, which are their main addressees, or of other parties to an armed conflict. In order for a serious violation of IHL to become a war crime, it is necessary that the violation be also criminalized by international law. In other words, it is necessary for the law to attach to breaches of IHL the consequence that—in addition to the international responsibility of the state (or other party to an armed conflict)—the criminal liability of the individual (be he a state agent or a private individual) perpetrating that breach also arises. The question then becomes one of how to determine whether this is the case.

The point of departure is that only the relevant provisions enshrined in the four 1949 Geneva Conventions and Additional Protocol I concerning the so-called 'grave breaches' (see 4.3), expressly indicate the violations of the rules that, in addition to the international responsibility of the party to the conflict, also entail criminal responsibility of the individual for war crimes. Leaving aside these provisions, usually rules of IHL fail to provide expressly for the criminalization of their violations, or for the need for criminal proceedings in the event of the rule being breached. This is not, however, determinative of the

---

[7] This point was clarified in *Pilz* by the Dutch Special Court of Cassation (for a comment see *Cassese's Companion*, at 872). A young Dutchman in the occupied Netherlands had enlisted in the German army and while attempting to escape from his unit had been fired upon and wounded. Pilz, a German doctor serving in the German army with the rank of *Hauptstürmführer*, prevented medical and other aid or assistance being given by a doctor and hospital orderly to the wounded Dutchman, and in addition, 'in abuse of his authority as a superior', 'ordered or instructed a subordinate to kill the wounded [man] by means of a firearm' (at 1210), as a result of which the Dutchman died. The Court held that the offence was not a war crime, for 'the wounded person was part of the occupying army and the nationality of this person is therefore irrelevant, given that, by entering the military service of the occupying forces, he removed himself from the protection of international law and placed himself under the laws of the occupying power' (at 1210): consequently, the offence constituted a crime 'within the province of the internal law of Germany' (at 1211).

See also the decision in *Motosuke* delivered by a Temporary Court Martial of the Netherlands East Indies, at Amboina (for a comment on the case, see *Cassese's Companion*, at 816). Motosuke, a Japanese officer, had been accused, among other things, of having ordered the execution by shooting of a Dutch national named Barends, who, during the occupation of Ceram by Japanese armed forces, had joined the Gunkes, a corps of volunteer combatants composed mainly of Indonesian natives serving with the Japanese army. The Court held that by joining the Japanese forces, Barends had lost his nationality. His killing by Japanese forces was not considered a war crime (at 682–4).

issue. What matters is that criminal or military courts have in fact adjudicated breaches of IHL as war crimes. Various courts rightly held this view.[8]

A second, general and preliminary, remark concerns the need to avoid the following simplistic proposition: to determine whether a particular act may be termed a war crime, one need only establish that the act breaches IHL, since all violations of the laws of war are war crimes under national law and military manuals. The Judge Advocate at a Canadian Military Court pronouncing in 1946 on a war crime in *Johann Neitz* took this view.[9] This approach is not convincing, as not all violations of IHL amount to war crimes, as pointed out in *Tadić* (*Interlocutory Appeal*) (§ 94), although they may give rise to international responsibility of the party to the conflict to which the violation can be attributed.

These points having been established, several situations need to be distinguished. First, it may be that a violation has been consistently considered a war crime by national or international courts (this is, for example, true for the most blatant violations, such as unlawfully killing prisoners of war or innocent civilians, shelling hospitals, refusing quarter, killing shipwrecked or wounded persons, and so on). The existence of war crimes cases on a particular matter may sometimes be considered sufficient for holding the breach to be a war crime. However, strictly speaking, the existence of a few (possibly isolated) war crimes decisions may not be enough. It would be better if it were possible to show that the breach is considered a war crime under customary international law, in which case there would have to be widespread evidence that states customarily prosecute such breaches as war crimes and that they do so because they believe themselves to be acting under a binding rule of international law (*opinio juris*).

A second possible instance is that a breach is termed a war crime by the Statute of an international criminal court. In this case, even if the breach has never been brought before a national or international criminal court, it may justifiably be regarded as a war crime—or, at least, as a war crime falling under the jurisdiction of that international court.

A third, and more difficult, category is when the case law and statutes of international criminal courts are absent or silent on the matter.[10] In such a case, can one determine whether violating a prohibition of international humanitarian law amounts to a war crime? In light of the case law (see *List and others* (Hostages case), *John G. Schultz*, *Tadić* (*Interlocutory Appeal*), and *Blaškić*, to which I will presently return) and the general principles of ICL, in seeking an answer to the question one should examine: *i*) military manuals; *ii*) the national legislation of states belonging to the major legal systems of the world; or, if these elements are lacking, *iii*) the general principles of criminal justice common to domestic legal systems; and *iv*) the legislation and judicial practice of the state to which the accused belongs or on whose territory the crime has allegedly been committed.

---

[8] See e.g. the Nuremberg Tribunal in *Göring and others* (at 220–1), a US Military Tribunal sitting at Nuremberg in *List and others* (the so-called *Hostages* case) (at 635), and in *Ohlendorf and others* (the so-called *Einsatzgruppen* case) (at 658), as well as the US Supreme Court in *Ex parte Quirin* (at 465). For comments on all these cases, see the relevant entries in *Cassese's Companion*.

[9] After noting that, under Canadian law, a war crime was any 'violation of the laws and usages of war committed during any war in which Canada had been or may be engaged at any time', the Judge Advocate added, 'The test of criminal responsibility is therefore not properly applicable, and the issue upon any charge is not "did the accused commit a crime?" as we understand the word "crime" under our criminal law, but "did he violate the laws and usages of war"?' (195–6)

[10] An example is the prohibition on the use of weapons that are inherently indiscriminate or cause unnecessary suffering.

Let us now take a look at how courts have gone about this matter.

In *List and others* (*Hostages* case) the defendants were high-ranking officers in the German armed forces charged with war crimes and crimes against humanity. They were accused of offences committed by troops under their command during the occupation of Greece, Yugoslavia, Albania, and Norway, these offences mainly being reprisal killings (purportedly carried out in an attempt to maintain order in the occupied territories in the face of guerrilla opposition), or wanton destruction of property not justified by military necessity. They claimed that Control Council Law no. 10, on the basis of which they stood accused, was an *ex post facto* act and retroactive in nature. The Tribunal rejected the contention, holding that the crimes defined in that Law were crimes under pre-existing rules of international law, 'some by conventional law and some by customary law'. It went on to state that the war crimes at issue were such under the Hague Regulations of 1907 and then added

> In any event, the practices and usages of war which gradually ripened into recognized customs with which belligerents were bound to comply, recognized the crimes specified herein as crimes subject to punishment. It is not essential that a crime be specifically defined and charged in accordance with a particular ordinance, statute or treaty if it is made a crime by international convention, recognized customs and usages or war, or the general principles of criminal justice common to civilized nations generally. (634–5)

The Tribunal then noted that the acts at issue were traditionally punished, adding that, although no courts had been established nor penalties provided for the commission of these crimes, 'this is not fatal to their validity. The acts prohibited are without deterrent effect unless they are punishable as crimes' (635).

It was the Appeals Chamber of the ICTY that best addressed the issue under discussion, in *Tadić* (*Interlocutory Appeal*). The question in dispute was whether the accused could be held criminally liable for breaches of IHL allegedly committed in an internal armed conflict; in other words, whether he could be held responsible for war crimes perpetrated in a civil war. The Appeals Chamber first considered whether there were customary rules of IHL governing internal armed conflicts, and answered in the affirmative (§§ 96–127). It then asked itself whether violations of those rules could entail individual criminal responsibility. For this purpose, the Appeals Chamber examined national cases, military manuals, national legislation, and resolutions of the UN Security Council. It concluded in the affirmative (§§ 128–34) and then added that in the case at issue this conclusion was fully warranted 'from the point of view of substantive justice and equity', because violations of IHL in internal armed conflicts were punished as criminal offences in the countries concerned; that is, both the old Socialist Federal Republic of Yugoslavia and in Bosnia and Herzegovina. As the Appeals Chamber noted, 'Nationals of the former Yugoslavia as well as, at present, those of Bosnia-Herzegovina were therefore aware, or should have been aware, that they were amenable to the jurisdiction of their national criminal courts in cases of violation of international humanitarian law' (§ 135; see also § 136).

An ICTY Trial Chamber returned to the question in *Blaškić*. The defence contended that violations of common Article 3 of the four 1949 Geneva Conventions (on internal armed conflict)[11] did not entail criminal liability. The Trial Chamber dismissed this contention by noting, first, that those violations were envisaged in Article 3 of the ICTY Statute, conferring jurisdiction on the Tribunal, and second, that the criminal code of Yugoslavia, taken over in 1992 as the criminal code of Bosnia and Herzegovina (the place

---

[11] For the text of this provision see n. 20.

where the alleged offences had been committed), provided that war crimes perpetrated either in international or in internal armed conflicts involved the criminal liability of the perpetrator (§ 176).[12]

4.3 THE OBJECTIVE ELEMENTS

4.3.1 GENERAL

In order to identify the main legal features of the prohibited conduct, it is necessary to consider in each case the content of the substantive rule that has been allegedly breached. This should not be surprising. No authoritative and legally binding list of conducts that can constitute war crimes exists in customary international law. The 1949 Geneva Conventions and the First Additional Protocol of 1977 contain an enumeration of a sub-category of war crimes, namely those acts that are provided for in terms and defined by the Conventions and the First Additional Protocol themselves as 'grave breaches'. A broader enumeration can also be found in Article 8 of the ICC Statute, which is not, however, intended to codify customary international law. It should also be noted, more generally, that the principle of legality or *nullum crimen sine lege* (traditionally laid down in national legal systems) is upheld in ICL only in a limited way (see 2.2–2.4). Hence in each case (and with only the exception of grave breaches) the objective element of the crime must essentially be inferred from the substantive rules of IHL.

As for grave breaches, a further requirement is provided for by the 1949 Geneva Conventions and the First Additional Protocol: such acts must be committed within the context of an international armed conflict. The ICTY Appeals Chamber held in *Tadić*

---

[12] The question was also dealt with, albeit in less compelling terms, by a US Court of Military Appeals in *John G. Schultz* (already quoted Chapter 3, n. 28). The accused, a former captain of the US Air Force who had returned to civilian life, had killed two Japanese pedestrians in Japan in 1950. He was tried by a US General Court Martial on charges of involuntary manslaughter and drunken driving, in violation of Articles of War (respectively, 93 and 96). The Judge Advocate General of the Air Force appealed the case on, among other grounds, the issue of whether the Court Martial had jurisdiction over the accused and the offences charged. The Court of Appeals, having found that the accused was neither a 'retainer to the camp' nor a 'person accompanying or serving with the US Armies', hence not amenable to a US Court Martial's jurisdiction on these grounds, asked itself whether he fell under the category of 'any other person who by the law of war is subject to trial by military tribunals'. To answer this question it noted, among other things, that US jurisdiction extended to two types of offences: first, crimes committed against the civilian population made 'punishable by the penal codes of all civilized nations', namely war crimes; second, 'crimes condemned by local statute which the military occupying power must take cognizance of inasmuch as the civil authority is superseded by the military'. The court first looked into the first category, to establish whether the offence at issue fell within such category. Having reached a negative conclusion, it turned to the second category, and concluded that the offence came within its purview. Let us now briefly see how the court discussed the class of war crimes in a lengthy *obiter dictum*.

The court noted that this category 'finds its basis in the customs and usages of civilized nations'. It then went on to say that, 'It is [...] no obstacle to finding a particular offence to be a violation of the law of war that it has not yet been precisely labelled as such. On the other hand, of course, we are not free to add offences at will. In deciding whether an offence comes within the common law of war, we must consider the international attitude towards that offence. The power to define such offences is derived from Articles of War 12 and 15 [...] and it is no objection that Congress has not codified that branch of international law or defined the acts which that law condemns [...] We shall assume that a crime may become a violation of the law of war if universally recognized as an offence even though it contains no element of specific criminal intent. A careful perusal of the penal codes of most civilized nations leads us to the conclusion that homicide involving less than culpable negligence is not universally recognized as an offence' (114–16).

(*Interlocutory Appeal*) that a rule of customary international law was *in statu nascendi*—that is, in the process of forming, whereby 'grave breaches' could also be perpetrated in internal armed conflicts; instead, according to Judge Abi-Saab's Separate Opinion in that case, such a rule had already evolved. At present, in light of the recent trends in the legislation or practice of states,[13] the contention is perhaps warranted that a customary rule has indeed emerged. However, it is plausible to contend that this rule only confers on states the *power* to search for and bring to trial or extradite alleged authors of grave breaches committed in internal armed conflicts; the rule does not go so far as to also impose upon states an *obligation* to seek out and try or extradite those alleged authors (as is instead the case for grave breaches perpetrated in international armed conflicts).

4.3.2 CLASSES OF WAR CRIME

On the basis of their contextual element, war crimes can be classified under two different headings: *i)* war crimes committed in *international* armed conflicts—that is, between two or more states, or between a state and a national liberation movement, pursuant to Article 1(4) of the First Additional Protocol of 1977; and *ii)* war crimes perpetrated in internal (*rectius*: non-international) armed conflicts (these can be defined as large-scale armed hostilities, other than internal disturbances and tensions, or riots or isolated or sporadic acts of armed violence, between state authorities and rebels, or between two or more organized armed groups within a state). Traditionally, states and courts have held that war crimes may only be committed during wars proper. Violations of IHL committed in the course of internal armed conflicts were not criminalized. Thus, a glaring and preposterous disparity existed. As stated above, in 1995, a seminal judgment of the ICTY Appeals Chamber in *Tadić* (*Interlocutory Appeals*) (§§ 97–137) signalled a significant advance: the Appeals Chamber held that custom had evolved to provide that war crimes could be committed not only in international armed conflicts but also in internal armed conflicts. Since then the view has been generally upheld and the ICC Statute definitively consecrates it in Article 8(2)(c)–(f).

On account of their objective elements, both classes include the following:

i) Crimes committed *against persons not taking part, or no longer taking part, in armed hostilities.* In practice by far the most numerous crimes are committed against civilians,[14] or armed resistance movements in occupied territory,[15] and include sexual violence

---

[13] For instance, Art. 8 of the Netherlands Criminal Law in Time of War Act (1952) provides that national courts have jurisdiction over all violations of the laws and customs of war. The law has been interpreted to apply to internal armed conflicts as well (Art. 1(3) states that the term 'war' includes civil war). Art. 3 of that law provides that courts may exercise universal jurisdiction over violations of the laws and customs of war. In Switzerland an amendment to the Criminal Code of 13 December 2002 provides for criminal jurisdiction over violations of IHL in internal armed conflict as well. In Germany Section 1 of the Code of Crimes Against International Law applies the universality principle to all international crimes such as genocide, war crimes, and crimes against humanity, whether or not committed in Germany. This provision is strengthened by Sections 153ff. of the Code of Criminal Procedure, which also lays down a duty of investigation and prosecution for international crimes committed abroad.

[14] See e.g. *von Falkenhausen and others* (at 867–93), *Bellmer* (at 541–4), *Lages* (at 2–3), *Wagener and others* (at 148), *Sch. O.* (at 305–7), *Sergeant W.* (decision of 18 May 1966, at 1–3; decision of 14 July 1966, at 2). For fairly recent cases see, for instance, *Major Malinky Shmuel and others* (at 10–137), *Calley* (at 1164–84), *Tzofan and others* (*Yehuda Meir* case) at 724–46, *Sabli and others* (at 37–135).

[15] See e.g. the *SIPO Brussels* case (at 11518–26), *Allers and others* (at 225–47). For comments on these cases, see *Cassese's Companion*, at 926 and 582, respectively.

against women.[16] In particular, they are perpetrated against persons detained in internment or concentration camps.[17] They are also committed against prisoners of war.[18]

In the case of international armed conflicts, serious war crimes against one of the 'protected persons' (i.e. those persons whose status is expressly defined by the four Geneva Conventions of 1949: wounded, shipwrecked persons, prisoners of war, civilians on the territory of the Detaining Power or subject to the belligerent occupation of an Occupying Power) or 'protected objects' (again those provided for in the 1949 Geneva Conventions, as well as the First Additional Protocol) are termed 'grave breaches'. Grave breaches are defined in the following provisions: Articles 50, 51, 130, and 147 of the First, Second, Third, and Fourth Geneva Conventions, respectively, as well as in Article 85 of the First Additional Protocol. They include wilful killing, torture, or inhuman treatment, including biological experiments, wilfully causing great suffering or serious injury to body or health, extensive destruction and appropriation of property, not justified by military necessity and carried out unlawfully and wantonly. The essential feature of 'grave breaches' is that, under the system envisaged by the 1949 Geneva Conventions and the First Additional Protocol, they are subject to 'universal jurisdiction' of all states parties to the Convention and the Protocol: any contracting state is authorized as well as obliged to search for and bring to trial—or, alternatively, extradite to a requesting state—any person suspected or accused of a grave breach (whatever his or her nationality and the territory where the grave breach has allegedly been perpetrated) who happens to be on its territory.

In the case of non-international armed conflict,[19] the same violations are prohibited and may amount to a war crime if they are serious. In this connection reference should be

---

[16] In this respect it is worth mentioning two cases brought after the Second World War before the Dutch Temporary Court Martial in Batavia (Indonesia). The first is *Washio Awochi*. The accused, a Japanese civilian who managed a club for Japanese civilians in Indonesia, had procured or arranged the procurement of girls and women for the club's visitors, forcing them into prostitution; they were not free to leave the part of the club where they had been confined. The Court held that the defendant was guilty of the war crime of 'forcing into prostitution' and sentenced him to ten years' imprisonment (at 1–15). In *Takeuchi Hiroe* the accused, a Japanese national, had used violence or threats of violence against a young Indonesian woman, and had forced her to have sexual intercourse with him. The Court found him guilty of the war crime of rape and sentenced him to five years' imprisonment (at 1–5).
See also some cases of rape brought before the ICTY: *Furundžija*, TC, §§ 165–89, and *Kunarac and others*, TC, §§ 436–64 and 630–87, 717–45, 785–98, 806–22.

[17] Among the numerous cases on this matter, one may recall various ones concerning the ill-treatment of persons detained in the concentration camps instituted in Poland, such as Auschwitz (see *Mulka and others*), in Germany; at Dachau (see *Martin Gottfried and others*); by the German occupying troops in Majdanek (see *Götzfrid*, at 2–70); in camps in Belgium (see e.g. *Köpperlmann* as well as *K.W.* (at 565–7) and *K.* (at 653–5); in Amersfoort (Netherlands) (see e.g. *Kotälla*); or in Bolzano (Italy) (see e.g. *Mittermair*, at 2–5, *Mitterstieler*, at 2–7, *Lanz*, at 2–4, *Cologna*, at 2–9, *Koppelstätter and others*, at 3–7) or in the Italian camp of Fossoli (see *Gutweniger*, at 2–4); or in internment camps in the former Yugoslavia (see e.g. *Sarić*, 2–6). Such crimes may even be perpetrated by internees against other internees (see e.g. *Tarnek*, at 3–11, and *Enigster*, at 5–26). (For comments on some of these cases, see the relevant entries in *Cassese's Companion*.)

[18] See, for instance, some cases brought after the First World War before the Leipzig Supreme Court: *Heynen* (at 2543–7), *Müller* (at 2549–52), and *Neumann* (at 2553–6). See also other cases, relating to the Second World War: *Mälzer* (at 53–5), *Feurstein and others* (at 1–26), *Krauch and others* (at 668–80), *Weiss and Mundo* (at 149), *Gozawa Sadaichi and others* (at 195–228), *General Seeger and others* (*Vosges* case), at 17–22; *St Die* case, at 58–61; *La Grande Fosse* case, at 23–7; *Essen Lynching* case, at 88–92. For comments on some on these cases, see the relevant entries in *Cassese's Companion*.

[19] For a case where a court has endeavoured to define the notion of 'internal armed conflict' see *Ministère public and Centre pour l'égalité des chances et la lutte contre le racism v. C. and B.* (at 5–7). Other cases where courts had to pronounce on whether or not the conflict was internal, include: *Osvaldo Romo Mena* (decision of the Supreme Court of Chile of 26 October 1995, at 3, and decision of 9 September 1998, at 2–5), *Chilean state of emergency* case (at 1–3), and *G.* (Swiss Military Tribunal, at 7).

made to Article 3 common to the four 1949 Geneva Conventions,[20] the Second Additional Protocol (especially Article 4 thereof),[21] as well as Article 4 of the ICTR Statute.[22] As noted above, there is no treaty provision characterizing violations of these rules as 'grave breaches' and consequently attaching to such classification all the ensuing consequences at the procedural level (power and duty to exercise universal jurisdiction over the alleged offender). Nor, it would seem, has a rule of customary international law evolved imposing upon states (and the rebellious group engaged in a civil war) the obligation to search for and bring to trial (or extradite) persons suspected or accused of a grave breach perpetrated in an internal armed conflict.

ii) Crimes against enemy combatants or civilians, committed by resorting to *prohibited methods of warfare*. Examples include intentionally directing attacks against the civilian population in the combat area or individual civilians in the combat area not taking part in hostilities; committing acts or threats of violence the primary purpose of which is to spread terror among the civilian population; intentionally launching an indiscriminate attack affecting the civilian population or civilian objects in the knowledge that such attack will cause excessive loss of life, injury to civilians, or damage to civilian objects; intentionally making non-defended localities or demilitarized zones the object of attack; intentionally making a person the object of attack in the knowledge that he is *hors de combat*; intentionally attacking medical buildings, material, medical units and transport, and personnel; intentionally using starvation of civilians as a method of warfare by depriving civilians of objects indispensable to their survival, including wilfully impeding relief supplies; intentionally launching an attack in the knowledge that such attack will cause widespread, long-term, and severe damage to the natural environment; utilizing the presence of civilians or other protected persons with a view to rendering certain points, areas, or military forces immune from military operations;

---

[20] Common Art. 3 provides: 'In the case of armed conflict not of an international character occurring in the territory of one of the High Contracting Parties, each Party to the conflict shall be bound to apply, as a minimum, the following provisions:

(1) Persons taking no active part in the hostilities, including members of armed forces who have laid down their arms and those placed hors de combat by sickness, wounds, detention, or any other cause, shall in all circumstances be treated humanely, without any adverse distinction founded on race, colour, religion or faith, sex, birth or wealth, or any other similar criteria. To this end the following acts are and shall remain prohibited at any time and in any place whatsoever with respect to the above-mentioned persons:

    (a) violence to life and person, in particular murder of all kinds, mutilation, cruel treatment and torture;

    (b) taking of hostages;

    (c) outrages upon personal dignity, in particular, humiliating and degrading treatment;

    (d) the passing of sentences and the carrying out of executions without previous judgment pronounced by a regularly constituted court affording all the judicial guarantees which are recognized as indispensable by civilized peoples.

(2) The wounded and sick shall be collected and cared for.

An impartial humanitarian body, such as the International Committee of the Red Cross, may offer its services to the Parties to the conflict.

The Parties to the conflict should further endeavour to bring into force, by means of special agreements, all or part of the other provisions of the present Convention. The application of the preceding provisions shall not affect the legal status of the Parties to the conflict.'

[21] For a case where a court has held that the Second Additional Protocol was applicable, see *Applicability of the Second Additional Protocol to the Conflict in Chechnya* (*Chechnya* case) (at 2–3). See also *Constitutional Conformity of Protocol II* (§ 25).

[22] For a case of war crimes in civil war, see *Nwaoga* (at 494–5).

declaring that no quarter will be given—that is, that enemy combatants will be killed and not taken prisoner.[23]

It should be noted that, the substantive rules of IHL on this matter being purposely loose, so far very few cases have been brought before national or international courts concerning alleged violations of rules on the conduct of hostilities entailing the criminal liability of the perpetrators.[24] Strikingly, more cases involving the alleged breach of rules of IHL on the conduct of hostilities have been brought before interstate courts, pronouncing on state responsibility.[25]

iii) Crimes against enemy combatants and civilians, involving the use of *prohibited means of warfare*. Examples include employing weapons, projectiles, and materials which are of a nature to cause superfluous injury or unnecessary suffering; employing poison or poisoned weapons, or asphyxiating, poisonous, or other gases, and all analogous liquids, materials, or devices; using chemical or bacteriological weapons; employing expanding bullets or weapons, the primary effect of which is to injure by fragments not detectable by X-rays, or blinding laser weapons;[26] employing booby-traps or land mines indiscriminately—that is, in such a way as to hit both combatants and civilians alike, or anti-personnel mines which are not detectable; employing napalm and other incendiary weapons in a manner prohibited by the 1980 Protocol III to the aforementioned Convention (for instance, by making a military objective 'located within a concentration of civilians the object of attack by air-delivered incendiary weapons').

What I have pointed out with regard to breaches of international rules on methods of war, a fortiori applies to violations of rules on means of warfare, the latter category of rules being even more difficult to apply than the legal standards on the conduct of hostilities.

---

[23] See ICTY, *Kordić anad Cerkez*, TC, § 328; *Galić*, TC, § 62; *Strugar*, TC, § 283.

[24] For instance, see the *General Jacob H. Smith* case, decided by a US Court Martial on 3 May 1902, concerning the order that no quarter should be given (at 799–813). Before the Nuremberg Tribunal Admirals Dönitz and Reeder were charged with, but acquitted of, waging unrestricted submarine warfare (see *Trial of the Major War Criminals*, vol. I, 311–12 and 316–17). See also the *Calley* case, revolving around the killing of Vietnamese civilians in the village of My Lai (see the Instructions of the Military Judge to the Court Martial, March 1971, at 1703–27, as well as the decision of 16 February 1973 of the US Army Court of Military Review, 1131). The *van Anraat* case, brought before the Hague District Court and subsequently the Hague Appeal Court, relates to complicity in a war crime (the accused sold chemicals for the manufacture of prohibited chemical weapons to Iraqi authorities).

As for international criminal courts, see ICTY, *Blaškić*, TC (unlawful attacks against civilians and civilian property; destruction of institutions dedicated to religion); *Galić*, TC (on sniping and shelling at civilians in Sarajevo); *Strugar*, TC (on the shelling of Dubrovnik); *Martić*, TC (on the shelling of Zagreb).

[25] For instance, see some cases brought before the Eritrea–Ethiopia Claims Commission, *Partial Award, Central front, Ethiopia's Claim 2*, as well as *Partial Award, Western and Eastern Fronts, Ethiopia's Claims 1 and 2*. See also a few cases brought before the European Court on Human Rights: *Isayeva, Ysupova and Bazaieva v. Russia*, *Isayeva v. Russia*, and *Khatsiyeva and others*. See also some cases brought before the Inter-American Court of Human Rights: *Plan de Sanchez Massacre v. Guatemala*; *case Las Palmeras v. Colombia*; *case of the massacre of Mapiripán v. Colombia*. See also the decision of the Inter-American Commission of Human Rights on *Juan Carlos Abella Argentina*.

Seldom have national courts pronounced upon the conduct of hostilities, and always within the context of civil, not criminal, action. See e.g. *Shimoda and others* (on the atomic bombing of Hiroshima and Nagasaki), at 1688–1702.

[26] According to the definition of the 1995 Protocol IV to the Convention on Prohibitions or Restrictions on the Use of Certain Conventional Weapons Which May be Deemed to be Excessively Injurious or to Have Indiscriminate Effects, adopted at Geneva on 10 October 1980, the latter are 'laser weapons specifically designed, as their sole combat function or as one of their combat functions, to cause permanent blindness to un-enhanced vision, that is to the naked eye or to the eye with corrective eyesight devices'.

iv) Crimes *against specially protected persons and objects* (such as medical personnel units or transport, personnel participating in relief actions, humanitarian organizations such as the Red Cross, or Red Crescent, or Red Lion and Sun units, UN personnel belonging to peacekeeping missions, etc.).

v) Crimes consisting of *improperly using protected signs and emblems* (such as a flag of truce; the distinctive emblems of the Red Cross, or Red Crescent, or Red Lion and Sun, plus the emblem provided for in the Third Additional Protocol of 8 December 2005 (the emblem 'composed of a red frame in the shape of a square on edge on a white ground'); perfidious use of a national flag or of military uniform and insignia, etc.).

vi) Conscripting or enlisting *children under the age of 15 years* or using them to participate actively in hostilities (in either international or internal armed conflicts). According to the Appeals Chamber of the SCSL in *Norman* (*Decision on Preliminary Motion Based on Lack of Jurisdiction*, § 53) 'child recruitment was criminalised before it was explicitly set out as a criminal prohibition in treaty law and certainly by November 1996, the starting point of the time frame relevant to the indictment' (against the defendants in that case). This proposition was restated by a Trial Chamber of the SCSL in *Brima and others* (§§ 727–8), where the elements of the crime were set out (§ 729).

4.4 THE SUBJECTIVE ELEMENTS

The subjective—or mental—element (mens rea) of the crime is sometimes specified by the international rule prohibiting a certain conduct.

Thus, for instance, Article 130 of the Third Geneva Convention of 1949 (on prisoners of war) enumerates among the 'grave breaches' of the Convention the 'wilful killing [of prisoners of war], torture or inhuman treatment, including biological experiments' as well as 'wilfully causing great suffering or serious injury to body or health' of a prisoner of war, or 'wilfully depriving a prisoner of war of the rights of fair and regular trial prescribed in [the] Convention'.

The word 'wilful' obviously denotes *criminal intent*, namely the intention to bring about the consequences of the act prohibited by the international rule (for instance, in the case of 'wilful killing' proof must be produced of the intention to cause the death of the victim; in the case of 'wilfully causing great suffering' it must be proved that the perpetrator had the intention to cause great suffering, etc.). The same holds true for other similar provisions, such as Article 147 of the Fourth Geneva Convention (on civilians), as well as provisions of other treaties, such as Article 15 of the 1999 Second Hague Protocol for the Protection of Cultural Property in the Event of Armed Conflict. (This provision, in enumerating the serious violations of the Protocol entailing individual criminal liability, makes such liability contingent upon the fact that the author of the 'offence' has perpetrated it 'intentionally'.)

One can also mention Article 85(3) of the First Additional Protocol of 1977. This provision subordinates the criminalization of such acts as attacking civilians or undefended localities, or demilitarized zones, or perfidiously using the distinctive emblem of the Red Cross, Red Crescent, or Red Lion and Sun, to three conditions: *i*) the acts must be committed 'wilfully'; *ii*) they must be carried out in violation of the relevant provisions of the Protocol; and *iii*) they must cause death or serious injury to body or health. Thus, the provisions clearly require intent or at least *recklessness* (so-called *dolus eventualis* or indirect intent), which exists whenever somebody, although aware of the likely pernicious consequences of his conduct, knowingly takes the risk of bringing about such consequences (see 3.5).

For other acts, the same provision also requires 'knowledge' as a condition of criminal liability. This, for instance, applies to 'launching an indiscriminate attack affecting the civilian population or civilian objects in the knowledge that such attack will cause excessive loss of life, injury to civilians or damage to civilian objects' (Article 85(3)(b)); or to 'launching an attack against works or installations containing dangerous forces in the knowledge that such attack will cause excessive loss of life, injury to civilians or damage to civilian objects' (Article 85(3)(c)). As we have seen (see 3.6), in criminal law 'knowledge' is normally part of 'intent' (*dolus*) and refers to awareness of the circumstances forming part of the definition of the crime. However, in the context of the provision at issue, 'knowledge' must be interpreted to mean 'predictability of the likely consequences of the action' (recklessness or *dolus eventualis*, see 3.5). Therefore, for an act such as that just mentioned to be regarded as a war crime, evidence must be produced not only of the intention to launch an attack, for instance an attack on a military objective normally used by civilians (e.g. a bridge, a road, etc.), but also of the foreseeability that the attack was likely to cause excessive loss of life or injury to civilians or civilian objects. In other instances, international rules require knowledge in the sense of awareness of a circumstance of fact, as part of criminal intent (*dolus*). Thus, Article 85(3)(e) of the same Protocol makes it a crime to wilfully attack a person 'in the knowledge that he is *hors de combat*'.

When international rules do not provide, not even implicitly, for a subjective element, it would seem appropriate to hold that what is required is the intent or, depending upon the circumstances, recklessness as prescribed in most legal systems of the world for the underlying offence (murder, rape, torture, destruction of private property, pillage, etc.). Often, international criminal courts and tribunals have gradually identified the requisite mental element based on the nature of the underlying offence. Thus, for instance, in the case of murder as a war crime, the jurisprudence of the ICTR and the ICTY has consistently held that what is required is that 'the death of the victim must result from an act or omission of the accused committed with the intent either to kill or to cause serious bodily harm in the reasonable knowledge that it would likely result in death' (*Krstić*, TC, § 483; *Blaškić*, TC, § 217; *Kvocka and others*, TC, § 132; *Stakić*, TC, §§ 584–6; *Martić*, TC, § 60). In other words, either intent or at least *dolus eventualis* or recklessness are required.[27]

Generally speaking, it appears admissible to contend that, for at least some limited categories of war crimes, gross or *culpable negligence* (*culpa gravis*) may be sufficient; that is, the author of the crime, although aware of the risk involved in his conduct, is nevertheless convinced that the prohibited consequence will not occur (whereas in the case of 'recklessness' or *dolus eventualis* the author knowingly takes the risk). Indeed, the consequent broadening of the range of acts amenable to international prosecution is in keeping with the general object and purpose of IHL. This modality of mens rea may, for instance, apply to cases of command or superior responsibility (see 10.2), where the commander should have known that war crimes were being committed by his subordinates. Also, it could be contended that it may apply to such cases as wanton destruction of private property. In contrast, it may seem difficult to consider culpable negligence a sufficient subjective element of the crime in cases involving the taking of human life.

---

[27] As an ICTY Trial Chamber held in *Stakić*, 'both a *dolus directus* and a *dolus eventualis* are sufficient to establish the crime of murder under Article 3. In French and German law, the standard form of criminal homicide (*meurtre, Totschlag*) is defined simply as intentionally killing another human being. German law takes *dolus eventualis* as sufficient to constitute intentional killing' (*Stakić*, TC, § 587).

4.5 THE NEXUS WITH THE ARMED CONFLICT

Not all crimes committed during an armed conflict constitute war crimes. It is widely held in case law[28] and legal literature[29] that, in order to qualify as a war crime, criminal conduct must be 'closely related to the hostilities'. This relationship (which clearly exists in relation to all crimes consisting of violations of the rules on the conduct of hostilities, i.e. those consisting of recourse to illegal methods and means of warfare) serves to distinguish between war crimes, on the one side, and 'ordinary' criminal conduct that therefore falls under the law applicable in the relevant territory.[30]

The question of 'nexus' applies in particular to offences committed by civilians against other civilians or against combatants, although courts have also required the link or nexus with an armed conflict in the case of crimes perpetrated by members of the armed forces. In addition, it should be noted that identifying a nexus between a criminal offence and an armed conflict is relatively easy in the case of *international* armed conflict: there, normally two or more belligerents face each other, and offences committed by combatants or civilians of one party to the conflict against combatants and civilians of the opposing party will usually be considered as 'linked' to the armed conflict. In contrast, things are less clear in *non-international* armed conflict, in particular with respect to crimes committed by civilians not taking part in hostilities (or during such time as they do not take part in hostilities) against other civilians. Here, since there is no legal status as combatants, rebels are civilians who take up arms against another group or against the government: they all have the same nationality. In addition, civilians who do not belong to any rebellious group might attack other civilians—despite the fact that they have the same nationality—on the assumption that the latter 'belong to' the opposed faction (that is, owe

---

[28] See the following decisions by Trial Chambers of the ICTY and the ICTR: *Akayesu* (§§ 630–4, 638–44), *Kayishema and Ruzindana* (§§ 185–9, 590–624), *Musema* (§§ 259–62, 275, and 974). In all these cases the Chambers eventually found that the link required was lacking. See also ICTY, *Tadić*, TC, § 573; *Delalić and others*, TC, § 193).

[29] E.g., G. Mettraux, 'Nexus with Armed Conflict', in *Cassese's Companion*, at 435.

[30] The Swiss Appellate Military Tribunal aptly confirmed this proposition in *Niyonteze*. The accused was a Rwandan arrested in Switzerland and accused of having instigated, and in some cases ordered, the murder of civilians in Rwanda in 1994 in his capacity as mayor of a local 'community' (*commune*). The Tribunal could not apply the Genocide Convention since Switzerland had not yet ratified it. The Tribunal held, therefore, that it would apply the laws of warfare and the provisions of the Geneva Conventions applicable to internal armed conflicts as well as the Second Protocol of 1977. Faced with the question whether a civilian could be held responsible for war crimes where he had instigated or ordered the murder of other civilians, the Tribunal held: 'Anyone, whether military or civilian, who attacks a civilian protected by the Geneva Conventions [...] breaches these Conventions and consequently falls under Article 109 of the Swiss Penal Military Code [providing for the punishment of war crimes]. This Appellate Tribunal thus differs from the judgments of the ICTR, which require a close link between the breach and an armed conflict and confine the application of the Geneva Conventions to persons discharging functions within the armed forces or the civilian government (*Musema* §§ 259[–62] and *Akayesu* §§ 642–3). Nevertheless this Tribunal considers that in any case there must exist a link between the breach and an armed conflict. If, within the framework of a civil war, where civilians of the two sides are both protected by the Geneva Conventions, a protected person commits a breach against another protected person, it is necessary to establish a link between this act and the armed conflict. If such link is lacking, the breach does not constitute a war crime but an ordinary offence (*infraction de droit commun*)' (39–40). In the case at bar, the Tribunal found this link in the fact that the accused was the mayor of the *commune*, and exercised *de jure* and *de facto* authority over the local citizens; it was thus in his capacity as a 'public official' or civil servant that he committed the crimes (40–1).

The Tribunal Militaire de Cassation upheld the ruling in its decision of 27 April 2001 on the same case (§ 9).

allegiance to the military and political structure of the opposed faction).[31] Furthermore, technically speaking, in a civil war civilians are not 'protected persons' pursuant to the Geneva Conventions and Protocols. These problems affecting *non-international* armed conflicts should be borne in mind when considering the various issues that accompany the question of pinpointing the nature and scope of the 'nexus'.

The ICTY and ICTR considered the following criteria of assistance when assessing whether an offence qualifies as a war crime: the fact that the perpetrator is a combatant; the fact that the victim is a non-combatant; the fact that the victim is a member of the opposing party; the fact that the act may be said to serve the ultimate goal of a military campaign; and the fact that the crime is committed as part of or in the context of the perpetrator's 'official duties'.[32]

However, one could argue that the following two requirements must be met for an offence to be considered a war crime. The offence must have been *i*) perpetrated against persons who do not take direct part in hostilities or who no longer take part in such hostilities; and *ii*) it must have been committed to pursue the aims of the conflict or, alternatively, it must have been carried out with a view to somehow contributing to attaining the ultimate goals of a military campaign or, at a minimum, in unison with the military campaign. These two requirements are consonant with the rationale behind the punishment of war crimes, i.e. that all those who, during an armed conflict, seriously contravene rules of IHL against persons protected by such rules should be personally accountable for such breaches (here persons protected by IHL must be understood *lato sensu*; that is, as a term embracing both protected persons under the four Geneva Conventions and civilians in internal armed conflict who do not take direct part in the hostilities).

The two conditions must exist *cumulatively*. Thus, an offence (murder, torture, rape, etc.) committed by a combatant against a civilian of the opposing party, or an offence against an enemy combatant (e.g. by using unlawful weapons) in breach of a rule of IHL is generally classified as a war crime: such offence has been perpetrated to (wrongly) pursue the purposes of war. By the same token, an offence (theft, murder, rape, etc.) committed by a combatant against another combatant belonging to the same belligerent (e.g. the rape of a member of an army by a fellow officer or private), is not a war crime, although the armed conflict may have been the occasion for the offence (for instance, it is possible that if there was no armed conflict they would not happen to serve in the same battalion or to meet in the barracks). Similarly, an offence (e.g. murder or rape) committed by a civilian against another civilian of the same party to the conflict is not a war crime, even when the opportunity for the commission of the offence has been created by the armed conflict (for example, a civilian murders or rapes a neighbour, knowing that he is likely to enjoy impunity on account of the collapse of public order caused by the armed conflict).

Instead, an offence perpetrated during a non-international armed conflict by a civilian against a civilian belonging to the opposing party to the conflict may amount to a war crime (for instance, the rape of a Muslim woman by a Croat in a civil war opposing Croats to Muslims). If the offender identifies with the party to which the civilian victim belongs to (or to which she owes allegiance), the crime may be regarded as carried out in unison with the ultimate goals of the military campaign. These circumstances would make it clear that the armed conflict created the situation for the crime to be perpetrated. Indeed, the offence is committed because, and within the context, of the armed conflict, and is carried out in consonance with the ultimate goals of the military

---

[31] On the notion of allegiance to a party to the conflict as a possible alternative to nationality of that party, see *Tadić* (*Interlocutory Appeal*), §§ 164–6.

[32] See ICTY, *Kunarac*, TC, § 402, and ICTR, *Nyiramasuhuko and others*, TC, §§ 6153–4.

campaign, and against a protected person. The same applies to the case of an offence (e.g., murder) committed, in breach of IHL, by a civilian against a combatant belonging to the opposing party to the conflict.

In contrast, if a crime committed by a combatant against an enemy civilian does not pursue the ultimate goals of the military campaign nor is at least consonant with the military campaign, it can be classified as an ordinary crime. Take the case of a group of militias or combatants intent on profiting from the confusion caused by an internal armed conflict by stealing goods from the wealthy, who engage in armed robbery of the house or a jewellery store of a rich civilian who happens to belong to the enemy party. In this case, unless prosecuting authorities show some other specific link with the armed conflict, the robbery should be characterized as a common crime and not as looting as a war crime.

Importantly, the 'nexus' standard is objective in linking the armed conflict *with the crime*, not the criminal. The fact that the offender is a soldier, does not, in and of itself, provide the necessary link. Rather, it is the inference regarding the conduct taken by the combatant that establishes the link. The very same link can be proved between a crime committed by a civilian and the armed conflict. Thus, the conduct is objectively a war crime—even if in other respects the nexus is proven by looking at the personal (subjective) qualification of the perpetrator and the victim. The application of the standard as such avoids two unwanted outcomes. First, opportunistic crimes that are unrelated to the conflict will not be characterized as war crimes merely because of the existence of an armed conflict (for example, where a civilian who holds a personal vendetta against his neighbour takes advantage of lawlessness created by the conflict to murder his neighbour). Second, an inquiry into the state of mind of the offender is not necessary to establish a nexus.[33]

4.6 WAR CRIMES IN THE ICC STATUTE

Generally speaking, the ICC Statute appears to be praiseworthy in many respects as far as substantive criminal law is concerned. Many crimes have been defined with the

---

[33] It may happen that doubts arise as to the classification of a criminal offence, for instance because there is no compelling evidence that the aforementioned requirements are met in a given situation, and one finds oneself in that type of 'penumbral' situation or area discussed by H. A. Hart (*Essays in Jurisprudence and Philosophy* (Oxford: Clarendon Press, 1983), at 68) with regard to any body of law. In such cases, I submit that a *teleological interpretation* of IHL and ICL may lead to the proper classification of the offence. Indeed, the aim of the whole corpus of rules of IHL is to safeguard as much as possible the life and limb of persons caught in the maelstrom of armed violence. ICL supports and enforces this aim, by providing for the prosecution and punishment of all those who, by their conduct, run counter to that aim and imperil persons involved in armed conflict. ICL is indeed a branch of criminal law that specializes in penalizing those who breach, among other things, rules of IHL. This branch of criminal law is intended to attach a strong stigma to the perpetrators of those breaches (a war criminal is normally more seriously reprehended than a common murderer or thief). In addition, ICL often grants jurisdiction over such crimes to special military courts, and may provide a heavier penalty for those crimes because of the stronger moral and social reprobation they meet. If this is so, characterizing as a war crime an offence somehow linked to war and which clearly and indisputably may not be classified as an ordinary criminal offence, may serve to implement the object and purpose of IHL. The maxim *in dubio pro reo* should not stand in the way of this legal construction because that maxim normally affects the weight of the penalty, not the characterization of a crime, lest to comply with the maxim one were to deprive criminal law of its value in moral condemnation of contraventions of legal commands. The maxim could be taken into account by making the penalty more lenient, while maintaining the stronger legal labelling of the offence as a war crime. Similarly, the *lex mitior* principle would not apply, on obvious grounds.

required degree of specificity, and the general principles of criminal liability have been set out in detail.

As far as war crimes more specifically are concerned, it is no doubt commendable that they have been regulated in such a detailed manner. Furthermore, the notion of war crimes has rightly been extended to offences committed in time of internal armed conflict.

At the outset it should, however, be underlined that Article 8(1) of the ICC Statute provides:

> The Court shall have jurisdiction in respect of war crimes in particular when committed as part of a plan or policy or as part of a large-scale commission of such crimes.

This provision should be construed to the effect that the jurisdiction of the Court is limited to those war crimes which are not isolated events but constitute part of a policy or a large-scale practice. Plainly, the drafters of the ICC Statute intended to limit the Court's jurisdiction over war crimes to those offences that are more conspicuous and may involve a plurality of persons or constitute part of a general practice. This limitation affects the scope of the Court's jurisdiction. However, it has no impact on the notion of war crimes as established under international customary law or as defined in the case law of other international criminal courts such as the ICTY or the ICTR, where war crimes embrace any serious violation of IHL criminalized under customary law.

The regulation of war crimes in the ICC Statute, while meritorious in so many respects, can be faulted in other respects; indeed, it would seem that such regulation marks a retrograde step with regard to existing international law.

First of all, there is a perplexing phrase, 'within the established framework of international law', that appears in Article 8(2)(b) and (e), dealing with crimes likely to be perpetrated while in combat (that is, crimes involving the wrongful use of means or methods of combat), respectively in international armed conflicts and in non-international armed conflicts. These two provisions are worded as follows:

> [For the purpose of this Statute 'war crimes' means] Other serious violations of the laws and customs applicable in international armed conflict [in armed conflicts not of an international character: litt. (e)], *within the established framework of international law*, namely, any of the following acts [. . .]

It is notable that in the other provisions of Article 8 no mention is made of 'the established framework of international law'. Hence one could argue that there is only one possible explanation of this odd phrase: the offences listed in the two aforementioned provisions are to be considered as war crimes for the purpose of the Statute only if they are regarded as such by customary international law. In other words, whilst for the other classes of war crimes the Statute confines itself to setting out the content of the prohibited conduct, and the relevant provision can thus be directly and immediately applied by the Court, in the case of the two provisions under consideration things are different. The Court may consider that the conduct envisaged in these provisions amounts to a war crime only if and to the extent that general international law already regards the offence as a war crime. It would follow, for example, that 'declaring that no quarter will be given' (Article 8(2)(b)(xii)) will no doubt be taken to amount to a war crime, because indisputably denial of quarter is prohibited by customary international law and, if effected, amounts to a war crime. By contrast, offences such as 'The transfer, directly or indirectly, by the Occupying Power of parts of its own civilian population into the territory it occupies, or the deportation or transfer of all or parts of the population of the occupied territory within or outside this territory' (Article 8(2)(b)(viii)) cannot *ipso facto* be regarded as war crimes. The Court will first have to establish whether: *i*) under general international law they are considered as breaches of the international humanitarian law of armed conflict; and, in addition, *ii*) whether under customary international law their commission amounts to a war crime.

Were the above explanation regarded as sound, it would follow that for two broad categories of war crime the Statute does not set out a self-contained legal regime, but presupposes a mandatory examination, by the Court, on a case-by-case basis, of the current status of general international law. This method, while commendable in some respects, may, however, entail that the Statute's provisions eventually constitute only a tentative and interim regulation of the matter, for the final say rests with the Court's determination. Whether or not such a regulation is considered satisfactory, it seems indisputable that it leaves greater freedom to sovereign states or, to put it differently, makes the net of international prohibitions less tight and stringent.

Second, the legal regulation of means of warfare seems to be narrower than that laid down in customary international law.

The use in international armed conflict of modern weapons which cause superfluous injury or unnecessary suffering, or are inherently indiscriminate, is not banned per se and therefore does not amount to a crime under the ICC Statute—whereas arguably such use constitutes a war crime under customary international law, at least in those instances where the weapon at issue or the way it is used indisputably infringes those two principles or one of them.[34] Thus, in the event the two principles are deprived of their overarching legal value, at least with regard to individuals (the principles still act as standards applicable to states, with the consequence that those states that breach them incur international responsibility). This seems all the more questionable because even bacteriological weapons, which undoubtedly are already prohibited by general international law, might be used without entailing the commission of a crime falling under the jurisdiction of the Court. (It would seem that the use of this category of weapons is not covered by the ban on 'asphyxiating, poisonous or other gases and all analogous liquids, materials or devices', contained in Article 8(2)(b)(xviii) and clearly relating to chemical weapons only.)

A similar criticism may be made of the sub-article on damage to the environment. Under Article 8(2)(b)(iv) 'Intentionally launching an attack in the knowledge that such attack will cause [...] widespread, long-term and severe damage to the natural environment which would be clearly excessive in relation to the concrete and direct overall military advantage anticipated' constitutes a war crime. It should be noted that Article 55(1) of Additional Protocol I—to which any provision on environmental war crimes must accord a sort of 'precedential' value—provides

> Care shall be taken in warfare to protect the natural environment against widespread, long-term and severe damage. This protection includes a prohibition on the use of methods or means of warfare which are intended or may be expected to cause such damage to the natural environment and thereby to prejudice the health or survival of the population.

Article 55 makes no mention of the 'excessive' or disproportionate character of the attack nor of 'anticipated military advantage' (let alone of the 'direct overall military advantage anticipated', a phrase that gives belligerents a very great latitude and renders judicial scrutiny almost impossible). Moreover, in paragraph 2 it prohibits reprisals by way of attack against the natural environment. Article 8 of the ICC Statute therefore takes

---

[34] The ban will only take effect, and its possible breach amount to a crime, if an amendment to this end is made to the Statute pursuant to Arts 121 and 123. In practice, as it is extremely unlikely that such amendment will ever be agreed upon, those weapons may eventually be regarded as lawful.

a huge leap backwards by allowing the defence that 'widespread, long-term and severe damage to the natural environment' caused by the perpetrator—not just damage, but widespread, long-term and severe damage, intentionally caused—was not 'clearly excessive' (perhaps it was excessive, but not 'clearly excessive') in relation to the concrete and direct overall military advantage anticipated. This seems indefensible.

Thirdly, one may entertain some misgivings concerning the distinction, upheld in Article 8, between the regulation of *international* armed conflict, on the one side, and *non-international* armed conflicts on the other. Insofar as Article 8 separates the law applicable to the former category of armed conflict from that applicable to the latter category, it is somewhat retrograde, as the current trend has been to abolish the distinction and to have simply one corpus of law applicable to all conflicts. It can be confusing—and unjust—to have one law for international armed conflict and another for internal armed conflict.

More specific flaws may be discerned. For instance, when it comes to crimes in internal armed conflicts perpetrated against *adversaries hors de combat* (combatants who have laid down their weapons), the wounded, the sick, as well as civilians, the relevant provision (Article 8(2)(c)) admits that such crimes may be perpetrated in broad categories of armed conflict (any 'armed conflict not of an international character', excluding 'situations of internal disturbances and tensions, such as riots, isolated and sporadic acts of violence or other acts of a similar nature'). In contrast, the threshold required by the provision for crimes committed in combat is higher: Article 8(2)(f)) stipulates that the relevant provisions only apply 'to armed conflicts that take place in the territory of a state when there is *protracted* armed conflict between governmental authorities and organized groups or between such groups' (emphasis added). It follows that for a crime belonging to the second class to be perpetrated, an added requirement is envisaged, namely that the internal armed clash be 'protracted'. Allegedly the main reason for this distinction is that in the first class, there already existed a set of provisions laid down in Article 3 common to the four Geneva Conventions and that furthermore these provisions are held to have turned into customary international law. On the contrary, no previous treaty or customary rule existed regulating methods of combat in internal armed conflict. While making progress in this area, the majority of states gathered at the Rome Conference preferred to tread gingerly, so the explanation goes, so as to take due account of states' concerns. Assuming that this explanation is correct, the fact remains that a dichotomy was created, which appears contrary to the fundamental object and purpose of international humanitarian law.

Furthermore, the prohibited use of weapons in internal armed conflicts is not regarded as a war crime. This regulation does not reflect the current status of general international law.[35]

The above ICC Statute restrictions on modern regulation of armed conflict are compounded by two more factors: *i*) allowance has been made for superior orders to relieve subordinates of their responsibility for the execution of orders involving the commission of war crimes (whereas under the ICC Statute for crimes against humanity or genocide

---

[35] As the ICTY Appeals Chamber stressed in *Tadić* (*Interlocutory Appeal*), in modern warfare it no longer makes sense to distinguish between international and internal armed conflicts: 'Why protect civilians from belligerent violence, or ban rape, torture or the wanton destruction of hospitals, churches, museums or private property, as well as *proscribe weapons causing unnecessary suffering* when two sovereign States are engaged in war, and yet refrain from enacting the same bans or providing the same protection when armed violence has erupted "only" within the territory of a sovereign State?' (§ 97, emphasis added).

The Appeals Chamber rightly answered this question by finding that the prohibition of weapons causing unnecessary suffering, as well as the specific ban on chemical weapons, also applies to internal armed conflicts (§§ 119–24).

superior orders a priori may not be pleaded); *ii*) Article 124 allows states to declare, upon becoming parties to the Statute, that the Court's jurisdiction shall not become operative for a period of seven years with regard to war crimes (committed by their nationals or on their territory), whereas no similar allowance is made for other categories of international crime.[36]

One is therefore left with the impression that the framers of the ICC Statute were eager to shield their servicemen as much as possible from being brought to trial for war crimes.

To summarize, a tentative appraisal of the provisions on war crimes of the ICC Statute cannot but be chequered: in many respects the Statute marks a great advance in ICL, in others it proves instead faulty; in particular, it is marred by being too obsequious to state sovereignty.

---

[36] One should also note an odd provision, which applies to all the crimes envisaged in the ICC Statute. While children may be conscripted or enlisted as from the age of 15 (Art. 8(2)(b)(xxvi), and (e)(vii)), the Court has no jurisdiction over persons under the age of 18 at the commission of the crime (Art. 26). Thus a person between 15 and 17 is regarded as a lawful combatant and may commit a crime without being brought to court and punished. A commander could therefore recruit minors into his army expressly for the purpose of forming terrorist units whose members would be immune from prosecution. Moreover, in modern warfare, particularly in developing countries, young persons are more and more involved in armed hostilities and thus increasingly in a position to commit war crimes and crimes against humanity.

5

CRIMES AGAINST HUMANITY

The notion of crimes against humanity was propounded for the first time in 1915, on the occasion of mass killings of Armenians in the Ottoman Empire. On 28 May 1915 the French, British, and Russian governments decided to react strongly. They therefore jointly issued a declaration stating that

> In view of these new *crimes* of Turkey *against humanity and civilisation*, the Allied governments announce publicly to the *Sublime Porte* that they will hold personally responsible [for] these crimes all members of the Ottoman Government and those of their agents who are implicated in such massacres.[1]

The expression 'crimes against humanity' was not in the original proposal emanating from the Russian Foreign Minister, Sazonov. He had suggested instead a protest against 'crimes against Christianity and civilisation'. However, the French Foreign Minister Delcassé took issue with the reference to crimes against Christianity. He feared that the Muslim populations under French and British colonial domination might take umbrage at that expression, because it excluded them; consequently, they might feel discriminated against. Hence, he proposed, instead of 'crimes against Christianity', 'crimes against humanity'. This proposal was accepted by the Russian and British Foreign Ministers, and passed into the joint Declaration.[2]

It would seem that the three states were neither aware of, nor interested in, the general philosophical implications of the phrase they had used. Indeed, they did not ask themselves, nor did they try to establish in practice, whether by 'humanity' they meant 'all human beings' or rather 'the feelings of humanity shared by men and women of modern nations' or even 'the concept of humanity propounded by ancient and modern philosophy'. It is probable that, although they used strong language criminalizing the perpetrators of

---

[1] Emphasis added. For the full text of the note, see the dispatch of the US Ambassador in France, Sharp, to the US Secretary of State, Bryan, of 28 May 1915, in *Papers Relating to the Foreign Relations of the United States, 1915, Supplement* (Washington: US Government Printing Office, 1928), at 981.

[2] See the Russian dispatch of 11 May 1915, published in A. Beylerian, *Les Grandes Puissances, l'Empire Ottoman et les Arméniens dans les archives françaises (1914–1918)—Recueil de documents* (Paris, 1983), at 23 (doc. no. 29). The Russian draft referred to 'crimes against Christianity and civilisation' ('crimes de la Turquie contre la chretienté et la civilisation'). The French Foreign Minister, Delcassé, changed the expression to 'crimes against humanity' ('crimes contre l'humanité'), in addition to making another, minor change (*Les Grandes Puissances*, at 23, footnotes with an asterisk).

The political reasons for this change, in particular for dropping any reference to Christianity, were set out by the French Ministry in a Note of 20 May 1915 to the British Embassy (*Les Grandes Puissances*, at 26, doc. 34: 'L'intérêt qu'il y a à ménager le sentiment des populations musulmanes qui vivent sous la souveraineté de la France et de l'Angleterre fera sans doute estimer au gouvernement britannique comme au gouvernement français qu'il convient de s'abstenir de spécifier que l'intérêt des deux puissances paraît ne se porter que du côté des éléments chrétiens'). The two French suggestions were eventually accepted by Great Britain and Russia and the text of the note was changed accordingly.

the massacre, in fact they were only intent on solving a short-term political problem, as is shown by the lack of any practical follow-up to their joint protest.[3]

In any event, various initiatives to act diplomatically on behalf of humanity subsequently failed.[4] Similarly, the special Commission set up after the First World War proposed in its report to the Versailles Conference that an international criminal tribunal be created and that its jurisdiction extend to 'offences against the laws of humanity'.[5] However, the 'Memorandum of Reservations' submitted by the two distinguished representatives of the United States, Robert Lansing and James Brown Scott, paralysed any action by the Conference. They emphasized that while war crimes should be punished because 'the laws and customs of war are a standard certain' (at 64), the 'laws and principles of humanity are not certain, varying with time, place and circumstance, and according, it may be, to the conscience of the individual judge. There is no fixed and universal standard of humanity' (at 73). This, the US delegates said, 'if for no other reason, should exclude them from consideration in a court of justice, especially one charged with the administration of criminal law' (at 64). As a result of the American opposition, no provision was made for crimes against humanity.

It is notable that in 1919 a few Extraordinary Courts Martial were established in the Ottoman Empire to try the presumed authors of the 1915–16 deportation, massacres, and looting of Armenians. According to a distinguished author,[6] between 28 and 63 Court Martial trials were held. Judging from the verdicts that are available, those courts tried between 1919 and mid-1922 officials of the Ottoman Empire under the Ottoman Criminal Code,[7] and found many of them responsible for massacres, deportation, and looting,[8] or massacres 'for the purpose of destroying and annihilating' (*ifnâ' ve imhâ'si emrinde*) Armenians.[9]

---

[3] On 11 August 1915, during the massacre of Armenians, the American Ambassador to Turkey, Morgenthau, had proposed to the US Secretary of State, Robert Lansing, among other things, that 'The United States Government on behalf of humanity urgently request the Turkish Government to cease at once the present campaign and to permit the survivors to return to their homes if not in the war zones, or else to receive proper treatment.' However, the Secretary of State did not adopt this suggestion, contenting himself merely with asking whether the protest of the German Ambassador to the Turkish Government had 'improved conditions'. See *Papers Relating to the Foreign Relations of the United States*, n. 1, at 986.

[4] The Peace Treaty of Sèvres of 10 August 1920 provided in Article 230 that the 'Ottoman Government' undertook to hand over to the Allies the persons requested by these Powers as responsible for the massacres perpetrated, during the war, on territories which constituted part of the Ottoman Empire; the Allies reserved the right to 'designate' the tribunal which would try those persons. However, the Treaty was never ratified, and its replacement, the Peace Treaty of Lausanne, of 24 July 1923, provided in an annexed Declaration for an amnesty for crimes committed between 1914 and 1922.

[5] See 'Report presented to the preliminary Peace Conference by the Commission on the Responsibility of the Authors of the War and on the Enforcement of Penalties', in Carnegie Endowment for International Peace, Division of International Law, Pamphlet No. 32, *Violations of the Laws and Customs of War, Report of Majority and Dissenting Reports of American and Japanese Members of the Commission of Responsibilities, Conference of Paris 1919* (Oxford: Clarendon Press, 1919), at 25–6.

[6] T. Akcam, *Armenien und der Völkermord: Die Istanbuler Prozesse und die Türkische Nationalbewegung* (Hamburg: Hamburger Edition, 1996), at 162–5, where he mentions 28 trials. In another book (*A Shameful Act: The Armenian Genocide and the Question of Turkish Responsibility* (New York: Henri Holt and Co., 2007), at 4–5) the same author mentions 63 trials.

[7] They applied in particular Arts 102 (negligence in the execution of one's duties or failure to carry out a superior order), 130 (undue interference with civilian or military officials), 170 (murder) and 171 (premeditated coercion to destroy or rob supplies or goods) or 172 (abuse of an official position), together with Articles 45 (aiding and abetting), and 55 (co-perpetration).

[8] See in particular *Talât Paşa and others*, at 106–16; *Kemâl Bey and others*, at 155–8 (or 171–5); *Kerim Bey and others*, at 166–8.

[9] See in particular *Ahmed Mithad Bey and others*, at 147–53; *Mehmed 'Alz Bey and others* (at 159–65 or 177–84); *Bahâeddin Şâkir and others*, at 169–73. See also *Talât Paşa and others* (at 106–16).

5.1 THE NUREMBERG CHARTER AND JUDGMENT

During the Second World War, the Allies became aware that some of the most heinous acts of barbarity perpetrated by the Germans were not prohibited by customary international law. The laws of warfare only proscribed violations involving the adversary or the enemy populations, whereas the Germans had also performed inhuman acts for political or racial reasons against their own citizens (Jews, trade union members, social democrats, communists, gypsies, members of the church), as well as other persons not covered by the laws of warfare.[10] In addition, in 1945 persecution for political or racial purposes was not prohibited, even if perpetrated against civilians of occupied territories.

In 1945, at the strong insistence of the USA, the Allies thus decided that a better course of action than simply to execute all the major war criminals would be to bring them to trial. The London Agreement embodying the Charter of the Nuremberg Tribunal included a provision under which the Tribunal was to try and punish persons guilty, among other things, of 'crimes against humanity' (the use of this specific term was suggested by a leading scholar, Hersch Lauterpacht, to Robert Jackson, the US delegate to the London Conference, who was subsequently appointed chief US prosecutor at Nuremberg).[11] These crimes were defined as

> murder, extermination, enslavement, deportation, and other inhuman acts committed against any civilian population, before or during the war, or persecutions on political, racial, or religious grounds in execution of or connexion with any crimes within the jurisdiction of the Tribunal [i.e. either 'crimes against peace' or 'war crimes'], whether or not in violation of the domestic law of the country where perpetrated.

One major shortcoming of this definition is that it closely linked crimes against humanity to the other two categories of offences. Article 6(c) indeed required, for crimes against humanity to come under the jurisdiction of the Nuremberg Tribunal, that they be perpetrated 'in execution of or in connection with' war crimes or crimes against peace. This link was not spelled out, but it was clear that it was only within the context of a war or of the unleashing of aggression that these crimes could be prosecuted and punished. As rightly pointed out by Schwelb,[12] this association meant that only those criminal activities were punished which 'directly affected the interests of other States' (either because these activities were connected with a war of aggression or a conspiracy to wage such a war, or because they were bound up with war crimes; that is, crimes against enemy combatants or enemy civilians). Plainly, in 1945 the Allies did not feel that they should 'legislate' in such a way as to prohibit inhuman acts *regardless of their consequences or implications for third states*. At that stage, what happened within a national system, even if contrary to fundamental values of humanity, was still of exclusive concern to that state if it had no spill-over effects on other states: it fell within its own 'domestic jurisdiction'.

---

[10] For instance, citizens of the Allies (e.g. French Jews under the Vichy regime (1940–4)); nationals of states not formally under German occupation and, therefore, not protected by the international rules safeguarding the civilian population of occupied territories: this applied to Austria, annexed by Germany in 1938, and Czechoslovakia (following the Munich Treaty in 1938, the Sudeten territory was annexed by Germany, and the rest of the country became the so-called Protectorate of Bohemia and Moravia, in 1939). The Germans also harassed and murdered stateless Jews and gypsies.

[11] See on this point M. Koskenniemi, 'Hersch Lauterpacht and the Development of International Criminal Law', 2 JICJ (2004), at 811.

[12] E. Schwelb, 'Crimes against Humanity', 23 BYIL (1946), at 207.

Despite this limitation, the creation of the new category marked a great advance. First, it indicated that the international community was widening the category of acts considered of 'meta-national' concern. This category came to include all actions running contrary to those basic values that are, or should be, considered inherent in any human being (in the notion, humanity did not mean 'mankind' or 'human race' but 'the quality' of being humane).

Second, inasmuch as crimes against humanity were made punishable even if perpetrated in accordance with domestic laws, the 1945 Charter showed that in some special circumstances there were limits to the 'omnipotence of the State' (to quote the British Chief Prosecutor, Sir Hartley Shawcross) and that 'the individual human being, the ultimate unit of all law, is not disentitled to the protection of mankind when the State tramples upon his rights in a manner which outrages the conscience of mankind'.[13]

A number of courts have explicitly or implicitly held that Article 6(c) of the London Agreement simply crystallized or codified a nascent rule of customary international law prohibiting crimes against humanity. It seems more correct to contend that that provision constituted *new* law. This explains both the limitations to which the new notion was subjected (and to which reference has already been made above) and the extreme caution and indeed reticence of the Nuremberg Tribunal in applying the notion.

The reticence and what could be viewed as the embarrassment of the Nuremberg Tribunal on the matter are striking. Six points, in particular, should be stressed.

First, the Nuremberg Tribunal tackled the issue of *ex post facto* law only with regard to crimes against peace (in particular, aggression), whereas it did not pronounce at all upon the no less delicate question of whether or not crimes against humanity constituted a new category of offence. (However, the reason for this omission may also be found in the fact that the German defence counsel, in the joint motion of 19 November 1945 by which they complained about the retroactive application of criminal law by the Nuremberg Tribunal,[14] only referred to crimes against peace; this probably occurred because they felt that the underlying offences comprising crimes against humanity, such as murder, extermination, and so on, were proscribed by the national criminal law in most countries of the world and in any case had been committed by Nazi authorities on a very large scale.)

Second, when dealing with *ex post facto* law, the Nuremberg Tribunal was rather reticent and indeed vague, as is apparent from, *inter alia*, the glaring discrepancy between the English and the French text of the judgment,[15] both authoritative.

Third, the Nuremberg Tribunal held that no evidence had been produced to the effect that crimes against humanity had been committed *before* the war, in execution of or in connection with German aggression.[16] The Nuremberg Tribunal thus markedly narrowed

---

[13] Sir Hartley Shawcross, in *Speeches of the Chief Prosecutors at the Close of the Case against the Individual Defendants* (London: HM Stationery Office, Cmd. 6964, 1946), at 63.

[14] See *Trial of the Major War Criminals*, vol. I, at 168–70.

[15] In the English text, the Nuremberg Tribunal stated that 'the maxim *nullum crimen sine lege* is not a limitation of sovereignty, *but is in general a principle of justice*' (at 219; emphasis added), while in the French text it is stated that '*Nullum crimen sine lege* ne limite pas la souveraineté des États; *elle ne formule qu'une règle généralement suivie*' (at 231; emphasis added). Furthermore, the phrase in the English text, 'On this view of the case alone, it would appear that the maxim has no application to the present facts' (at 219) does not appear in the French text.

[16] The Tribunal stated that: 'To constitute crimes against humanity, the acts relied on before the outbreak of war must have been in execution of, or in connection with, any crime within the jurisdiction of the Tribunal. The Tribunal is of the opinion that revolting and horrible as many of these crimes were, it has not been satisfactorily proved that they were done in execution of, or in connection with, any such crime. The Tribunal therefore cannot make a general declaration that the acts before 1939 were crimes against humanity within the meaning of the Charter' (at 254).

the scope, *in casu*, of the category of crimes against humanity, although it asserted that it did so on grounds linked to the evidence produced.

Fourth, probably aware of the novelty of that class of crimes and hence of the possible objection that the *nullum crimen* principle was being breached by applying criminal law retroactively, the Nuremberg Tribunal tended to find that some defendants accused of various classes of crime were guilty both of war crimes and of crimes against humanity (this was the case with fourteen defendants): in other words, the Tribunal avoided clearly identifying the distinction between the two classes, preferring instead to find that in many cases the defendant was answerable for both.

Fifth, in the only two cases where the Nuremberg Tribunal found a defendant guilty exclusively of crimes against humanity (*Streicher* and *von Schirach*), the Tribunal did not specify the nature, content, and scope of the link between crimes against humanity and war crimes (in the case of *Streicher*) or crimes against humanity and crimes against peace (in the case of *von Schirach*); rather, the Tribunal confined itself to a generic reference to the connection between the classes of crimes, without any further elaboration.

Finally, it is striking that in the part of the judgment referring to Streicher, the English text is markedly different from the French.[17]

In summary, in all probability the Nuremberg Tribunal applied new law, or substantially new law, when it found some defendants guilty of crimes against humanity alone or of these crimes in conjunction with others. However, this was not in breach of a general norm strictly prohibiting retroactive criminal law. As noted (see 2.2), immediately after the Second World War, the *nullum crimen sine lege* principle could be regarded as a moral maxim destined to yield to superior exigencies whenever it would have been contrary to justice not to hold persons accountable for appalling atrocities. The strict legal prohibition of *ex post facto* law had not yet found expression in international law; nor did it constitute a general principle of law universally accepted by all states. The Nuremberg Tribunal set out the view that 'the maxim *nullum crimen sine lege* [. . .] is in general a principle of justice'

---

[17] In the English text it is stated that 'Streicher's incitement to murder and extermination at the time when Jews in the East were being killed under the most horrible conditions clearly constitutes persecution on political and racial grounds in connection with War Crimes, as defined in the Charter, and constitutes a crime against humanity' (at 304). By contrast, in the French text it is stated that Streicher's persecution of Jews was itself a war crime as well as a crime against humanity ('Le fait que Streicher poussait au meurtre et à l'extermination, à l'époque même où, dans l'Est, les Juifs étaient massacrés dans les conditions les plus horribles, réalise "la persécution pour des motifs politiques et raciaux" prévue parmi les crimes de guerre définis par le Statut, et constitue également un crime contre l'Humanité' (at 324)). Clearly, this wording reflects the position of the French Chief Prosecutor, François de Menthon (see his opening statement, of 17 January 1946, in Nuremberg Tribunal, vol. V, at 371. The French prosecutor stated that 'This horrible accumulation and maze of Crimes against Humanity both include and go beyond the two more precise juridical notions of Crimes against Peace and War Crimes. But I think—and I will revert later separately to Crimes against Peace and War Crimes—that this body of Crimes against Humanity constitutes, in the last analysis, nothing less than the perpetration for political ends and in a systematic manner, of common law crimes such as theft, looting, ill treatment, enslavement, murders, and assassinations, crimes that are provided for and punishable under the penal laws of all civilized states. No general objection of a juridical nature, therefore, appears to hamper your task of justice. Moreover, the Nazis accused would have no ground to argue on alleged lack of written texts to justify the penal qualification that you will apply to their crimes.') The wording at issue also reflected the reservations and misgivings of the French judge, H. Donnedieu de Vabres, who in 1947 set forth his views in scholarly papers in which he argued that crimes against humanity simultaneously constituted war crimes and hence the Tribunal did not breach the *nullum crimen, nulla poena sine lege* principle (see H. Donnedieu de Vabres, 'Le Jugement de Nuremberg et le principe de légalité des délits et des peines', in 27 *Revue de droit pénal et de criminologie* (1946–7), 826–7; see also his Hague Academy lectures: 'Le Procès de Nuremberg devant les principes modernes du droit pénal international', HR (1947–I), 525–7 (in particular n. 1 at 526)).

allowing the punishment of actions not proscribed by law at the time of their commission, when it would be 'unjust' for such wrongs to be 'allowed to go unpunished' (at 219).[18]

5.2 SUBSEQUENT DEVELOPMENTS

In the wake of the major war trials, momentous changes in international law took place. On 11 December 1946 the UN General Assembly unanimously adopted a resolution 'affirming' the principles of the Charter of the Nuremberg Tribunal and its judgment. On 13 February 1946 it passed resolution 3(1) recommending the extradition and punishment of persons accused of the crimes provided for in the Nuremberg Charter. These resolutions show that the category of crimes against humanity was in the process of becoming part of customary international law.[19]

---

[18] However, as pointed out above, the Nuremberg Tribunal expressed this view only with regard to aggressive war; in addition it hastened to add (at 219–23) that in any event, under international law, such wars were already regarded as criminal before the outbreak of the Second World War.

Interestingly, the first of the two propositions referred to in the text was repeatedly set forth, with specific regard to crimes against humanity, by the German Supreme Court in the British Occupied Zone. According to this Court, '[r]etroactive punishment is unjust when the action, at the time of its commission, falls foul not only of a positive rule of criminal law, but also of the moral law. This is not the case for crimes against humanity. In the view of any morally-oriented person, serious injustice was perpetrated, the punishment of which would have been a legal obligation of the state. The subsequent cure of such dereliction of a duty through retroactive punishment is in keeping with justice. This also does not entail any violation of legal security but rather the re-establishment of its basis and presuppositions' (case against *Bl.*, at 5). See also the following judgments: *B. and A.* case, at 297; *H.* case (18 October 1949), at 232–3; *N.* case, at 335; *H.* case (11 September 1950), at III, 135. Other judgments include elaborate reasoning concerning the distinction to be drawn between law enacted by the Occupying Powers and German law: see, for example, *G.* case, at 362–4; *M. et al.* case, at 378–81 (this judgment sets out important reasons in support of the view that crimes against humanity could be punished retroactively: see 380–1).

[19] Strikingly, the French Court of Cassation, in *Sobanski Wladyslav* (also called the *Boudarel* case), in 1993 placed a patently flawed interpretation on the second resolution and the Charter of the Nuremberg Tribunal, to which the resolution referred. It held that the resolution and Art. 6(c) of the Tribunal's Statute only related to 'offences perpetrated on behalf of the Axis European States', hence it could not apply to atrocities committed elsewhere. The specific question brought to the Court revolved around the scope of the French law of 26 December 1964. (Under this law, crimes against humanity by their nature are not covered by any statute of limitation; the law stated that such crimes were those referred to in the UN resolution of 13 February 1946, which in turn adverted to the definition set out in the Statute of the Tribunal.) In the case at bar the question was whether such law applied to the accused Boudarel, a French serviceman who, after deserting the French army, had sided with the Viet Minh and allegedly committed atrocities against French prisoners of war in 1952–4. By interpreting the General Assembly resolution and the Nuremberg Tribunal Statute as recalled above, and consequently by also restrictively construing the French law of 1964, the Court concluded that the law did not apply to the accused, who consequently could not be tried. According to the Court, his alleged crimes were covered by a law of 1966 granting amnesty for all crimes committed in Indochina before 1 October 1957 (at 354–5).

To refute the legal grounds set forth in the judgment, it may suffice to quote the sort of 'authentic interpretation' of Art. 6 of the Nuremberg Tribunal Statute, propounded by Robert H. Jackson, the protagonist of the London Conference that led to the adoption, on 8 August 1945, of that Statute. After the Conference he wrote that 'The most serious disagreement [at the Conference], and one on which the United States declined to recede from its position even if it meant the failure of the Conference, concerned the definition of crimes. The Soviet Delegation proposed and until the last meeting pressed a definition which, in our view, had the effect of declaring certain acts crimes only when committed by the Nazis. The United States contended that the criminal character of such acts could not depend on who committed them and that international crimes could only be defined in broad terms applicable to statesmen of any nation guilty of the proscribed conduct. At the final meeting the Soviet qualifications were dropped and agreement was reached on a generic definition acceptable to all' (*International Conference on Military Trials*, at vii–viii).

In addition to the Charter of the Tokyo Tribunal, a number of international instruments were then drawn up embodying the prohibition of crimes against humanity, some of which improved and expanded the provisions of the London Agreement, for instance, the Peace Treaties with Italy, Romania, Hungary, Bulgaria, and Finland, each of which included terms providing for the punishment of these crimes.[20]

In particular, after 1945 the link between crimes against humanity and war was gradually dropped. This is evidenced by Article II(1)(c) of such 'multinational' legislation as Control Council Law no. 10 passed by the four victorious Powers four months after the London Agreement; that is, on 20 December 1945, by national legislation (such as the Canadian[21] and the French[22] criminal codes), case law,[23] as well as international treaties such as the 1948 Genocide Convention, the 1968 Convention on the Non-Applicability of Statutory Limitations to War Crimes and Crimes against Humanity, and the 1973 Convention on Apartheid. This evolution gradually led to the abandonment of the nexus between crimes against humanity and war: at present, as stated above, customary international law bans crimes against humanity whether they are committed in time of war or peace.[24] The same holds true for the ICC Statute, which confirms the rupture of the link between these crimes and armed conflict.

On the other hand, some treaties and other binding international instruments enshrining the Statutes of international courts and tribunals restrict the scope of customary rules. To be more accurate (because strictly speaking those Statutes do not lay down substantive rules of criminal law but only provide for the definition of those crimes over which each relevant court or tribunal is endowed with jurisdiction), such treaties and other instruments may *indirectly contribute* to the restriction of the customary rules. Thus, for instance, the Statute of the ICTY refers to crimes against humanity committed in armed conflict, although the need for such contextual element is not required by customary international law.

5.3 THE NOTION TODAY

Under customary international law the category of crimes against humanity is sweeping but sufficiently well defined. It covers actions that share a set of common features.

i) They are particularly odious offences in that they constitute a serious attack on human dignity or a grave humiliation or degradation of one or more persons.

---

[20] See e.g. Art. 45 of the Peace Treaty with Italy, Art. 6 of the Treaty with Romania, and Art. 5 of that with Bulgaria.

[21] Para. 7 (3.76) of the Canadian Criminal Code provides that: ' "[C]rimes against humanity" means murder, extermination, enslavement, deportation, persecution or any other inhumane act or omission that is committed against any civilian population or any identifiable group of persons, whether or not it constitutes a contravention of the law in force at the time and in the place of its commission, and that, at that time and in that place, constitutes a contravention of customary international law or conventional international law or is criminal according to the general principles of law recognized by the community of nations.'

[22] Art. 212-1, para. 1 of the French Criminal Code (enacted by Law no. 92-1336 of 16 December 1992, modified by Law no. 93-913 of 19 July 1993), which entered into force on 1 March 1994, provides: 'La déportation, la réduction en esclavage ou la pratique massive et systématique d'exécutions sommaires, d'enlèvements de personnes suivis de leur disparition, de la torture ou d'actes inhumains, inspirés par des motifs politiques, philosophiques, raciaux ou religieux et organisés en exécution d'un plan concerté a l'encontre d'un groupe de population civile sont punies de la réclusion criminelle à perpétuité.'

[23] See e.g. the *Einsatzgruppen* case, at 49; *Altstötter and others* (*Justice* case), at 974. See, however, the *Flick* case, at 1213 and the *Weizaecker* case, at 112. For comments on these cases, see the relevant entries in *Cassese's Companion*.

[24] See on this point the dictum of the ICTY, *Tadić* (*Interlocutory Appeal*), AC, § 141.

ii) They are not isolated or sporadic events, but are part of a widespread or systematic practice that either forms part of a policy by a government, a *de facto* political authority, or an organized political group, or is tolerated, condoned, or acquiesced in by the aforementioned government, authority, or group. Clearly, it is required that a single crime be an instance of a repetition of similar crimes or be part of a string of such crimes (widespread practice), or that it be the manifestation of a policy or a plan of violence worked out, or inspired by, state authorities or by the leading officials of a *de facto* political authority, or of an organized political group (systematic practice). However, this contextual element does not necessarily mean that the individual act amounting to crime against humanity (murder, torture, rape, persecution, etc.) be repeated in time and space or, in other words that the *same* underlying offence be committed on a large scale. It may also be sufficient for the underlying offence at issue (murder, torture, persecution, etc.) to be part of a massive attack on the civilian population, whatever the form taken by such large-scale violence. This conclusion is warranted by the very rationale behind the prohibition and criminalization of this category of heinous conduct (international rules intend to proscribe and make punishable any offence against humanity, whatever its features, which is part of massive despicable violence against human beings, for they consider that such attacks, in whatever form, offend against humanity). It is also borne out by case law.[25]

iii) They are prohibited and may consequently be punished regardless of whether they are perpetrated in time of war or peace. While in 1945 a link with an armed conflict was required, at present customary international law no longer attaches any importance to such nexus. Thus, while in 1945 the 'contextual element' of the crime was the existence of an armed conflict, such element now resides in a 'widespread or systematic' attack on the population.

iv) The victims of the underlying offence may be civilians or, where crimes are committed during armed conflict, persons who do not take part (or no longer take part) in armed hostilities, as well as, under customary international law (but not under the Statute of the ICTY, ICTR, and the ICC), enemy combatants. It is, however, necessary that the widespread or systematic attack which is made out of the various underlying

---

[25] See the German cases in denunciations, etc., mentioned in nn. 26, 37, and 38.The same conclusion is also indirectly corroborated by more recent case law relating to the elements from which one can infer the existence of a policy. For instance, in *Blaškić* an ICTY Trial Chamber, in addressing the issue of the 'systematic' character of the crimes at issue, held that 'The systematic character refers to four elements which for the purposes of this case may be expressed as follows:—the existence of a political objective, a plan pursuant to which the attack is perpetrated or an ideology, in the broad sense of the word, that is, to destroy, persecute or weaken a community—the perpetration of a criminal act on a very large scale against a group of civilians or the repeated and continuous commission of inhumane acts linked to one another—the preparation and use of significant public or private resources, whether military or other—the implication of high-level political and/or military authorities in the definition and establishment of the methodical plan. This plan, however, need not necessarily be declared expressly or even stated clearly and precisely. It may be surmised from the occurrence of a series of events, inter alia—the general historical circumstances and the overall political background against which the criminal acts are set—the establishment and implementation of autonomous political structures at any level of authority in a given territory—the general content of a political programme, as it appears in the writings and speeches of its authors—media propaganda—the establishment and implementation of autonomous military structures—the mobilisation of armed forces—temporally and geographically repeated and co-ordinated military offensives—links between the military hierarchy and the political structure and its political programme—alterations to the "ethnic" composition of populations—discriminatory measures, whether administrative or other (banking restrictions, laissez-passer [. . .]—the scale of the acts of violence perpetrated—in particular, murders and other physical acts of violence, rape, arbitrary imprisonment, deportations and expulsions or the destruction of non-military property, in particular, sacral sites' (ICTY, *Blaškić*, TC, §§ 203–4).

offences be committed against *a civilian population*, which must be the ultimate target of crimes against humanity.

To a large extent many concepts underlying this category of crimes derive from, or overlap with, those of human rights law (the rights to life, not to be tortured, to liberty and security of the person, etc.), laid down in provisions of international human rights instruments (e.g. the Universal Declaration of Human Rights, the UN Covenant on Civil and Political Rights). Indeed, while ICL concerning war crimes largely derives from, or is closely linked with, IHL, ICL concerning crimes against humanity is to a great extent predicated upon international human rights law. IHL (which traditionally regulates warfare between or within states), and international human rights law (which regulates what states may do to their own citizens and, more generally, to individuals under their control), are in essence two distinct bodies of law, each arising from separate concerns and considerations. The former is largely rooted in notions of *reciprocity*—one need not be a great humanist to be in favour of laws of war for international conflicts, as it is simple self-interest for a state to ensure that its soldiers are treated well in exchange for treating enemy soldiers well and that its civilians are spared the horrors of war. The latter is more geared to *community concerns*, as it intends to protect human beings per se, regardless of their national or other allegiance.

5.4 THE OBJECTIVE ELEMENTS

The conduct prohibited was loosely described in the London Agreement of 1945, and similarly in Control Council Law no. 10 and the Charter of the Tokyo Tribunal, as well the ICTY and the ICTR. Gradually case law has contributed to defining the legal contours of the actus reus. In the event, the various categories have been largely spelled out in the ICC Statute, Article 7, of which may be held to a large extent either to crystallize nascent notions or to codify the bulk of existing customary law (see 5.8).

5.4.1 THE CONTEXTUAL ELEMENT

First of all, crimes against humanity are of a *large-scale* or *massive nature*. That this feature is a necessary ingredient of the crimes may be inferred from the first provisions setting out a list of such offences. They clearly, if implicitly, required that the offence, to constitute an attack on humanity, be of extreme gravity and not be a sporadic event but part of a pattern of misconduct. Subsequent case law has consistently borne out that this is a major feature of the crimes.[26] In summary, criminal acts such as murder, extermination,

---

[26] In 1949, in *Ahlbrecht*, the Dutch Special Court of Cassation delivered one of the first decisions on crimes against humanity, after the Nuremberg Judgment of the International Military Tribunal (for a comment on the case, see *Cassese's Companion*, at 576). The defendant, a German *Sturmscharführer* (commander of a storm company) of the *Waffen SS* (German state Security Police), had been accused of killing a Dutch national and ill-treating five others. The Court was called upon to decide whether the offences perpetrated by Albrecht were to be regarded as war crimes or as crimes against humanity. It opted for the first category, adding that they could not also be classified as crimes against humanity. Addressing this last class of crimes the Court stated that: '[C]rimes of this category are characterised either by their seriousness and their savagery, or by their magnitude, or by the circumstance that they were part of a system designed to spread terror, or that they were a link in a deliberately pursued policy against certain groups of the population' (at 750). A judgment of the Dutch Court of Cassation in 1981 substantially supported this view (see *Menten* at 362–3; for a comment, see *Cassese's Companion*, at 807).

torture, rape, political, racial, or religious persecution, and other inhumane acts reach the threshold of crimes against humanity only if they are part of a practice.[27] Isolated inhumane acts of this nature may constitute grave infringements of human rights or, depending on the circumstances, war crimes, but fall short of the stigma attaching to crimes against humanity. On the other hand, an individual may be guilty of crimes

The link or connection with a systematic policy of a government or a *de facto* authority was emphasized by the German Supreme Court in the British zone of occupation, in the numerous and significant decisions on crimes against humanity it delivered in the years 1948–52. By way of illustration, one can mention *J. and R.*, summarized in 1950 by the Court of Assizes of Hamburg in *Veit Harlan*. In *J. and R.*, a trial court had sentenced for crimes against humanity a German who had denounced to the police two other Germans for listening to a foreign radio, which amounted under German law to national treason; as a consequence the two persons had been arrested and sentenced to imprisonment; they had died as a result of harsh prison conditions. The Supreme Court overruled the acquittal pronounced by the trial court and the appeals court. It pointed out, among other things, that the aggressive behaviour of the agent and the inhuman injury to the victim had to be objectively connected with the Nazi system of violence and tyranny. 'This connection does not need [. . .] to lie in support for the tyranny, but may, for example, also consist of the use of the system of violence and tyranny. [Furthermore], the agent need not act systematically; it is sufficient that his single action be connected with the system and thereby lose the character of an isolated occurrence.' The Court went on to explain that the denunciation by the accused was closely linked with the arbitrary and violent Nazi system, that there existed no freedom, and the state suppressed any deviant behaviour by violence and harsh punishment. The denunciation at issue had been intended to achieve the handing over of two persons to an arbitrary police system based on terror: hence 'he who caused such a consequence through his denunciation, objectively committed a crime against humanity' (167–71). *Veit Harlan* dealt with a charge of complicity in a crime against humanity. (The accused, a film director, had contributed to the persecution of Jews by his film *Jud Süss*, produced in 1940.) The Court of Assizes, basing itself on numerous judicial precedents on the matter, gave the following definition of crimes against humanity: 'One must regard as a crime against humanity any conscious and willed attack that, in connection with the Nazi system of violence and arbitrariness, harmfully interferes with the life and existence of a person or his relationships with his social sphere, or interferes with his assets and values, thereby offending against his human dignity as well as humanity as such' (52).

However, when the atrocities are part of a governmental policy, the perpetrators need not identify themselves with this policy, as the District Court of Tel-Aviv held in 1951 in *Enigster* (a case concerning a Jew imprisoned in a Nazi concentration camp, who persecuted his fellow Jewish inmates; for a comment, see *Cassese's Companion*, at 658). The Tel-Aviv Court rightly stated: '[A] person who was himself persecuted and confined in the same camp as his victims can, from the legal point of view, be guilty of a crime against humanity if he performs inhumane acts against his fellow prisoners. In contrast to a war criminal, the perpetrator of a crime against humanity does not have to be a man who identified himself with the persecuting regime or its evil intention' (542).

[27] In *Limaj and others* an ICTY Trial Chamber held that, as a rule, the widespread or systematic attack required for crimes against humanity occurs at the behest of a state: 'Due to structural factors and organisational and military capabilities, an "attack directed against a civilian population" will most often be found to have occurred at the behest of a State. Being the locus of organised authority within a given territory, able to mobilise and direct military and civilian power, a sovereign State by its very nature possesses the attributes that permit it to organise and deliver an attack against a civilian population; it is States which can most easily and efficiently marshal the resources to launch an attack against a civilian population on a "widespread" scale, or upon a "systematic" basis. In contrast, the factual situation before the Chamber involves the allegation of an attack against a civilian population perpetrated by a non-state actor with extremely limited resources, personnel and organisation' (ICTY, *Limaj and others*, TC, § 191). This statement is acceptable to the extent that it is intended merely to reflect what happens in practice, not as the formulation of a legal requirement (plainly, a widespread or systematic attack on the population can be carried out by non-state groups or paramilitary units with the acquiescence of state authorities or in circumstances where such authorities lack the effective power to put an end to such attacks).

For insistence on the notion that the context of a 'widespread or systematic' attack is a fundamental requirement for crimes against humanity, see a string of recent Indonesian cases concerning East Timor: *Abilio Soares* (at 98–9), *Herman Sedyono and others* (at 66–8), *Endar Priyanto* (at 32.3); *Eurico Guterres* (at 27–8); *Asep Kuswani* (at 45); *Letkol Inf. Soedjarwo* (at 22–3); *Yayat Sudrajat* (at 6–7).

against humanity even if he perpetrates one or two of the offences mentioned above, or engages in one such offence against only a few civilians, provided those offences are part of a consistent pattern of misbehaviour by a number of persons linked to that offender (for example, because they engage in armed action on the same side, or because they are parties to a common plan, or for any other similar reason) and the perpetrator is aware that his conduct is part of this pattern.

At present, ICL always requires for the crimes under discussion a *general context* of criminal conduct, consisting of a widespread *or* systematic practice of unlawful attacks against the civilian population.

5.4.2 THE UNDERLYING OFFENCES

If the aforementioned contextual element does exist, crimes against humanity consist of two distinct categories of crimes: *i*) inhumane acts such as murder, extermination, enslavement, and deportation of *any* civilian population, i.e. *any group of civilians* whatever their nationality—these largely constitute offences already covered by all national legal systems, and also are committed against civilians; and *ii*) persecution on political, racial, or religious grounds—this can embrace actions that at the time of their commission may not be prohibited by national legal systems, for persecution may take the form of acts other than murder, extermination, enslavement, or deportation. It is therefore customary to refer to the underlying offences of crimes against humanity by distinguishing between the so-called 'murder-type' offences and the 'persecution-type' offences.

Let's examine each of them in more detail.

i) Murder: as a rule, the mental element of this conduct is the intent to bring about the death of another person; intentional killing may or may not be premeditated; that is, planned and willed in advance of the act of killing (with the mental status persisting over time between the first moment when the intention took shape and the later physical act of killing). However, for murder as a crime against humanity a lesser mental element is required by case law: it is sufficient for the perpetrator 'to cause the victim serious injury with reckless disregard for human life'.[28]

ii) Extermination: that is mass or large-scale killing, as well as 'the intentional infliction of conditions of life, *inter alia* the deprivation of access to food and medicine, calculated to bring about the destruction of part of a population' (Article 7(2)(b) of the ICC Statute). The ICTR has defined the notion of extermination in a few cases.[29] A Chamber of the ICTY offered a better definition in *Krstić*. It held that:

> for the crime of extermination to be established, in addition to the general requirements for a crime against humanity, there must be evidence that a particular population was targeted and that its members were killed or otherwise subjected to conditions of life

---

[28] ICTR, *Akayesu*, TC, §§ 589–90, and *Rutaganda*, TC, § 80; ICTY, *Kupreškić*, TC, § 561; ICTR, *Musema*, TC, § 215.

[29] ICTR: *Akayesu*, TC, §§ 591–2; *Kambanda*, TC, §§ 141–7; *Kayishema and Ruzindana*, TC, §§ 141–7; *Rutaganda*, TC, §§ 82–4; *Musema*, TC, §§ 217–19; *Rukundo*, AC, § 185; *Seromba*, AC, § 189; *Gacumbitsi*, AC, § 86; *Ndindabahizi*, AC, § 135; *Ntakirutimana & Ntakirutimana*, AC, §§ 516, 522; *Nyiramasuhuko and others*, TC, § 6048.

The ICTR has held that the requisite elements of the offence are as follows: *i*) the accused or his subordinate participated in the killing of certain named or described persons; *ii*) the act or omission was unlawful and intentional; *iii*) the unlawful act or omission must be part of a widespread or systematic attack; and *iv*) the attack must be against the civilian population. This definition does not seem to be satisfactory, for it is loose and does not indicate the unique objective features of the crime.

calculated to bring about the destruction of a numerically significant part of the population. (§ 503)[30]

It is submitted that one ought not to exclude from this class of crimes extermination carried out by groups of terrorists *for the purpose of spreading terror.* (Of course, the necessary condition that the terrorist attack exterminating a group of persons be part of a widespread or systematic attack, must be fulfilled.)

iii) Enslavement: this notion was gradually elaborated upon by case law, notably by two US Military Tribunals sitting at Nuremberg, in *Milch* (at 773–91) and in *Pohl and others* (at 970), and then refined by a Trial Chamber of the ICTY in *Kunarac and others* (§§ 515–43). According to the ICC Statute, which crystallizes a nascent notion, enslavement 'means the exercise of any or all of the powers attaching to the right of ownership over a person and includes the exercise of such power in the course of trafficking in persons, in particular women and children' (Article 7(2)(c)). The ICTY Trial Chamber in *Kunarac and others* convincingly propounded a set of elements that clarify this definition (§§ 542–3). In addition, the Trial Chamber set out clearly the reasons for which it found two of the defendants guilty of enslavement (§§ 728–82).

iv) Deportation or forcible transfer of population: that is, the 'forced displacement of the persons concerned by expulsion or other coercive acts from the area in which they are lawfully present, without grounds permitted under international law' (Article 7(2)(d)). An ICTY Trial Chamber emphasized in *Krstić* that:

> Both deportation and forcible transfer relate to involuntary and unlawful evacuation of individuals from the territory in which they reside. Yet the two are not synonymous in customary international law. Deportation presumes transfer beyond State borders, whereas forcible transfer relates to displacement within a State. (§ 521)

In that case the Trial Chamber found that, on 12–13 July 1995, about 25,000 Bosnian Muslim civilians were forcibly bussed outside the enclave of Srebrenica to the territory under Bosnian Muslim control, always within the same state (Bosnia and Herzegovina). The transfer was compulsory and was carried out 'in furtherance of a well organised policy whose purpose was to expel the Bosnian Muslim population from the enclave'. The Chamber concluded that the civilians transported from Srebrenica were not subjected to deportation but to forcible transfer, a crime against humanity (§§ 527–32).[31]

v) Imprisonment or other severe deprivation of physical liberty in violation of fundamental rules of international law. An ICTY Trial Chamber, in *Kordić and Čerkez*, was the first international court to offer a definition of this offence. It held that imprisonment as a crime against humanity must 'be understood as arbitrary imprisonment, that is to say, the deprivation of liberty of the individual without due process of law, as part of a widespread or systematic attack directed against a civilian population' (§§ 302–3).

vi) Torture: that is, 'the intentional infliction of severe pain or suffering, whether physical or mental, upon a person in the custody or under the control of the accused', except

---

[30] The TC also specified that 'In accordance with the *Tadić* (AC), [. . .] it is unnecessary that the victims were discriminated against for political, social or religious grounds' (§ 499). In the same case the Trial Chamber found that the accused was guilty of extermination (*Krstić*, TC, §§ 504–5).

[31] In *Popović and others*, an ICTY Trial Chamber considered as an additional element of deportation that the persons must be forcibly displaced by the accused across a *de jure* or *de facto* border (§ 895). It held that it was insufficient to prove force on the part of the accused and displacement across a border without establishing a link between the two elements (ICTY, *Popović and others*, TC, § 893). This interpretation—the Trial Chamber held—was further supported by the plain meaning of the word 'deport', which 'clearly imports an action of movement across a border' (at § 894).

when pain or suffering is inherent in or incidental to lawful sanctions (Article 7(2)(e) of the ICC Statute). In *Delalić and others* an ICTY Trial Chamber noted that the definition of torture contained in the 1984 Torture Convention was broader than, and included, that laid down in the 1975 Declaration of the UN GA and in the 1985 Inter-American Convention, and considered it to reflect a consensus which the Trial Chamber regarded as 'representative of customary international law' (§ 459). Another Trial Chamber of the ICTY, ruling in *Furundžija*, shared that conclusion, although on different legal grounds. It held that, as shown by the broad convergence of international instruments and international jurisprudence, there was general acceptance of the main elements contained in the definition set out in Article 1 of the Torture Convention (see 7.1). It considered, however, that some specific elements pertained to torture as considered from the specific viewpoint of ICL relating to armed conflicts. Subsequently, in *Kunarac and others*, another Trial Chamber of the ICTY broadened that definition. Starting from the correct assumption that one ought to distinguish between the definition of torture under international human rights law and that applicable under ICL, the Trial Chamber held, among other things, that 'the presence of a State official or of any other authority-wielding person in the torture process is not necessary for the offence to be regarded as torture under IHL' (§ 496). Another TC shared this view in *Kvočka and others* (§§ 137–41). The ICC Elements of Crimes also do not require torture as a crime against humanity be committed by, or perpetrated with the tolerance, acquiescence, or support of a state official or any other authority-wielding person. (On torture as a crime against humanity, see also 7.1.2.)

In *Brđanin* the ICTY Appeals Chamber made an interesting contribution to the delineation of the notion. The appellant had submitted that the Trial Chamber had erred in law in its determination of what acts constitute torture; in his view torture, to amount to an international crime, must involve physical pain equivalent in intensity to the pain accompanying serious physical injury, such as organ failure, impairment of bodily function, or even death. To support his contention, the appellant had stressed that this notion of torture was that recently propounded by the US Department of Justice in a legal memorandum. The Appeals Chamber dismissed the submission. After noting that 'no matter how powerful or influential a country is, its practice does not automatically become customary international law' (§ 247), the Chamber held that 'acts inflicting physical pain may amount to torture even when they do not cause pain of the type accompanying serious injury' (§ 251).

Finally, in *Naletilić and Martinović* the ICTY Appeals Chamber added an important specification, given the general purport of the definition of torture eventually set out in international case law. It clarified that the concrete and specific determination of whether an act causing severe mental or physical pain amounts to torture must be made on a case-by-case basis.[32]

vii) Sexual violence. This class of offence includes: (a) *rape*, a category of crime that was not defined in international law until a Trial Chamber of the ICTR set out a rather terse definition in *Akayesu* (rape is 'a physical invasion of a sexual nature, committed under

---

[32] 'As stated in the *Kunarac et al.* Appeal Judgment, torture 'is constituted by an act or an omission giving rise to "severe pain or suffering, whether physical or mental", but there are no more specific requirements which allow an exhaustive classification and enumeration of acts which may constitute torture. Existing case-law has not determined the absolute degree of pain required for an act to amount to torture.' Thus, while the suffering inflicted by some acts may be so obvious that the acts amount *per se* to torture, 'in general allegations of torture must be considered on a case-by-case basis so as to determine whether, in light of the acts committed and their context, severe physical or mental pain or suffering was inflicted. Similar case-by-case analysis is necessary regarding the crime of wilfully causing great suffering' (ICTY, *Naletilić and Martinović*, AC, § 299).

circumstances which are coercive', § 597), taken up by a Trial Chamber of the ICTY in *Delalić and others* (§ 479). Subsequently, two ICTY Trial Chambers delivered important judgments, in *Furundžija* and *Kunarac and others*;[33] (b) *sexual slavery*; (c) *enforced prostitution*; (d) *forced pregnancy*, namely 'the unlawful confinement of a woman forcibly made pregnant, with the intent of affecting the ethnic composition of any population or carrying out other grave violations of international law' (Article 7(2)(f) of the ICC Statute (perhaps this sub-category is not yet contemplated by customary international law: see 5.8); (e) *enforced sterilization*; and (f) any other form of *sexual violence of comparable gravity*.

viii) *Persecution* against any identifiable group or collectivity on political, racial, national, ethnic, cultural, religious, gender, or other grounds, that are universally recognized as impermissible grounds of discrimination under international law; persecution 'means the intentional and severe deprivation of fundamental rights contrary to international law by reason of the identity of the group or collectivity' (Article 7(2)(g) of the ICC Statute). An ICTY Trial Chamber propounded an elaborate definition of this crime in *Kupreškić and others* (§§ 616–27). It found that the defendants were guilty of persecution, for:

> the 'deliberate and systematic killing of Bosnian Muslim civilians' as well as their 'organised detention and expulsion from Ahmici [the village where the crimes were committed]' can constitute persecution. This is because these acts qualify as murder, imprisonment, and deportation, which are explicitly mentioned in the Statute under Article 5. (§ 629)

The Trial Chamber also found that the comprehensive destruction of Bosnian Muslim homes and property constituted 'a gross or blatant denial of fundamental human rights', and, being committed on discriminatory grounds, amounted to persecution (§§ 630–1).[34]

ix) *Enforced disappearance of persons*, namely 'the arrest, detention or abduction of persons by, or with the authorization, support or acquiescence of, a state or a political organization, followed by a refusal to acknowledge that deprivation of freedom or to give information on the fate or whereabouts of those persons, with the

---

[33] In *Furundžija*, the Trial Chamber held that neither international customary or treaty law, nor general principles of ICL, nor general principles of international law offered any possible definition of rape. It therefore resorted to the principles of criminal law common to the major legal systems of the world, deriving them, with caution, from national laws. It concluded that the objective elements of rape are as follows: '(i) the sexual penetration, however slight: (a) of the vagina or anus of the victim by the penis of the perpetrator or any other object used by the perpetrator; or (b) of the mouth of the victim by the penis of the perpetrator; (ii) by coercion or force or threat of force against the victim or a third person' (ICTY, *Furundžija*, TC, § 185).

Subsequently, in *Kunarac and others*, another Trial Chamber of the same ICTY placed a different interpretation on one of the elements of the definition set out in *Furundžija*; that is the element of 'coercion, or force, or threat of force'. According to this Trial Chamber that element must be taken to mean that there is rape whenever sexual autonomy is violated, or in other terms the person subjected to the act has not freely agreed to it or is otherwise not a voluntary participant. Therefore, that element may be set out as follows: 'sexual penetration occurs without the consent of the victim. Consent for this purpose must be consent given voluntarily, as a result of the victim's free will, assessed in the context of the surrounding circumstances' (*Kunarac and others*, TC, § 460, and see §§ 438–60).

It would appear that the two definitions are in substance equivalent, for 'coercion, or force, or threat of force' in essence imply or mean 'lack of consent'.

The *Kunarac* definition has been taken up by the ICTR in *Gacumbitsi*, AC, § 151 and then in *Nyiramasuhuko and others*, TC, at § 6075.

[34] In *Brđanin* the ICTY Appeals Chamber rejected the Appellant's submission that the dismissal of Bosnian Muslims and Bosnian Croats by the Bosnian Serb authorities had been justified by the security reasons provided for in Art. 27 of the IVth Geneva Convention of 1949. It held that, as such dismissals were based on the ethnicity of the individuals concerned, they amounted to persecution as a crime against humanity (*Brđanin*, AC, §§ 166–7).

intention of removing them from the protection of the law for a prolonged period of time'
(Article 7(2)(i) of the ICC Statute). It may be noted that with respect to this crime the ICC
Statute has not codified existing customary law but contributed to the crystallization of a
nascent rule, evolved primarily out of treaty law (that is, the numerous treaties on human
rights prohibiting various acts falling under this heading), as well as the case law of the
Inter-American Commission and Court of Human Rights, in addition to a number of
UN General Assembly resolutions. These various strands have been instrumental in the
gradual formation of a customary rule prohibiting enforced disappearance of persons.
The ICC Statute has upheld and laid down in a written provision of the criminalization
of this conduct.

   x) *Other inhumane acts of a similar character and gravity*, intentionally causing great
suffering, or serious injury to body or to mental or physical health. This notion harks
back to Article 6(c) of the Statute of the Nuremberg Tribunal, which simply criminalized
'other inhumane acts', by a provision lacking any precision and therefore at odds with the
principle of specificity proper to criminal law (see 2.3.1). The provision was subsequently
interpreted in such cases as *Tarnek*[35] on the strength of the *ejusdem generis* principle,
thereby acquiring some degree of precision, as well as in *Kupreškic and others*, where an
ICTY Trial Chamber dwelt at length on the interpretation of the clause (§§ 563–6). The
rule was recently restated in Article 7(1)(k) of the ICC Statute, which to a large extent
codifies and in some respects develops customary international law.

   In spite of its relatively loose character (which, however, has been rightly narrowed
down by the case law, as just noted), the rule is important for it may function as a 'residual
clause' covering and criminalizing instances of inhuman behaviour that do not neatly fall
under any of the other existing categories of crimes against humanity (for instance, it can
cover acts of terrorism not falling under the sub-category of murder, torture, etc; see 8.6).
Of course, the clause may serve this purpose only subject to strict conditions concerning
the gravity of the inhuman conduct.[36]

5.5 THE SUBJECTIVE ELEMENTS

The relevant rules of international law require two mental elements for the crimes under
discussion: *i*) the mens rea proper to the underlying offence (murder, rape, torture, deportation, etc.); and *ii*) awareness of the existence of a widespread or systematic practice.

   In most cases the first mental element is *intent*; that is, the intention to bring about
a certain result. However, as noted above (see 5.4.2) in the case of murder, case law has
considered that what is required for such conduct to amount to a crime against humanity
is *inter alia* either the intent to kill, proper to murder, or a different intentional element,
namely 'the intent to inflict serious injury in reckless disregard of human life'. More

---

[35] The District Court of Tel-Aviv held in a decision of 14 December 1951 that the definition of 'other
inhumane acts', was to apply only to such other inhumane acts as resembled in their nature and their gravity
those specified in the definition (at § 7 or p. 538).

[36] The ICTY has dealt with this notion in *Galić*, AC, §§ 155, 157; *Stakić*, AC, §§ 315–16, 362; *Kordić and
Čerkez*, AC, § 117.

   The ICTR has pronounced on this notion in *Bagosora et al.*, TC, § 2218 and in *Nyiramasuhuko and others*,
where an ICTR TC held: 'For an act or an omission to be "inhumane" under this Article, the victim must
have suffered serious bodily or mental harm or must have been the subject of a serious attack on human dignity. Moreover, the suffering must be the result of an act or omission of the accused or his or her subordinate,
and the accused or subordinate must have been motivated by the intent to inflict serious bodily or mental
harm upon the victim when the offence was committed' (ICTR, *Nyiramasuhuko and others*, TC, § 6127).

generally, where an accused, acting as an 'agent of a system', does not directly and immediately cause the inhumane acts, it is not necessary that he anticipate all the specific consequences of his misconduct; it is sufficient for him to be *aware of the risk* that his action might bring about serious consequences for the victim, on account of the violence and arbitrariness of the system to which he delivers the victim.[37] Thus, recklessness (or *dolus eventualis*) may be sufficient.

When crimes against humanity take the form of *persecution*, another mental element is also required: a persecutory or discriminatory animus. The intent must be to subject a person or group to discrimination, ill-treatment, or harassment, so as to bring about great suffering or injury to that person or group on religious, political, or other such grounds. This added element for persecution amounts to a *special criminal intent* (*dol spécial*).

Finally, courts have not required, as part of the mens rea, that the perpetrator should have a specifically racist or inhuman frame of mind.[38]

The second requirement is that the agent be *cognizant of the link* between his misconduct and a widespread or systematic practice (the 'contextual' practice may refer either to offences of the same category or to other large-scale attacks on the civilian population directed to offend the dignity and humanity of the population, as long as a link exists between the crime against humanity at issue and the practice). As the ICTY AC held in *Tadić* (AC, 1999), the perpetrator needs to know that there is an attack on the civilian population and that his acts comprise part of the attack (§ 248); a Trial Chamber held in *Blaškić* that the perpetrator needs at least to be aware of the *risk* that his act is part of the attack, and then takes that risk (TC §§ 247, 251). This does not, however, entail that he needs to know the details of the attack (*Kunarac and others*, TC, § 434). The rationale behind this requirement is clear: ICL intends to punish persons who, being aware of the fact that the crimes they are perpetrating (or plan to perpetrate) are part of a general framework of criminality, are thereby encouraged to misbehave and also hope subsequently to enjoy impunity (if this requirement is lacking, depending on the circumstances misconduct will amount to either a war crime or an ordinary criminal offence under domestic law).

---

[37] This point was particularly stressed by the German Supreme Court in the British Occupied Zone, with particular reference to cases of denunciation of Jews or political opponents to the police or Gestapo, for instance in *T. and K.*, in which the accused had been charged with burning down a synagogue in 1938 (at 198–202). See also *Finta*, decisions by the Ontario Court of Appeal (at 1–153) and the Supreme Court of Canada (at 701–877). For a comment on these cases, see the relevant entries in *Cassese's Companion*.

[38] On this point, a number of cases brought before the German Supreme Court in the British Occupied Zone are also relevant. Most of these cases concern denunciations by Germans to the police or military authorities of Jews or political opponents, with the consequence that the denounced persons were arrested and imprisoned or severely ill-treated; some such cases concern the burning of synagogues in 1938.

In the *Sch.* Case (for a comment, see *Cassese's Companion*, at 903), in 1943 a person had denounced his landlord to the Gestapo for his statements against Hitler; as a result the man had been arrested and sentenced to death. It is notable that the German Supreme Court held that the existence of a link or nexus between an offence against humanity and a general policy or a systematic practice of abuses did not necessarily imply that the author of the crime against humanity intended by his action to further or promote the violent and brutal practice of the regime within which the crime had been committed. Nor was it required that the agent should approve the final result of his action. In other words, the Court simply required an *objective link* between that act and the policy or practice, as well as the awareness of the policy or practice, not necessarily the intention to commit the crime for the purpose of pursuing that policy or practice, or a state of mind that approved the outcome of the crime (at 124). In *K.* (at 50) the German Supreme Court in the British Occupied Zone held that for the mens rea in a crime against humanity to exist, it is not necessary for the agent to have acted 'out of inhumane convictions'.

The *Barbie* (at 137–41 and 331–7) and *Touvier* (at 337) cases, brought before the French Court of Cassation, confirm this approach. For a comment on these cases, see the relevant entries in *Cassese's Companion*.

To sum up, the requisite subjective element or mens rea in crimes against humanity is not simply limited to the *criminal intent* (or recklessness) *required for the underlying offence* (murder, extermination, deportation, rape, torture, persecution, etc.).[39] The viciousness of these crimes goes far beyond the underlying offence, however wicked or despicable it may be. This additional element—which helps to distinguish crimes against humanity from war crimes—consists of awareness of the broader context into which this crime fits.

5.6 THE AUTHORS

Normally it is state organs, i.e. individuals acting in an official capacity such as military commanders, servicemen, etc. who perpetrate crimes against humanity. Is this a necessary element of the crimes; that is, must the offence be perpetrated by organs or agents of a state or a governmental authority or on behalf of such bodies, or may such crimes be committed by individuals not acting in an official capacity? In the latter case, must the offence be approved or at least condoned or countenanced by a governmental body for it to amount to a crime against humanity?

The case law seems to indicate that the crimes we are discussing may be committed by individuals acting in their private capacity, provided they behave in unison, as it were, with a general state policy and find support for their misdeeds in such policy. This is clearly shown by the numerous cases brought after 1945 before the German Supreme Court in the British Occupied Zone and concerning denunciations to the German authorities of Jews or political opponents by private German individuals.[40]

An interesting problem that may arise is whether crimes against humanity may be committed by state officials acting in a private capacity. It would seem that in such cases some sort of explicit or implicit approval or endorsement by state or governmental authorities is required, or else that it is necessary for the offence to be clearly encouraged by a general governmental policy, or at least to *fit clearly within such a policy*. This is best illustrated by the *Weller* case. This case, which seems to have been unknown until it was cited by the ICTY in *Kupreškić* (§ 555), gave rise to six different judgments by German courts after the Second World War.[41]

---

[39] In some cases courts have held that the subjective element may be *culpable negligence* (see 3.7): see *Hinselmann and others* (at 58–60). In some German cases it was held that instead mere negligence or *Fahrlässigkeit* was not sufficient (see e.g. *R.*, at 45–9).

[40] See e.g. the judgments in *B.* (at 6–10); in *P.* (at 11–18); in *V.* (at 20–5); in *R.* (at 46–9); in *K.* (at 49–52); in *M.* (at 91–5); in *H.* (at 385–91); in *P.*, decision of 10 May 1949 (at 17–19); in *Ehel. M.* (at 67–9); in *A.* (at 144–7); in *S.* (at 56–7).

[41] Given its significance (and its historical value as well), it may be useful to dwell on it at some length. The facts, as set out in almost all the six judgments, are as follows. In early 1940, in the small German town of Mönchengladbach (near Düsseldorf), various Jewish families were obliged to move together into one house; eventually 16 persons lived there. One night, in May 1940, three (probably drunken) persons broke into the house. One of them was the accused Weller, a member of the SS, who was in civilian clothing; another wore the SA uniform, and the third wore the blue uniform of the German Navy. They obliged all 16 inhabitants to assemble in their night clothes in the basement, then went to the kitchen, where they summoned the 16 persons, one by one. There, 11 (or 10, according to some of the judgments) of the 16 inhabitants of the house were beaten with a 'heavy leather whip' and verbally abused. The next day the injured parties reported to the Jewish community (*Jüdische Gemeinde*), which turned to the local Gestapo. The head of the Gestapo informed the wronged Jews that 'Weller's and the other persons' actions were an isolated event, which would in no way be approved' (judgment of 16 June 1948, at 3). Thereafter Weller was summoned by the Gestapo and strongly taken to task by the district leader of the NSDAP (the national socialist party). It is not clear (nor was it established by the various German courts dealing with the case after 1945) whether in 1940 Weller had

5.7 THE VICTIMS

Article 6(c) of the Charter of the Nuremberg Tribunal expressly mentions *any civilian population* as the target of murder-type crimes against humanity (see 5.4.2). The words 'any' and 'civilian' need careful interpretation. As for 'any', it is apparent, both from the text of the provision and from the legislative history of Article 6(c), that it was intended to cover civilian populations other than those associated with the enemy, who were already protected by the traditional rules of the law of warfare. In other words, by using 'any', the

---

in fact been fined 20RM for bodily harm, as alleged, instead of imprisonment for not less than two months (this being the penalty which was usually imposed by German law for bodily harm). After the war, the case was brought before the District Court (*Landgericht*) of Mönchengladbach. The Court found Weller guilty of grievous bodily harm and sentenced him to 18 months' imprisonment. While admitting that he had acted out of racist motives, the Court ruled that his action could nevertheless not be regarded as a crime against humanity. In this connection the Court held that three requirements were to be met for such a crime to exist: *i)* a significant breach of human dignity (this the Court held to have been established in the case at issue, and lay in the ill treatment of Jews); *ii)* the racial motivation of the offence (this could also be found in this case); and *iii)* the action must be perpetrated 'by abusing the authority of the state or of the police' (at 7–12). The Court found that this third element was lacking. It held that a crime against humanity must be 'either systematically organized by the government or carried out with its approval' (at 10). In the case at issue, one was faced with the 'occasional persecution of various persons by one person', not with abuses perpetrated by the 'holder of political power or at least by a person acting under the protection of or with the approval of [those holding] political power' (at 10). In short, the necessary 'link between crimes against humanity and State authority' was lacking.

On appeal, the case was passed on, 'to ensure uniform jurisprudence' (at 5), by the Court of Appeal in Düsseldorf to the Supreme Court (Oberster Gerichtshof) for the British Occupied Zone. This Court overturned the decision of the District Court and held that the offence did indeed constitute a crime against humanity. According to the Supreme Court, it was sufficient for the attack on human dignity to be *connected* to the national socialist system of power and hegemony (at 7–9). The same Supreme Court, when again seized with the case (the prosecutor contending that the sentence newly passed by the Court of Assize was too light), emphasized that the offence amounted to a crime against humanity, although it had been committed by Weller 'on his own initiative and out of racial hatred' (decision of 10 October 1949, at 2, or 150). The Court also pointed out that the 'punishment' (fine of 20RM) allegedly inflicted in 1940 and on which the accused so much insisted, was a measure that, assuming it had been taken, 'would not serve justice, but only scorn the victims' (at 5, or 153).

The Supreme Court pointed out the following: 'The national-socialist leadership often, and quite readily, utilized for its criminal goals and plans actions which appeared to have, or actually had, originated from quite personal decisions. This was true even of actions that were outwardly disapproved of, perhaps because it was felt that some sort of consideration should be shown and it was inappropriate openly to admit such actions [. . .] The link, in this sense, with the national-socialist system of power and tyranny does in the case at issue manifestly exist. The state and the party had long before the action at issue made Jews out to be subhumans, not worthy to be respected as human beings [. . .] Also the action of the accused fitted into the numerous persecutory measures which then affected the Jews in Germany, or could at any time affect them. As the trial court established, the accused, influenced by official propaganda, acted from racial hatred. In the decision [of the Düsseldorf Court of Appeal] [. . .] it is rightly pointed out that the link with the national-socialist system of power and tyranny exists not only in the case of those actions which are ordered and approved by the holders of hegemony. That link also exists when those actions can only be explained by the atmosphere and condition created by the authorities in power. The trial court was wrong when it attached decisive value to the fact that after his action the accused was "rebuked" and that even the Gestapo disapproved of the excess as an isolated infringement. This action nevertheless fitted into the persecution of Jews carried out by the state and the party. This is proved by the fact that the accused, assuming he was the subject of an order for summary punishment (*Strafbefehl*) or a criminal measure (*Strafverfügung*) for the payment of 20RM—a matter that in any case has not been clarified—was in any event not held criminally accountable in a manner commensurate to the gravity of his guilt [. . .] Given the gravity of the abuse, the harm caused to the victims brought about consequences extending beyond the single individuals and affecting the whole of humanity' (at 206–7).

draftsmen intended principally to protect the civilian population of the state committing crimes against humanity, as well as the civilian population of its allied countries or of countries under its control, although formally under no military occupation. As for the word 'civilian', it is apparent that it does not cover combatants.[42]

Interestingly, exclusion of combatants as possible targets of crimes against seems not to apply to persecution, therefore the inference is warranted that not only any civilian population but also the armed forces may be the target of this class of crime. There is an obvious rationale for this regulation: traditional laws of warfare, while they protected combatants against murder-type offences if captured by the enemy (and therefore as prisoners of war) or against other illegal actions by the enemy such as treachery and use of prohibited means or methods of warfare, did not safeguard them against *persecution* either by the enemy, or by the Allies or by the very authorities to which military personnel belonged. The textual and logical construction of Article 6(c) was confirmed implicitly in *Pilz*[43] by the Dutch Special Court of Cassation and explicitly by French courts in *Barbie* and *Touvier*.[44]

It is worth noting, however, that the requirement that murder-type crimes against humanity must target the civilian population does not exclude that the individual victims of the underlying offences might be non-civilians. In other terms, while a civilian population must be the ultimate object of the attack amounting to crimes against humanity, it is possible that some of the underlying offences be committed against military people or captured combatants if it is proven that those offences are part of the general attack. For instance, the Supreme Court of Germany in the British Occupied Zone held in at least three cases that military persons could be the victims of crimes against humanity even in situations where the crime did not take the form of persecution.[45] After the Second

---

[42] See the categories of combatants envisaged in the Regulations annexed to the Fourth Hague Convention of 1899/1907 (subsequently supplemented by Article 4 of the Third Geneva Convention of 1949 and Articles 43–4 of the First Additional Protocol of 1977).

[43] As recalled above, *Pilz* was a German medical doctor serving with the German army occupying the Netherlands. He had prevented a young Dutchman, who had enlisted in the German army and been wounded while attempting to escape from his unit, from being treated and had then ordered a subordinate to kill the Dutchman. The Dutch Special Court of Cassation held that the offence did not amount to a war crime, because the victim, even if still a Dutch national, belonged to the German army. It then asked itself whether it could amount to a crime against humanity, and answered in the negative, noting that the victim 'was not part of the civilian population of occupied territory, nor [could] the acts with which he [was] charged be seen as forming part of a system of persecution on political, racial or religious grounds' (at 1211). Clearly, it can be deduced from this reasoning that had the victim, a member of the military, been the object of persecution on one of those grounds, the offence might have amounted to a crime against humanity.

[44] In *Barbie*, in a decision rendered on 20 December 1985 the French Court of Cassation held that crimes against humanity in the form of persecution had been perpetrated against members of the French Resistance movements (at 136). Subsequently, the Paris Court of Appeal took the same view in a judgment of 9 July 1986, again in *Barbie*, followed by the Chambre d'Accusation of the same Court of Appeal in a judgment of 13 April 1992 in *Touvier* (at 352). In this last decision the Chambre d'Accusation held that: 'Jews and members of the Resistance persecuted in a systematic manner in the name of a state practising a policy of ideological supremacy, the former by reason of their membership of a racial or religious community, the latter by reason of their opposition to that policy, can equally be the victims of crimes against humanity' (at 352). For a comment on both cases, see the relevant entries in *Cassese's Companion*.

[45] These three cases will be briefly summarized.

In a decision of 27 July 1948 in *R.*, the Court pronounced upon the guilt of a member of the Nazi Party and Nazi commandos (NSKK), who in 1944 had denounced a non-commissioned officer in uniform and member of the Nazi Party and the SA (assault units), for insulting the leadership of the Party. As a result of this denunciation, the victim had been brought to trial three times and eventually sentenced to death (the sentence had not been carried out because in the interim the Russians had occupied Germany). The Court

World War other courts, with the notable exception of the French Court of Cassation in *Barbie*,[46] tended instead to place a strict interpretation on the prohibition of murder-type crimes against humanity and consequently to rule out from the notion of victims persons who belonged, or had belonged, to the military.[47] The trend towards loosening the strict requirement that the victims of murder-type crimes against humanity be civilians also continued, however, in more recent times. It is significant that the ICTY has placed a liberal interpretation on the narrow notion of victims of crimes against humanity set out in

held that the denunciation could constitute a crime against humanity if it could be proved that the agent had intended to hand over the victim to the 'uncontrollable power structure of the [Nazi] party and State', knowing that as a consequence of his denunciation, the victim was likely to be caught up in an arbitrary and violent system (at 47).

In 1948, in *P. and others* (for a comment, see *Cassese's Companion*, at 868) the same court applied the notion of crimes against humanity to members of the military. In the night following Germany's partial capitulation (5 May 1945), four German marines had tried to escape from Denmark back to Germany. The next day they were caught by Danes and delivered to the German troops, who court-martialled and sentenced three of them to death for desertion; on the very day of the general capitulation of Germany (10 May 1945), the three were executed. The German Supreme Court found that the five members of the Court Martial were guilty of complicity in a crime against humanity. According to the Supreme Court, the glaring discrepancy between the offence and the punishment proved that the execution of the three marines had constituted a clear manifestation of the Nazis' brutal and intimidatory justice, which denied the very essence of humanity in blind deference to the superior exigencies of the Nazi state. In this case as well, there had taken place 'an intolerable degradation of the victims to mere means for the pursuit of a goal, hence the depersonalisation and reification of human beings' (at 220); consequently, by sentencing to death those marines, the members of the Court Martial had also injured humanity as a whole. With regard to the wording of the relevant provision on crimes against humanity (namely, Article II(1)(c) of Control Council Law no. 10, which referred only to offences 'against civilian populations'), the Court observed the following:

> Whoever notes the expressly emphasized illustrative character of the instances and classes of instance mentioned there, cannot come to the conclusion that action between soldiers may not constitute crimes against humanity. [Admittedly], a single and isolated excess would not constitute a crime against humanity pursuant to the legal notion of such crimes. [However], it has already been shown [in the judgment] that the action at issue *can* belong to the criminal system and criminal tendency of the Nazi era. For the offence to be a crime against humanity, it is not necessary that the action should support or sustain Nazi tyranny, or that the accused should intend so to act. (228)

Finally, in its decision of 18 October 1949 in *H.* (for a comment, see *Cassese's Companion*, 708), the Court dealt with a case in which a German judge had presided over two trials by a Naval Court Martial against two officers of the German Navy: one against a commander of submarines who had been accused of criticizing Hitler in 1944, the other against a lieutenant-commander of the German naval forces, charged with procuring two foreign identity cards for himself and his wife in 1944. The judge had initially sentenced both officers to death (the first had been executed, while the sentence against the second had been commuted by Hitler to ten years' imprisonment). The Supreme Court held that the judge could be held guilty of crimes against humanity to the extent that his action was undertaken deliberately in connection with the Nazi system of violence and terror (at 233–4, 238, 241–4).

[46] In 1985 the French Court of Cassation in *Barbie* held that the victims of crimes against humanity could include 'the opponents of [a] policy [of ideological supremacy, manifesting itself in inhumane acts and persecution committed in a systematic manner], whatever the form of their "opposition"' (at 137 and 139–40).

[47] Indicative in this respect is *Neddermeier* (for a comment, see *Cassese's Companion*, 840), brought before a British Court of Appeal established under Control Council Law no. 10. The accused had been convicted by the High Court of Brunswick of crimes against humanity, pursuant to Article II(1)(c) of Control Council Law no. 10. The Court had found that he had caused a number of Polish workers to be beaten (the Poles, originally brought to Germany as prisoners of war, had subsequently been compelled to sign agreements to surrender such status and be treated as civilians). Before the Appeal Court the defence claimed among other things that the offence did not amount to a crime against humanity because 'there was no element of cruelty'. The prosecution admitted that, if the victims of ill-treatment were to be considered as prisoners of war, a conviction under the label of war crimes 'could be substituted' for the conviction for crimes against humanity. The Court held that the victims had the status of prisoners of war 'and not civilians'. It consequently set aside the conviction for crimes against humanity and substituted for it that for war crimes (at 58–60).

Article 5 of its Statute (according to which those crimes can only be committed against 'any civilian population'). In its decision in *Mrkšić and others* (rendered under Rule 61 of the Rules of Procedure and Evidence), the Court held that crimes against humanity could be committed even where the victims at one time bore arms.[48]

Clearly, because of the gradual disappearance in customary international law of the nexus between crimes against humanity and armed conflict, the emphasis on the civilian population as the exclusive target of such crimes dwindled, if not disappeared. For if crimes against humanity may be committed *in time of peace* as well, it no longer makes sense to require that such crimes be perpetrated against the civilian population alone. Why should military forces be excluded, since they in any case would not be protected by IHL in the absence of any armed conflict? Plainly, in times of peace military personnel too may become the object of crimes against humanity at the hands of their own authorities. By the same token, *in time of armed hostilities*, there is no longer any reason for excluding servicemen, whether or not *hors de combat* (wounded, sick, or prisoners of war), from protection against crimes against humanity (chiefly persecution), whether committed by their own authorities, by allied forces, or by the enemy.

In addition, the broadening of the category of persons safeguarded by the international prohibition of crimes against humanity is consonant with the overall trend in IHL towards expanding the scope of protection of the basic values of human dignity, regardless of the legal status of those entitled to such protection. This trend has manifested itself in, *inter alia*, the adoption of international treaties protecting human rights and treaties prohibiting crimes such as genocide, apartheid, or torture, in the passing of some significant resolutions by the United Nations General Assembly, and in certain pronouncements of the ICJ. Nowadays, international human rights standards also clearly protect individuals against abuses and misdeeds of *their own* governmental authorities. It follows that there no longer exists any substantial reason for refusing to apply the notion of crimes against humanity to vicious and inhumane actions undertaken on a large scale by governments against the human dignity of their own military or the military personnel of allies or other non-enemy countries (or even of the enemy). It is worth noting that, had this expansion of the notion of crimes against humanity not occurred, a strict interpretation of the notion of civilians would lead in times of armed conflict to a questionable result. Some categories of combatants who, in modern armed conflicts (particularly in internal conflicts) often find themselves in a twilight area, would remain unprotected—or scantily protected—against serious atrocities. Consider, for example, members of paramilitary forces or members of police forces who occasionally or sporadically take part in hostilities. These are persons whose legal status may be uncertain, as one may not be sure whether they are to be regarded as combatants or civilians.[49] It could therefore follow that, under a strict and traditional interpretation of the crimes at issue, and assuming

---

[48] In *Kupreškić and others*, a Trial Chamber held that 'the presence of those actively involved in the conflict should not prevent the characterization of a population as civilian and those actively involved in a resistance movement can qualify as victims of crimes against humanity' (ICTY, *Kupreškić and others*, TC, § 549). In *Kunarac and others*, an ICTY Trial Chamber held that 'as a minimum, the perpetrator must have known or considered the possibility that the victim of his crime was a civilian [. . .] in case of doubt as to whether a person is a civilian, that person shall be considered to be a civilian. The Prosecution must show that the perpetrator could not reasonably have believed that the victim was a member of the armed forces' (*Kunarac and others*, TC, § 435).

[49] Under Art. 43(3) of the First Additional Protocol of 1977, 'Whenever a Party to a conflict incorporates a paramilitary or armed law enforcement agency into its armed forces it shall so notify the other Parties to the conflict.' If such notification has not been made, the status of the paramilitary or police force may be uncertain.

that these persons were at the same time regarded as combatants, they would ultimately be unprotected by the prohibition against such crimes.

A *different* issue that arose in cases brought before the US Military Tribunals sitting at Nuremberg is whether victims of extermination through euthanasia as a crime against humanity may be nationals of the state concerned, or whether such victims must perforce be foreigners. In these cases some defendants had been accused of participating in euthanasia programmes for the chronically disabled or terminally ill. The Tribunals wrongly held that euthanasia amounted to a crime against humanity only if carried out against *foreigners*, i.e. non-nationals of the state practising euthanasia.[50]

5.8 ARTICLE 7 OF THE ICC STATUTE AND CUSTOMARY INTERNATIONAL LAW

Article 7 of the ICC Statute contemplates crimes against humanity as one of the categories of criminal conduct over which the Court has jurisdiction. A comparison between this provision and customary international law shows that by and large the former is based on the latter. However, many differences may be discerned. In some respects, Article 7 elaborates upon and clarifies; in other respects it is narrower than, customary international law; in others, it instead broadens customary rules.

5.8.1 AREAS WHERE ARTICLE 7 SETS FORTH ELEMENTS OF CUSTOMARY INTERNATIONAL LAW

Article 7 specifies and elaborates upon customary international law in many respects. First, it specifies that a crime against humanity must be committed 'with knowledge of the attack'. The provision thus makes it clear that the requisite mens rea must include the awareness that the individual criminal act is part of a widespread or systematic attack on a civilian population.

Second, Article 7 clarifies the objective elements of some of the underlying offences, by making explicit notions that, until set out in this Article, were only implicit and could therefore be determined only by way of interpretation. These notions are further elaborated upon in the 'Elements of Crimes' adopted by the Preparatory Commission.[51]

---

[50] In *Karl Brandt*, the Tribunal found that the defendant had participated in a programme for the extermination of disabled persons, and that this programme had quickly been extended to Jews and then to concentration camp inmates (those inmates deemed to be unfit for labour were ruthlessly weeded out and sent to extermination camps in great numbers). The Tribunal stressed that it was difficult to believe Brandt's assertion that he was not implicated in the extermination of Jews or of concentration camp inmates; however, even if it were true, 'the evidence [was] conclusive that almost at the outset of the programme *non-German nationals* were selected for euthanasia and extermination' (at 197–8). The same Tribunal also took this restrictive (and undisputedly fallacious) view in *Greifelt and others* (at 654–5).

[51] This applies to the following notions: *i*) 'Extermination', which, pursuant to Art. 7(2)(b), 'includes the intentional infliction of conditions of life, inter alia, the deprivation of access to food and medicine, calculated to bring about the destruction of part of a population'; *ii*) 'Enslavement', which under Art. 7(2)(c) refers to 'the exercise of any or all the powers attaching to the right of ownership over a person and includes the exercise of such power in the course of trafficking in persons, in particular women and children'. This notion is made more specific in the 'Elements of Crime', where it is stated that the conduct at issue takes place when 'the perpetrator exercised any or all of the powers attaching to the right of ownership over one or more persons, such as purchasing, selling, lending or bartering such a person or persons, or by imposing on them a similar deprivation of liberty', and it is added (in a footnote) that deprivation of liberty may include 'exacting

Finally, one should emphasize that the 'Elements of Crime' have clarified an important aspect of mens rea. In commenting on the need for the offender to have knowledge of a widespread or systematic attack on a civilian population, it is stated there that: 'The perpetrator knew that the conduct was part of or intended the conduct to be part of a widespread or systematic attack against a civilian population.' However, the last element should not be interpreted as requiring proof that the perpetrator had knowledge of all characteristics of the attack or the precise details of the plan or policy of the state or organization. In the case of an emerging widespread or systematic attack on a civilian population, the intent clause of the last element indicates that this mental element is satisfied if the perpetrator intended to further such attack.

5.8.2 AREAS WHERE ARTICLE 7 IS NARROWER THAN CUSTOMARY INTERNATIONAL LAW

On some points, Article 7 departs from customary law by setting out notions at odds with that body of law.

First, Article 7(1) defines the victim or target of crimes against humanity as 'any civilian population'. This provision, if narrowly interpreted, could exclude non-civilians (i.e. the military) from the victims of the crimes under discussion. Thus, any of the acts enumerated in Article 7(1)(c) to (k), if perpetrated against an enemy combatant, would only amount to a war crime or a grave breach of the 1949 Geneva Conventions. The question arises whether the term 'civilian population' includes belligerents *hors de combat* who have laid down their weapons, either because they are wounded or because they have been captured. The question also arises whether crimes against humanity could be committed against the military people as the main target of the attack. As we have seen above, the

---

forced labour or otherwise reducing a person to a servile status'; *iii*) 'Deportation or forcible transfer of population', which under Art. 7(2)(d) is defined as 'forced displacement of the persons concerned by expulsion or other coercive acts from the area in which they are lawfully present, without grounds permitted under international law'. In the 'Elements of Crime' the important specification is added that the persons deported or forcibly transferred 'were lawfully present in the area from which they were so deported or transferred' and that 'the perpetrator was aware of the factual circumstances that established the lawfulness of such presence'; *iv*) 'Torture': Art. 7(2)(e) sets out a definition of torture that, rightly, is broader than that laid down in customary international law with regard to torture as an international crime per se as established by an ICTY Trial Chamber in *Kunarac and others*. In general international law, for the torture as a discrete crime to have occurred, it is necessary, amongst other things, that a public official be involved, either as the perpetrator or as one of the participants or accomplices (see 7.1). By contrast, under Art. 7, torture may amount to a crime against humanity even if committed by civilians against other civilians without any involvement of public officials or military personnel. Indeed, Art. 7(2)(e) defines torture as 'the intentional infliction of severe pain or suffering, whether physical or mental, upon a person in the custody or under the control of the accused'. Consequently, as long as the single act of torture is part of a widespread or systematic practice, even torture inflicted without any participation of a public official is punishable as a crime against humanity. The only involvement of public authorities is required by the 'Elements of Crime': it is necessary for the widespread or systematic practice constituting the general context of the crime to take place 'pursuant to or in furtherance of a state or organizational policy' of torture; *v*) 'Imprisonment', which under Art. 7(1)(e) embraces 'other severe deprivation of physical liberty in violation of fundamental rules of international law'; *vi*) 'Rape', which under Art. 7(1)(g) is not the sole form of sexual violence punishable under international law; as spelled out by an ICTY Trial Chamber in *Furundžija*, in addition to the violent physical penetration of the victim's body, other forms of serious sexual violence are criminalized by international law: 'sexual slavery, enforced prostitution [. . .] enforced sterilization, or any other form of sexual violence of comparable gravity'; *vii*) 'Other inhumane acts' are defined in Art. 7(1)(k) as acts 'of a similar character [to those listed in Art. 7(1), from (a) to (j)] intentionally causing great suffering, or serious injury to body or to mental or physical health.'

question should be answered in the affirmative. It would seem to be consonant with the humanitarian object and purpose of Article 7 to suggest the same solution with regard to this provision.

Second, Article 7, in defining 'attack directed against any civilian population' narrows the scope of the notion of 'widespread or systematic practice' required as a context of a specific offence, for the offence to amount to a crime against humanity. Indeed, in paragraph 2(a) that provision stipulates that 'attack' means 'a course of conduct involving the multiple commission of acts referred to in paragraph 1 against any civilian population, pursuant to or in furtherance of a state or organizational policy to commit such attack'. It would seem that the Statute requires that the offender, in committing a crime against humanity, pursue or promote such a practice. It would follow that any practice simply tolerated or condoned by a state or an organization would not constitute an attack on the civilian population or a widespread or systematic practice. For instance, in the case of murder, or rape, or forced pregnancy, why should it be required that the general practice constitute a policy pursued by a state or an organization? Would it not be sufficient for the practice to be accepted, or tolerated, or acquiesced in by the state or the organization, for those offences to constitute crimes against humanity? Clearly, this requirement goes beyond what is required under international customary law and unduly restricts the notion under discussion. The 'Elements of Crime' make this restriction even broader and more explicit. There it is stated that 'the policy to commit such attack' 'requires that the state or organization *actively promote or encourage* such an attack against a civilian population' (emphasis added).

Thirdly, Article 7 is less liberal than customary international law with regard to one element of the definition of persecution. Under Article 7(1)(h), persecution, in order to fall under the jurisdiction of the ICC, must be perpetrated 'in connection with any act referred to in this paragraph or any crime within the jurisdiction of the Court'. Instead, under customary international law no such link is required. In other words, it is not necessary for persecution to consist of (a) conduct defined as a war crime or a crime against humanity or linked to any such crime; plus (b) a discriminatory intent. Under general international law, persecution may also consist of acts not punishable as war crimes or crimes against humanity, as long as such acts (a) result in egregious violations of fundamental human rights; (b) are part of a widespread or systematic practice; and (c) are committed with a discriminatory intent. Article 7(1)(h) imposes a further burden on the prosecution: it must be proved that, in addition to discriminatory acts based on one of the grounds described in this provision, the actus reus consists of one of the acts prohibited in Article 7(1) or of a war crime or genocide (or aggression, if this crime is eventually accepted as falling under the jurisdiction of the Court), or must be 'connected' with such acts or crimes. Besides adding a requirement not provided for in general international law, Article 7 uses the phrase 'in connection with', which is unclear and susceptible to many interpretations.

5.8.3 AREAS WHERE ARTICLE 7 IS BROADER THAN CUSTOMARY INTERNATIONAL LAW

Article 7 expands general international law in at least two respects.

First, it broadens the classes of conduct amounting to crimes against humanity. Thus, it includes within this category 'forced pregnancy' (Article 7(1)(g) and (2)(f)); 'enforced disappearance of persons' (Article 7(1)(i) and (2)(i)); and 'the crime of apartheid' (Article 7(1)(j) and (2)(h)) (it could be argued that the ICC Statute has, however, contributed to the recent formation of a customary rule on the matter).

Second, in dealing with the crime of persecution, it greatly expands the category of discriminatory grounds. While under customary international law these grounds may be political, racial, ethnic, or religious, Article 7(1)(h) adds 'cultural' grounds, 'gender as defined in paragraph 3 [of the same provision]', as well as 'other grounds that are universally recognized as impermissible under international law'.

6

GENOCIDE

The intention to destroy entire groups, whether national, racial, religious, cultural, and so on, is by all evidence an ancient phenomenon in the history of mankind. The word 'genocide', which etymologically describes it, however, was coined only in 1944, by the Polish lawyer R. Lemkin.[1] This explains why the word 'genocide' itself, which is now commonly used also to describe the Holocaust of the Jews before and during the Second World War, cannot be located within the Statute of the Nuremberg Tribunal, nor in its final judgment.[2] As a matter of fact the Holocaust was punished by the Nuremberg Tribunal under the charges of persecution, which constituted one of the underlying offences of crimes against humanity (*Göring and others*, at 247–55).

The extermination of Jews as a crime against humanity was discussed in a few other cases: *Hoess*, decided by a Polish court in 1947 (at 12–18), and *Greifelt and others*, heard in 1948 by a US Military Tribunal (at 2–36). In the latter judgment (and in *Altstötter and others*, at 1128, 1156), the word 'genocide' was used to describe the criminal conduct without, however, elevating genocide to a distinct category of criminality. In other cases (for instance, *Kramer and others* (the Belsen trial), at 4, 117–21; and see 106) the killing of Jews in concentration camps was dealt with as a war crime.

Thus, at this stage prosecution and punishment of massacres of ethnic or religious groups did not require evidence of the 'special intent' typical of genocide (see 6.4), but simply proof of the subjective and objective elements of either crimes against humanity or war crimes.

Genocide acquired autonomous significance as a specific crime in 1948, when the UN General Assembly adopted the Genocide Convention, whose substantive rules may largely be considered as declaratory of customary international law. Among those, one can certainly mention Article II, which provides the legal definition for the crime of genocide. This definition has been reproduced literally in any subsequent instrument establishing an international or hybrid criminal court.

This chapter analysis the main features of the Genocide Convention and subsequently examines the legal ingredients of the crime of genocide, as also clarified in international and national case law.

[1] R. Lemkin, *Axis Rule in Occupied Europe: Laws of Occupation, Analysis of Governments, Proposals for Redress* (Washington, DC: Carnegie Endowment for International Peace, 1944), at 79.

[2] The word 'genocide' was neither used in the Charter establishing the Tokyo Tribunal nor in the final judgment issued by this Tribunal. It was, however, used in the indictment before the Nuremberg Tribunal, in some of the speeches of the prosecutors before such a Tribunal, and in the *Justice* case before a US military court sitting at Nuremberg and operating under Control Council Law no. 10. See Y. Shany, 'The Road to the Genocide Convention and Beyond', in P. Gaeta (ed.), *The UN Genocide Convention: A Commentary* (Oxford: Oxford University Press, 2009), 7–26.

6.1 THE GENOCIDE CONVENTION

6.1.1 THE DEFINITION OF GENOCIDE

In accordance with the definition contained in Article II of the Genocide Convention, the crime of genocide consists of five specific enumerated acts, which are listed in an exhaustive manner. It is also requested that the acts in question be carried out with a specific intent, namely to destroy in whole or in part, 'a national, ethnical, racial or religious group as such'. [3]

Article II of the Genocide Convention can certainly be commended for having provided a legal definition to 'crime without a name'. [4] Nonetheless, the exhaustive enumeration of the protected groups and the prohibited acts has rendered the evolution of a parallel, and potentially wider, definition of the crime of genocide through customary international law more difficult. Yet, one has not to forget that Article II, and the definition of genocide it enshrines, is merely the outcome of a negotiating process that reflects the views on genocide prevailing at the specific time of the adoption of the Genocide Convention. Such a process, involving representatives from a plethora of states, inevitably results in the formation of a text based on compromise. It must be stated that since this time, international law has undergone significant transformation, most noticeably the development of the doctrine of human rights. Therefore it is conceptually more difficult to understand why today attacks against members of groups other than those listed in the Genocide Convention cannot be considered as amounting to genocide. Furthermore, it is even more difficult to understand why genocide can be carried out only through one of the enumerated acts, since there may be other acts that can be resorted to with a view to destroying one of the protected groups.

The 'rigidity' of the definition of genocide, however, has been softened down by way of judicial interpretation. In particular, the ICTR has adopted specific criteria to widen the categories of groups protected by the definition, and has considered that some acts, such as rape, can fall within the purview of the enumerated genocidal acts (see 6.3).

---

[3] 'In the present Convention, genocide means any of the following acts committed with intent to destroy, in whole or in part, a national, ethnical, racial or religious group as such:

(a) killing members of the group;
(b) causing serious bodily or mental harm to members of the group;
(c) deliberately inflicting on the group conditions of life calculated to bring about its physical destruction, in whole or in part;
(d) imposing measures intended to prevent births within the group;
(e) forcibly transferring children of the group to another group.'

This definition has been reproduced *verbatim* in the Statutes of international criminal courts, such as the ICTY (Article 4), the ICTR (Article 2), and the ICC (Article 6).

[4] 'Prime Minister Winston Churchill's Broadcast to the World about the Meeting with President Roosevelt', 24 August 1941, available http://www.ibiblio.org/pha/timeline/410824awp.html (accessed 27 October 2012), speaking of the mass killings committed by the Nazis in the occupied Russia: 'The aggressor [...] retaliates by the most frightful cruelties. As his Armies advance, whole districts are being exterminated. Scores of thousands—literally scores of thousands—of executions in cold blood are being perpetrated by the German police-troops upon the Russian patriots who defend their native soil. Since the Mongol invasions of Europe in the sixteenth century, there has never been methodical, merciless butchery on such a scale, or approaching such a scale. And this is but the beginning. Famine and pestilence have yet to follow in the bloody ruts of Hitler's tanks. We are in the presence of a crime without a name.'

6.1.2 MAIN FEATURES OF THE GENOCIDE CONVENTION

A careful look at the Genocide Convention shows that it pursued two goals: *i*) to oblige contracting parties to criminalize genocide and punish their authors within the legal system of each party; and accordingly *ii*) to provide for the judicial cooperation of those contracting states for the suppression of the crime. This is already made clear by the Preamble, where the draughtsmen, after declaring that genocide is a crime under international law, set out their conviction that 'in order to liberate mankind from such an odious scourge, international cooperation is required'. The various provisions of the Convention bear out that this is its main purpose. In Article I it is stipulated that the contracting parties 'undertake to prevent and punish' genocide. Article III imposes upon contracting parties the obligation to punish not only the perpetration of genocide but also conduct somehow linked to the crime, which the provision defines by using criminal law categories: conspiracy, incitement, attempt, and complicity. By Article IV states assume the obligation to punish persons committing genocide or related conduct even if they are 'constitutionally responsible rulers' or 'public officials'. Article V provides for the enactment of the necessary criminal legislation, with particular regard to penalties. Article VI deals with criminal jurisdiction over the offence, and Article VII addresses the issue of extradition.

It thus seems clear, both from the text and the preparatory works,[5] that the Genocide Convention is very much like some previous international treaties such as the 1926 Convention on Slavery (followed by the Protocol of 1953), the 1929 International Convention for the Suppression of Counterfeiting Currency, or the more recent UN Convention Against Torture of 1984, which provide for a set of international obligations that contracting states are required to implement within their own domestic legal systems, and in addition arrange for judicial cooperation in the matter regulated by the treaty (see 1.3).

It was perhaps the naive assumption of the Convention's draughtsmen that, after the horrendous genocide of European Jews in the Second World War and the stiff punishment of many of its planners and perpetrators at the hands of criminal courts, contracting states themselves would not dare to engage in genocide. Plausibly it is this assumption that to some extent accounts for the odd (or, rather, ingenuous) provision in Article VI stipulating that persons accused of genocide must be prosecuted and tried by the judicial

---

[5] For the preparatory work, see N. Robinson, *The Genocide Convention—A Commentary* (New York: Institute of Jewish Affairs, 1960). It is crystal clear, for instance with regard to Article III, that the authors of the Convention only had in mind action to be taken by each contracting state at the domestic level. This is also apparent from the statement of the Swedish delegate: 'The discussion at the beginning of this meeting seems to me to have shown that the significance of the terms corresponding to the French and English expressions here in question [used in Article III]—incitement, conspiracy, attempt, complicity, etc.—is subject to certain variations in many systems of criminal law represented here. *When these expressions have to be translated in order to introduce the text of the Convention into our different criminal codes in other languages*, it will no doubt be necessary to resign ourselves to the fact that certain differences in meaning are inevitable. It would therefore be advisable to indicate in the Committee's report that Article IV of the Convention does not bind signatory States to punish the various types of acts to a greater extent than the corresponding acts aimed at the most serious crimes, as, for example, murder and high treason, already recognized under national law' (A/760, at 4 and A/C.6 SR.84, at 7, reported in Robinson, *Genocide Convention*, at 70; emphasis added).

For the drafting of the Genocide Convention see also W. Schabas, *Genocide in International Law*, 2nd edn (Cambridge: Cambridge University Press, 2009), at 59–90. The preparatory works of the Genocide Convention are now available thanks to the much-needed work edited by H. Abtahi and P. Webb under the title *The Genocide Convention: The Travaux Préparatoires* (The Hague: Martinus Nijhoff, 2008). The two documents quoted above are reproduced in this two-volume book, namely in vol. II, at 2021 and 1519, respectively.

authorities of the territory in which 'the act was committed' (plus a future international criminal court that in 1948 looked like a radiant daydream).[6]

6.1.3 THE DUAL REGIME OF RESPONSIBILITY FOR GENOCIDE, ACCORDING TO THE ICJ

In the judgment delivered on 26 February 2007 in the *Bosnia v. Serbia and Montenegro* case, the ICJ chose to place an expansive interpretation on the Convention. It preferred to look upon it as a treaty that also imposes on contracting states as such, that is as international subjects, the obligation not to commit genocide as defined by the Convention. This led the Court to propound the notion that the Convention upholds 'a duality of responsibility' for genocide: according to the Court the same acts may give rise both to individual criminal liability and state responsibility (§§ 163 and 173).

The Court first of all construed Article I as imposing not only a duty to prevent and punish genocide, but also an obligation for contracting states to refrain from engaging in genocide (§§ 162–6). This interpretation, as the Court rightly noted, is fully warranted having regard to the object and purpose of the Convention. It broadens the scope of Article I and also makes the set of obligations it is designed to impose more consistent: it would be 'paradoxical' for states to be obliged to prevent and punish genocide, while being free themselves to engage in genocide (§ 166). The interpretation 'is also supported by the purely humanitarian and civilizing purpose of the Convention' (§ 162). I would add that this obligation, as set out by the Court, does not remain unchecked: it is the ICJ that can ensure the judicial safeguard of compliance with such obligation, pursuant to Article IX of the Convention. However, the Court did not stop here. It interpreted Article III as implying that contracting states are also under the obligation to refrain from engaging in any of the sets of conduct envisaged in that provision: conspiracy, direct and public incitement, attempt to commit genocide, or complicity in genocide.[7]

Thus the Court ended up contemplating the same prohibited conduct both with regard to individuals and with respect to states. Both individuals and states may incur, respectively, criminal liability and state responsibility for the same unlawful behaviour (acts of genocide, conspiracy, incitement, attempt, or complicity). This view has been criticized by a number of commentators.[8] According to a more convincing view, the Convention (and the customary rules evolved as a result of its broad acceptance by states and the passing of national legislation along the same lines) chiefly provides for *criminal liability of individuals* for any of the acts of genocide enumerated in Article III of the Convention (and in addition imposes on contracting states only the obligation to prevent and repress

---

[6] That the 1948 Convention was conceived of as a treaty having the scope I have just described, can also be inferred from another circumstance: both in 1947–8 and subsequently, states have consistently shied away from the notion that they—as such—might be held criminally accountable for genocide. In their view, states as international subjects may not commit *crimes* proper: they can only incur state responsibility for *internationally wrongful acts*. Hence, it would be inappropriate to apply criminal law categories to their conduct.

[7] In the view of the Court, 'although the concepts used in paragraphs *(b)* to *(e)* of Article III, and particularly that of "complicity", refer to well known categories of criminal law and, as such, appear particularly well adapted to the exercise of penal sanctions against individuals [...] it would however not be in keeping with the object and purpose of the Convention to deny that the international responsibility of a State—even though quite different in nature from criminal responsibility—can be engaged through one of the acts, other than genocide itself, enumerated in Article III' (§ 167).

[8] See P. Gaeta, 'Génocide d'État et responsabilité pénale individuelle', 111 RGDIP (2007), 272–84; 'On What Conditions Can a State Be Held Responsible for Genocide?', 18 EJIL (2007), 631–48; A. Cassese, 'On the Use of Criminal Law Nations in Determining State Responsibility for Genocide', 5 JICJ (2007), 875–87.

genocide by individuals, be they state officials or private individuals). As for state responsibility for genocide, it arises in the event of a breach of the customary rule of international law obliging states to refrain from engaging in genocide as a conduct involving a genocidal policy pursued or tolerated by the state.[9] Thus, as has been rightly noted,[10] the subjective and objective conditions on which the arising of, respectively, state and individual responsibility for genocide is contingent, may and indeed do differ.

6.1.4 MERITS AND FLAWS OF THE CONVENTION

The Convention has numerous merits. Among other things, *i*) it sets out a careful definition of the crime; *ii*) it punishes other acts connected with genocide (conspiracy, complicity, etc.); *iii*) it prohibits genocide regardless of whether it is perpetrated in time of war or peace; *iv*) thanks to the Convention and its very broad acceptance by states, at the level of state responsibility it is now widely recognized that customary rules on genocide impose *erga omnes* obligations; that is, lay down obligations towards all other member states of the international community, and at the same time confer on any state the right to require that acts of genocide be discontinued. Furthermore, those rules now form part of *jus cogens* or the body of peremptory norms; that is, they may not be derogated from by international agreement (nor a fortiori by national legislation).

One should, however, be mindful of the flaws or omissions of the Convention. These are the most blatant ones.

First, the definition of genocide does not embrace cultural genocide (that is, the destruction of the language and culture of a group).[11] Probably it was felt that cultural genocide is a rather nebulous concept. Similarly, genocide does not encompass the extermination of a group on political grounds. This was a deliberate omission. One may wonder whether the elimination of political groups fits with the notion of genocide. Killing all the communists in a country is extermination, but is it genocide? Many would think not. The Convention confined itself to the physical destruction of relatively stable groups to which persons in most instances belong 'involuntarily' and, often, by birth (clearly, in the case of religious groups, membership may be voluntary).

Second, the four classes of protected groups (national, ethnical, racial, and religious) are not defined, nor are criteria for their definition provided.

Third, the enforcement mechanism envisaged in the Convention is ineffective. In Article IV the Convention contemplates trials before the courts of the state on the territory of which genocide has occurred, or before a future 'international penal tribunal'. This is a flaw because it is the territorial state authorities (or persons supported by such authorities) that normally tend to commit acts of genocide; so national prosecutors will be reluctant to bring prosecutions; furthermore, no international penal tribunal existed at the time, nor for fifty years afterwards. Moreover, Article VIII provides that any contracting party

---

[9] This is the approach substantially underpinning the section on genocide of the Report of the UN International Commission of Inquiry on Darfur, UN Doc. S/2005/60, §§ 439–522.

[10] P. Gaeta, 'Génocide d'État', cit. n. 8, and 'On What Conditions', cit. n. 8.

[11] See e.g. the decision of the High Court of Australia in *Kruger* v. *Commonwealth* (at 32). It should be noted that some countries, in passing legislation on genocide, have broadened the category of protected groups. For instance, in Ethiopia Art. 281 of the 1957 Penal Code also uses genocide with regard to 'political groups'. Other countries include 'social groups' within the definition of genocide: Peru (Art. 129, Criminal Code); Paraguay (Art. 308, Criminal Code); Lithuania (Art. 71, Criminal Code). For other countries that have expanded the notion of genocide by including other protected groups in the definition of the crime, see M. J. Ventura, 'Terrorism According to the STL's Interlocutory Decision on Applicable Law', 9 JICJ (2011), 1021–42, notes 46 to 54.

'may call upon the competent organs of the United Nations to take such action' under the Charter 'as they consider appropriate' for the prevention or suppression of genocide, whereas Article IX confers on the ICJ jurisdiction over disputes between states concerning the interpretation, application, or fulfilment of the Convention.

Indeed, at the enforcement level the Convention has long proved a failure. Only once did a United Nations body pronounce on a specific instance of massacres, that it defined as genocide: this occurred in the case of *Sabra and Shatila*, when the UN General Assembly characterized the mass killing of Palestinians perpetrated there by Christian falangist troops as 'an act of genocide' in its resolution 37/123 D of 16 December 1982. (However, the General Assembly did not set out the legal reasons for this 'finding', nor did it draw any legal consequences from it.) Subsequently in 1993, for the first time a state brought a case of genocide before the ICJ (*Bosnia and Herzegovina* v. *Serbia and Montenegro*). In 1999 Croatia also instituted before the ICJ proceedings against Serbia for violations of the Genocide Convention.

6.2 DEVELOPMENTS IN THE CASE LAW ON GENOCIDE

If we leave aside a few decisions handed down by the Extraordinary Courts Martial of the Ottoman Empire in 1920 and dealing with 'the massacres of Armenians carried out with the goal of annihilating them'[12] (at that time the notion of genocide had not yet been fully developed), it is striking that, until the 1990s, only a few cases of genocide were brought before national courts. Chief among them is *Eichmann* (decided in 1961 by the District Court of Jerusalem and subsequently, in 1962, by the Israeli Supreme Court). Eichmann was tried for 'crimes against the Jewish people', an offence under Israeli law, which incorporated all the elements of the definition of genocide (and the Supreme Court of Israel held that 'the crimes against the Jewish People' corresponded to genocide, *Eichmann*, Supreme Court, at 287).

By contrast, much headway has been made both at the level of prosecution and punishment of genocide by international criminal courts (which have prodded national courts also to deal with this crime) and at the normative level.

Genocide as a crime of individuals began to be punished following the establishment of the ICTY and the ICTR. Genocide having been provided for in the Statutes of both Tribunals as well as the ICC (followed by provisions relating to the Special Panels for East Timor (SPET) and the Extraordinary Chambers for Cambodia (EEC)),[13] the first two courts have had the opportunity to try quite a few persons accused of this crime. They have delivered important judgments on the matter: the ICTR, particularly in *Akayesu* (TC, §§ 204–28) and *Kayishema and Ruzindana* (TC, §§ 41–9); the ICTY in *Jelisić* (TC, §§ 78–83); and *Krstić* (TC, §§ 539–69).

After the establishment of the ICTY and the ICTR, some national courts began to institute criminal proceedings against persons accused of serious crimes in the former Yugoslavia. German courts have thus pronounced on some cases of genocide.[14] Trials on

---

[12] For instance, see in particular *Ahmed Mithad Bey and others*, at 147–53; *Mehmed Alī Bey and others*, at 159–65; *Bahâeddîn Şâkir and others*, at 169–73.

[13] See ICTY Statute, Art. 4; ICTR Statute, Art. 2; Art. 4 of Regulation 2000/15, s. 4 (as amended by regulation 2001/30) of the SPET; as well as Art. 4 of the law establishing the ECC.

[14] See *Jorgić*, decided in 1997 by the Higher State Court (*Oberlandsgericht*) of Düsseldorf. The Court found the defendant guilty of genocide and sentenced him to life imprisonment. The most significant part of

genocide have also been conducted in other countries (for instance, in Ethiopia, where the High Court tried former President Mengistu in absentia; see *Mengistu and others*) and in Rwanda.[15]

At the norm-setting level, some major advances stand out. The major substantive provisions of the Convention gradually turned into customary international law. In its Advisory Opinion on *Reservations to the Convention on Genocide*, the ICJ held that 'the principles underlying the Convention are principles which are recognized by civilized nations as binding on states, even without any conventional obligation' (at 24). This view was confirmed by the Court in *Bosnia and Herzegovina v. Serbia and Montenegro* (§§ 161). It is notable that the UN Secretary-General took the same view of the customary status of the Genocide Convention (or, more accurately, of the substantive principles it lays down), a view that was endorsed implicitly by the UN Security Council,[16] and explicitly by the ICTR in *Akayesu* (TC, § 495) and by the ICTY in *Krstić* (TC, § 541).

6.3 THE OBJECTIVE ELEMENTS

Article II of the Genocide Convention, and the corresponding rule of customary law, clearly defines the conduct that may amount to genocide:

(a) killing members (hence more than one member) of what we could term a 'protected group', namely a national or ethnical, racial, or religious group;

(b) causing serious bodily or mental harm to members of a 'protected group';

(c) deliberately inflicting on the group conditions of life calculated to bring about its physical destruction in whole or in part;

(d) imposing measures intended to prevent birth within the group; or

(e) forcibly transferring children of the group to another group.

While the definition of the four classes of group is an intricate problem that requires serious interpretative efforts (see 6.5), the various classes of action falling under genocide seem to be relatively clear. They were to a large extent spelled out by the ICTR in *Akayesu*, as well as by other judgments of the ICTR and the ICTY.

As for killing members of the group, 'killing' must be interpreted as 'murder', i.e. voluntary or intentional killing.[17] As for causing serious bodily or mental harm, these terms

---

the judgment is that relating to mens rea. The Court held that the intent to destroy a group 'means destroying the group as a social unit in its specificity, uniqueness and feeling of belonging: the biological-physical destruction of the group is not required' (section III, para. 1). The Court's findings about the factual and psychological elements from which one can infer the existence of 'intent' are extremely interesting. The judgment was upheld by the Federal High Court (*Bundesgerichtshof*) in 1999, followed by the Constitutional Court in 2000. See also *Sokolović* and *Kušljić* in 2001. On these cases, see K. Ambos and S. Wirth, 'Genocide and War Crimes in the Former Yugoslavia before German Criminal Courts' in H. Fischer, C. Kress, and S. R. Lüder (eds), *International and National Prosecution of Crimes under International Law* (Berlin: Arno Spitz, 2001), 783–97; R. Rissing-van Saan, 'The German Federal Supreme Court and the Prosecution of International Crimes Committed in the Former Yugoslavia', 2 JICT (2005), 381–99.

[15] For a comment on the Rwandan cases, see V. Thalmann, 'Rwandan Genocide Cases', in *Cassese's Companion*, 498–505.

[16] See Report of the Secretary-General Pursuant to Para. 2 of Security Council Resolution 808 (1993), UN Doc. S/25704, § 45.

[17] *Akayesu*, TC, §§ 500–1. See also *Semanza*, TC, § 319, and *Kayishema and Ruzindana*, AC, § 151. Various arguments have been put forward to support this interpretation, including the fact that the French text refers to *meurtre*, and therefore clearly exclude unintentional homicide.

'do not necessarily mean that the harm is permanent and irremediable' (*Akayesu*, TC, §§ 502–4; *Gacumbitsi*, TC, § 291; *Krstić*, TC, § 513), 'but it must involve harm that goes beyond temporary unhappiness, embarrassment or humiliation. It must be harm that results in a grave and long-term disadvantage to a person's ability to lead a normal and constructive life' (*Krstić*, TC, § 513). The harm caused can be bodily *or* mental, and must be serious. The seriousness of the harm 'must be assessed on a case by case basis and with due regard for the particular circumstances' (*Krstić*, TC, § 513). The harm may include acts of bodily or mental torture, sexual violence, and persecution (*Rutaganda*, TC, § 51).

'Deliberately inflicting on the group conditions of life calculated to bring about its physical destruction' include the so-called 'slow death measures'. In *Akayesu* the ICTR Trial Chamber held that this expression includes among other things, 'subjecting a group of people to a subsistence diet, systematic expulsion from homes and the reduction of essential medical services below minimum requirement[s]' (*Akayesu*, TC, §§ 505–6), or the 'deliberate deprivation of resources indispensable for survival, such as food or medical services' (*Kayishema and Ruzindana*, TC, § 115); according to an ICTY Trial Chamber in *Brđanin*, 'also included is the creation of circumstances that would lead to a slow death, such as lack of proper housing, clothing and hygiene or excessive work or physical exertion' (*Brđanin*, TC, § 691). It is not required that those conditions of life actually bring about the physical destruction of the group, in whole or in part; it is only required that 'they are calculated to bring its destruction', namely that they intended to achieve this result.[18]

'Imposing measures intended to prevent births within the group' intends to cover conduct whose aim is to prevent the biological reproduction of the group. This result can usually be achieved through the sterilization of women (when the transmission of the distinguishing features of the group is matriarchal, as it was in the case of the sterilization of the Jewish women). It can also be accomplished through the rape of women of the group by members of another group, when rape aims at changing the ethnic composition of the group whose characteristics are transmitted following the patriarchal line. Other measures intended to achieve the same objective can include segregation of sexes, prohibition of marriage, or forced birth control. In *Akayesu* it was held that these measures could consist of 'sexual mutilation, the practice of sterilization, forced birth control [and the] separation of the sexes and prohibition of marriages' (*Akayesu*, TC, § 507); in addition, the measures at issue may be not only physical but also mental (*Akayesu*, TC, § 508); they may include rape as an act directed to prevent births when the woman raped refuses subsequently to procreate (*Akayesu*, TC, § 508); see also ICTR, *Rutaganda*, TC, § 53 and *Musema*, TC, § 158. As in the preceding hypothesis, it is not required that the measures achieve the desired goal, being only necessary that they are carried out for that particular purpose.

'Forcibly transferring children of the group to another group' skirts along the borderline of 'cultural genocide'.[19] The forcible transfer of the children of the targeted group

---

[18] The relevant comment in the UN Secretariat Draft of the Genocide Convention explains that '[i]n such cases, the intention of the author of genocide may be less clear. Obviously, if members of a group of human beings are placed in concentration camps where the annual death rate is thirty per cent to forty per cent, the intention to commit genocide is unquestionable. There may be borderline cases where a relatively high death rate might be ascribed to lack of attention, negligence or inhumanity, which, though highly reprehensible, would not constitute evidence of intention to commit genocide. At all events, there are such borderline cases which have to be dealt with on their own merits.' (See the Draft of the Convention prepared by the Secretary-General of the UN: Secretariat Draft E/447, reproduced in Abtahi and Webb, *The Genocide Convention*, cit. n. 5, vol. I, at 233.)

[19] In this regard, also for additional reference, see F. Jessberger, 'The Definition and the Elements of the Crime of Genocide', in P. Gaeta (ed.), *The UN Genocide Convention*, cit. n. 5, at 102–3.

to another group may not result in the biological or physical destruction, but cause the disappearance of the group through the severance of the links of the youngest generation with the group of origin. In this way, the children will lose their original cultural identity and their original group will be destroyed. This conduct may embrace threats or intimidation leading to the forcible transfer of children to another group (*Akayesu*, TC, § 509).

Another interesting problem relating to actus reus is whether genocide may also include the killing, with the required intent, of only *one single member* of a protected group. In *Akayesu* the Trial Chamber, when dealing with the constituent elements of genocide, held the view that there may be genocide even if one of the acts prohibited by the relevant rules on this matter is committed 'against one' member of a group (*Akayesu*, TC, § 521). Arguably, this broad interpretation is not consistent with the text of the norms on genocide, which speak instead of 'members of a group'. Furthermore, with respect to the conduct under (c) ('deliberately inflicting on the group conditions of life, etc.'), which deals with acts against the group as such, the prohibited conduct by necessity must be carried out against a plurality of members of the group.

It would seem that Article II does not cover the conduct currently termed in non-technical language 'ethnic cleansing'; that is, the forcible expulsion of civilians belonging to a particular group from an area, a village, or a town. (In the course of the drafting of the Genocide Convention, Syria proposed an amendment designed to add a sixth class of acts of genocide: 'Imposing measures intended to oblige members of a group to abandon their homes in order to escape the threat of subsequent ill-treatment'. However, the draughtsmen rejected this proposal.)[20]

Some courts have indeed excluded the forced expulsion of persons belonging to a particular ethnic, racial, or religious group from the notion of genocide.[21] However, in other

---

[20] For the Syrian proposal see UN Doc. A/C6/234, incorporated in A/C6/SR.81, in Abtahi and Webb, *The Genocide Convention*, cit. n. 5, at 1479.

[21] See e.g. *Jelišić*, TC, §§ 107–8. The prosecution had alleged that Jelišić had contributed to the campaign of ethnic cleansing in Brčko in eastern Bosnia and had, for a period, acted as the principal executioner at the Luka camp 'with the intent to destroy, in whole or in part, a racial, ethnic or religious group' (*Jelišić*, TC, oral ruling, 19 October 1999). The prosecution asserted that the accused demonstrated considerable authority, that he had received instructions to kill as many Muslims as possible, and that his genocidal intent could be shown by the accused's own words, as was reported to the judges by the witnesses. In this regard, they characterized Jelišić as 'an effective and enthusiastic participant in the genocidal campaign' and noted, in addition, that the group targeted by Jelišić was significant, 'not only because it included all the dignitaries of the Bosnian Muslim community in the region but also because of its size'. The Trial Chamber ruled, however, that Jelišić could not be found guilty of the crime of genocide. Although he had pleaded guilty to both war crimes and crimes against humanity (*Jelišić*, TC, §§ 24–58), with respect to the crime of genocide the Trial Chamber issued the following pronouncement: 'In conclusion, the acts of Goran Jelišić are not the physical expression of an affirmed resolve to destroy in whole or in part a group as such. All things considered, the Prosecutor has not established beyond all reasonable doubt that genocide was committed in Brčko during the period covered by the indictment. Furthermore, the behaviour of the accused appears to indicate that, although he obviously singled out Muslims, he killed arbitrarily rather than with the clear intention to destroy a group. The Trial Chamber therefore concludes that it has not been proved beyond all reasonable doubt that the accused was motivated by the *dolus specialis* of the crime of genocide. The benefit of the doubt must always go to the accused and, consequently, Goran Jelišić must be found not guilty on this count' (*Jelišić*, TC, §§ 107–8).

On ethnic cleansing it is also worth mentioning the decision delivered on 31 August 2001 by the Supreme Court of Kosovo in *Vucković*: 'Indeed, the essential characteristic of the criminal act of genocide is the intended destruction of a national, ethnical, racial or religious group. However, the appealed verdict only considered that the accused, forcefully expelling population from their houses in unbearable living conditions, was ready to accept the consequence that the part or entire group of Albanian population of these villages will be exterminated. Such motivation does not characterize the intent to destroy an ethnic group in whole or in part. More generally, according to the Supreme Court, the exactions committed by the Milošević

cases courts have asserted that that expulsion, under certain circumstances, could be held to amount to genocide.[22] Probably the better view is that upheld by the German Constitutional Court in *Jorgić*, namely that 'systematic expulsion can be a method of destruction and therefore an indication, though not the sole substantiation, of an intention to destroy' (at § 24). (A similar view was propounded by the ICTY Trial Chamber in *Krstić*, at §§ 589–98.)

6.4 THE SUBJECTIVE ELEMENTS

It is necessary to distinguish between first, the mental element required for each of the underlying acts (murder, etc.) and, second, the specific mental element that is necessary to consider those acts as amounting to genocide.

All the prohibited acts must be accomplished *intentionally*, i.e. they require *intent* on the part of the perpetrator. This is also the case, as has been already pointed out above, for the killing of members of the group. Premeditation, i.e. the planning and preparation of the prohibited act, is not required, except—in the opinion of a distinguished commentator—in the case of the act listed under (c), because of the use of the word 'deliberately'.[23] It logically follows that other categories of mental element are excluded: recklessness (or *dolus eventualis*) and gross negligence.

Genocide is a typical crime based on the 'depersonalization of the victim'; that is, a crime where the victim is not targeted on account of his or her individual qualities or characteristics, but only because he or she is a member of a group. As the German Federal Court of Justice rightly held in *Jorgić* in 1999, the perpetrators of genocide do not target a person 'in his capacity as an individual'; they 'do not see the victim as a human being but only as a member of the persecuted group' (at 401).[24] Therefore, to the general intent of the underlying act an additional specific mental element must be added, namely 'the intent to

regime in 1999 cannot be qualified as criminal acts of genocide, since their purpose was not the destruction of the Albanian ethnic group in whole or in part, but its forceful departure from Kosovo as a result of a systematic campaign of terror including murders, rapes, arsons and severe mistreatments' (at 2–3).

See also *Kušljić* (decision of the German *Bundesgerichtshof* of 21 February 2001), at 7–10.

[22] In the confirmation of the second indictment of 16 November 1995 (pertaining to the fall of the UN safe area of Srebrenica) against Radovan Karadžić and Ratko Mladić, for instance, Judge Riad expressly characterized 'ethnic cleansing' as a form of genocide: *Karadžić and Mladić*, confirmation of indictment of 16 November 1995. An ICTY Trial Chamber observed in the *Karadžić and Mladić (Rule 61 Decision)* that the character of the acts in question may permit the inference of genocidal intent: *Karadžić and Mladić (Rule 61 Decision)*, TC, § 94. See also ICTY *Nikolić (Rule 61 Decision)*, TC, § 34. However, a subsequent judgment of the Trial Chamber suggests a retreat from the Trial Chamber's abovementioned and relatively expansive stance (see *Jelišić*, TC, §§ 107-8).

[23] Robinson, *Genocide Convention*, cit. n. 5, 63–4.

[24] In the same case the German Federal Constitutional Court held the following view: 'The Higher State Court and Federal Constitutional Court take the view that para. 220(a) of the StGB [the German Criminal Code] protects the group. They have unanimously interpreted the intention of StGB para. 220a as meaning that the destruction of the group as a social entity in its specificity and particularity and sense of togetherness, or even geographically limited part of the group, need not extend to its physical and biological extermination [...] It is enough if the culprit takes upon himself the intent of the central controlling structure that inevitably must be in place for the elements of the crime to be met, even if toward a part of the group [...] the statutory definition of genocide defends a supra-individual object of legal protection, i.e. the social existence of the group [...] The text of the law does not therefore compel the interpretation that the culprit's intent must be to exterminate physically at least a substantial number of the members of the group [...] the intent can be deduced as a rule from the circumstances of an attack carried out under a structurally organized central control on the group, of which the culprit is aware, and which he wills' (Germany, *Jorgić*, Federal Constitutional Court, §§ 19–22).

destroy, in whole or in part' one of the enumerated group 'as such', which is provided for in Article II(1) of the Convention on Genocide (and in the corresponding customary rule). This is the *dolus specialis* (specific intent) of genocide, also known as genocidal intent. It is an aggravated form of intent that does not demand realization through the material conduct, but that is nonetheless pursued by the perpetrator. In other words, it is not required that the perpetrator should actually manage to destroy a member of a protected group by carrying out one of the five acts prohibited under the Convention. It is only necessary that the perpetrator harbour the specific intent to destroy the group while carrying out one of those acts, regardless of whether by accomplishing the act the intended ultimate objective is achieved. The requirement of the specific intent, therefore, has a preventative function, since it allows the criminalization of genocide before the perpetrator achieves the actual destruction of the group.

The question, however, arises of whether the specific intent harboured by the perpetrator has to be 'realistic'; must the perpetrator believe that the intended goal can be achieved through the commission of one of the prohibited acts? The case law of the ICTR and ICTY has not expressly tackled this issue.[25] In *Mpambara*, however, an ICTR Trial Chamber stressed that 'even a single instance of one of the prohibited acts' can amount to genocide, 'provided that the accused genuinely intends by that act to destroy at least a substantial part of the group' (ICTR, *Mpambara*, TC, § 8). The reference to the *genuine* intent to destroy the group is explained by the Trial Chamber in a footnote to the judgment: 'The perpetrator of a single, isolated act of violence could not possess the requisite intent based on a delusion that, by his action, the destruction of the group, in whole or in part, could be effected' (ICTR, *Mpambara*, TC, n. 7). It seems therefore that for the Trial Chamber the genocidal intent can be 'genuine' only to the extent that the perpetrator considers it possible that the destruction of the group can eventually be achieved.

6.5 THE PROTECTED GROUPS

The genocidal intent of the perpetrator must be directed towards one of the enumerated groups ('protected groups' or 'targeted groups'). The list of the protected groups provided in Article II(1) of the Genocide Convention is exhaustive. During the preparatory works of the Genocide Convention, an attempt was made to include in the list also cultural and political groups, but to no avail. The exclusion was grounded in the volatile membership of these two categories of groups and the desire to instead afford protection to groups characterized by a certain degree of stability.[26]

---

[25] The ICC Pre-Trial Chamber, in its decision on Al Bashir, has considered that the case law of the ICTR and ICTY, by excluding that the existence of a genocidal policy constitutes a legal ingredient of genocide (on this issue, see text *supra* n. 41), entails that 'for the purpose of completing the crime of genocide, it is irrelevant whether the conduct in question is capable of posing any concrete threat to the existence of the targeted group, or a part thereof'. For the ICC Pre-Trial Chamber, this case law implies that 'the protection offered to the targeted groups by the penal norm defining the crime of genocide is dependent on the existence of an intent to destroy, in whole or in part, the targeted group. As soon as such intent exists and materialises in an isolated act of a single individual, the protection is triggered, regardless of whether the latent threat to the existence of the targeted group posed by the said intent has turned into a concrete threat to the existence in whole or in part of that group.' See Al Bashir (*Decision on Prosecutor's Application for a Warrant of Arrest*), §§ 119–20.

[26] This is the interpretation put forward by the ICTR Trial Chamber in *Akayesu*, TC, § 511: 'On reading through the *travaux préparatoires* of the Genocide Convention, it appears that the crime of genocide was allegedly perceived as targeting only "stable" groups, constituted in a permanent fashion and membership of which is determined by birth, with the exclusion of the more "mobile" groups which one joins through individual voluntary commitment, such as political and economic groups. Therefore, a common criterion

Two major problems arise with respect to the targeted groups of genocide: *i*) the notion of the group that is targeted; and *ii*) the identification of the four groups enumerated in the rule (national, ethnical, racial, religious). The former problem may be framed as follows: what do the Convention and the corresponding customary rule mean by 'group'? In other words, when can one state with certainty that one is faced with a group protected by the Convention? The latter question, which is obviously closely related to the former, is 'By what standards or criteria can one identify each of the four groups?' Can one rely upon an objective test for each group? If so, where does one find such a test?

The case law of the ICTR and ICTY has contributed considerably to clarifying the notion of 'group', moving from an objective to a subjective evaluation. The importance of *Akayesu* in particular needs to be stressed. In this case, an ICTR Trial Chamber not only emphasized that genocide is the most grave international crime or, as it put it, 'the crime of crimes' (*Akayesu*, TC, § 16), but also, and more importantly, set out a definition of 'group'. In its view, this word, in the provisions on genocide, refers only to 'stable groups',

> constituted in a permanent fashion, and membership of which is determined by birth, with the exclusion of the more 'mobile' groups which one joins through individual voluntary commitment, such as political and economic groups. Therefore, a common criterion in the four types of groups protected by the Genocide Convention is that membership in such groups would seem to be normally not challengeable by its members, who belong to it automatically, by birth, in a continuous and often irremediable manner. (*Akayesu*, TC, § 511)

According to the Trial Chamber, the groups protected against genocide should not be limited to the four groups envisaged in the relevant rules, but—in order to respect the intention of the draughtsmen of the Genocide Convention, who clearly intended to protect any identifiable group—should include 'any stable and permanent group' (*Akayesu*, TC, § 516). This proposition without further elaboration appears unconvincing, given that the framers of the Convention, as clearly expressed in the text of that instrument, evinced an intention to protect only the four groups explicitly indicated there. The Chamber then propounded a definition of each of the four groups envisaged in the relevant rules. It defined 'national groups' as 'a collection of people who are perceived to share a legal bond of common citizenship, coupled with reciprocity of rights and duties' (*Akayesu*, TC, § 512),[27] an 'ethnic group' as 'a group whose members share a common language or culture' (§ 513), a 'racial group' as a group 'based on the hereditary physical traits often identified with a geographical region, irrespective of linguistic, cultural, national or religious factors' (§ 514), and a 'religious group' as a group 'whose members share the same religion, denomination or mode of worship' (§ 515).

It is important to stress, however, that the reference to the four enumerated groups is made to the groups as social entities. It would therefore be useless to try to describe the protected groups by applying rigorous scientific or objective notions, also because

---

in the four types of groups protected by the Genocide Convention is that membership in such groups would seem to be normally not challengeable by its members, who belong to it automatically, by birth, in a continuous and often irremediable manner.'

[27] This definition of 'national group' has been criticized, among others, by Schabas, who rightly observes that the ICTR TC mixed up the notion of 'nationality' with that of membership in a national group by referring, as it did, to the decision of the ICJ in *Nottembohm* to ground the definition of 'national group'. Schabas correctly underlines that in the *Nottembohm* case the Court focused on the effectiveness of the nationality, in the sense of citizenship, of an individual, and did not examine at all the question of individuals who, while sharing cultural, linguistic, and other bonds of a particular 'nation', have in fact the citizenship of another State or have even stateless: see Schabas, *Genocide*, cit. n. 5, 134–5.

by so doing one may find that some groups do not scientifically and objectively exist.[28] In the particular case of the genocide of Tutsis by Hutus in Rwanda, the question of how to identify a protected group played a major role. Indeed, these two groups shared language, religion, and culture, lived in the same areas, and in addition there was a high rate of mixed marriages. The ICTR stressed that the two terms of Tutsi and Hutus before colonization by the Germans (1885–1916) and then by the Belgians (1916–62) referred to individuals and not to groups, the distinction being based on lineage rather than ethnicity (*Akayesu*, TC, § 81). (Furthermore, Tutsis were originally shepherds, whereas Hutus were farmers.) However, in 1931 Belgians introduced a permanent distinction by dividing the population into three ethnic groups (Hutu, Tutsi, and Twa), making it mandatory for each Rwandan to carry an identity card that mentioned his or her ethnicity (*Akayesu*, TC, § 83). The Trial Chamber concluded that thus in fact the members of the various groups ended up considering themselves as distinct from members of the other groups.[29]

It is for that reason that the question of the identification of a given group as a group protected by the prohibition of genocide has eventually been solved by the ICTR by applying a subjective test. Thus, it has considered that the Tutsis in Rwanda constituted an ethnic group distinct from the Hutus and the Twa, since the official classifications referred to them as an ethnic group and the Rwandans themselves, without hesitation, answered questions regarding their ethnicity (*Akayesu*, TC, § 702). This so-called subjective approach in the identification of the protected groups was also followed by the ICTY Trial Chambers,[30] and by the UN International Commission of Inquiry on Darfur.[31]

As far as the specific individual victim of the genocidal conduct, and the question of whether he or she belongs to the targeted group, it is sufficient that the perpetrator believes that the victim is a member of the group he or she seeks to destroy.

The genocidal intent must be directed at one of the listed groups 'in whole or in part'. This means that it is not required that the perpetrator seeks to destroy the group in its entirety, since the intent to attain only a 'partial' destruction would suffice. It is, however, not clear what 'in part' exactly means. If one applies a quantitative approach 'in part' can describe the numeric size of the group with respect to its totality. By contrast, if one uses a qualitative approach, the intrinsic characteristic of the selected part of the group would count, i.e. the leadership of the targeted group. In any case, it has been contended that 'in part' seems to mean 'a substantial part'[32] of the group, and that both a quantitative and

---

[28] The paradigmatic example is that of 'racial group', since the notion of race or racial group does not find room from a scientific point of view.

[29] The Trial Chamber noted that 'in Rwanda, in 1994, the Tutsi constituted a group referred to as "ethnic" in official classifications. Thus, the identity cards at the time included a reference to "*ubwoko*" in Kinyarwnda or "*ethnie*" (ethnic group) in French which, depending on the case, referred to the designation Hutu or Tutsi, for example [...] [In addition] all the Rwandan witnesses who appeared before it [the Trial Chamber] invariably answered spontaneously and without hesitation the questions of the Prosecutor regarding their ethnic identity' (*Akayesu*, TC, § 702).

[30] See *Jelisić*, TC, §§ 70–1, and *Krstić*, TC, §§ 556–7 and 559–60.

[31] In 2005 the UN International Commission of Inquiry on Darfur shared this approach when discussing whether the so-called African tribes (essentially consisting of sedentary farmers) in Darfur made up an ethnic group distinct from the so-called Arab tribes (essentially consisting of nomadic shepherds), in spite of their sharing the same language (Arabic) and religion (Muslim) and not distinguishing themselves from one another as far the colour of their skin was concerned (§§ 498–501 and 508–12).

[32] See the Commentary on Article 17 (on genocide) of the Draft Code of Crimes against the Peace and Security of Mankind, adopted in 1996 by the UN International Law Commission (ILC), p. 45, para. 8., where the ILC observes: 'the intention must be to destroy a group "in whole or in part". It is not necessary to intend to achieve the complete annihilation of a group from every corner of the globe. None the less the crime of genocide by its very nature requires the intention to destroy at least a substantial part of a particular group.'

a qualitative approach can be used to establish whether or not part of the targeted group constitutes a substantial part.[33]

In *Krstić* the ICTY Trial Chamber clarified the actus reus by defining the notion of the destruction of a group 'in part'. The prosecution had accused the defendant of genocide for having planned and participated in the massacre in a limited locality (the area of Srebrenica), of between 7,000 and 8,000 Bosnian Muslims, all of them men of military age. The question arose of whether the 'protected group' was constituted by the 'Bosnian Muslims of Srebrenica' or instead by 'Bosnian Muslims'. The Chamber answered the query by noting that the group was that of Bosnian Muslims, and the Bosnian Muslims of Srebrenica constituted 'a part of the protected group' under Article 4 of the ICTY Statute (*Krstić*, TC, § 560) (which was based on Article II of the Genocide Convention and was held by the Chamber to be declaratory of customary international law: *Krstić*, TC, §§ 541–80). The Chamber added that 'the intent to eradicate a group within a limited geographical area such as the region of a country or even a municipality' could be characterized as genocide (§ 589).[34] As for the fact that the persons systematically killed at Srebrenica were 'only men of military age', the Trial Chamber emphasized that, while these men were being massacred, at the same time the rest of the Bosnian Muslim population was being forcibly transferred out of the area.[35]

---

[33] *Kayishema and Ruzindana*, TC, §§ 96–7. On this issue and for further reference see Jessberger, 'The Definition and the Elements of the Crime of Genocide' (cit. n. 19), 108–9.

[34] It then pointed out the following: 'the intent to destroy a group, even if only in part, means seeking to destroy a distinct part of the group as opposed to an accumulation of isolated individuals within it. Although the perpetrators of genocide need not seek to destroy the entire group protected by the Convention, they must view the part of the group they wish to destroy as a distinct entity which must be eliminated as such. A campaign resulting in the killings, in different places spread over a broad geographical area, of a finite number of members of a protected group might not thus qualify as genocide, despite the high total number of casualties, because it would not show an intent by the perpetrators to target the very existence of the group as such. Conversely, the killing of all members of the part of a group located within a small geographical area, although resulting in a lesser number of victims, would qualify as genocide if carried out with the intent to destroy the part of the group as such located in this small geographical area. Indeed, the physical destruction may target only a part of the geographically limited part of the larger group because the per-petrators of the genocide regard the intended destruction as sufficient to annihilate the group as a distinct entity in the geographic area at issue. In this regard, it is important to bear in mind the total context in which the physical destruction is carried out' (*Krstić*, TC, § 590).

[35] In this respect it stressed that 'The Bosnian Serb forces could not have failed to know, by the time they decided to kill all the men, that this selective destruction of the group would have a lasting impact upon the entire group. Their death precluded any effective attempt by the Bosnian Muslims to recapture the territory. Furthermore, the Bosnian Serb forces had to be aware of the catastrophic impact that the disappearance of two or three generations of men would have on the survival of a traditionally patriarchal society, an impact the Chamber has previously described in detail. The Bosnian Serb forces knew, by the time they decided to kill all of the military aged men, that the combination of those killings with the forcible transfer of the women, children and elderly would inevitably result in the physical disappearance of the Bosnian Muslim population at Srebrenica. Intent by the Bosnian Serb forces to target the Bosnian Muslims of Srebrenica as a group is further evidenced by their destroying homes of Bosnian Muslims in Srebrenica and Potocari and the principal mosque in Srebrenica soon after the attack. Finally, there is a strong indication of the intent to destroy the group as such in the concealment of the bodies in mass graves, which were later dug up, the bodies mutilated and reburied in other mass graves located in even more remote areas, thereby preventing any decent burial in accord with religious and ethnic customs and causing terrible distress to the mourn-ing survivors, many of whom have been unable to come to a closure until the death of their men is finally verified. The strategic location of the enclave, situated between two Serb territories, may explain why the Bosnian Serb forces did not limit themselves to expelling the Bosnian Muslim population. By killing all the military aged men, the Bosnian Serb forces effectively destroyed the community of the Bosnian Muslims in Srebrenica as such and eliminated all likelihood that it could ever re-establish itself on that territory' (*Krstić*, TC, §§ 595–7).

The Chamber concluded that the killing of all the Bosnian Muslim men of military age in Srebrenica accompanied by the intent to destroy in part the Bosnian Muslim group within the meaning of Article 4 of the ICTY Statute must qualify as genocide. Before making this ruling, the Trial Chamber had also discussed the question of the extent to which, while appraising whether or not genocide had been perpetrated in the case at issue, it could take into account evidence or facts relating to the cultural or social destruction of a group, as opposed to its physical or biological destruction.[36]

Finally, the genocidal intent must aim at the destruction of the group 'as such'. This requirement makes it clear that the ultimate intended victim of genocide is the group, whose destruction is sought by the perpetrator through carrying out the prohibited acts against its individual members or the group itself.[37]

6.6 TWO PROBLEMATICAL ASPECTS OF GENOCIDE

There are at least two issues concerning genocide that are at the same time intricate and controversial, and which therefore deserve our attention: *i*) whether acts of genocide always require an underlying genocidal policy by a state or organized authority; *ii*) how to discern genocidal intent.

6.6.1 WHETHER GENOCIDE ALWAYS REQUIRES A GENOCIDAL POLICY OR CONTEXT

The word 'genocide' reminds us of the extermination of thousands, if not millions of people, on account of their membership of a particular group and in the pursuance of a state policy. The definition of genocide enshrined in the Genocide Convention, however, does not expressly require the existence of such a policy, and as a matter of fact does not even consider the number of the victims of the prohibited acts as relevant. The fact that historically genocide coincides with the actual destruction of a protected group, carried out in furtherance of a genocidal policy, has not been mirrored in the legal definition of genocide, which is aimed at punishing some enumerated acts as genocide on account of the specific intent harboured by the perpetrator. The ICTR and the ICTY have clearly confirmed this view (*Kayishema and Ruzindana*, TC, § 94; *Jelisić*, AC, § 48), although they have admitted that the existence of a genocidal plan may be useful to establish whether the perpetrator of one of the prohibited acts of genocide possess the required genocidal intent.

---

[36] On this point it set out the following interesting remarks (which it then applied in the ruling just cited): 'The Trial Chamber is aware that it must interpret the Convention with due regard for the principle of *nullum crimen sine lege*. It therefore recognises that, despite recent developments, customary international law limits the definition of genocide to those acts seeking the physical or biological destruction of all or part of the group. Hence, an enterprise attacking only the cultural or sociological characteristics of a human group in order to annihilate these elements which give to that group its own identity distinct from the rest of the community would not fall under the definition of genocide. The Trial Chamber however points out that where there is physical or biological destruction there are often simultaneous attacks on the cultural and religious property and symbols of the targeted group as well, attacks which may legitimately be considered as evidence of an intent to physically destroy the group. In this case, the Trial Chamber will thus take into account as evidence of intent to destroy the group the deliberate destruction of mosques and houses belonging to members of the group' (*Krstić*, TC, § 580).

[37] *Akayesu*, TC, § 521. For further reference in international case, see Jessberger, 'The Definition and the Elements of the Crime of Genocide', 109, n. 135.

Some distinguished commentators consider this stand to be incorrect and argue that a contextual element, in the form of a genocidal campaign, or at least of a pattern of collective violence against the group, is necessary.[38] To bolster this proposition, it is maintained that it would be unrealistic for a single individual to aim at the destruction of a group; therefore the genocidal intent must perforce be directed to the result of a collective endeavour to which the single individual contributes.[39] This view has also been echoed in the case law.[40] It also finds some support in the Elements of Crimes of the ICC, according to which the conduct must take place 'in the context of a manifest pattern of similar conduct directed against the group' or must be conduct 'that could itself effect [the] destruction [of the group]'.

Clearly, the question of the need for the existence of a genocidal policy is closely intertwined with whether the specific intent to destroy one of the protected group, in whole or in part, must be 'genuine' (to use the expression of the ICTR Trial Chamber in *Mpambara*). The existence of a genocidal policy or campaign against the targeted group will in fact make it possible for the perpetrator to form a 'realistic' intent to attain the destruction of the group; the conduct of the perpetrator will indeed aim at the same result pursued by others, thus creating a genuine threat to the existence of the group. Nonetheless, it would be incorrect to conclude that the genocidal policy or campaign is one of the legal ingredients of genocide. Even admitting that historically genocide has been perpetrated within a genocidal context, still it is theoretically possible that a lone perpetrator may realistically aim at the destruction of a targeted group in the absence of such context. An example is one mentioned before, namely that of the individual who possesses a weapon of mass destruction. Another example is the attack, by a single individual, against the leadership of the group, that may realistically endanger its existence, at least in part.

It is on account of these considerations that one may perhaps understand why the ICC Elements of Crimes provide, with respect to genocide, that the conduct either must take place in the context of a manifest pattern of similar conduct directed against the group, *or* must be of a kind that *could itself effect* the destruction of the targeted group. If a *single* conduct may pose a concrete risk to the existence of the group regardless of the existence of a genocidal policy, the act carried out by the perpetrator can amount to genocide. As the Pre-Trial Chamber of the ICC has put it in Al Bashir, the presence of one of these two requirements clarifies that

> the crime of genocide is only completed when the relevant conduct presents a concrete threat to the existence of the targeted group, or a part thereof. In other words, the protection offered by the penal norm defining the crime of genocide—as an ultima ratio mechanism to preserve the highest values of the international community—is only triggered when the threat against the existence of the targeted group, or part thereof, becomes concrete and real, as opposed to just being latent or hypothetical.[41]

---

[38] See e.g. Schabas, *Genocide*, cit. n. 5, 243–56. See also, among others, A. K. A. Greenawalt, 'Rethinking Genocidal Intent: The Case for a Knowledge-Based Interpretation', 99 *Columbia Law Review* (1999), 2259; C. Kress, 'The Darfur Report and Genocidal Intent', 3 JICJ (2005), 562.

[39] As Kress put it: 'An individual perpetrator cannot realistically *desire* the destruction of a protected group to occur *as a result* of his or her *individual genocidal conduct*. The perpetrator's desire must rather be related to the *results* to be brought about by the *collective activity* to which he or she contributes' (Kress, 'The Darfur Report', at 566).

[40] In *Krstić*, TC, § 682, the Trial Chamber has stated that the genocidal acts must be committed 'in the context of a manifest pattern of similar conduct, or themselves [must] constitute a conduct that could in itself effect the destruction of the group, in whole or in part, as such'. What is requested here, as it is clear, is the systematic or widespread attack against a protected group, to use two expressions that describe the contextual element of crimes against humanity.

[41] *Al Bashir* (*Decision on Prosecutor's Application for Warrant of Arrest*), § 124.

Admittedly, however, three categories of genocide perforce not only presuppose, but necessarily take the shape of, some sort of collective or even organized action, namely *i*) deliberately inflicting on a protected group or members thereof conditions of life calculated to bring about its physical destruction in whole or in part; *ii*) imposing measures intended to prevent births within a protected group; *iii*) forcibly transferring children of a protected group to another group). Plainly, actions such as deliberate deprivation of resources indispensable for the survival of members of a protected group, e.g. food or medical supplies, or such action as systematic expulsion from home with a view to bringing about conditions of life leading to the destruction of the group, constitute actions that are necessarily carried out on a large scale and by a multitude of individuals in pursuance of a common plan, possibly with the support or at least the acquiescence of the authorities. Similarly, such measures designed to prevent births as prohibition of marriages, separation of the sexes, forced birth control, sterilization, large-scale sexual mutilation, are all activities that only state organs or other official authorities may undertake, or authorize to undertake, or at least approve or condone.

6.6.2 HOW TO IDENTIFY GENOCIDAL INTENT

The ICTR Trial Chamber has significantly contributed to elucidating the subjective element of genocide. As noted, in *Akayesu* the ICTR Trial Chamber held that intent 'is a mental factor which is difficult, even impossible to determine' (*Akayesu*, TC, § 523).[42]

Indeed, normally to prove the existence of genocidal intent one has to infer such intent from factual circumstances. Only seldom can one find documents or statements by which one or more persons explicitly declare that they intend to destroy a whole group. An instance of such statements can be found in the minutes (drafted by Eichmann) of the discussion held at Wannsee (Berlin) on 20 January 1942 to plan the extermination of the European Jews,[43] as well as in the speech Heinrich Himmler (head of the SS) made on 4 October 1943 in Poznan to SS officers[44] to the same effect.

In other instances utterances against a particular group expressing the intent to destroy (or to contribute to destroy) the group, were not taken to express genocidal intent proper. A case in point is *Jelisić*. The ICTY Trial Chamber held that his repeated statements against Muslims and the consequent criminal offences perpetrated by him against many Muslims did not manifest genocidal intent but were expression of 'a disturbed personality' (*Jelisić*, TC, §§ 102–7). The Appeals Chamber took a different (and a more correct) view, ruling that the accused had instead entertained genocidal intent (*Jelisić*, AC, §§ 55–72), although it then oddly declined to reverse the acquittal for genocide entered by the Trial Chamber and remit the case for further proceedings.

In *Krstić* the ICTY Trial Chamber made a considerable contribution, in various respects, to the identification of mens rea of genocide. The prosecution, as noted above, accused the defendant of genocide for having planned and participated in the massacre in a limited locality (the area of Srebrenica), of between 7,000 and 8,000 Bosnian Muslims, all of them men of military age. The following question then arose: was this intent present in this case where only men of military age were systematically killed? The Chamber answered

---

[42] The approach taken in *Akayesu* has to a very large extent been followed by the ICTR Trial Chambers: in *Kayishema and Ruzindana*, TC, §§ 87–118, as well as in *Rutaganda*, TC, §§ 44–63, and in *Musema*, TC, §§ 884–941.

[43] See the English translation online: http://avalon.law.edu/imt/wannsee.asp.

[44] He insisted in that speech on the 'extermination [*Ausrottung*] of the Jewish people' (German text and English translation online: http://www.holocaust-history.org/himmler-poznan/speech-text.shtml).

the query in the affirmative. It emphasized that the rest of the Bosnian Muslim population had been forcibly transferred out of the area, with the inevitable result of the physical
disappearance of the whole Muslim population of Srebrenica (*Krstić*, TC, §§ 593–7). The
Chamber concluded that the intent to kill all the Bosnian Muslim men of military age in
Srebrenica evinced the intention to destroy in part the Bosnian Muslim group and therefore must qualify as genocidal intent.

As pointed out above, the special intent under discussion is normally deduced from
the factual circumstances. Hence, in those cases where the actus reus is murder or bodily
or mental harm the question whether those acts were part of a plan or policy or of widespread or systematic practice may eventually acquire importance from an *evidentiary*
viewpoint (although, as noted above, not as a legal ingredient of the crime), as an *element*
capable of proving (or confirming) that there was indeed genocidal intent.

This is clear from what an ICTR Trial Chamber held in some cases, for instance in
Akayesu and in *Kayishema and Ruzindanda*. In the former case the Trial Chamber
inferred the special intent from the speeches by which the accused called, 'more or less
explicitly', for the commission of genocide (*Akayesu*, TC, § 729). It also deduced intent
from the very high number of deliberate and systematic atrocities committed against the
Tutsis (§ 730) and the numerous and systematic acts of rape and sexual violence against
Tutsi women (§§ 731–3). Also in *Kayishema and Ruzindanda* the Trial Chamber inferred
genocidal intent from the high number of Tutsis killed (*Kayishema and Ruzindanda*, TC,
§§ 531 and 533), the fact that they had been massacred regardless of gender or age (§ 532),
as well as the fact that the attacks had been carried out in a consistent and methodical way
(§§ 534–6 and 543). The utterances of the two defendants were also taken into account
(for instance, Tutsis had been called 'cockroaches', had been referred to as 'dirt' or 'filth'
(§ 538)); in particular, Ruzindana had stated that babies whose mothers had been killed
must not be spared 'because those attacking the country initially left as children' (§ 542).

Similarly, in *Musema* the ICTR Trial Chamber inferred special intent to destroy
Tutsis from the numerous atrocities committed against them (*Musema*, TC, § 928), from
large-scale attacks launched against Tutsi civilians (§ 930) and, more generally, from the
widespread and systematic perpetration of other criminal acts against members of the
Tutsi group (§ 931) in which the defendant participated. These acts were accompanied by
humiliating utterances.[45]

When the objectively genocidal act is part of a whole pattern of conduct taking place in
the same state (or region or geographical area), or, a fortiori, of a policy planned or pursued by the governmental authorities (or by the leading officials of an organized political
or military group), then it may become easier to deduce not only the intent[46] but also *lack*

---

[45] According to the TC such humiliating utterances 'clearly indicated that the intention underlying each
specific act was to destroy the Tutsi group as a whole. The Chamber notes, for example, that during the rape
of Nyiramusugi Musema declared: "The pride of the Tutsis will end today." In this context, the acts of rape
and sexual violence were an integral part of the plan conceived to destroy the Tutsi group. Such acts targeted
Tutsi women, in particular, and specifically contributed to their destruction and therefore that of the Tutsi
group as such. Witness N testified before the Chamber that Nyiramusugi, who was left for dead by those who
raped her, had indeed been killed in a way. Indeed, the Witness specified that "what they did to her is worse
than death"' (*Musema*, TC, § 933).

[46] As the Hague Court of Appeal held in the *van Anraat* case with regard to the Iraqi genocide of Kurds
in 1987–8. The Court stated that 'From a number of documents, including the aforementioned reports and
statements in the case file, it appears that the offences put forward in the charges refer to the air attacks that
were carried out partly during the so-called Anfal Campaign by or under the command of the perpetrators.
Moreover, they show that those attacks, however horrifying and shocking they were, formed part of a considerably larger complex of many years of actions against the Kurds in the Northern Iraqi territory, which is
mainly inhabited by the Kurdish population. Apparently these actions involved the systematic destruction

of intent from the facts of the case. Thus, the UN Commission of Inquiry on Darfur held that a range of acts or conducts by the Sudanese governmental authorities committed in breach of international rules evinced that the intent to destroy an ethnic group in whole or in part was lacking.[47]

If instead no policy or plan or widespread practice may be discerned, it may turn out to be extremely difficult to prove the required intent. The Commission of Inquiry on Darfur stated that the fact that no genocidal intent could be imputed to the Sudanese authorities did not exclude that such special intent might be entertained by single individual Sudanese servicemen or militias fighting on behalf of or together with the Sudanese armed forces. To establish the existence of such intent in specific cases was, according to the Commission, a task falling to a competent court of law (§§ 520–1).

6.7 GENOCIDE AND CRIMES AGAINST HUMANITY

As emphasized above, large-scale massacres of ethnic or religious groups were first criminalized as a subclass of the category of crimes against humanity. However, after the adoption of the Genocide Convention of 1948 and the gradual transformation of its main substantive provisions into customary international law, genocide became a category of crimes per se, with its own specific actus reus and mens rea.

True, both categories share at least three elements: *i*) they encompass very serious offences that shock our sense of humanity in that they constitute attacks on the most fundamental aspects of human dignity; *ii*) they do not constitute isolated events, but are

---

of hundreds of Kurdish villages. Hundreds of thousands of Kurdish civilians were chased from their home towns and deported to other places and tens of thousands of Kurds were killed. In one of his reports, Van der Stoel described the policy that constituted the basis for the so-called Anfal Campaign, as a policy that without a doubt had the characteristics of a genocidal design. In view of the said facts and circumstances, the Court believes that the actions taken by the perpetrators, in any case even the ones that have not been included in the charges, as outlined in the above, as to their nature at least produce strong indications that the leaders of the Iraqi regime, also regarding the actions that have been put down in the charges, let themselves be guided by a genocidal intention with regards to at least a substantial part of the Kurdish population group in (Northern) Iraq' (§7). The Court however held that 'Nevertheless, [...] a final judicial judgment regarding the important as well as internationally significant question whether certain actions by certain persons as mentioned in the charges should be designated as genocide, deserves a better motivated judgment (which should be based on conclusive evidence) than the one on which the Court was able to establish its observation' (§ 7).

[47] The Commission scrutinized various elements and concluded that the attacks by Arab militias (under governmental control) on villages inhabited by so-called African tribes did not disclose genocidal intent. As it put it: 'the intent of the attackers was not to destroy an ethnic group as such, or part of the group. Instead, the intention was to murder all those men they considered as rebels, as well as forcibly expel the whole population so as to vacate the villages and prevent rebels from hiding among, or getting support from, the local population' (§ 514).The Commission went on to note that 'Another element that tends to show the Sudanese Government's lack of genocidal intent can be seen in the fact that persons forcibly dislodged from their villages are collected in IDP camps. In other words, the populations surviving attacks on villages are not killed outright, so as to eradicate the group; they are rather forced to abandon their homes and live together in areas selected by the Government. While this attitude of the Sudanese Government may be held to be in breach of international legal standards on human rights and international criminal law rules, it is not indicative of any intent to annihilate the group. This is all the more true because the living conditions in those camps, although open to strong criticism on many grounds, do not seem to be calculated to bring about the extinction of the ethnic group to which the IDPs [Internally Displaced Persons] belong. Suffice it to note that the Government of Sudan generally allows humanitarian organizations to help the population in camps by providing food, clean water, medicines and logistical assistance (construction of hospitals, cooking facilities, latrines, etc.)' (§ 515).

instead always part of a larger context, either because they are large-scale and massive infringements of human dignity or because they are linked to a broader practice of misconduct; and *iii*) although they need not be perpetrated by state officials or by officials of entities such as insurgents, they are usually carried out with the complicity, connivance, or at least the toleration or acquiescence of the authorities.

However, the objective and subjective elements of the two crimes differ in many respects. As for the objective element, the two crimes may undoubtedly overlap to some extent: for instance, killing members of an ethnic or religious group may as such fall under both categories; the same holds true for causing serious bodily or mental harm to members of a racial or religious group, or even for the other classes of protected group. However, crimes against humanity have a broader scope, for they may encompass acts that, as such, do not come within the purview of genocide (for instance, imprisonment and torture)—unless they amount to acts inflicting on members of a group conditions of life calculated to bring about the physical destruction of the group. By the same token, there may be acts of genocide that are not normally held (at least under the Statutes of the ICTY, ICTR, and the ICC) to fall within the other category of crime (for instance, killing detained military personnel belonging to a particular religious or racial group, by reason of their membership of that group). Thus, from the viewpoint of their objective elements, the two categories are normally 'reciprocally special', in that they form overlapping circles which nevertheless intersect only tangentially.

By contrast, from the perspective of the mens rea, the two categories do not overlap at all. In the case of crimes against humanity, international law requires the intent to commit the underlying offence plus knowledge of the widespread or systematic practice constituting the general context of the offence. For genocide, what is required is instead the special intent to destroy, in whole or in part, a particular group, in addition to the intent to commit the underlying offence. From this viewpoint, the two categories are therefore 'mutually exclusive'. They form two circles that do not intersect. The only exception is the case where the underlying actus reus is the same—for instance, murder; in this case, the intent to kill is required in both categories. Nevertheless genocide remains an autonomous category, for it is only genocide that *also* requires the intent to destroy a group. Similarly, it is only for crimes against humanity that knowledge of the widespread or systematic practice is required. As for persecution, the intent of seriously discriminating against members of a particular group is shared by both crimes against humanity and genocide. For persecution-type crimes against humanity, however, it is sufficient to prove that the perpetrator intentionally carried out large-scale and severe deprivations of the fundamental rights of a particular group, whereas for genocide it is necessary to prove the intent to destroy a group, in whole or in part.[48]

I should add that, depending on the group targeted and the accompanying intent, the same objective conduct may give rise to a combination of both genocide and crimes against humanity. For instance, the Hutus' massacres of Tutsis in Rwanda in 1994 amounted to genocide, whereas their simultaneous or concomitant killing of moderate Hutus constituted a crime against humanity.

---

[48] It should be noted that in *Kayishema and Ruzindana* the majority of the ICTR Trial Chamber dismissed the charge of crime against humanity by wrongly holding that it was already covered and indeed 'completely absorbed' by genocide (*Kayishema and Ruzindana*, TC, §§ 577–9); Judge Khan dissented.

6.8 ARTICLE 6 OF THE ICC STATUTE AND CUSTOMARY INTERNATIONAL LAW

Article 6 of the ICC Statute reproduces word for word Article II of the Genocide Convention and the corresponding customary rule. In contrast, Article III of the Convention (and the corresponding customary rule) on responsibility for forms of participation in the crime other than perpetration, namely conspiracy, incitement, attempt, and complicity, have not been taken up in the provision on genocide, either because the notion has not been accepted by the Rome Diplomatic Conference (as was the case with conspiracy, a concept that has not found the support of all the civil law countries present at Rome), or because the relevant notion is laid down in general terms (i.e. in terms applicable to other crimes as well) in other provisions of the ICC Statute: this applies to incitement (at present envisaged in Article 25(3)(e)), attempt (which is provided for in Article 25(3)(f)), and complicity (which is contemplated in Article 25(3)(c) and (d)).

It follows that in at least one respect there is an inconsistency between customary international law and the ICC Statute. The former prohibits and makes punishable 'conspiracy to commit genocide'; that is, an inchoate crime consisting of the planning and organizing of genocide not necessarily followed by the perpetration of the crime, whereas Article 6 does not contain a similar prohibition.

It should be noted that in the process of drafting Article 6, in February 1997 it was suggested in the Working Group of the Preparatory Committee that 'the reference to "intent to destroy in whole or in part [...] a group as such" was understood to refer to the specific intention to destroy more than a small number of individuals who are members of a group'.[49] This suggestion was aptly assailed by two commentators, who noted that nothing in the Genocide Convention could justify such a restrictive interpretation and that, in addition, international practice belied this interpretation, for 'successful counts or prosecutions of crimes against humanity, of which genocide is a species, have involved relatively small numbers of victims'.[50] It would seem that the customary international rule, as codified in Article 6, does not require that the victims of genocide be numerous. Arguably, the only thing that can be clearly inferred from the rule is that genocide cannot be held to occur when there is only one victim. However, as long as the other requisite elements are present, the killing or commission of the other enumerated offences against more than one person may amount to genocide.

Finally, one should note a further view put forth with regard to the mens rea element of genocide. According to the proponent of this view, under Article 28 of the ICC Statute (providing for superior responsibility: see 10.2), 'it is possible to participate in the commission of genocide even despite real knowledge that the crime is being committed'.[51]

It may be objected that an individual can be responsible for genocide under the doctrine of superior responsibility only with regard to the case where the superior knows that genocide is about to be perpetrated, or is being committed, and deliberately refrains from forestalling the crime or stopping it. Indeed in this case, according to a widespread opinion, the superior may be equated to a co-perpetrator, or at least an aider and abettor (see 10.1). Instead, one could not accuse a superior of genocide (as a co-perpetrator or

---

[49] UN Doc. A/AAC.249/1997/L.5 Annex I, p. 3, n. 1.
[50] L. Sadat Wexler and J. Paust, in 13(3) *Nouvelles Études pénales* (1998), at 5.
[51] W. A. Schabas, 'Article 6' in Triffterer, *ICC Commentary*, at 156.

an accomplice) when the superior fails to punish the subordinates who have engaged in genocide; or when, although he has information that should enable him to conclude that genocide is being committed or may be committed, fails to act, in breach of his supervisory obligations (see Article 28(1)(a) and (2)(a) of the ICC Statute). In these cases the superior would be guilty of a different offence: intentional, reckless, or grossly negligent breach of his supervisory duties. It follows that, with regard to such cases, it would not be correct to assert that he should be held responsible for genocide, although with a subjective element lower than specific intent.

7

TORTURE AND AGGRESSION

In this chapter we will discuss two classes of international crimes—torture and aggression—that have repeatedly drawn international attention and condemnation but have not been adjudicated as stand-alone crimes. Both torture and aggression are recurring challenges for civilization. Politically charged allegations are faced by powerful states as well as the less mighty. The evolution of the definitions of the crimes has taken different paths. Well defined as a discrete crime by the UN Torture Convention, torture is normally adjudicated as an underlying aspect of a larger core crime such as a war crime or crime against humanity. Aggression is far less well defined. The lack of a consensus definition stymies prosecution and jurisprudential elaboration of what constitutes the crime of aggression.

It may prove useful briefly to dwell on the different reasons for the treatment—in practice, if not always in theory—of these two crimes as outside the 'core crimes' involving the most heinous offences: war crimes, crimes against humanity, and genocide.

With respect to torture as a discrete international crime, the fact that to date no international criminal court has been authorized to exercise its jurisdiction over such crime may probably be explained by noting that torture as a crime connected with armed conflicts (a war crime) or as large-scale or widespread criminal conduct (a crime against humanity) has been considered more in need of attention. In contrast, in the opinion of states, torture *i)* practised by state officials or with their connivance or complicity; and *ii)* disconnected from a wider context (armed conflict, or widespread or systematic practice), is a matter pertaining to their domestic domain, where international intrusions are not welcome. Hence torture in principle falls under national criminal jurisdiction. This state of affairs is not altogether salutary. It is common knowledge that despite the major merits of the UN Torture Convention, state prosecutors and courts are still somewhat loath to prosecute torturers allegedly committing offences *abroad* against foreigners.

As for aggression, the Nuremberg and Tokyo Tribunals' Statutes provided for prosecution of aggression and the crime is currently prohibited at the national level in some instances (see 7.2.1–7.2.2, nn. 16 and 17). While Article 5 of the ICC Statute also counts aggression as a 'core crime' and contemplates jurisdiction over it some day, that day may be years away for lack of a definition until recently. As discussed in this chapter (see 7.2.2) delegates at the 2010 Review Conference of the ICC Statute adopted a definition of the crime after years of groundwork and two weeks of debate. Jurisdiction will not vest, however, unless and until two-thirds of state parties decide to activate jurisdiction after 1 January 2017, *and* at least thirty state parties ratify or accept the amendments containing the definition. The jurisprudence of aggression has been slow to develop because the offence is too politically charged to be defined in sufficiently clear and exhaustive criminal provisions that permit international independent judicial bodies to adjudicate.

Whatever the reasons for the present legal condition, the failure to extend international criminal adjudication to these two classes of crimes is a matter of regret. Indeed, entrusting an international criminal court with the task of pronouncing upon torture as a crime per se and aggression would offer at least two major advantages. First, it would significantly contribute, at a judicial level, to rein in impunity for these odious crimes. Second, it would ensure—more and better than any national criminal court can do—full respect both for the principle of impartiality of courts and for the fundamental rights of the accused.

7.1 TORTURE

Torture is prohibited by a number of international instruments. While some earlier instruments were not legally binding, they contributed to the formation of a customary law rule banning this odious practice, and paved the way for the conclusion of international treaties on the matter.[1] The existence of such a variety of international rules demonstrates the willingness of the international community to outlaw torture in all its manifestations formally at least, though the problem recurs in reality (ICTY, *Furundžija*, TC § 146).

7.1.1 TORTURE AS A DISCRETE CRIME

The definition of torture as a crime per se (i.e. as a criminal act that is punishable regardless of whether it is committed in connection with an armed conflict, and therefore constituting a war crime; or as part of widespread or systematic attack against a civilian population, and therefore as a crime against humanity) is laid down in Article 1(1) of the UN Torture Convention. As held by the ICTY,[2] 'there is now general acceptance [in the world community] of the main elements contained' in that definition.

According to the UN Torture Convention's definition, the objective elements of torture consist of: *i*) 'any act by which severe[3] pain or suffering, whether physical or mental, is [...] inflicted on a person'; and *ii*) such pain or suffering does not arise 'only from' nor is it 'inherent in or incidental to lawful sanctions'.

As to the mens rea of the crime, the UN Torture Convention provides that the infliction of pain or suffering must be 'intentional'. It appears, therefore, that criminal intent (*dolus*) is always required for torture to be an international crime. Other less stringent

---

[1] See e.g. Art. 5 of the Universal Declaration of Human Rights, Art. XXVI of the American Declaration of the Rights and Duties of Man (1948), Art. 7 of the UN International Covenant on Civil and Political Rights, Art. 3 of the European Convention of Human Rights, Art. 5(2) of the American Convention on Human Rights, and Art. 5 of the African Charter on Human and Peoples' Rights. See also the 1975 UN Declaration on the Protection of All Persons from Being Subjected to Torture and other Cruel, Inhuman or Degrading Treatment or Punishment, that led to the conclusion of the UN Torture Convention, and the 1985 Inter-American Convention to Prevent and Punish Torture. In international humanitarian law, torture is prohibited by the four Geneva Conventions and the 1977 Additional Protocols (see common Art. 3; Arts 12 and 50 of Geneva Convention; Arts 12 and 51 of Geneva Convention II; Arts 13, 14, and 130 of Geneva Convention III; Art. 75 of the First Additional Protocol and Art. 4 of the Second Additional Protocol). In addition torture as a crime against humanity was subject to the jurisdiction of the tribunals acting under Control Council Law no. 10 (Art. II(1)(c)), and constitutes a crime against humanity both under the ICTY and the ICTR Statute (Art. 5(f) and Art. 3(f), respectively). The ICC Statute expressly provides that torture can constitute a crime against humanity and a war crime (see Arts 7(1)(f), 8(2)(a)(ii), and 8(2)(c)(i)).

[2] See *Delalić and others* (§§ 455–74), in *Furundžija* (§§ 257), and *Kunarac and others* (§§ 483–97).

[3] The broadest definition of torture in the Inter-American Convention to Prevent and Punish Torture does not require that the physical or mental suffering be 'severe' (see Art. 2 of the Inter-American Convention; for an interpretation, see Colombia, Remedy of Unconstitutionality, Art. 101 of L.599–2000, Crim. Code., in 49 *Digest of Latin American Jurisprudence on International Crimes* (2010)).

subjective criteria (recklessness, culpable negligence) are not sufficient (except where superior responsibility is at stake).

Moreover, to constitute torture, the UN Torture Conventions provides that the infliction of severe mental or physical pain or suffering must have been committed for an instrumental purpose, namely *i*) to obtain from the victim or a third person a confession or an information; *ii*) to punish the victim or a third person for an act the victim or the third person has committed or is suspected of having committed; *iii*) to intimidate or coerce the victim or a third person; *iv*) for any reason based on a discrimination of any kind. The instrumental purpose requirement distinguishes the phenomenon of torture from isolated sadism more properly the concern of domestic law.

Finally, under the UN Torture Convention, the 'pain or suffering' that is a necessary ingredient of torture must be inflicted 'by or at the instigation of or with the consent or acquiescence of a public official or other person acting in an official capacity'. The need for this sort of participation of a *de jure* or *de facto* state official stems from: *i*) the fact that in this case torture is punishable under international rules even when it constitutes a single or sporadic episode; and *ii*) the consequent necessity to distinguish between torture as a common or 'ordinary' crime (for example, torture of a former intimate partner by a sadist) and torture as an international crime covered by international rules on human rights.[4] The official actor requirement can pose puzzles in light of the contemporary fragmentation of authority. For example, is the Palestinian Authority an official actor? The US Court of Appeals for the DC Circuit in *Ali Shafi* v. *Palestinian Authority* recently concluded that customary international law lacks consensus on the question of whether non-state actors such as the Palestinian Authority can constitute a 'public official' and declined to decide the question (at 7–8).

Torture as a discrete crime may be perpetrated either in time of peace or in time of armed conflict, as was rightly held in 2001 by the ICTY in *Kunarac and others* (TC, §§ 488–97) with a slight departure from the previous judgments of the ICTR in *Akayesu* (TC, § 593) and the ICTY in *Furundžija* (TC, § 162).

The ban on torture perpetrated in the above circumstances has had a long evolution. Significant contributions to this process, at the norm-setting level, were made by an important Declaration passed by the UN GA (Res. 3452 (XXX) of 9 December 1975), by the increasing importance of the 1984 UN Convention on Torture and by general treaties on human rights. Interpretation and adjudication by judicial bodies have advanced the law in practice. Examples from national case law include, for example, *Pinochet*, *Filártiga* v. *Peña-Irala*, and *United States* v. *Belfast*, in which Chuckie Taylor, son of former Liberian President Charles Taylor, became the first person prosecuted under the US Torture Act and received a 97-year sentence for his crimes. International case law has also made much progress, such as in the judgments of the ICTY (for example, *Furundžija* (TC, § 111) and *Kunarac* (TC, § 146)) and the European Court of Human Rights (for example, *Aksoy* (§ 62) and *Selmouni* (§§ 96–105)).

Suffice it to mention that in *Filártiga* the US Court of Appeals for the Second Circuit held that 'the torturer has become, like the pirate or the slave trader before him, *hostis humani generis*, an enemy of all mankind' (at 980). And in 1998 in *Furundžija* the ICTY, after mentioning the human rights treaties and the resolutions of international organizations prohibiting torture, stated that

the existence of this corpus of general and treaty rules proscribing torture shows that the international community, aware of the importance of outlawing this heinous

---

[4] In this regard see P. Gaeta, 'When Is the Involvement of State Officials a Requirement for the Crime of Torture?', in 6 JICJ (2008), 183–93.

phenomenon, has decided to suppress any manifestation of torture by operating both at the interstate level and at the level of individuals. No legal loopholes have been left. (TC, § 146)

By now a rule of customary international law has evolved in the international community *i*) prohibiting individuals from perpetrating torture, regardless of whether it is committed on a large scale; and *ii*) authorizing all states to prosecute and punish the alleged author of such acts, irrespective of where the acts were perpetrated and the nationality of the perpetrator or the victim.

7.1.2 TORTURE AS A WAR CRIME AND A CRIME AGAINST HUMANITY

Torture may be a predicate offence underlying a *war crime*, provided that all the general requirements for this class of crimes are met. In other words, to qualify as a war crime torture must be committed in connection with an armed conflict. Thus for instance, acts of torture performed by a civilian against another civilian fall under the category of 'ordinary crimes' if committed without any nexus to the armed conflict (for example, torture practised by a civilian on a neighbour out of sadism, or on another civilian to take vengeance for a previous personal wrong). In addition, torture as a war crime must be committed against a protected person in international armed conflict or, more generally, against persons not taking part in hostilities or captured fighters in non-interntaional armed conflict.

One may wonder whether torture, as a war crime, retains two of the requirements set forth by the UN Torture Convention concerning: *i*) the instrumental purposes of the criminal act; *ii*) the need for torture to be committed by, or with the involvement of, a state official.

As for the first requirement, it is interesting to note that the ICC Elements of Crimes provide that for the war crime of torture (Articles 8(2)(a)(ii)-1 and 8(2)(c)(i)-(4)) the perpetrator must have 'inflicted the pain or suffering for such purposes as: obtaining a confession, punishment, intimidation or coercion, or for any reason based on any discrimination of any kind', reproducing almost literally the purposes of the UN Torture Convention. The need for the same instrumental purposes was also asserted by the ICTY Appeals Chamber in *Kunarac* (AC, §§ 142, 144), which, however, clarified that there is no requirement that the severe pain or suffering be inflicted exclusively for one or more of the purposes mentioned, but only that such a purpose or purposes be part of the motivation behind the conduct (§ 155). Where applicable, the instrumental purpose requirement has been broadly construed (see, among other cases, *Furundžija* (TC, § 162), which held that humiliation is a cognizable purpose).

As for the state official requirement, initially the ICTY asserted that this is demanded also in the case of torture as a war crime, although it clarified that in IHL 'this requirement must be interpreted to include officials of non-State parties to a conflict, in order for the prohibition to retain significance in situations of internal armed conflicts or international conflicts involving some non-State entities' (*Delalić*, TC, § 473). In *Furundžija*, the Trial Chamber took a more explicit stand on the matter and held that the person inflicting torture 'must be a public official or must at any rate act in a non-private capacity, e.g. a *de facto* organ of a State or any other authority-wielding entity' (TC, § 162). In *Kunarac*, however, the ICTY reversed this position and held that 'the presence of a State official or of any other authority-wielding person in the torture process is not necessary for the offence to be regarded as torture under international humanitarian law' (TC, § 459;

AC, §§ 145–8). It is worth noticing that under the ICC Elements of Crimes, the definition of torture as a war crime does not require the involvement of a state official either. The stand taken by the ICTY in *Kunarac* seems to be sound, although on grounds different from those stated by the Trial Chamber.

As noted, the UN Torture Convention's definition contains a state official require-ment to leave out infliction of severe pain or suffering by a private individual for personal purposes. Such conduct was considered a matter of domestic rather than international concern. In other words, the state official requirement constitutes what one could term the *quid pluris* transforming an 'ordinary' criminal offence into an international crime. It simply serves the purpose of precluding every single wicked act carried out by private individuals against other private individuals being elevated to a crime of international concern. Clearly, the state official requirement is not needed any more when other ele-ments are present capable of 'upgrading', an individual conduct of 'merely' internal con-cern to the level of an international crime. This is certainly the case for the infliction of severe pain and suffering during an armed conflict upon a person not taking part in the hostilities or captured by the enemy belligerent, for reasons linked to the conflict. In this instance (and, as we shall see, in the case of torture as a crime against humanity), torture can be punished regardless of the involvement or participation of a state official because another factor elevates the conduct to a matter of international concern. The *quid pluris* that turns the infliction of such pain or suffering into an international crime is the partic-ular *context* of violence surrounding the act, coupled with the necessity to protect the dig-nity and integrity of human beings when a situation of armed conflict puts them at great risk. It is therefore not necessary that a state official be involved in the torture process for a war crime to occur, though there has been confusion on the matter, as demonstrated by the contrary suggestions by the German Federal Court of Justice in *Sokolović*.[5]

In peace and in times of armed conflict, torture may also amount to a *crime against humanity* when committed as part of a widespread or systematic practice or attack on a civilian population, the general requirement of *all* crimes against humanity. Moreover, the accused must know that his acts of torture form part of a widespread or systematic pattern of violence against the civilian population. As in the case of torture as a war crime, private persons may commit torture as a crime against humanity; again, there is no need for the participation of a state official in the specific act of torture, as the ICTY and ICTR Appeals Chamber has clarified (see, e.g., *Kvočka*, TC, § 284; *Semanza*, TC, § 248). The *quid pluris* that turns the infliction of severe pain and suffering into a crime of international concern is the fact that it takes place in a context of a widespread or system-atic attack against a civilian population.

Indeed, Article 7(1)(f) of the ICC Elements of Crimes dispenses with the instrumental purpose requirement when it comes to torture as a predicate for crimes against humanity. This makes sense because torture committed as part of a widespread or systematic attack directed against civilians is certainly a matter of international concern.

---

[5] The Court required, for a war crime to exist, that, among other things, torture be practised 'by a state organ or with state approval' (at 16). The Court therefore expressed misgivings about the notion of torture laid down in Article 7(1)(f) of the ICC Statute (at 17–18). On the state official requirement for torture as a discrete crime, see P. Gaeta, 'When is the Involvement of a State Official a Requirement for the Crime of Torture?', in JICJ (2008), 183-93.

7.2 THE CRIME OF AGGRESSION

7.2.1 THE EMERGENCE OF THE NOTION AND ITS FALLING INTO LETHARGY

Aggression was first considered as an international crime of individuals in 1945, when the London Agreement establishing the Nuremberg Tribunal was adopted[6] and punished as such in 1946–7 by the Nuremberg Tribunal, the Tokyo Tribunal, by courts acting on the basis of Control Council Law no. 10 and by US military tribunals in the US zone of occupation of Germany.[7] On 11 December 1946 the UN General Assembly unanimously adopted resolution 95(I), by which it 'affirmed' the 'principles of international law recognized by the Charter of the Nuremberg Tribunal and the judgment of the Tribunal'. Thus, all the states that at that stage were members of the UN eventually approved of both the definition of crimes against peace and its application by the Nuremberg Tribunal. At that stage the crime fell into oblivion.

In 1974, when the UN General Assembly adopted a resolution containing the famous Definition of Aggression, the existence and punishability of aggression as a crime was substantially glossed over.[8] The resolution began with a broad definition of aggression based on the Nuremberg Charter and proffered a list of examples that was left deliberately incomplete so as to leave the Security Council broad discretion in characterizing other acts as aggression under the UN Charter. Article 1 of the resolution defined aggression as 'the use of armed force by a state against the sovereignty, territorial integrity or political independence of another state, or in any other manner inconsistent with the Charter of the United Nations, as set out in this Definition'. The resolution did not specify whether aggression entails both state responsibility and individual criminal liability. Article 5(2) of the Definition simply provided that war of aggression is a crime against international law, adding that it 'gives rise to international responsibility'.

---

[6] Article 6(a) of the IMT Charter, annexed to the Agreement, provided as follows: 'The following acts, or any of them, are crimes coming within the jurisdiction of the Tribunal for which there shall be individual responsibility: (a) CRIMES AGAINST PEACE: namely planning, preparation, initiation or waging of a war of aggression, or a war in violation of international treaties, agreements or assurances, or participation in a Common Plan or Conspiracy for the accomplishment of any of the foregoing.'

[7] The Nuremberg Tribunal dwelt at some length in its judgment on this category of crimes to prove that: *i)* it had already been established before 1945; and *ii)* consequently punishing the Nuremberg defendants for having committed these crimes did not fall foul of the *nullum crimen sine lege* principle. The Nuremberg Tribunal went so far as to define aggression as the 'supreme international crime' (at 186). Twelve defendants were found guilty on this count and sentenced either to death or to long terms of imprisonment. Subsequently the Tokyo International Military Tribunal found 25 defendants guilty of aggression.

Control Council Law no. 10 provided for aggression in Art. II (1)(a).

Some of the US Military Tribunals established at Nuremberg also pronounced on aggression (see *Krauch and others* (so-called *IG Farben* case), at 1081ff.; *Krupp and others*, 1327ff.; *von Weizsäcker and others* (so-called Ministries trial), 308ff.; *Wilhelm von Leeb and others* (so-called High Command trial), 462ff.), as well as the French Tribunals that adjudicated the *Röchlingen and others* case (at 1–7 and 404–12).

[8] See Res. 3314 (XXIX) of 14 December 1974. The definition propounded in the Draft Code of Crimes against Peace and Security of Mankind, adopted by the ILC in 1996, although it specifically dealt with criminal liability for aggression, was rather circular and in fact did not provide any definition. Article 16 of the Draft Code provided that 'An individual, who, as leader or organizer, actively participates in or orders the planning, preparation, initiation or waging of aggression committed by a state, shall be responsible for a crime of aggression' (UN Doc. A/51/332)).

Since 1947 in many instances states have engaged in acts of aggression in serious breach of Art. 2(4) of the UN Charter, and in a few cases the Security Council has determined that such acts were committed by states.[9] Before the ICJ, allegations of aggression as an international wrongful act of states have been raised in disputes between states.[10] The ICJ has analysed the claims on the basis of the principles of non-use of force in international relations, non-intervention, and self-defence.[11] However, none of the array of ad hoc and hybrid international criminal courts that have developed the jurisprudence of ICL since the 1990s has been vested with jurisdiction over the crime of aggression, and therefore there have been no international criminal trials for alleged crimes of aggression.

Only recently have alleged cases of aggression as a crime been brought before some national courts,[12] or have national prosecutors been requested to open investigations into alleged instances of aggression. Such requests, however, have not been granted.[13] Although some national criminal codes provide for the crime of aggression,[14] no criminal action at the judicial level is being initiated. Similarly, although the Statute of the Iraqi

---

[9] The Security Council defined as 'acts of aggression' certain actions or raids by South Africa and Israel; see, for example, resolution 573 of 4 October 1985, on Israeli attacks on PLO targets, and Resolution 577 of 6 December 1985, on South Africa's attacks on Angola.

[10] In *Case Concerning Armed Activities on the Territory of the Congo (Democratic Republic of the Congo v. Uganda)*, the Democratic Republic of the Congo filed suit against the Republic of Uganda alleging acts of armed aggression in violation of the United Nations Charter and the Charter of the Organization of African Unity. (ICJ, § 23(a)). In *Nicaragua (Case Concerning Military and Paramilitary Activities in and against Nicaragua)*, the United States justified its Cold War-era military intervention in Nicaragua on the ground that it was responding to requests from El Salvador, Honduras, and Costa Rica for assistance in self-defence against alleged Nicaraguan aggression. (ICJ, §§ 126, 161, 163, 189, 195).

[11] *Case Concerning Armed Activities on the Territory of the Congo (Democratic Republic of the Congo v. Uganda)*, ICJ, § 345(1); *Nicaragua (Case Concerning Military and Paramilitary Activities in and against Nicaragua)*, ICJ, §§ 190–6.

[12] See *R. v. Jones et al.*, decided by the House of Lords on 29 March 2006. The appellants, who in 2003 had unlawfully entered British or NATO military bases in the UK to prevent what they considered to be preparations for a war of aggression against Iraq, had been charged with or convicted of causing criminal damage or aggravated trespass in British military bases. The House of Lords held that aggression is criminalized in international law; however, absent any statutory enactment in the UK incorporating the international customary law criminalizing aggression, the appellants were not entitled to rely upon that criminalization as a defence for the illegality of their action. On this decision, see C. Villarino Villa, in 4 JICJ (2006), 866–77.

[13] Pursuant to Article 80 of the German Criminal Code (which criminalizes 'whoever prepares a war of aggression' in which Germany 'is supposed to participate') Germany's Chief Federal Prosecutor was requested in 1999 to initiate prosecution into the alleged aggression against the Federal Republic of Yugoslavia (Serbia and Montenegro), in which German forces participated. He was then again requested to act in 2003, on account of the use of force in Iraq by US and British forces (German officials were allegedly responsible for allowing US bases in Germany to be used for activities related to military actions against Iraq). In both cases the Prosecutor declined to initiate investigations. On this matter, see C. Kress, in 2 JICJ (2004), 245–64.

[14] See e.g. the following provisions of criminal codes: Art. 80 of the German Criminal Code ('Whoever prepares a war of aggression ([envisaged in Art. 26(1) of the Basic Law] in which the Federal Republic of Germany is supposed to participate and thereby creates a danger of war for the Federal Republic of Germany, shall be punished with imprisonment for life or for no less than ten years'); of Bulgaria (Art. 409), the Russian Federation (Art. 353); Ukraine (Art. 437); Armenia (Art. 384); Uzbekistan (Art. 151); Tajikistan (Art. 395); Latvia (§ 72); Moldova (Art. 139); Macedonia (Art. 415); Montenegro. See www.legislationonline.org.

See also Art. 1 of the Iraqi Law no. 7 of 17 August 1958 (which criminalizes 'Using the country's armed forces against the brotherly Arab countries threatening to use such forces or instigating foreign powers to jeopardize its security or plotting to overthrow the existing regime or to interfere in their internal affairs against its own interest, or spending money for plotting against them or giving refuge to the plotters against them or attacking in international fields or through publications their heads of state').

High Tribunal (IHT) granted jurisdiction over the crime of aggression against other Arab countries,[15] nobody was tried for the crime.

All this is compounded by the fact that the Statute of the ICC, while envisaging the crime of aggression in Article 5, stipulates that the Court shall exercise jurisdiction over the crime once a provision defining it is adopted through an amendment of the Statute. It is striking that in the negotiations leading to the adoption in 1998 of the Statute of the ICC, no agreement was reached on the definition of aggression. Indeed, many African and Arab countries wanted to hold to the 1974 Definition, and even broaden it, while other states such as Germany proposed solutions better tailored to suit the needs of criminal law. It would seem, however, that the main bone of contention was about the role to be reserved to the UN Security Council. It was a matter of discussion whether its determinations were binding upon the Court, whether it could thus stop the Court from prosecuting alleged cases of aggression, or whether the Court should instead be free to make its own findings, whatever the deliberations of the supreme UN body.

Not until the 2010 ICC Review Conference in Kampala, Uganda, was a consensus definition reached (for an overview, see 7.2.2). Jurisdiction over the crime will not vest unless and until at least thirty state parties have ratified or accepted the amendments *and* two-thirds of the state parties agree to activate jurisdiction after 1 January 2017. These limitations arose, in part, because of intense debate over whether the UN Security Council would have the exclusive power to refer a situation of alleged aggression to the ICC. Ultimately, the amendments did not give the UN Security Council a monopoly on referrals. Because of controversy over the matter, the vesting of jurisdiction was delayed pending state party vote and ratifications.

Why there was no international follow-up to the criminalization of aggression after 1947 while other crimes were spelled out in various conventions, is not difficult to grasp. There are many reasons.

First, in 1945–7 it was easy to penalize the leaders of the vanquished states: the war was over, it was patent that it had been initiated in blatant disregard of international treaties; it was felt necessary to react to it not only by resorting to the normal means used by victors (reparation of the wrongful acts; that is, payment by the vanquished states of huge sums of money as war reparations), but also more dramatically, by making criminally accountable the single individuals that in some way had willingly participated in the planning and waging of the war. The written provisions of the Tribunals' Statutes criminalizing aggression were held to be sufficient, supplemented by general notions of criminal law (intent or knowledge as subjective ingredients of the crime).

Second, in 1945 the UN Charter established for the future a system of bans and permissions in the area of use of armed force. Such force was prohibited in international relations (Article 2(4)); it was instead allowed if used or authorized by the UN Security Council (Articles 42–9 and 53 of the UN Charter) or in self-defence (Article 51). However, while the ban was crystal clear, the permission was in some respects fuzzy. In particular, it soon became controversial whether anticipatory self-defence was allowed, and if so, under what conditions. True, the better interpretation of Article 51 seems to be that self-defence is lawful when an armed attack by another state is imminent (*pre-emptive* self-defence, as in the case of Israel in 1967, when the international community did not object to Israel's

---

[15] Art. 14(3) of the 2005 Law establishing the Tribunal confers on the Tribunal jurisdiction over 'The abuse of position and the pursuit of policies that may lead to the threat of war or the use of the Iraqi armed forces against an Arab country, in accordance with Art. 1 of Law 7 of 1958'. For the text of that Article 1, see n. 14.

For a view different from that set out here, see C. Kress, 'The Iraqi Special Tribunal and the Crime of Aggression', in 2 JICJ (2004), 347–52.

attack to forestall the impending invasion by some Arab countries); instead, anticipatory self-defence is unlawful when the attack is launched to prevent a possible future aggression (*preventative* self-defence, as in the case of the Israeli 1981 attack on Iraq to destroy the Osirak nuclear reactor, an attack the Security Council condemned by Res. 487/1981). The fact, however, remains that this interpretation is not upheld by all members of the international community. This looseness of the international legal regulation of the exception to the ban perforce impinged upon the ban: obviously, when self-defence is allowed, the prohibition on military force is not breached and therefore a state may not be termed 'aggressor'. This grey area of international legal regulation, calculated to give states much leeway in practice, a fortiori rendered the criminalization of aggression problematic, given that ICL, as any corpus of criminal law, requires legal precision in the interest of the accused.

Thirdly, the Cold War prompted members of the two blocs to refrain from fleshing out the rules on the crime of aggression for fear that they might be used in the ideological and political struggle between the blocs. Furthermore, there was a general hesitancy by all major powers to elaborate upon aggression, so as to retain as much latitude as possible in the application of the rules on self-defence. Thus, the definition of aggression remained to a large extent in abeyance until the ICC Kampala Review Conference, after years of preparatory groundwork and two weeks of intense debate.[16]

7.2.2 THE ELEMENTS OF THE CRIME

A. Objective Elements

The definition of aggression in new Article 8 *bis* adopted at the ICC Kampala Review Conference builds on the language of the London Charter, the UN Charter, and General Assembly Resolution 3314's list of what qualifies as an 'act of aggression'. The new article defines the crime of aggression as

> the planning, preparation, initiation or execution, by a person in a position effectively to exercise control over or to direct the political or military action of a state, of an act of aggression which, by its character, gravity and scale, constitutes a manifest violation of the Charter of the United Nations.

Section 2 defines an 'act of aggression' as 'the use of armed force by a State against the sovereignty, territorial integrity or political independence of another State, or in any other manner inconsistent with the Charter of the United Nations'. The requirement of 'manifest' violations of the UN Charter excludes borderline or grey-area cases in an area of law with a lot of blurry regions and focuses on conduct that warrants criminal condemnation.

Generally speaking, customary international law essentially prohibits some traditional forms of aggression as either international wrongful acts of states or as the actus reus of a crime entailing individual responsibility, or both. These instances of aggression, constituting the core of the notion normally valid for *both categories* of international responsibility, are basically those envisaged in terms in the 1974 Definition[17] (and confirmed,

---

[16] For accounts of the long road to the ICC Kampala Review Conference, see, for example, C. Kress and L. von Holtzendorff, 'The Kampala Compromise on the Crime of Aggression', 8 JICJ (2010), 1183–217; J. Trahan, 'The Rome Statute's Amendment on the Crime of Aggression: Negotiations at the Kampala Review Conference', 11 *International Criminal Law Review* (2011), 54–87.

[17] The objective element of aggression as an international crime may comprise various instances, if they exhibit the necessary character of massiveness. Mention can be made of some instances, substantially based

at least in part, by the ICJ in *Nicaragua*,[18] albeit solely with respect to the international responsibility of states).

Customary international law appears to consider as an international *crime* giving rise to the international responsibility of individuals the planning, organizing, preparing, or participating in the first use of armed force by a state against the territorial integrity and political independence of another state in contravention of the UN Charter, provided the acts of aggression concerned are large-scale and produce serious consequences. It follows that single attacks that are limited in scope and time, though very serious in nature (such as, for example, that of Israel on Iraq in 1981), do not reach the necessary threshold to be considered as acts of aggression. They may constitute, however, blatant breaches of the ban on the use of force by the attacking state and consequently give rise to its international responsibility.

Arguably, international criminal liability for aggression might also arise where the armed attack against a state is planned, organized, initiated, or executed by individuals belonging to a non-state organization or other organized entity. Nothing precludes non-state organizations from being able to use massively armed force against a foreign state, as the attack of 11 September 2001 by Al Qaeda members against the US clearly demonstrated. This attack, which in principle cannot be considered as a breach of the ban on the use of force set forth in Article 2(4), of the UN Charter (which arguably only concerns the use of armed force by states in their international relations), but can give rise to the international criminal responsibility for aggression of the individuals involved in the attack. While there are sound arguments for extending criminal responsibility for aggression to instances of massive use of armed force by non-state actors, the ICC Kampala Review Conference took a different approach: the definition of the crime of aggression finally adopted restricts criminal liability persons 'in a position effectively to exercise control over or to direct the political or military action of a state' because of questions over whether current customary international law supported an extension of the crime to non-state or minor official actors.[19] Aggression thus retains its connotation as a leadership crime.

---

on the 1974 Definition: 1. The invasion of or the attack on the territory of a state, or any military occupation, however temporary, resulting from such invasion or attack, or any annexation by the use of force of the territory or part of the territory of a state. 2. Bombardment, or use of any weapon or lethal device, by the armed forces of a state or a non-state entity, against the territory of another state (as long as such bombardment or use of weapons is not isolated or sporadic). 3. Blockade of the ports or coasts of a state by the armed forces of another state or a non-state entity. 4. Large-scale attack on the land, sea, or air forces, or marine and air fleets of a state. 5. The massive use of the armed forces of a state or a non-state entity, which are within the territory of another state with the agreement of the receiving state, in blatant contravention of the conditions provided for in the agreement and the customary rules on the use of force. 6. The sending by or on behalf of a state or a non-state entity of armed bands, groups, irregulars, or mercenaries, which carry out acts of armed force against a state of such gravity as to amount to the acts listed above, or its substantial involvement therein. While the list in the 1974 Definition was left open, the list in new Article 8 *bis* is 'semi-open' or 'semi-closed' in the sense that any other act not enumerated must meet the standard in the definition. J. Trahan (cit. n. 16), at 60.

[18] In addressing the element of aggression defined in Article 3(g) of the Definition, whereby aggression includes the case where a state 'sends or is substantially involved in sending into another state armed bands with the task of engaging in armed acts against the latter state of such gravity that they would normally be seen as aggression', the Court held that 'This description [...] may be taken to reflect customary international law. The Court sees no reason to deny that, in customary law, the prohibition of armed attacks may apply to the sending by a state of armed bands to the territory of another state, if such an operation, because of its scale and effects, would have been classified as an armed attack rather than as a mere frontier incident had it been carried out by regular armed forces' (§ 195).

[19] See Kress and von Holtzendorff, cit. n. 16, at 1190.

Be that as it may, it is clear from the intrinsic features of aggression that such crime: *i*) is never perpetrated by single individuals acting severally; instead, it always results from some sort of collective action of a plurality of persons; and *ii*) is certainly an offence attributable to political and military leaders and other senior state officials (or leading organs of a non-state entity); that is, those who mastermind, plan, or organize the crime. It may not involve the personal criminal liability of low-level perpetrators. For instance, it would seem difficult to charge with aggression the pilots carrying out air raids in foreign territory in execution of an aggressive plan because they are not in a position to effectively exercise control over, or direct, the political or military action.

B. Subjective Elements

While the ICC Kampala Review Conference definition is blurry regarding mens rea, history instructs that the crime also requires criminal intent. It must be shown that the perpetrator intended to participate in planning or waging aggression, was aware of the scope, significance, and consequences of the action taken, and substantially contributed to 'shaping' or 'influencing' the planning or waging of aggression. A leader or high-ranking military officer or senior state officials or leading private (for instance, an industrialist) may also bear responsibility if he has *knowledge* of other leaders' plans and willingly pursues the criminal purpose of furthering the aggressive aims. International case law on this matter is clear and consistent.[20]

---

[20] See *Göring and others*, 279–80 (Göring), 282–4 (Hess), 285–6 (von Ribbentropp), 288–9 (Keitel), 291 (Kaltenbrunner), 294–5 (Rosenberg), 296 (Frank), 299–300 (Frick), 302 (Streicher), 304–5 (Funk), 307–10 (Schacht), 310–11 (Dönitz), 315–16 (Raeder), 317–18 (von Schirach), 320 (Sauckel), 322–4 (Jodl), 325–7 (von Papen), 328–30 (Seyss-Inquart), 330–1 (Speer), 333–6 (von Neurath), 336–7 (Fritzsche), 338–9 (Bormann).

In *Krupp and others* another US Military Tribunal noted that 'the defendants were private citizens and non-combatants [they were industrialists]'. The Tribunal went on to emphasize that 'None of them had any voice in the policies that led their nation into aggressive war; nor were any of them privies to that policy. None had any control over the conduct of the war or over any of the armed forces; nor were any of them parties to the plans pursuant to which the wars were waged and so far as appears, none of them had any knowledge of such plans' (at 488).

In *Krauch and others* (*IG Farben* case), a US Military Tribunal sitting at Nuremberg held that: 'If the defendants [senior staff or managers of the German company I. G. Farben specializing in synthetic rubber, gasoline, nitrogen, and light metals, as well as explosives], or any of them, are to be held guilty under either count one [planning, preparation, initiation, and waging of wars of aggression] or five [formulation and execution of a common plan or conspiracy to commit crimes against peace] or both on the ground that they participated in the planning, preparation, and initiation of wars of aggression or invasions, it must be shown that they were parties to the plan or conspiracy, or, knowing of the plan, furthered its purpose and objective by participating in the preparation for aggressive war' (1108). The Court concluded that none of the defendants were guilty of the crimes set forth in counts one and five (at 1128; see also 1124–7). The Court concluded that the accused lacked the required mens rea (at 1306). In his Concurring Opinion Judge Hebert insisted on the need for knowledge and criminal intent for criminal liability for aggressive wars to arise. He stated: 'We are thus brought to the central issue of the charges insofar as the aggressive wars charges are concerned. Acts of substantial participation by certain defendants are established by overwhelming proof. The only real issue of fact is whether it was accompanied by the state of mind requisite in law to establish individual and personal guilt. Does the evidence in this case establish beyond reasonable doubt that the acts of the defendants in preparing Germany for war were done with knowledge of Hitler's aggressive aims and with the criminal purpose of furthering such aims?' (1217)

In *von Leeb and others* (so-called *High Command* case) a US Military Tribunal held that 'There first must be actual knowledge that an aggressive war is intended and that if launched it will be an aggressive war. But mere knowledge is not sufficient to make participation even by high-ranking military officers in the war criminal. It requires in addition that the possessor of such knowledge, after he acquires it shall be in a position to shape or influence the policy that brings about its initiation or its continuance after initiation, either by furthering, or by hindering or preventing it. If he then does the former, he becomes criminally responsible; if he does the latter to the extent of his ability, then his action shows the lack of criminal intent

As convincingly argued by a commentator, [21] aggression requires in addition a *special intent*; that is, the will to achieve territorial gains, or to obtain economic advantages, or deliberately to interfere with the internal affairs of the victim state (for instance, by toppling its government or bringing about a change in its political regime or ideological leanings or in its international political alignment). It would seem that the standard by which to evaluate whether an individual harbours that special intent can be found in the General Treaty of Paris for the Renunciation of War (or Kellogg–Briand Pact) of 27 August 1928, which banned war as 'an instrument of national policy'. In short, any unlawful large-scale attack against a state intentionally carried out as an instrument of national policy (hence, to acquire territory; or coerce the victim state to change its government or its political regime, or else its domestic or foreign policy; or to appropriate assets belonging to the victim state) amounts to aggression as a criminal act.

The above considerations bear out that, as in the case of genocide (see 6.1.3), the notion of aggression is split into two separate concepts, one valid for the internationally wrongful acts of states (where no special intent would be required, for the purpose of banning armed attacks amounting to a serious breach of Article 2(4) of the UN Charter), the other for individuals' criminal offences (where instead the requisite subjective element of crime includes special intent).

7.2.3 THE NEED TO DISENTANGLE CRIMINAL LIABILITY OF INDIVIDUALS FROM STATE RESPONSIBILITY: THE TWO DIFFERENT LEGAL REGIMES

Now that there seems to be a broad interest in reviving the notion and spelling out its legal contours, it may be of some interest to draw attention to some of the '*acquis*' of the past experience, so as to build on them.

To my mind it would be fallacious to hold the view that, since no general agreement has been reached in the world community on a *treaty definition* of aggression, and the ICC Kampala Review Conference amendments have yet to be formally ratified or agreed to by the necessary number of parties, perpetrators of this crime may not be prosecuted and punished. The ruling in *R. v. Jones et al.* issued in 2006 by the House of Lords bears out this view. The House unanimously held that aggression is criminalized under customary

---

with respect to such policy' (68). The Tribunal then noted the following: 'The acts of commanders and staff officers below the policy level, in planning campaigns, preparing means for carrying them out, moving against a country on orders and fighting a war after it has been instituted, do not constitute the planning, preparation, initiation and waging of war or the initiation of invasion that international law denounces as criminal' (490–1). The Tribunal also noted that 'mere knowledge is not sufficient to make participation even by high-ranking military officers in the war criminal. It requires in addition that the possessor of such knowledge, after he acquires it, shall be in a position to shape or influence the policy that brings about its initiation or its continuance after initiation, either by furthering, or by hindering or preventing it' (488). 'It is not a person's rank or status, but his power to shape or influence the policy of his state, which is the relevant issue for determining his criminality under the charge of crimes against peace' (489). A US Military Tribunal took up the notion that it is necessary to show that a culprit has the power to shape or influence the policy of an aggressor state, in *Weizsäcker and others* (*Ministries case*), at 425.

See also *Araki and others* (Tokyo trial), at 456–7, as well as the *Röchling* case (for the accused T, at 4, 7, 10; for the accused ST, at 406–8).

[21] S. Glaser, 'Quelques remarques sur la définition de l'agression en droit international pénal', in *Festschrift für Th. Rittler* (Aalen: Verlag Scientia, 1957), 388–93; S. Glaser, 'Culpabilité en droit international pénal', 99 HR 1960–I, 504–5. Glaser's views are taken up by G. Werle, *Principles of International Criminal Law* (The Hague: Asser Press, 2005), 395.

international law. Lord Bighman of Cornhill,[22] as well as Lord Hoffmann (§ 59) and Lord Mance (at § 99) explicitly stated that, contrary to what the Court of Appeals had held in the same case (§§ 24–30), the crime of aggression does not lack the certainty of definition required for a criminal offence.[23] True, as pointed out above, this is an area where states deliberately want to retain a broad margin of discretion. Nevertheless, a few points are clear.

The basic point is that the rules of customary international law and the treaty provisions (Articles 2(4) read in conjunction with Articles 42–9, 51, and 53 of the UN Charter) that prohibit the unlawful use of force as an international wrongful act are *different from and broader than* the customary international rules that criminalize aggression. The two legal regimes of responsibility for aggression are different not only because each notion is linked to a different 'primary' or substantive international rule of customary international law, but also with regard to the preconditions of responsibility and the legal consequences of such responsibility.

First of all, aggression as an international wrongful act of a state embraces any serious and large-scale breach of Article 2(4) of the UN Charter not justified by Articles 51 and 53 (and the corresponding customary international law rules). As such, aggression is subject to the legal regime governing the so-called aggravated responsibility of states.[24]

In contrast, the following are breaches of the ban on the use of armed force that, while constituting international wrongful acts giving rise to state responsibility, do not amount to state aggression: *i*) breaching Article 2(4) of the UN Charter by violating through the use of force the territory or the air space or the independence of a state by means of acts that are sporadic or in any event not large scale; *ii*) engaging in an armed conflict in violation of international treaties proscribing resort to armed violence; *iii*) using force under the authority of the resolution of an international body or on humanitarian grounds but in contravention of the UN Charter; or *iv*) resorting to self-defence in disregard of the

---

[22] His Lordship wrote the following: 'It was suggested, on behalf of the Crown, that the crime of aggression lacked the certainty of definition required of any criminal offence, particularly a crime of this gravity. This submission was based on the requirement in Article 5(2) of the Rome Statute that the crime of aggression be the subject of definition before the international court exercised jurisdiction to try persons accused of that offence. This was an argument which found some favour with the Court of Appeal (in para. 43 of its judgment). I would not for my part accept it. It is true that some states parties to the Rome statute have sought an extended and more specific definition of aggression. It is also true that there has been protracted discussion of whether a finding of aggression against a state by the Security Council should be a necessary pre-condition of the court's exercise of jurisdiction to try a national of that state accused of committing the crime. I do not, however, think that either of these points undermines the appellants' essential proposition that the core elements of the crime of aggression have been understood, at least since 1945, with sufficient clarity to permit the lawful trial (and, on conviction, punishment) of those accused of this most serious crime. *It is unhistorical to suppose that the elements of the crime were clear in 1945 but have since become in any way obscure*' (§ 19; emphasis added).

[23] If the above remarks are correct, it would follow that the contrary view propounded by a US delegate in 2001 would be erroneous from the legal viewpoint (see 95 AJIL (2001), 400–1). The US representative of the US State Department noted that 'the [1974] Definition neither restated existing customary international law' nor generated such law, due to lack of subsequent practice and *opinio juris*. After noting that there was no '*opinio juris generalis*', the US representative pointed out that there was no practice: 'Obviously, there has been no concordant practice based on the [General Assembly Resolution 3314 on the definition of aggression]. Just look at the records of the Security Council. And if anyone still had any doubts, the controversy about Resolution 3314 in our own discussions, has clearly demonstrated the absence of *opinio juris generalis*' (at 400). Arguably this view is immaterial to the existence of the customary rules at issue, for it is an isolated statement not supported by similar views of other states.

[24] On the notion of 'aggravated state responsibility', see A. Cassese, *International Law*, 2nd edn (Oxford: Oxford University Press, 2005), 262–77.

conditions laid down in Article 51 of the UN Charter (for instance, individual self-defence not followed by a report to the Security Council, or collective self-defence initiated without a request by the victim state nor followed by such state's consent). All these acts would be illegal state conduct not amounting to aggression proper.

Second, international rules on aggression as a wrongful act of state only envisage and ban aggression by a state against another state. This is because traditionally, international rules tend to govern interstate dealings.

As for criminal law, international practice, particularly as evinced by the views set forth by states within the UN (in particular on the occasion of the adoption of the 1970 Declaration on Friendly Relations[25] and of the 1974 Definition), seems to bear out the following propositions. First, customary rules have evolved to the effect that only serious and large-scale instances of use of force (not legitimized by the UN Charter as collective enforcement or collective or individual self-defence) may be regarded as amounting to an international crime involving the criminal liability of those who planned, organized, and masterminded the aggression. For example, it would seem difficult to deny that the attack by Iraq on Kuwait in 1990 was not only an inter-state breach of Article 2(4) of the UN Charter, not justified by self-defence, and thus constituted aggression involving the responsibility of the state, *as well as* an international *crime* of aggression.

Second, ICL rules that prohibit and criminalize aggression also penalize aggressive acts by non-state actors (such as terrorist armed groups, organized insurgents, liberation movements, and the like) against a state. Since this body of law is geared to penalizing individuals' misconduct, one cannot see what would stand in the way of extending criminal liability for aggression to individuals who do not belong to, or act on behalf of, a state. If the purpose of the relevant international rules is to protect the world community from serious breaches of the peace, one fails to see why individuals operating for non-state entities should be immune from criminal liability for aggressive conduct.

Third, an additional *subjective* element is required by international criminal rules for aggression, which instead is not envisaged for aggression as an international state delinquency.

There is another difference between the two classes of responsibility. Under the UN Charter the UN Security Council is empowered to determine whether a state or non-state entity has engaged in aggression, and also to adopt all the necessary measures to counter such aggression. It can also adopt or authorize sanctions against either the delinquent state or non-state entity, or against individuals participating in the aggression. The Security Council thus enjoys considerable latitude in this matter. However, being a political body, its determinations may not amount to a judicial finding of the criminal liability of individuals for the crime of aggression. It follows that a decision of the SC condemning actions by a state as aggression may have no *direct* legal effect on courts empowered to adjudicate crimes of aggression. Courts are free to make any finding in this matter regardless of what is decided by the Security Council.

It is thus clear that one of the merits of the distinction between two different regimes of responsibility lies in, among other things, enabling courts that try persons accused of aggression legitimately to embrace a judicial approach, which may differ from the political stand taken by international political bodies such as the UN Security Council. There may be cases where one of those bodies does not consider that aggression has materialized, while a national or international court may take a contrary position and consequently find individuals criminally responsible for aggression. It remains nonetheless true, that

---

[25] GA Res. 2625 (XXV). Principle I (2) states that 'A war of aggression constitutes a crime against peace, for which there is responsibility under international law.'

when the Security Council concludes that in a particular instance acts committed by a state amount to aggression as an international wrongful act, it may sometimes prove easier for a national or international court to find that aggression as a crime was perpetrated and, therefore, to pronounce on the issue of whether the individuals involved are criminally liable. For courts, pronouncements of the Security Council constitute important elements that may count, along with relevant evidence, for their making judicial findings on criminal liability for the conduct at issue.

7.2.4 WHETHER CONSPIRACY TO WAGE AGGRESSION IS CRIMINALIZED

The Statutes of both the Nuremberg and the Tokyo Tribunals provided that, in addition to aggression (planning, preparation, initiation, or waging of a war of aggression), also participation in a conspiracy to wage such a war was criminalized. The indictments in both cases charged separately aggression and conspiracy to wage aggression.

The Nuremberg Tribunal merged conspiracy with planning a war of aggression (at 225–6). It acquitted some defendants (e.g. Funk and Speer) of conspiracy (because they had not participated in the early stages of the planning of aggression) and found no defendant guilty solely of conspiracy. The Tokyo Tribunal tended instead to envisage the two charges as separate, and indeed found one defendant (foreign minister Shigemitsu) guilty of waging a war of aggression but acquitted him of conspiracy, whereas it held another defendant (ambassador Shiratori) guilty of conspiracy but acquitted him of aggressive war.

In spite of the different attitudes taken by the two Tribunals and the lack of any follow-up in subsequent case law, it would seem that conspiracy to wage a war of aggression may be regarded as a separate crime in ICL. Aggression is such a devastating crime, with grave consequences for peace and the whole international community, that it seems warranted to infer from the present system of ICL the criminalization of the early stages of preparation of the crime, when a plurality of persons get together and agree to put in place the necessary measures to engage in a war of aggression. It is also notable that there is a parallel prohibition in the field of *state* responsibility: that, laid down in Article 2(4) of the UN Charter, relating to the mere *threat* of force. If such a threat has been proscribed in interstate dealings so as to quell any attempt or preliminary steps toward the actual use of force, it is only natural for ICL to also criminalize the 'preliminaries' to the crime of aggression; that is, the getting together of leaders and their agreeing to engage in aggression.

However, this inchoate crime (that is, preliminary offence that has not been completed and has not yet caused any harm (see 11.6) is only criminalized per se if it is *not* followed up by the actual undertaking of aggression. If the incursion actually ensues, then aggression as a crime should 'absorb' the crime of conspiracy because the concept of aggression includes the harm of a plurality of persons working toward the crime.

8

TERRORISM

As in the case of torture and aggression, terrorism is also usually considered to fall foul of the notion of 'core crimes' deserving international criminal adjudication. Many states still feel that on practical grounds terrorism is better investigated and prosecuted at the state level by individual or joint enforcement and judicial action. This view is strengthened by the feeling that the concept of terrorism is still controversial at the international level because it is widely held that there is no agreement yet on what some states deem to be a necessary exception to the crime. As a consequence, even in the only Statute of international tribunal envisaging such crime (that of the Special Tribunal for Lebanon, STL) no international definition of the offence is laid down, and instead a reference to Lebanese law is made.

This chapter examines the reasons why the traditional wisdom is that a generally agreed definition on terrorism as an international crime is lacking; it will argue instead that many factors point to the existence of such agreed definition, at least for terrorism in time of peace. The legal ingredients of terrorism as an international crime will therefore be analysed.

8.1 THE FREEDOM FIGHTERS' PROBLEM

Interminable polemical arguments have been exchanged between states since the 1970s over what should be meant by terrorism. The main bone of contention is the following: could 'freedom fighters' engaged in national liberation movements be classified as terrorists?[1] Three different positions of states and other authorities may be identified, positions that do not necessarily exclude one another, and in some instances overlap.

The first is that of states stubbornly insisting on any act by peoples or organizations engaged in wars of self-determination *being exempt from the label of terrorism* (even when they engage in attacks against civilians). These states, however, do not clarify what law would govern such acts or whether, and more simply, these acts should be held to be *authorized* under international law. This stand was taken, for instance, by Pakistan in 2002 when acceding to the 1997 Convention for the Suppression of Terrorist Bombing. The Convention excludes from its scope activities of armed forces, including freedom fighters, in armed conflict, keeping such activities subject to the legal regulation of

---

[1] The other main problematic issue is whether the working out of international rules on terrorism be made contingent upon delving into the root causes of this phenomenon. It would appear that, generally speaking, the question of investigating the historical, social, and economic causes of terrorism has instead been put on the backburner, although very recently the UN Security Council has again drawn attention to the need to 'address conditions conducive to exploitation by terrorists'. See his Report to the General Assembly of 27 April 2006 (A/60/825), *Uniting against Terrorism: Recommendations for a Global Counter-Terrorism Strategy*, at §§ 20–37.

international humanitarian law. Pakistan made a declaration that can be held to be at least ambiguous:

> The Government of the Islamic Republic of Pakistan declares that nothing in this Convention shall be applicable to struggles, including armed struggle, for the realization of right of self-determination launched against any alien or foreign occupation or domination, in accordance with the rules of international law. This interpretation is consistent with Article 53 of the Vienna Convention on the Law of Treaties 1969 which provides that an agreement or treaty concluded in conflict with an existing *jus cogens* or preemptory norm of international law is void and, the right of self-determination is universally recognized as *a jus cogens*.

A very similar position is taken by other states, which purport to exclude the application of anti-terrorist conventions to armed conflict, without, however, clarifying whether the use of force by freedom fighters against civilians in such conflicts must be covered by international humanitarian law. This stand was taken by Egypt, Jordan, and Syria in 2003–5 when ratifying, or acceding to, the Convention for the Suppression of the Financing of Terrorism.[2]

The second position is that of states or authorities which hold that, while any act performed by freedom fighters in wars of national liberation is not covered at all by the body of international law on terrorism, it remains nevertheless governed by the international humanitarian law of armed conflict. The member states of the Islamic Conference participating in the UN negotiations for the elaboration of a Comprehensive Convention on Terrorism have proposed a draft provision encapsulating the famous exception to the notion of terrorism. However, this time the proposal spells out the hitherto ambiguous formula used by Arab and Islamic countries. It is now specified that actions undertaken in the course of an armed conflict 'including in situations of foreign occupation' are not covered by the Convention, hence may not be classified as 'terrorist acts'. Nevertheless—and here comes the novelty—it is now added that those actions remain covered by other rules of international law (in particular, international humanitarian law). It logically follows that, if such actions are contrary to those rules, their authors may be prosecuted under other relevant rules of international law. Translated into 'contemporary' terms, this means that, for instance, Palestinians' deliberate attacks on Israeli civilians in the West Bank (occupied territory), while they could not be termed terrorist acts, would amount to war crimes (see 8.5), in particular to 'crimes the primary purpose of which is to spread terror among the civilian population'; their perpetrators would be liable to be punished under national and international law for such crimes. If this is so, it becomes clear that now the intent of Islamic states is simply to remove the label of 'terrorism' from any action of 'freedom fighters' contrary to international law. The fact remains however, that even those states now concede—or, at least, it would seem so—that the authors of those actions may be prosecuted and punished for their criminal conduct. The diplomatic contention

---

[2] See the explanatory declaration by Egypt: 'Without prejudice to the principles and norms of general international law and the relevant United Nations resolutions, the Arab Republic of Egypt does not consider acts of national resistance in all its forms, including armed resistance against foreign occupation and aggression with a view to liberation and self-determination, as terrorist acts within the meaning of article 2, paragraph 1, subparagraph (b), of the Convention.' See also the declaration by Jordan: 'The Government of the Hashemite Kingdom of Jordan does not consider acts of national armed struggle and fighting foreign occupation in the exercise of people's right to self-determination as terrorist acts within the context of paragraph 1(b) of article 2 of the Convention.' Syria entered a reservation, concerning the provisions of Article 2, paragraph 1 (b) of the Convention, 'inasmuch as the Syrian Arab Republic considers that acts of resistance to foreign occupation are not included under acts of terrorism'.

then boils down to an essentially ideological dispute over how to further term an act that is undisputedly criminal as a terrorist act or as a war crime.

This difference in ideology and social psychology is not, however, the end of the matter. For, classifying an act as terrorist may trigger the use by the relevant national police of a set of investigative powers normally not authorized for any ordinary crime or for any war crime. It follows that, if agreement emerges on assigning acts performed by freedom fighters in armed conflict to the regulation of international humanitarian law alone, the whole range of investigative powers and consequent measures accruing to enforcement agencies under domestic law may no longer be applied with regard to them.

A third, middle-of-the-road position, has also emerged, which combines the application of international rules on terrorism with international humanitarian law. This view is enshrined in the UN Convention for the Suppression of the Financing of Terrorism and is shared by 171 out of the 174 current parties to the Convention. The same view is laid down in Canadian legislation on terrorism and has also been put forward by some Italian courts, as well as the Israeli foreign minister. It would seem plausible to contend that this stand is shared by the UN Secretary-General. The supporters of this position hold that attacks by freedom fighters and other combatants in armed conflict, if directed at military personnel and objectives in keeping with international humanitarian law, are lawful and may not be termed terrorism. If instead they target civilians, they amount to terrorist acts (not, therefore, to war crimes) if their purpose is to terrorize civilians. Thus the conduct of hostilities is not left to the exclusive legal dominion of international humanitarian law. Principles and rules on terrorism reach out to armed conflict, in that they apply to acts that are not consonant with international humanitarian law.

8.2 ELEMENTS POINTING TO THE EXISTENCE OF A GENERALLY AGREED DEFINITION OF TERRORISM IN TIME OF PEACE

Many states have asserted that as long as no agreement is reached on the freedom fighters' contentious issue, no consent could evolve on the very notion of terrorism either. As a consequence, treaty rules laying down a comprehensive and all-embracing definition have not yet been agreed upon.

However, over the years, under the strong pressure of public opinion and also in order to come to grips with the spreading of terrorism everywhere, in fact widespread consensus on a generally acceptable definition of terrorism has evolved in the world community, so much so that the contention can be made—based on the arguments set forth in this chapter—that indeed a rule of customary international law on the objective and subjective elements of the international crime of terrorism in time of peace has evolved. The requisite practice (*usus*) lies in, or results from, the converging adoption of national laws, the handing down of judgments by national courts, the passing of UN General Assembly resolutions, as well as the ratification of international conventions by a great number of states (such ratifications evincing the attitude of states on the matter). In contrast, disagreement continues to exist on a possible *exception* to such definition: whether to exempt *in time of armed conflict* from the scope of the definition acts that, although objectively and subjectively falling within the definition's purview, according to a number of states are nevertheless *legitimized* in law by their being performed by 'freedom fighters' engaged in liberation wars.

In 2011 the Appeals Chamber of the STL has confirmed this view. In its *Interlocutory Decision on the Applicable Law* of 16 February 2011, it held that a number of treaties, UN resolutions, and the legislative and judicial practice of States evince the formation of a general *opinio juris* in the international community, accompanied by a practice consistent with such opinion, to the effect that a customary rule of international law regarding the international crime of terrorism, at least in time of peace, has indeed emerged. This customary rule requires the following three key elements: (i) the perpetration of a criminal act (such as murder, kidnapping, hostage-taking, arson, and so on), or threatening such an act; (ii) the intent to spread fear among the population (which would generally entail the creation of public danger) or directly or indirectly coerce a national or international authority to take some action, or to refrain from taking it; (iii) when the act involves a transnational element. (§ 85)

The Appeals Chamber went on to note that the banning of terrorism as laid down in customary international law did not necessarily entail that terrorism was also criminalized under international law, in addition to being prohibited vis-à-vis states and other international subjects:

According to the legal parameters suggested by the ICTY Appeals Chamber in the *Tadić* Interlocutory Decision with regard to war crimes, to give rise to individual criminal liability at the international level it is necessary for a violation of the international rule to entail the individual criminal responsibility of the person breaching the rule. The criteria for determining this issue were again suggested by the ICTY in that seminal decision: the intention to criminalise the prohibition must be evidenced by statements- of government officials and international organisations, as well as by punishment for such violations by national courts. Perusal of these elements of practice will establish whether States intend to criminalise breaches of the international rule. (§ 103)

According to the STL Appeals Chamber the criminalization of terrorism is undisputed. It began at the domestic level, 'with many countries of the world legislating against terrorist acts and bringing to court those allegedly responsible for such acts'. This practice was 'internationally strengthened by the passing of robust resolutions by the UN General Assembly and Security Council condemning terrorism, and the conclusion of a host of international treaties banning various manifestations of terrorism'. The STL Appeals Chamber then concluded that

the customary rule in question has a twofold dimension: it addresses itself to international subjects, including rebels and other non-State entities (whenever they exhibit such features as to enjoy international legal personality), by imposing or conferring on them rights and obligations to be fulfilled in the international arena; at the same time, it addresses itself to individuals by imposing on them the strict obligation to refrain from engaging in terrorism, an obligation to which corresponds as correlative the right of any State (or competent international subject) to enforce such obligation at the domestic level. (§ 105)

The position according to which there exists a generally agreed definition of terrorism in time of peace has been taken by the UK Court of Appeal (Criminal Division) in *Regina* v. *Mohammed Gul* (the Court explicitly referred to the STL *Interlocutory Decision on Applicable Law*).

8.3 THE INGREDIENTS OF TERRORISM AS AN INTERNATIONAL CRIME IN TIME OF PEACE

8.3.1 THE OBJECTIVE ELEMENT

A first element of terrorism as an international crime (as distinguished from, i.e. not necessarily coinciding with, terrorism as a domestic crime) relates to conduct. The terrorist act consists of conduct that is already criminalized under any national body of criminal law: murder, mass killing, serious bodily harm, kidnapping, bombing, hijacking, and so on.

Furthermore, the conduct must be transnational in nature; that is, not limited to the territory of one state with no foreign elements or links whatsoever (in which case it would exclusively fall under the domestic criminal system of that state).[3]

As for the victims of criminal conduct, they may embrace both private individuals or the civilian population at large and also state officials, including members of state enforcement agencies.

8.3.2 THE SUBJECTIVE ELEMENT

A second distinguishing trait of terrorism is the *purpose* of terrorist acts. A number of international instruments and national laws provide that terrorists pursue the objective of *either* spreading terror among the population *or* compelling a government or an international organization to perform or abstain from performing an act.[4] Other instruments also envisage a third possible objective: to destabilize or destroy the structure of a country.[5]

One can understand that, both for descriptive purposes and also in order to cover the whole range of possible criminal actions, these treaties, laws, or other legal instruments enumerate a wide set of terrorist aims. In addition, expressly contemplating various alternative purposes pursued by terrorists may prove useful to prosecutors and other enforcement agencies when the demands of terrorist groups are not clear or are not made with regard to a specific terrorist attack. In these cases, in order to classify the conduct as terrorist, it may suffice to determine that at least the immediate aim of terrorists was to spread panic among the population. This indeed may greatly facilitate the action of prosecutors in applying national laws against terrorism. However, close scrutiny and legal logic demonstrate that in fact the *primary goal* of terrorists is always that of coercing a public (or private) institution to take a certain course of action or to spread deep fear or anxiety in the population. The destabilization of the political structure of a state is a means of making the incumbent government take a certain course of action. To be sure, in some instances the terrorists' goal is not set forth in so many words either before or after the terrorist action. For instance, the 11 September attack on the Twin Towers and the Pentagon was not accompanied by specific demands of the terrorist organization that had planned the attack. Yet, even in these cases the murder, bombing, kidnapping is not made for its own sake; it is instrumental in inducing a public or private authority to do or refrain from doing something. The 11 September attack was clearly intended to prompt the US government to change its overall policy in the Middle East, in particular by pulling out its military forces there and reversing its policy vis-à-vis Israel.

Hence it can be said that ultimately terrorism always pursues one primary and essential purpose, that of spreading fear and anxiety (for instance, by blowing up a theatre,

---

[3] The transnational nature of international terrorism is pithily caught in Art. 3 of the Convention for the Suppression of the Financing of Terrorism ('This Convention shall not apply where the offence is committed within a single State, the alleged offender is a national of that State and is present in the territory of that State and no other State has a basis [. . .] to exercise jurisdiction [. . .]').

[4] See, for instance, § 3 of SC Res. 1566 (2004) adopted on 4 October 2004; Art. 83.01(1) (B) of the Canadian Criminal Code.

[5] See e.g. Art. 1(2) of the 1999 Convention of the Organization of the Islamic Conference on Combating International Terrorism; Article 1 of the EU Framework Decision on Combating Terrorism (which refers to the aim of 'seriously destabilising or destroying the fundamental political, constitutional, economic or social structures of a country or an international organization').

kidnapping civilians, planting a bomb in a train, in a bus, or in a public place such as a school, a museum, a bank) and/or of coercing a public authority (a government or an international organization) or a transnational private organization (for instance, a multinational corporation) to take (or refrain from taking) a specific action or a certain policy (e.g. blowing up, or threatening to blow up, the premises of Parliament, the Ministry of Defence, or a foreign embassy) or else against a leading personality of a public or private body (for instance, the head of government, a foreign ambassador, the president of a multinational corporation, and so on). This is the hallmark of any terrorist action.

It should be added that terrorism as an international crime has an ideological or political underpinning. As the STL Appeals Chamber put it

> the terrorist's intent to coerce an authority or to terrorise a population will often derive from or be grounded in an underlying political or ideological purpose, which thus differentiates terrorism from criminal acts similarly designed to spread fear among the civilian population but pursuing merely private purposes (such as personal gain, revenge, and so on). (§ 106)

In other words, the criminal conduct is not taken for a personal end (for instance, gain, revenge, or personal hatred). It is based on political, ideological, or religious motivations, which are important because they serve to differentiate terrorism as a manifestation of *collective criminality* from criminal offences (murder, kidnapping, and so on) that are instead indicative of *individual criminality*. Terrorist acts are normally performed by groups or organizations, or by individuals acting on their behalf or somehow linked to them. A terrorist act, for instance the blowing up of a disco, may surely be performed by a single individual not belonging to any group or organization. However, that act is terrorist if the agent was moved by a collective set of ideas or tenets (a political platform, an ideology or a body of religious principles), thereby subjectively identifying himself with a group or organization intent on performing similar acts. It is this factor that transforms the murderous action of an individual into a terrorist act.[6]

---

[6] Hence, if it is proved that a criminal action (for instance, blowing up a building) has been motivated by non-ideological or non-political or non-religious considerations, the act can no longer be defined as terrorism as an international crime, although it may of course fall under a broader notion of terrorism upheld in the state where the act has been accomplished. This, for instance, holds true for cases similar to the *McVeigh* case: in this case Timothy McVeigh blew up in 1995 a public building in Oklahoma City, with the consequent death of 168 persons; reportedly that action was carried out in revenge for the killing, by the FBI, of members of a religious sect at Waco, Texas. Similarly, if bandits break into a bank, kill some clients, and take others hostage for the purpose of escaping unharmed with the loot, this action cannot be classified as terrorism, although the killing and hostage-taking are also intended to spark terror among civilians and compel the authorities to do or not to do something. Here the ideological or political motivation is lacking. Consequently, the offence is one of armed robbery aggravated by murder and hostage-taking, not terrorism. Let us take another example, namely the episode at the Los Angeles International airport (where on 4 July 2002 an Egyptian fired at and killed some tourists who were about to take a plane bound for Israel, and was eventually shot down by enforcement officers). To determine whether this was a terrorist act or simply multiple murder, one ought to inquire into the possible motives of the killer (in that case motives could have been inferred from his life, his possible statements, his criminal record, any links he might have had with terrorist groups, and so on).

Another example can also be useful for illustration purposes, although it relates to terrorist groups that were not involved in transnational terrorism. In the 1970s some terrorist groups in Italy and Germany (respectively, the Red Brigades and the *Rote Armee Fraktion*) carried out armed robberies against banks to replenish the organization's funds. Here the motivation of the criminal act was not personal (to acquire a private gain), but collective (to boost the organization's cash). Yet the action was not terrorist in nature, but an ordinary criminal offence, because another crucial element proper to terrorism was lacking (the purpose of spreading terror or compelling through criminal conduct an authority to take a certain stand). However, this conclusion does not exclude that individual national criminal systems may consider that, since the

In summary, for terrorism to materialize, two subjective elements (mens rea) are required: first, the subjective element (*intent*) proper to any underlying criminal offence: the requisite psychological element of murder, wounding, kidnapping, hi-jacking, and so on (*dolus generalis*); second, the *specific intent* of compelling a public or a prominent private authority to take, or refrain from taking, an action (*dolus specialis*).

8.4 SPECIFIC SUB-CATEGORIES OF TERRORISM AS AN INTERNATIONAL CRIME

At the time when ideological clashes mired the international discussion on terrorism, preventing the achievement of general consensus on the matter, in order to break the deadlock states opted for the passing of international conventions on specific categories of conduct. They thus agreed upon a string of conventions through which they imposed on contracting parties the obligation to make punishable and to prosecute in their domestic legal orders certain classes of actions. These actions were defined in each convention by indicating the principal outward elements of the offence. The conventions refrained from terming the conduct terrorist, nor did they point to the purpose of the conduct or motive of the perpetrators. Instead, they confined themselves to setting out the *objective elements* of prohibited conduct.

This applies to *i*) acts that, whether or not they are offences under national law, may or do jeopardize the safety of aircraft, or of persons or property therein, or which jeopardize good order and discipline aboard;[7] *ii*) the unlawful taking control, by force or threat thereof or by any other form of intimidation, of an aircraft in flight;[8] *iii*) acts of violence against persons on board an aircraft in flight or against the aircraft;[9] *iv*) murder and other violent acts against internationally protected persons or their official premises, private accommodation, or means of transport;[10] *v*) unlawful possession, use, transfer, or theft of nuclear material as well as threat to use it;[11] *vi*) taking control of a ship by force or threat thereof or any other form of intimidation or acts of violence against persons aboard or against the ship;[12] *vii*) taking control over a fixed platform by force or threat thereof or any other form of intimidation, or acts of violence against persons on board or against the platform;[13] *viii*) acts of violence against persons at an airport serving international civil aviation or against the facilities of the airport;[14] *ix*) the manufacture, or the movement

aforementioned acts were performed to support a terrorist organization, the crimes involved must be characterized as terrorist at least for such purposes as jurisdiction, the use of special investigative methods, and so on.

[7] Art. 1(b) of the 1963 Tokyo Convention on Offences and Certain Other Acts Committed on Board Aircraft.

[8] Art. 1 (a) of the 1970 Hague Convention for the Suppression of Unlawful Seizure of Aircraft.

[9] Art. 1(1) of the 1971 Montreal Convention for the Suppression of Unlawful Acts against the Safety of Civil Aviation.

[10] Art. 2(1) of the 1973 Convention on the Prevention and Punishment of Crimes against Internationally Protected Persons, Including Diplomatic Agents.

[11] Art. 7 of the 1979 Vienna Convention on the Physical Protection of Nuclear Material.

[12] Art. 3(1) of the 1988 Rome Convention for the Suppression of Unlawful Acts against the Safety of Maritime Navigation.

[13] Art. 2 of the 1988 Rome Protocol for the Suppression of Unlawful Acts against the Safety of Fixed Platforms Located on the Continental Shelf.

[14] Art. II of the 1988 Montreal Protocol for the Suppression of Unlawful Acts of Violence at Airports Serving International Civil Aviation.

into or out of a territory, of unmarked plastic explosives;[15] x) the delivery, placing, discharging, or detonation of explosive or other lethal device in a place of public use, a state or government facility, a public transportation system, or an infrastructure facility.[16]

Other Conventions, instead, besides setting out the objective elements of criminal conduct, also place emphasis on the *purpose* pursued by the perpetrators. This holds true for the 1979 Montreal Convention against the Taking of Hostages, as well as the 1999 Convention for the Suppression of the Financing of Terrorism. Both legal instruments characterize the terrorist actions they deal with as intended to compel a state or an international organization to do or to abstain from doing any act; in addition, the latter Convention contemplates the purpose of intimidating a population.[17]

It is warranted to contend that for the whole range of aforementioned conduct the hallmarks of terrorism as an international crime in time of peace, outlined above, were considered *implicit* in the banning of such conduct. Indeed, the primary purpose of those Conventions was to put a stop to terrorist conduct belonging to each category of action banned by the Conventions and increasingly ubiquitous when those legal texts were drafted.

Nevertheless, as the classes of action prohibited by the first ten Conventions mentioned above are very broad, one cannot exclude from the scope of such Conventions conduct that, although clearly banned by them, does not fall under the category of terrorism for lack of the requisite elements. For instance, the hijacking of a plane by a robber that aims at obtaining a huge sum of money as a ransom or the release of some fellow criminals in exchange for saving the passengers, plainly falls under the 1970 Hague Convention, without, however, constituting an act of international terrorism proper.

8.5 TERRORISM IN ARMED CONFLICT: A SUB-CATEGORY OF WAR CRIMES

8.5.1 THE PROHIBITION OF RESORT TO TERRORISM IN ARMED CONFLICT AND THE CRIMINALIZATION OF ITS VIOLATION

At present, both IHL and ICL already cover acts of terrorism performed during an international or internal armed conflict.

International rules indisputably ban terrorism in time of armed conflict. Art. 33(1) of the Fourth Geneva Convention of 1949 prohibits 'all measures [...] of terrorism' against

---

[15] Arts II and III of the 1991 Montreal Convention on the Marking of Plastic Explosives for the Purpose of Detection.

[16] Art. 2(1) of the 1998 International Convention for the Suppression of Terrorist Bombings.

[17] Art. 1(1) of the Convention on the Taking of Hostages provides that 'Any person who seizes or detains or threatens to kill, to injure or to continue to detain another person (hereinafter referred to as the "hostage") in order to compel a third party, namely a State, an international intergovernmental organization, a natural or juridical person, or a group of persons, to do or abstain from doing any act as an explicit or implicit condition for the release of the hostage commits the offence of taking hostages ("hostage-taking") within the meaning of this Convention.'

Art. 2 (1) (b) of the Convention on the Financing of Terrorism provides that a person commits an offence within the meaning of the Convention if that person provides or collects funds to carry out among other things any act 'intended to cause death or serious bodily injury to a civilian, to any other person not taking an active part in the hostilities in a situation of armed conflict, when the purpose of such act, by its nature or context, is to intimidate a population, or to compel a government or an international organization to do or to abstain from doing any act'.

civilians. Although the provision was primarily calculated to forestall terrorism by Occupying Powers or, more generally, by belligerents,[18] terrorist acts are also prohibited if perpetrated by civilians or organized groups in occupied territories or in the territory of a party to the conflict. Thus, Article 33(1) is a provision of general purport, applicable in any situation (whether terrorism is resorted to in the territory of one of the belligerents, in the combat area, or in an occupied territory).

A similar provision is contained in the Second Additional Protocol of 1977. Article 4(2)(d) prohibits 'acts of terrorism' against 'all persons who do not take a direct part or have ceased to take part in hostilities, whether or not their liberty has been restricted' (Article 4(1)).

The two Protocols also spell out the general prohibition of terrorism. Article 51(2) of the First Protocol prohibits 'acts or threats of violence the primary purpose of which is to spread terror among the civilian population'. Article 13(2) of the Second Protocol repeats this prohibition word for word. It can be safely contended that all these provisions reflect, or have turned into customary law.[19]

Thus, IHL proscribes terrorism both in international and non-international armed conflict. The question, however, arises of whether, in addition to addressing its prohibition to states, customary international law and treaty law also *criminalize* terrorism in armed conflict as a war crime. An ICTY Trial Chamber convincingly proved in 2003 in *Galić* that already in 1992 (when the facts at issue in that case occurred) a serious violation of the prohibition against terrorizing the civilian population entailed, at least under treaty law, the individual criminal responsibility for war crimes of the person breaching the rule (§§ 113–29).[20] The ICTY, however, preferred to use the term the war crime at issue 'crime of spreading terror', instead of 'terrorism'.

Contrary to this holding one could object that the Statute of the ICC, which carefully and extensively lists in Article 8 the various classes of war crimes subject to the ICC jurisdiction, fails to mention resort to terror against civilians. This argument would not, however, be compelling. Indeed, as noted (see 1.2) the various provisions of the ICC Statute are not intended to codify existing customary rules; this is borne out by Article 10 of the Statute ('Nothing in this Part shall be interpreted as limiting or prejudicing in any way existing or developing rules of international law for purposes other than this Statute'), as well as by the fact that some specific provisions of the Statute concerning the crimes over

---

[18] According to the ICRC Commentary, Art. 33(1) was aimed primarily at forestalling a common practice, that of belligerents resorting to 'intimidatory measures to terrorise the population' with a view to preventing hostile acts (see ICRC, *Commentary, Fourth Geneva Convention* (Geneva, ICRC, 1958), at 225–6).

[19] In *Strugar and others (Interlocutory Appeal)* the ICTY Appeals Chamber held that 'the principles prohibiting attacks on civilians and unlawful attacks on civilian objects stated in Articles 51 and 52 of Additional Protocol 1 and Article 13 of Additional Protocol II are principles of customary international law' (§ 10).

It is notable that in 1977, at the close of the Geneva Diplomatic Conference on the Reaffirmation of International Humanitarian Law, the United Kingdom stated that Art. 51(2) was a 'valuable reaffirmation of existing customary rules of international law designed to protect civilians (CDDH, *Official records*, vol. VI, at 164, § 119).

The 2004 British *Manual of the Law of Armed Conflict*, in referring to the prohibition of 'terror attacks', seems clearly based on the assumption that this rule is general in nature (§ 5.21.1).

The important research work undertaken by the ICRC on customary law also concludes that a customary rule has evolved on this matter (see J.-M. Henckaerts and L. Doswald-Beck, *Customary International Humanitarian Law*, vol. I (Cambridge: Cambridge University Press, 2005), at 8).

[20] It would seem, however, that the Trial Chamber's finding that the prohibition of terror in armed conflict was criminalized was essentially limited to the case at issue and to the accused standing trial. In addition, the Trial Chamber left open the question of the possible criminalization of terror under *customary* international law (see § 138).

which the Court has jurisdiction go beyond customary or previous treaty rules, whereas others only partially take account of customary law.

Support for the criminalization of terrorist acts as war crimes in the course of armed conflict can be found in various normative developments. The relevant provisions of the Statutes of the ICTR and the SCSL, in granting these two criminal tribunals jurisdiction over violations of international rules of humanitarian law, include 'acts of terrorism'.[21] This proves that the drafters of those Statutes took the view that such acts may amount to war crimes. Also Article 20(f)(iv) of the 1996 ILC Draft Code of Crimes against Peace and Security of Mankind considers that 'acts of terrorism' committed in non-international armed conflict constitute war crimes. Furthermore, it seems significant that Art. 2(1)(b) of the 1999 Convention of the Financing of Terrorism explicitly refers to 'a situation of armed conflict', thus implying that terrorist acts can be committed in such a 'situation'. Of course the Convention is only binding on the contracting parties. Nevertheless, so far the Convention has been ratified or acceded to by almost all states of the world, namely 174. Only three of these states—Egypt, Jordan, and Syria—entered reservations to the relevant treaty stipulation, reservations to which numerous other contracting parties objected that they were incompatible with the object and scope of the Convention. The provision at issue is therefore indicative of the generally held view that terrorism is also criminalized in time of armed conflict.

In summary, attacks on civilians and other 'protected persons' in the course of an armed conflict, aiming at spreading terror, may amount to war crimes (although not to grave breaches of the Geneva Conventions,[22] with the consequence that the specific system of criminal repression envisaged by the Geneva Conventions over such crimes do not apply[23]).

8.5.2 LEGAL INGREDIENTS OF TERRORISM AS A WAR CRIME

Let us now consider the constitutive elements of terrorism as a war crime. It would seem that in IHL terrorism as a war crime has a narrower scope than the notion contemplated by the whole body of international law in time of peace.

First of all, the prohibited conduct arguably consists of any violent action or threat of such action against civilians or other persons not taking a direct part in armed hostilities (wounded, shipwrecked, prisoners of war). It can be inferred both from the whole spirit and purpose of international humanitarian law and also from the wording of Articles 4(1) and (2)(d) of the Second Additional Protocol (a rule that, it is submitted, codifies a general principle applicable to any armed conflict),[24] which attacks on combatants not being

---

[21] Art. 4(d) of the 1994 Statute of the ICTR provides that the Tribunal has jurisdiction over violations of common Article 3 of the Geneva Conventions and the Second Additional Protocol and explicitly provides for jurisdiction over 'acts of terrorism'. Art. 3(d) of the 2000 Statute of the Special Court for Sierra Leone grants the Court jurisdiction over 'acts of terrorism'.

[22] The relevant provisions of the 1949 Geneva Conventions (Articles 50/51/130/147) do not include 'acts or measures of terrorism' among the offences amounting to grave breaches.

[23] As rightly held, with regard to the war crime of torture in armed conflict, by the Hague District Court in the *Afghani* cases. The Court rightly emphasized the importance of the common provision of the Conventions (Articles 49(3); 50(3); 129(3); 146(3)) stipulating that 'Each High Contracting Party shall take measures necessary for the suppression of all acts contrary to the provisions of the present Convention other than the grave breaches defined in the following Article.'

[24] This provision is simply an expansion and elaboration of common Art. 3 of the four Geneva Conventions of 1949, which the International Court of Justice held in 1986 in *Nicaragua (merits)* to constitute 'a minimum yardstick' applicable to any armed conflict (at § 218). For the state practice and the practice of international organizations that can corroborate the proposition set out above in the text, see the wealth

actively engaged in armed hostilities can also amount to terrorism: for instance, attacks (or threats of attack) on officers attending a mass or praying in a mosque, a church, or a synagogue, or military personnel taking their children to the cinema. This proposition is borne out by the aforementioned Article 2(1)(b) of the Convention for the Suppression of the Financing of Terrorism, which includes among the possible victims of terrorist acts in time of armed conflict 'any other persons [than civilians] not taking an active part in the hostilities'. Furthermore, as rightly stressed by the Italian Court of Cassation in *Bouyahia and others* (at 18–19), acts may be held to be terrorist if they are carried out against servicemen engaged not in warlike actions but humanitarian operations, or if such acts are performed against civilians and military alike (for instance, if an attack is made against a military vehicle in a crowded market, with the consequence that both civilians and military are among the victims).

The violent action or threat thereof can also be directed against a civilian object, even if it is empty (for instance, a square, a private building, a theatre), as long as the goal pursued in taking such action is that of terrorizing the population. As rightly noted in the 2004 British Manual, the rule prohibiting terror attacks 'would apply, for instance, to car bombs installed in busy shopping streets, even if no civilians are killed or injured by them, their object being to create panic among the population' (§ 5.21.1). As for threats, again the British Manual rightly pointed out that 'threats of violence would include, for example, threat to annihilate the enemy's civilian population' (§ 5.21.1). In contrast, the prohibition on terror does not cover terror caused as a by-product of attacks on military objectives 'or as a result of genuine warning of impending attacks on such objectives'.[25]

We can thus move to the *subjective element* of the action or threat of action. Articles 51(2) of the First Additional Protocol and 13(2) of the Second Additional Protocol, which, as I stated above, can be taken to spell out in many respects the terse content of other provisions on IHL, make it clear that terrorist acts in armed conflict are acts calculated to 'spread terror' among the civilian population or other protected persons. Here, then, the purpose of coercing a public (or private) authority to take a certain course of action disappears or, at least, wanes. The only conspicuous purpose appears to be that of *terrorizing the enemy*. In other words, in IHL terrorist acts are performed within the framework of the general goal of defeating the enemy. Their ultimate purpose is to contribute to the war effort. Instead of simply attacking civilians, a belligerent carries out actions (for instance, random killing of persons passing through a bridge, or haphazard blowing up of civilian installations, or systematic shelling of an empty place in a populated area) designed to beget profound insecurity and anxiety in the population (and consequently in the enemy belligerent).

It is thus clear that also in time of armed conflict international criminal law requires *intent*, with the consequence that, as rightly emphasized in *Galić*, simple *dolus eventualis* or recklessness must be ruled out.[26]

In sum, during an armed conflict, belligerent acts of terrorism, being prohibited and criminalized, are covered both by IHL and ICL. They may also be covered by rules on

of material collected in J.-M. Henckaerts and L. Doswald-Beck, *Customary International Humanitarian Law*, vol. I, at 306–83. See also the *Report of the International Commission of Inquiry on Darfur*, UN doc. S/2005/60 (25 January 2005), at §§ 154–67.

[25] See M. Bothe, K.-J. Partsch, and W. Solf, *New Rules for the Victims of Armed Conflicts* (The Hague, Boston, London: M. Nijhoff Publishers, 1982), at 301; *The Manual of the Law of Armed Conflict*, at § 5.21.1.

[26] The Trial Chamber noted that 'the Prosecution is required to prove not only that the Accused accepted the likelihood that terror would result from the illegal acts—or, in other words, that he was aware of the possibility that terror would result—but that that was the result which he specifically intended. The crime of terror is a specific-intent crime' (§ 136).

terrorism as a discrete crime to the extent that a state fighting terrorism is bound by an international convention that addresses terrorism both in time of peace and in time of war. In this event there would be a twofold legal characterization of the same conduct or the combined simultaneous application of two different bodies of law to the same conduct or set of acts. A case in point is the Convention on the Financing of Terrorism. If a state is party to such Convention, it may apply its provisions to the financing of terrorist acts performed or planned in a foreign country where an armed conflict is under way. It would consequently punish the financing of violent acts abroad directed against persons not taking an active part in armed hostilities (whereas it would not consider unlawful the financing of groups solely aimed at attacking enemy armed forces in the foreign country concerned). It may also bring to trial for war crimes the perpetrators of terrorist actions abroad, who benefited from the financing in question.

8.6 TERRORISM AS A CRIME AGAINST HUMANITY

Terrorist acts can amount to crimes against humanity, subject to a number of conditions.

First of all, it can be inferred from the relevant international rules and case law on crimes against humanity that terrorist acts may fall under this category of crimes, whether they are perpetrated in time of war or peace. Furthermore, they must cause (or consist of) the following *conduct: i)* murder; or *ii)* great suffering; or *iii)* serious injury to body or to mental or physical health; or else take the form of *iv)* torture; *v)* rape; or even *vi)* enforced disappearance of persons; namely arrest, detention, or abduction of persons by, or with the authorization, support, or acquiescence of, a state or a political organization, followed by a refusal to acknowledge that deprivation of freedom or to give information on the fate or whereabouts of those persons, with the intention of removing them from the protection of the law for a prolonged period of time.[27]

Terrorist acts must also meet the contextual requirements of the category of crimes under discussion. Consequently terrorist action must be part of a widespread or systematic attack against a civilian population conducted with the support or tolerance or acquiescence of a state or a non-state entity (even if terrorist acts are performed against persons or state officials in *another* state).

Finally, as for the mental element, the perpetrator, in addition to mens rea required for the underlying offence (murder, torture, etc.) must also have *knowledge* that his action is part of a widespread or systematic attack.

It would seem that, as in the case of terrorism as a discrete international crime, also when terrorist acts are such as to amount to crimes against humanity, the *victims* may embrace both civilians and state officials, including members of armed forces. Admittedly, the Statutes of international criminal tribunals, in granting jurisdiction to these tribunals over crimes against humanity, stipulate that they must be perpetrated against a civilian population. In other words, the widespread or systematic attack required as the necessary *context* of a crime against humanity must be one that targets the civilian population.

---

[27] This is the definition of 'enforced disappearance of persons' set out in Article 7(2)(i) of the ICC Statute, which can be taken to be declaratory of an existing (or emerging) rule of customary international law banning and criminalizing that offence. See also Art. 2 of the International Convention for the Protection of All Persons from Enforced Disappearances.

This does not mean, however, that the victims of the underlying offences must perforce be civilians (see 5.7). This is also true in the case of terrorism as a crime against humanity.

Some examples can illustrate the above propositions. In time of peace a group of terrorists, in addition to conducting attacks on civilians, engages in such atrocities against military or police personnel as bombing barracks, blowing up police stations, destroying a major building of the defence ministry, or else kidnapping servicemen and subjecting them to torture or rape. These acts (murder, imprisonment, torture, rape, and so on) should be classified as crimes against humanity. Similarly, it may happen that in time of armed conflict an armed group or organization (or even a state), besides indiscriminately and violently attacking on a large scale civilians and other persons not taking an active part in hostilities, captures, rapes, or tortures enemy combatants for the purpose of spreading terror among the enemy belligerents or to obtain from them the release of imprisoned members of the group or organization (or state). These acts, which normally would be classified as war crimes, may acquire the magnitude of a crime against humanity.

It is clear from the above that, in addition to the aforementioned objective elements, it is also necessary for the author of terrorist acts to entertain the *specific intent* required for terrorism as a discrete crime, namely the purpose of compelling a public or private authority to take, or refrain from taking, a certain course of action, a purpose that may be achieved either by generating fear and anxiety among the public or by other criminal actions.

In summary, terrorism as a crime against humanity substantially constitutes an aggravated form of terrorism as a discrete crime.

SECTION II

MODES OF CRIMINAL LIABILITY

9

PERPETRATION: IN PARTICULAR JOINT AND INDIRECT PERPETRATION

Just as in any national legal system, criminal responsibility in ICL arises not only when a person physically commits a crime but also when he or she is involved in criminal conduct in other ways. In ICL perpetration (or commission) at its most basic level—i.e. involving only a single perpetrator—is the physical carrying out of the prohibited conduct, accompanied by the requisite mental element for the crime. As we shall discuss in Chapter 10, a person can also be held liable for *commission by omission* in ICL where he was under a duty to act and had the ability to do so, but did not. In addition, ICL may impose criminal liability under the theory of indirect perpetration, where the accused uses another person to commit a crime (see 9.3). As for group criminality, it is perhaps trivial to note that international crimes are typically committed on a scale that would be virtually impossible for a single person to achieve on his or her own. As the *Tadić* Appeals Chamber put it:

> Most of the time these crimes do not result from the criminal propensity of single individuals but constitute manifestations of collective criminality: the crimes are often carried out by groups of individuals acting in pursuance of a common criminal design. Although only some members of the group may physically perpetrate the criminal act (murder, extermination, wanton destruction of cities, towns or villages, etc.), the participation and contribution of the other members of the group is often vital in facilitating the commission of the offence in question. It follows that the moral gravity of such participation is often no less—or indeed no different—from that of those actually carrying out the acts in question. (*Tadić*, AC, 1999, § 191)

National legal systems converge in holding that when a crime is committed by an individual person acting alone, then this person is guilty as a principal perpetrator. Likewise, when a crime is committed by more than one person, each performing the same act, all are equally liable as co-perpetrators or principals. In contrast, national legal systems differ when it comes to the conviction and punishment of two or more persons who contribute to a crime in different ways.

For instance, in the classic bank robbery hypothetical, each participant plays a different role: A draws up plans for a bank robbery; B provides the weapons; C performs the actual robbery; D acts as a lookout; E drives the getaway car; and F hides the loot and gives shelter to the robbers. Legal commentators and courts use *descriptive terms* to distinguish between these 'modes of liability': A is an 'accessory before the fact' (he is not a 'principal' for he was not present when the robbery was committed); B is an aider and abettor (or an 'accessory before the fact'); C is a 'first degree principal'; D and E are 'second degree principals' (or 'accomplices'); and F is an 'accessory after the fact'. However, when it comes to establishing the legal consequences attaching to these different roles, national legal systems generally follow two different approaches, termed the *unitary* and *differentiated models* of criminal responsibility.[1] In a unitary system (followed, for instance, in the USA, France, Italy, and Uruguay) all the main participants in a crime face the same charges and the same penalties, regardless of their particular role in the commission of the crime. In practice, however, judges may still draw a distinction between the modes of liability when describing the accused's participation in the crime and meting out the sentence. One participant who is still likely to be singled out in a unitary system is the 'accessory after the fact', who is generally subjected to a statutorily lesser sentence. In differentiated systems (for instance, Germany and Russia) the law draws a *normative* distinction between principals on the one hand and accomplices (or accessories) on the other and provides that persons falling under the latter category must be punished less severely. Thus, for instance, in German law, the scale of penalties for accomplices (at least in the case of aiders and abettors, *Gehilfe*) is less harsh than for the perpetrator (*Täter*). It is not unusual, however, for a legal system to incorporate aspects of both models.

Interestingly, although it is not strictly required by any of the statutes of the modern international criminal courts, the judicial practice has been to classify every charge and conviction by mode of liability. Thus, the discussion of the mode of liability—whether it is, for example, commission, aiding and abetting, ordering, or command responsibility—is a focus of almost every judgment. Such a discussion is more characteristic of a differentiated system. On the other hand, like a unitary system, the statutes of international criminal courts and tribunals do not impose any strict legal consequence to this determination, at least as far as penalties are concerned. Thus, although the judges might have invested a lot of effort in determining the particular mode of liability, this does not result in any automatic sentencing distinction. Of course, to the extent that the mode of liability is descriptive of a greater or lesser role or degree of culpability, this may affect the sentence. For example, in considering the gravity of the offence, the judges take into account the form and degree of responsibility of the convicted person. For this reason, although there is no agreed scale of penalties, the general trend is that perpetration is at the high end of the sentencing range and forms of accomplice liability (such as aiding and abetting) are at the lower end.

We will now discuss the two major theories that are currently in use in ICL to address group criminality, i.e. *i*) joint criminal enterprise; and *ii*) co-perpetration by control over the crime. Under these theories, each participant will be treated as a *principal*,[2] provided that he played a sufficiently important role in the commission of the crime.

---

[1] The *unitary* v. *differentiated* labels are also respectively referred to as *monistic* v. *dualistic*. These terms should not be confused with the terms 'monism' and 'dualism' in public international law used to denote different relationships between international and domestic law.

[2] However, some courts of common law countries have taken the view that participants in a common criminal design may play the role of, and be regarded as, accessories. Thus, for instance, in *Einsatzgruppen*, with regard to common design, the prosecutor T. Taylor, in his closing statement noted that 'the elementary principle must be borne in mind that neither under Control Council Law no. 10 nor under any known system of criminal law is guilt for murder confined to the man who pulls the trigger or buries the corpse. In line with recognized principles common to all civilized legal systems, § 2 of Art. II of Control Council Law no. 10 specifies a number of types of connection with crime which are sufficient to establish guilt. Thus, not only are principals guilty but also accessories, those who take a consenting part in the commission of crime or are connected with plans or enterprises involved in its commission, those who order or abet crime, and those who belong to an organization or group engaged in the commission of crime. These provisions embody no harsh or novel principles of criminal responsibility' (at 372). For a comment on the case, see *Cassese's Companion*, at 863.

Gradations of culpability may be taken into account at the sentencing stage. In addition, although—as we shall see below—joint criminal enterprise focuses on shared intention and co-perpetration focuses on shared action, the application of either theory will yield the same result in most cases. We will then analyse indirect perpetration.

9.1 JOINT CRIMINAL ENTERPRISE

Joint criminal enterprise (JCE) addresses the criminal liability of participants in a common criminal plan. The rationale behind this mode of liability is clear: if those who take part in a common criminal act are aware of its purpose and share its requisite criminal intent, they must share criminal liability, whatever the role and position they may have played in the commission of the crime. JCE requires the prosecution to prove: *i*) the involvement of a plurality of persons in the commission of the crime; *ii*) the existence of a common plan, design, or purpose which amounts to or involves the commission of a crime; and *iii*) the participation of the accused in the JCE in the form of a significant contribution to the crime.

The three categories of JCE will be discussed in more detail below. The distinction between them is based primarily on the required mental element: JCE I, where, as held by the ICTY in *Tadić*, 'all co-defendants, acting pursuant to a common design, possess the same criminal intention' (*Tadić*, AC, § 196); JCE II, substantially a variation of JCE I, where the crimes are committed within the framework of a concentration or detention camp (§ 202); and JCE III, which embraces 'cases involving a common design to pursue one course of conduct where one of the perpetrators commits an act which, while outside the common design, was nevertheless a natural and foreseeable consequence of the effecting of that common purpose' (§ 204).

The element of *significant contribution* distinguishes JCE from the related concepts of conspiracy and membership in a criminal organization (*Milutinović and others* (*Decision on Dragoljub Ojdanić's Motion Challenging Jurisdiction—Joint Criminal Enterprise*), AC, §§ 23–6). Unlike JCE, conspiracy requires only an agreement to commit a crime and is punishable regardless of whether the crime is eventually completed. JCE, on the other hand, is a mode of liability in a completed crime, requiring—in addition to the common criminal purpose—the accused's significant contribution to its commission. For JCE, mere membership in an institutional framework or organization, without more, is insufficient for conviction. Thus, JCE is distinguishable from the *crime* of membership in a criminal organization laid down in the Nuremberg Charter annexed to the London Agreement of 8 August 1945 (Articles 9–11) and addressed in certain respects by the Nuremberg Tribunal.

JCE, a principal perpetrator mode of responsibility, is also distinct from aiding and abetting (see 10.1). The material element, or actus reus, of aiding and abetting requires a substantial contribution to another's crime. This is more than the 'significant' contribution required for JCE. The mental element, however, is higher for JCE. For aiding and abetting the accused merely needs to know that the contribution assists in the commission of the crime. In contrast, to be a principal perpetrator through JCE, the accused must share the common criminal purpose. This difference in mens rea explains why aiding and abetting 'generally involves a lesser degree of individual criminal responsibility than co-perpetration in a joint criminal enterprise' (*Kvočka and others*, AC, § 92; see also *Krnojelac*, AC, § 75 and *Vasiljević*, AC, § 102). According to the ICTY, it is inaccurate to speak of 'aiding and abetting a JCE' because the JCE is not a crime in itself; instead, the aider and abettor aids the principal perpetrator in committing the crime (*Kvočka and others*, AC, § 91).

JCE is widely recognized in ICL. In the *Tadić*, the ICTY Appeals Chamber articulated the doctrine, based on customary international law, particularly as evidenced by the jurisprudence of domestic and international courts. JCE has been applied by the ICTY, ICTR, SCSL,[3] and by national courts adjudicating international crimes such as the War Crimes Chamber of the Court of Bosnia and Herzegovina[4] and the East Timorese Special Panel for Serious Crimes.[5] The STL has also judicially recognized JCE as a mode of liability in ICL.[6] The ECCC accepted the first two categories of JCE, discussed below, but has questioned whether the third category was established in customary international law in 1975 to 1979, the time period of interest to that court.[7]

9.1.1 JCE I: LIABILITY FOR A COMMON PURPOSE

The first category of JCE liability requires the participants to share a common criminal plan, design, or purpose (JCE I or JCE in its 'basic' form). It imposes criminal responsibility on all participants in the JCE for crimes committed pursuant to the common criminal purpose, even though only some of the participants physically perpetrate the crime.

What is important for JCE I is that all participants share the same intent to commit the crime. This common intent necessarily includes the specific intent requirement for crimes such as persecution or genocide. Shared criminal intent is distinct from motive in that it does not require personal satisfaction or enthusiasm. The common criminal purpose can be expressly criminal or it can amount to or involve the commission of crimes (see, for instance, *Brima and others*, AC, §§ 76–80). For example, the shared goal to take control of territory may not be criminal in itself, yet it may form the shared intent for a JCE if it involves the ethnic cleansing of the territory by deporting all people of other ethnicities. The shared intent does not need to be manifested in any formal agreement. It can arise extemporaneously. However, the intent must be shared in the sense that it is common to all the participants; it is not sufficient for the participants to each have formed an independent, yet identical, intent. The requirement of shared intent limits the scope of the crimes for which each individual can be criminally responsible. For this reason, it is difficult to imagine shared intent in the type of 'vast joint criminal enterprise' contemplated by the ICTR Appeals Chamber in the *Karemera* case (*Karemera and others* (*Decision on Jurisdictional Appeals: Joint Criminal Enterprise*), AC, §§ 11–18; see also, *Brđanin*, AC, §§ 420–5).

All the participants in a JCE I are treated as criminally responsible for the crime if they made a *significant* (though not necessarily substantial) contribution to the commission of a crime (*Brđanin*, AC, § 430). The contribution is not limited to fulfilling elements of the crime; it can also include various means of supporting the other members of the JCE to commit the crime. For example, in a JCE to murder, all the participants can be convicted even if only one of them actually shoots the gun that kills the victim. The other participants who share the common criminal purpose—for example, the participant who brings

---

[3] See e.g. *Brima and others*, AC, §§ 72–5.

[4] See e.g. *Prosecutor's Office of Bosnia and Herzegovina* v. *Milorad Trbić*, First Instance Verdict, §§ 203–14 (reading JCE I and II into Art. 180(1) of the Bosnia and Herzegovina Criminal Code), *affirmed*, Second Instance Verdict; *Rašević and Todović*, Second Instance Verdict, at 26-7.

[5] See *Cardoso*, 04/2001, Special Panel for the Trial of Serious Crimes in the District Court of Dili, East Timor, Judgment 5 April 2003, §§ 367–76; *De Deus* 2a/2004, Special Panel for the Trial of Serious Crimes in the District Court of Dili, East Timor, Judgment, 12 April 2005, at 13.

[6] STL, *Interlocutory Decision on the Applicable Law*, AC, § 237.

[7] Ieng and others (Decision on Appeals against the Co-Investigative Judges Order on Joint Criminal Enterprise (JCE)), §§ 69-83.

the victim to the scene of the crime or the participant who drives the getaway car—are also criminally responsible for the murder. Moreover, the contribution need not be criminal in itself. For example, public statements protected by freedom of speech were considered to be part of Momčilo Krajišnik's contribution to ethnically cleansing Bosnian-Serb territory (*Krajišnik*, AC, §§ 218, 695–6). An accused can also make a significant contribution to the crimes of the JCE through omission. General Gotovina, for example, was found to have made a significant contribution to the common purpose of deporting Serbs from Croatia by failing to prevent the troops under his control from committing crimes (*Gotovina and others*, TC, § 2370; see also *Kvočka and others*, AC, § 187; *Milutinović and others*, TC, vol. I, § 103). The extent of the contribution can be reflected in sentencing (*Brđanin*, AC, § 432).

Individual criminal liability based on a common plan finds its customary international law origins in the post-Second World War jurisprudence.[8] The *Ponzano* case, for instance, concerned the unlawful killing of four British prisoners of war by German troops. The Judge Advocate explained that in order to convict, the accused must have knowledge of the intended purpose of the criminal enterprise and stressed that

> [T]o be concerned in the commission of a criminal offence [...] does not only mean that you are the person who in fact inflicted the fatal injury and directly caused death, be it by shooting or by any other violent means; it also means an indirect degree of participation [...] [I]n other words, he must be the cog in the wheel of events leading up to the result which in fact occurred. He can further that object not only by giving orders for a criminal offence to be committed, but he can further that object by a variety of other means (at 6).[9]

9.1.2 JCE II: LIABILITY FOR PARTICIPATION IN A COMMON CRIMINAL PLAN WITHIN AN INSTITUTIONAL FRAMEWORK

The second form of JCE liability (JCE II or JCE in its 'systemic' form) addresses criminal responsibility for participation in a criminal design that is implemented in an institution such as an internment, detention, or concentration camp. In a camp, or similar criminal system, all participants bear responsibility for the crimes committed within the system. Unlike the first category, JCE II does not require proof of an express or implied

---

[8] In the case of *Georg Otto Sandrock et al.* (*Almelo Trial*) a British court convicted three Germans under the doctrine of 'common enterprise' for murdering a British prisoner of war. Each had the intention to kill, although each of them played a different role (at 35, 40–1). In *Hölzer and others*, tried before a Canadian military court, the Judge Advocate emphasized that the three accused (Germans who had killed a Canadian prisoner of war) knew that the purpose of taking the Canadian to a particular area was to kill him. The Judge Advocate spoke of a 'common enterprise' with regard to that murder (at pp. 341, 347, 349), summarized in *Cassese's Companion*, at 726. In *Jepsen and others*, before a British court, the prosecutor argued (and the Judge Advocate did not rebut) that '[I]f Jepsen was joining in this voluntary slaughter of eighty or so people, helping the others by doing his share of killing, the whole eighty odd deaths can be laid at his door and at the door of any single man who was in any way assisting in that act' (at 241). In *Schonfeld and others* the Judge Advocate stated that: 'if several persons combine for an unlawful purpose or for a lawful purpose to be effected by unlawful means, and one of them in carrying out that purpose, kills a man, it is murder in all who are present [...] provided that the death was caused by a member of the party in the course of his endeavours to effect the common object of the assembly' (at 68). See also *Krauch and others* (*I. G. Farben* trial), 39–40; *Buhler) Krupp and others*, at 391–3; *USA* v. *Josef Altstötter and others*, at 1195–9; *Einsatzgruppen*, at 369–73, 578, 584. For a comment on all these cases, see the relevant entries in *Cassese's Companion*.

[9] Reported in 5 JICJ (2007), at 238. For a comment on the case, see *Cassese's Companion*, at 670.

agreement to commit a crime. Instead, proof of the accused's participation in the system of ill-treatment serves the same legal function as an agreement.

The mental element required for JCE II is knowledge of the criminal system and the intent to further its criminal purpose. Each participant in the criminal institutional framework who is aware of the crimes in which the institution or its members engage must implicitly or expressly share the criminal intent to commit such crimes. It cannot be otherwise, because any person discharging a task of some consequence in the institution could refrain from participating in its criminal activity by leaving. Knowledge of the criminal nature of the system can be inferred, for example, from the accused's position within the camp, time spent in the camp, contact with detainees, and the opportunity of the accused to observe the ill-treatment or its effects (see, e.g., *Kvočka and others*, TC, § 324; see also AC, § 201).

As with JCE I, criminal liability arises if the participant makes a *significant contribution* to the joint criminal enterprise. In addition to the camp's leaders and the physical perpetrators, JCE II responsibility extends, for example, to those who discharge administrative duties indispensable to the achievement of the camp's main goals such as registering the incoming inmates, recording their deaths, or providing medical treatment. It bears noting that the requirement of a significant contribution was not explicitly articulated by the ICTY Appeals Chamber in *Tadić* (§ 227). However, it is particularly important in a JCE II because there will be many people peripherally involved in the system (for example, those who merely clean the laundry in a prison camp) who should not ordinarily incur criminal liability because their contribution to the enterprise is insufficient.

Institutional participants in a JCE constitute an indispensable cog in the criminal machinery. By fulfilling their administrative or other operational tasks, they contribute to the commission of crimes. Without their willing support, crimes could not be perpetrated. The man who, upon arrival of new trains at Auschwitz, separated the men and women from the children and the elderly, knowing that this determined who should be a forced labourer and who should instead be sent immediately to gas chambers, was instrumental in the perpetration of extermination. To avoid criminal responsibility, he should have asked to be relieved of his duties. This decision was possible and was sometimes permitted, although it often involved being sent to combat zones on the Eastern Front. Similarly, the driver of a train carrying hundreds of detainees to Auschwitz could have been held criminally liable for his participation in extermination, so long as he knew what would happen to the people he was transporting and was shown to share the intent to exterminate them by willingly continuing to fulfil his role.

The customary international law status of JCE II liability is grounded in the post-Second World War jurisprudence.[10] One can find a particularly clear illustration of this category of criminality in *Alfons Klein and others* (the *Hadamar* trial), heard by a US Military Commission sitting at Wiesbaden. The accused were seven Germans who killed over 400 Polish and Russian forced labourers who were brought to the 'hospital' for supposed treatment but were instead killed by lethal injection. Afterwards, their medical records and death certificates were falsified. The prosecution alleged that the seven accused 'acting jointly and in pursuance of a common intent' 'did [...] wilfully, deliberately and

---

[10] See e.g. *Dachau Concentration Camp Martin Gottfried Weiss*, brought before a US Tribunal under Control Council Law no. 10 (at 5, 14–16); *Nadler and others*, also discussing *Mauthausen Concentration Camp Case*; decided by a British Court of Appeal under Control Council Law no. 10 (pp. 132–4), commented upon in *Cassese's Companion*, at 833; *Auschwitz Concentration Camp*, decided by a German court (at 882), commented upon in *Cassese's Companion*, at 825; *Belsen*, decided by a British military court sitting in Germany (at 120, 121).

wrongfully, aid, abet and participate in the killing of human beings of Polish and Russian nationality' (LRTWC, I, at 47). In his Opening Argument the prosecutor emphasized that all those who participate in a common criminal enterprise are equally guilty as 'co-principals', whatever the role played by each single participant. He offered an eloquent illustration of the rationale behind the legal notion he was invoking:

> At this Hadamar mill there was operated a production line of death. Not a single one of these accused could do all the things that were necessary in order to have the entire scheme of things in operation. For instance, the accused Klein, the administrative head, could not make the initial arrangements, receive those people, attend to undressing them, make arrangements for their death chamber, and at the same time go up there and use the needle that did the dirty work, and then also turn around and haul the bodies out and bury them, and falsify the records and the death certificates. No, when you do business on a wholesale production basis as they did at the Hadamar Institution, that murder factory, it means that you have to have several people doing different things of that illegal operation in order to produce the results, and you cannot draw a distinction between the man who may have initially conceived the idea of killing them and those who participated in the commission of those offences. Now, there is no question but that any person who participated in that matter, no matter to what extent, technically is guilty of the charge that has been brought [...] every single one of the accused has overtly and affirmatively participated in this entire network that brought about the illegal result. (205–7)

The Court upheld the charges, sentencing the administrative head of the hospital and two nurses to death, the physician to life imprisonment and hard labour, the book-keeper to 35 years and hard labour, the third nurse to 25 years and hard labour; the doorman and caretaker to 30 years and hard labour LRTWC, I, at 51–2).

Courts also applied JCE II in cases where members of military or administrative units running concentration camps committed crimes. In such cases the accused held some position of authority within the hierarchy of the concentration camps. Normally, the defendants were charged with having acted in pursuance of a common design to kill or mistreat prisoners and hence to commit war crimes.[11] When found guilty, they were regarded as co-principals in the various crimes of ill-treatment, because of their objective 'position of authority' within the concentration camp system and because they had 'the power to look after the inmates and make their life satisfactory' but failed to do so (Belsen, § 121).

In these cases, as the ICTY Appeals Chamber in *Tadić* indicated,

> the required actus reus was the active participation in the enforcement of a system of repression [...] The *mens rea* element comprised: *i*) knowledge of the nature of the system; and *ii*) the intent to further the common concerted design to ill-treat inmates. It is important to note that, in these cases, the requisite intent could also be inferred from the position of authority held by the camp personnel. Indeed, it was scarcely necessary to prove intent where the individual's high rank or authority would have, in and of itself, indicated an awareness of the common design and an intention to participate therein. All those convicted were found guilty of the war crime of ill-treatment, although of course the penalty varied according to the degree of participation of each accused (*Tadić*, AC, § 203).

In *Kvočka and others*, an ICTY Trial Chamber found a JCE II at the Omarska camp in Bosnia and Herzegovina. According to the Chamber, the Omarska camp was a JCE,

---

[11] In his summing up in the *Belsen* case, the Judge Advocate took up the three requirements set out by the prosecution as necessary to establish guilt in each case: (i) the existence of an organized system to ill-treat the detainees and commit the various crimes alleged; (ii) the accused's awareness of the nature of the system; and (iii) the fact that the accused in some way actively participated in enforcing the system, i.e. encouraged, aided, and abetted or in any case participated in the realization of the common criminal design (120–1).

'a facility used to interrogate, discriminate against, and otherwise abuse non-Serbs from Prijedor and which functioned as a means to rid the territory of or subjugate non-Serbs' (*Kvočka and others*, TC, § 323). The Chamber held that the continuous perpetration of crimes in the camp was common knowledge to anybody working there (§ 324). It convicted the five defendants, four of whom occupied positions at the camp: Kvočka was the camp commander's assistant; Kos was a guard shift commander; Radić was a shift commander; Prcać was *de facto* a deputy camp commander. Zigić, a local taxi driver and thug, held no official position at the camp. He visited the camp on, at most, ten occasions, during which he twice mistreated detainees. The Trial Chamber convicted him of participating in the JCE and held him accountable for all the crimes that occurred in Omarska. The Appeals Chamber overturned this conviction, finding that although there is no requirement that a JCE member hold an official position, Zigić's contributions to the JCE were insufficient to qualify him as a JCE member. His contributions were 'only mosaic stones in the general picture of violence and oppression' (*Kvočka and others*, AC, § 599). In later cases the Appeals Chamber has stressed that although an accused's contribution to a JCE need not be 'necessary or substantial', it must at least be 'significant' (*Brđanin*, AC, § 430).

9.1.3 JCE III: CRIMINAL LIABILITY BASED ON FORESIGHT AND VOLUNTARY ASSUMPTION OF RISK

The third form of JCE responsibility (JCE III or the 'extended' form of JCE) arises when one or more members of a JCE I or II commits an additional crime that was not part of the common criminal design. For instance, in a JCE I to forcibly expel civilians from an occupied territory, one member of the JCE kills a civilian during the expulsion. If the other JCE members could foresee the possibility of this crime, then they can also be held accountable for the murder. The ICTY Appeals Chamber has explained that the possibility standard 'is not satisfied by implausibly remote scenarios'. The risk must be 'sufficiently substantial' to allow the accused to foresee the crime.[12] An example in domestic criminal law of this mode of liability is that of a gang who agree to rob a bank without killing anyone, carrying only fake weapons. One of the members, however, takes a real gun with him to the bank with the intent to kill, if need be. Suppose another participant in the common criminal plan sees this gang member stealthily carrying the real gun. If the armed man then kills a bank teller during the robbery, the one who knew that he was carrying a real gun may be held liable for robbery and murder, like the killer. He was in a position to anticipate that the robber who was armed with a real gun would use it to kill if something went wrong during the robbery. Although he did not share the mens rea of the murderer, he foresaw the event and willingly took the risk that it might come about. If he did not accept the risk, then he had a number of options available. For example, he could have told the other robbers that there was a serious danger of a murder being committed; taken the weapons away from the armed robber; withdrawn from the bank robbery; or even dropped out of the gang. The other robbers, who did not know that their colleague was carrying a real gun, would only be liable for armed robbery because the murder would not have been foreseeable to them.

JCE III only arises if the participant who did not have the intent to commit the 'incidental' offence, was nevertheless in a position to foresee its commission and willingly took

---

[12] *Karadžić* (*Decision on Prosecution's Motion Appealing Trial Chamber's Decision on JCE III Foreseeability*), AC, § 18 (confirming that the correct standard is awareness of a 'possibility'. Awareness of a 'probability' is not required.)

that risk by continuing to participate in the criminal enterprise. JCE III responsibility is thus premised on the execution of a common criminal purpose; that is, a JCE I or II. All of the participants have already joined together to commit international crimes of extreme gravity. Under these circumstances society can legitimately expect the participants in an existing JCE to be particularly alert to the possible consequences of their concerted criminal actions and hold them criminally accountable if additional crimes are committed in the execution of the common purpose.

Some commentators have argued that this third category of JCE breaches the principle of culpability (*nullum crimen sine culpa*) and amounts to guilt by association. The concern is that under JCE III the 'secondary offender' (who foresaw the additional crimes of another JCE member) is treated as equally culpable as the 'primary offender' (who committed the additional offence). This approach, it is argued, places the person who deliberately brought about the death of the victim on an equal footing with another who did not have the intent to kill. The STL Appeals Chamber responded directly to this concern (STL, AC, *Interlocutory Decision on the Applicable Law*, 244–9). It explained that although the secondary offender may not have had the intention (*dolus*) to commit the additional crime, this crime was rendered possible by his continued participation in the JCE, despite his ability to foresee the additional crime. The STL Appeals Chamber also noted that the differences in culpability should be addressed in sentencing, with the secondary offender receiving a lower sentence than the primary offender. Finally, as the STL Appeals Chamber explained, JCE III is founded on considerations of public policy. When people work together to commit crimes, there is a heightened danger to society. These policy considerations were aptly spelled out in a domestic setting by the English House of Lords in *R v. Powell (Anthony) and English*. In Lord Steyn's view, by punishing the 'secondary offender' the law intends to convey the message that he should have opposed or impeded the crime of the 'primary offender':

> It is just that a secondary party who foresees that the primary offender might kill with the intent sufficient for murder, and assists and encourages the primary offender in the criminal enterprise on this basis, should be guilty of murder. He ought to be criminally liable for harm which he foresaw and which in fact resulted from the crime he assisted and encouraged. [...] The criminal justice system exists to control crime. A prime function of that system must be to deal justly but effectively with those who join with others in criminal enterprises. Experience has shown that joint criminal enterprises only too readily escalate into the commission of greater offences. (§ 14)

Moreover, at least some of the concern about using JCE III results from the rudimentary nature of ICL. In a mature legal system, it would be possible to take account of the lesser degree of culpability of the 'secondary offender' by qualifying his culpability with a charge less than that against the 'primary offender'. For example, in the classic bank robbery scenario, if the 'primary offender' commits a murder, the 'secondary offender' might be found guilty of the *lesser included offence* of manslaughter based on his lack of direct intention to kill. Such sophisticated distinctions are not available in international criminal law. Each category of international crimes (such as genocide, crimes against humanity, or war crimes) has developed independently in customary international law. Although certain trends can be observed, there is no formal hierarchical relationship between the different crimes; one crime is not included in the other. Since there is no lesser offence, it is not possible for the court to recognize a lesser offender by convicting him of a different category of crimes (for example, by substituting a war crime for a crime against humanity). In relation to a small number of crimes, it may be possible to find a lesser offence within the same class of crimes. In crimes against humanity, for example, it might be possible to convict a lesser offender of the crime of 'other inhumane acts'. A lower sentence can also be imposed to recognize the lower intent.

The critics who oppose JCE III by arguing that it comes close to a form of 'strict liability' generally neglect a crucial factor: incidental criminal liability based on foresight and risk is a mode of liability that depends on the prior existence of a JCE I or II. The additional crime we are discussing is the outgrowth of the previously agreed or planned criminal conduct for which each participant in the common purpose already shares the criminal intent and has already made a contribution. This additional crime is rendered possible by the prior joint purpose to commit the agreed crime. Thus, what is at stake here is not the responsibility arising when members of a group (for instance, a military unit) engage in *lawful* action (for example, overpowering an enemy fortification by military force) and in the course of combat one of the combatants deliberately targets a civilian—a crime for which he alone must bear criminal responsibility. Our discussion here turns, rather, on cases where a plurality of persons agrees to perpetrate one or more crimes for which they all bear responsibility and *in addition* one of them commits a further crime. In these circumstances, the additional crime is premised on the existence of the original shared criminal purpose. In other words, there exists a causal link between the concerted crime and the additional crime: the former constitutes the preliminary *sine qua non* condition and the basis of the latter.

JCE III is firmly established in customary international law.[13] The historical roots of this mode of responsibility date back to the post-Second World War era case law, which recognized individual criminal responsibility for additional foreseeable crimes in the context of group criminality in a number of cases.[14] In the *Essen Lynching* case, for example, three British prisoners of war were killed by a mob of Germans in Essen West on 13 December 1944. Two soldiers and three civilians were convicted for being 'concerned in the killing'. The Captain instructed his soldiers to take three British prisoners of war to a Luftwaffe unit for interrogation. He ordered the escort to refrain from interfering if civilians molested the prisoners. En route, a crowd attacked and murdered the prisoners. The prosecutor argued that 'every person in that crowd who struck a blow is both morally and criminally responsible for the deaths' (at 89). It can be inferred from the verdicts that not all of the convicted accused shared the intent to kill; some merely intended to ill-treat the prisoners.

Although the ICTY Appeals Chamber articulated the test for JCE III in its first case, the ICTY Appeals Chamber has only affirmed (or entered) four convictions for JCE III

---

[13] When faced with the question of whether JCE III was recognized in customary international law prior to 1975 when the relevant crime occurred, the ECCC Pre-trial Chamber concluded that 'the authorities relied on by the ICTY Appeals Chamber in *Tadić* do not 'constitute a sufficiently firm basis to conclude that JCE III formed part of customary international law at the time relevant to Case 002' (ECCC, *Ieng (Decision on Appeals against the Co-Investigative Judges Order on Joint Criminal Enterprise* (JCE)), § 83). As the STL Appeals Chamber observed, the modern acceptance of JCE III in customary international law includes a consideration of jurisprudence and legal developments unavailable to the STL (*Interlocutory Decision on the Applicable Law*, AC, n. 360).

[14] For example, *RuSHA*, at 117–20 (finding the Chief of the SS Race and Resettlement Main Office guilty of crimes against humanity relating to the illegal punishment of 'racially inferior' foreigners who had sexual intercourse with German women because he knew that the decree prescribing the punishment of 'special treatment' might result in hanging); See also additional cases cited in STL, *Interlocutory Decision on the Applicable Law*, AC, n. 355.

to date.[15] In *Tadić*, the Appeals Chamber found that the defendant had taken part in a common plan to commit inhumane acts against the non-Serb civilian population in the Prijedor region in 1992. He was an armed member of the armed group that took part in the attack and committed several crimes. He must have been aware 'that the actions of the group of which he was a member were likely to lead to [...] killings, but he nevertheless willingly took that risk' (*Tadić*, AC, § 232). The Appeals Chamber therefore found the defendant guilty of murder as a crime against humanity pursuant to JCE III and inhumane acts pursuant to JCE I.

The Appeals Chamber affirmed Krstić's JCE III conviction for the murders, beatings, and other abuses arising out of his participation in a joint criminal enterprise to forcibly transfer civilians, finding that they were the natural and foreseeable consequences of the JCE (*Krstić*, AC, § 151). The victims of the additional crimes were Muslims fleeing from the massacre in Srebrenica. The Trial Chamber reasoned that these crimes were not an 'agreed upon objective' of the JCE, but found that there was 'no doubt that these crimes were natural and foreseeable consequences of the ethnic cleansing campaign'. In relation to Krstić's awareness of the risk that these further crimes would be committed in the execution of the JCE, the Trial Chamber found that:

> [G]iven the circumstances at the time the plan was formed, General Krstić must have been aware that an outbreak of these crimes would be inevitable given the lack of shelter, the density of the crowds, the vulnerable condition of the refugees, the presence of many regular and irregular military and paramilitary units in the area and the sheer lack of sufficient numbers of UN soldiers to provide protection. In fact, on 12 July, the VRS organised and implemented the transportation of the women, children and elderly outside the enclave; General Krstić was himself on the scene and exposed to firsthand knowledge that the refugees were being mistreated by VRS or other armed forces. (§ 616)

The Appeals Chamber emphasized that it is unnecessary to show that the accused was actually aware that the opportunistic crimes were being committed; rather 'it was sufficient that their occurrence was foreseeable to him and that those other crimes did in fact occur' (§ 150).

In the third case, *Stakić*, the ICTY Appeals Chamber imposed JCE III responsibility after reversing the TC's application of the notion of 'co-perpetratorship'. The Appeals Chamber held that the accused had participated in a JCE I to commit crimes of persecution, deportation, and forcible transfer of Muslims in the Prijedor area in Bosnia-Herzegovina (*Stakić*, AC, §§ 84–5). The Appeals Chamber concluded that the accused was responsible under the third category of JCE for the crimes of murder, as a war crime and a crime against humanity, and extermination as a crime against humanity for additional killings of non-Serbs in detention camps, transportation convoys, and municipalities. It relied on the TC's factual findings to conclude that the required intent was proven (*Stakić*, AC, §§ 93–8).

In the final case, *Martić*, the Trial Chamber found that the accused participated in a JCE, the common purpose of which was the establishment of an ethnically Serb territory in the Serbian Autonomous District (SAO) Krajina and the Republic of Serbian Krajina (RSK) in between August 1991 and December 1995 through the displacement of the non-Serb population. He incurred JCE III liability for additional crimes, including murder,

---

[15] In *Popović and others* (TC); *Milutinović (Šainović) and others* (TC); *Gotovina others* (TC), Trial Chambers have entered convictions for JCE III that are currently under appeal.

torture, imprisonment, destruction, and plunder, that occurred in the course of the discriminatory forcible displacement of the non-Serb population. The Trial Chamber's findings were upheld on appeal (*Martić*, AC, §§ 187, 195, 205–6, 210).

9.1.4 DEFINING THE LIMITS OF JCE RESPONSIBILITY

A. The evolving relationship between JCE I/II and JCE III

A JCE is not necessarily static and may evolve over time. The intention of the JCE members may expand to include additional crimes, which at the beginning of the enterprise
were only foreseeable. If, over time, the JCE members accept the foreseeable crimes and
embrace them as part of their intentional conduct, then these crimes move from JCE III
to JCE I. The STL Appeals Chamber (*Interlocutory Decision on the Applicable Law*, § 246)
explained that

> when a participant in a JCE foresees an additional crime he originally had not subscribed
> to and nevertheless agrees to continue providing his significant contribution to the JCE,
> the only reasonable inference might be that he has come to agree to that additional crime,
> therefore bringing his liability back into the fold of JCE I.

In *Krajišnik*, for example, the President of the Bosnian Serb Assembly was found to have
participated in a JCE to permanently remove Bosnian Muslims and Bosnian Croats from
large areas of Bosnia and Herzegovina. From its inception, the common purpose included
the crimes of deportation, forcible transfer, and persecution by forced displacement. Over
time, Krajišnik and the other leading members of the JCE learned of murders, extermination, and other forms of persecution being committed during the implementation of
the common purpose. They took no measures to prevent these crimes and continued to
pursue their objective. The Trial Chamber found that the JCE had expanded. Although
the ICTY Appeals Chamber quashed Krajišnik's conviction for the expanded crimes
because the Trial Chamber had failed to make all the necessary factual findings, the
Appeals Chamber affirmed that the criminal means of realizing the common objective of
the JCE may evolve over time (*Krajišnik*, AC, § 163).

B. JCE III and specific intent crimes

Resorting to JCE III would be intrinsically ill-founded when the crime committed requires
'special' or specific intent. It would thus be inappropriate to apply the extended form of
JCE to charges, for example, of genocide, persecution, or aggression. In these cases the
'secondary offender' does not share—by definition—that 'special' intent (otherwise liability would fall under the first or second category of JCE). As noted by the STL Appeals
Chamber, the application of JCE III liability to 'special' intent crimes leads to a serious
legal anomaly: the accused becomes a principal perpetrator of a 'special intent' crime
for which he lacks the 'special intent' (*Interlocutory Decision on the Applicable Law*, AC,
§§ 248–9). A conviction for 'committing' genocide, for example, should be reserved for
those who have genocidal intent. To hold otherwise risks watering down the gravity and
stigma of the crime. In such circumstances, the secondary offender should be charged
with a form of accomplice liability such as aiding and abetting.

Another way of approaching this problem is through the lens of foreseeability. For
criminal liability to be imposed under JCE III, the additional crime should be objectively
foreseeable in the sense that it is connected to or in line with the agreed-upon offence of the
foundational JCE I. A crime that requires 'special' intent is so unique that it cannot be said
to be a legally foreseeable consequence of an unconnected JCE I. The 'distance' between
the subjective elements of the two offences is too great. In such cases, the causal connection

between the agreed-upon crime and the additional crime is too tenuous. To convict in these circumstances would be inconsistent with the principal of personal culpability.

The ICTY Appeals Chamber views this issue differently. In answering an interlocutory appeal of the defence challenging an indictment charging genocide pursuant to JCE III, the ICTY Appeals Chamber reasoned that JCE III is a mode of liability that can apply to any of the crimes, even crimes of specific intent (*Brđanin* (*Decision on Interlocutory Appeal* dated 29 March 2004), §§ 7–10).

C. Does the JCE need to include the physical perpetrator?

In a classic JCE, such as a bank robbery, involving a small number of JCE members operating at the same level but in different capacities, each member is responsible for the concerted criminal action, even if the criminal act is performed only by another member of the JCE.

In ICL, however, many cases involve larger groups, working together through institutions or organizations. The problem becomes more complicated in a leadership JCE, consisting of high-level superiors who control political or military structures. What happens when, instead of carrying out the criminal acts themselves, these leaders use their power to control soldiers or others within their organizations to carry out the common criminal purpose? In this situation, who bears criminal responsibility for these crimes? First, the physical perpetrators would be criminally responsible for committing the crimes. The JCE member who used the physical perpetrators to commit the crimes would be criminally responsible for his participation in the crimes. For example, he may have planned, ordered, instigated, or co-perpetrated the crimes of the physical perpetrator.

The more difficult question, however, is what responsibility should the other members of the JCE bear for these crimes. The ICTY faced this question in the *Brđanin* case. Radoslav Brđanin, a civilian leader of the Serb-run Autonomous Region of Krajina (ARK) in north-western Bosnia and Herzegovina, was convicted of a range of crimes, including persecutions as a crime against humanity, willful killing and torture as grave breaches of the Geneva Conventions, and wanton destruction and destruction of religious institutions as violations of the laws and customs of war. The Trial Chamber noted that for a JCE to materialize, it was required to prove not only that a common criminal plan existed, but also that the crimes were committed by one or more participants in the common plan. The challenge in this case arose because the crimes were physically committed by members of the army, police, and para-military groups who were not participants in the JCE (§ 345).[16] The Trial Chamber therefore dismissed the applicability of the notion of JCE to those crimes (§§ 351, 355). The Trial Chamber explained that

> JCE is not an appropriate mode of liability to describe the individual criminal responsibility of the Accused, given the extraordinarily broad nature of this case, where the Prosecution seeks to include within a JCE a person as structurally remote from the commission of the crimes charged in the Indictment as the Accused. (*Brđanin*, TC, § 355)

The ICTY Appeals Chamber reversed this position, finding that JCE members could be held responsible for crimes committed by non-members, where the crime could be 'imputed' to a member of the JCE who was using the non-member in accordance with the common plan. After reviewing post-Second World War case law, the AC concluded that

---

[16] The Trial Chamber had set out the same view in a previous decision in the same case (*Brđanin, Form of Further Amended Indictment and Prosecution Application to Amend*, § 44).

international law recognizes the imposition of liability for participation in a common criminal purpose, where the conduct that comprises the criminal actus reus is perpetrated by persons who do not share the common purpose:

> [W]hat matters in a first category JCE is not whether the person who carried out the *actus reus* of a particular crime is a member of JCE, but whether the crime in question forms part of the common purpose. In cases where the principal perpetrator of a particular crime is not a member of the JCE, this essential requirement may be inferred from various circumstances, including the fact that the accused or any other member of the JCE closely cooperated with the principal perpetrator in order to further the common criminal purpose. (§ 410)

The Appeals Chamber clinched the point by adding, always in light of post-Second World War jurisprudence, that when the principal perpetrator is not part of the JCE, for the accused to be held liable for the crime perpetrated, an understanding or an agreement between the accused and the principal perpetrator of the crime is not necessary. It may suffices that the crime at issue is part of the common criminal purpose (§§ 415–19) and the accused 'uses' the principal perpetrator to further that purpose (§§ 430–1).

The *Brđanin* Appeals Chamber left open the question of what kind of factual link is required to show that the crimes can be imputed to a JCE member, stating only that the existence of the link is a matter to be assessed on a case-by-case basis (*Brđanin*, AC, § 413). Subsequent case law has provided further guidance. In *Krajišnik*, the Appeals Chamber indicated that the link between the JCE member and the physical perpetrators might be established on the basis of evidence showing that the JCE member requested, instigated, ordered, encouraged, or 'otherwise availed himself' of the non-JCE member to commit the crime (*Krajišnik*, AC, § 226). In *Martić*, the ICTY Appeals Chamber found a sufficient link where the physical perpetrators belonged to or were acting in concert with a hierarchical organization controlled by a JCE member (*Martić*, AC, §§ 187–8, 195).

Judge Shahabudden disagreed with the majority's position in *Brđanin* and would have required the physical perpetrator to be a member of the JCE. However, he argued for a broad approach to determining membership. According to his analysis, 'a physical perpetrator, who acquiesces in the JCE and perpetrates a crime within its common purpose, thereby becomes a member of the JCE, if he is not already a member' (§§ 2–4). Likewise, when the JCE member uses a physical perpetrator as a tool to commit a crime, then 'the *actus reus* was, in law, perpetrated by the member of the JCE in the same way as if he had used an inanimate instrument to accomplish his will; so the real perpetrator was in any event a member of the JCE' (§ 13). Judge Shahabudden also noted that in the event that JCE members agreed to order subordinates to commit crimes, then the crimes of the non-JCE members could be attributed to the JCE (§ 11).

In my view, this is the preferable approach, since it best accords with the general principles of international criminal law, in particular the principle of personal criminal responsibility. In accordance with these principles, the JCE members should only be held responsible for the crimes of non-members if *i*) there was a prior understanding between the relevant JCE members that the execution of the common criminal purpose would involve physical perpetration of crimes by persons outside of the JCE (a JCE I); or *ii*) they *anticipated the risk* that a JCE member might order or instigate persons outside the JCE to perpetrate crimes and willingly ran that risk (JCE III). It would not be sound to hold a JCE member liable for crimes committed by other non-JCE perpetrators if this possibility was not known or anticipated. The basic precondition of liability for JCE would be lacking, and to hold the member responsible for the crimes committed by the physical perpetrator would be contrary to the principle of personal criminal responsibility.[17] Moreover, the Appeals Chamber's ruling in *Brđanin* seems all the more objectionable because in the same case the Chamber also held that the doctrine of the JCE extends to 'large-scale cases', covering instances where crimes are perpetrated on a large scale by individuals who are remote from the accused (§§ 420–5).[18]

In a separate opinion, Judge Meron pointed out a further concern with the *Brđanin* Appeals Chamber's approach. He raised the question of whether a JCE using outside perpetrators should still be a form of 'commission'. In his view, the nature of the link between the JCE member and the physical perpetrators is the limiting factor: 'where a JCE member uses a non-JCE member to carry out a crime in furtherance of the common purpose, then all other JCE members should be liable via the JCE under the same mode of liability that attaches to this JCE member' (*Brđanin*, AC, Separate Opinion of Judge Meron, § 6). Thus if a JCE member ordered his subordinates to physically commit the crimes, then all JCE members would be convicted of ordering the crimes.

9.1.5 JCE AT THE ICC

JCE liability is implicitly permitted by Article 25(3)(a) of the ICC Statute, which generically states that criminal responsibility for any of the crimes covered by the Statute is incurred by anybody 'committing a crime' 'jointly with another person'.

One argument against JCE liability at the ICC is based on the general provision of Article 30 of the ICC Statute, which states that criminal responsibility requires 'intent and knowledge'. If the ICC finds that intent is always required, then this would likely rule out the application of the third category of JCE, which is based on the acceptance of a foreseeable risk.[19] However, Article 30 also states that it applies 'unless otherwise provided'.[20] This leaves open the possibility that a mental element lower than intent and knowledge might be sufficient in particular situations, such as in cases of JCE III.

Contrary to what various authors, including the present one, have either implicitly or expressly contended,[21] Article 25(3)(d) of the ICC Statute does not introduce JCE. Rather, it addresses the 'residual form of accessory liability' of a person who '[i]n any other way contributes to the commission or attempted commission of such a crime by a group of persons acting with a common purpose'.

Although the pre-trial and trial decisions of the ICC to date indicate a preference for co-perpetration based on joint control over the act (see 9.2), it remains possible that other ICC Chambers will apply JCE theory.[22]

---

[17] For a similar view, see the Partly Dissenting opinion of Judge Shahabuddeen in *Brđanin* (AC, §§ 4–13). The contrary view is advanced by Judge Meron in his Separate Opinion in the same case (§§ 3–8).

[18] See also *Rwamakuba* (*Decision on Interlocutory Appeal Regarding Application of Joint Criminal Enterprise to the Crime of Genocide*), AC.

[19] See *Bemba* (*Decision Pursuant to Article 61(7)(a) and (b) of the Rome Statute on the Charges of the Prosecutor Against Jean-Pierre Bemba Gombo*) § 369 (rejecting *dolus eventualis* and explaining that intent requires that the suspect 'was at least aware that, in the ordinary course of events, the occurrence of such crimes was a virtually certain consequence of the implementation of the common plan'); compare *Lubanga* (*Decision on the Confirmation of Charges*), §§ 350–5.

[20] See G. Werle and F. Jessberger, 'Unless Otherwise Provided', in 3 JICJ (2005), 35–55.

[21] See e.g. W. A. Schabas, *An Introduction to the International Criminal Court*, 3rd edn (Cambridge: Cambridge University Press, 2007), at 211–13; A. Cassese, 'The Proper Limits of Individual Responsibility under the Doctrine of Joint Criminal Enterprise', 5 JICJ (2007), 132. See also *Tadić*, AC, § 222. On Art. 25(3)(d) see K. Ambos, Triffterer, *ICC Commentary*, at 757–65, A. Eser, 'Individual Criminal Responsibility', in Cassese, Gaeta, Jones, *ICC Commentary*, vol. I, 802–3.

[22] See e.g. *Lubanga*, TC, Separate Opinion of Judge Adrian Fulford, §§ 6–18 (arguing that the control over the crime theory is unsupported by the Rome Statute and advocating an interpretation similar to JCE theory).

9.2 CO-PERPETRATION BASED ON JOINT CONTROL

In contrast to JCE liability, co-perpetration based on joint control over the crime focuses on the criminal acts rather than the mental element. This mode of criminal liability, drawn primarily from German legal theory, has been applied at the ICC, when interpreting the reference in Article 25(3)(a) of the ICC Statute Article to committing 'jointly with another'.[23] In adopting this model of co-perpetration, the *Lubanga* Pre-Trial Chamber explained that 'principals to a crime are not limited to those who physically carry out the objective elements of the offence, but also include those who, in spite of being removed from the scene of the crime, control or mastermind its commission because they decide whether and how the offence will be committed' (*Lubanga (Decision on the Confirmation of Charges)*, § 330). Thus, co-perpetration based on joint control is thus principal, rather than accessory, liability for the crime. It is

> rooted in the idea that when the sum of co-ordinated individual contributions of a plurality of persons results in the realisation of all the objective elements of a crime, any person making a contribution can be held vicariously responsible for the contributions of all the others and, as a result, can be considered as a principal to the whole crime. (*Lubanga (Decision on the Confirmation of Charges)*, § 326)

The *Lubanga* Pre-Trial Chamber rejected both purely objective and purely subjective approaches to distinguishing between principal perpetrators and accessories. It reasoned that an objective approach, which would require a principal to physically carry out an element of the offence, was incompatible with Article 25(3)(a) of the ICC Statute's reference to committing an offence through another person. The Pre-Trial Chamber similarly rejected a subjective approach based on shared intent, finding that did not fit with the ICC Statute's explicit recognition of a residual form of accessory liability similar to JCE liability in Article 25(3)(d). Thus, the Pre-Trial Chamber opted for a mixed subjective and objective approach requiring objective joint control plus awareness of the factual circumstances enabling the accused to jointly control the crime.

According to this model, co-perpetrators share control over the commission of the offence. Joint control does not imply exclusive control or even overall control over the offence. Instead, each co-perpetrator depends on the others to complete the crime. A participant is in joint control when he or she has been assigned essential tasks and thus has the ability to frustrate the commission of the crime by not performing the assigned functions. Co-perpetration is not limited to those who participate directly in the execution of the crime; it may also extend to those who participate in its preparatory stages. According to the ICC's first Trial Judgment in the *Lubanga* case, co-perpetration requires the following material elements: *i)* the involvement of at least two individuals in the commission of the crime (*Lubanga*, TC, § 980); *ii)* the existence of an agreement or common plan between the co-perpetrators involving criminality, in that its implementation embodied at least a risk that, if events follow the ordinary course, the crime will be committed (§§ 981, 984); *iii)* an 'essential' contribution by the co-perpetrator, including by controlling or masterminding its commission, which is not limited to physically perpetrating elements of the crime (§§ 999, 1003).

Co-perpetration based on joint control also requires that the co-perpetrators possess the requisite mens rea elements for the crime. According to the *Lubanga* Judgement, the

---

[23] *Lubanga (Decision on the Confirmation of Charges)*, §§ 330–40; *Katanga and Chui Decision on the Confirmation of Charges*, §§ 520–6; *Bemba (Decision Pursuant to Article 61(7)(a) and (b) of the Rome Statute on the Charges of the Prosecutor Against Jean-Pierre Bemba Gombo)*, §§ 347–50; *Banda and Jerbo (Decision on the Confirmation of Charges)*, § 126.

mental elements can be summarized as *i*) the co-perpetrator's mutual awareness and acceptance of the risk that implementing the common plan may result in the crime in the ordinary course of events (§§ 1012, 1013);[24] and *ii*) the co-perpetrator's awareness that he provided an essential contribution to the implementation of the common plan (§ 1013).

The ICC model of co-perpetration is similar to that applied by the ICTY Trial Chamber in *Stakić*. The Trial Chamber explained that for co-perpetration

> [I]t suffices that there was an explicit agreement or silent consent to reach a common goal by coordinated co-operation and joint control over the criminal conduct. For this kind of co-perpetration it is typical, but not mandatory, that one perpetrator possesses skills or authority which the other perpetrator does not. These can be described as shared acts which when brought together achieve the shared goal based on the same degree of control over the execution of the common acts. (*Stakić*, TC, § 440)

The ICTY Appeals Chamber overturned this approach, finding that co-perpetration based on joint control did not find support in customary international law or in the jurisprudence of the ICTY (*Stakić*, AC, §§ 58–62). Instead, the Appeals Chamber re-analysed the facts under the rubric of JCE.

In recent cases, however, the ICTY and ICTR have started to employ another form of co-perpetration based on the notion of 'essential contribution'. Although the judges are not calling this new mode 'co-perpetration', it displays many of the hallmarks of the *Stakić* indirect co-perpetration model.

Non-JCE joint commission first appeared in the *Gacumbitsi* case, where the ICTR Appeals Chamber found that the accused had 'committed' genocide because his acts formed an 'integral part' of the crime. The Appeals Chamber reasoned that, in the context of genocide, commission does not necessarily require physical participation in killing because other acts could constitute direct participation in the actus reus of the crime (*Gacumbitsi*, AC, § 60). The ICTR Appeals Chamber found that Sylvestre Gacumbitsi was present at the crime scene to supervise and direct the massacre. It held that his active participation in separating the Tutsi refugees to be killed 'was as much an integral part of the genocide as were the killings which it enabled' (§ 60). Accordingly, he was to be treated as a principal perpetrator for committing the crime (see also *Karera*, TC, § 543; *Ndindabahizi*, AC, § 123). Having agreed with the Trial Chamber's assessment that the indictment did not properly plead JCE liability, the Appeals Chamber was not able to assess this participation under a JCE model. As Judge Güney pointed out in his Partially Dissenting Opinion in *Gacumbitsi*, however, the Appeals Chamber adopted this new form of responsibility without any explicit consideration of whether this approach was consistent with customary international law and without providing any cogent reasons for departing from the established JCE jurisprudence (§§ 4–6).

In *Seromba*, the ICTR Appeals Chamber again invoked a non-JCE model of co-perpetration. Anathase Seromba, a Catholic priest, was convicted of committing genocide and extermination as a crime against humanity after he instructed a bulldozer driver to destroy his church where 1,500 Tutsi refugees were seeking shelter. Again, the AC found that the actions of the accused formed an integral part of the crime (*Seromba*, AC, §§ 161, 171-2). In a strong dissenting opinion, Judge Liu questioned the application of this new mode of responsibility, noting that

> The Majority's extension of the definition of 'committing' is not only inconsistent with the jurisprudence of this Tribunal and that of the ICTY, but has been applied by the Majority

---

[24] See *Lubanga* (*Decision on the Confirmation of Charges*), § 362 (explaining that this awareness and acceptance justifies the mutual attribution of the contributions and the resulting responsibility for the whole crime).

without any indication of the criteria or legal basis. This Judgement marks a turning point in the jurisprudence of this Tribunal. It has opened the door for an accused to be convicted of committing an offence, where there is no direct perpetration of the *actus reus* of the offence, and where the essential elements of JCE have not been pleaded and proved by the Prosecution, as the accused's acts can in any case be subsumed by this new definition of 'committing'. Not only is it regrettable for the accused, but it is against his right to legal certainty, particularly at this point in the Tribunal's existence. (§ 18)

In *Lukić and Lukić*, this jurisprudence was picked up by an ICTY Trial Chamber, which reasoned that 'a person who plays a central role in the commission of the crime of murder and embraces and approves as his own the decision to commit murder is not adequately described as an aider and abettor but qualifies as a direct perpetrator who committed the crime' (§ 899). Milan Lukić and two other soldiers fired at a group of Muslim men lined up on the riverbank. Based on evidence that one of the men was shot with a silenced gun, the TC was able to conclude that Lukić personally killed one of the men. Lukić was also convicted for the four other murders because, whether or not he fired the shots, he 'embraced these shootings as his own' (§ 908).

9.3 INDIRECT PERPETRATION

Indirect perpetration occurs when the indirect perpetrator uses another person to physically commit the crime. This form of commission is specifically enumerated in Article 25(3)(a) of the ICC Statute, which covers indirect perpetration regardless of whether the physical perpetrator is criminally responsible. In indirect perpetration, the principal (the 'perpetrator-by-means') uses the physical perpetrator as a tool to commit the crime. In a typical domestic case, the physical perpetrator is an innocent agent who is not fully criminally responsible for his actions because he is acting under a mistaken belief, duress, or incapacity. The concept extends, however, to indirect perpetration where the physical perpetrator is criminally responsible ('perpetrator behind the perpetrator').

For the purposes of ICL the most important example of this type of 'perpetrator behind the perpetrator' liability is based on control over a hierarchical organization (*Organisationsherrschaft*[25]). In setting out the requirements of indirect perpetration based on control over an organization, the ICC Pre-Trial Chamber explained that the organization must be based on a hierarchical structure comprising sufficient fungible subordinates ensuring automatic compliance with the leader's will (*Katanga and Chui (Decision on the Confirmation of Charges)*, § 511). In this way, the perpetrator-behind-the-perpetrator is able to achieve his criminal aims by using subordinates as a 'mere gear in a giant machine' (§ 515).

In *Katanga and Chui*, the ICC Pre-Trial Chamber noted that the combination of co-perpetration based on joint control and indirect perpetration through other persons results in a mode of liability that is especially suited to cases of 'senior leaders' (*Katanga and Chui (Decision on the Confirmation of Charges)*, § 492). Germain Katanga and Mathieu Ngudjolo Chui were military leaders in Eastern Congo. Together, they are alleged to have hatched a plan to 'wipe out' the village of Bogoro and their troops jointly executed the plan. The Pre-Trial Chamber held that when a group of senior leaders works together to

---

[25] T. Weigend, 'Perpetration through an Organization: The Unexpected Career of a German Legal Concept', 9 JICJ (2011), 91–111.

commit criminal acts (co-perpetration), each using the organizations under their control (indirect perpetration), these crimes can be mutually attributed amongst them through 'indirect co-perpetration'.

Indirect co-perpetration was applied by the ICTY Trial Chamber in the *Stakić* case. The Chamber convicted Stakić, a physician and civilian leader in the Prejidor municipality of Bosnia and Herzegovina, of extermination, persecution, and other crimes through indirect co-perpetration. The Chamber reasoned that he shared joint control over the crimes with his co-perpetrators who were in charge of political bodies, the police, and the army. As an indirect co-perpetrator, Dr Stakić's criminal responsibility encompassed the crimes committed by or attributed to his co-perpetrators. Although the Appeals Chamber overturned the Trial Chamber's analysis of co-perpetration based on control over the crime, substituting a JCE analysis, it implicitly accepted the TC's findings on indirect perpetration.

Both the *Gacumbitsi* and *Seromba* judgments of the ICTR Appeals Chamber also demonstrate aspects of indirect co-perpetration theory. The AC found that Seromba

> [A]pproved and embraced as his own the decision [...] to destroy the church in order to kill the Tutsi refugees. It is irrelevant that Athanase Seromba did not personally drive the bulldozer that destroyed the church. What is important is that Athanase Seromba fully exercised his influence over the bulldozer driver who, as the Trial Chamber's findings demonstrate, accepted Athanase Seromba as the only authority, and whose directions he followed. (§ 171)

In a similar vein, the ICTY's acceptance that JCE members can use non-member 'tools' to achieve the common purpose can involve an indirect perpetration analysis. A popular way of linking the crimes to a JCE member is through a leader's control over a hierarchical organization (see e.g. *Martić*, AC, § 187–8; *Krajišnik*, AC, §§ 239, 241, 262; *Stakić*, AC, §§ 68–70). For example, when a JCE member controls an army a Trial Chamber may be satisfied that crimes within the common purpose committed by soldiers of that army are attributable to the JCE.

10

OMISSION LIABILITY AND SUPERIOR RESPONSIBILITY

International criminal liability may arise not only as a result of a positive act but also from an omission; that is, the failure to take required action. Omission is only criminalized when the law imposes a clear obligation to act and the person fails to do what is legally required.

It took a long time for a general rule on omission liability to evolve in ICL. Traditionally, IHL tended to prohibit action; it imposed on combatants the obligation not to engage in conduct contrary to international standards (killing civilians, raping, shelling hospitals, etc.). Generally speaking, it refrained from imposing positive obligations to do something. The purpose of this body of law was to ensure that belligerents respect minimum legal standards. After the Second World War, the focus of IHL shifted from state sovereignty towards protecting victims of war. Many provisions of the 1949 Geneva Conventions laid down duties to act.[1] The failure to fulfil some of these duties could result in individual criminal responsibility.[2]

The post-Second World War tribunals recognized that both action and omission to act in accordance with a legal duty could fulfil the physical element (actus reus) of a crime.[3] Additionally, the doctrine of superior responsibility (also referred to as command

---

[1] For example, some provisions of the 1949 Geneva Conventions lay down *unconditional* positive obligations: Art. 118 Geneva Convention III imposes positive obligations concerning release and repatriation of prisoners of war at the close of hostilities, the violation of which amounts to a grave breach, pursuant to Art. 85(4)(b) of the First Additional Protocol. For other *unconditional* positive obligations see e.g. GCI Arts 16, 17, 32; GCII Art 19; GCIII Arts 69–77, 121–2. Other provisions lay down broader positive obligations leaving Contracting States a *margin of appreciation*: see e.g. GCIII Art. 13 concerning the duty to protect prisoners of war against acts of violence or intimidation. See also, GCIII Arts 15, 29. Other provisions contain *qualified* obligations. For instance, Art. 12 of GCI provides that a party to the conflict compelled to abandon wounded or sick to the enemy must leave with them a part of its medical personnel as well as material, 'as far as military considerations permit'. For further examples of qualified obligations see e.g. GCII Art. 12, GCIII Art. 60, GCIV, Arts 55–6. Examples of positive obligations can also be found in the Additional Protocols: see e.g. API, Arts 36, 69(1), 70, 76, 77, 82, 83.

[2] See e.g. *Sumida Haruzo and others* (at 228–9, 278, and 280–2) for the breach of the duty to provide food and care to detained civilians as a war crime. In *Gozawa Sadaichi and others* it was held that the poor conditions, including lack of food and medical supplies, for prisoners of war, amounted to a crime (at 200–1, 210–11, 222–3, and 227–31). See also *Schmitt* (decision of the Antwerp Court Martial, at 751–2, and the subsequent decision of the Cour Militaire de Bruxelles, at 752, n. 89 *bis*) and *Köppelmann Ernst* (decision of the Brabant Court Martial, at 753–4, and of the Belgian Court of Cassation, at 185–6). In both cases the courts dealt with the positive obligations of the commanders of detention camps for prisoners of war. For a comment on these cases, see the relevant entries in *Cassese's Companion*.

[3] See e.g. *High Command* case (finding that a commander of occupied territory had the duty to protect prisoners of war and civilians, emphasizing that 'inaction with knowledge that others within his area are violating this duty which he owes, constitute[s] criminality'; Vol. XI, at 632); *Essen Lynching* case, at 88–92 (convicting a soldier of a war crime for failing to protect a prisoner in his custody from the attack of a crowd). See also *Fire Brigade*, at 316–17; *Heinrich Gerike and others*, at 76–81.

responsibility, since it originally developed in a military context) emerged in its modern form as a discrete and important type of omission liability in the post-war case law. Pursuant to this doctrine, a superior who omits to prevent or punish his subordinate's criminal acts may be held criminally responsible.

10.1 CULPABLE OMISSION

Where there is a legal duty to act, an omission to do what is legally required may result in criminal responsibility.[4] Although Article 7(1) of the ICTY Statute does not specifically mention omissions, the ICTY Appeals Chamber was the first of the modern international criminal tribunals to recognize that individual criminal responsibility may nevertheless be imposed for both acts and culpable omissions (*Tadić*, AC 1999, § 188). Notwithstanding the fact that a proposed general provision on omission was ultimately left out of the ICC Statute, the ICC has also accepted that criminal liability can be based on either acts or omissions.[5]

Criminal responsibility for omission may only be imposed when there is a failure to comply with a legal duty. The nature and origin of the duty to act has been a source of uncertainty. In *Tadić*, the Appeals Chamber specified that the duty needed to be 'mandated by a rule of criminal law' (*Tadić*, AC, § 188). This important requirement implements the legality principle (*nullum crimen sine lege*). Although the issue is not settled in the jurisprudence, the preferable view is that the duty to act must be found in international law. A duty based solely on domestic law is an insufficient basis for international criminal responsibility. To hold otherwise would allow for an unacceptable variation in the rules of ICL in different places.

For an omission to constitute the physical element of a crime, the accused must not only be under a duty to act, he must also possess the *ability to act*.[6]

In *Ntagerura and others*, the ICTR Trial Chamber set out the elements of commission of a crime by omission:

> [I]n order to hold an accused criminally responsible for an omission as a principal perpetrator, the following elements must be established: (a) the accused must have had a duty to act mandated by a rule of criminal law; (b) the accused must have had the ability to act; (c) the accused failed to act intending the criminally sanctioned consequences or with awareness and consent that the consequences would occur; and (d) the failure to act resulted in the commission of the crime. (§ 659)

Omissions may constitute the physical element of other modes of liability, such as aiding and abetting (see 11.1); the elements of aiding and abetting are identical whether the alleged conduct is an act or an omission[7]) and instigation (see 11.3) (see e.g. *Galić*, TC, § 168).

---

[4] *Mrkšić and Šljivančanin*, AC, § 134; *Orić*, AC, § 43; *Galić*, AC, § 175; *Ntagerura and others*, AC § 334, 370; *Blaškić*, AC, § 663.

[5] See e.g. *Lubanga Decision on the Confirmation of Charges*, §§ 152, 351–2; *Katanga and Chui*, §§ 287, 310, 315, 357, 368–9, 529.

[6] *Mrkšić and Šljivančanin*, AC, §§ 49, 82, 154; *Ntagerura and others*, AC, § 335.

[7] *Orić*, AC, § 43; *Mrkšić and Šljivančanin*, AC, § 146. In determining if an omission constituted the requisite 'substantial assistance' for aiding and abetting, the ICTY Appeals Chamber assessed whether the murder of the prisoners of war would have been 'substantially less likely' to occur if the accused had acted in accordance with his duties (*Mrkšić and Šljivančanin*, AC, §§ 97, 100).

Omissions have also been recognized as contributions to a JCE.[8] However, the ICTY Appeals Chamber has indicated that ordering (see 11.2) by omission is not possible because this mode requires a positive act (*Galić*, AC, § 176; *Milošević D.*, AC, § 267). It is likely that the same reasoning applies to planning (see 11.4) a crime. As in the case of participation in crimes through positive conduct, omissions are only punished if accompanied by the required criminal state of mind (*Mrkšić and Šljivančanin*, AC, § 159; *Ntagerura*, TC, § 659).

10.2 SUPERIOR RESPONSIBILITY

ICL imposes criminal liability on superiors, both civilian and military, who fail to prevent or punish the criminal activities of their subordinates. It bears noting that it is not necessary for the subordinates to have physically perpetrated the crimes themselves; they may have engaged in criminal conduct under any head of liability; for example perpetration, co-perpetration, JCE, aiding and abetting, etc. (*Blagojević and Jokić*, AC, §§ 280–1).

10.2.1 THE EMERGENCE AND EVOLUTION OF THE DOCTRINE

Although it was discussed after the First World War,[9] it was in the aftermath of the Second World War that the notion of criminal responsibility of superiors for failure to prevent or punish crimes perpetrated by their subordinates evolved in international law. The gradual development of superior responsibility can be roughly divided into five phases.

A. Command Responsibility as a Form of Complicity

At the outset lawmakers and courts considered that military commanders should be held criminally liable for failure to prevent or punish, for in so acting they in some way aided and abetted the crimes of their underlings. Some national laws set out the notion tersely and conceived of such responsibility as a form of complicity. For instance, the French Order on War Crimes of 28 August 1944[10] provided in Article 4 that

> where a subordinate is prosecuted as the actual perpetrator of a war crime, and his superiors cannot be indicated as being equally responsible, they shall be considered as accomplices in so far as they have organized or tolerated the criminal acts of their subordinates.

Here the notion was clearly set out that a military commander is criminally liable as an aider and abetter, if he tolerated—that is, failed to stop or repress—the commission of war crimes by his subordinates. A slightly broader notion was embodied in the Chinese law of 24 October 1946 on the trial of war criminals. Like the French, the Chinese regarded culpable commanders as accomplices of the subordinates committing crimes.[11] In 1949–50, two Belgian Courts Martial took the same approach in *Schmitt*, although they stressed

---

[8] See e.g. *Kvočka*, AC, § 187; *Milutinović and others*, TC, Vol. 1, § 103.

[9] See 1919 International Commission on the Responsibility of the Authors of the War and on Enforcement of Penalties, 14 AJIL (1920), 95, at 121.

[10] Quoted in the *Notes on the case of General Yamashita*, in LRTWC, vol. IV, at 87.

[11] Quoted in the *Notes on the case of General Yamashita*, vol. IV, at 88 citing Article IX of the Chinese Law of 24 October 1946 Governing the Trial of War Criminals, 'Persons who occupy a supervisory or commanding position in relation to war criminals and in their capacity as such have not fulfilled their duty to prevent crimes from being committed by their subordinates shall be treated as the accomplices of such war criminals.'

the notion that a commander is under a set of obligations, the breach of which may entail his criminal liability.[12]

B. *Yamashita*

A second step in the evolution of the doctrine can be seen in the leading, if controversial, US case of *Yamashita* (1946). The *Yamashita* judgment was the first to fully enunciate the modern doctrine with regard to *military* commanders. The Court did not base itself on the notion of complicity, stressing instead that command responsibility is a consequence of the breach of the duties incumbent upon commanders. Given the importance of the case, a few words of explanation are necessary.

The Japanese general Yamashita was Commanding General of the Japanese Army in the Philippines between 1943 and 1945. His soldiers had massacred a large part of the civilian population of Batangas Province and inflicted acts of violence, cruelty, and murder upon the civilian population and prisoners of war, as well as wholesale pillage and wanton destruction of religious monuments in the occupied territory. The US authorities accused the General, before a US Military Commission, of breaching his duty as an army commander to control the operations of his troops 'by permitting them to commit' extensive and widespread atrocities. The Commission upheld these submissions by setting out a new doctrine as follows:

> Clearly, assignment to command military troops is accompanied by broad authority and heavy responsibility. This has been true in all armies throughout recorded history. It is absurd, however, to consider a commander a murderer or rapist because one of his soldiers commits a murder or a rape. Nevertheless, where murder and rape and vicious, revengeful actions are widespread offences, and there is no effective attempt by a commander to discover and control the criminal acts, such a commander may be held responsible, even criminally liable, for the lawless acts of his troops, depending upon their nature and the circumstances surrounding them. (LRTWC, Vol. IV, p. 35)

The US Supreme Court—to which the case had been brought by the defendant by way of a petition for habeas corpus—agreed. It held that commanders had a duty to take such appropriate measures as are within their power to control the troops under their command for the prevention of violations of the laws of warfare. It derived this duty from a number of provisions of such laws: Articles 1 and 43 of the Regulations annexed to the Fourth Hague Convention of 1907 (under the former, combatants, to be recognized as legitimate belligerents, must 'be commanded by a person responsible for his subordinates'; pursuant

---

[12]   The Antwerp Court Martial convicted the German head of the Breendonck prisoners of war camp as co-perpetrator for deaths of 32 inmates who were killed by guards. For the deaths of other inmates, resulting from exhaustion from forced labour or starvation he was liable as an accomplice, 'since he had rendered such assistance that without it the crimes could not be committed'. Applying Art. 66 of the Belgian Penal Code (which made liable for a crime both the perpetrators and aiders and abetters), the Court stressed that the defendant 'had the positive duty to protect prisoners in his custody' (at 751) and reasoned that 'he had seriously breached his duty as head of the camp and hence voluntarily and consciously cooperated to the criminal activity of the *Sicherheitsdienst* [the SS branch whose members were in charge of the camp at his orders]. A Military Court of Appeal upheld the decision and noted that the defendant's action was twofold: 'positive', where he imposed exhausting labour and ordered the destruction of food parcels, and 'negative', where he refrained to step in to prevent cruel acts. The appellant, the Court went on to hold, must be punished for both classes of conduct. As for the latter, he was punishable for the breach of his duty to see to it that 'the inmates in his camp be adequately nourished and treated' so as not to 'become physically exhausted and unable to work'. This duty, the Court noted, was similar to 'that incumbent upon a person charged with nourishing another person unable to attend to himself, and who gets him to starve'. In this case, 'the failure to act constitutes the material act sufficient to evidence criminal intent' (at 752). For a comment, see *Cassese's Companion*, at 904.

to the latter, the commander of a force occupying enemy territory 'shall take all the meas-ures in his power to restore, and ensure, as far as possible, public order and safety, while respecting, unless absolutely prevented, the laws in force in the country'); Article 19 of the Tenth Hague Convention of 1907, relating to bombardment by naval vessel and providing that commanders-in-chief of the belligerent fleets 'must see that the above Articles are properly carried out'; Article 26 of the 1929 Geneva Convention on the wounded and sick, which made it the duty 'of the commanders-in-chief of the belligerent armies, to arrange for the details of execution of the Articles [of the Convention] as well as for unforeseen cases. The Court's majority held that these provisions made it clear that the accused had

> an affirmative duty to take such measures as were within his power, and appropriate in the circumstances, to protect prisoners of war and the civilian population. This duty of a commanding officer has heretofore been recognized, and its breach penalized by our own military tribunals. (at 16)

However, two judges, Murphy and Rutledge, forcefully (and rightly) disagreed and set forth their views in important Dissenting Opinions. They noted among other things that the Court's majority had not shown that Yamashita had 'knowledge' of the gross breaches perpetrated by his troops (at 28, 34, 39, 50–1, 53) or had any 'direct connection with the atrocities' (at 36), or could be found guilty of 'a negligent failure [...] to discover' the atrocities (at 49) or in other words, had 'personal culpability' (at 39).[13]

This is therefore a case where the principle was affirmed, based (as the two dissent-ing judges rightly noted), on a novel interpretation of existing rules of IHL, as well as a questionable application of the principles to the case, in addition to total disregard for the required mental element for the crime.

C. The Requirement of Knowledge and Extension of the Doctrine to Civilian Leaders

Although the case law thus started off on the wrong foot, soon other decisions handed down after the Second World War fleshed out the doctrine. Unlike *Yamashita*, these deci-sions, which can be considered as a third step in the formation of the doctrine at issue, emphasized the need for the commander to have knowledge of the crimes committed by his underlings, in some instances also requiring criminal intent for the commander's liability to arise. None of these cases viewed superior responsibility as a form of compli-city. Furthermore, in some cases the doctrine was extended to *civilian* leaders.

In *Karl Brand and others* (*Doctors* case), a US Military tribunal sitting at Nuremberg under Control Council Law no. 10 held the leadership of the German medical staff liable for the killings perpetrated by their subordinate doctors, stressing that those leaders had knowledge of what was going on.[14] In *Pohl and others*, a US Military Tribunal held that

---

[13] Justices Murphy and Rutledge did not only dissent on the application of the law to the facts by the Commission—they also objected to the whole notion of command responsibility as a matter of law. Justice Murphy stated: 'The recorded annals of warfare and the established principles of international law afford not the slightest precedent for such a charge. This indictment in effect permitted the military commission to make the crime whatever it willed, dependent on its biased view as to the petitioner's duties and his disregard thereof, a practice reminiscent of that pursued in less respected nations in recent years' (327 US, at 28).

[14] After citing the *Yamashita* case, the Prosecution argued: 'This decision is squarely in point as to the criminal responsibility of those defendants in this dock who had the power and authority to control the agents through whom these crimes were committed. It is not incumbent upon the prosecution to show that this or that defendant was familiar with all of the details of all of these experiments. Indeed, in the *Yamashita* case, there was no charge or proof that he had knowledge of the crimes [...] But we need not discuss the require-ment of knowledge on the facts of this case. It has been repeatedly proved that those responsible leaders of

'[t]he law of war imposes on a military officer in a position of command an affirmative duty to take such steps as are within his power and appropriate to the circumstances to control those under his command for the prevention of acts which are violations of the law of war' (at 1011). The Tribunal required 'actual knowledge' of the misdeeds of subordinates (at 1011–12). The same doctrine was set out in a subsequent case, *Wilhem List and others* (*Hostages* case), where another US Military tribunal sitting at Nuremberg applied it to twelve high-ranking German officers charged, among other things, with the unlawful killing of hostages by way of reprisal. In this case the Tribunal stressed that, to pronounce a guilty verdict, it required 'proof of a causative, overt act or omission from which a guilty intent can be inferred' (at 1261). Turning to the liability of the defendants for their failure to prevent or punish, the Tribunal noted that, for this form of criminal liability to arise, knowledge by the army commander of the crimes committed by the subordinates was required. Furthermore, the Tribunal emphasized that a commander has the duty to require reports about occurrences taking place in the area under his control, failing which he may be accused of 'dereliction of duty' (at 1271–2).[15] These notions were taken up and elaborated on by another US Tribunal sitting at Nuremberg in *Wilhelm von Leeb and others* (*High Command* case). The Tribunal noted that a commander's 'criminal responsibility is personal. The act or neglect to act must be voluntary and criminal' (at 543). It went on to note that

> there must be a personal dereliction. That can occur where the act is directly traceable to him [the commander] or where his failure to properly supervise his subordinates constitutes criminal negligence on his part. In the latter case it must be a personal neglect amounting to a wanton, immoral disregard of the action of his subordinates amounting to acquiescence. [...] the occupying commander must have knowledge of these offenses [by his troops] and acquiesce or participate or criminally neglect to interfere in their commission and [...] the offences committed must be patently criminal. (543–5)[16]

The doctrine was not only embraced by US tribunals. The Tokyo Tribunal also accepted superior responsibility in *Araki and others* (at 29–31). In dealing with responsibility for war crimes against prisoners of war, the Tribunal insisted on the liability of commanders on account of their 'negligence or supineness' (at 30) if a commander who had the duty to know 'knew or should have known' about the commission of crimes but failed to stop them or to take 'adequate steps' 'to prevent the occurrence of [...] crimes in the future'

---

the German medical services in this dock not only knew of the systematic and criminal use of concentration camp inmates for murderous medical experiments, but also actively participated in such crimes. [...] No, it was not lack of information as to the criminal program which explains the culpable failure of these men to destroy this Frankenstein's monster. Nor was it lack of power' (934–5).

[15] 'If he fails to require and obtain complete information, the dereliction of duty rests upon him and he is in no position to plead his own dereliction as a defence' (at 1271).

[16] The Tribunal also noted the following: 'Military subordination is a comprehensive but not conclusive factor in fixing criminal responsibility. The authority, both administrative and military, of a commander and his criminal responsibility are related but by no means coextensive. Modern war such as the last war entails a large measure of decentralization. A high commander cannot keep completely informed of the details of military operations of subordinates and most assuredly not of every administrative measure. He has the right to assume that details entrusted to responsible subordinates will be legally executed. The President of the United States is Commander in Chief of its military forces. Criminal acts committed by those forces cannot in themselves be charged to him on the theory of subordination. The same is true of other high commanders in the chain of command. Criminality does not attach to every individual in this chain of command from that fact alone. There must be a personal dereliction. That can occur only where the act is directly traceable to him or where his failure to properly supervise his subordinates constitutes criminal negligence on his part' (at 543).

(at 31).[17] Similarly, the doctrine was enunciated by an Australian–US Military Tribunal, in *Soemu Toyoda* (at 5005–6) and by a Chinese War Crimes Tribunal in *Takashi Sakai* (at 1–7). It is notable that in *Soemu Toyoda* the Tribunal, in addition to insisting on the need for knowledge as a requirement of command responsibility, also held that such knowledge may be either *actual* ('as in the case of an accused who sees' the commission of the subordinates' crimes or 'is informed thereof shortly after') or *constructive*, for example when

> the commission of such a great number of offences within his command that a reasonable man could come to no other conclusion than that the accused must have known the offences or of the existence of an understood and acknowledged routine of their commission. (5005–6)

D. Crystallization of the Customary Rule

In a matter of only a few years after the Second World War, the doctrine of command responsibility crystallized into a rule of customary international law *i)* imposing on military commanders as well as civilian leaders[18] the obligation to prevent or repress crimes by their subordinates if they knew or should have known that their troops were about to commit or were committing or had committed crimes; and *ii)* criminalizing the culpable failure to fulfil this obligation, albeit without clearly outlining the mental element of such criminal liability. That such a rule (the existence of which was authoritatively explored in *Delalić and others*, TC, § 343) evolved so quickly should not be a surprise. In modern times, international criminality increasingly tends to be planned, organized, ordered, condoned, or tolerated by superior authorities. In other words, a clear trend is emerging towards commission of crimes involving the participation or acquiescence of the military and political leadership. Hence, the issue of superior responsibility has acquired enormous importance in international criminal law.

It is striking that in this area there has been an inversion of the normal law-making process. In the normal course of the development of international law, states first adopt an international rule binding upon them and then this rule gradually evolves as a penal rule criminalizing individuals violating the inter-state rule. The doctrine of superior responsibility, in contrast, emerged first as a criminal law rule (admittedly based on a general principle of IHL concerning 'responsible command') that addressed itself to individuals (military commanders or civilian or political leaders). From this case law, states then agreed upon a rule requiring states to ensure that their commanders prevent or repress crimes by their subordinates. Together, Articles 86 and 87 of the First Additional Protocol, addressed to the Contracting Parties and to the Parties to a conflict, codify the principle on responsible command mentioned above and restate the customary criminal law rule.

---

[17] The Tribunal found the highest-ranking defendant, prime minister Hideki Tojo, guilty of omissions in that 'He took no adequate step to punish offenders [who had ill-treated prisoners and internees] and to prevent the commission of similar offences in the future. His attitude towards the Bataan Death March gives the key to his conduct towards these captives. He knew in 1942 something of the conditions of that march and that many prisoners had died as a result of these conditions. He did not call for a report on the incident. When in the Philippines in 1943 he made perfunctory inquiries about the march but took no action. No one was punished. [...] Thus the head of the Government of Japan knowingly and wilfully refused to perform the duty which lay upon the Government of enforcing performance of the Laws of War' (at 462).

[18] See *Araky and others*; *Flick and others* (at 1202–12); and *Delalić and others* (TC, §§ 370, 377–8).

E. Modern Superior Responsibility

Article 7(3) of the Statute of the ICTY, which is in substance identical to the corresponding provision of the Statute of the ICTR, provides:

> The fact that any of the [...][crimes within the Tribunal's jurisdiction, including war crimes, crimes against humanity and genocide] was committed by a subordinate does not relieve his superior of criminal responsibility if he knew or had reason to know that the subordinate was about to commit such acts or had done so and the superior failed to take the necessary and reasonable measures to prevent such acts or to punish the perpetrators thereof.

The ICTY and ICTR have convicted a number of military and civilian leaders under this provision. The Tribunals have also affirmed that superior responsibility applies in non-international armed conflicts, since 'military organization implies responsible command and [...] responsible command in turn implies command responsibility'.[19]

In dealing with superior responsibility, Article 28 of the ICC Statute distinguishes between military and non-military superiors. Military superiors are held to a more exacting mens rea standard: they may be liable if they 'either knew or, owing to the circumstances at the time, should have known' about subordinate's criminal activity. The mental element for non-military superiors is articulated as 'either knew, or consciously disregarded information which clearly indicated, that the subordinates were committing or about to commit' crimes within the jurisdiction of the Court.

The ICC Statute also diverges from the practice of the ICTY and ICTR by requiring an element of causation.[20] According to Article 28 of the ICC Statute, the subordinate's crimes must have occurred 'as a result of' the superior's failure to exercise control properly over his subordinates. This does not require a direct causal link or a *conditio sine qua non*; the superior's omission must be shown to have 'increased the risk of the commission of the crimes' (*Bemba (Decision pursuant to Article 61(7)(a) and (b) of the Rome Statute on the Charges of the Prosecutor against Jean-Pierre Bemba Gombo)*, § 425).

At the same time, the ICC Statute limits the scope of superior liability for failing to punish the crimes of subordinates. Article 28 requires the superior to have knowledge or constructive knowledge of the subordinate's crimes before or during their commission. In relation to both military and non-military superiors it requires knowledge 'that the subordinates were committing or about to commit such crimes'. This language appears to rule out any responsibility for a superior who learns of the crimes *after* they were committed.

10.2.2 ELEMENTS OF SUPERIOR RESPONSIBILITY

In order to hold a superior criminally responsible for crimes committed by a subordinate, the following elements must be proven: *i)* the existence of relationship of subordination between the accused and those who are about to commit or have committed the crimes, which requires that the superior has effective control over the subordinates; *ii)* knowledge or constructive knowledge of the accused of the involvement of the subordinates in a crime; *iii)* failure by the accused to prevent the commission of the crimes or to punish the subordinates; *iv)* as noted above, the ICC Statute also requires that the commission of the crimes resulted from the superior's failure to exercise control.

---

[19] *Hadzihasanović and others (Decision on Interlocutory Appeal Challenging Jurisdiction in Relation to Command Responsibility)*, AC, § 17; TC (*Decision on Joint Challenge to Jurisdiction*), §§ 67–179.

[20] Contrast *Blaškić*, AC, § 77 (rejecting a requirement of 'causality between a commander's failure to prevent subordinates' crimes and the occurrence of these crimes', finding 'it is more a question of fact to be established on a case by case basis, than a question of law in general').

A. Subordination and Effective Control

The superior-subordinates relationship can be either *de jure* (such as in the case of officially appointed military commanders) or *de facto* (such as in the case of 'persons effectively acting as a military commander'). In both cases liability under the doctrine of superior responsibility requires that the superior's control over the subordinates is *effective*.[21] A superior has 'effective control' over a subordinate when he has the material ability to prevent or punish subordinate criminality.[22] As an ICTY Trial Chamber explained in the *Blagojević and Jokić* case:

> A commander vested with *de jure* authority who does not, in reality, have effective control over his or her subordinates would not incur criminal responsibility pursuant to the doctrine of command responsibility, while a *de facto* commander who lacks formal letters of appointment, superior rank or commission but does, in reality, have effective control over the perpetrators of offences could incur criminal responsibility under the doctrine of command responsibility. (§ 791)

Effective control is more than mere influence or ability to persuade.[23] As the ICC Pre-Trial Chamber observed in *Bemba*, effective control is usually a manifestation of a hierarchical relationship of subordination.[24] Both the ICC and the ICTY/ICTR have emphasized that determining whether a superior has effective control is 'more a matter of evidence than of substantive law'.[25] The ICTY and ICTR have stressed that effective control cannot be presumed from de jure authority. As the ICTR Appeals Chamber explained in the *Media* (*Nahimana and others*) case, '[p]ossession of de jure authority may obviously imply such material ability, but it is neither necessary nor sufficient to prove effective control' (§ 625).

The indicators of effective control are facts which demonstrate that the accused 'had the power to prevent, punish or initiate measures leading to proceedings against the alleged perpetrators where appropriate'.[26] Drawing on the experience of the ICTY and ICTR, the ICC Pre-Trial Chamber in *Bemba* listed the following factors as indicative of effective control of a military superior:

> (i) the official position of the suspect; (ii) his power to issue or give orders; (iii) the capacity to ensure compliance with the orders issued (i.e., ensure that they would be executed); (iv) his position within the military structure and the actual tasks that he carried out; (v) the capacity to order forces or units under his command, whether under his immediate command or at a [*sic*] lower levels, to engage in hostilities; (vi) the capacity to re-subordinate units or make changes to command structure; (vii) the power to promote, replace, remove or discipline any member of the forces; and (viii) the authority to send forces where hostilities take place and withdraw them at any given moment.(§ 417)

The SCSL Trial Chamber in *Brima and others* noted that although the ability to issue orders and mete out discipline is always important in assessing effective control, some of

---

[21] *Delalić and others*, TC, §§ 377–8 and AC, §§ 197–8; *Bemba* (*Decision pursuant to Article 61(7)(a) and (b) of the Rome Statue on the Charges of the Prosecutor against Jean-Pierre Bemba Gombo*), §§ 408–19; *Gacumbitsi*, AC, § 143.

[22] *Delalić and others*, AC, § 256; *Bemba* (*Decision pursuant to Article 61(7)(a) and (b) of the Rome Statute on the Charges of the Prosecutor against Jean-Pierre Bemba Gombo*), § 415.

[23] *Delalić and others*, AC, § 266; see also *Hadžihasanović and Kubura*, AC, § 214 (finding that cooperation between units was insufficient to establish effective control of the 3rd Corps commander over members of the *El Mujahedin* detachment); *Bemba* (*Decision pursuant to Article 61(7)(a) and (b) of the Rome Statute on the Charges of the Prosecutor against Jean-Pierre Bemba Gombo*), § 415.

[24] *Bemba* (*Decision pursuant to Article 61(7(a) and (b)) of the Rome Statute on the Charges of the Prosecutor against Jean-Pierre Bemba Gombo*), § 414; see also *Delalić and others*, AC § 303; *Halilović*, AC, §§ 59, 210.

[25] *Blaškić*, AC, § 69; *Bemba* (*Decision pursuant to Article 61(7)(a) and (b) of the Rome Statute on the Charges of the Prosecutor against Jean-Pierre Bemba Gombo*), § 416.

[26] *Blaškić*, AC, § 69. See also *Nahimana and others*, AC, § 788; *Strugar*, AC, § 254.

the 'traditional criteria' of effective control may not be appropriate or useful in a context involving an irregular army or rebel group (*Brima and others*, TC, §§ 787–9). The Chamber offered an additional set of indicia that might be suited to less formal military hierarchies.[27]

Civilian leaders do not need to be in a military-like structure, but they must possess a similar degree of effective control over their subordinates.[28] For example, in the *Media* case (*Nahimana and others*), the ICTR Appeals Chamber upheld the Trial Chamber's finding that Jean Bosco Barayagwiza, a founder and member of the steering committee of RTLM radio station, was the superior of the employees and journalists at the radio station (§§ 606–9).

It is important to note that a superior can exercise effective control through both direct and indirect subordination. All superiors in a chain of command who exercise effective control may thus incur criminal responsibility for the same conduct of a subordinate, so long as they each exercise effective control over their common subordinate.[29]

B. Actual or Constructive Knowledge

The doctrine of superior responsibility does not impose strict liability on a superior for the acts of subordinates (*Bemba* (*Decision pursuant to Article 61(7)(a) and (b) of the Rome Statute on the Charges of the Prosecutor against Jean-Pierre Bemba Gombo*), § 427). The superior must have had actual or constructive knowledge that his subordinates were going to commit, or were committing (or, except at the ICC, had committed) crimes.

At the ICTY and ICTR, constructive knowledge is proven when the superior is shown to have 'had reason to know' of subordinate crimes.[30] The superior who possesses information providing notice of the risk of subordinate crimes must take steps to determine whether his subordinates are involved in crimes. Inquiry notice is sufficient to hold a superior criminally responsible for failing to prevent or punish subordinates' crimes (*Delalić and others*, TC, § 383; and AC, § 241). According to the ICTY Appeals Chamber in the seminal *Delalić and others* case:

> A showing that a superior had some general information in his possession, which would put him on notice of possible unlawful acts by his subordinates would be sufficient to prove that he 'had reason to know' [...] This information does not need to provide specific information about unlawful acts committed or about to be committed. For instance, a military commander who has received information that some of the soldiers under his command have a violent or unstable character, or have been drinking prior to being sent on a mission, may be considered as having the required knowledge. (§ 238)

The assessment of whether the information is 'sufficiently alarming to justify further inquiry' (see *Hadžihasanović and Kubura*, AC, § 28; *Strugar*, AC, § 298)) must be grounded in the specific situation of the superior at the time. In *Strugar*, the ICTY Appeals Chamber overturned the Trial Chamber's interpretation of the necessary level of risk as being 'strong' or 'a clear possibility' and instead emphasized that the superior only needs

---

[27] According to the Trial Chamber, such indicia include 'that the superior had first entitlement to the profits of war, such as looted property and natural resources; exercised control over the fate of vulnerable persons such as women and children; the superior had independent access to and/or control of the means to wage war, including arms and ammunition and communications equipment; the superior rewarded himself or herself with positions of power and influence; the superior had the capacity to intimidate subordinates into compliance and was willing to do so; the superior was protected by personal security guards, loyal to him or her, akin to a modern praetorian guard; the superior fuels or represents the ideology of the movement to which the subordinates adhere; and the superior interacts with external bodies or individuals on behalf of the group'; *Brima and others*, TC, § 788.

[28] *Nahimana and others*, AC, § 605; *Bagilishema*, AC, §§ 51–5; *Kajelijeli*, AC, § 87.

[29] *Blaškić*, AC, § 67; *Delalić and others*, AC, §§ 251–2; *Orić*, TC, § 313; *Halilović*, TC, § 63.

[30] See First Additional Protocol, Art. 86(2) ('had information which should have enabled them to conclude in the circumstances at the time' that a subordinate was committing or was going to commit a breach).

to be on notice of a risk *sufficient to justify further inquiry* (*Strugar*, AC, §§ 303–4). As a result, the Appeals Chamber found that Strugar had reason to know of his subordinate's crimes seven hours earlier than the Trial Chamber had found (§ 308).

Information triggering a duty to investigate might include reports of crimes, the past criminal behaviour of the subordinates and the superior's reaction to it, the subordinate's level of training, or the tactical situation.[31] In some circumstances, a superior's knowledge of and failure to punish past offences might be sufficiently alarming information to justify further inquiry.[32] Knowledge of the occurrence of a crime is insufficient; the superior must also know that his subordinates are involved (*Orić*, AC, § 50–60; *Bagilishema*, AC, § 42). However, the superior need not know the exact identity of the subordinates engaging in criminal conduct; it is sufficient that he knows the 'category' of the subordinates.[33]

This standard is similar to the standard applied at the ICC for civilian superiors, which requires that the accused 'consciously disregarded information which clearly indicated that the subordinates were committing or about to commit' crimes within the jurisdiction of the Court. In contrast, the ICC Statute employs a lower 'should have known' standard to establish constructive knowledge for military superiors. In *Bemba*, the Pre-Trial Chamber accepted that this formulation was a type of negligence (§ 429). This imposes an 'active duty on the part of the superior to take the necessary measures to secure knowledge of the conduct of his troops and to inquire, regardless of the availability of information at the time on the commission of the crime' (§ 433). This standard was rejected by the ICTY and ICTR Appeals Chambers on the basis that it would approach negligence or strict liability (*Delalić and others*, AC, § 226; *Bagilishema*, AC, § 37).

C. Failure to Take Necessary and Reasonable Measures

To be found criminally responsible, the superior must have failed to take the necessary and reasonable measures to prevent or punish the subordinate's crimes. What is necessary and reasonable depends on the circumstances (*Blaškić*, AC, §§ 72, 417).[34] Although a superior cannot be required to do the impossible, he must take all measures within his material ability (*Blaškić*, AC, § 417). This may require the superior to go beyond his formal powers (*Krajišnik, AC*, §§ 193–4; *Kayishema and Ruzindana*, AC, § 302). A superior may fulfil his duty to punish by personally implementing disciplinary measures or, where appropriate, by reporting the crimes to the competent authorities.[35]

The ICTY and ICTR have treated the duty to prevent and the duty to punish as two separate and legally distinct obligations:

> The failure to punish and failure to prevent involve different crimes committed at different times: the failure to punish concerns past crimes committed by subordinates, whereas the failure to prevent concerns future crimes of subordinates. (*Blaškić*, AC, § 83; see also *Hadžihasanović and Kubura*, AC, § 260)

---

[31] See e.g. *Krnojelac*, AC, §§ 154–5); compare *Delalić and others*, TC, § 386, citing the UN Commission of Experts Report, UN Doc. S/1994/674, finding that the following indicia are relevant to providing actual knowledge: by circumstantial evidence (a) the number of illegal acts; (b) the type of illegal acts; (c) the scope of illegal acts; (d) the time during which the illegal acts occurred; (e) the number and type of troops involved; (f) the logistics involved; (g) the geographical location of the acts; (h) the widespread occurrence of the acts; (i) the tactical tempo of the operations; (j) the modus operandi of similar illegal acts; (k) the officers and staff involved; and (l) the location of the commander at the time.

[32] *Hadžihasanović and Kubura*, AC, §§ 30, 267; *Strugar*, AC, § 301; see also *Krnojelac*, AC, § 169.

[33] *Orić*, AC, § 35; *Hadžihasanović and Kubura*, TC, § 90.

[34] For an attempt to distinguish between 'necessary' and 'reasonable' measures, *see Halilović*, AC § 63.

[35] *Blaškić*, AC, §§ 68, 632; *Boškoski and Tarčulovski*, AC, §§ 233–4; *Bemba* (*Decision pursuant to Article 61(7)(a) and (b) of the Rome Statute on the Charges of the Prosecutor against Jean-Pierre Bemba Gombo*), § 440; see also ICC Statute, Art. 28(a)(ii) and (b)(iii).

A superior is obliged to both prevent and punish. If he learns of the crimes prior to commission, he cannot avoid responsibility for failing to prevent merely by imposing punishment after the fact (*Semanza*, TC, § 407). The ICC Pre-Trial Chamber in the *Bemba* case drew on the experience of the ICTY and ICTR to provide a non-exhaustive list of the type of measures required to discharge the duty to prevent:

> (i) to ensure that superior's forces are adequately trained in international humanitarian law; (ii) to secure reports that military actions were carried out in accordance with international law; (iii) to issue orders aiming at bringing the relevant practices into accord with the rules of war; (iv) to take disciplinary measures to prevent the commission of atrocities by the troops under the superior's command. (§ 438)

The ICC Pre-Trial Chamber also observed that the duty to repress includes both a duty to stop ongoing crimes from being repeated and a duty to punish forces after the crimes are completed (§ 439). However, under the ICC Statute, criminal responsibility only arises when the superior has actual or constructive knowledge of subordinate crimes prior to or during their commission. This temporal limitation rules out criminal liability for the superior who learns about subordinate crimes after they have been perpetrated. It remains to be seen whether the ICC will view a failure to punish as dependent on the failure to prevent.

10.3 IS SUPERIOR RESPONSIBILITY A MODE OF LIABILITY OR A CRIME PER SE?

Superior responsibility has a *sui generis*, unique nature. The superior did not personally commit the underlying offences; he performed a different actus reus with a different mens rea. His criminal responsibility is therefore of a different type from that of the person who committed the offence. Yet both the charging practice of international prosecutors and the convictions of international tribunals generally treat superior responsibility as a mode of liability through which the accused is guilty of the underlying offence. Some more recent judgments of the ICTY have challenged this assumption and raised questions about the nature of superior responsibility as a mode of liability.[36]

In order to fully understand the special nature of superior responsibility, it is useful to draw a distinction between failure to prevent and failure to punish.[37] When a superior knows or has reason to know that a subordinate is about to or is committing a crime and fails to prevent it, he should be legally treated as participating in the crime. Whether or not causation is legally required, there is at least a connection between the omission of the superior and the crimes.[38] Arguably this view was reflected in the French and Chinese laws mentioned above and in *Araki and others* (at 30–1) and in the German Law on Crimes against International Law 2002.[39]

---

[36] See e.g. *Halilović*, TC, §§ 54, 78; *Hadžihasanović and Kubura*, TC, § 75; *Orić*, TC, § 293.

[37] See e.g. *Blaškić*, AC, §§ 76–7 (noting the Trial Chamber's reasoning that causation could not be an element of superior responsibility under the ICTY Statute because it was impossible to link a failure to punish with the commission of the crime).

[38] *Delalić and others*, TC, § 399 ('the superior may be considered to be causally linked to the offences, in that, but for his failure to fulfil his duty to act, the acts of his subordinates would not have been committed').

[39] Section 4(1) of the Code provides that the commander who fails to prevent subordinate crimes 'shall be punished in the same way as the perpetrator of the offence committed by [the] subordinate'. The Explanatory Memorandum of the German Government states that 'from a theoretical viewpoint' 'the negligence' of the superior 'could be classified as mere complicity' (at 39). Compare Section 14 of the same act,

On the other hand, a superior who breaches his *duty to punish* is in a different situation. A superior who only learns of the crime after its commission, cannot be said to have participated in the criminal offence. In this case, the superior's responsibility should be conceptualized as a distinct crime, consisting of the failure to discharge supervisory duties, rather than any form of participation in the underlying offence of the subordinate. To hold otherwise risks infringing the culpability principle (*nulla poena sine culpa*);[40] the superior would be held responsible for a crime that he had no knowledge of and nothing to do with at the time of its commission.

The outcome of this discussion is not merely academic; it has consequences for the analysis of the so-called 'successor commander' issue, a topic that has divided judges at the international criminal courts and tribunals.[41] In *Hadzihasanović, Alagić and Kubura*, the Appeals Chamber held that a commander could not be held responsible for failing to report crimes committed *before* he took command of the relevant unit.[42] The majority considered that there was no practice or *opinio juris* to support this proposition. As was opined by Judges Hunt and Shahabuddeen in their dissenting opinions, however, it is not necessary to search for a specific rule of customary international law on the matter. Once the new commander has effective control, he has a duty to punish the crimes committed by the subordinates before he took command as soon as he acquires knowledge or constructive knowledge about them. If one considers that the failure of the duty to punish is nothing other than the actus reus of a distinct crime committed by the superior, in the form of violation of supervisory duties, the position of Judges Hunt and Shahabuddeen appears to be sound. One of the consequences of the majority's ruling is that the subordinates' prior crimes may go unpunished. This would be contrary to the notion that superiors are legally bound to make their subordinates criminally accountable. The issue of successor commander liability is unlikely to arise at the ICC because its Statute only covers failures to punish that follow a failure to prevent.

The nature of superior responsibility also affects sentencing. If a failure to prevent a subordinate's criminal activity is conceived as a form of participation in the underlying offence, then the subordinate's crimes should be the starting point of the sentencing analysis. Depending on the circumstances, the fact that a superior is under a duty to prevent crimes may warrant a higher sentence than the principal perpetrator. In contrast, when dealing with a failure to punish, the starting point for sentencing should be the seriousness of the superior's breach of duty. While the gravity of the underlying offence may play a part in sentencing, it is a more remote factor in the sentencing equation for failure to punish.

---

which sets out the separate offence of 'Omission to report a crime', punishable with a maximum sentence of five years.

[40] *Mpambara*, TC, § 26, suggesting that failure to punish is an exception to the culpability principal.

[41] *Bemba (Decision pursuant to Article 61(7)(a) and (b) of the Rome Statute on the Charges of the Prosecutor against Jean-Pierre Bemba Gombo)*, §§ 418–19. In *Hadžihasanović and others (Decision on Interlocutory Appeal Challenging Jurisdiction in Relation to Command Responsibility)*, a 3:2 majority of the ICTY Appeals Chamber held that customary international law required the superior to have effective control at the time of the offences, thus excluding criminal liability for 'successor commanders' who came into control after the crimes were committed. Although subsequent cases have followed this ruling, a number of ICTY judges and an SCSL Trial Chamber have pointed out that this decision creates a gap in the law: see e.g. *Orić*, AC, Declaration of Judge Shahabuddeen; Partially Dissenting Opinion and Declaration of Judge Liu; Separate and Partially Dissenting Opinion of Judge Schomburg; *Sesay and others*, TC, § 299.

[42] *Hadžihasanović and others (Decision on Interlocutory Appeal Challenging Jurisdiction in Relation to Command Responsibility)*, AC, §§ 37–57.

11

OTHER MODES OF CRIMINAL LIABILITY AND INCHOATE CRIMES

Individual criminal responsibility under ICL extends beyond commission or personal perpetration. It encompasses a number of other modes of liability; some are well known in national jurisdictions (such as aiding and abetting) and some are more unique to ICL (such as planning or ordering). ICL also covers a limited number of inchoate crimes (preparatory criminal acts that are punishable regardless of whether the crimes are actually committed). This chapter provides a brief overview of some of the most important modes of criminal liability and of inchoate offences in ICL.

11.1 AIDING AND ABETTING

Aiding and abetting consists of giving practical assistance, encouragement, or moral support with knowledge that it assists the perpetrator in the commission of the crime. The assistance given by the accessory to the principal must have a substantial effect on the perpetration of the crime.

The objective element of aiding and abetting is a positive action or omission (on omission liability see 10.1) that has a substantial effect on the perpetration of the crime (*Blaškić*, AC, § 46). The assistance may be physical (sometimes described in the case law as 'tangible') or psychological (in the sense of providing moral support or encouragement) (*Blaškić*, AC, § 46). The aider and abetter does not need to be present at the scene of the crime (*Blaškić*, AC, § 48). The assistance may be given before, during, or after the principal perpetrator's crime (*Blaškić*, AC, § 48). Where the act of assistance follows the completion of the crime, it must still be shown that it had a substantial effect on the perpetration of the crime. This may be demonstrated, for example, when the aider and abettor makes a promise before the crime to perform an act after the crime's completion.

The subjective element of aiding and abetting requires the aider and abettor to have knowledge that 'his actions assist the perpetrator in the commission of the crime'.[1] As the SCSL Trial Chamber summarized in *Brima and others*, knowledge may include an awareness of a risk:

> [T]he *mens rea* required for aiding and abetting is that the accused knew that his acts would assist the commission of the crime by the perpetrator or that he was aware of

---

[1] *Mrkšić and Šlijivančanin*, AC, §§ 49, 63; *Simić*, AC, § 86; *Vasiljević*, AC, § 102; *Blaškić*, AC, §§ 45, 49; *Furundžija*, TC, §§ 236–49.

the substantial likelihood that his acts would assist the commission of a crime by the perpetrator. (§ 776)[2]

This mental element presupposes that the aider and abettor knows of the principal perpetrator's crime. He must have knowledge of the 'essential elements of the crime which was ultimately committed by the principal', including any special requirements such as specific intent (*Simić*, AC, § 86). In other words, the aider and abettor is not required to possess the mental element for the crime. It is sufficient that he has knowledge that the principal is committing the crime. For example, to be convicted of aiding and abetting genocide, the defendant needs to know that he is substantially assisting the principal perpetrator in committing genocide. He does not need to share the specific genocidal intent to destroy the group.[3]

Although the aider and abettor has to have knowledge of the principal's crime, he does not have to predict the exact crime that will be committed. According to the ICTY Trial Chamber in the *Furundžija* case:

> [I]t is not necessary that the aider and abettor should know the precise crime that was intended and which in the event was committed. If he is aware that one of a number of crimes will probably be committed, and one of those crimes is in fact committed, he has intended to facilitate the commission of that crime, and is guilty as an aider and abettor. (§ 246)[4]

By way of example, if someone lent a gun to a well-known armed robber without knowing what specific crime he intended to perpetrate but aware that he would use it to engage in criminal conduct (murder, armed robbery, serious bodily harm, etc.), that person is answerable for aiding and abetting whichever of these crimes the armed robber may later have committed by using that weapon. It is not necessary for the lender to have been fully aware of the specific crime the well-known armed robber intended to perpetrate and the required mental element of that crime, so long as the lender was aware of the crimes that the armed robber was likely to commit and one of those crimes was committed.

This issue arose in the Dutch case of *van Anraat* before The Hague Court of Appeal. Between 1980 and 1988, the accused supplied the chemical raw material TDG (Thiodiglycol) necessary for the manufacture of mustard gas, which was then used by the Iraqi government against the Kurds. Applying Article 48 of the Dutch Criminal Code, the Court found that the accused *knew* that the chemicals he provided would be used to produce mustard gas and was aware of the high risk of use of mustard gas in war (*van Anraat*, Hague Court of Appeal, § 11.16). The Dutch Supreme Court (*Hoge Raad der Nederlanden*) upheld Van Anraat's conviction for aiding and abetting violations of the laws or customs of war, but reduced the sentence from 17 to 16.5 years' imprisonment because a delay in rendering the judgment violated the accused's right to an expeditious trial.

---

[2] Confirmed on appeal, *Brima and others*, AC, § 243.

[3] *Krstić*, AC, § 140; *Krnojelac*, AC, § 52; *Vasiljević*, AC, § 142; *Semanza*, AC, § 316. When, however, the defendant possesses genocidal intent, this does not compel the conclusion that he is also a principal. In *Kalimanzira*, the ICTR Appeals Chamber affirmed the Trial Chamber's finding that the accused was an aider and abettor, notwithstanding the fact that he possessed the specific intent required for genocide (*Kalimanzira*, AC, § 220). Likewise, an accessory is not required to share any common purpose with the principal. As stated by the ICTY Appeals Chamber in *Tadić*, 'the principal may not even know about the accomplice's contribution' (*Tadić*, AC, § 229).

[4] See also *Haradinaj and others*, AC, § 58; *Blaškić*, AC, § 50; *Simić*, AC, § 86.

Although ICL does not prescribe a mandatory lower sentence for an aider and abettor as opposed to the principal perpetrator, in practice aiding and abetting has attracted lower sentences.[5]

11.1.1 AIDING AND ABETTING AT THE ICC

Aiding and abetting is set out in Article 25(3)(c) of the ICC Statute, which provides:

> In accordance with this Statute, a person shall be criminally responsible and liable for punishment for a crime within the jurisdiction of the Court if that person [...] (c) For the purpose of facilitating the commission of such a crime, aids, abets or otherwise assists in its commission or its attempted commission, including providing the means for its commission.

Based on this language, it is possible that the ICC will interpret Article 25(3)(c) as introducing an additional requirement that the aider and abettor act 'for the purpose' of facilitating the principal's crime. This would narrow the concept of aiding and abetting as currently established in ICL.[6] Arguably this is an unfortunate outcome: a person who sells a gun to a known thug with knowledge that he is going to commit a crime should be criminally responsible for aiding and abetting. He should not be able to avoid conviction by showing that he sold the gun for a 'purpose' other than facilitating the crime, such as profit. Requiring the aider and abettor to act with purpose to facilitate the crime is tantamount to requiring shared intent.

11.1.2 THE 'APPROVING SPECTATOR' AIDER AND ABETTOR

Physical presence of an authority figure at the scene of a crime may provide moral and psychological encouragement resulting in aiding and abetting liability (the 'approving spectator' scenario).[7] As the ICTR Trial Chamber explained in the *Mpambara* case, the liability of an approving spectator should not be analysed as omission liability because:

> by choosing to be present, the accused is taking a positive step which may contribute to the crime. Properly understood, criminal responsibility is derived not from the omission alone, but from the omission combined with the choice to be present. (§ 22)[8]

The *Synagogue* case (at § 56), decided in 1948 under the terms of Control Council Law no. 10 by the German Supreme Court in the British Occupied Zone is a good example of an 'approving spectator' whose mere presence involved his aiding and abetting a crime. One of the defendants was found guilty of a crime against humanity for the devastation of a synagogue, although he had not physically participated in its destruction. The Court of First Instance and then the Supreme Court held that his

---

[5] For example, when the ICTY Appeals Chamber set aside Radislav Krstić's conviction for participating in a JCE and substituted a conviction for aiding and abetting genocide and murder, it reduced his sentence from 46 years' to 35 years' imprisonment (*Krstić*, AC, § 275). Similarly, when the ICTY Appeals Chamber replaced Mitar Vasiljević's convictions for JCE participation in the crimes of persecution and murder with aiding and abetting, it reduced his sentence from 20 to 15 years' (§ 159) imprisonment (*Vasiljević*, AC, 182). In imposing a sentence of 50 years on Charles Taylor mainly for aiding and abetting, the SCSL Trial Chamber explained that his sentence would have been much longer if he had been found to have been a principal perpetrator (*Taylor* (*Sentencing Judgement*), TC, §§ 94, 100).

[6] In *Mrkšić and Šlijivančanin*, the ICTY Appeals Chamber rejected a similar proposition, affirming that the accused is not required to 'specifically direct' his assistance to the crime (§ 159).

[7] *Brđanin*, AC, § 273; *Aleksovski*, AC, § 87; *Kayishema and Ruzindana*, AC, §§ 201–2.

[8] See also *Brđanin*, AC, § 273.

intermittent presence at the crime scene, together with his status as a long-time militant of the Nazi party, as well as his knowledge of the criminal enterprise, were sufficient to convict him.

However, the approving spectator must meet the legal test for aiding and abetting. Silent approval that does not make a substantial contribution to the offence does not fulfil the requirements for criminal liability. In the *Pig-cart parade* case (*L. and others* case), also from the German Supreme Court in the British Occupied Zone, the defendant P. attended a 'parade' of Nazi troops in which two political opponents of the Nazi party were exposed to public humiliation. P. followed the 'parade' as a spectator dressed in civilian attire. According to the Court, P.'s conduct could not 'even with certainty be evaluated as objective or subjective approval'. Hence he was acquitted.[9]

11.2 ORDERING

Ordering is a mode of responsibility whereby a person in a position of authority is held criminally responsible for instructing a perpetrator to commit a crime. The order must have a direct and substantial effect on the commission of the crime.[10]

Ordering does not require a formal superior–subordinate relationship (*Kordić and Čerkez*, AC, § 28). The ICTR Appeals Chamber explained, '[i]t is sufficient that there is proof of some position of authority on the part of the accused that would compel another to commit a crime in following the accused's order'.[11] This is distinct from the hierarchical relationship required for superior responsibility. The ICTR Appeals Chamber emphasized that 'Ordering requires no such relationship—it requires merely authority to order, a more subjective criterion that depends on the circumstances and the perceptions of the listener' (*Gacumbitsi*, AC, § 182). For example, in *Semanza*, the ICTR Appeals Chamber found that the Trial Chamber had erred in qualifying Semanza's role in relation to certain crimes as 'instigating'. Although Semanza, a former *bourgmestre* (mayor), no longer held any formal government position, he was still a highly respected authority figure in the community. The Appeals Chamber substituted ordering as the correct mode of responsibility (*Semanza*, AC, § 363). Since the person who issues the order is not required to have any formal position, it follows that the order need not be legally binding on the perpetrator (*Milutinović and others*, TC, vol. I, § 86).

There is no need for the order to be given in writing or in any other particular form.[12] Its existence can be proved by inference from the circumstances. For example, in the *Meyer* case before a Canadian Military Court in Aurich, Germany, the Judge Advocate explained that

> There is no evidence that anyone heard any particular words uttered by the accused which would constitute an order, but it is not essential that such evidence be adduced. The giving of the order may be proved circumstantially. (108)

Applying a similar approach, the ICTY Appeals Chamber upheld General Stanislav Galić's conviction for ordering the shelling campaign against the besieged city of Sarajevo, notwithstanding the fact that there was no such written order in evidence (*Galić*, AC, §§ 239–40).

---

[9] See also *Furundžija*, TC, § 199–209; *Kayishema and Ruzindana*, AC, §§ 201–2.
[10] See e.g. *Kamuhanda*, AC, § 75.
[11] *Semanza*, AC, § 361, referring to *Kordić and Čerkez*, AC, § 28. See also *Kamuhanda*, AC, § 75.
[12] *Kamuhanda*, AC, § 76; *Galić*, AC, §§ 239–40. See also *Brima and others*, TC, § 772.

Ordering requires a positive act and cannot be committed by an omission.[13] Presence at the scene of the crime is not required for ordering.[14] If the order issued by a superior authority is passed by a subordinate authority down the chain of command, the latter authority may, depending upon the circumstances, also be held criminally responsible (*Boškoski and Tarčulovski*, AC, §§ 166–7).

The person giving the order must do so with either direct intent or with the awareness of the substantial likelihood that a crime will be committed in execution of the order and acceptance of that risk. Thus, a conviction can be entered even when the order does not explicitly direct any criminal act. Of course, if an official issues a lawful order (for example, bombing military installations near civilian houses, after taking all the necessary precautions imposed by international humanitarian law) and the subordinates, in partial non-compliance with the order and without any prior notice to the superior, commit a war crime (for instance, deliberately bombing some civilian dwellings as well, or else failing to take the necessary precautions), the official is not criminally liable for ordering that war crime.

11.3 INSTIGATING

Instigating, that is prompting another to commit a crime—is closely related to other modes of liability such as aiding and abetting and ordering. Instigating is listed as a mode of responsibility in Article 7(1) of the ICTY Statute and Article 6(1) of the ICTR and SCSL Statutes. This type of conduct will likely be adjudicated under Article 25(3)(b) of the ICC Statute, which refers to soliciting and inducing.

The prompting of the instigator must make a substantial contribution to the conduct of the principal perpetrator who commits the crime (*Kordić and Čerkez*, AC, § 27). The instigator can act with direct intent or advertent recklessness, in the sense of an awareness of the substantial likelihood that a crime will be committed and acceptance of that risk (§ 112).

In the *Nahimana and others*, the ICTR Appeals Chamber drew a distinction between RTLM radio broadcasts that made a substantial contribution to murders and those that did not. It found that one reason why the denunciations of certain Tutsi individuals in broadcasts before the start of the genocide on 6 April 1994 were not instigating was because 'the longer the lapse of time between a broadcast and the killing of a person, the greater the possibility that other events might be the real cause of such killing' (*Nahimana and others*, AC, § 513). The Appeals Chamber also noted that there was no evidence that the killers heard the specific broadcast. In contrast, certain radio broadcasts after 6 April 1994 were found to be acts of instigation because they were 'designed to facilitate the killing of Tutsi' and substantially contributed to the killings of the named victims (§ 515).

11.4 PLANNING

Planning consists of devising, preparing, and arranging for the commission of a crime. It can be done alone or together with others. One may think, for instance, of planning an air attack on civilians or the use of prohibited chemical weapons, or the indiscriminate killing of civilians as part of a widespread or systematic attack.

---

[13] *Galić*, AC, § 176; *Milošević D.*, AC, § 267.
[14] *Boškoski and Tarčulovski*, AC, § 125; *Milošević D.*, AC, § 290.

The objective element is established when one or more persons design the commission of a crime, which is then carried out.[15] The planning has to contribute substantially to the crime.[16] The subjective element for planning is the direct intent to commit the crime or have it committed by others pursuant to the plan.[17] It is also sufficient if the planner acted with advertent recklessness; that is, with an awareness of the substantial likelihood that a crime will be committed in the execution of the plan and an acceptance of that risk.[18]

Given the nature and features of international crimes, it is often the higher military or civilian authorities that carry out the planning. However, planning is not limited to those who are the originators or architects of a master plan. The ICTY Appeals Chamber confirmed the conviction of Johan Tarčulovski (a police officer acting as an Escort Inspector in the President's Security Unit in the Ministry of the Interior of the former Yugoslav Republic of Macedonia) for planning, despite the possible involvement of higher authorities, finding that more than one person may be responsible for planning the same crime (*Boškoski and Tarčulovski*, AC, § 154).

Although planning is frequently charged as one of many possible modes of criminal responsibility, it is rarely relied on as the sole basis for conviction. One explanation for this is that planning, particularly as interpreted by the ICTY and ICTR, overlaps to a great extent with other modes such as aiding and abetting and ordering. It is difficult to imagine a scenario that would result in planning responsibility that is not also encompassed by aiding and abetting liability. This lack of distinction may be one of the reasons why planning is not specifically enumerated in the ICC Statute. It is likely that conduct categorized as planning at the ICTY and ICTR will be treated by the ICC under the general provisions of Article 25(3)(c) covering aiding and abetting and 'otherwise assisting'.

11.5 RESIDUAL ACCESSORY LIABILITY IN THE ICC STATUTE

Article 25(3)(d) of the ICC Statute introduces a novel mode of criminal responsibility at the crossroads of joint criminal enterprise and aiding and abetting. It provides for criminal responsibility when a person, who, while not necessarily[19] belonging to a group, '[i]n any other way contributes to the commission or attempted commission of such a crime by a group of persons acting with a common purpose'. The *Lubanga* Pre-Trial Chamber explained that this serves as a 'residual form of accessory liability' (*Lubanga (Confirmation Decision)*, § 337).

The objective element requires that the accused has contributed to a crime carried out by a group sharing a common purpose in any way other than those set out in Article 25(3)(a) to (c) of the Statute. In the first decision that discussed this mode of criminal liability in detail, the *Mbarushimana* Pre-Trial Chamber explained that in light of the residual nature of this type of liability and its focus on group criminality, the required contribution to the commission or attempted commission of a crime must be at least a *significant* one, a standard not met in that case (*Mbarushimana (Confirmation Decision)*,

---

[15] See e.g. *Milošević D.*, AC, § 268; *Kordić and Čerkez*, AC, § 26.

[16] *Milošević D.*, AC, § 268; *Kordić and Čerkez*, AC, § 26.

[17] *Milošević D.*, AC § 268; *Kordić and Čerkez*, AC, §§ 29, 33; *Media case (Nahimana and others)*, AC, § 479; *Brima and others*, TC, § 766.

[18] *Milošević D.*, AC, § 268; *Kordić and Čerkez*, AC, §§ 29, 31; *Media case (Nahimana and others)*, AC, § 479.

[19] *Mbarushimana (Confirmation Decision)*, § 275 (noting that liability under 25(3)(d) 'must apply irrespective of whether the person is or is not a member of the group acting with a common purpose').

§ 283). Article 25(3)(d) may include contributions after the crime as occurred, provided that there was a prior agreement between the group and the accused (§ 287).

As for the subjective elements, the ICC Statute distinguishes between the situations in Article 25(3)(d)(i), where the accused aims to further the criminal intent of the group and Article 25(3)(d)(ii), where the accused is merely aware of (but does not share) the group's intention to commit a crime. In either case, the accused's contribution must be linked with the crime in the sense that the accused must mean to engage in the conduct and be aware that his conduct contributes to the group's activities (*Mbarushimana* (*Confirmation Decision*), § 288).

11.6 INCHOATE CRIMES

Many legal systems punish not only consummated criminal offences (for instance, murder, theft, etc.), but also 'inchoate' crimes ('*crimes formels*'), meaning preliminary or incomplete criminal wrongdoings. These are acts that: *i*) are preparatory to prohibited offences; *ii*) have not been completed, therefore have not yet caused any harm; and *iii*) are punished on their own.

The rationale behind criminalization of inchoate offences is clear: the criminal law is aimed at protecting society. Therefore, in addition to punishing offences already perpetrated, the criminal law also endeavours to prevent the commission of future crimes. It consequently intervenes with its prohibitions at an early stage, before crimes are completed; that is, at the stage of their preparation, so as to forestall the consummation of the harmful consequences of actual crimes.

In many national legal systems (particularly in common law countries) three main categories of inchoate crimes are envisaged: attempt, conspiracy, and incitement. In ICL, while attempts are regarded as admissible as a *general class* of inchoate crimes, conspiracy and incitement are only prohibited when connected to the most serious crime: genocide.[20] Arguably, ordering and planning should also be considered as inchoate crimes.

11.6.1 ATTEMPT

Attempt as a distinct criminal offence occurs when a person acts with the intent to commit a crime, but fails. This can happen when the perpetrator takes the initial steps but is then apprehended or when the perpetrator's actions do not produce the intended results because of intervening external circumstances. An example of the first category is when a soldier starts to beat a prisoner of war with the intention of killing him and is only prevented from so doing by an officer. An example of the second category is when a soldier shoots a prisoner of war, intending to execute him, but the intended victim is not fatally wounded and manages to escape.[21] Attempt is considered a completed crime even though the intended harm is not caused to the victim.

---

[20] It could also be argued that threatening is another inchoate offence recognized by international criminal law. ICTR Art. (4)(h) refers to '[t]hreats to commit any of the foregoing acts', which include murder, rape, pillage, and other violations of Common Article 3 to the Geneva Conventions or the Second Additional Protocol. The ICTY has also recognized threats of violence in the limited context of the war crime of spreading terror: see *Milosevic D.*, AC, § 31. It is questionable whether threats in the terror context are technically inchoate because the prohibited harm may be caused by threat alone.

[21] In *Charles W. Keenan* the accused had been ordered by his superior to 'finish off' a civilian woman at whom the superior had already shot. A US Court of Military Appeal held that attempted murder was to be ruled out only because Keenan knew that she was no longer alive when he fired at her. The accused and

For an attempt to be punishable, the accused must take a significant step towards initi-ating the criminal action that is interrupted by intervening circumstances. The subjective element for attempt is direct intent. This is consistent with the approach in most common law countries, as well as in many civil law systems, which require the *intention* to carry out the offence. Recklessness (or indirect intent, as it is called in the ICTY case law) is not enough.[22]

The existence of a rule of customary international law on attempt can be inferred from the fact that all penal systems of the world provide for attempt as a separate mode of criminal liability[23] or a distinct offence.[24] National courts have repeatedly relied upon the notion of attempt (normally attempted murder) in connection with international crimes. There are numerous cases brought before German courts concerning the attempted kill-ing of prisoners of war, civilians, or inmates in concentration camps.[25] Other key exam-ples of attempted murder include the Canadian case of *Johann Neitz*, which involved the attempted murder of a prisoner of war, and the US case of *Charles W. Keenan* (at § 113).[26] In these cases, national courts adjudicated the war crime of attempted murder (or manslaughter).

The rule under discussion has been codified in Article 25(3)(f) of the ICC Statute, whereby a person is criminally responsible if he 'attempts to commit [a crime under the Court's jurisdiction] by taking action that commences its execution by means of a sub-stantial step, but the crime does not occur because of circumstances independent of the person's intentions'. Article 25(3)(f) goes on to provide for the possibility that the attempt might be abandoned by the accused:

> However, a person who abandons the effort to commit the crime or otherwise prevents the completion of the crime shall not be liable for punishment under this Statute for the attempt to commit that crime if that person completely and voluntarily gave up the crimi-nal purpose.

Surprisingly, attempt has not played any significant role at the ICTY or ICTR. In early cases at both Tribunals, Trial Chambers determined that the Tribunals' Statutes did not

---

two witnesses testified that they believed the woman was dead before the accused fired, absolving him of attempted murder (at 112–13). For a comment on the case, see *Cassese's Companion*, at 756.

[22] For a contrary view, see *Katanga and Chui (Confirmation Decision)*, §§ 458–60), holding that 'the *dolus* that embodies the attempt is the same than that one that embodies the consummated act'.

[23] See e.g. the laws cited in LRTWC, vol. XV, at 89 (Norway, Yugoslavia, the Netherlands).

[24] See the cases reported in LRTWC, vol. VI, at 120; vol. VII, at 73.

[25] See e.g. *Friedrich Otto Köhler*, at 274 (the defendant was a police officer charged with killing German and foreign detainees in 1945); *Kurt Köllner*, at 682 (the accused, a member of the SS and head of the secu-rity police, committed war crimes in 1942 against persons detained in a concentration camp in Poland); *Otto Haupt and others*, at 604 (the defendants committed war crimes against prisoners of war detained in a concentration camp); *Karl Dietrich*, at 485 (ill-treatment of Jews in occupied territory; the Court of Assize ruled out attempted murder on the facts). Some cases concern aiding and abetting attempted murder: see e.g. *W. J. F. Kleinhenn*, at 9 (in 1942 the accused committed war crimes against sick detainees in a concentra-tion camp). Other cases concern attempted manslaughter; see for instance *S.* case, at 505 (in early 1945 the defendant committed war crimes against foreign workers).

[26] In the *Neitz* case, the accused Johann Neitz, a German soldier, shot twice at a member of the Royal Canadian Air Force, who had been taken prisoner. As a result of the shooting the Canadian prisoner fell down but did not die. Neitz was charged both with committing a war crime, for shooting with the intent to kill, and, alternatively, with a war crime for wounding the prisoner of war in violation of the laws and usages of war (see prosecutor's opening address, at 13, and Judge Advocate's summing-up, at 195–205). The Court found Neitz guilty of the first charge and sentenced him to be imprisoned for life (at 209). For a comment see *Cassese's Companion*, at 841.

contemplate attempt as a general mode of responsibility or an inchoate crime.[27] It is possible that this narrow view is partly due to the fact that attempt as an inchoate offence rarely occurs in the context of the most serious crimes. It may also be due to the practical fact that instead of charging attempt, which is not specifically enumerated in the Tribunals' Statutes (except in relation to genocide), prosecutors charged other completed offences.

A case in point is *Vasiljević*.[28] The accused, a Bosnian Serb member of a paramilitary group, together with three others took seven Bosnian Muslim civilians to the bank of the river Drina, forced them to line up, and then shot at them. Five men were killed. Two, pretending to be dead, jumped into the river and escaped. The prosecution charged the defendant with murder (as a war crime and a crime against humanity) for the killing of the five men. For the attempted murder of the survivors, the prosecution charged him with inhumane acts as a crime against humanity and violence to life and persons as a war crime. The Trial Chamber convicted the defendant of 'other inhumane acts' as a crime against humanity.[29]

Although the ICTY Statute does not explicitly provide for 'attempt', it would have been preferable for the Trial Chamber to analyse these events under the law of attempted murder, rather than that of inhumane acts. Instead of focusing on the shooters' intent to kill, the Trial Chamber had to measure the harm suffered by the surviving victims against the legal standard for inhumane acts. This approach does not fully capture the gravity of the crime because it fails to account for the intention to kill, a mens rea standard far above the intention to cause serious physical or mental harm required for inhumane acts as a crime against humanity. The Appeals Chamber found that Vasiljević was an aider and abettor, rather than a participant in a JCE, but left the inhumane acts analysis untouched.

Attempt to commit genocide is listed as a punishable act in Article 4(3)(d) of the ICTY statute and Article 2(3)(d) of the ICTR Statute. To date, no cases have been tried on these provisions.

11.6.2 CONSPIRACY

Conspiracy is a form of criminality punished in common law systems, but either unknown to or accepted only to a very limited extent by civil law countries.[30] Conspiracy is a group offence, consisting of the *agreement of two or more persons to commit a crime*. It is punishable even if the crime is never perpetrated. The mens rea element of conspiracy is twofold: (i) *knowledge* of the facts or circumstances making up the crime the group intends to commit; (ii) *intent* to carry out the conspiracy and thereby perpetrate the substantive offence. The rationale behind the prohibition of this crime is the need to prevent offences, especially when they involve several persons and are thus more dangerous to the community.

In ICL no customary rule has evolved on conspiracy on account of the lack of support from civil law countries for this category of crime. In the *Hamdan* case (2006), the US

---

[27] See e.g. *Akayesu*, TC, § 473; *Krnojelac*, TC, § 432, n. 129, stating 'The existence of a mistaken belief that the intended victim will be discriminated against, together with an intention to discriminate against that person because of that mistaken belief, may in some circumstances amount to the inchoate offence of *attempted* persecution, but no such crime falls within the jurisdiction of this Tribunal'.

[28] See also *Mrda* (*Amended Indictment*, Count 3); TC, § 31.

[29] On the decision, see the critical remarks of A. Cassese, 'Black Letter Lawyering v. Constructive Interpretation', 2 JICJ (2004), 265–74.

[30] In most civil law systems, entering into agreement to commit a crime is not punishable per se, unless it leads to the perpetration of the crime. Conspiracy as an inchoate offence is only recognized in exceptional circumstances, particularly for serious crimes concerning state security or organized crime.

Supreme Court, per Justice Stevens, rightly held that conspiracy is not criminalized as a war crime under international law (at 601–13).

However, treaty rules on conspiracy can be found in the Charter of the Nuremberg Tribunal annexed to the London Agreement of 1945. Article 6 made punishable persons 'participating in a common plan or conspiracy for the accomplishment' of any crime against peace, and in addition made 'leaders, organizers, instigators or accomplices participating in the formulation or execution of a common plan or conspiracy to commit any of the foregoing crimes [that is, crimes against peace, war crimes, and crimes against humanity] responsible for all acts performed by any persons in execution of such plan'. This provision laid down *ex post facto* law. By referring to conspiracy to commit a crime against peace, it punished persons who had conspired to wage the war that had just ended. In addition, to the extent that it referred to other crimes, it also made conspiracy punishable for acts already accomplished. In other words, conspiracy was held to be punishable to the extent that any plan or agreement to commit an international crime *had been actually carried out*. Interestingly, Control Council Law no. 10 only referred to conspiracy to commit crimes against peace: see Article 2(1)(a). Understandably, both the Nuremberg Tribunal and the US Military Tribunals sitting at Nuremberg took a restrictive view of conspiracy: see, in particular, *Göring and others* (at 224–6) and *Altstötter and others* (at 956). In the former case, the influence of the French Judge Donnedieu de Vabres, and his insistence on the novel nature of conspiracy in international law, were indisputably decisive.[31]

The only treaty rule on conspiracy currently in force is Article 3(b) of the 1948 Genocide Convention, which makes 'conspiracy to commit genocide' punishable. Genocide is such an odious crime that the international community decided that even the mere agreement to commit genocide should be criminalized. Like most other substantive provisions of the Convention, the prohibition of conspiracy to commit genocide has crystallized into customary international law. Conspiracy to commit genocide is an enumerated crime in the ICTY and ICTR Statutes. It is not included in the ICC Statute, which consequently differs in this respect from customary international law.

According to the ICTR Appeals Chamber, a conspiracy to commit genocide is 'an agreement between two or more persons to commit the crime of genocide' (*Ntagerura and others*, AC, § 92). The actus reus is the act of entering the agreement to commit genocide. This does not require proof of a formal agreement, for example in the form of a contract or a specific meeting where the agreement was devised. Instead, the agreement can be inferred from the circumstances, in particular from the coordinated actions of the conspirators.[32] The required mental element is the intention to form an agreement coupled with the specific intent of the crime of genocide, the intent to destroy, in whole or in part, a national, ethnical, racial, or religious group, as such (*Nahimana and others*, AC, § 894). The *Popović* Trial Chamber confirmed that conspiracy to commit genocide is a continuing crime, and thus additional people can join the conspiracy after the initial agreement has been made (*Popović*, TC, § 876).

As an inchoate offence, the crime of conspiracy to commit genocide is punishable even if it fails to lead to genocidal results; that is, even if no member of the targeted group has been harmed. But what happens when genocide does follow the conspiracy? International case law is inconsistent on the question of whether the conspiracy *merges*

---

[31] H. Donnedieu de Vabres, 'Le Procès de Nuremberg devant les principes modernes du droit pénal international', 70 HR (1947–I), 528–42, reprinted in English as 'The Nuremberg Trial and the Modern Principles of International Criminal Law' in G. Mettraux (ed.), *Perspective on the Nuremberg Trial* (Oxford: Oxford University Press, 2008), 213–73. Among other things, he held the view that Art. 6 of the Nuremberg Charter expressed the French notion of '*complicité*' (at 541). He also emphasized that, with regard to crimes against peace, the IMT ultimately avoided holding that there was a general conspiracy (at 541–2).

[32] See e.g. *Nahimana and others*, AC, §§ 896–8; *Niyitegeka*, TC, § 428.

with the completed crime. In some cases, ICTR trial chambers have convicted for both conspiracy to commit genocide and genocide itself. In *Gatete*, the ICTR Appeals Chamber confirmed that a person may be convicted for both conspiracy to commit genocide and genocide itself.[33] The better view, advanced by the *Musema* Trial Chamber, is that it is unnecessary to convict for conspiracy when the completed offence has been perpetrated because it would no longer serve any preventative purpose (*Musema*, TC, §§ 195–8).

11.6.3 DIRECT AND PUBLIC INCITEMENT TO COMMIT GENOCIDE

Incitement to genocide is prompting of others to commit the crime of genocide. According to the ICTR Appeals Chamber, hate propaganda or even 'propaganda tending to provoke genocide' is insufficient; only specific acts of direct and public incitement to commit genocide are criminalized (*Nahimana and others*, AC, § 726). The required intent to incite others to commit genocide includes the genocidal intent to destroy the group (§ 677). As an inchoate crime, incitement to commit genocide is punishable whether or not genocide is perpetrated as a result of the incitement. Genocide's extreme gravity justifies punishing preparatory acts of incitement.

In order to be punishable, incitement to genocide must be both *direct* and *public*. These requirements serve to limit the scope of the inchoate crime. They also distinguish the crime of direct and public incitement from modes of liability involving the prompting of another to commit a crime, such as instigation. Whereas direct and public incitement to genocide is a crime in itself, instigation is a mode of participation in the completed crime and does not need to be either direct or public (§§ 678–9).

Incitement must be *direct*; that is, it must specifically provoke or induce other persons to engage in genocide. In other words, it must not consist of vague suggestions. Nevertheless, the meaning of the message must be assessed in its cultural and linguistic context (§§ 700–1).[34] Even implicit messages may amount to direct incitement, as long as the audience can immediately understand the message in context.[35] For instance, the use of coded language employing the pejorative term 'cockroaches' to refer to Tutsi as the targets of the genocide in Rwanda was found to amount to 'direct' incitement (*Akayesu*, TC, §§ 556–7).

Incitement must also be *public*: the act of inducing or provoking other persons to engage in acts of genocide must be performed in a public place or gathering or through the mass media capable of reaching the general public at large.[36] In *Muvunyi*, an ICTR Trial Chamber explained:

> There is no requirement that the incitement message be addressed to a certain number of people or that it should be carried through a specific medium such as radio, television, or a loudspeaker. However, both the number and the medium may provide evidence in support of a finding that the incitement was public. (*Muvunyi*, TC, § 503)

In *Kalimanzira*, the ICTR Appeals Chamber found that the supervision of people at a roadblock did not qualify as direct and public incitement because it was more akin to a private conversation in that it 'did not involve any form of mass communication such as public speech'.[37]

---

[33] See e.g. *Gatete*, AC, § 260–4.
[34] See also *Mugesera*, Supreme Court of Canada, §§ 87, 94.
[35] *Nahimana and others*, AC, §§ 698–700, 703; *Akayesu*, TC, §§ 557–8.
[36] See e.g. *Akayesu*, TC, § 555; *Bikindi*, TC, § 389; *Nahimana and others*, TC, §§ 1011–15; *Kajelijeli*, TC, § 851.
[37] *Kalimanzira*, AC, § 159 and §§ 156–65; *Nahimana and others*, AC, § 862.

The ICTR case against Simon Bikindi, a popular Rwandan composer and singer, provides a good example of incitement that is both *direct and public*. The Trial Chamber found that Bikindi 'deliberately, directly and publicly incited the commission of genocide with the specific intent to destroy the Tutsi ethnic group' (*Bikindi*, TC, § 424), based on the following facts:

> [T]owards the end of June 1994, in Gisenyi *préfecture*, Bikindi travelled on the main road between Kivumu and Kayove in a convoy of *Interahamwe* and broadcast songs, including his own, using a vehicle outfitted with a public address system. When heading towards Kayove, Bikindi used the public address system to state that the majority population, the Hutu, should rise up to exterminate the minority, the Tutsi. On his way back, Bikindi used the same system to ask if people had been killing Tutsi, who were referred to as snakes. (§ 281)

11.6.4 ORDERING AND PLANNING

Although the ICTY and ICTR have treated ordering and planning exclusively as modes of liability for participating in a completed crime, there is considerable historical authority supporting ordering and planning as inchoate crimes.

When ordering is conceived of as an inchoate offence, an authority figure issuing an illegal order may be found guilty even if the order is not carried out by the subordinates if the superior intended the order to be executed and knew that the order was illegal, or else the order was manifestly illegal. Ordering makes most sense as an inchoate crime when it is limited to situations of formal authority, such as the military context. A good example of inchoate ordering is the case of *General Jacob H. Smith*. In 1902, a US Court Martial held that General Smith was guilty of ordering that no quarter should be given to the enemy in the Philippines, even though in fact his troops did not comply with this order (§§ 799–813).[38] In many other cases courts have convicted officers for issuing criminal orders, even if such orders were not executed.[39] For this category of criminality the requisite mental element is the *intent* to have the crime committed.[40]

According to an ICTR Trial Chamber, treating planning exclusively as a mode of participation in a completed crime is consistent with the conclusions of the International Law Commission and the relevant rule of the ICTR Statute (Article 6(1)) laying down the principle of individual criminal responsibility, which 'implies that the planning or preparation of the crime actually leads to its commission (*Akayesu*, TC, § 472). Arguably, however, the gravity of international crimes (or at least the most serious among them)

---

[38] For a comment on the case, see *Cassese's Companion*, at 926.

[39] See e.g. *High Command* (at 118–23): *The Hostages Trial* (vol. VIII, at 90); *Falkenhorst* (at 18, 23, 29–30), *Hans Wickmann* (at 133). In *Tzofan and others v. IDF Advocate and others* (*Meir* case), Judge D. Levin (concurring) held that 'the higher the rank of the commanding officer and the more comprehensive and more decisive his authority, the greater the responsibility incumbent upon him to examine and determine the justification and legality of the order' (at 745).

[40] In *Jung and Schumacher*, decided by a Canadian Military Court sitting at Aurich, Germany, the Judge Advocate, in discussing the position of the defendant Jung, who had ordered the other defendant to shoot and kill a Canadian war prisoner, noted: 'The Court may find that the accused uttered the words or some words to do harm to the prisoner, but it must be found that he uttered them with the expectation and intention that they should be acted upon by someone who heard them, including Schumacher. In this event he would have either incited, counseled or procured the acts to have been done, and so be concerned [in the crime]. Now, if you find that the accused Jung handed the prisoner over to Schumacher, knowing or expecting he would be killed, then again he would be concerned [in the killing of the Canadian POW]' (at 219–20). For a comment on the case, see *Cassese's Companion*, at 739.

warrants the conclusion that planning their commission should be punishable even if the crime is not actually perpetrated. The rationale is that ICL aims not only to punish persons for completed crimes, but also to prevent persons from engaging in criminal conduct preparatory to serious crimes. The law should therefore be interpreted as much as possible in a manner that is designed to prevent crime.

SECTION III

CIRCUMSTANCES EXCLUDING CRIMINAL LIABILITY

12

JUSTIFICATIONS AND EXCUSES

Circumstances can sometimes arise that either justify criminal conduct, or excuse the perpetrator for engaging in it. A justification is a circumstance that makes the accused's conduct preferable to even worse alternatives, such as self-defence; an excuse, such as duress, involves an action that, while voluntary, nevertheless was produced by an impairment of a person's autonomy to such a degree as to negate their blameworthiness. Mistakes of law, mental incapacity, or intoxication are also usually categorized as excuses, although strictly speaking, these are cognitive impairments that preclude the formation of a guilty mental state in the first place. All of these are commonly referred to as 'defences', although this term is misleading to the extent that it implies a shifting of the burden of proof. These doctrines are 'defences' only in the sense that it is the accused who is normally expected to raise them.

Justifications and excuses are, by their nature, exceptional occurrences. The concepts are therefore relatively underdeveloped in international criminal jurisprudence and have not always been scrupulously distinguished from each other in the cases where they have arisen. This in no way detracts from the need to distinguish the foundations and consequences arising from these two concepts.

As noted above, a justification affirms that conduct normally deemed criminal may, in exceptional circumstances, be appropriate or at least permissible, if not legally authorized. Thus, homicide committed in self-defence or in execution of a legal sentence of death is no crime.[1] An excuse, by contrast, does not negate that the crime has taken place, but recognizes a circumstance that makes it unjust or inappropriate to hold the perpetrator criminally responsible for the action. Justifications affirm the rightness, or at least permissibility, of the action; excuses preserve the wrongness of the action, while at the same time recognizing the injustice of punishing the actor.

Some situations may arise that straddle this distinction. Self-defence, for example, is characterized as a justification in that the innocent defender has a superior interest to that of the culpable attacker, but self-protection is also an overpowering psychological inducement to action. Both considerations can arise from the same circumstances, as where the interests that need to be protected so dramatically outweigh the interests damaged by committing the crime that the action may be both justified (as representing the less evil choice) and excused (because the better choice is so important to the accused that the actor is psychologically constrained). The former may be described as 'necessity'

---

[1] US Manual for Courts Martial (1951), § 197(b): 'A homicide committed in the proper performance of a legal duty is justifiable. Thus executing a person pursuant to a legal sentence of death, killing in suppression of a mutiny or riot, killing to prevent the escape of a prisoner if no other reasonably apparent means are adequate, killing an enemy in battle, and killing to prevent the commission of an offence attempted for force or surprise such as burglary, robbery, or aggravated arson, are cases of justifiable homicide.'

(as justification); whereas the latter has been variously described as 'duress by circumstances' or as 'excused necessity'.[2]

Justifications and excuses are distinguished by their rationales and consequences. A justification legitimizes certain conduct as lawful, whereas an excuse merely precludes imposing liability. A first consequence is that other persons participating in the crime, for example as accessories or co-perpetrators, are not necessarily excused because the perpetrator is excused. For example, any accessory to the excused perpetrator may be convicted of aiding and abetting (unless they themselves also benefit from an excuse). Second, self-defence is not a justified reaction against actions that are themselves justified, but is a justified reaction to actions that may be excused. Third, while it may be unjust to punish a person where his conduct is excused, it may not always be unjust to require the payment of *compensation* for any resulting damage. No such obligation would arise, on the other hand, if the action is deemed legally justified.

Caution should be exercised in transplanting certain features of domestic law commonly associated with justifications and excuses. Consent of the victim, for example, will be irrelevant in respect of most international crimes prohibiting attacks on the life, body, or dignity of human beings, most of which have the rank of *jus cogens* i.e. peremptory norms, and are therefore not derogable by either states or individuals.[3] The Elements of Crimes and the Rules of the ICC limit, but do not entirely exclude, the possibility of claiming consent in response to a charge of rape or other forms of sexual violence.[4] On the other hand, some property-related war crimes are expressly predicated on lack of consent.[5] Consent, to the extent it is permissible, constitutes a full justification because it negates an essential condition for the existence of the crime, and renders lawful conduct that would otherwise be criminal.

12.1 JUSTIFICATIONS

Among the circumstances that negate unlawfulness of what would otherwise be a criminal act are: *i*) self-defence; *ii*) necessity (as justification); and *iii*) *belligerent reprisals* (for war crimes).

---

[2] UK Ministry of Defence's Manual of the Law of Armed Conflict (2004) (Oxford: Oxford University Press, 2004), §§ 16.42.1 and 16.42.2. See also A. Eser, 'Article 31', Triffterer, *ICC Commentary*, 884–4.

The dual meaning of 'necessity' has caused ambiguity in the case law and amongst commentators, which the discussion below will seek to clarify and avoid. Despite the terminological confusion, the conceptual distinction is clear: necessity as justification asserts that the perpetrator's action was morally correct because it averted a harm greater than the criminal act; duress by circumstances (or 'excused necessity') depends on the circumstances of threat or danger creating a psychological pressure on the perpetrator tantamount to duress. A second situation of duress, 'duress by threats', arises when the perpetrator is directly threatened as an inducement to commit a criminal act. The mental process is dramatically different than in the case of 'duress by circumstances', but the conduct may be excused on essentially the same ground. See J. Ohlin, 'The Bounds of Necessity', 6 JICJ (2008), 289, at 292–5; J. Pradel, *Droit pénal comparé* (Dalloz: Paris, 2008), at 140–1. In national legislation see the French Criminal Code, Art. 122-7; and the US Model Penal Code, s. 3.02.

[3] Consent is expressly excluded as a defence to the war crime of mutilation. ICC Elements of Crimes, Art. 8(2)(b)(x)-1. The unique reference to consent in respect of this crime does not reflect that consent is available for all other war crimes, but probably arose as a response to the special role played by informed consent in respect of medical procedures.

[4] Rule 70 of the ICC Rules excludes, in effect, evidence of any words or conduct as showing consent where the perpetrator has allegedly committed rape by taking advantage of a coercive environment.

[5] The war crime of pillage is said to be conditioned on appropriation 'without the consent of the owner': ICC Elements of Crimes, Art. 8(2)(b)(xvi). The crime against humanity of forcible transfer is also inherently predicated on the absence of genuine consent arising from coercion.

12.1.1 SELF-DEFENCE

The commission of an international crime may be justified as self-defence when perpetrated to prevent, or put an end to, a crime being, or about to be, perpetrated against himself or a third person. Self-defence is lawful provided it fulfils the following requirements: *i*) the action in self-defence is taken in response to an imminent or actual unlawful attack on the life of the person or of another person; *ii*) there is no other way of preventing or stopping the unlawful attack; *iii*) the unlawful attack has not been caused by the person acting in self-defence; *iv*) the conduct in self-defence is proportionate to the unlawful attack to which the person reacts.[6]

Self-defence as a justification in criminal law shall not be confused with acts of self-defence by states under public international law. The latter relates to the legality of the resort to force by states (and arguably state-like entities), whereas the former concerns a plea that a defendant may raise to escape criminal liability. The ICTY has repeatedly held that whether an armed attack is characterized as 'self-defence' against another attack is legally irrelevant to the claim of self-defence by a defendant.[7] In the context of armed conflict, this is no more than an application of the well-established distinction between the international rules on the legality of resort to armed force (the so-called *jus ad bellum*) and the rules that apply within armed conflict (the *jus in bello*) (*Boskoski and Tarculovksi*, AC, § 44). The last sentence of Article 31(1)(c) of the ICC Statute ('the fact that the person was involved in a defensive operation conducted by forces shall not in itself constitute a ground for excluding criminal responsibility under this subparagraph') does not imply the contrary.[8]

Post-Second World War courts have frequently discussed, though seldom accepted, a claim of self-defence.[9] The plea did succeed in *Erich Weiss and Wilhelm Mundo*, before a US Military Court in Ludwigsburg. An American airman who in May 1944 had safely parachuted from his military aircraft over Germany was captured and turned over to two policemen. When, during an air raid, a crowd gathered around them demanding that the prisoner be killed, he suddenly moved his right hand in his pocket; the two policemen fired at him and he was instantly killed. The two defendants pleaded that they had

---

[6] The *Kordić and Čerkez* Trial Chamber held that self-defence as a ground for excluding criminal responsibility is one of the defences that 'form part of the general principles of criminal law which the International Tribunal must take into account in deciding the cases before it' (*Kordić and Čerkez*, TC, § 449). It went on to note that the 'principle of self-defence' enshrined in Article 31(1)(c) of the Statute of the ICC 'reflects provisions found in most national criminal codes and may be regarded as constituting a rule of customary international law' (§ 451).

[7] *Martić*, AC, § 268; *Kordić and Čerkez*, AC, § 812; *Kordić and Čerkez*, TC, §§ 448–52.

[8] The provision could be misread as implying that the defensive character of the operation is at least a relevant, through not decisive, consideration. But at least the commentator rejects that view: Eser, 'Article 31', cit. n. 2, 879–80.

[9] See *Krupp and others* (US Tribunal sitting at Nuremberg, at 1438); *Willi Tessmann and others* (Opinion of Judge Advocate, British Military Court, Hamburg, at 177). In *Krupp and others*, the Tribunal in the former case acknowledged, *obiter*, that 'self-defence excuses the repulse of a wrong', and insisted that 'the mere fact cit. n. 2, that [...] a danger was present is not sufficient. There must be an actual *bona fide* belief in danger by the particular individual' (for a comment on the case see *Cassese's Companion*, at 779). The plea was also recognized in principle, but failed on the facts, in *Yamamoto Chusaburo*, before a British Military Court sitting in Kuala Lumpur. A Japanese sergeant claimed, amongst other things, that he had acted in self-defence in killing a civilian whom he had placed under arrest on suspicion of stealing rice from a military store, because he had been surrounded by a hostile crowd at night and feared grave danger to life and property, the more so because he was in pitch darkness. The claim was rebutted on the ground that the act had not been committed in defence of property or person while the civilian was in the process of looting; it had been committed after the civilian had been taken from his house into custody (at 76–9).

felt threatened by the prisoner's movement of his hand in his pocket and had fired in self-defence. The US Court upheld the plea (149–50).[10]

A recent ICTY case rejected a claim of self-defence on the grounds that the persons killed had not been attacking the perpetrators, and that the response was 'disproportionate' as there were 'other ways of thwarting any possible danger instead of firing lethal shots'.[11]

Article 31(1)(c) of the ICC Statute reflects (*Kordić and Čerkez*, TC, § 451), but also broadens, the customary international law definition of self-defence:

> A person shall not be criminally responsible if, at the time of that person's conduct [...] [t]he person acts reasonably to defend himself or herself or another person or, in the case of war crimes, property which is essential to the survival of the person or another person or property which is essential for accomplishing a military mission, against an imminent and unlawful use of force in a manner proportionate to the degree of danger to the person or the other person or property protected.

The requirements of imminence and proportionality are undoubtedly sensible articulations of existing customary international law, as is the clarification that the perception of the threat must be objectively justified, even if it later turns out to be mistaken.[12] The extension to acts in defence of 'property which is essential for accomplishing a military mission' is, however, problematic. An officer would apparently be able to claim self-defence for having ordered his unit to commit a war crime against enemy combatants that were about to unlawfully attack and blow up a weapons depot or a military compound containing tanks and other military equipment needed for an imminent expedition. Similarly, with a view to saving from an impending unlawful enemy attack a military compound containing food, water, and other supplies indispensable to the survival of servicemen, an officer could lawfully order to launch an otherwise unlawful attack against the enemy combatants and, arguably, the civilian population.

The provision lends itself to a number of major objections.[13] First, it unjustifiably departs from customary international law, which arguably does not cover these and similar eventualities. That body of law only affords self-defence as a justification for saving the *life and limb* of the person acting in self-defence or other persons whose life and limb was in imminent danger.

Similarly, in *Schultz*, a US marine claimed that he had killed a Vietnamese villager believing him to be a member of the Viet Cong who was in the process, or had been, of signalling the enemy and attempting to lead him and his patrol into an ambush. He claimed that he had done 'what he felt he had to do to survive'. The Court rejected the defence, noting that 'self-defence is unavailable for it is a plea of necessity not available, normally speaking, to one who is an aggressor' (at 136–8; for a comment on the case, see *Cassese's Companion*, at 906). The decision relied on another, *Carl D. O'Neal*, where the same Court had ruled that 'a person cannot provoke an incident, and then excuse himself from responsibility for injury inflicted by him upon another in the course thereof, on the ground of self-defence [...] A plea of self-defence is a plea of necessity [...] It is generally not available to one who engages with another in mutual combat' (at 193).

[10] For a comment on the case, see *Cassese's Companion*, at 828.

[11] *Gotovina and others*, TC, vol. II, § 1730. The case also illustrates that self-defence is, indeed, a justification: the accused were alleged to have been responsible as members of a JCE and through superior responsibility, neither of which would have been extinguished if the actions of the direct perpetrators were merely excused, rather than justified.

[12] Mistaken perceptions of threats may still be excused under the rubric of mistake of fact, but cannot constitute a justification.

[13] According to K. Ambos ('Other Grounds for Excluding Criminal Responsibility', in Cassese, Gaeta, Jones, *ICC Commentary*, I, at 1033), 'The *property* defence was promoted by the United States and Israel, the former invoking constitutional provisions and insisting that "the defence of one's home can be perfectly legitimate". The US delegation even proposed an equal treatment of defence of life and physical integrity,

Second, there is no rule in international humanitarian law prohibiting attacks against property which is essential for accomplishing a military mission or indispensable for the survival of combatants. International humanitarian law only contains rules protecting objects indispensable to the survival of the civilian population (customary rules on the matter evolved out of Article 54 of the First Additional Protocol). The provision under discussion admittedly requires that the imminent enemy attack be unlawful (as a US Tribunal sitting at Nuremberg pithily put it in *Krupp and others*, 'self-defence excuses [*sic*] the repulse of a *wrong*' (at 1438; emphasis added)). Hence the clause of Article 31(1)(c) we are discussing may chiefly refer to an attack by the enemy that is unlawful either because it involves the use of prohibited weapons (for instance, chemical or bacteriological means of warfare) or because it causes disproportionate casualties among civilians. It is difficult to see how a disproportionate attack could be foreseen, particularly according to the 'objective' reasonably standard. The provision must either be viewed as having only a very narrow application, or as likely to lead to serious abuses.

Third, the clause at issue serves to justify through a defence war crimes committed solely to pursue military objectives. It is contrary to the very spirit of ICL, for it eventually 'covers' and legitimizes crimes perpetrated for the sole sake of protecting military exigencies, whereas in ICL justifications are provided for with a view to taking into account fundamental values such as human life and dignity—values that under certain circumstances ICL regards as such as to override military requirements.

Fourth, the clause is unsustainable, for in fact it tries surreptitiously to introduce, through a criminal rule, a new *substantive* legal standard into IHL; this standard aims at protecting property that serves the military or military operations, a property that traditionally is instead a legitimate military objective. However, since the provisions of the ICC Statute, as those of the statute of any other tribunal, only apply to the judicial institution at issue and to its jurisdiction (in this case to the ICC), the introduction of the provision under discussion into IHL or even ICL could only occur through a possible gradual turning of the provision into customary international law. I hope this process will not materialize, on the grounds set out above.

12.1.2 NECESSITY AS JUSTIFICATION

Domestic jurisdictions recognize that occasions may arise, albeit very rarely, when the harm occasioned by the commission of a criminal act is less than some other harm thereby avoided. Doctrinal formulations differ, but a representative example asserts that a criminal act is justified if the actor subjectively 'believes [it] to be necessary to avoid a harm or evil to himself or to another', and the harm or evil avoided by the act is objectively greater than that 'sought to be prevented by the law defining the offense charged'.[14]

---

on the one hand, and property, on the other. This position did not find much sympathy, and the final text of subparagraph (c) shows that protection of property is limited to war crimes situations in which the property is "essential for the survival of the person or another person" or "essential for accomplishing a military mission". Even in this limited form, the protection of property was difficult to accept for many delegations; it became the "real cliff-hanger" in the negotiations of the Working Group.' See also Eser, cit. *supra* n. 2, at 881–2.

[14] United States Model Penal Code, s. 3.02(1)(a); French Criminal Code, Art. 122-7 ('A person is not criminally liable who, faced with an existing or imminent danger to himself, another or property, carries out an act necessary to safeguard the person or property, except if there is a disproportion between the means employed and the gravity of the danger'); German Penal Code, s. 34 ('Whoever, faced with an imminent

The principle overlaps with, but is broader than, self-defence to the extent that it encompasses not only actions defending against an aggressor, but also actions seeking to avoid harm from natural or external forces.

Necessity was recognized to be a part of customary international law in *Orić*, upon the existence of four conditions: *i*) a present or imminent threat of severe and irreparable harm to life; *ii*) the crime committed 'must have been the only means to avoid the aforesaid harm'; *iii*) it must not be 'disproportionate'; and iv) it must not have been 'voluntarily brought about by the perpetrator himself.' (*Orić, Oral Decision Rendered Pursuant to Rule 98bis*, TC, pp. 9027–31).[15]

12.1.3 BELLIGERENT REPRISALS

A controversial source of justification is the scope for a belligerent in armed conflict to violate the laws of war as a counter-measure against previous violations. The scope for lawful reprisals appears to be narrowing, given the progressive absolute prohibition of certain classes of weapons, and the progressive absolute elimination of certain objects of targeting, even in reprisal. Thus, the 1949 Geneva Conventions prohibit, and this must be taken as reflecting customary international law, reprisals against the wounded, medical personnel, prisoners of war, and other protected persons and their property.[16] The list has been extended in the First Additional Protocol to targeting civilians, historic monuments, the natural environment, and other protected objects, although some states have entered reservations against this extension in respect of reprisals.[17] Some states have also asserted that nuclear weapons could be used as lawful reprisal (ICJ, *Legality of the Threat or Use of Nuclear Weapons*, § 46).

Even to the extent that scope remains for lawful reprisals under customary international law, they are subject to a variety of strict conditions, including that *i*) they may only be a reaction to previous serious violations by the adversary; *ii*) protests or other efforts must have been undertaken to secure compliance that have been fruitless, and that no other lawful measures are available to suppress or deter the violation; *iii*) they are proportionate; *iv*) they have been approved at the highest levels of government, and not

---

danger to life, limb, freedom, honor, property or another legal interest which cannot otherwise be averted, commits an act to avert the danger from himself or another, does not act unlawfully, if, upon weighing the conflicting interests, in particular the affected legal interests and the degree of danger threatening them, the protected interest substantially outweighs the one interfered with. This shall apply, however, only to the extent that the act is a proportionate means to avert the danger').

[15] The accused was alleged to be responsible for plunder of cattle around the besieged enclave of Srebrenica, though there was no suggestion that he was himself starving or acting out of psychological compulsion at the time. The claim of necessity succeeded on the ground that those who needed to be fed were 'surrounded and isolated and starving', thus making the plunder of cattle 'indispensable for the survival of the population of Srebrenica'.

A dissenting judge in another case, though not referring expressly to the concept of necessity, asserted that the accused would have not been convicted for assisting a forcible transfer operation where, at the time of the assistance, the evacuees 'were so desperate that the only viable solution on the ground was to evacuate the Bosnian Muslim population [...] as soon as possible [...] I find it unacceptable that, according to the reasoning of the majority, the only way for [the accused] to have complied with the law on that day was to have stood back and done nothing.' *Popović*, TC, Dissenting and Separate Opinions of Judge Kwon, § 33.

Both these cases involved crimes—plunder and forcible transfer—that may be said to reflect values of distinctly lower importance than life; where an irreducible choice between the two must be made, the hierarchy of values is relatively easy to judge.

[16] GC I, Art. 46; GC II, Art. 13; GC IV, Art. 33.

[17] UK Military Manual, s. 16.19.1.

a field commander, and the issuance of a public warning of impending reprisals; and *v*) immediate cessation upon compliance by the adversary.[18]

12.2 EXCUSES

12.2.1 DURESS

Duress can arise either from threats by a third party against the perpetrator, or from circumstances that exert tremendous pressure on the perpetrator to commit a crime. The latter situation, as previously mentioned, is sometimes described as 'necessity', in the sense of 'excused necessity'.[19] The difference between justified and excused necessity depends on whether the claim is that the criminal act led to a less evil outcome (and is therefore justified) or was the product of psychological coercion (and is therefore excused). The term 'duress' will be used for the remainder of this chapter as encompassing 'duress by circumstances', also known as 'excused necessity'.

The key criterion in assessing duress is whether the circumstances 'eliminated the actor's autonomy by asking him to sacrifice something (such as his family or himself), that he was not capable of doing'.[20] In other words, even though the person possesses the mens rea for the action, his or her capacity to choose is so impaired as to require excusing their liability.[21]

Duress is well established in customary international law,[22] albeit under strict conditions:[23] *i*) the crime is committed under an immediate threat of severe and irreparable

---

[18] See e.g. Y. Dinstein, *The Conduct of Hostilities under the Law of International Armed Conflict* (Cambridge: Cambridge University Press, 2010), at 254–6; *Martić*, TC, §§ 466–7.

[19] Most definitions of duress seem to encompass both duress by direct threats and duress by circumstances. Article 19(1)(d) of UNTAET Regulation 2000/15 of 6 June 2000 on the 'Establishment of Panels with Exclusive Jurisdiction over Serious Criminal Offences' sets out a definition of duress that encompasses both duress and necessity as excuse: '[A person shall not be criminally responsible if, at the time of that person's conduct] the conduct which is alleged to constitute a crime within the jurisdiction of the panels has been caused by duress resulting from a threat of imminent death or of continuing or imminent serious bodily harm against that person or another person, and the person acts necessarily and reasonably to avoid this threat, provided that the person does not intend to cause a greater harm than the one sought to be avoided. Such a threat may either be: (i) made by other persons; or (ii) constituted by other circumstances beyond that person's control.'

National systems appear to differ on this, however: French Code Penal, Art. 122-2 (referring generally to a person acting under 'the influence of a force of a constraint'); German Penal Code, § 35 (referring to a 'present risk to life, health or liberty', though restricting the objects of that risk specifically to 'himself, or a relative or another person standing in a close relationship to him or her'); cf. US Model Penal Code, § 13.03 (referring specifically to the source of the duress as 'unlawful force by the coercer').

[20] J. Ohlin, 'Necessity and Duress', *Cassese's Companion*, at 432. See K. Ambos, 'Other Grounds for Excluding Criminal Responsibility', in Cassese, Gaeta, and Jones, *ICC Commentary*, I, at 1037: 'the underlying rationale of duress is not the balancing of competing legal interests but the criterion of Zumutbarkeit (could it fairly be expected that the person concerned resisted the threat?)'.

[21] Involuntary acts, such as where a person's finger is forcibly pressed onto a trigger against their will causing death by gunshot, are not duress. As set out in the 2004 UK Manual, 'criminal responsibility is not incurred by a person for such acts as he is physically compelled to perform against his will and despite his resistance', § 16.46.

[22] The law on necessity (and duress, treated on the same footing) is summarized in vol. XV of LRTWC, at 174. For the relevant case law see, in particular, *Einsatzgruppen*, at 471 and 480–1; the *High Command*, at 509; *Jepsen*, at 357; *Fullriede*, at 549; *Eichmann*, Supreme Court, at 318; *Götzfrid*, at 68–70; *Zühlke*, at 134–5; and *Finta*, at 837.

[23] For these conditions see *Erdemović*, AC, 1997 Dissenting Opinion of Judge Cassese, §§ 14–16.

harm to life or limb; *ii*) the harm threatened cannot be averted other than through commission of the crime; *iii*) the crime committed is not disproportionate to the harm threatened; and *iv*) the situation leading to duress must not have been voluntarily brought about by the person coerced.

Article 31(1)(d) of the ICC Statute encompasses both duress by threat and duress by circumstances. The provision adopts the customary international law definitions of intensity of threat required to constitute duress, but also imposes objective and subjective limitations on the range of actions that could be so excused:

> [A person shall not be criminally responsible if, at the time of that person's conduct], The conduct which is alleged to constitute a crime within the jurisdiction of the Court has been caused by duress resulting from the threat of imminent death or of continuing or imminent serious bodily harm against that person or another person, and the person acts necessarily and reasonably to avoid this threat, provided that the person does not intend to cause a greater harm than the one sought to be avoided. Such a threat may either be (i) made by another person; or (ii) constituted by other circumstances beyond that person's control.

Article 31(3) of the ICC Statute leaves the door open to further 'grounds for excluding criminal responsibility' being developed through jurisprudence, wisely recognizing that such exclusions are by their very nature reserved for exceptional cases, not all of which are foreseeable.

A. Unavailability of Duress where a Person has Knowingly Joined a Criminal Organization

Duress cannot be invoked as an excuse where a person freely and knowingly chooses to become a member of a unit, organization, or group institutionally intent upon actions contrary to IHL.[24] In other words, if a person has voluntarily joined a military or paramilitary unit whose main purpose is to engage in criminal action, he is not allowed to plead in defence to the crimes perpetrated in that capacity that he acted under threat to his life or limb. Indeed, when he chose to acquire membership in that unit he knew or should have known that its primary purpose was to perpetrate criminal offences.[25]

---

[24] In addition to *Einsatzgruppen* (at 91) and *Erhard Milch* (at 40), both decided by US courts sitting at Nuremberg, some cases brought after the Second World War before German courts are particularly significant in this respect, for those courts also acted on the strength of Control Council Law no. 10. Thus, in *T. and K.*, a case decided by the German Supreme Court in the British Zone (for a comment, see *Cassese's Companion*, at 943), the two accused had been members of the National-Socialist party, one being Colonel (*Standartenführer*) of the SA, the other a committee member of the NSDAP (Nazi party). They had participated in attacks on synagogues on 10 November 1938 (*Kristallnacht*), and in arson. They claimed that they acted upon superior orders and in addition under duress (*Notstand*). The Court dismissed the claim, pointing out that: 'As an old member of the [National-Socialist] Party T. knew the programme and the fighting methods of NSDAP. If he nevertheless made himself available as official *Standartenführer*, he had to count from the start that he would be ordered to commit such crimes. Nor, in this condition of necessity for which he himself was to blame, could he have benefited from a possible misapprehension of the circumstances that could have misled him as to the condition of necessity or compulsion' (at 200–1).

See also the decision of the *Oberlandesgericht* of Freiburg im Breisgau in the *Gestapo informer* case, at 200–3 (for a comment, see *Cassese's Companion*, at 693), as well as the decision of the German Supreme Court in the British Occupied Zone in *H. and others* (at 129–30; for a comment, see *Cassese's Companion*, at 708).

A number of cases brought before the Italian Court of Cassation can also be mentioned: see e.g. the decision in *Spadini* (at 354; for a comment on the case, see *Cassese's Companion*, at 930), in *Toller* (at 920), and in *Fumi* (at 380; for a comment, see *Cassese's Companion*, at 682). The same position was taken by the Court of Appeal of Versailles in *Touvier* (at 341; for comment, see *Cassese's Companion*, at 956).

[25] Interestingly, in the *Sipo–Brussels* case (for a comment, see *Cassese's Companion*, at 926) the Brussels Court Martial took into account voluntary participation in a criminal organization, not from the viewpoint

B. May Duress be a Defence to Killing?

In some cases, under the influence of English criminal law going back to Blackstone[26] and eloquently reaffirmed by J. F. Stephen in 1883,[27] domestic courts have taken the view that duress may never excuse homicide, though it may be urged in mitigation. The principle is grounded in the notion that human life is such a sacred asset that its taking may never be excused, not even when the person that takes the life of another is under a very serious threat to his own life. The harshness of the rule may nonetheless be substantially mitigated by meting out a very lenient sentence, as occurred in the celebrated case of *Dudley* v. *Stephens* (also called the *Mignonette* case),[28] where the court set out the basic rationale for this attitude.[29] This balancing of values has been called 'moralistic' and 'hypocritical'[30] and assailed for absurdly requiring men to act as heroes. According to one distinguished Nigerian criminal lawyer, 'To require a person to die so that another (though innocent) man may be saved will be to invoke in him a standard of heroism that can hardly be expected.'[31] In the case of killing, a choice between the two

of duress, but with regard to the relevance of superior orders. In restating a decision in previous cases, it held that 'superior orders cannot be considered to provide extenuating circumstances, at least in the case where the accused has voluntarily and consciously joined such an organization [i.e. a criminal organization such as the Gestapo or the SD]' (at 1519). On superior orders given within a 'criminal organization', see also *Sch. O.*, at 306–7 (for a comment, see *Cassese's Companion*, at 903).

[26] *Commentaries*, Book IV, at 30.

[27] J. F. Stephen, *History of the Criminal Law of England* (1883), ii (New York: B. Franklin, 1964), at 107–9. He wrote the following: 'It is of course a misfortune for a man that he be placed between two fires but it would be a much greater misfortune for society at large if criminals confer immunity upon their agents by threatening them with death or violence if they refuse to execute their commands. If immunity could be so secured a wide door would be open to collusion and encouragement would be given to male-factors secret or otherwise [...] these reasons lead me to think that compulsion by threats ought in no case whatever be admitted as an excuse for crime though it may and ought to operate in mitigation of punishment in most, though not all, cases' (at 108–9).

[28] Three seamen and a cabin boy of 17 or 18 had been cast away in a storm on the high seas, and compelled to put into an open boat that soon went drifting on the ocean; after eighteen days, being without food and water, two of the seamen, namely Dudley and Stephens, decided to kill the boy and eat him, while the third dissented; one of the two then killed the boy, and they, with the third seaman, fed on his flesh for four days. On the fourth day a passing vessel picked up the boat, and the men were rescued, still alive but 'in the lowest state of prostration'. They were carried to a British port and committed for trial. The Court held that the defendants were guilty of murder and sentenced them to death. However, the Crown afterwards commuted the sentence to six months' imprisonment (*Dudley* v. *Stephens*, at 608).

[29] The Court, among other things, stated that 'Though law and morality are not the same, and many things may be immoral which are not necessarily illegal, yet the absolute divorce of law from morality would be of fatal consequence; and such divorce would follow if the temptation to murder in this case were to be held by law an absolute defence of it. It is not so. To preserve one's life is generally speaking a duty, but it may be the plainest and the highest duty to sacrifice it [...] The duty, in case of shipwreck, of a captain to his crew, of the crew to the passengers, of soldiers to women and children [...]; these duties impose on men the moral necessity, not of the preservation, but of the sacrifice of their lives for others, from which in no country, least of all, it is to be hoped, in England, will men ever shrink, as indeed they have not shrunk. It is not correct, therefore, to say that there is any absolute or unqualified necessity to preserve one's life' (at 607).

[30] See e.g. H. L. Packer, *The Limits of Criminal Sanction* (Stanford, Calif.: Stanford University Press, 1968), at 118.

[31] See K. S. Chkkol, *The Law of Crimes in Nigeria* (Zaria: Kola, 1989), at 152, as well as, more generally, the sharp reflections set out at 150–8. This author also notes the following: 'True, the notion of sacrifice of one's own life has in fact some religious foundations when it is remembered that according to Christian theology it was the sacrifice made by Jesus of his own life that has redeemed mankind so that as the Bible tells us "whoever believeth in him shall not perish but have everlasting life". However, no matter how grandiose the notions of sacrifice or heroism may sound it must be realized that an average man or woman can hardly be expected to be overwhelmed by them when faced with the threat of death' (at 152).

possible options (duress as a defence or as an extenuating circumstance) may, of course, only be based on policy considerations.

The issue of whether duress is available as a defence for international crimes involving killing was addressed by the ICTY in the *Erdemović* case and led to a majority decision accompanied by two strong dissents (by Judge Stephen and Judge Cassese). In July 1995 the accused, a member of a Bosnian Serb military unit, had participated in the shooting and killing of many unarmed Bosnian Muslims as a member of an execution squad. Before the ICTY he pleaded guilty, but claimed that he had refused to shoot at the civilians because he felt sorry for them, but his commander had told him 'If you are sorry for them, stand up, line up with them and we will kill you too.' This statement amounted to a plea of duress. The Appeals Chamber had to decide whether the guilty plea was invalidated by this statement (since one cannot plead guilty for the commission of a crime and at the same time refer to a circumstance that, if proven at trial, would amount to an admissible defence). The Appeals Chamber's majority was unable to find either a customary international rule or a general principle of criminal law ruling out the defence of duress in case of killing. However, the pedagogical role of the International Tribunal required to decide that 'duress does not afford a complete defence to a soldier charged with crimes against humanity and/or a war crime involving the killing of innocent human beings' (*Erdemović*, AC, § 19). The same majority consequently held that in such cases duress could only be used in mitigation of punishment.[32]

Criminal courts have frequently struggled with this issue, reaching opposing conclusions.[33] In spite of this contradictory case law, it would seem that, generally speaking, the customary rule of on duress does not exclude the applicability of this defence to war crimes and crimes against humanity whose underlying offence is murder

---

[32] The view propounded in *Hölzer and others* and taken up in *Erdemović* by the majority of the ICTY Appeals Chamber had already been upheld in the provisions of two military manuals. One is the British Military Manual, § 629 of which provides: 'No criminal responsibility is incurred by a person for an act performed by him under an immediate and well-grounded fear for his own life, provided that the act does not involve the taking of innocent life. Otherwise threats afford no defence to a person accused of a war crime but may be considered in mitigation of sentence.' The other is the United States Manual for Courts Martial, of 1984, whereby duress is a defence 'to any offence except killing an innocent person'.

[33] In *Hölzer and others*, a Canadian Military Court sitting at Aurich, Germany, in March 1945, applying Canadian law, considered a plea of duress by three German soldiers who had killed Canadian airmen. They claimed that they had been compelled at gunpoint by Lieutenant Schaefer (not among the accused) to kill the wounded airman. Their advocates relied on the definition of duress set out in Arts 52 and 54 of the German Criminal Code. The prosecutor assailed the validity of the plea, citing English law excluding duress as a defence in the case of the taking of innocent lives. The Judge Advocate took the same position. The Court sentenced both Hölzer and another accused (Weigel) to death, while it sentenced the third accused (Ossenbach) to 15 years' imprisonment (Vol. I, at 289–99, 304, 312, 315, 338, 345–6; vol. II, 1–4). The case arguably reflected the common law tradition as a whole, although its precedential significance is ambiguous in light of the Judge Advocate's assertion that the Court should apply the Canadian War Crimes Regulations and Canadian law, *not* international law. Other cases support the opposite view: see e.g. the *Einsatzgruppen* case, at 56–9, 61–82, 462–3, 471–2, 480–1 (in the event, the defence of duress was rejected on the facts and all but one of the accused were convicted); *Jepsen and others*, at 222–4, 233–51, 357–9, 363, and some judgments of German and Italian courts (they are quoted in Judge Cassese's Dissenting Opinion in *Erdemović*, AC, 1997). Finally, one should mention other cases, where the court conceded the possibility of raising duress as a defence to a charge of killing innocent people, although the defence failed *on the facts*. See e.g. *Llandovery Castle* (at 722–3); *Eichmann* (at 340); *Müller and others* brought first before the Belgian Military Court of Brussels and then the Belgian Court of Cassation (see 400–3); *Touvier* (at 340–1) and *Papon* (at 151); *Priebke* (at 55–7); *Retzlaff and others* (at 118–20), as well as a string of German cases and a case recently dealt with by a Military Court of Belgrade (*Sablić and others*, at 73, 126). For references to these cases see *Erdemović*, AC, 1997, Judge Cassese's Dissenting Opinion, §§ 31–4.

or unlawful killing. However, as the right to life is the most fundamental human right, the rule demands that the general requirements for duress be applied particularly strictly in the case of killing of innocent persons. The following propositions seem to commend themselves.

First, it is extremely difficult to meet the requirements for duress where the offence involves killing of innocent human beings. Indeed, courts have rarely allowed the defence to succeed in those cases, even where they have in principle admitted its applicability. But for the two cases cited above, plus some Italian and German decisions,[34] which stand out as exceptional, the only cases where national courts have upheld the plea in relation to violations of IHL relate to offences other than killing. This bears out the strong reluctance of national courts to make duress available for offences involving killing. The reason for this restrictive approach no doubt has its roots in the fundamental importance of human life to law and society. As the Court of Assize of Arnsberg (Germany) pointed out in *Wetzling and others* (at 623), the right to life is one of the most fundamental and precious human rights, and any legal system is keen to safeguard it at the utmost. It follows that any legal excusing of attacks on this right must be strictly construed and only exceptionally admitted.

Second, it is relevant to examine whether a crime would have been committed *in any case* by a person other than the one acting under duress, in which case duress seems admissible as a defence. In fact, where the accused has been charged with participation in a collective killing which would have proceeded irrespective of whether the accused was a participant, the defence has in principle been allowed. Thus the case law makes an exception for those instances where—on the facts—it is highly probable, if not certain, that if the person acting under duress had refused to commit the crime, the crime in any event would have been carried out by persons other than the accused. The best example is where an execution squad has been assembled to kill the victims, and the accused participates, in some form, in the execution squad, either as an active member or as an organizer, albeit only under the threat of death. In this case, if an individual member of the execution squad first *refuses to obey* but has then to comply with the order as a result of duress, he may be excused: indeed, whether or not he is killed or instead takes part in the execution, the civilians, prisoners of war, etc., *would be shot anyway*. Were he to comply with his legal duty not to shoot innocent persons, he would forfeit his life for no benefit to anyone and no effect whatsoever apart from setting a heroic example for mankind (a task that the law cannot demand him to fulfil). His sacrifice of his own life would be to no avail.

12.2.2 MISTAKE OF LAW

ICL, like in most national legal systems, does not consider ignorance of the law to be a ground for excluding criminal responsibility. As stated in the first sentence of Article 32(2) of the ICC Statute: 'A mistake of law as to whether a particular type of conduct is a crime within the jurisdiction of the Court shall not be a ground for excluding criminal responsibility.'

The rationale behind the principle *ignorantia legis non excusat* (ignoring the law may not excuse the commission of a crime) is self-evident. The law is a body of rules that are normally fairly deep-rooted (for in most legal systems legal rules are consonant with the fundamental moral or religious values prevalent in society). In addition, legal rules are

---

[34] For detailed references to these cases see *Erdemović*, AC, 1997, Judge Cassese's Separate and Dissenting Opinion, §§ 35–9.

normally accessible to everybody. Hence all those living under a legal system are bound to know the law; were one allowed to successfully plead that he committed a crime because he did not know that the conduct was prohibited, the road would be open to general non-compliance with the law. The foundations of society would be undermined. In addition, if ignorance of law were admitted as a defence, *i*) the applicability of criminal norms would differ from person to person, depending on their degree of knowledge of law; *ii*) the admission of such a defence would eventually constitute an incentive for persons to break the law, by simply proving thereafter that in fact they were not aware of the existence of a legal ban.

Post-Second World War case law has frequently affirmed the proposition that ignorance of the law is no excuse.[35]

Domestic legal systems, however, widely recognize that there are exceptional circumstances cases where mistake of law can be successfully raised as an excuse. The Swiss, French, and German criminal codes stipulate that this is the case when the mistake could not have been avoided;[36] the American Model Penal Code restricts such errors to situations where the law has not been 'published or otherwise reasonably made available' or there are official pronouncements of the erroneous view on which the accused relied.[37]

An argument could be made that the character of IHL and ICL merits a limited recognition of mistake of law. Some areas of law are still evolving, ambiguous, or highly technical, and may not be fully or accurately reflected in national laws. These factors were given prominent place in the Judge Advocate's summing up in *Peleus*: 'no sailor and no soldier can carry with him a library of international law'.[38] They also had a strong influence in

---

[35] In *Jung and Schumacher*, a case brought before a Canadian Military Court sitting at Aurich in Germany, the Judge Advocate, after discussing the legal position of the two defendants (one had ordered the other to execute a Canadian prisoner of war), noted: 'Both Jung and Schumacher have admitted that they knew the killing of a prisoner to be wrong. If I am wrong in this, the Court will correct me since they find the facts. In any event, ignorance of the law is no excuse' (at 221; for a comment on the case, see *Cassese's Companion*, at 739). Similarly, in *Buhler*, the accused (Secretary of State and Deputy Governor General of that part of Poland occupied by German armed forces and known as the Government-General), charged with war crimes and crimes against humanity, had pleaded ignorance of international law; the Polish Supreme National Tribunal sitting in Cracow rejected the plea on the grounds that as a doctor of laws the accused must have possessed sufficient knowledge of the rights and duties of an Occupying Power and of the general principles of criminal law common to all civilized countries (at 682; for a comment on the case, *Cassese's Companion*, at 626). In *Enkelstrohth* a Dutch Special Court at Arnhem held that the accused, a German police officer, must know that the shooting without previous trial even of a spy caught red-handed was contrary to the Hague Regulations, the more so because several German Ordinances promulgated in occupied Netherlands had enacted precise rules for the trial of saboteurs; according to the Court the shooting in question was so clearly at variance with international law that even a police officer of inferior rank must have known that it was unlawful (at 685–6; for a comment, *Cassese's Companion*, at 659).

Similarly, in *Calley* a US Court of Military Review held that the accused could not rely upon the defence of mistake of law for he willingly had summarily executed enemy civilians in custody. The Court stated that 'Mere absence of a sense of criminality is [...] not mitigating, for any contrary view would be an excrescent exception to the fundamental rule that ignorance of the very law violated is no defence to violating it. The maxim *ignorantia legis neminem excusat* applies to offences in which intent is an element [...] "It matters not whether appellant realized his conduct was unlawful. He knew exactly what he was doing; and what he did was a violation [...] of a nature which had to be shown to be knowing and wilful. He intended to do what he did, and that is sufficient" (*United States* v. *Gris*, at 864)' (at 1180).

[36] Swiss Penal Code, Art. 21; German Penal Code, § 17; French Penal Code, Art. 122-3.

[37] Model Penal Code, § 2.04(3).

[38] Addressing the question of superior orders, he stated the following: 'It is quite obvious that no sailor and no soldier can carry with him a library of International law, or have immediate access to a professor in that subject who can tell him whether or not a particular command is a lawful one' (at 129). With specific

the German Supreme Court's decision in the *Llandovery Castle* case, though the excuse was still rejected on the facts:

> The fact that his [the Captain's] deed is a violation of international law must be well-known to the doer [...] In examining the question of the existence of this knowledge, the ambiguity of many of the rules of international law, as well as the actual circumstances of the case, must be borne in mind, because in war time decisions of great importance have frequently to be made on very insufficient material. This consideration, however, cannot be applied to the case at present before the court. The rule of international law, which is here involved, is simple and is universally known. No possible doubt can exist with regard to the question of its applicability. The court must in this instance affirm [Captain] Patzig's guilt of killing contrary to international law. (2585/721)

Second World War cases also tended to give prominence to these considerations. In *Wintgen*, the Dutch Special Court of Cassation upheld the defence in the case of a member of the German Security Police in occupied Netherlands who, under orders, set fire to a number of houses near Amsterdam as a reprisal for acts of sabotage perpetrated by unknown persons on a nearby railway line. The Court held that his action amounted to a war crime for it was contrary to Article 50 of the Hague Regulations of 1907 providing that 'No general penalty, pecuniary or otherwise, shall be inflicted upon the population on account of the acts of individuals for which they cannot be regarded as jointly and severally responsible.' Nevertheless, according to the Court the accused could not be punished for he was not aware that his conduct constituted a war crime. The Court held that the force of the plea of mistake of law depended on the intellectual status and military position of the individual concerned and on the nature of the acts committed. The accused held a very subordinate rank in the Security Police and the destruction of property was generally held to be morally a less grave offence than, for example, the killing of innocent civilians or prisoners of war (at 484–6).[39]

A more dubious application of mistake of law is to be found in the Dutch Court Martial case of *B*.[40]

---

regard to the case at bar (alleged killing of shipwrecked persons), the Judge Advocate noted that 'If this were a case which involved the careful consideration of questions of International Law as to whether or not the command to fire at helpless survivors struggling in the water was lawful, you might well think it would not be fair to hold any of the subordinates accused in this case responsible for what they are alleged to have done; but it was not fairly obvious to you that if in fact the carrying out of Eck's command involved the killing of these helpless survivors, it was not a lawful command, and that it must have been obvious to the most rudimentary intelligence that it was not a lawful command, and that those who did that shooting are not to be excused for doing it upon the ground of superior orders?' (129)

[39] For a comment on the case, see *Cassese's Companion*, at 973.

[40] For a comment on the case, see *Cassese's Companion*, at 591. The accused, a commander of a unit of the Dutch Resistance movement which, by royal decree, had been granted the status of armed forces as part of the Royal Dutch Army, had ordered the execution of four Dutch Nazis whom they had taken prisoner in April 1945. The executions were ordered after another prisoner had escaped and apparently rejoined German forces in the vicinity, and was believed might be able to reveal their location. Regarding the prisoners as *franc-tireurs* and traitors, and after being tacitly encouraged to do so by French soldiers with whom the Dutch were operating, B. ordered v. E. to kill the prisoners with the assistance of other members of the unit. The prosecutor argued that the accused's claim that he had been mistaken as to the unlawfulness of his conduct was 'not in itself sufficient to relieve him of responsibility; for that, the error must also have been pardonable. Only if there was no intent and no negligence as to the unlawfulness, is the accused not liable criminally.' The Court disagreed, observing that it was 'general knowledge that the broadcasts of Radio Orange from England were intended to give the impression that members of the NSB were to be regarded as traitors and that it was unnecessary to show them any consideration, nor would they be shown any'. The accused 'had to take his decision without being able to consult a superior, he was placed in a position for which he was not trained and in circumstances in which it was practically impossible quietly to consider the

The progression of certainty in ICL since the Second World War has substantially reduced the scope for the accused to claim that a failure to know the law was legitimate or unavoidable. Various doctrines, including *nullem crimen sine lege* and the standard of customary international law, ensure that it is hard for a norm to reach the status of a criminal prohibition without being well-established through practice.

Article 32(2) of the ICC Statute allows for only two exceptions to the prohibition on claiming mistake of law as a defence: mistakes of law that 'negate [...] the mental element requirement by such a crime, or as provided in article 33' (concerning superior orders). The first category appears to relate to the evaluation of facts that are themselves imbued with a legal assessment such as, for example, the consequence of a flag of truce or the minimum standard of due process required for lawful sentence to be passed against a prisoner of war.[41] This may therefore merely be viewed as a special type of mistake of fact. The second exclusion is discussed below.

12.2.3 MISTAKE OF FACT

Mistake of fact is not properly viewed as either an excuse or a justification, it refers to instances where the person, though possessed of his individual autonomy, is under a non-culpable misapprehension of the facts and therefore is not aware of the circumstances making his or her action criminal. Mistake of fact negates the very existence of mens rea and culpability. Since it concerns an element of the crime that must be proven, the burden of showing that the mistake did not exist rests always with the prosecution.

A mistake of fact arises only if it 'negates the mental element required by the crime'.[42] That can occur only if the person is mistaken *i*) about facts upon which an element of the

---

relative merits of the various interests'. The Court therefore accepted that the accused was 'mistaken as to the unlawfulness of his actions', hence was 'not criminally liable' and must be acquitted (at 516–25).

See also *Zimmermann*, at 30–2, where the Court excluded mistake of law (the accused was a German official responsible for the deportation of many Dutch workers to Germany for forced labour). For a comment on the case, *Cassese's Companion*, at 981.

[41] For instance, an Occupying Power may not, under Art. 56 of the Hague Regulations, appropriate the produce of public immovable property where: *i*) it has been set aside for religious purpose, for the maintenance of charitable or educational institutions, or for the benefit of art and science; or *ii*) it belongs to municipalities. Whether this is the case might require fine assessments of law, in respect of which mistake of law might be a viable claim depending on the position, and knowledge, of the accused. Another example may be taken from *Hinrichsen*, brought before the Dutch Special Court of Cassation in 1950. Art. 53(2) of the Hague Regulations of 1907 provides that the Occupant may seize 'all the appliances [...] adapted [...] for the transport of persons or things, even if they belong to private individuals', but then must 'restore' them and 'fix compensation' when peace is made. In the spring of 1945 Hinrichsen, a member of the German Frontier Customs Guard, seized in occupied Netherlands two privately owned motorcycles without payment or receipt. After the war he pleaded before a Dutch Criminal Court that his action was not at variance with international law. The Special Court of Cassation held, on the contrary, that his action was contrary to Art. 53(2), for the accused did not provide the means for later verification of the seizure. It added, however, that in determining the penalty it was appropriate to take into consideration the fact that, unlike the case of requisition under Art. 52 of the Regulations, giving a receipt was not expressly prescribed for seizure of means of transport; consequently, the punishment must not be severe (at 486–7). This is clearly a case where international law is not absolutely clear and unambiguous and therefore invocation of the defence at issue might be regarded as admissible.

[42] ICC Statute, Art. 32(1): 'A mistake of fact shall be a ground for excluding criminal responsibility only if it negates the mental element required by the crime.'

crime is based; and *ii*) in a way that deprives the person of the required mental state in respect of that element. If a hunter kills a man in the woods genuinely believing that the man is a gorilla, the hunter will not be guilty of murder; but his mistake would not negate a crime with a lower mental state, such as negligent homicide, if it could be shown that the mistake, though genuine, was not reasonable.[43] In any event, few triers of fact would be likely to accept that a person genuinely mistook a man for a gorilla in the absence of some specific indication as to why that may have been the case.

The US Manual for Air Forces gives the following example:

> A pilot attacks, admittedly in a negligent manner, and consequently misses his target, a military objective, by several miles. The bombs fall on civilian objects unknown to the pilot. No deliberate violation of international law has occurred. However, he might be subject to possible criminal punishment under his own state's criminal code for dereliction of duty. He could not be charged with a violation of the law of armed conflict. (AFP 110–31, 19 November 1976, 15–16)

The plea of mistake of fact was partially accepted by a US Court Martial in *Schwarz*. The accused, as part of a five-man night patrol team, had entered the small hamlet of Son Thang in South Vietnam on 19 February 1970. The team killed sixteen civilians in sequence in three different huts. After four women had been ordered out of the first hut and lined up outside, the accused was ordered to go inside and search it. While inside he heard the team leader yell 'Shoot them, shoot them all, kill them.' He claimed that he had run outside and participated in killing the four women, mistakenly believing that they were attacking. The Military Judge instructed the jury that if they found that the accused genuinely believed that he was returning fire, they must acquit.[44] The Court Martial accepted the plea in respect of the killings in front of the first hut, but rejected the claim in respect of the second and third huts, by which time the circumstances negated the claim of a genuine mistake.[45]

Mistake of fact was rejected in *Calley*, where the accused had sought acquittal of an aggravated charge of homicide requiring 'malice' on the basis that he had killed the victims in the genuine, but mistaken, belief that the villagers had no right to live where they

---

[43] German Penal Code, § 16.1 ('Whoever upon commission of the act is unaware of a circumstance which is a statutory element of the offense does not act intentionally. Punishability for negligent commission remains unaffected.')

[44] The Military Judge stated the following: 'The court is advised that if the accused was of the honest belief that he and his team-mates were being attacked by enemy forces he cannot be found guilty of any offence charged or the lesser included offences thereto. Such belief no matter how unreasonable will exonerate the accused. In determining whether the accused was of the belief that enemy forces were attacking him and his team-mates you should consider the accused's age, education, military training, and combat experience together with all the other evidence bearing upon this issue. The burden is upon the prosecution to establish the accused's guilt of each offence charged by legal and competent evidence beyond a reasonable doubt. The accused committed no crime unless he knew that the enemy forces were not attacking him.' (Reported in *Schwarz*, at 862–3.)

[45] On appeal, defence counsel argued that the aforementioned instructions unduly restricted the members of the Court, for they limited the defence to the case where the accused believed that he was under enemy attack, without extending it to the case where he believed that the 'killer team' was attacking the enemy. The Court of Military Review rejected the argument, ruling that: 'In the setting of this case we are certain that the instructions conveyed to the court the direction that the accused must be acquitted unless they found beyond a reasonable doubt that he did not honestly believe that he was in immediate contact with the enemy either offensively or defensively' (*Schwarz*, at 862–3).

were killed. The plea was properly rejected, because the mistake did not affect the mental state in respect of any element of the crime.[46]

12.2.4 MENTAL INCAPACITY

Mental incapacity arises where the accused's psychological condition deprives the person of the capacity to assess the nature or wrongfulness of his actions. This may be a transient condition, as in the case of intoxication, or relatively continuous, as with insanity or age. The mental incapacity may be so severe as to negate mens rea entirely, but some national legal systems nevertheless refer to the actions as 'criminally not imputable'.

A. Intoxication

Intoxication as a result of alcohol, drugs, or other intoxicants may amount to an excuse only under very strict conditions: *i*) the intoxication is so serious as to negate mens rea (that is, it alters the agent's mental state to such a point that he is not in a position to be aware of his actions and to appraise the unlawfulness of his conduct); and *ii*) in the case of voluntary intoxication, the person has not become voluntarily intoxicated knowing the risk that, as a result of his state, he was likely to engage in criminal action.[47]

In *Yamamoto Chusaburo*, a British Military Court sitting at Kuala Lampur rejected a plea of drunkenness.[48] In *Kvočka and others*, the ICTY Trial Chamber not only rejected drunkenness as an excuse for the accused's beating and brutalization of inmates (*Kvočka and others*, TC, §§ 616 and 680); it even seemed prepared to find it to be an aggravating factor, but as the prosecutor had not previously raised the matter, it was disregarded (§ 748).

B. Insanity or Serious Mental Disorder

Insanity or serious mental disorder or disturbance may be invoked, as in many national legal systems, as a defence whenever it deprives a person of the capacity to understand or control his own otherwise criminal acts, or to understand whether those actions are right or wrong. The condition or state must be so extreme, as articulated in Art. 31(1)(a) of the ICC Statute, as to 'destroy that person's capacity to appreciate the unlawfulness or nature of his or her conduct, or capacity to control his or her conduct to conform to the requirements of law'.

---

[46] The US Army Court of Military Review held that 'To the extent this state of mind reflects a mistake of fact, the governing principle is: to be exculpatory, the mistaken belief must be of such a nature that the conduct would have been lawful had the facts actually been as they were believed to be [...] An enemy in custody may not be executed summarily' (at 1180).

[47] ICC Statute, Art. 31(1)(b): a person shall not be criminal responsible if the 'person is in a state of intoxication that destroys that person's capacity to appreciate the unlawfulness or nature of his or her conduct, or capacity to control his or her conduct to conform to the requirements of law, unless the person has become voluntarily intoxicated under such circumstances that the person knew, or disregarded the risk, that, as a result of the intoxication, he or she was likely to engage in conduct constituting a crime within the jurisdiction of the Court').

[48] The accused, a sergeant of the Japanese Army, had been charged with a war crime for killing a civilian who had stolen rice from the army store. He pleaded, among other things, that he had acted under the influence of alcohol. According to the summary of the UN War Crime Commission, the prosecutor said that 'drunkenness in itself was not an excuse for crime, but where intention was of the essence of the offence, drunkenness might justify a court in awarding a lesser punishment than the offence would otherwise have deserved or it might reduce the offence to one of a less serious character. In such a case the man must be in such a state of drunkenness as to make him incapable of formulating any intention to commit the offence, and such a state would clearly affect the degree of killing of which the Court would find the accused guilty' (at 78).

A case that illustrates the concept is *Stenger and Crusius*, decided by the German Supreme Court in 1921. The German Captain Crusius, commander of a company, had been accused of passing on to his subordinates an order from Major General Stenger to take no prisoners during fighting with French forces near Sainte Barbe (Alsace) on 26 August 1914. The Court found that he had misunderstood that order, and hence could not invoke it as a defence. The Court found, however, that the accused's mental condition, under the pressures of particularly horrifying combat and a 'psychopathic disposition', had, at some point prior to the order to his subordinates, triggered 'a complete mental and psychological collapse, that is a state of utter mental confusion [...] which would unequivocally preclude responsibility pursuant to criminal law' and which 'render[ed] him incapable of forming a rational intention' (at 2571–2).[49] The Court therefore acquitted Crusius on that count (2568–72). The Court rejected the same plea in respect of a previous episode, however, where the accused's mental state amounted only to 'extreme agitation and psychological suffering'. Since that mental state did not preclude his 'free determination of will,' Crusius was found guilty on that count (at 2567). The plea was rejected on similar grounds in *Kotälla*, by a Special Criminal Court of Amsterdam,[50] as well as in *Schultz*, a case heard by a US Court of Military Appeal.[51]

An impaired mental condition may be more likely to affect specific mental states. An illustrative national case is the 1971 US Court Martial case of *Calley*, in which the accused was charged with premeditated murder in violation of Article 118 of the Uniform Code of Military Justice (for killing Vietnamese civilians in My Lai, South Vietnam). The defence raised, among other things, the issue of mental capacity. The Judge Advocate, in his instructions to the Court, accepted that a soldier could be found to be 'suffering from a mental impairment or condition of such consequence and degree that it deprived him of

---

[49] For a comment on the case, see *Cassese's Companion*, at 935. The Court admitted that this mental state only emerged gradually in the afternoon: 'at around the time when the accused, distraught, with a bright red face and swollen eyes, came running out of the forest, screaming and rushing towards Dr. Döhner [another German serviceman, who testified in court], grabbing his arm, desperately uttering calls, and leaving the overall impression of a maniac [...] this state did not occur suddenly and abruptly but rather gradually worsened after having developed from an already existing nervous condition induced by a psychopathic disposition and by the particular disturbance' of the battles of the previous days. The Court found that when the supposed superior order was passed on to his subordinates 'the accused was suffering from a mental disorder rendering him incapable of forming a rational intention' (at 2572). After suffering from 'so-called diminished responsibility' (*verminderte Zurechnungsfähigkeit*, at 2572), he then found himself in a state of mind 'precluding responsibility'.

[50] For a comment on the case, see *Cassese's Companion*, at 767. The Court rejected the plea of mental disorder invoked by the accused (who had been charged with war crimes and crimes against humanity). It held that it had established, 'on the basis of its own observations at the hearing and further information presented [...] at the hearing, that the accused [did] not suffer from such a limited development of his mental faculties or mental disorder which could result in the offences committed by him not being attributed to him or being attributed to him to a lesser extent' (at 6). See also the decision delivered in the same case by the Dutch Special Court of Cassation on 5 December 1949 (at 13).

[51] For a comment on the case, see *Cassese's Companion*, at 906. The defence had raised the issue of insanity. The appellant had been accused and then convicted of premeditated murder, for having killed an innocent Vietnamese civilian. The Court rejected the plea of insanity. After noting that the testimony of two psychiatrists, one for the government, the other for the defence, showed that the accused had suffered from probable mental impairment, the Court referred to two previous cases unrelated to war crimes, *Michael F. Kunak* (354–66) and *Vadis Storey* (426–30), and approvingly cited their holding whereby 'More than partial mental impairment must be shown in order to raise the issue. There must be evidence from which a court-martial can conclude that an accused's mental condition was of such consequences and degree as to deprive him of the ability to entertain the particular state of mind required for the commission of the offence charged' (138). See also *Sergeant W.* (decision of the Military Court, at 2; for a comment on this case, *Cassese's Companion*, at 913).

the ability to entertain the premeditated design to kill required in the offence of premedi-tated murder'.[52] The US Army Court of Military Review adopted the same standard, but rejected the application to the fact.[53]

Some mental conditions may not be sufficient to meet the threshold for excusing liabil-ity, but can be serious enough to be taken into account for sentencing. In some states (in particular common law countries, notably the UK) the plea, if successful, entails reducing the gravity of the offence with which a defendant might be charged (for instance, reduc-ing murder to manslaughter, whenever there is a mandatory sentence for murder, namely death or life imprisonment). In other states (chiefly civil law countries), if the plea is suc-cessful, the accused qualifies for mitigation of sentence.

The latter approach is reflected in the case of *Gerbsch* before a Special Court in Amsterdam. Between 1944 and 1945, the accused was a guard at a penal camp in Zoeschen, Germany, where he ill-treated many detainees, in particular Dutchmen and other persons transferred from the Netherlands. The Court found him guilty of a crime against humanity, but took into account as a mitigating circumstance the fact that his 'mental faculties were defective and undeveloped' when the crime was committed, as well as at the time of trial (at 492).[54]

---

[52] The Judge Advocate stated the following: 'The law recognizes that an accused may be sane and yet, because of some underlying mental impairment or condition, be mentally incapable of entertaining a pre-meditated design. You should therefore consider, in connection with all other relevant facts and circum-stances, all evidence tending to show that Lt. Calley may have been suffering from a mental impairment or condition of such consequence and degree that it deprived him of the ability to entertain the premeditated design to kill required in the offence of premeditated murder. The burden of proof is upon the government to establish the guilt of Lt. Calley beyond a reasonable doubt. Unless, in light of all the evidence, you are satis-fied beyond a reasonable doubt that Lt. Calley, on 16 March 1968, in the village of My Lai (4), at the time of each of the alleged offences, was mentally capable of entertaining, and did in fact entertain, the premeditated design to kill required by law, you must find him not guilty of each premeditated murder offence for which you do not find premeditated design. You may, however, find Lt. Calley guilty of any of the lesser offences in issue [unpremeditated murder or voluntary manslaughter], provided you are convinced beyond a reasonable doubt as to the elements of the lesser offence to which you reach a guilty finding, bearing in mind all these instructions' (at 1716).

[53] The two defence psychiatrists had asserted that the accused was acting automatically and did not have capacity to premeditate because he was effectively without ability to reflect upon alternative courses of action and choose from them; he did not have the mental capacity to 'contrive' the deaths of the villagers. The Court noted, however, that both psychiatrists agreed that Calley had 'capacity to perceive and predict, the two functions essential to the pertinent *mens rea*. Appellant knew he was armed and what his weapon would do. He had the same knowledge about his subordinates and their arms. He knew that if one aimed his weapon at a villager and fired, the villager would die. Knowing this, he ordered his subordinates to "waste" the villagers at the trail and ditch, to use his own terminology; and fired upon the villagers himself. These bare facts evidence intent to kill, consciously formed and carried out' (1178). The Court concluded (at 1178–9) that Calley had acted with premeditation.

[54] Some international cases can also be mentioned. In *Delalić and others* the ICTY Trial Chamber, based on national legislation, admitted that there might be an impairment of mind affecting criminal liability (*Delalić and others*, TC, §§ 1166 and 1186). The Appeals Chamber convincingly clarified the matter in the same case: 'The Appeals Chamber recognises that the rationale for the partial defence provided for the offence of murder by the English *Homicide Act* 1957 is inapplicable to proceedings before the Tribunal. There are no mandatory sentences. Nor is there any appropriate lesser offence available under the Tribunal's Statute for which the sentence would be lower and which could be substituted for any of the offences it has to try. The Appeals Chamber accepts that the relevant general principle of law upon which, in effect, both the common law and the civil law systems have acted is that the defendant's diminished mental responsibility is relevant to the sentence to be imposed and is not a defence leading to an acquittal in the true sense. This is the appropriate general legal principle representing the international law to be applied in the Tribunal. Rule 67(A)(ii)(b) [of the ICTY Rules of Procedure and Evidence] must therefore be interpreted as referring to diminished mental responsibility where it is to be raised by the defendant as a matter in mitigation of

Uncontrollable fits of temper would not normally qualify as negating or excusing responsibility. At the most, and under strict conditions, it might prove appropriate to take them into account, as extenuating circumstances.[55]

C. Minors

Persons under a certain age are in many national legal systems deemed not to possess full individual autonomy and, normally, are considered exempt from criminal responsibility if they engage in criminal conduct. The threshold varies from country to country: in Britain, children aged 10 and above may be held accountable in some respects and liable to conviction.

No customary international rule can be said to have emerged on this matter. Article 26 of the ICC Statute, declaring that the Court 'shall have no jurisdiction over any person who was under the age of 18 at the time of the alleged commission of a crime,' constitutes merely a jurisdictional limitation, not a substantive definition of capacity. Art. 8(2)(e)(vii) of the ICC Statute elsewhere recognizes that adolescents as young as 15 years of age may lawfully join armed forces or groups and participate actively in hostilities. The concept of responsible command would not be compatible with a recognition that members of armed groups between 15 and 18 years of age are immune from prosecution.

---

sentence. As a defendant bears the onus of establishing matters in mitigation of sentence, where he relies upon diminished mental responsibility in mitigation, he must establish that condition on the balance of probabilities—that more probably than not such a condition existed at the relevant time' (*Delalić and others*, AC, § 590).

[55] In *Erhard Milch* one of the judges serving on a US Military Tribunal sitting at Nuremberg, Judge Phillips, in his concurring opinion implicitly conceded that uncontrollable temper might be taken into account, although he did not specify for what legal purposes. Nonetheless, in the case at issue he rejected a defence claim that the accused (Field-Marshal in the German *Luftwaffe*, Aircraft Master General, Member of the Central Planning Board and State Secretary in the Air Ministry), who had been charged with war crimes and crimes against humanity involving deportations of civilian populations, forced labour and illegal experiments, had made violent statements due to uncontrollable temper, overwork, and head injuries. The judge noted that: 'If but only a few of such remarks could be attributed to the defendant, his protestations might be given some credence; but when statements such as appear in the documents have been persistently made over a long period of time, at many places and under such varying conditions, the only logical conclusion that can be reached is that they reflect the true and considered attitude of the defendant toward the Nazi foreign labour policy and its victims and are not mere aberrations brought on by fits of uncontrollable anger' (47).

13

OBEDIENCE TO SUPERIOR ORDERS AND OFFICIAL CAPACITY

Individuals who committed international crimes were once able to rely on the expansive doctrines of superior orders, or acting in an official capacity, to excuse their liability. These doctrines, at least in their widest versions, were firmly repudiated in the London Charter. As Justice Jackson eloquently explained in his Opening Speech at the Nuremberg Trial:

> The Charter [establishing the Nuremberg Tribunal] recognizes that one who has committed criminal acts may not take refuge in superior orders nor in the doctrine that his crimes were acts of states. These twin principles working together have heretofore resulted in immunity for practically everyone concerned in the really great crimes against peace and mankind. Those in lower ranks were protected against liability by the orders of their superiors. The superiors were protected because their orders were called acts of state. Under the Charter, no defense based on either of these doctrines can be entertained.

This approach now generally prevails and the doctrines of superior orders and official capacity have been largely superseded. The two defences, or at least the policy factors underlying them, nevertheless continue to be asserted in residual or modified form. Superior orders may debatably be the basis of an excuse based on mistake of law (see 13.2) or where they are part of a climate of coercion that is so severe as to rise to the level of duress (see 12.2.1).

13.1 SUPERIOR ORDERS

The law of armed conflict in its earliest incarnations recognized a principle known as *respondeat superior*, by which the commander, and the commander alone, would be criminally responsible for orders to commit a crime. The scope and status of this doctrine was uncertain from the outset, however. A US military commission case in the Civil War case of *Wirz* seemed to deny the existence of the doctrine entirely, holding that actions were equally criminal whether undertaken pursuant to orders or not.[1] Section 47 of the 1872 German Military Penal Code limited the defence by imposing accomplice liability for the subordinate who had committed a criminal offence pursuant to a superior order if

---

[1] Captain Henry Wirz, a Swiss doctor who had emigrated to Louisiana, joined the Confederate army having been, as he later wrote, 'carried away by the maelstrom of excitement'. He was given command of the Andersonville prison camp in Georgia, which became notorious for its appalling conditions. After the defeat of the Confederacy, he was tried by a Military Commission in Washington. He defended himself by saying that he had acted on superior orders, being merely 'the medium, or better, the tool in the hands of his superiors'. The Judge Advocate objected that when an order is illegal both the superior officer and his subordinate are guilty. As he put it: 'A superior officer cannot order a subordinate to do an illegal act, and if the subordinate obey such an order and disastrous consequences result, both the superior and the subordinate

'he knew that the order of the superior concerned an act which aimed at a civil or military crime or offence'. The *Llandovery Castle* case interpreted this provision to mean that, in practice, although a subordinate must generally be able to 'count upon' the legality of superior orders, this presumption must give way when the order is 'universally known to everybody, including the accused, to be without any doubt whatever against the law'.[2] British and American military manuals, however, continued to assert a blanket exclusion of liability for violations of the law of armed conflict right up until the Second World War, but not in respect of violations of their own domestic law. But Hersch Lauterpacht was already arguing in 1944, however, that these provisions did not reflect 'the existing position in international law' which, according to him, imposed liability either when the subordinate *i)* knew the act he was committing pursuant to an order was criminal; or *ii)* ought to have known that it was.[3]

State practice moved decisively towards the elimination of any vestige of superior orders as a defence after the Second World War. The Nuremberg and Tokyo Statutes as well as Control Council Law no. 10 excluded the doctrine as a basis for relief from liability.[4] This approach was followed in the Statutes of all the ad hoc international courts created so far—ICTY, ICTR, SCSL, STL, and ECCC alike—where superior orders are confined to a potential factor in mitigation of sentence.[5]

The elimination of superior orders as a defence to criminal conduct reflects several important trends, including: an awareness of the massive scale of crimes that would

must answer for it. General Winder [the officer above Wirz] could no more command the prisoner [Wirz] to violate the laws of war than could the prisoner do so without orders. The conclusion is plain, that where such orders exist both are guilty [...]' (at 796). The Military Commission accepted the argument and sentenced Wirz to death by hanging (at 797–8).

[2] The two defendants had fired on the lifeboats of the British steamer *Llandovery Castle* (a naval hospital that, according to the Germans, had in fact been used for the transport of troops and had thus been sunk by the German submarine) following the orders of their superior, Captain Patzig. The Court rejected the claim: '[the commander]'s order does not free the accused from guilt. It is true that according to Section 47 of the Military Penal Code, if the execution of an order in the ordinary course of duty involves such a violation of the law as is punishable, the superior officer issuing such an order is alone responsible. According to para. 2, however, the subordinate obeying an order is liable to punishment, if it was known to him that the order of the superior involved the infringement of the civilian or military law. This applies in the case of the accused. It is certainly to be urged in favour of the military subordinates that they are under no obligation to question the order of their superior officer, and they can count upon its legality. But no such confidence can be held to exist; if such an order is universally known to everybody, including the accused, to be without any doubt whatever against the law. This happens only in rare and exceptional cases. But this case was precisely one of them, for, in the present instance, it was perfectly clear to the accused that killing defenceless people in the lifeboats could be nothing else but a breach of the law. As naval officers by profession they were well aware, as the naval expert Saalwächter has strikingly stated, that one is not legally authorised to kill defenceless people. They well knew that this was the case here. They quickly found out the facts by questioning the occupants in the boats when these were stopped. They could have gathered, from the order given by Patzig, that he wished to make use of his subordinates to carry out a breach of the law. They should, therefore, have refused to obey. As they did not do so, they must be punished' (at 2586/721–2).

[3] See H. Lauterpacht, 'The Law of Nations and the Punishment of War Crimes', 21 *British Year Book of International Law* (1944), 58, 70–2.

[4] Charter of the International Military Tribunal, Art. 8 ('The fact that the Defendant acted pursuant to order of his Government or of a superior shall not free him from responsibility, but may be considered in mitigation of punishment if the Tribunal determines that justice so requires'). In the same vein, Art. 6 of the Charter of the Tokyo Tribunal. See also *Hostages Case*: '[T]he general rule is that members of the armed forces are bound to obey only the lawful orders of their commanding officers and they cannot escape criminal liability by obeying a command which violated international law and outrages fundamental concepts of justice' (at 1236).

[5] ICTY Statute, Art. 7(4) ('The fact that an accused person acted pursuant to an order of a Government or of a superior shall not relieve him of criminal responsibility, but may be considered in mitigation of

be excused by such a defence in the case of a thoroughly criminal regime; the primacy of international humanitarian and criminal law over any domestic military doctrines or orders that might purport to exclude responsibility; and the direct responsibility of individuals as actors under international law. The first of these considerations was articulated eloquently by the Nuremberg Tribunal in response to the argument of counsel Nelte that his client Keitel and the other accused had been 'merely mouthpieces or tools of an overwhelming will' (vol. XVIII, at 6). The Tribunal dismissed the argument:

> Hitler could not make aggressive war by himself. He had to have the co-operation of statesmen, military leaders, diplomats, and business men. When they, with knowledge of his aims, gave him their co-operation, they made themselves parties to the plan he had initiated. They are not to be deemed innocent because Hitler made use of them, if they knew what they were doing. That they were assigned to their tasks by a dictator does not absolve them from responsibility for their acts. The relation of leader and follower does not preclude responsibility here any more than it does in the comparable tyranny of organised domestic crime. (at 226)

The potential conflict between orders and international humanitarian and criminal law has also been substantially reduced by the incorporation of relevant international law norms, directly or by reference, into national military doctrine. Most national military manuals or laws now expressly recognize that international humanitarian and criminal law must at all times be obeyed. Although this eliminates the clash at a normative level between international and domestic law, or between orders and crime, soldiers on the ground are also normally required to obey all legal orders promptly, and they are trained to do so without question. As a practical matter, this may raise a serious dilemma for a soldier who may have doubts, but is unsure, about the legality of an order. As the great English constitutionalist Dicey put it, a soldier may thus be caught in a grievously conflictual situation: he 'may be liable to be shot by a court-martial if he disobeys an order, and to be hanged by a judge and jury if he obeys it'.[6]

The problem arises not only from uncertainty, but from retrogressive and despotic regimes that still require soldiers to follow orders that may be lawful under their domestic law, but illegal under IHL and ICL (think of a national law imposing the use of weapons prohibited by IHL to repress a rebellion). Individual soldiers may, in these circumstances, be constrained to commit crimes or risk harsh punishment, if not death.

The sections that follow discuss these two circumstances where superior orders may still have some vitality as an excuse: mistake of law or duress. The overall position appears to be, however, that there is now little scope for mistake of law even in respect of superior orders, and that while duress certainly is a well-founded defence in principle, it is very rarely accepted in practice. Mistake of fact, it must be emphasized, involves a different issue: non-awareness of certain facts that show the absence of mens rea. Superior orders may indeed be the source of such misleading information, but then the proper claim is properly the absence of mens rea that negates criminal liability, not excuse. That distinction is described in more detail in 13.1.3.

---

punishment if the International Tribunal determines that justice so requires'); ICTR Statute, Art. 6(4); SCSL Statute, Art. 6(4); STL Statute, Art. 3(3). In case law, see *Mrksić*, AC, n. 331.

[6] A. V. Dicey, *Introduction to the Study of Law of the Constitution*, 10th edn (London: Macmillan, 1959), at 303.

13.1.1 SUPERIOR ORDERS AND MISTAKE OF LAW

A. The ICC Statute

Article 33 of the ICC Statute provides that superior orders 'shall not relieve [a] person of criminal responsibility unless: (a) The person was under a legal obligation to obey [the] orders [. . .] (b) The person did not know that the order was unlawful; and (c) The order was not manifestly unlawful.' Article 33(2) of the ICC Statute deems that orders to commit genocide or crimes are 'manifestly unlawful'.

The provision does not renew *respondeat superior* or a broad exclusion of liability merely because a person acts according to orders. It does, however, appear to open the door to, and define the standard for, a claim of mistake of law when a person commits a crime pursuant to superior orders.

Even the narrow resuscitation of superior orders for this purpose appears to be at odds with customary international law, discussed in 13.2.2, and incoherent with the ICC Statute itself. First, it seems strange that the ICC Statute would purport in Article 32 to abolish mistake of law (which presumably existed at least in principle as a matter of customary law, if seldom in practice), but then to carve out a specific situation in which mistake of law could be accepted. Both measures, in effect, would appear to go against customary international law. Second, Article 33 is incongruous with the progressive clarification of IHL, to which the ICC Statute and the ICC Elements of Crimes themselves significantly contribute. Any serviceman is expected and required to *know* whether the act he is about to commit falls under the category of war crimes; he therefore must (or is expected to) be aware of whether or not the execution of a superior order involves the commission of such crime. Besides, the ICC Statute provides in its Preamble that it addresses 'the most serious crimes of concern to the international community as a whole'. In addition, Article 8(1) of the ICC Statute stipulates that, with regard to war crimes, the Court has jurisdiction over such crimes 'in particular when committed as part of a plan or policy or as part of a large-scale commission of such crimes'. One can hardly see how, given all these limitations on the class of war crimes over which the ICC may pronounce, there might be cases where a defendant could validly claim that he was not aware of the illegality of the order and that the order was not 'manifestly unlawful'. Finally, the exclusion of the defence for crimes against humanity and genocide gives rise to an unacceptable and arbitrary distinction. The content of many war crimes overlaps with the content of crimes against humanity: why should mistake of law be available in the former case but not the latter? This distinction is all the more incongruous considering that war crimes are defined with much *greater* specificity in the Statute than crimes against humanity.

B. The 'Manifestly Unlawful' Standard in Domestic Law and Military Manuals

National legislation frequently states that a subordinate is not 'liable to punishment' or not 'criminally responsible' unless the unlawfulness of the order is 'manifest' or 'obvious',[7] or unless the person 'should have known' that it was unlawful.[8]

---

[7] See e.g. French Penal Code (Art. 122-4 ('N'est pas pénalement responsable la personne qui accomplit un acte commandé par l'autorité légitime, sauf si cet acte est manifestement illégal')); Peruvian Code of Military Justice (Art. 19(7)); the Spanish Military Criminal Code of 1985 (Art. 21), the Criminal Code of Sweden (1999) (Chapter 24, s. 8), the Israeli law (s. 19(B) of the Criminal Code Ordinance, 1936).

[8] South Africa Law of Armed Conflict, s. 44 ('A person who commits a war crime pursuant to an order is guilty of a war crime if that person knew or should have known that the order was unlawful'). See P. Gaeta, 'The Defence of Superior Orders: The Statute of the International Criminal Court versus Customary International Law', 10 EJIL (1999), 172, at 176–7.

This approach, described as 'the conditional liability approach' by one commentator,[9] is adopted also by some national military manuals[10] and is frequently applied in national case law (starting with a case decided by the Austrian Supreme Military Tribunal on 30 March 1915 (case of the *Russian prisoner of war J. K.*, at 20)).

One could argue that Article 33 of the ICC Statute is defensible on the basis of these national codes. But as one commentator has conclusively argued, the illegality to which a subordinate may otherwise be subject at the national level is not limited to violations of the IHL or other prohibitions of ICL, but also includes 'very broad categories of offences, including ordinary crimes such as theft, military offences and minor violations of the laws of warfare'.[11] International rules, by contrast, regulate a more limited number of norms, almost all of which are notorious crimes that may, in themselves, be understood as manifestly unlawful. Indeed, the standard of reception of an international crime in state practice requires a high level of clarity and consistency, as does the principle *nullem crimen sine lege*. It is difficult to see how the definition of any crime could clear these hurdles, and yet founder on the basis of mistake of law. The 'manifestly unlawful' standard in state practice, therefore, cannot be simplistically transferred to the international realm.

C. Case Law Rejecting the Plea of Superior Orders

National courts and international criminal courts have dismissed the plea of superior orders in numerous cases, in particular those concerning the killing or ill-treatment of: *i*) defenceless shipwrecked persons;[12] *ii*) innocent civilians in occupied territory;[13] *iii*) prisoners of war;[14] *iv*) non-combatants detained in the combat area;[15] and also in cases concerning *v*) the taking of illegitimate reprisals against civilians;[16] or *vi*) unlawfully

---

[9] P. Gaeta, cit. n. 8 at 174.

[10] See e.g. the US Field Manual of 1956 (§509), the Canadian Manual for Courts Martial (1999, at 16–5) and the US Manual for Courts Martial (2002 edn), Rule 916(d).

[11] P. Gaeta, cit. n. 8, at 172–91. See also *Hass and Priebke (Appeal)*. Discussing the acts of German military in Rome in 1943, and the claim of the defendants that they had executed civilians as a reprisal and upon superior order, the Court noted that Article 40 of the Italian Military Penal Code in Time of Peace was applicable, whereby an order must be executed unless it is manifestly illegal. The Court went on to state that 'Article 8 of the Statute establishing the Nuremberg Tribunal had not derogated from that provision; indeed, by laying down that a superior order could not excuse an order, [Article 8] simply took away from the judge the task of verifying the concrete manifest illegality of the order and was based on the presumption that such illegality existed whenever the offence ordered and executed amounted to a war crime or at any rate to a crime subject to the jurisdiction of the Tribunal. This standard of appraisal was patently grounded on the very essence of war crimes: these crimes are envisaged for the purpose of protecting fundamental values endowed with absolute character and valid for the whole of mankind; hence they are laid down regardless of any particular viewpoint, are clear in their essence and intend to criminalize highly condemnable conduct' (at 52–3).

[12] See e.g. *Llandovery Castle* (at 2580–6); *Peleus* (at 128–9).

[13] See e.g. *Schintholzer and others* (Military Tribunal of Verona, 21 February 1989, unpublished, p. 44 of the typescript); *Josef Kramer and others* (the Belsen trial), at 631–2; *Heinrich Gerike and others* (the *Velpke Baby Home* trial), at 338; *Sipo-Brussels* case (at 3–10); *Götzfrid* (at 62–6).

[14] See e.g. *Gozawa Sadaichi and others* (at 225, 229, 231); *Sumida Haruzo and others* (at 232, 240–1, 258); *Strauch and others* (at 562–3).

[15] See e.g. *Lages* (at 2); *Zühlke* (at 133–4); *Rauter* (at 157–9); *Zimmermann* (at 30–1); *Bellmer* (at 543); *Thomas L. Kinder* (at 770–4); *Walter Griffen* (at 587–91); *Frank C. Schultz* (at 137); *Charles W. Keenan* (at 114–19); *Michael A. Schwarz* (at 859–61); *William L. Calley* (US Army Court of Military Review, at 1180–2); US Court of Military Appeals, at 541–5); *Sergeant W.* (Brussels War Council, at 3, and Military Court, at 2); *Sablić and others* (at 120–1); *M. and G.* (at 989–90); *Major Shmuel Malinki and others* (at 88–132).

See also a case where, in an *obiter dictum*, the Court held that the plea was not applicable in a civil war (*Nwaoga*, at 3).

[16] See *Wagener and others* (Rome Military Tribunal, at 52–3; High Military Tribunal, at 746); *Neubacher Fritz* (at 39–41).

punishing civilians who are acting on behalf of, or collaborating with, the enemy;[17] or
vii) refusing quarter.[18] In *Calley*, the Court of Military Appeals, *per* Judge Quinn, nevertheless recognized that the accused's mental state must be assessed according to actual
conditions, not with the benefit of hindsight:

> In the stress of combat, a member of the armed forces cannot reasonably be expected to
> make a refined legal judgment and be held criminally responsible if he guesses wrong on a
> question as to which there may be considerable disagreement. (at 543–4).[19]

Even under those extraordinary circumstances, however, a soldier is required to appraise
the legality or illegality of the order, both as a matter of fact and law.[20]

Other cases rejecting the plea have affirmed its existence in principle. The Italian High
Military Tribunal upheld the plea in theory, but rejected it on the facts, in *Wagener and
others* in 1950.[21] Another case worth mentioning is *Grumpelt* (*Scuttled U-Boats* case).[22]

---

[17] See e.g. *Wolfgang Zeuss and others* (at 206–7, 216).

[18] Seee.g. *Nikolaus von Falkenhorst* (at 226–7, 237).

[19] In the war crime case of *Major Shmuel Malinki and others*, an Israeli court, in applying para. 19(B) of
the Israeli Criminal Law, drew a distinction between 'sudden and unexpected orders' and 'other orders'. It
stated that 'A soldier [...] is educated and trained to use his weapon in two types of activities—independently and in a group framework. In a group framework he is trained to act most mechanically with general
reliance on the commander's order, without hesitation. He is trained to act quickly and immediately, as
automatically as possible, in order to fulfil his task in the framework suitably. In training and in the daily
routine the soldier is educated towards battle activity, where there is no time for deliberation, no place for
independent thoughts on the part of the private who forms part of a unit, where the results of the battle and
the fate of the soldier and his comrades might depend on his unquestioned obedience to his commander's
orders and his speed in operating his weapon before the enemy. The modern and sophisticated weapon of
our era adds and obliges educating the soldier in speed and maximum automatism in its use [...] The soldier
who operates within a framework and obeys a sudden and unexpected order to fire from his commander,
will in general be relieved of criminal responsibility for the results in taking a man's life through his actions,
since the necessary training of the soldier to respond immediately and almost automatically to orders of this
kind deprives him of the possibility that he consider the circumstances under which the order was given and
forces him to rely on the commander regarding the reason for using his weapon' (at 134–5).

[20] See the *Instructions* from the military judge to the Court Martial, March 1971 (at 1720–4). See also
Schwarz (for a comment, see *Cassese's Companion*, at 907). In 1970 a five-man US Marines patrol in South
Vietnam had been sent out, overnight, to search out, locate, and kill Viet Cong. In a small hamlet called Son
Thang they came across sixteen civilians, women, and children, in three huts, and killed all of them upon
order of the team leader. The plea entered by two members of the team, to have acted upon orders and under
conditions of extreme tension and stress for fear of ambushes, was rejected. In the first case (*Schwarz*), the
Navy Court of Military Review held that 'the accused could not have honestly and reasonably believed that
Herrod's [the team leader's] order to kill the apparently unarmed women and children was legal [...] The
record [...] before us shows beyond any doubt that Herrod's orders to kill the unarmed women and children
were patently illegal and were recognized as being so by members of the patrol including private Schwarz' (at
860, 863).

[21] According to defence counsel, General Wagener, when obeying the order to take reprisals against
Italian internees in territory occupied by Germany, had erred, not, however, about criminal law, but about
international law (as far as the lawfulness of reprisals was concerned) and constitutional and international
law (with regard to the power to issue military proclamations). The Court, while implicitly conceding the
admissibility of the defence, rejected it in the case at bar, noting first, that the violation of the laws of warfare
entailed criminal punishment and, second, that 'a military may not invoke as a defence ignorance of the
duties inherent in his military status. The commander of a big unit in time of war may not ignore international obligations deriving from the laws of war, the more so when these obligations coincide with the
principles, prevailing in any law, directed to safeguard the life and limb of individuals' (at 763).

[22] In this case Grumpelt, an officer in the German Navy, had scuttled two German U-boats after the belligerents had signed the terms of surrender, providing, among other things, that all German vessels would
be handed over to the British Command on 5 May 1945. A few hours after the signature of the Instrument of

Some other cases mentioning superior orders do not, in fact, stand for the proposition that the orders themselves offer any defence, but an acquittal was entered for other reasons. For example, in some cases the orders themselves have been adjudged lawful and, hence, the actions taken in pursuit of the orders were also lawful.[23] As long as the execution of the orders did not go beyond the legally permissible orders themselves, no crime had taken place.[24] Another type of case involves a subordinate whose mental state was somehow impaired, or who was under duress, because of circumstances related to the chain of command. These cases do not, however, stand for the proposition that

Surrender but before the cessation of hostilities, the German Naval Command had issued a coded order that all U-boats must be scuttled. A few hours later the same Command issued another order countermanding the first. The accused claimed that *i*) he had received the first order but not the second; and *ii*) when he had decided to scuttle the two submarines he was not apprised of the terms of surrender; had he known them, he would have been able to refrain from obeying the first order. He thus implied that he lacked mens rea, for, ignoring the terms of surrender, he honestly believed that the (first) order was legal. The Judge Advocate put the question to the Military Court as follows: 'Are you satisfied that the man's state of mind at the time in question was this: "I honestly believed I had an order: I did not know anything about any surrender; it was not for me to inquire why the higher command should be scuttling submarines; I honestly, conscientiously and genuinely believed I had been given a lawful command to scuttle these submarines and I have carried out that command and I cannot be held responsible"? Gentlemen, that is a matter for you to consider' (at 70). The Court found the accused guilty of the charge of committing a war crime.

[23] See e.g. *Neumann*. Upon the orders of a superior officer, the accused had taken part in an attack on prisoners of war who had refused to work, and had in addition 'belaboured a prisoner with his fists and feet'. The German Supreme Court at Leipzig held that the accused could not be held responsible for these events, for there could be no doubt as to the legality of the order (at 2554). The Court went on to state that 'Unless there is to be irreparable damage to military discipline, even in a body of prisoners, disorderly tendencies have to be nipped in the bud relentlessly and they have to be stamped out by all the means at the disposal of the commanding officer and if necessary even by the use of arms. It is of course understood that the use of force in any particular case must not be greater than is necessary to compel obedience. It has not been established that there was any excessive use of force here. The accused has been charged with having continued to belabour [the Scottish prisoner of war] Florence when he was lying on the ground and after the resistance of the prisoners generally had already been overcome. For this, however, no adequate proof has been forthcoming' (at 2553–4; at 699 for the English translation). It is notable that in the same case the Court also ruled out the defence being available to the accused with regard to other instances where he had ill-treated prisoners of war using what the Court held to be excessive force, not justified by the order (at 2554–6 and 699–704, for the English translation).

In *von Falkenhausen* the Brussels Court Martial (Conseil de Guerre) held that the superior orders concerning the execution of reprisals against the population could amount to an admissible plea to the extent that the reprisals were necessary to ensure the security of the Occupant; indeed, according to the Court at the time these reprisals were carried out, under international law such reprisals could not be regarded as a 'flagrant violation of the laws of warfare' (at 868–70).

[24] Reference can be made to *V. J. F. G.* (*Korad Khalid* v. *Paracommando soldier*), brought in 1995 before a Belgian Military Court. In 1993 a member of the Belgian military troops in Somalia had wounded a Somali child who was trying to enter the safety area, through barbed wire fencing guarded by the accused. The Court found that the order 'to defend and prevent anyone from penetrating into the cantonment of various Belgian military units' was lawful (at 1064–6). It then considered how the defendant had carried it out. It noted that 'on observing the child creep through the concertina and thus arrive in the immediate vicinity of the bunker, he [the defendant] first gave the necessary verbal warning in both Somali and English [...] he then fired two warning shots into the ground about 50 cm away from the child, who still showed no reaction, [...] he finally decided to fire an aimed shot [...] at non-vital organs, viz. the legs [...] the procedure followed by the accused was the only possible one to fulfil his defensive duties [...] he was physically incapable of catching the intruder (in view of the special position of the bunker, which was accessible only from the rear along an aperture in the cantonment wall) [...] and [in addition] it was unrealistic to call upon other reserve facilities, e.g. the picket; [furthermore] in view of the possible imminent attack, the reaction had to be prompt and this reaction was also commensurate; [...] all being considered, there was no other action suitable in the circumstances which could be taken to prevent further penetration [...and] the force used was unmistakably proportional to the nature and extent of the threat' (at 1066–7).

A similar case is *D. A. Maria Pierre* (*Osman Somow* v. *Paracommando Soldier*). A Belgian Military Court held that the order was lawful and that, in accidentally causing the death of a Somali civilian, the Belgian

superior orders offers a separate defence that does not already exist. A case in point is *Caroelli and others*, decided by the Italian Court of Cassation on 10 May 1947. In northern Italy, in the area under the control of the Republic set up in 1943–5 by Italian fascists with the support and under the control of Germans (the so-called Repubblica Sociale Italiana), the provincial representative of the government (*prefetto*) had ordered the head of the National Guard, Mr Caroelli, to execute ten partisans by way of reprisal following the killing of a National Guard officer. The reprisal, in addition to being unlawful, was absolutely arbitrary (the *prefetto* had been informed by one of his subordinates that the killing of the National Guard officer was due more to jealousy than to political motives, and at any rate the police were about to ferret out the perpetrator). The case was brought before the Court of Assize of Padua which acquitted Caroelli, his deputy, and another officer, on the strength of Article 51, last paragraph, of the Italian Criminal Code, whereby 'whoever executes an unlawful order is not punishable, whenever the law does not allow him to scrutinize the lawfulness of the order'. On appeal from the Prosecutor, the Court of Cassation held that reliance upon that provision was wrong, because the order was patently unlawful and arbitrary, and the subordinates were not bound to carry it out, pursuant to Article 40 of the Military Criminal Code applicable in time of war. Nevertheless, the three accused were acquitted, because they 'lacked freedom of will, in the conduct ordered by their superior'. The Court emphasized that, when the order was given, Caroelli tried to oppose it 'in two agitated talks' with the *prefetto* and, when he left the *prefetto*'s office, he had 'a cadaverous appearance' and 'could hardly stand on his feet'. According to the Court, this showed that the order brought about in Caroelli a state of 'psychic confusion that was also accompanied by clear physical manifestations' and this 'confusion was transmitted to his aides'.[25]

The above reasoning does not comport with the relevant rules and principles of international law. In any event, assuming that the legal grounds set out by the court were correct, it remains that in this and similar cases the excuse the defendant might validly raise is not superior order, but *mental disorder* (see 12.2.4). In addition, in all such cases, it would of course be necessary for the courts to be extremely cautious in establishing the facts and the credibility of witnesses, lest the plea of superior orders should become a general pretext for negating criminal responsibility.

D. Case Law Accepting the Plea of Superior Orders

The plea of superior orders has rarely been successful on the basis of a permissible mistake of law. In *Wilhelm von Leeb and others* (*High Command* case), the Tribunal discussed the question of whether the field commanders under trial, by obeying an order issued by their superior authorities to use prisoners of war for the construction of fortifications, had complied with an unlawful order and were therefore guilty. The Tribunal held that the order was not patently illegal because the law on the matter was unclear; consequently, the accused were not responsible under this count.[26]

---

soldier on guard duty who had executed the order was not responsible for he had not failed 'to exercise foresight and care' when firing a warning shot which by ricochet had fatally wounded the Somali (at 1069–71).

[25] According to the Court, 'when the manifestation of will contrary to the criminal action ordered by the superior is such as to cause clear physical troubles and a psychic confusion that nullifies the subordinate's freedom of decision, clouding a clear vision of hierarchical relations, evidently there does not exist that integrity of awareness and will required for making up a generic criminal intent, and even more the specific criminal intent necessary for the crime at issue' (at 2).

[26] It is worth quoting the Tribunal's reasoning: 'One serious question that confronts us arises as to the use of prisoners of war for the construction of fortifications. It is pointed out that the [IV] Hague

In *Kappler and others* (1948), the Rome Military Tribunal dealt with the unlawful reprisals ordered by Hitler for the partisans' attack in Rome, which killed 32 members of an SS unit. The SS Lieutenant Colonel Kappler, besides carrying out those orders, decided to kill ten more Italians because meanwhile another SS had died as a result of the attack. In addition, he had five more Italians killed by mistake: a total of 335 persons. The Court held that the reprisals were unlawful, and Kappler was guilty of ordering the shooting of ten persons plus the additional five people. However, it found that he was not guilty for the killing of 320 persons ordered by Hitler.[27] It held:

> The mental habit of prompt obedience that the accused had developed working in an organization based on very strict discipline, the fact that orders with the same content had been previously executed in the various areas of military operation, the fact that an order from the Head of State and Supreme Commander of the armed forces, owing to the great moral force inherent in it, cannot but diminish, especially in a serviceman, that freedom of judgment which is necessary for an accurate appraisal, all these are elements which lead this Court to believe that it may not be held with certainty that Kappler was aware and willed to obey an unlawful order. (30)

The Court's reasoning is highly questionable and, indeed, was 'reversed' in subsequent judgments of Italian courts.[28] If one were to share this approach, the subordinate would be relieved of responsibility in all cases where a superior gives an unlawful order. Indeed, one could easily prove that the superior authorities' widespread practice of issuing unlawful orders, together with the great clout of such authorities, bring about a frame of mind whereby the subordinate forfeits his awareness and will, and hence lacks the requisite mental element for the commission of the crime.

Convention [of 1907] specifically prohibited the use of prisoners of war for any work in connection with the operation of war, whereas the later Geneva Convention [of 1929] provided that there shall be no *direct* connection with the operations of war. This situation is further complicated by the fact that when the proposal was made to definitely specify the exclusion of the building of fortifications, objection was made before the [Geneva] conference to that limitation, and such definite exclusion of the use of prisoners was not adopted. There is also much evidence in this case to the effect that Russia used German prisoners of war for such purposes. It is no defence in the view of this Tribunal to assert that international crimes were committed by an adversary, but as evidence given to the interpretation of what constituted accepted use of prisoners of war under international law, such evidence is pertinent. At any rate, it appears that the illegality of such use was by no means clear. The use of prisoners of war in the construction of fortifications is a charge directed against the field commanders on trial here. This Tribunal is of the opinion that in view of the uncertainty of international law as to this matter, orders providing for such use from superior authorities, not involving the use of prisoners of war in dangerous areas, were not criminal upon their face, but a matter which a field commander had the right to assume was properly determined by the legal authorities upon higher levels' (at 534; see also 535).

Another case in point is *E. van E.*, decided after the Second World War by a Dutch Special Court of Cassation. In April 1945 a Dutch unit of resistance fighters in occupied Netherlands, recognized by Royal decree as members of the Dutch armed forces, shot and killed four members of the Dutch Nazis (NSB) they had captured. The order to kill them, given by the commander B., was executed by van E. with two other members of the unit. The Court found that 'given the circumstances in which the order was given, the accused was entitled to assume in good faith that his commanding officer was authorized to give that order for the liquidation of the prisoners, and that this order was within the scope of his subordination'. The Court therefore found van E. not criminally liable and acquitted him (at 514–16). To better grasp the purport of this decision, it must be recalled that in the case against the commander, B., the same Court held that he was not guilty for ordering to shoot and kill the prisoners, because the law was unclear and he committed a pardonable error of law.

[27] The Supreme Military Tribunal upheld the judgment by a decision of 25 October 1952, at 97–118.

The Court applied the same reasoning to the four other accused, who had executed Kappler's order, and found them not guilty (at 51).

[28] See, in particular, *Hass and Priebke (Appeal)*, 15 April 1998, at 52–4.

The plea of superior order was raised in conjunction with mistake of law in *Thomas L. Kinder*. The defence counsel urged on behalf of the accused a mistake of law both as to *i*) the legality of the order of the superior officer; and *ii*) whether or not the airman was required to obey all orders without exception. The US Air Force Board of Review, on appeal from the General Court Martial, admitted the plea in principle, but dismissed it on the facts. It first cited paragraph 154*a*(4) of the 1951 Manual for Courts Martial, whereby 'As a general rule, ignorance of law [...] is not an excuse for a criminal act. However, if a special state of mind on the part of the accused, such as specific intent, constitutes an essential element of the offence charged, an honest and reasonable mistake of law, including an honest and reasonable mistake as to the legal effects of known facts, may be shown for the purpose of indicating the absence of such a state of mind' (at 775). The Court then went on to say that

> As the offence of murder charged in the instant case involves a specific intent to kill, 'mistake of law' is in principle an applicable defence to negative the unlawfulness of the element of the specific intent to kill.

Turning to the case at issue, the Court pointed out the following:

> However, viewing the defence of mistake of law as based on a claim in the instant case that the accused was mistaken in law as to the legality of the order of the superior officer, the defence fails for a prerequisite of such defence is that the mistake of law was an honest and reasonable one and as pointed out in the preceding paragraph the evidence not only does not raise a reasonable doubt as to whether or not the accused possessed an honest and reasonable belief that the order was legal, but justifies the inference that the accused was aware of the illegality of the order. Viewing the defence of mistake of law as based on a claim that the accused mistakenly believed the law to be that a soldier must without exception obey every order of a superior officer, we must also reject the defence for not [only] is such a view unreasonable, but is so absurd as to render unbelievable an honest belief by the accused that he entertained such an opinion of the law. The absurdity of such a belief can be illustrated by innumerable examples such as a superior officer's orders to commit rape, to steal for him, for the subordinate to cut off his own head, etc. Accordingly, under the circumstances of the instant case, we find no merit to a defence based on the principle of mistake of law. (775–6)

13.1.2 SUPERIOR ORDERS AND DURESS

Obedience to superior orders is commonly raised in conjunction with a claim of duress. However, there is no necessary connection between the two, nor does the existence of an order necessarily satisfy the threshold for duress. Superior orders may be issued without being accompanied by *any* threats to life or limb. In these circumstances, if the superior order involves the commission of an international crime (or, under the different heading referred to above, is manifestly illegal under international law), the subordinate is under a duty to refuse to obey the order. If, following such a refusal, the order is reinforced by a threat to life or limb, then the defence of duress may be raised, and the superior order loses any legal relevance. Equally, duress may be raised independently of superior order, for example, where the threat issues from a fellow serviceman, or even a subordinate.[29]

---

[29] One of the first cases where the issue of duress was raised in connection with superior orders is *Llandovery Castle*. After finding that the two defendants were guilty of a war crime for they had carried out the illegal order of their captain Patzig to fire on shipwrecked persons, the Court noted that 'the defence finally points out that the accused must have considered that Patzig would have enforced his orders, weapon

13.1.3 SUPERIOR ORDER AND MISTAKE OF FACT

Individual soldiers often have to rely on information given to them by others about the circumstances in which they are acting, and often have to rely on information implicitly or expressly conveyed to them in orders given to them by their superiors. Soldiers are generally entitled to presume that the orders they receive are based on an assessment of the facts that ensures that the action they are committing is not criminal. The UK Manual of the Law of Armed Conflict offers an illustration:

> If an artillery commander is ordered to fire at an enemy command post in a particular building and he does so believing that it is a command post but it later turns out that, unbeknown to him, it was a school, he would not be guilty of a war crime because he did not intend to attack a school. (§ 16.45.1)

The US Manual for Air Forces similarly explains: if a hospital is selected as a target for attack, '[a]lthough the person making the selection would be criminally responsible, a pilot given such coordinates would not be criminally responsible unless he knew the nature of the protected target' (AFP 110–31, 19 November 1976, 15–16).

The defence has been raised by soldiers who executed enemy persons on the alleged basis that they thought that the victims had been properly tried and sentenced to death, whereas this was not the case. The claim, in effect, was that they were under a mistake of fact about the presence of a justification that would have made their acts lawful. Though accepted in principle, the defence was rejected as unproven in, for example, *Almelo*,[30] *Stalag Luft III*,[31] and *Wagener and others*.[32]

in hand, if they had not obeyed them. This possibility is rejected. If Patzig had been faced by refusal of the part of his subordinates, he would have been obliged to desist from his purpose, as then it would have been impossible for him to attain his object, namely, the concealment of the torpedoing of the *Llandovery Castle*. This was also quite well known to the accused, who had witnessed the affair. From the point of view of necessity (Section 52 of the [German] Penal Code) they can thus not claim to be acquitted' (at 2586/ 722–3). See also *José Valente*, at 10.

[30] Four German members of a special security detachment had arrested a British pilot who had parachuted from his burning Lancaster and had taken refuge in a house in the Dutch village of Almelo, along with a Dutch civilian who was hiding from the Germans to avoid compulsory labour service in Germany. The German officer in charge of the detachment (not on trial) had told the four accused that the British officer had been sentenced to death and was to be executed, together with the Dutchman. The two were then shot dead. Defence counsel argued that, so far as the accused knew, it was quite possible that the two victims were in fact liable to be shot. The Judge Advocate stated that if the Court found that the accused honestly believed, or that *a reasonable man might have believed*, that the British officer had been tried according to the law, and that they were carrying out a lawful execution, they must acquit the accused. The Court found, however, that the accused were guilty (March 1945 at 41 and 45).

[31] In *Stalag Luft III*, tried by a British Court Martial in 1947, the accused were charged with killing some fifty British officers who had escaped in March 1944 from a German internment camp (Stalag Luft III). Some of the accused pleaded that they had shot the British officers upon superior orders and without knowing that they were prisoners of war on the run, in the belief that they were liable to punishment and were to be lawfully executed. Thus, in the case of the accused Jacobs, he claimed that he had been told that the British officers were 'parachute sabotage agents' who had been sentenced to death but had then escaped and killed two German officials during the break-out. The Judge Advocate admitted that this defence was based on mistake of fact and regarded it as admissible if the facts alleged by the accused were proved (at 15–16). In the case of the accused Preiss, his plea, regarded as admissible by the Judge Advocate, was that 'he thought this was a legal execution and [...] he did not know for certain that Cochran [the British prisoner he shot dead] was actually an escaped prisoner-of-war' (at 23). Similarly, in the case of the accused Schulz, according to the Judge Advocate his defence was that 'he really believed that this was a legal shooting which was being carried out in secret for some special purpose and that it was the shooting of two spies, although he knew they might have been officers, on the orders of some high authority' (at 27).

[32] The Italian High Military Tribunal in *Wagener and others* admitted that this defence may be invoked and found valid on its merits; it held that 'a military, notwithstanding the manifest criminal nature of an

The Norwegian Supreme Court upheld the defence in *Hans*, overturning a contrary decision of the Court of Appeal. The accused, an officer of the German Security Police, had been charged with executing without trial Norwegian nationals during the belligerent occupation of Norway by Germany during the Second World War. He had claimed that the execution took place on the orders of his superior, who had acted pursuant to a secret decree issued by Hitler in June or July 1944 abolishing German tribunals in occupied territories and vesting in the German secret police the authority to carry out executions for offences considered to be of a political character. The Court of Appeal of Eidsivating (Norway) found the accused guilty, on the basis that he had failed to establish the legality of the execution orders. However, on appeal the Supreme Court of Norway reversed the decision, among other things because 'it was not sufficient to support a conviction for wilful murder, [to hold] that the accused *ought to have known* the circumstances which made his act unlawful' (at 306); in addition, the decision of the Court of Appeal 'did not disclose sufficiently clearly whether the accused had been aware of the unlawfulness of his acts, a fact which the Court seemed to have taken for granted' (at 306).[33]

German courts have upheld the defence in a number of cases. For instance, in *Wülfing and K.*, an officer and a sergeant in the German army's Special Service were accused of murder as a crime against humanity for having killed a German civilian who was opposed to national socialism and whom they considered guilty of instigation to desertion, as American troops approached the German town where they were stationed. The officer, Wülfing, had ordered Sergeant, K. and a non-commissioned officer to execute the civilian; the officer then finished him off with his pistol. The District Court of Hagen, in a decision of 4 August 1947 pursuant to Control Council Law no. 10, convicted Wülfing of 'murder' (*Mord*) (at 613–21), whereas K. was acquitted outright (even of the lesser crime of 'criminal homicide' (*Totschlag*)[34] on the basis that he had acted under mistake: he had believed that he was participating in the execution of a death sentence passed by a regular court (the Court held in addition that he had acted under duress (*Notstand*) for he had feared that, if he did not carry out the order to shoot, he himself would be killed by the officer who was standing by, pistol in his hand; at 618–20).

Similarly, in a decision of 12 December 1950, the German Federal Court of Justice (*Bundesgerichtshof*) upheld the excuse in the *Polish prisoner of war* case. On 10 October 1940 the accused, commander of a detachment of border guards also entrusted with assignments by the Gestapo, on the orders of the Gestapo officer superior to him commanded the execution squad that carried out a death sentence by hanging of K., a Polish prisoner of war (who in fact had not been court-martialled and duly sentenced). The Court of Assize of Flensburg acquitted the accused. It found that he lacked the intent or culpable negligence required for the charge of 'deliberate killing' (*vorsätzliche Tötung*). The Federal Court of Justice dismissed the Prosecutor's appeal and upheld the acquittal. It noted that the accused had not entertained any doubt that a death sentence had been

---

order, may be relieved of responsibility when he makes a culpable mistake of fact' (in the case at issue the Tribunal found, however, that the defence was not available to the accused) (at 763–4). See also *Buck and others* (at 39–44).

[33] Interestingly, in another case, *Flesch*, both the Court of Appeal of Frostating (Norway) and the Supreme Court of Norway convicted an officer of the German Security Police because he knew that the executed persons (Norwegian nationals and Russian prisoners of war) had not been sentenced to death by a court (at 307).

[34] In Germany s. 212 of the Criminal Code provides for *Totschlag* as distinguished from *Mord* (murder), provided for in s. 211. *Totschlag* is roughly equivalent to the second-degree murder of the US.

issued by a competent authority; hence, he was not aware of the unlawfulness of his act and could not be held accountable.[35]

13.2 THE IRRELEVANCE OF OFFICIAL CAPACITY

One of the possible obstacles to prosecution for international crimes may be constituted by rules intended to protect the accused by granting him immunity from prosecution for the acts accomplished in an official capacity. Under international law, there exists one category of immunities that may in principle come into play and be relied upon, i.e. the so-called immunities *ratione materiae*, also called *functional immunities*. This class of immunities apply, to all state agents discharging their official duties. Their rationale

---

[35] The Federal Court noted that 'at the time of the offence the accused knew that offices of the Gestapo imposed and executed penalties against nationals of eastern peoples. At the time of the offence he also assumed that K. had been sentenced to death in this manner. As the Court of Assize explicitly stated, 'the accused had no doubt that the judgment had been issued by the competent and appropriate authority in accordance with properly conducted proceedings and was legally binding and final'. The accused had based his conviction on a telex he had received in October 1944 from the Regional office (*Gau*) of the Gestapo. The telex was signed by the head of the office, a senior governmental official (*Regierungsrat*) and stated more or less that the Polish K. had been sentenced to death for a violation of the 'Order for the Protection of Law Enforcement Agents' and that the main office of the Reich Security Service had ordered that the execution should take place in the district where the offence had been committed. Such an Order did not in fact exist; but that is immaterial. The crucial fact is that the accused [...] had believed in some type of 'judgment' based on legal requirements (even if not rendered by a regular court). Furthermore, he knew that fully qualified lawyers were employed at the higher office of the Gestapo. In a prior conversation in the Gestapo office it had been explicitly pointed out that the conviction of foreigners by the Gestapo occurred with the participation of fully qualified lawyers in something akin to 'Chamber of Judges' (at 234).

The Federal Court also dismissed the Prosecution's ground of appeal against the lower court's finding that the accused had not acted 'negligently in either a factual or legal sense' in his assumption that the Pole had been legally sentenced to death and that the task of executing the sentence, entrusted upon him, was lawful. The Federal Court concluded that the accused was not guilty, because he lacked either intent (*Vorsatz*) or negligence (*Fahrlässigkeit*). It stated that the international law question of whether or not the legal Regulations issued by the Nazi authorities (on the punishment of Polish war prisoners by Gestapo officers, outside of any regular trial proceedings) were valid, could be left undecided. In any case, at least at the time of the offence, the legal issue was still dubious, as was held by a United States Military Tribunal at Nuremberg in the *Wilhelm von Leeb and others* case (see *Law Reports of Trials of War Criminals* 1949, vol. XII, at 86, where a contrary conclusion is reached). Rather, what really mattered was to establish whether the accused, 'based on his personal circumstances, could and should have recognized the possible legal invalidity' of those Regulations.

The Court of Assize had answered this question in the negative, after admitting the illegality of those Regulations. It had pointed out that at the time of the offence one could not expect that the accused, 'based on his personal circumstances' 'could recognize that possibly those Regulations were contrary to international law and consequently the death sentence issued by the Gestapo, with whose execution he had been tasked, was legally invalid'. This was all the more true because the accused, based on the record of police interrogation of the Pole, 'was convinced and could be convinced that the Pole had attacked the Police Superintendent Sch. and seized him by the neck, thereby committing a criminal offence punishable by death. Although the accused may have been a particularly capable, knowledgeable and experienced official within the group of criminal investigators to which he had belonged for 24 years, nevertheless, according to the legally incontrovertible evidence presented to the Court of Assize, he did not have the knowledge necessary for appraising these legal issues of public law and international law. There are no indications that, at the time of the offence, the accused had any reason to mistrust the academically trained head of the Gestapo office. Moreover, the accused had learned from experience prior to the offence that the administration of criminal justice against Poles had passed from the hands of the judiciary to the offices of the Gestapo and that, according to his observations, generally Public Prosecutors and ordinary courts had not opposed this development' (at 234–5). See also *Scheiner Z.*, at 712–15.

is that an individual performing acts on behalf of a sovereign state may not be called to account before *foreign courts* for a violation of international law he may have committed while acting in an official function. Only the state may be held responsible at the international level.[36]

Is the international rule on functional immunities also applicable with respect to acts amounting to international crimes? To answer this question one must of course establish whether there are international customary or treaty rules that cover this matter.

13.2.1 THE INAPPLICABILITY OF THE DOCTRINE OF FUNCTIONAL IMMUNITIES WITH RESPECT TO INTERNATIONAL CRIMES

A. The Pre-Nuremberg Phase

Traditionally, international customary rules only authorized the removal of functional immunities in time of war for war crimes perpetrated by low-level members of the armed forces.[37] By contrast, it would seem that political leaders as well as military commanders enjoyed functional immunities. Indeed, no case can be found where any such leader or commander was brought to trial for war crimes. In 1919, an attempt was made to lay down and implement the doctrine of criminal responsibility of senior state officials for both war crimes and the new category of 'crimes against the laws of humanity'. The Commission on Responsibilities relating to the war (created by the Preliminary Peace Conference of Paris) recommended that

> all persons belonging to enemy countries, *however high their position may have been*, without distinction of rank, *including chiefs of States*, who have been guilty of offences against the laws and customs of war or the laws of humanity, are liable to criminal prosecution.[38]

This proposal was strongly opposed by the American representatives, who took issue both with the notion that heads of states should be liable to criminal prosecution and with the concept of crimes against humanity.[39] The upshot was the adoption in the 1919 Treaty of Versailles of Article 227 on the responsibility of the former German Emperor for 'a supreme offence against international morality and the sanctity of treaties'[40] and

---

[36] Functional immunities must be distinguished from personal (or *ratione personae*) immunities (see 17.4) See also P. Gaeta, 'Official Capacity and Immunities', in Cassese, Gaeta, Jones, *ICC Commentary*, vol. 1, 975–1002 (on which the revision of the present section also relies), at 975–8.

[37] It has been argued that the power of a belligerent state to punish war criminals was initially limited to the time of the armed conflict and, in any case, could only be exercised within occupied territory. It was envisaged that armistice or peace treaties could contain a clause whereby the victorious belligerent imposed upon the defeated states the obligation to surrender alleged war criminals for trial (see UN War Crimes Commission, *History of the UN War Crimes Commission and the Development of the Laws of War* (1948), at 29–30).

[38] The Report of the Commission can be read in 14 AJIL (1920), at 95ff.

[39] According to the American representatives, 'the Head of the State, whether he be called emperor, king, or chief executive [...] is responsible not to the judicial but to the political authority of his country. His act may and does bind his country and render it responsible for the acts which he has committed in its name and its behalf, or under cover of its authority; but he is, and it is submitted that he should be, only responsible to his country, as otherwise to hold would be to subject to foreign countries a chief executive, thus withdrawing him from the laws of his country, even its organic law, to which he owes obedience, and subordinating him to foreign jurisdictions to which neither he nor his country owes allegiance or obedience, thus denying the very conception of sovereignty'; see UN War Crimes Commission, *History of the UN War Crimes Commission*, at 39–40. With regard to the position of the American representatives on the concept of crimes against humanity see *History of the UN War Crimes Commission*, at 36.

[40] Art. 227 provided for the establishment of a special tribunal for the trial of Wilhelm II of Hohenzollern. This Tribunal was to be guided 'by the highest motives of international policy, with a view of vindicating the solemn obligations of international undertakings and the validity of international

Articles 228–9 providing for the trial by the Allied and Associated Powers of 'all persons accused of having committed acts in violations of law and customs of war'.[41] Since no reference was made to the rank of the accused, the inference is warranted that Articles 228–9 also provided for the criminal responsibility of senior military commanders, thus ruling out the applicability to them of customary rules on functional immunities.

It is well known that the former German Emperor was never brought to trial on account of the refusal of the Netherlands to extradite him (on grounds of national law: Dutch legislation allowed extradition only on the basis of a treaty, and the Netherlands was not party to the Versailles Treaty; in addition, the offences provided for in Article 227 did not constitute crimes under Dutch law). In addition, the high-ranking German military officers indicted under Articles 228–9 were never tried either by the Allies or by Germany.[42] These developments support the view that in the period under consideration no customary rule had yet evolved to the effect of removing the functional immunities senior state officials enjoyed under customary international law.

B. A Watershed: Nuremberg and Tokyo

A turning point can be seen in the London Agreement of 8 August 1945 establishing the Nuremberg Tribunal. Article 7 provided as follows:

> The official position of the defendants, whether as Heads of States or responsible officials in Government Departments, shall not be considered as freeing them from responsibility or mitigating punishment.

This provision clearly made the international law doctrine of functional immunities unavailable to senior officials accused of one of the categories of crimes envisaged in Article 6 of the London Agreement. The same provision, slightly changed, can also be found in Article 6 of the Charter of the Tokyo.[43] In their judgments, both Tribunals applied the provisions under discussion without, however, addressing whether they were in keeping with customary international law.[44]

---

morality'. It must be underlined that Wilhelm II was charged with offences against *moral* rather than *legal* provisions.

[41] It should be noted that these articles only deal with violations of law and customs of war; the American view prevailed and no reference was to made to the 'laws of humanity'.

[42] Under Article 229, persons charged with war crimes against the nationals of one of the Allied and Associated Powers, should have been brought before the military tribunals of the relevant Power, while persons accused of war crimes against nationals of more than one of these Powers should have been brought before military tribunals composed of members of the military tribunals of the Powers concerned. However, Germany refused to surrender the 896 persons requested by the Allies (among those persons there were many senior military and naval officers). As a compromise solution, it was decided that instead of handing the accused persons over to the Allies, the German government would have brought to trial those persons before the Supreme Court of Leipzig. Only 45 persons, against whom the most serious charges had been brought, were tried by the Leipzig court (see UN War Crimes Commission, *History of the UN War Crimes Commission*, at 46–52).

[43] 'Neither the official position, at any time, of an accused, nor the fact that an accused acted pursuant to order of his government or of a superior shall, of itself, be sufficient to free such accused from responsibility for any crime with which he is charged, but such circumstances may be considered in mitigation of punishment if the Tribunal determines that justice so requires.' Article 6 did not refer specifically to the position of the head of State, probably because of the political decision not to try the Japanese Emperor Hirohito (O. Triffterer, 'Art. 27', in Triffterer, *ICC Commentary*, at 781).

[44] The Nuremberg Tribunal stated: 'The principle of international law, which under certain circumstances, protects the representatives of a state, cannot be applied to acts which are condemned as criminal by international law. The authors of these acts cannot shelter themselves behind their official position

Subsequent developments included numerous restatements of the principle affirmed by the Statutes of the two Tribunals, both at the international and national level.[45] Therefore, the contention can be made that a customary rule has evolved in the international community to the effect that all state officials, including those at the highest level, are not immune from criminal jurisdiction—either of a national or international nature—if charged with war crimes and other international crimes.[46]

National case law supports the inapplicability to international crimes of the customary rule on functional immunities to international crimes. Many cases where state military officials were brought to trial demonstrate that state agents accused of war crimes, crimes against humanity, or genocide may not invoke before national courts their official capacity as a valid defence. Even if we leave aside cases where tribunals adjudicated on the strength of international treaties or Control Council Law no. 10, a string of significant judgments where courts applied national law should be mentioned.[47] It can be conceded that most of the cases under discussion deal with *military* officers. However, it would be untenable to infer from this fact that the customary rule only applies to such persons. It would indeed be odd that a customary rule should have evolved only with regard to members of the military and not for all state agents, including former senior political leaders, who are accused of having committed international crimes. A recent case, concerning the former Algerian Minister of Defence, Khaled Nezzar, confirms this stand. In a landmark decision delivered in 2012, the Swiss Federal Court found that the accused could not claim immunity for acts allegedly amounting to war crimes and crimes against humanity committed during his office, thus paving the way for a trial in

in order to be freed from punishment in appropriate proceedings. Article 7 of the Charter expressly declares: "The official position of the Defendants, whether as heads of State, or responsible officials in Government departments, shall not be considered as freeing them from responsibility, or mitigating punishment." On the other hand, the very essence of the Charter is that individuals have international duties which transcend the national obligations of obedience imposed by the individual State. He who violates the laws of war cannot obtain immunity while acting in pursuance of the authority of the State if the State in authorizing action moves outside its competence under international law' (*Göring and others*, at 223).

[45] See e.g. Art. II(4)(a) of the 1945 Control Council Law no. 10; Art. IV of the 1948 Genocide Convention, Principle III of the Nuremberg Principles adopted in 1950 by the UN General Assembly; Art. III of the 1973 Apartheid Convention; Art. 7(2) of the ICTY Statute; Art. 6(2) of the ICTR Statute; Art. 27 of the ICC Statute, and so on.

[46] One commentator has tried to demonstrate that, even if one considers that the above instances of international practice do not persuasively demonstrate the existence of a customary rule on the matter, the denial of functional immunities in cases of international crimes can be affirmed on the basis of logic. As this author has maintained, 'International Law cannot grant immunity from prosecution in relation to acts which the same international law condemns as criminal and as an attack on the interests of the international community as a whole. Nor can the principle of sovereignty, of which immunity is clearly a derivative, be persuasively set forth to defeat a claim based on an egregious violation of human rights' (A. Bianchi, 'Immunity versus Human Rights: The *Pinochet* Case', 10 EJIL (1999), 237–77, at 261).

[47] One may recall, for instance, *Eichmann* in Israel (at 277–342); *Barbie* in France (see the various judgments in 78 ILR, 125ff., and 100 ILR 331ff.), *Kappler* (193–9), and *Priebke* in Italy (959ff.); *Rauter* (526–48); *Albrecht* (747–51); and *Bouterse* in the Netherlands (Amsterdam Court of Appeal); *Kesserling* (9ff.) before a British Military Court sitting in Venice, and *von Lewinski* (called *von Manstein*) before a British Military Court in Hamburg (523–4), *Pinochet* in the UK; *Yamashita* in the USA (1599ff.); *Buhler* before the Supreme National Tribunal of Poland (682); *Pinochet* and *Scilingo* in Spain (at 4–8 and 2–8, respectively); and *Miguel Cavallo* in Mexico (by Judge Jesus Guadalupe Luna authorizing the extradition of Ricardo Miguel Cavallo to Spain).

Switzerland under universal jurisdiction.[48] The Supreme Court of Israel in *Eichmann* (at 311), and more recently various Trial Chambers of the ICTY have held that the provisions of, respectively, Article 7 of the Charter of the Nuremberg Tribunal and Article 7(2) of the Statute of the ICTY (both of which relate to *any person* accused of one of the crimes provided for in the respective Statutes) 'reflect a rule of customary international law'.[49] In 2002 in *Letkol Inf. Soedjarwo*, the Indonesian Ad Hoc Court on Human Rights held that the relevant provision of the ICC Statute has 'developed' into 'a legal principle' (at 23). Furthermore, Lords Millet and Phillips of Worth Matravers in the House of Lords' decision of 24 March 1999 in *Pinochet* took the view, with regard to any senior state agent, that functional immunity cannot excuse international crimes.[50] The ICTY Appeals Chamber had already set out this legal proposition in *Blaškić* (*Subpoena*) (§ 41) (see also SCSL, TC, *Taylor* (*Decision on the immunity from prosecution*), §§ 52–3). In addition, important national Military Manuals, for instance those issued in 1956 in the USA and in 1958 (and then in 2004) in the UK,[51] expressly provide that the fact that a person who has committed an international crime was acting as a government official

---

Admittedly, in most of these cases the accused did not challenge the court's jurisdiction on the ground that he had acted as a state official. The fact remains, however, that the courts did pronounce on acts performed by those officials in the exercise of their functions. The defendants' failure to raise the 'defence' of acting on behalf of their state shows that they were aware that such defence would have been of no avail. In addition, in some cases the defendant did plead that he had acted in his official capacity and hence was immune from prosecution. This, for example, happened in *Eichmann*, where the accused raised the question of 'Act of State'. Although the Court used that terminology, which could be misleading, in essence it took the right approach to the question at issue and explicitly held that state agents acting in their official capacity may not be immune from criminal liability if they commit international crimes (at 309–12).

[48] The Tribunal stated the following: 'Il reste à décider si l'immunité *ratione materiae* [...] couvre tous les actes commis pendant [la] fonction et prévaut sur la nécessité de dégager les responsabilités éventuelles du recourant sur de prétendues violation graves des droits humains. Selon les principes qui ressortent des courants de doctrine et de jurisprudence [...] une réponse affirmative à cette question ne fait plus l'unanimité. Il est en effet généralement reconnu que l'interdiction des crimes graves contre l'humanité, notamment en cas de torture, a un caractère coutumier. Cette approche est partagée par le législateur suisse, pour qui "l'interdiction du génocide, des crimes contre l'humanité et des crimes de guerre est de nature impérative (*jus cogens*) ". Selon ce même législateur, "les Etats sont tenus de faire respecter cette interdiction indépendamment de l'existence de règles conventionnelles et de leur validité. Ce devoir vise à préserver les valeurs fondamentales de l'humanité et doit être accompli indépendamment de l'attitude des autres Etats (*erga omnes*)" (Message relatif à la mise en œuvre du Statut de Rome; FF 2008 3474). Eu égard à la valeur fondamentale du bien juridique protégé, le législateur suisse a décidé "d'assurer une répression sans faille de ces actes" (Message relatif à la mise en œuvre du Statut de Rome; FF 2008 3468). Or, il serait à la fois contradictoire et vain si, d'un côté, on affirmait vouloir lutter contre ces violations graves aux valeurs fondamentales de l'humanité, et, d'un autre côté, l'on admettait une interprétation large des règles de l'immunité fonctionnelle (*ratione materiae*) pouvant bénéficier aux anciens potentats ou officiels dont le résultat concret empêcherait, *ab initio*, toute ouverture d'enquête. S'il en était ainsi, il deviendrait difficile d'admettre qu'une conduite qui lèse les valeurs fondamentales de l'ordre juridique international puisse être protégée par des règles de ce même ordre juridique. Une telle situation serait paradoxale et la politique criminelle voulue par le législateur vouée à rester lettre morte dans la quasi-totalité des cas. Ce n'est pas ce qu'il a voulu. Il en découle qu'en l'espèce le recourant ne saurait se prévaloir d'aucune immunité *ratione materiae*.' (*A. c. Ministère Public de la Confédération*, § 5.4.3.)

[49] See *Karadžić and others* (§ 24); *Furundžija* (§ 140); and *Milošević Slobodan* (*Decision on Preliminary Motions*) (§ 28).

[50] See at 171–9 (Lord Millet) and 186–90 (Lord Phillips of Worth Matravers). Instead, according to Lord Hope (at 152), Pinochet lost his immunity *ratione materiae* only because of Chile's ratification of the Torture Convention. In other words, for him the unavailability of functional immunity did not derive from customary law; it stemmed from treaty law.

[51] See the US Department of the Army Field Manual, *The Law of Land Warfare* (July 1956), §§ 498 and 510. See also the British manual, *The Law of War on Land* (1958), at § 632 and the 2004 *Manual of the Law*

(and not only as a serviceman) does not constitute an available defence. It is also signifi-cant that, at least with regard to one of the crimes at issue—genocide, the ICJ implicitly admitted that under *customary* law official status does not relieve responsibility (see *Reservations to the Convention on Genocide*, at 24).[52]

Arguably, while each of these elements of practice, on its own, cannot be regarded as indicative of the crystallization of a customary rule,[53] taken together they may be deemed to evidence the formation of such a rule (a rule, it should be added, on whose existence legal commentators seem to agree, although admittedly without producing compel-ling evidence concerning state or judicial practice,[54] and which the Institut de Droit International recently restated).[55]

The logic behind the rule regarding the irrelevance of official capacity was forcefully set out as early as 1945 by Justice Robert H. Jackson:

> Nor should such a defence be recognized as the obsolete doctrine that a head of state is immune from legal liability. There is more than a suspicion that this idea is a relic of the doctrine of the divine right of kings. It is, in any event, inconsistent with the posi-tion we take toward our own officials, who are frequently brought to court at the suit of citizens who allege their rights to have been invaded. We do not accept the paradox that legal responsibility should be the least where power is the greatest. We stand on the principle of responsible government declared some three centuries ago to King James by Lord Justice Coke, who proclaimed that even a King is still 'under God and the law'. [56]

of Armed Conflict (UK Ministry of Defence, London: Oxford University Press, 2004), at 16.38.1. ('Heads of State and their ministers are not immune from prosecution and punishment for war crimes. Their liability is governed by the same principles as those governing the responsibility of civilian authorities.')

[52] One should also recall that on 11 December 1946 the UN General Assembly unanimously adopted resolution 95, whereby it 'affirmed' 'the principles recognized by the Charter of the Nuremberg Tribunal and the judgment of the Tribunal'. These principles include Principle III as formulated in 1950 by the UN International Law Commission. This Principle provides as follows: 'The fact that a person who committed an act which constitutes a crime under international law acted as Head of State or responsible Government official does not relieve him from responsibility under international law.' See YILC (1950–II), 192. All the Nuremberg Principles, Israel's Supreme Court noted in *Eichmann*, 'have become part of the law of nations and must be regarded as having been rooted in it also in the past' (at 311). It is notable that the UN SG took the same view of the customary status of the Genocide Convention (or, more accurately, of the substantive principles it lays down), a view that was endorsed implicitly by the UN Security Council (see Report of the Secretary-General Pursuant to Para. 2 of Security Council Resolution 808 (1993), UN Doc. S/25704, § 45) and explicitly by the ICTR Trial Chamber in *Akayesu*, § 495, and by the ICTY Trial Chamber in *Krstić*, § 541.
A further element supporting the existence of a customary rule having a general purport can be found in the pleadings made by the two states (the Congo and Belgium) that were in dispute before the International Court of Justice in the aforementioned *Arrest Warrant case*. In its *Mémoire* of 15 May 2001, the Congo explicitly admitted the existence of a principle of ICL, whereby the official status of a state agent cannot exonerate him from individual responsibility for crimes committed while in office; the Congo also added that on this point there was no disagreement with Belgium (*Mémoire*, at 39, §60).

[53] A contrary view has, however, been put forward by the Special Rapporteur of the International Law Commission, Roman Anatolevich Kolodkin, in his Second Report on immunity of State officials from for-eign criminal jurisdiction, 10 June 2010, A/CN.4/631.

[54] See e.g. S. Glaser, 'L'Acte d'État et le problème de la responsabilité individuelle', *Revue de droit pénal et de criminologie* (1950), 1ff.; Glaser, *Introduction*, 71–6;; Y. Dinstein, 'International Criminal Law', 5 IYHR (1975), 82–3; A. Bianchi, 'Immunity versus Human Rights: The *Pinochet* Case', 10 EJIL (1999), 237–77.

[55] See the Resolution adopted at the *Naples* session (2009) on *Immunity from Jurisdiction of the State and of Persons Who Act on Behalf of the State in Case of International Crimes* (Art. III (1)).

[56] *International Conference on Military Trials*, 47.

Today, more so than in the past, it is state officials, and in particular senior officials, that commit international crimes. Most of the time they do not perpetrate crimes directly. They order, plan, instigate, organize, aid and abet, or culpably tolerate or acquiesce, or willingly or negligently fail to prevent or punish international crimes. To allow these state agents to go scot free only because they acted in an official capacity, except in the few cases where an international criminal tribunal has been established or an international treaty is applicable, would mean to bow to traditional concerns of the international community (chiefly, respect for state sovereignty). Respect for human rights and the demand that justice be done whenever human rights have been seriously and massively put in jeopardy is now recognized in the international community as overriding the traditional principle of respect for state sovereignty. The new thrust towards protection of human dignity has shattered the shield that traditionally protected state agents.[57]

C. The ICC Statute

Article 27(1) of the ICC Statute provides that it

> shall apply equally to all persons without any distinction based on official capacity. In particular, official capacity as a Head of State or Government, a member of a Government or Parliament, an elected representative or a government official shall in no case exempt a person from criminal responsibility under this Statute, nor shall it, in and of itself, constitute a ground for reduction of sentence.

It therefore restates the customary rule whereby for the purpose of establishing criminal responsibility for crimes under international law the plea of acting in an official capacity is of no avail.[58]

As has been correctly stated, this provision constitutes 'one of the clearest manifestations in the Statute of the determination in paragraph 5 of the Preamble to "put an end to impunity for the perpetrators of these crimes and thus to contribute to the prevention of such crimes"'.[59] Article 27(1) of the ICC Statute enshrines the principle whereby even those who abuse their official position and the powers flowing from it cannot avail themselves of that position to obtain impunity from crimes committed while exercising public functions.

Interestingly, in illustrating the official functions that cannot be relied upon to exclude prosecution and punishment for the crimes laid down in Article 5, Article 27(1) provides a list that is not exhaustive, but simply illustrative. It first of all explicitly mentions heads of states or government, thus establishing the principle that even those individuals who hold the highest state positions may be prosecuted and tried. Second, the list in Article 27(1) includes both the members of government and those of parliament, as well as any other 'elected representative or [...] government official'. As is apparent, Article 27(1) of the ICC Statute provides a fairly detailed list. It is warranted to submit

---

[57] A recent deviation from the rule should, however, be stressed. In 2007, in *Ibrahim Matar and others v. Avraham Dichter*, the US District Court for the Southern District of New York dismissed a civil action brought before US courts under the Alien Torts Statute against a former Israeli agent who, in his capacity as head of the Shin Beth, had allegedly authorized, planned, and directed the bombing on 22 July 2002 of an apartment building in Gaza City housing a Palestinian terrorist (the bombing caused many deaths and other casualties among civilians, and was termed in the petition a war crime). The US District Court, applying the US Foreign Sovereign Immunities Act, held that that action was covered by immunity (at 4–15).

[58] On the drafting process of this rule see Triffterer, cit. n. 48, at 783–6.

[59] Triffterer, cit. n. 43, at 786.

that the accurate and detailed nature of this list is not primarily motivated by the need to reject the international doctrine of functional immunities with regard to international crimes. If it were so, it would have been sufficient to lay down by way of illustration the possibility *also* for heads of states or government and members of parliament to be prosecuted and punished. In fact the *raison d'être* of the long list in Article 27(1) can be found in the existence, in national law, of 'functional immunities' covering certain state officials.[60] Within the framework of, and with reference to, complementarity, the provision makes it clear that—whenever a state exercises its jurisdiction over one of the crimes under Article 5, the possible application of national legislation on functional immunities runs counter to the Statute. Consequently the Court is entitled to exercise its jurisdiction.

Finally, it should be stressed that, although Article 27(1) does not expressly mention the issue, the unavailability—in case of charges of international crimes—of the plea of acting in one's official capacity also applies to officials of international intergovernmental organizations.

13.2.2 SOME MISUNDERSTANDINGS ON FUNCTIONAL IMMUNITIES AND INTERNATIONAL CRIMES

It is worth noting that, in tackling the issue of functional immunities and international crimes, the question is posed in the following terms: does customary international law provide for an exception to the applicability of the rules on functional immunities in cases of charges of international crimes? Discussing functional immunities as an exception to otherwise applicable rules, however, could be misleading. Functional immunities in international law serve to determine the 'irresponsibility' of the agent of the state for acts accomplished in the exercise of his function before foreign domestic jurisdiction, to make only the state responsible under international law. The very birth of international criminal law is based on the rejection of such a paradigm, since—as the Nuremberg Tribunal forcefully put it—'crimes against international law are committed by men, not by abstract entities, and only by punishing individuals who commit such crimes can the provisions of international law be enforced'. In other words, in Nuremberg the principle of irrelevance of having acted in an official capacity was asserted as the necessary postulate for the assertion of personal criminal liability for serious violations of international law amounting to international crimes. The impact of the new paradigm set forth in Nuremberg is that, at least for some specific conduct, states are not the exclusive duty-bearers under international law, and that also individuals must be internationally liable. In a way, the Nuremberg paradigm partially responds to what is one of the main criticisms raised against the theory of international responsibility as a form of 'collective' responsibility, namely that of its ineffectiveness in promoting compliance with international obligations: why should a state agent be induced to comply with international parameters and values if he knows that he will never personally incur any sanction, at the international level, for his illegal behaviour?[61]

---

[60] National legislation may also grant immunities to some state officials, for the acts accomplished in discharging their official function. These are normally granted to the head of state, members of cabinet, and members of parliament and they involve exemption from national jurisdiction (think, for example, of the so-called principle of unaccountability, laid down in many Constitutions, and covering these state officials for acts performed in the exercise of their functions).

[61] See P. Allot, 'State Responsibility and the Unmaking of International Law', 29 Harv Int'l L Rev (1988), 14, and the remarks by J. Crawford and J. Watkins, 'International Responsibility', in S. Besson and J. Tasioulas (eds), *The Philosophy of International Law* (Oxford: Oxford University Press, 2010), 283, who

In light of the above, it is apparent that to describe the principle of the irrelevance of having acted in an official capacity as an exception of, or a derogation from, the customary rules of international law on functional immunities, is patently wrong. In international law states are free to dispose of the scope of their criminal and civil jurisdiction, and of many other aspects related to their sovereignty, with the only exception of respect for *jus cogens* rules. This means that states are at liberty, if they wish, not to exercise their criminal and civil jurisdiction beyond what is imposed on them by customary international law. To maintain that, in cases of international crimes, there is an exception to or derogation from the rules of international law on functional immunities could lead to the contention or belief that states retain their freedom not to exercise it in relation to claims concerning the commission of crimes committed by foreign state officials in the exercise of their official capacity, as a matter of self-restraint, act of courtesy, or in application of treaties concluded to that effect. This construction would be incorrect. It would run counter to the fabric of international criminal law, which is based on the assumption that for given acts amounting to international crime every individual can be held liable, regardless of whether he has acted qua state official. If states were at liberty to dispose of this basic postulate, the whole logic of the system of international criminal justice would simply collapse.

This is the reason why, far from constituting a derogation from or an exception to the rules of international law on functional immunities, the proper interpretation of the principle of the irrelevance of official capacity for international crimes is that it gives rise to an international obligation. Consequently, states cannot claim or obtain respect for the rules of international law of functional immunities when their state officials are accused of having committed an international crime in the exercise of their function. On the other hand, states having jurisdiction over the crime cannot refuse to exercise it on account of the official nature of the act.[62]

---

correctly observe that this criticism has radical implications, since it would require that 'states should surrender their standing as principal duty-bearer under international law in favour of individuals' (at 291).

[62] In addition, if construed with the meaning propounded above, the principle of the irrelevance of official capacity would also imply the obligation for states not to apply the national rules on immunity sheltering some categories of state officials from criminal responsibility for acts committed in an official capacity. This is an obligation that already stems from the ICC Statute and other treaties, such as the Genocide Convention. However, it is submitted that it also constitutes an obligation stemming from international criminal law as such, and from its basic principle of the irrelevance of official capacity. Indeed, it would be illogical to contend that this principle only applies with respect to the exercise of criminal jurisdiction over foreign state officials, leaving the states of nationality and/or of territoriality (which are usually the states to which the state official responsible for international crimes belongs) free to shelter from criminal responsibility the alleged authors of international crimes before their own courts. See P. Gaeta, 'Immunity of States and State Officials: A Major Stumbling Block to Judicial Scrutiny?', in A. Cassese (ed.), *Realizing Utopia. The Future of International Law* (Oxford: Oxford University Press, 2012), at 237. The views expressed in the present section partially rely upon this paper.

PART III

PROSECUTION AND PUNISHMENT

SECTION I

INTERNATIONAL AND NATIONAL CRIMINAL JURISDICTION

14

INTERNATIONAL CRIMINAL COURTS

The idea of setting up an international criminal court to punish crimes of international concern goes back to the aftermath of the First World War. The attainment of that goal has been slow and painstaking. The process toward the eventual adoption of a Statute for a permanent International Criminal Court and the adoption of Statutes of various ad hoc international criminal courts (which in some cases have a mixed or hybrid nature; that is, composed both of national and international judges), can be conceptualized in terms of various distinct phases: *i*) abortive early attempts (1919–45); *ii*) the establishment of the Nuremberg and Tokyo Tribunals in the aftermath of the Second World War (1945–7); *iii*) the post-Cold War 'new world order' and the establishment by the UN Security Council of the ICTY and ICTR (1993–4); *iv*) the drafting and adoption of the ICC Statute (1994–8); *v*) the establishment of ad hoc hybrid criminal courts.

As we shall see, although the prosecution and punishment of international crimes by international courts has its merits, it is not flawless.

14.1 ABORTIVE EARLY ATTEMPTS (1919–1945)

The period immediately following the First World War is notable for numerous attempts to establish a variety of international criminal institutions, all of which ended in failure. For instance, in 1919 the 'Commission on the Responsibility of the Authors of the War and on Enforcement of Penalties' proposed the establishment of a 'high tribunal composed of judges drawn from many nations'.[1]

In the same year the victors had agreed upon a few provisions of the peace treaty with Germany, signed at Versailles, which provided for the punishment of the leading figures responsible for war crimes committed during the war and went so far as to lay down in Article 227 the responsibility of the German Emperor (Wilhelm II) for 'the supreme offence against international morality and the sanctity of treaties' (see 13.2.1). The same provision envisaged the establishment of 'a special tribunal' composed of five judges (to be appointed by the USA, Great Britain, France, Italy, and Japan) and charged with trying the Emperor. The Allies were clearly motivated by their outrage at the atrocities perpetrated by the vanquished Powers, in particular Germany, and wished to set an example. However, the accused would have been judged by their erstwhile opponents; this would have thrown doubt on the fairness of the proceedings and the impartiality of the tribunal. In any case, the Netherlands, where the German Emperor had taken refuge, refused to

---

[1] See the Report of the Commission, in 14 AJIL (1920), at 116. As for the objections of the US delegates, see at 129, 139ff.

extradite him, chiefly because the crimes of which he was accused were not contemplated in the Dutch Constitution (see 13.2.1).[2] In addition, the aforementioned provisions of the Versailles Treaty were harshly criticized by some eminent publicists, among them the Italian leading jurist and politician V. E. Orlando.[3]

As for the trials of German military personnel alleged to have committed war crimes, no international court was set up, nor were they tried by courts of the Allies, as had been envisaged in Articles 228–30 of the Versailles Treaty (see 13.2.1). Eventually, out of the 895 Germans accused (who comprised various generals and admirals including the Chief of Staff of the Army, General E. Ludendorff, General Paul von Hindenburg, later Chief of Staff of the Army, as well as the former Chancellor Bethmann-Hollweg), the Allies selected only 45 cases for prosecution.[4] Ultimately, twelve minor indictees were brought to trial in 1921, and before a German court, the 'Imperial Court of Justice' (*Reichsgericht*, sitting at Leipzig). Six of the twelve indictees were acquitted. Thus, the attempts to establish some sort of international criminal justice ended in failure. However, some of the judgments delivered by the Leipzig Court set significant precedents, chiefly because of their high legal quality. The attempts to bring to justice the 'Young Turks' responsible for the massacres of the Armenians in 1915–16 were generally partial failures; some Extraordinary Courts Martial in Istanbul brought to trial a few minor accused (plus major defendants, but in absentia).[5]

In 1920, the 'Advisory Committee of Jurists', summoned to prepare the project for the Permanent Court of International Justice, proposed that the 'High Court of International Justice' to be established should also 'be competent to try crimes constituting a breach of international public order or against the universal law of nations, referred to it by the Assembly or by the Council of the League of Nations'.[6] However, a few months later

---

[2] On the non-implementation of Art. 227, see, *inter alia*, A. Merignhac and E. Lemonon, *Le Droit des gens et la guerre de 1914–1918*, II (Paris: Pedone, 1921), 580ff.

The Dutch diplomatic note of 21 January 1920 to the Allies stated: 'Or, ni les lois constituantes du Royaume qui sont basées sur des principes de droit universellement reconnus, ni une respectable tradition séculaire qui a fait de ce pays de tout temps une terre de refuge pour les vaincus des conflits internationaux, ne permettent au Gouvernement des Pays-Bas de déférer au désir des Puissances en retirant à l'ex-empereur le bénéfice de ces lois et cette tradition' (see the text of the Dutch diplomatic notes in A. Mérignhac, 'De la responsabilité pénale des actes criminels commis au cours de la guerre 1914–1918', 47 *Revue de droit international et de législation comparée* (1920), 37–45. According to a distinguished author, B. Swart, 'Arrest and Surrender', in Cassese, Gaeta, and Jones, *ICC Commentary*, II, at 1643, 'Given the fact that the former Article 4 of the Dutch Constitution permitted extradition on the basis of a treaty only, that the acts alleged did not constitute criminal offences according to Dutch law or to extradition treaties concluded with the Allied and Associated Powers, and that the Constitution did not permit the conclusion of an extradition treaty for the surrender of one person only, it is hard to see that the Dutch government could have reacted in a different way.'

[3] V. E. Orlando, 'Il processo del Kaiser' (1937), reprinted in *Scritti vari di diritto pubblico e scienza politica* (Milan: Giuffrè, 1940), 97ff. For the English translation of this paper see ID., 'On the Aborted Decision to Bring the German Emperor to Trial', in 5 JICJ (2007), at n. 1015–28.

[4] See C. Mullin, *The Leipzig Trials—An Account of the War Criminals' Trials and a Study of German Mentality* (London: Witherby, 1921), at 27.

[5] See, in particular, *Kemâl and Tevfik* (at 1–7); *Bahâeddîn Şâkir* (at 1–8); *Mehmed 'Alî Bey and others* (at 177–84); *Sa'îd Halîm Paşa and others* (at 353–64), as well as the other cases cited in Chapter 4. More generally, see T. Akcam, *Armenien und der Völkermord: die Istanbuler Prozesse und die Türkische Nationalbewegung* (Hamburg: Hamburger Edition, 1996), 192–207, 353–64; V. N. Dadrian, 'The Documentation of the World War I Armenian Massacres in the proceedings of the Turkish Military Tribunal', in 23 *International Journal of Middle East Studies* (1991), 549–76; V. N. Dadrian, 'The Turkish Military Tribunal's Prosecution of the Authors of the Armenian Genocide: Four Major Court-Martial Series', in 7 *Holocaust and Genocide Studies* (Spring 1997), 28–59. See also G. Lewy, 'Revisiting the Armenian Genocide, in *Middle East Quarterly* (2005), online: www.meforum.org/article/748.

[6] See the text of the Second Resolution adopted by the Advisory Committee in Lord Phillimore, 'An International Criminal Court and the Resolutions of the Committee of Jurists', 3 BYBIL (1922–3), at 80.

the Assembly of the League of Nations rejected the proposal out of hand as being 'premature'.[7] Thereafter, draft statutes of an international criminal court were adopted by non-governmental organizations such as the Inter-Parliamentary Union, in 1925,[8] and by scholarly bodies such as the International Law Association, in 1926.[9] None of these drafts, however, led to anything concrete.[10]

Such early attempts were laudable for their far-sighted recognition of the need for an international organ of criminal jurisdiction. Nevertheless, these initiatives could not bear fruit in a period which placed an exceptionally high premium upon considerations of national sovereignty. Although new values had emerged which transcended narrow nationalistic concerns (such as the gradual elaboration of principles seeking to limit the methods of warfare, or the protection of workers through the establishment of the International Labour Organization, or the protection of minorities through the numerous treaties entered into after the First World War), state sovereignty was nevertheless still very much the bedrock of the international society. The practical import of this was that no feasible mechanism could be brought into being enabling a state official—let alone a head of state—accused of war crimes or other outrages to be tried.

14.2 THE NUREMBERG AND TOKYO TRIBUNALS (1945-1947)

It was nevertheless this scenario (an international society dominated by state sovereignty) that led to the successful establishment, in the immediate post-war period, of the Nuremberg and Tokyo Tribunals. These Tribunals were a response to the overwhelming horrors of the Nazi genocide in Europe and the Japanese crimes perpetrated during the wartime occupation of large parts of many South East Asian nations (for instance, the so-called rape of Nanking, biological experiments in Manchuria, the fall of Singapore and the extensive loss of life there, and other crimes). It took the full extent of the atrocities committed during the war to demonstrate the pernicious consequences that could follow from the pursuit of extreme notions of state sovereignty and to jolt the international community out of its complacency. The conviction gradually emerged that tyranny and the attendant disregard for human dignity could no longer be allowed to go unchecked and unpunished.

It is worthwhile to consider what, in particular, induced the Allies to hold trials of the Germans and their collaborators after the Second World War and what, more recently, has persuaded governments to hold similar trials for war crimes and crimes against humanity.

After the defeat of Germany, the British, led by Churchill, stated that it was enough to arrest and hang those primarily responsible for determining and applying Nazi policy, without wasting time on legal procedures; minor criminals, they suggested, could be tried by specially created tribunals.[11] However, neither President F. D. Roosevelt, nor Henry

---

[7] 3 BYBIL (1922–3), at 84.

[8] See the text of the draft in B. Ferencz (ed.), *An International Criminal Court—A Step Toward World Peace—A Documentary History and Analysis*, vol. I (London, Rome, New York: Oceana, 1980), at 244ff.

[9] Text reproduced in Ferencz, cit. n. 8, at 252ff.

[10] A Convention for the creation of an International Criminal Court to try terrorist offences was also adopted on 16 November 1937 by the League of Nations, but never entered into force. See generally V. V. Pella, 'Towards an International Criminal Court', in 44 AJIL (1950), 37–68.

[11] See F. Smith (ed.), *The American Road to Nuremberg: The Documentary Record, 1944–1945* (Stanford, Calif.: Hoover Institution Press, 1982), at 31–3, 155–7.

Stimson, the US Defense Secretary, agreed; nor, indeed, did Stalin. In the end, they prevailed, and the International Military Tribunal was set up in Nuremberg to try the 'great Nazi criminals', while lesser Allied tribunals in the four occupied zones of Germany were to deal with minor criminals. The Americans advanced various arguments to support their view, later accepted by the other Allies.

First, how could a defeated enemy be condemned without due process of law? To hang them without trial would mean to do away with one of the mainstays of democracy: no one can be considered guilty until his crimes have been proved in a fair trial. To relinquish such a fundamental principle would have put the Allies on a par with the Nazis, who had ridden roughshod over so many principles of justice and civilization, when they had held mock trials, or punished those allegedly guilty without even the benefit of judicial process.

Second, those who set up the Nuremberg Tribunal felt that the dramatic rehearsal of Nazi crimes—and of racism and totalitarianism—would make a deep impression on world opinion. Thus, the trial was designed to render tragic historical phenomena plainly visible.

The third reason was a desire on the part of the Allied powers to act for posterity. The crimes committed by the Third Reich and its Nazi officials were so appalling that some detailed record had to be left. A trial held on a grand scale would allow the Tribunal to assemble a massive archive useful not only in court, but also to historians and to the generations to come. The trial would also serve as a lesson in history for future generations.

In addition, for the Americans there was a particular motivation behind the establishment of an international criminal court. It was eloquently set forth by Justice Robert H. Jackson (the special representative of the US President to the London Conference and later the US Chief Prosecutor at Nuremberg) in 1945, when he stressed that the trial would have rendered visible and indeed 'authenticated' the Nazi crimes in the USA, a country not devastated by war.[12]

A further rationale for the Nuremberg trial was the collective character of the Nazi crimes. The massacre of civilians and prisoners of war, the persecution of Jews, gypsies, and political opponents were not only large-scale phenomena but, in addition, indicative of a policy pursued assiduously by the highest echelons of the Nazis and applied by the whole military and bureaucratic apparatus. The crimes commissioned by the directives of the Nazi leaders belonged to 'collective or system criminality': such was their nature that it would have been impossible to punish them by using the courts of the state to which the perpetrators belonged. In consequence, and as mentioned above, only an adversary (together with neutral states, as had been suggested)[13] could have made sure that justice was done, upon winning the war.

---

[12] In a Memorandum he submitted on 30 June 1945, together with a redraft of the US proposals for the new international tribunal, to the representatives of the UK, France, and the Soviet Union participating in the London Conference on military trials, he wrote the following: 'The United States [...] has conceived of this case as a broad one. It must be borne in mind that Russian, French, English and other European peoples are familiar with the Hitlerite atrocities and oppressions at first-hand. Our country, three thousand miles away, has known of them chiefly through the press and radio and through the accusations of those who have suffered rather than through immediate experience. German atrocities in the last war were charged. The public of my country was disillusioned because most of these charges were never authenticated by trial and conviction. If there is to be continuing support in the United States for international measures to prevent the regrowth of Nazism, it is necessary now to authenticate, by methods which the American people will regard as of the highest accuracy, the whole history of this Nazi movement, including its extermination of minorities, its aggressions against neighbors, its treachery and its barbarism' (International Conference on Military Trials, at 126).

[13] See e.g. C. C. Hyde, 'Punishment of War Criminals', *Proceedings of the American Society of International Law, Thirty-Seventh Annual Meeting, 1943* (1943), at 43–4. See also H. Kelsen, *Peace through Law*

In the summer of 1945, the 'Big Four' (the United Kingdom, France, the United States, and the Soviet Union) convened the London Conference to decide by what means the world was to punish the high-ranking Nazi war criminals. The resultant Nuremberg Charter established the Nuremberg Tribunal to prosecute individuals for 'crimes against peace', 'war crimes', and 'crimes against humanity'. The Nuremberg Tribunal met from 14 November 1945 to 1 October 1946. In addition, in occupied Germany, the four major Allies, pursuant to Control Council Law no. 10, prosecuted through their own courts sitting in Germany, in their respective zones of occupation, the same crimes committed by lower-ranking defendants.

On 26 July 1945, two weeks before the conclusion of the London Conference, the 'Big Four' issued the Potsdam Declaration announcing, to the surprise of many, their intention to prosecute leading Japanese officials for these same crimes.[14] Subsequently, on 19 January 1946, General Douglas MacArthur, Supreme Commander for the Allied Powers in Japan, approved, in the form of an executive order, the Tokyo Charter, setting forth the constitution, jurisdiction, and functions of the Tokyo Tribunal. Like the Nuremberg Charter, the Tokyo Charter, which was issued on 26 April 1946, included the newly articulated crimes against peace and humanity.[15]

By and large, the Tokyo Charter was modelled on the Nuremberg Charter. However, there were some differences between the two texts and the way they regulated the structure of the Tribunals and the charges that could be brought against the defendants.[16] It is also notable that the bench comprised persons from newly independent countries, such as India and the Philippines.

The Tokyo Trial (which commenced on 3 May 1946, and lasted for approximately two-and-a-half years) was the source of much controversy both during and after the event. Some have claimed that the trial was either a vehicle for America's revenge for the treacherous attack on Pearl Harbor, or a means of assuaging American national guilt over the use of atomic weapons in Japan. Others, defence counsel at the trial included, attacked the trial's legitimacy on legal grounds.[17]

Whereas the post-First World War experience showed the extent to which international criminal justice can be compromised for the sake of political expedience, the post-Second World War experience revealed, conversely, how effective it could be when there is political will as well as the necessary resources. These sets of experiences were nevertheless one-sided, as everybody knows. They imposed 'victors' justice' over the defeated. The major drawback of the two 'international' military Tribunals was that they were composed of judges (4 and 11, respectively) appointed by each of the victor Powers; the prosecutors too were appointed by each of those Powers and acted under the instructions of each appointing state (at Tokyo there was a chief prosecutor, or 'Chief of Counsel' as he was called, namely the American Joseph B. Keenan, and ten associate prosecutors). Thus,

---

(Chapel Hill: University of North Carolina Press, 1944), at 111; H. Kelsen, 'Will the Judgment in the Nuremberg Trial Constitute a Precedent in International Law?', 1 *International Law Quarterly* (1947), at 170.

[14] Some of the Allies in the Pacific theatre prosecuted the Japanese for 'war crimes' under their respective military laws: see, *inter alia*, R. John Pritchard, 'War Crimes Trials in the Far East', in R. Bowring and P. Kornick (eds), *Cambridge Encyclopedia of Japan* (Cambridge: Cambridge University Press, 1993), at 107.

[15] The Charter had been drafted by the Americans only, essentially by Joseph B. Keenan, Chief Prosecutor at the Tokyo Trial, and the other Allies were only consulted after it was issued: B. V. A. Röling and A. Cassese, *The Tokyo Trial and Beyond* (Cambridge: Polity Press, 1993), at 2.

[16] For a summary of the principal differences see Röling and Cassese, cit. n. 15, at 2–3.

[17] For instance, the legal categories of the crimes against peace and humanity have been criticized as *ex post facto* legislation, in that these crimes did not exist in international law prior to 1945 (Röling and Cassese, cit. n. 15, at 3–5).

the view must be shared that the two military Tribunals were not independent international courts proper, but judicial bodies acting as organs common to the appointing states.[18]

However, the two Tribunals were important in many respects. First, they broke the 'monopoly' over criminal jurisdiction concerning such international crimes as war crimes, until that moment firmly held by states. For the first time non-national, or multinational, institutions were established for the purpose of prosecuting and punishing crimes having an international dimension and scope.

Second, new offences were envisaged in the London Agreement and made punishable: crimes against humanity and crimes against peace. Whether or not this was done in breach of the principle of *nullum crimen sine lege*, it is a fact that since 1945 those crimes gradually became proscribed by customary international law.

Third, while until that time only servicemen and minor officers had been prosecuted, now for the first time military leaders as well as high-ranking politicians and other prominent civilians were brought to trial.

Fourth, the statutes and the case law of the Nuremberg and Tokyo Tribunals contributed to the development of new legal norms and standards of responsibility, by providing, for example, for the elimination of the defence of 'obedience to superior orders'.

Finally, a symbolic significance emerged from these experiences in terms of their moral legacy.[19]

14.3 THE ESTABLISHMENT OF THE ICTY AND ICTR (1993–1994)

14.3.1 GENERAL

Various factors led to the establishment of the ICTY and ICTR in the early 1990s.

The end of the Cold War proved to be of crucial importance. It had significant effects. For one thing, the animosity that had dominated international relations for almost half a century dissipated. In its wake, a new spirit of relative optimism emerged, stimulated by the following factors: *i)* a clear reduction in the distrust and mutual suspicion that had frustrated friendly relations and co operation between the Western and the Eastern bloc; *ii)* the successor states to the USSR (the Russian Federation and the other members of the Confederation of Independent States) came to uphold greater respect for international law; *iii)* as a result the emergence of unprecedented agreement in the UN Security Council and increasing convergence in the views of the five permanent members, with the consequence that this organ became able to fulfil its functions more effectively.

Another effect of the end of the Cold War was no less important. Despite the problems of that bleak period, during the Cold War era the two power blocs had managed to guarantee a modicum of international order, in that each of the Superpowers had acted as a sort of policeman and guarantor in its respective sphere of influence. The collapse of this

---

[18] The Nuremberg Tribunal admitted this legal reality when it stated that 'The making of the Charter [of the IMT] was the exercise of the sovereign legislative power by the countries to which the German Reich unconditionally surrendered; and the undoubted right of these countries to legislate for the occupied territories has been recognised by the civilised world [...] The Signatory Powers created this Tribunal, defined the law it was to administer, and made regulations for the proper conduct of the Trial. In doing so, they have done together what any one of them might have done singly; for it is not to be doubted that any nation has the right thus to set up special courts to administer law' (at 218).

[19] M. Lippman, 'Nuremberg: Forty-Five Years Later', 7 *Conn. J. Int. L.* (1991), at 1.

model of international relations ushered in a wave of negative consequences. It entailed a fragmentation of the international community and intense disorder which, coupled with rising nationalism and fundamentalism, resulted in a spiralling of mostly internal armed conflicts, with much bloodshed and cruelty. The ensuing implosion of previously multi-ethnic societies led to gross violations of international humanitarian law on a scale comparable in some respects to those committed during the Second World War.

A further crucial factor contributing to an enlarged need for international criminal justice was the increasing importance of the human rights doctrine, which soon became a sort of 'secular' religion. As the few available international mechanisms for monitoring respect for human rights had proved deficient, the notion gradually took hold that the best way of ensuring compliance with those rights was to prosecute and punish those individually responsible for their breach. This begot the quest for, or at least gave a robust impulse to, international criminal justice.

This period is thus characterized by the development of institutions empowered to prosecute and punish serious violations of international humanitarian law.

14.3.2 THE TWO AD HOC TRIBUNALS FOR THE FORMER YUGOSLAVIA AND RWANDA

The conflicts that erupted in, amongst other places, the former Yugoslavia and Rwanda served to rekindle the sense of outrage felt at the closing stage of the Second World War.[20] Thus, the UN Security Council set up two ad hoc International Criminal Tribunals pursuant to its power to decide on measures necessary to maintain or restore international peace and security: in 1993 the International Criminal Tribunal for the former Yugoslavia (ICTY), and in 1994 the International Criminal Tribunal for Rwanda (ICTR).

The former was empowered to exercise jurisdiction over grave breaches of the Geneva Conventions, violations of the laws and customs of war, genocide, and crimes against humanity allegedly perpetrated in the former Yugoslavia since 1 January 1991. The latter was called upon to adjudicate genocide, crimes against humanity, and violations of Article 3 common to the Geneva Conventions and of the Second Additional Protocol, allegedly perpetrated in Rwanda (or in 'the territory of neighbouring states in respect of serious violations of international humanitarian law committed by Rwandan citizens') between 1 January and 31 December 1994.

The response of the international community to the conflict in Yugoslavia had been tardy and lukewarm, due to impotence at the military and political levels. The establishment of a Tribunal was thus seized upon during the conflict not only as a belated face-saving measure but also in the pious hope that it would serve as a deterrent to further crimes.[21] As the UN Security Council itself noted, the ICTY was established in the belief that an international criminal tribunal would 'contribute to ensuring that such violations are halted and effectively redressed'.[22]

---

[20] See e.g. the letters to A. Cassese of Lawrence Eagleburger of 8 May 1996 ('the United States could no longer remain silent on the issue of war crimes [...A]cts against humanity could not and would not be ignored') and Elie Wiesel of 28 June 1996 ('not to prosecute the criminals would amount to condoning their crimes. In extreme situations, speaking out is a moral obligation') reprinted in *The Path to the Hague: Selected Documents on the Origins of the ICTY* (UN: ICTY, 1996), at 89 and 91, respectively.

[21] See in this regard the letter of Lawrence Eagleburger of 8 May 1996 to A. Cassese: 'There can be—and are—arguments about the wisdom of external armed intervention in the tragedy that is Bosnia [...] Of far greater precedential significance is the UN's decision to try accused war criminals before an International Tribunal especially created for that purpose [...T]hese trials will serve to put potential future war criminals on notice that the international community will not tolerate crimes against humanity' (at 89, 91).

[22] See in this regard UNSC Resolution 827 of 25 May 1993.

The Security Council established the ICTY with resolution 827 of 25 May 1993.[23] A striking feature of this resolution was that the Security Council determined that the situation in the former Yugoslavia, and in particular in Bosnia and Herzegovina—where there were 'reports of mass killings, massive, organised and systematic detention and rape of women and […] the practice of "ethnic cleansing"'—constituted a threat to international peace and security under Chapter VII of the UN Charter.[24]

The setting up of the ICTY gave rise to many objections.[25] In brief, the principal criticisms were that: *i*) the Tribunal was established to make up for the impotence of diplomacy and politics; *ii*) by establishing the Tribunal the Security Council exceeded its powers under the Charter, adopting an act that was patently *ultra vires*; *iii*) by the same token, by creating a criminal court dealing only with crimes allegedly committed in a particular country, instead of granting to the new court jurisdiction over crimes committed everywhere in the world, the Security Council had opted for 'selective justice'.

The first criticism is right. The Tribunal's Appeals Chamber in *Tadić* (IA) proved the second criticism to be wrong (see §§ 9–40 of that judgment). As for the attack on 'selective justice', one could answer that such justice, however objectionable, is better than no justice at all. Half a loaf is better than pie in the sky. As long as an international criminal court endowed with universal jurisdiction was lacking, the establishment of ad hoc tribunals proved salutary.

The ICTR was established in like fashion to the ICTY in response to the civil war and genocide in Rwanda. The Security Council adopted the Statute of the ICTR by resolution 955 of 8 November 1994, after having determined that 'this situation continues to constitute a threat to international peace and security'.[26] While many of the factors mentioned above with regard to the former Yugoslavia were also motivations for the establishment

[23] The resolution was adopted following consideration of the Secretary-General's Report (S/25704, 3 May 1993), submitted pursuant to Security Council Resolution 808. The Secretary-General's Report proposed a Statute for the ICTY, which was unanimously adopted without amendment.
  In terms of the drafting of the Statute of the ICTY, it appears that the first draft was prepared by a group of three rapporteurs appointed by the Conference on Security and Cooperation in Europe (CSCE). In a letter of 24 November 1992 the British government, then holding the presidency of the European Union, proposed 'to draft a convention establishing an ad hoc tribunal to deal with war crimes and crimes against humanity committed in the former Yugoslavia'. The Ministers of Foreign Affairs of the CSCE, meeting in the CSCE Council, responded favourably on 15 December 1992. The three rapporteurs then produced a draft on 9 February 1993. On 16 January 1993 the French Foreign Minister, Roland Dumas, appointed a Commission of Experts with the task of drafting a statute of an ad hoc international tribunal. Various drafts were subsequently submitted by a number of states and international bodies to the UN Secretary-General and used by him in his drafting of the Statute of the ICTY after the Security Council, at the proposal of France, adopted on 22 February 1993 resolution 808 (1993), by which it decided to establish an international Tribunal (*The Path to the Hague*, cit. n. 20, at 13).

[24] In operative para. 2 of resolution 827 of 25 May 1993, the Security Council decided 'to establish an international tribunal for the sole purpose of prosecuting persons responsible for serious violations of international humanitarian law committed in the territory of the former Yugoslavia between 1 January 1991 and a date to be determined by the Security Council upon the restoration of peace and to this end to adopt the Statute of the International Tribunal annexed to the above-mentioned [Secretary-General's] report'. The Security Council amended the ICTY Statute by resolution 1166 (1998) on 13 May 1998 to add a third Trial Chamber and three new judges. Likewise, the Statute of the ICTR was amended by the Security Council in its resolution 1165 of 30 April 1998 to provide for a third Trial Chamber.

[25] See, in particular, G. Robertson, *Crimes against Humanity: The Struggle for Global Justice* (London: Penguin, 2000), at 300ff.

[26] Art. 1 of the Statute of the ICTR thus declared that the ICTR 'shall have the power to prosecute persons responsible for serious violations of international humanitarian law committed in the territory of Rwanda and Rwandan citizens responsible for such violations committed in the territory of neighbouring states, between 1 January 1994 and 31 December 1994, in accordance with the provisions of the present Statute'.

of the ICTR, the overwhelming magnitude of the crimes committed there and the fact that they assuredly amounted to genocide lent particular urgency to the setting up of the ICTR. Sensitive to criticism that the establishment of the ICTY represented yet another illustration of the disproportionate attention paid to the problems of Europe vis-à-vis those of the developing world, the international society was also anxious to establish a Tribunal for Rwanda so as to assuage its conscience and shield itself from accusations of double standards. An additional feature leading up to the establishment of the ICTR was that, in the early stages at least, the proposal to create an international tribunal was an initiative of the new Rwandan government. As they set about their task of post-war reconstruction, the new government had initially felt that one means of legitimizing and attracting international support to the new regime would be through an international judicial condemnation of the worst abuses committed during the civil war by the adversaries of the new government.[27]

Even though the Statutes for the ICTY and the ICTR differ, the Tribunals share an Appeals Chamber and (at least initially) a prosecutor. This scheme may appear to be a curious formula for distinct ad hoc Tribunals; but it demonstrates the need for ensuring some uniformity in administering international criminal justice.

Over the years the two ad hoc Tribunals have proved to be able to dispense fair justice, although they may be faulted for being somewhat slow and very costly. On 22 December 2010, the UN Security Council adopted resolution 1966, establishing the legal basis of the International Residual Mechanism for Criminal Tribunals. This Mechanism 'shall continue the jurisdiction, rights and obligations and essential functions of the ICTY and ICTR'. It is divided into two branches. The ICTR branch has commenced functioning on 1 July 2012, while the ICTY branch will begin functioning on 1 July 2013; both Tribunals are called to finish their work by 31 December 2014, in order to prepare closure and transition of cases to the Residual Mechanism. The Mechanism is to play an important role in ensuring that the completion strategies of the two ad hoc Tribunals do not result in impunity for fugitives and in unfairness to other stakeholders. As has been noted,[28] the compromise reached by UN member states also strikes a significant balance between, on the one hand, short-term financial and policy considerations and, on the other, the requirements of due process, acknowledging that ICTY and ICTY functions cannot simply be transferred to national authorities.

14.4 THE DRAFTING AND ADOPTION OF THE STATUTE OF THE ICC (1994–1998)

It was only in 1989, once the Cold War had drawn to a close, that the UN General Assembly once again requested the ILC 'to address the question of establishing an international

---

[27] In July 1994, the Security Council passed Resolution 935, using the precedent of the former Yugoslavia as a model, to establish a commission of experts to investigate violations committed during the Rwandan civil war (see SC Res. 935, UNSCOR, 49th Sess., 3400th mtg 1, UN Doc. S/RES/935 (1994)). The Rwandan commission lasted only four months, which was not long enough for it to perform its task effectively. On 1 October 1994, the Rwandan commission submitted its preliminary report to the Secretary-General, and a final report on 9 December 1994 (see *Preliminary Report of the Independent Commission of Experts Established in accordance with Security Council Resolution 935 (1994)*, UNSCOR, UN Doc. S/1994/1125 (1994); *Final Report of the Commission of Experts Established pursuant to Security Council Resolution 935 (1994)* and Annex, UNSCOR, UN Doc. S/1994/1405 (1994).

[28] G. Acquaviva, 'Was a Residual Mechanism for International Criminal Tribunals Really Necessary?, in 9 JICJ (2011), 789–96.

criminal court'.[29] This question came back on to the UN agenda by an unexpected route after a hiatus of thirty-six years, following a suggestion in the General Assembly by Trinidad and Tobago that a specialized international criminal court be established to deal with the problem of drug trafficking. In response to the General Assembly mandate arising out of the 1989 special session on drugs, the ILC in 1990 completed a report that was submitted to the 45th session of the General Assembly. Though that report was not limited to the drug trafficking question it was, nonetheless, favourably received by the General Assembly, which encouraged the ILC to continue its work. The ILC produced a comprehensive text in 1993, which was modified in 1994.[30]

The judicial institution envisaged in the 1994 ILC Draft to a very great extent took account of the concerns of states and in particular of major powers; it was thus markedly sovereignty-orientated. Among the salient features of the ICC delineated in the Draft, the following should be emphasized: *i*) the Court had 'automatic jurisdiction' (that is, jurisdiction following from the mere fact of ratifying the Statute) solely over genocide; for other crimes such as war crimes and crimes against humanity the Court could exercise its jurisdiction only if such jurisdiction had been accepted by the custodial state, the territorial state, as well as any other state seeking jurisdiction over the accused (Article 21); *ii*) only states parties or the Security Council could initiate proceedings (Articles 23 and 25); the prosecutor had no such power; *iii*) the Security Council had extensive powers with regard to prosecution of cases relating to situations falling under Chapter VII of the UN Charter (threat to the peace, breach of the peace, or act of aggression); under Article 23(3), in these cases a prosecution could not be commenced except in accordance with a decision of the Security Council.

Although the ICTY and ICTR were limited both temporally and geographically to the conflicts in the former Yugoslavia and Rwanda, respectively, their overall successes provided a final spur to the emergence of the ICC, an organ of global jurisdictional reach and thus potentially able to respond to violations occurring anywhere. Furthermore, much jurisprudence had accumulated regarding the interpretation of the offences punishable in terms of the new Statute. Those seeking a permanent, effective, and politically uncompromised system of international criminal justice drew upon all these factors.

The General Assembly established in 1996[31] a Preparatory Committee on the Establishment of an International Criminal Court (PrepCom). This Committee submitted to the Diplomatic Conference at Rome (15 June–17 July 1998) a Draft Statute and Draft Final Act consisting of 116 articles contained in 173 pages of text with some 1,300 words

---

[29] UN General Assembly Resolution 44/39 of 4 December 1989. In addition, a proposal to establish a criminal court dealing with international crimes such as aggression and war crimes did appear to be revived again in August 1990, in response to the Iraqi invasion of Kuwait and to hostage-taking of foreigners and atrocities allegedly committed in Kuwait (see various dispatches cited in *The Path to the Hague*, cit. n. 20, at 7, 9, 11). However, it is unclear to what extent it was envisaged that the court would have a truly international character (see *The Times*, 26 September 1990, 'Echo of Nuremberg Trials in Iraq'). In any case, these steps did not lead to any proposal at the international level, although moves towards the establishment of an international tribunal to prosecute and punish war crimes committed by Iraqi forces in Kuwait seems once more to be gaining momentum. (See in this regard A. Cassese, 'On Current Trends towards Criminal Prosecution and Punishment of Breaches of International Humanitarian Law', 9 EJIL (1998), 8–9.)

[30] *Report of the International Law Commission*, 46th Sess., 2 May–22 July 1994, UN GAOR, 49th Sess., Supp. No. 10, UN Doc. A/49/10 (1994).

[31] The 1994 ILC report on the Draft Statute for an International Criminal Court was submitted to the 49th session of the General Assembly, which resolved to consider it at its 50th Session, but first it set up an ad hoc committee to discuss the proposal. This committee, referred to as the 1995 Ad Hoc Committee for the Establishment of an International Criminal Court, met inter-sessionally for two sessions of two weeks each from April to August 1995.

in square brackets, representing multiple options either to entire provisions or to some words contained in certain provisions.

Both in the works of the PrepCom and in the Rome negotiations, three major group-ings of states emerged. The first was the group of so-called Like-Minded States, which included countries from all regions of the world and was to a large extent led by Canada and Australia. This group favoured a fairly strong court with broad and 'automatic juris-diction', the establishment of an independent prosecutor empowered to initiate proceed-ings, and a sweeping definition of war crimes embracing crimes committed in internal armed conflicts. A second group comprised the permanent members of the Security Council (P-5), however, minus the UK (which during the preparatory negotiations joined the Like-Minded States) and France (which also joined the Like-Minded States in Rome). The three remaining permanent members, and in particular the USA, were opposed to 'automatic jurisdiction' and to granting to the prosecutor the power to initiate proceed-ings. By the same token they were eager to assign extensive tasks to the Security Council. This body was to be empowered both to refer matters to the court and to prevent cases from being brought to the court. In addition, these states were opposed to envisaging aggression among the crimes subject to the court's jurisdiction and to including any reference to the use of nuclear weapons among the violations of humanitarian law over which the court was to exercise jurisdiction. The third grouping embraced members of the non-aligned-movement (NAM). They insisted on envisaging aggression among the crimes provided for in the Statute; some of them (Barbados, Dominica, Jamaica, and Trinidad and Tobago) pressed for the inclusion of drug trafficking, whereas others (India, Sri Lanka, Algeria, and Turkey) supported providing for terrorism. They strongly opposed the assignment of any role to the Security Council and opposed any jurisdiction over war crimes committed in internal armed conflicts. In contrast, they insisted on the inclusion of the death sentence among the possible penalties.

A group of distinguished diplomats, and in particular the Canadian Philippe Kirsch, who chaired the Committee of the Whole (where the major problems of the draft Statute were substantially thrashed out and settled) must be credited with having been able skil-fully to devise and suggest a number of compromise formulae that in the event permitted the Conference to adopt the Statute by 120 votes to 7 (USA, Libya, Israel, Iraq, China, Syria, Sudan) with 20 abstentions.

14.5 THE ESTABLISHMENT OF INTERNATIONALIZED OR MIXED COURTS

In the late 1990s and early 2000s the UN Security Council considered the situations in, among other places, Sierra Leone, Cambodia, and East Timor as being suitable for the establishment of ad hoc international courts.

In the case of Sierra Leone, it actively dealt with the matter. Eventually, in October 2000, at its request the Secretary-General drafted the statute of a Special Tribunal, which became part of the Agreement of 16 January 2002 between the UN and Sierra Leone.[32] The Special Court for Sierra Leone (SCSL) has a mixed composition (being made up of nation-als of Sierra Leone and international judges and staff) and has jurisdiction over crimes against humanity, violations of common Article 3 to the Geneva Conventions and the

---

[32] See UN Doc. S/2000/915. See also SC Res. 1315 (2000). For an overview, see M. Frulli, 'The Special Court for Sierra Leone: Some Preliminary Comments', 11 EJIL (2000), 857–69.

Second Additional Protocol, as well as other serious violations of IHL, and some criminal offences under Sierra Leonean law.

As for East Timor, Section 10 of UNTAET Regulation 2000/11 (as amended by Regulation 2001/25) conferred on the Special Panels for Serious Crimes (ETSP), which were a part of the Dili District Court, jurisdiction over genocide, war crimes, and crimes against humanity, as well as murder and sexual offences, provided that these offences were committed between 1 January 1999 and 25 October 1999.

Furthermore, following negotiations with the UN the Cambodian Parliament adopted in 2001 (and amended in 2004 in light of an agreement of 2003 with the UN) a law establishing the Extraordinary Chambers in the Courts of Cambodia (ECCC) for prosecuting crimes committed during the period of Democratic Kampuchea (1975–9). The various organs of the Court are composed partly of Cambodians, partly of international personnel.

In addition, following an agreement with the government of Bosnia and Herzegovina, in 2005 the High Representative for Bosnia and Herzegovina set up a Section for War Crimes in the Criminal and Appellate Divisions of the Court of Bosnia and Herzegovina; this section is mixed in composition. The establishment of the War Crimes Chamber (WCC) was considered necessary to enable effective war crimes prosecutions in Bosnia. The WCC is part of the State Court and exercises jurisdiction over the most serious war crimes in Bosnia, while the cantonal and district courts can handle other war crimes cases.[33]

On 30 May 2007 the UN Security Council imposed the entry into force of the provisions contained in agreement between the UN and Lebanon for the establishment of a Special Tribunal for Lebanon; it did so by virtue of resolution 1757 (2007), adopted on the strength of Chapter VII of the UN Charter. The Tribunal, which consists of a Trial Chamber and an Appeals Chamber, has jurisdiction over terrorist attacks committed in Lebanon since 14 February 2005 and applies Lebanese criminal law on terrorism. All the organs of the Tribunal have a mixed composition, the Lebanese nationals being, however, outnumbered by international professionals.[34]

---

[33] The WCC tries cases concerning lower- to mid-level perpetrators' referred to it by the ICTY pursuant to Rule 11 *bis* of the ICTY RPE. In this respect, the WCC represents an important component of the completion strategy of the ICTY. Furthermore, the WCC is responsible for those cases submitted to it by the Office of the Prosecutor (OTP) of the ICTY where investigations have not been completed. The ICTY Appeals Chamber referred the first case to the WCC on 1 September 2005 (*Radovan Stanković*). Mr Stanković was transferred to Bosnia on 29 September 2005, to stand trial before the WCC for charges of crimes against humanity, including enslavement and rape. The ICTY has since referred other cases to the WCC.

The WCC also has jurisdiction over 'Rules of the Road' cases. The 'Rules of the Road' procedure was first established in response to the widespread fear of arbitrary arrest and detention immediately after the conflict in Bosnia. Under this procedure, the authorities in Bosnia were required to submit every war crimes case proposed for prosecution in Bosnia to the OTP of the ICTY to determine whether the evidence was sufficient by international standards before proceeding to arrest. This process of review reduced incidents of arbitrary arrest in Bosnia. The ICTY ceased reviewing cases on 1 October 2004. The review function was subsequently assumed by the Special Department for War Crimes within the Office of the Prosecutor of the State Court.

The WCC includes national as well as international judges and prosecutors, defense counsel, experts in witness protection and support, as well as other officials engaged in providing substantive and administrative support.

[34] See UN Doc. S/2006/893 15 November 2006, containing the Report of the UN Secretary General to the Security Council as well as the Statute of the Tribunal and the Agreement between the UN and Lebanon on the establishment of the Tribunal.

As pointed out above, in recent years, faced with emergency situations involving the commission of large-scale atrocities, states have preferred to resort neither to national nor to international criminal courts, but rather to establish courts that are mixed in their composition, and the statutes and rules of which combine aspects of international law and municipal law. Such courts have been set up for Sierra Leone, East Timor, Kosovo, Cambodia, and Lebanon.[35]

These courts aim at improving on the two ad hoc Tribunals, which were perceived as being marred by four essential flaws: (i) their costly nature; (ii) the excessive length of their proceedings; (iii) their remoteness from the territory where crimes have been perpetrated and consequently the limited impact of their judicial output on the national populations concerned; (iv) the unfocused character of the prosecutorial targets resulting in trials of a number of low-ranking defendants. The attempt was therefore made to establish lean and agile courts sitting in the territory where crimes had been committed (and also including prosecutors and judges from this country), which would be relatively inexpensive and only tasked with prosecuting and trying those most responsible for the crimes perpetrated. Thus, some 'mixed' or, as they are often termed, 'internationalized' courts and tribunals were set up.

This notion encompasses judicial bodies that have *a mixed composition*. There may be two versions of these courts and tribunals. First, they may be organs of the relevant state, being part of its judiciary. This applies to the Cambodian Extraordinary Chambers as well as the courts in Kosovo and the 'Special Panels for Serious Crimes' in East Timor. Alternatively, the courts may be international in nature: they may be set up under an international agreement and not be part of the national judiciary. This holds true for the SCSL and the STL.

A multitude of historical and practical reasons combine to warrant the establishment of courts that are neither national nor international, but mixed.

First, these courts are predicated on the existence of *an emergency situation* (armed conflict, civil strife, strong religious and ethnic tension), in the course of which serious and widespread crimes are committed. When this situation is over, it is felt that bringing to trial those responsible for serious crimes may help in the post-conflict peace-building process and may also serve to deter the future commission of large-scale offences.

Second, as a result of the emergency situation a *breakdown of the judicial system* may have come about. This may have been caused by civil war (as in East Timor and Sierra Leone), possibly followed by an international conflict (as in Kosovo). Alternatively, even if

---

[35] In Cambodia, after years of pressure by the international community, and after a UN Commission had proposed the establishment of an international criminal tribunal, Cambodian authorities have opted for the creation of special Cambodian courts with mixed composition. On 2 January 2001 Cambodia's Parliament (the National Assembly) passed a Law on the Establishment of Extraordinary Chambers in the Courts of Cambodia for the Prosecution of Crimes Committed during the Period of Democratic Kampuchea.

In East Timor the UN provisional administration (UN Transitional Administration in East Timor, or UNTAET) adopted Regulation 2000/11 in 2000 setting up mixed panels within the District Court of Dili and Regulation 2000/15 established Panels with exclusive jurisdiction over 'serious criminal offences'.

In Sierra Leone, after the drafting of a Statute of a Special Court in 2000, on 16 January 2001 the UN and the Sierra Leone Government signed an agreement establishing a mixed court, accompanied by a Statute.

In Kosovo the UN provisional administration (UNMIK or UN Interim Administration in Kosovo) passed a Regulation on the appointment of international judges to serve on Kosovar courts (UNMIK Regulation no. 2000/64 of 15 December 2000). This Regulation provided for the establishment of panels of three judges, composed of two international judges (one of them presiding over the panel) and a local one. It also provided for the appointment of international prosecutors and investigating judges.

UNMIK has appointed international judges and prosecutors to district courts throughout Kosovo and to the Supreme Court. The international judges have worked on criminal cases involving alleged war crimes or inter-ethnic violence, and on property issues.

a very long time has elapsed since the crimes were perpetrated, and a stable government has taken root, as a result of a series of historical factors the judiciary may not be capable of administering justice in an unbiased and even-handed manner: this is what has happened in Cambodia, where the presence in the government of persons who allegedly are closely linked to the perpetrators of genocide, together with the lack of a really independent judiciary, might lead to unfair trials. It may also happen that the population prevents or hampers the conduct of fair trials. In Kosovo, the ethnic biases of Kosovo Albanians and Serbs rendered the presence of international judges indispensable for administering justice.[36]

Third, it is, however, considered that the judicial response *must not lie in the establishment of an international court.* This option is normally ruled out because of the combination of two factors: (i) lack of political will of the relevant organs of the international organization that should set up the international tribunal, for the country or the situation at issue are regarded as either inconsequential in geo-political terms, or likely to spawn further friction and thus to embroil the international organization in a never-ending conflict; and (ii) lack of will of major powers to fund the international court.

Fourth, it is felt that by holding trials *in the territory where the crimes have been perpetrated,* the local population is exposed to past atrocities, with the twofold advantage of making everybody cognizant of those atrocities, including those who sided with the perpetrators, and bringing about a cathartic process in the victims or their relatives, through public stigmatization of the culprits and just retribution; thus, exposure of past misdeeds to the local population contributes to the process of gradual reconciliation.

Finally, those in charge of finding a solution feel that *using the national judiciary* under some sort of international scrutiny, or even control, may prove advantageous and useful in many other respects.[37]

Nevertheless, one should not underestimate the practical problems and difficulties that may arise with mixed or hybrid, international–national courts.

The first problem is to ensure that the national and international components of the prosecution work in close, constructive, and constant agreement.[38] Another, no less

---

[36] As the UN Secretary General pointed out in his Report of 6 June 2000, 'Despite the appointment of more than 400 judges, prosecutors and lay judges [of whom 46 were non-ethnic Kosovo Albanians, 7 of whom Kosovo Serbs] and the increased capacity of the courts, the unwillingness of witnesses to testify and the ethnic bias and risk of intimidation of some judicial personnel have hampered the administration of justice' (see S/2000/538, § 57). The detainees of the Mitrovica detention centre who had gone on a hunger strike in protest over the length of their pre-trial detention, stopped the strike only when the UN Special Representative promised that he would ensure that a Kosovo Serb or an international judge would preside over their cases, in addition to Kosovo Albanian judges (S/2000/538, § 59).

[37] In short: (i) it assuages the nationalistic demands of local authorities, loath to hand over to international bodies an essential prerogative of sovereign Powers, the administration of justice; (ii) it involves, in rendering justice, persons (the local prosecutors and judges) familiar with the mentality, language, habits, and so on of the accused; (iii) it may expedite prosecution and trials without compromising respect for international standards and international law in general; (iv) it may produce a significant spill-over effect, in that it may contribute to gradually promoting the democratic legal training of local members of the prosecution and the judiciary.

[38] This may not prove easy, because the local prosecutors may either tend to be over-zealous, when the accused belong to an ethnic or religious group to which they are hostile, or instead to engage in dilatory tactics, or even to create obstacles to prosecution, when the accused belong to their own group. Article 20 of the Cambodian Draft Law provides that in case of disagreement between the two prosecutors (one national, the other international) the matter is referred to a Pre-Trial Chamber of five judges, two international and three national, deciding by an affirmative vote of at least four judges; if there is no majority, for a decision, 'the prosecution shall proceed'. The same procedure applies to possible disagreements between the two investigating judges (see Art. 23). At least in some respects this solution appears to be fairly

serious problem may be to ensure the smooth cooperation of the national and international components of the bench. There may be differences in mentality, language, experience, and legal philosophy.[39]

Two other practical problems may prove crucial: funding and security. Making *financial resources* available is a *sine qua non* for a court to function.[40] As for *security*, it is obvious that the dangers following from the hatred, resentment, and social conflict festering in those countries may pose a serious risk to those working in the judicial process. These seem to be the reasons why the trial against the former Liberian President Charles Taylor is being held before the SCSL, not at the seat of the Court (Freetown), but at The Hague, and why the STL is located in The Hague and not in Beirut.

14.6 MERITS AND FLAWS OF INTERNATIONAL CRIMINAL JUSTICE

International criminal courts present a number of advantages over domestic courts, particularly those sitting in the territory of the state where atrocities have been committed.

First, international criminal courts proper may be *more impartial* than domestic courts, for they are made up of judges having no link with the territory or the state where the crimes were perpetrated. When national courts conduct proceedings, national feelings, political ideologies, widespread resentment among the population, or possible public reaction to the verdict may seriously interfere with the task of judges. International judges may more easily ignore the possible future reaction of the public or the media to their judicial determinations. Even the so-called mixed or 'internationalized' courts (such as the SCSL, the ETSP, the Cambodian Extraordinary Courts or the STL) may avoid

---

sensible, for in the final analysis it ensures that a prosecution will be instituted. However, as has been pointed out, it is indeed unusual and contrary to the principled distinction between prosecution and bench, for a panel of judges to settle disputes between co-prosecutors concerning prosecutorial strategy at trial.

[39] Particularly where international members of the court are the majority (as is the case in Sierra Leone and East Timor), they may be perceived by the local judges as intrusive and overwhelming, with the consequence that the local judges may seek to obstruct or otherwise hamper the process of administering justice. On the other hand, the action of the international component may be thwarted by the attitude of the local judges. Probably the main reasons that the internationalized courts operating in Kosovo have been assailed for their alleged flaws in ensuring fair trials, and full respect for the rights of the defence, are linked to this problem. The matter is further complicated where, as in the case of Cambodia, the relevant law provides that the majority belongs to national judges (three to two), but a decision may only be taken if four judges are in favour. This entails that if two national judges are not agreeable, no decision is made, and the court becomes deadlocked.

Things may become even worse, for under Art. 46 of the Cambodian law, in cases of last resort Cambodians may be appointed to take the place of foreign judges (and prosecutors); hence, if there is a deadlock and the subsequent withdrawal of the international judges, judicial action may continue with all-Cambodian staff. It follows that ultimately the national component may gradually push the international component to withdraw, so as to take complete control of the judicial process.

[40] Money is needed not only to pay salaries to prosecutors and judges, but also to fund interpretation and translation from and to English and French, one of these two languages being the vehicular means of the international component. For instance, in his Report of 16 January 2001 on East Timor, the UN Secretary-General pointed out that a shortage of skilled translators had hampered efforts at all judicial levels (see S/2001/42, § 23). In his Report of 18 October 2001 the Secretary-General noted that the lack of resources, including interpreters, had led to delayed hearings and unduly prolonged detention of suspects (see S/2001/983, § 20).

Money is also needed to provide those authorities with books and documents. (For instance, in Kosovo, the destruction of law libraries among other things has resulted in a dearth of relevant legal texts.)

the pitfalls of national territorial tribunals: the international component in these courts ensures the needed impartiality. International judges are in a better position to be unbiased, or at any rate more even-handed, than national judges who have been caught up in the milieu in which the crime in question was perpetrated. This enables the internationalized courts to better resist the possible psychological pressure of the outside world and the reaction of the public or the media to their deliberations. The independence and impartiality of international courts is also guaranteed by their composition and the way judges are selected. Furthermore, the punishment by international tribunals of alleged authors of serious crimes normally meets with less resistance than national punishment, as it injures national feelings to a lesser degree.

True, international criminal courts can be faulted for not being vested with jurisdiction over the two classes of international crime that are now so widespread: terrorism and aggression. This, however, is a failing the blame for which should be laid at the door of the states that have set up those tribunals. It would be injudicious to assail the tribunals themselves for being deprived of jurisdiction over those two classes of crime. In addition, steps have been taken to partially fill this gap: in 2007 the STL was vested with jurisdiction over crimes of terrorism (albeit as defined by Lebanese criminal law), and at the ICC efforts have been made in 2010 at the Kampala Review Conference to reach a definition of aggression as an international crime acceptable to all and thus make Article 5(2) of the ICC Statute operational, albeit only in 2017.

Second, international judges, being selected on account of their competence in the area of international humanitarian and criminal law, are *better suited* to pass judgments over crimes that markedly differ from 'ordinary' criminal offences such as theft, murder, assault, etc. More than domestic courts, they are able to adjudicate on large-scale organized criminality (genocide, crimes against humanity, war crimes), as well as on the responsibility of military and political leaders. Domestic courts are often not well equipped to look into responsibility for 'system criminality'.

Also, international criminal courts, more easily than national judges, are able to try crimes with *ramifications in many countries*. Often witnesses reside in different states; other evidence may need to be collected, requiring the cooperation of several countries. In addition, special expertise is needed to handle the often complex legal issues arising both from the various national legislations involved and the relevant rules of international law.

Another merit of these courts is that they act on behalf of the whole international society and are therefore entitled to pronounce upon crimes that offend universal values; that is, values recognized and upheld by the whole society of states. Such crimes do not only run counter to moral and legal values prevailing in the local community directly affected by them. They also infringe *values that are transnational* and of concern to world order. Hence—as Jaspers had noted back in 1961—only international courts representing this community can appropriately pronounce on such crimes.[41]

Furthermore, such courts, as they apply international principles and rules, are not bound by national approaches and traditions. They may therefore ensure some kind of *uniformity* in the application of international law, whereas proceedings conducted before national courts may lead to disparity both in the interpretation and application of that law and the penalties given to those found guilty.

---

[41] K. Jasper, 'Karl Jasper zum Eichmann-Prozess-Ein Gespräch mit François Bondy', in 13 *Der Monat* (May 1961) at 16. English translation by A. Cassese ('Who should have Tried Eichmann?', 4 JICJ (2006)) 855–6.

Finally, as international criminal trials are by definition *more visible* than national criminal proceedings, holding international trials signals the will of the international society to break with the past, by punishing those who have deviated from acceptable standards of human behaviour. In delivering punishment, the international society's purpose is not so much retribution as stigmatization of deviant behaviour, in the hope that this may have a deterrent effect.

For all the merits of international trials, one should not, however, be blind to the numerous and grave problems plaguing, and indeed sometimes marring such trials.

The crucial problem international criminal courts face is the *lack of enforcement agencies* directly available to those courts for the purpose of collecting evidence, searching premises, seizing documents, or executing arrest warrants and other judicial orders. It follows that, international courts must rely heavily on the cooperation of states (see 16.4). They are totally dependent on international diplomacy and states' good will. As long as states refuse outright to assist these courts in collecting evidence or arresting the accused persons, or do not provide sufficient assistance, international criminal justice can hardly fulfil its role. This, of course, also applies to those cases, such as that of the ICTY, where a multilateral force established under the aegis of the UN provided or provides assistance in executing arrest warrants (I am referring, of course, to the NATO forces operating in Bosnia and Herzegovina and, more recently, to the EU forces operating in Kosovo). Indeed, these multilateral forces are under no international obligation to assist international criminal tribunals, and whenever they in practice assist the tribunals, they do so out of comity or expediency, or on practical grounds.

In addition, there exists a need for international criminal courts to *amalgamate* the approach of judges, each with a different cultural and legal background: some judges come from common law countries, others from states with a Romano-Germanic tradition; some are criminal lawyers, others are primarily familiar with international law; some have previous judicial experience, others do not.

Another serious problem is the *excessive length* of international criminal proceedings. It results primarily from the inherent difficulties of international criminal proceedings. These are linked, for instance, to the complexity of such crimes as genocide, war crimes, and crimes against humanity, which normally are a manifestation of collective criminality and involve more than one person; the difficulty of collecting evidence that may be scattered over large territories or more than one state; the need to prove some special ingredients of the crimes charged such as, for instance, the existence of a widespread or systematic practice (for crimes against humanity) or to look into numerous crimes perpetrated by troops in the field, to establish one of the objective elements of command responsibility; language problems, since international criminal proceedings are normally conducted courts in at least two, and possibly in three or more languages, with the consequence that documents and exhibits need to be translated into all these languages.

The substantial adoption of the adversarial system (see Chapter 18) further protracts international criminal proceedings. It requires that all the evidence be scrutinized orally through examination and cross-examination (whereas in many inquisitorial systems the evidence is selected and appraised beforehand by the investigating judge). The adversarial system was conceived of, and adopted, in most common law countries as a fairly exceptional alternative to the principal policy choice, namely avoidance of trial proceedings through plea-bargaining. In fact, on account of this feature, the adversarial model works sufficiently well in most countries. However, in international criminal proceedings defendants tend not to plead guilty and prefer to stand trial.

The excessive length of international trials is often coupled with and compounded by the need to uphold a feature of the inquisitorial system that can be found in a number of civil law countries, namely keeping the accused in custody both in the pre-trial phase and during trial and appeal. At the international level this need is warranted by the scant reliance that international criminal courts may have on the cooperation of the relevant states forcefully to ensure that the defendants will appear again in court, once summoned to resume their participation in trial or appellate proceedings.[42]

All this makes for a state of affairs that is hardly consistent with the right to a 'fair and expeditious trial' and the presumption of innocence accruing to any defendant.

Another major flaw of international trials is that international criminal courts must perforce confine themselves to prosecuting and trying *those who bear the heaviest responsibilities* for international crimes, the leaders or the high-ranking military officers. They may not or cannot try the thousands of people who have physically carried out murder, torture, rape, and other heinous acts. However, it is precisely these perpetrators that the survivors and the relatives of the victims would like to see in the dock.

Finally, some international criminal courts suffer from the 'Nuremberg syndrome': the tendency to try the 'vanquished', while the 'victors' remain sheltered from any judicial scrutiny. It is a fact that the accusations widely made against NATO airmen attacking Serbia in the 1999 war, or against some members of the Tutsi leadership for the crimes committed in Rwanda in 1994, have never been scrutinized through judicial inquiry nor even constituted the subject of preliminary investigation. It is, however, to be noted that other international courts do not seem to be marred by this deficiency. In particular, the way the ICC has been structured entails that in principle it should not be tainted by this notable drawback.

---

[42] It should, however, be noted that a new trend is emerging in ad hoc international tribunals towards granting provisional release to defendants. ICTY's judges have, for instance, granted requests for provisional release in different cases.

On 20 June 2007 the AC in the *Hadžihasanović and Kubura* case granted the motion on behalf of Enver Hadžihasanović for provisional release to Bosnia and Herzegovina pending the hearing of his appeal. The Appeals Chamber found that a series of conditions for provisional release, including the fact that the time he spent in detention amounted to approximately two-thirds of his sentence, had been met. His release was subject to specific terms and conditions, which included the obligation to surrender his passport and report to the local police regularly. On 15 March 2006, the Trial Chamber had sentenced Hadžihasanović to five years' imprisonment for murder and cruel treatment of Bosnian Croat and Bosnian Serb civilians and prisoners of war.

The Trial Chamber in the *Milutinović and others* case granted on 18 June 2007 the request by Vladimir Lazarević for temporary release to Serbia from 26 June to 2 July 2007 and the request by Nebojša Pavković for temporary release to Serbia from 4 July to 10 July 2007. Both provisional releases were subject to the specific terms and conditions as detailed in the TC's decision.

In the *Prlić and others* case the Trial Chamber ruled on 11 June 2007 to accept the defence motions to provisionally release Jadranko Prlić, Bruno Stojić, Slobodan Praljak, Milivoj Petković, Valentin Ćorić, and Berislav Pušić. The Trial Chamber decided to keep the dates and the specific terms and conditions confidential.

On 14 April 2008 the ICTY Appeals Chamber granted temporary provisional release on compassionate grounds to Pavle Strugar. On 26 June 2008 The ICTY Appeals Chamber ordered the temporary provisional release of Jovica Stanišić and Franko Simatović under terms and conditions outlined in the original decision of the Trial Chamber. Many other detainees were granted provisional release in 2008. On 9 February 2009 the Tribunal's Appeals Chamber ordered the provisional release of Bajrush Morina from the Tribunal's Detention Unit.

15

THE REPRESSION OF INTERNATIONAL CRIMES IN DOMESTIC JURISDICTIONS

To bring the alleged authors of international crimes to book, states need to have not only laws, statutes, or some sort of judge-made legal regulation punishing those crimes, but also legal provisions clarifying their ambit of applicability. These legal provisions normally provide that the criminal laws of the state apply if the offence has a specific link with the state. The most traditional link is that of *territoriality*, whereby criminal law applies with respect to acts or omissions taking place on the state's territory (the criterion here is the *locus commissi delicti*, i.e. the place where the alleged criminal behaviour has been committed). Another traditional link is *active nationality*, whereby national criminal laws are applicable extraterritorially, when the crime is committed abroad by a national of the prosecuting state.

The actual prosecution of international crimes on the basis of these two jurisdictional links, the legality of which under international law is indisputable, is however unlikely. International crimes, as noted above (see 1.3) express a sort of 'system criminality',[1] in that they are normally perpetrated by state officials with the acquiescence, tolerance, or support of the authorities of the state, which makes domestic prosecution in the state of the *locus commissi delicti* or of the nationality of the alleged perpetrators rare.[2] The concept of international crimes seems therefore to be ineluctably predicated on the necessity to expand the reach of national criminal jurisdiction beyond the traditional bases of territoriality and active nationality. It comes, therefore, as no surprise that the emerging culture of accountability with respect to international crimes increasingly necessitates the possibility of exercising criminal jurisdiction on the basis of extraterritorial principles other than active nationality.

However, one of the greatest difficulties in the field of international criminal law is establishing the scope and purpose of current international rules regarding jurisdiction over international crimes. To do so, one must take into account a network of international provisions

---

[1] B. V. A. Röling, 'The Significance of the Laws of War', in A. Cassese (ed.), *Current Problems of International Law* (Milan: Giuffrè, 1975), 137–9.

[2] When committed in the state's own territory (as could be the case for crimes against humanity, genocide, or war crimes in non-international armed conflicts), domestic prosecution grounded on the territoriality principle probably depends on a change of government, as well as on the lack of amnesty laws or other legal impediments expressly set out to avoid criminal repression. Similarly, when committed by a state's nationals abroad, e.g. in the context of an international armed conflict, it is unlikely that domestic courts will act on the basis of the active nationality principle, as state authorities would tend to shield their nationals (usually state officials) from criminal responsibility. In the last scenario, even the territorial state might tend to avoid prosecution of crimes committed by enemy belligerents, in particular at the end of hostilities, because of the necessity to restore peaceful relations with the former enemy. See P. Gaeta, 'The Need Reasonably To Expand National Criminal Jurisdiction over International Crimes', in A. Cassese (ed.), *Realizing Utopia. The Future of International Law* (Oxford: Oxford University Press, 2012) 585–95. See also ID., 'Les règles internationales

stemming from both customary and treaty law. Moreover, the status of customary law in this field is somewhat uncertain, at least with respect to criminal jurisdiction grounded on the universality principle. As for treaties, the relevant rules are not always clearly stated; they are therefore subject to different, and even contradictory, interpretations.

This chapter discusses briefly the relation between international law and criminal jurisdiction by states and examines the main heads of jurisdiction applied by states. It will then analyse the content of the relevant international rules dealing with domestic criminal jurisdiction for the repression of international crimes.

15.1 INTERNATIONAL LAW AND THE AMBIT OF STATES' CRIMINAL JURISDICTION

Back in 1927, in the Lotus case, the PCIJ delivered a judgment which still constitutes the inescapable starting point for any discussion about the relationship between public international law and states' jurisdiction in criminal matters, in particular the legality under international law of the exercise of extraterritorial criminal jurisdiction by domestic courts.[3]

As is well known, the Court started from the assumption that '[r]estrictions upon the independence of states cannot be...presumed' and stated as follows:

> Far from laying down a general prohibition to the effect that states may not extend the application of their laws and the jurisdiction of their courts to persons, property and acts outside their territory, it [international law] leaves them in this respect a wide measure of discretion which is only limited in certain cases by prohibitive rules; as regards other cases, every state remains free to adopt the principles which it regards as best and most suitable. (19)

This assertion was vigorously challenged by the dissenting judges. They opined that international law—far from being inspired by a laissez-faire approach—regulates directly the ambit of criminal jurisdiction of states and provides that it is mainly territorial. According to them, extraterritorial titles of jurisdiction could only be resorted to if this power was expressly provided for in an international rule, as was clearly the case for the active nationality principle.

Although the positivistic approach to international law, which inspired the majority in *Lotus*, seems to have been abandoned in contemporary legal thinking, the philosophical divide evinced in *Lotus* still persists in discussions concerning the ambit of states' jurisdiction. This divide is, of course, linked to one's own understanding of sovereignty

---

sur les critères de compétence des juges nationaux', in A. Cassese and M. Delmas-Marty (eds), *Crimes internationaux et juridictions internationales* (Paris: PUF, 2002), 191-213. The revision of the present chapter, which appeared in the first edition of this volume, is partially based on the content of these two papers.

[3] The case is well known. It concerns a collision in the high seas, off the coast of Turkey, between the French mail steamer *Lotus* and the Turkish collier *Boz-Kourt*, which resulted in the sinking of the latter and the death of eight Turkish nationals. Turkey started criminal proceedings against, among others, Lieutenant Demons, a French national, who was the officer of the watch on the *Lotus*. After rejecting the objection raised by Lieutenant Demons that Turkey had no jurisdiction, the Criminal Court of Istanbul convicted him for involuntary manslaughter and sentenced him to 80 days' imprisonment and a fine. France's reaction of diplomatic protection led the case to come before the PCIJ, which had to decide whether the criminal proceedings against Lieutenant Demons had breached Art. 15 of the 1924 Convention on Lausanne on Conditions of Residence and Business and Jurisdiction. This provision required 'all questions of jurisdiction shall [...] be decided in accordance with the principles of international law'. France contended, *inter alia*, that the exercise of criminal jurisdiction by Turkey, which asserted its criminal jurisdiction on the basis of its national criminal code provision on the passive personality principle, was not in accordance with international law.

and of the role and function of international law in a society whose primary subjects are sovereign states. A factual notion of sovereignty, according to which states are meta-legal entities whose formation is not regulated by international law, would lead one to believe that they were born free from obligations and rights, and that international law only intervenes to restrain their otherwise unfettered freedom. International law, however, would not attribute to them competences or powers (as Anzilotti put it, 'nothing is more repugnant to states than the notion that they exercise powers and authority granted to them by international law'[4]), let alone in criminal matters. By contrast, those (like Kelsen) who propound a legal notion of sovereignty consider that international law regulates the formation of states, and that it confers upon them rights and obligations in relation to their territories only in accordance with the principle of sovereign equality. According to this view, criminal jurisdiction is principally territorial; only exceptionally, namely once a rule of international law so establishes, can states assert their criminal jurisdiction over facts committed outside their territories.

Clearly, following the majority view in *Lotus*, the exercise of extraterritorial jurisdiction over international crimes would always be possible unless one can point to the existence of a rule of international law prohibiting it. In *Lotus*, the judges did not provide a list of possible rules to that effect. They confined themselves to demonstrating that the exercise of criminal jurisdiction in the case at stake, which was reclassified by the Court as a form of territorial jurisdiction, was not forbidden by international law. In the end, therefore, the Court did not offer any clue at all as regards the possible impediments placed upon the exercise of extraterritorial criminal jurisdiction. In addition, since it considered that after all the case concerned the exercise of territorial criminal jurisdiction, it could even have avoided the general statement concerning the restrictions to states' freedom that cannot be presumed. However, the fact remains that, from the point of view of the need to expand the jurisdictional reach of states for the repression of international crimes, the positivistic approach followed in *Lotus* would be the most suitable. According to this approach, there would exist a presumption in favour of the exercise of extraterritorial criminal jurisdiction, and it would be for the states challenging it to prove the existence of a specific prohibitive rule. This is perhaps rather paradoxical. The positivistic approach dominating the majority view in *Lotus* is indicative of a state-centric view of international law, which is at odds with the communitarianism that inspired the evolution of international criminal law.

The opposite (and one could say, more modern) approach, according to which criminal jurisdiction is principally territorial, obviously implies that in the matter of repression of international crimes one should point to a rule of international law allowing the exercise of extraterritorial jurisdiction. At the treaty law level, the task could be relatively easy since one can find rules allowing, if not obliging, the establishment of extraterritorial jurisdiction on the basis of specific heads. Nonetheless, a few problems still persist (see 15.3 and 15.4). The *punctum pruriens* concerns, therefore, the content of customary international law on the matter. In this regard, it seems undisputed that customary international law allows extraterritorial criminal jurisdiction, in addition to *active nationality*, on the basis of the so-called *protective* principle, whereby states possess jurisdiction over crimes committed abroad by nationals or foreigners when the crimes jeopardize or imperil the state's national interests (for instance, counterfeiting the national currency, planning attacks on the state's security, etc.). This principle, however, is normally not relevant with

---

[4] 'Niente più ripugna [agli Stati] dell'idea di esercitare una potestà loro concessa dall'ordinamento internazionale', in D. Anzilotti, *Corso di diritto internazionale*, vol. I, 4th edn (Padua: Cedam, 1955), 53.

respect to international crimes proper, on obvious grounds (states still tend to consider these crimes as not directly relevant to, or affecting, their national interests whenever a national or territorial link is lacking).

In addition, elements of state practice clearly indicate that the traditional opposition by common law countries to passive personality, at least as a basis to prosecute international crimes, has been overcome.[5] Things are more complex with respect to universal jurisdiction, as we shall see (at 15.2.4).

15.2 PRINCIPLES OF CRIMINAL JURISDICTION

15.2.1 THE PRINCIPLE OF TERRITORIALITY

The basic principle of criminal jurisdiction is that a crime committed in a state's territory is justiciable in that state. In the *Lotus* case, the PCIJ stated that 'in all systems of law the principle of the territorial character of criminal law is fundamental', although it also added that 'the territoriality of criminal law [...] is not an absolute principle of international law and by no means coincides with territorial sovereignty' (at 20). The latter legal proposition is a corollary of the principle of territoriality: even where a crime is committed outside the territory, if its effects will be felt in the territory, then it is amenable to the state's jurisdiction (for example, if, standing outside the territory, I shoot a pistol which kills someone in the territory; or if I manufacture drugs outside the territory and then smuggle them into the territory of the state. In both cases, I can be judged in the state where the effects of the crimes were felt, even though I committed the prohibited acts outside the territory.)

The principle of territoriality is grounded on ideological and political reasons: the need to affirm territorial sovereignty, which evolved in the age of reason and was linked to the consolidation of modern states. This need led states to replace the previous principle of 'personality of laws' (everybody is governed by his national law, wherever he resides) with that of territoriality (what matters is the law of the place where an act is performed).[6]

---

[5] Some common law countries have clearly accepted the application of the passive personality principle (traditionally perceived by them as an exorbitant title of jurisdiction for the repression of ordinary offences) over war crimes, crimes against humanity, and genocide. See in this regard P. Gaeta, 'Il principio di nazionalità passiva nella repressione dei crimini internazionali da parte delle giurisdizioni interne', in G. Venturini and S. Bariatti (eds), *Diritti individuali e giustizia internazionale, Liber Fausto Pocar* (Milan: Giuffrè, 2009), at 325.

[6] Montesquieu, Voltaire, Rousseau, and Beccaria insisted on the importance of territoriality in criminal law. The French Revolution confirmed it in the decree of 3–7 September 1792 ('foreigners charged with offences in their homeland may only be tried under the laws of their own country and by their own judges'; consequently, 'no foreigner will be retained on the galleys of France for crimes committed outside French territory'). In 1764 Beccaria, more than any other, developed the theory of territoriality. In his opinion, the adoption of this principle was warranted on two grounds. First of all, as state laws vary, one should only be punished in the place where one has infringed the law. Second, it is only just that a crime, which constitutes a violation of the social contract, be punished in the place where the contract was breached.

In his *Crimes and Punishments*, Beccaria wrote that 'There are those who think, that an act of cruelty committed, for example, at Constantinople, may be punished at Paris; for this abstracted reason, that he who offends humanity, should have enemies in all mankind, and be the object of universal execration; as if the judges were to be the knights errant of human nature in general, rather than guardians of particular conventions between men. The place of punishment can certainly be no other, than that where the crime was committed; for the necessity of punishing an individual for the general good subsists there, and there only.' C. Beccaria, *An Essay on Crimes and Punishments*, translated from the Italian, 4th edn (London: F. Newberry, 1775), repr. (Brooklyn Village: Branden Press Inc., 1983), at 64. (For the original text, which differs slightly, see C. Beccaria, *Dei delitti e delle pene*, ed. F. Venturi (Turin: G. Einaudi, 1965), at 71–2.)

The principle has numerous advantages. First, the *locus delicti commissi* (i.e. the place where the crime has been committed) is usually the place where it is easiest to collect evidence. It is therefore considered the *forum conveniens* (the appropriate place of trial), as was restated in *Eichmann* (at 302–3). Second, it is normally the place where the rights of the accused are best safeguarded, for—if he is not a foreigner fleetingly residing there—he is expected to know the law of the territory, hence he is likely to know the criminal law in force there as well as his rights as a defendant in a criminal trial. In addition, unless he is a non-resident foreigner, he knows and speaks the language in which the trial unfolds. Thirdly—and this applies in particular to international crimes, whose gravity may have serious repercussions on the society within which the crime has been committed—if the prosecution and punishment occur on the territory where the crime was perpetrated, it is more likely for the cathartic process of criminal trials to have effect: the victims and their families relive their tragedies, the whole society becomes aware of what has happened and is thus put in a position of better coming to terms with, hence of psychologically overcoming, past crimes. Moreover, the judges, jury, and advocates, being members of the community where the crimes took place, are aware of local feelings about the crimes and conscious of the press and public's close scrutiny of their administration of justice; they are thus broadly accountable to the community for the manner in which they dispense justice. Finally, by administering justice over crimes perpetrated in the territory, the territorial state affirms its authority over attacks on peace and security within its bounds; by the same token it helps to deter the commission of future offences.[7]

However, as noted already, in the case of international crimes, there may be a major obstacle to the exercise of criminal jurisdiction on the basis of the territoriality principle. These crimes are often committed by state officials or with their complicity or acquiescence: for example, war crimes committed by servicemen, or torture perpetrated by police officers, or genocide carried out with the tacit approval of state authorities. It follows that state judicial authorities may be reluctant to prosecute state agents or to institute proceedings against private individuals that might eventually involve state organs.

Whenever the territoriality principle is applicable, two problems may arise. First, what should be meant by 'territory' subject to the sovereignty of a state? Here one must turn to the international rules delimiting state territory, with the consequence that offences perpetrated in a state's territorial waters or on its ships or aircraft on the high seas are considered committed on the territory of that state. Similarly, territory comprises space under the control or 'under the jurisdiction' of a state, such as, for example, territory occupied following an international armed conflict. By contrast, crimes perpetrated in a state's embassy abroad are not carried out on national territory but abroad (hence the contrary view of the *Spanish Audiencia nacional* in the case of the Guatemalans (at 130), whereby crimes committed in the Spanish embassy in Guatemala were regarded as perpetrated in Spain, was wrong).

The second problem relates to the determination of the *locus commissi delicti* in the case of complex crimes: when the crime is planned in a country and committed in another

---

[7] In *Sawonjuk* the British Court of Appeal (Criminal Division) stated that: 'The criminal jurisdiction of the English courts is, generally speaking, territorial. Until enactment of the War Crimes Act 1991 [under which, proceedings may be brought in the UK "against a person in the United Kingdom irrespective of his nationality at the time of the alleged offence" for war crimes committed during the Second World War "in a place which at the time was part of Germany or under German occupation"] the appellant could not be tried here for an offence of murder or manslaughter committed in Byelorussia since he has never been a British subject and the exception made by Section 9 of the Offences against the Person Act 1861 to the ordinary rule of territoriality was confined to offences of murder or manslaughter committed outside the United Kingdom by British subjects' (at 4).

country, or the crime is committed in a country but takes its effects in another, which is the territory where trial proceedings may be instituted? The tendency of national legal systems is to give priority to the place of commission or to the place where the effects of the crime materialize. Many states have jurisdiction if one of the elements of the offence is committed in the state's territory, even if other elements occur abroad. It would seem that there are no international rules on this issue, nor may one infer from national legal systems a uniform regulation of the matter.

15.2.2 THE PRINCIPLE OF ACTIVE NATIONALITY

Normally the principle of active nationality is implemented in one of two forms. In some states, criminal laws apply over certain acts committed by their nationals abroad. This is so whether or not those acts are criminal under the law of the territorial state; that is, the state in which the conduct constituting the offences under the law of the state of nationality were committed. In this case, the underlying motivation is the will of a state that its nationals comply with its law, whether at home or abroad, regardless of what is provided for in the foreign state when the crime is committed. In other countries jurisdiction over crimes committed by nationals abroad is subordinated to the crime being punishable under the law of the territorial state as well. In this case, the essential rationale behind the principle is the desire—or constitutional prohibition in many cases—of the state of nationality not to extradite its nationals to the state where the crime has been perpetrated. Hence the law of the state of active nationality must provide for the possibility of trying the accused, so that he does not escape justice altogether.

All this holds true, generally speaking, for criminal offences. As for international crimes, states that uphold this ground of jurisdiction do so in order to bow to international dictates; that is, to make international law effective by complying with its commands. Thus, they normally do not require that the offence be also punishable by the territorial state, as it is sufficient for the offence to be regarded as an international crime by international rules (be they customary or treaty provisions).

A problem that may arise where jurisdiction is exercised on the basis of the active nationality principle concerns the moment at which the alleged perpetrator must possess the nationality of the prosecuting state: is it when the crime is perpetrated, or when criminal proceedings are instituted? It would seem that most states tend to accept that the nationality may be possessed at either moment, thus broadening the jurisdiction of the state and better ensuring the punishment of international crimes. One may also notice a tendency of states to broaden this ground by including residents (this applies, for instance, to the UK with regard to war crimes committed during the Second World War, as well as the crimes envisaged in the ICC Statute of the ICC; to Brazil with regard to genocide) or stateless persons residing on the territory of the prosecuting state (for instance, this applies to Italy and the Russian Federation).

Some states have passed legislation concerning crimes perpetrated during the Second World War, for the purpose of punishing persons who, whatever their nationality at the time of commission of crimes, have subsequently acquired their nationality, possibly with the hope of sheltering behind their newly acquired nationality.[8]

---

[8] Thus, §§ 1091 and 2342 of the US Code so provide with regard to genocide and war crimes. In the UK a law was passed in 1991 (the War Crimes Act) whereby proceedings may be brought for war crimes committed during the Second World War against persons who, whatever their nationality at the time of the alleged offence, are British citizens or residents as from 8 March 1990. (This cut-off date was chosen to prevent persons evading the Act by changing their nationality or residence.) Other states such as Australia and Canada have passed similar laws.

15.2.3 THE PRINCIPLE OF PASSIVE NATIONALITY

By virtue of the principle of passive nationality states possess jurisdiction over crimes committed abroad against their own nationals. Plainly, the principle is grounded both on: *i*) the need to protect nationals living or residing abroad; and *ii*) a substantial mistrust in the exercise of jurisdiction by the foreign territorial state.

Normally states invoking this ground of jurisdiction also provide that, whenever the accused is abroad, a 'double incrimination' is required for prosecuting a crime, namely that the offence be considered as such both in the territorial state and in the state of the victim. The requirement at issue is mainly intended to avoid prosecuting a person for an act that is not considered a criminal offence by the state where it has been performed. However, as far as international crimes are concerned, this requirement is replaced by the requirement that the offence be considered as an international crime by international law, whatever the content of the legal regulation in the territorial state. In this connection, the decision of the Supreme Court of Argentina delivered in *Priebke*, on 2 November 1995, concerning the extradition to Italy of a German national who had subsequently acquired Argentinian nationality, is pertinent: the Court explicitly held that as the offence of which the defendant stood accused, namely a war crime, was internationally regarded as an international crime, this sufficed for the purpose of the double incrimination principle.[9]

There has been frequent resort to this ground of jurisdiction to prosecute war crimes, particularly after the cessation of hostilities and by the victor state against the vanquished (former) enemies. More recently courts have relied upon this jurisdictional ground with regard to crimes against humanity and torture (see, for instance, *Astiz*, a case brought before French courts and concerning an Argentinian officer had tortured two French nuns in Argentina). Furthermore, this ground of jurisdiction has been laid down in national legislation with regard to terrorism; for instance, in the United States (see §§ 2331 and 2332 of the Federal Criminal Code), in France (Articles 113–17 of the Criminal Code), and in Belgium. It is also stipulated in a number of international conventions against terrorism and in the 1984 Convention against Torture (Article 5(1)).

Resort to the passive nationality principle is, however, particularly incongruous in the case of international crimes such as for instance those against humanity, and torture. By definition, these are crimes that injure humanity—that is, our sense of humanity—in other words our concept of respect for any human being, regardless of the nationality of the victims. As a consequence, their prosecution should not be based on the national link between the victim and the prosecuting state. This is indeed a narrow and nationalistic standard for bringing alleged criminals to justice, based on the interest of a state to prosecute those who have allegedly attacked one of its nationals. The prosecution of those crimes should instead reflect a universal concern for their punishment; it should consequently be based on such legal grounds as territoriality, universality, or active nationality.

It follows that, as far as such crimes as those against humanity, torture, and genocide are concerned, the passive nationality principle should only be relied upon as a fall-back, whenever no other state (neither the territorial state, nor the state of which the alleged criminal is a national, nor other states acting upon the universality principle) is willing or able to administer international criminal law. Conversely, the ground of jurisdiction under discussion may prove appropriate for such offences as war crimes or terrorism as a discrete offence, where the need to protect national interests and concerns acquires greater relevance.

---

[9] Fallos CSJN 318:2148, opinion of Judges Nazareno and O'Connor, § 77; opinion of Judge Bossert, § 91.

15.2.4 THE UNIVERSALITY PRINCIPLE

Under the principle of universality any state can apply its criminal law with respect to crimes committed abroad, by foreigners and against foreigners. The universality principle has been upheld in two different versions: the narrow notion (*conditional* universal jurisdiction) and the broad notion (*absolute* universal jurisdiction).

According to the more widespread version, i.e. conditional universal jurisdiction, only the state where the accused is in custody may acquire jurisdiction over him or her (the so-called *forum deprehensionis*, or jurisdiction of the place where the accused is apprehended). Thus, the presence of the accused on the territory is a condition for the existence of jurisdiction and consequently for its exercise.

Under a different version of the universality principle, a state may possess jurisdiction over persons accused of international crimes regardless of their nationality, the place of commission of the crime, the nationality of the victim, and even of whether or not the accused is in custody or at any rate present in the forum state. (However, if the legal system does not permit trials in absentia, the national legislation may require the presence of the accused on the territory as a condition for the initiation of trial proceedings.) Clearly, this conception of universality allows national authorities to commence criminal investigations of persons suspected of serious international crimes, and gather evidence about these alleged crimes, as soon as such authorities are seized with information concerning an alleged criminal offence; they can go so far as to issue an arrest warrant and a request of extradition to the relevant state where the suspect is found. They may thus exercise criminal jurisdiction over such persons, without requiring that the person first be present, even temporarily, in the country. In some countries, such exercise of jurisdiction is premised on the failure of the territorial or national state to take proceedings, and should therefore not be activated whenever one of those states initiates proceedings.

Although there is a trend towards considering that universal jurisdiction is allowed for the prosecution of international crimes generally speaking, strong disagreement persists among states and legal experts as regards the need for a jurisdictional link to the forum state, in particular the presence of the suspect in the territory of the state.[10]

This debate is, however, somewhat confused because the distinction between legislative and adjudicatory/enforcement jurisdiction is often not clearly maintained. As is well known, legislative jurisdiction indicates the authority of the state to determine the scope of application of its laws, in this case criminal legislation. Adjudicatory/enforcement jurisdiction refers to the ability of the state to apply its own laws to specific cases, through its courts and enforcement agencies. Clearly, legislative jurisdiction determines the scope of intervention of the judiciary and the enforcement agencies, since the latter cannot but intervene to apply and enforce a law that is applicable to a particular case. If adjudicatory/enforcement jurisdiction is by necessity territorial, in the sense that it can only be exercised within the territory of the state, legislative jurisdiction can extend to extraterritorial acts.

The issue with *absolute* universal jurisdiction is whether the criminal legislation of a state can regulate acts committed abroad by foreigners against foreigners, when the

---

[10] According to the 2010 UN Secretary-General's Report, 'The Scope and Application of the Principle of Universal Jurisdiction', as for the jurisdictional link, the uncertainty is greater since states adopt a variety of links for the assertion of universal jurisdiction and very few states, e.g. Spain, consider that 'unconditional' universal jurisdiction is allowed for the prosecution of international crimes. Disagreement also persists as regards the list of crimes: some states consider that universal jurisdiction is permitted under general international law over genocide, crimes against humanity, war crime, torture, and piracy, while other states deem that it is limited to piracy, genocide, and torture, or according to other states, to piracy only.

suspect has never entered the territory of the state after the commission of the crime and there is no prospect that he will, at least not voluntarily. This broad form of (legislative) jurisdiction would necessarily imply a corresponding form of adjudicatory/enforcement jurisdiction, in the sense that investigation and prosecution can be started without the presence of the accused in the territory of the state; in addition, the competent authorities could issue an arrest warrant and circulate it internationally (as was the case for *Yerodia*, subject to an arrest warrant by Belgium) and they can issue a request for extradition if they know where the accused is located (as was the case with *Pinochet*, subject to an arrest warrant by Spain). If the domestic system allows it, a trial *in absentia* could be held and, in case of a conviction, an extradition for the enforcement of the sentence could be requested.

A. Universal Jurisdiction and Respect for the Principle of Legality

One of the major concerns with the notion of absolute universality is respect for the principle of legality. True, one could contend that if the crimes with which the accused is charged were provided for in customary international law at the time of the commission of the offence this concern should not arise at all. However, respect for the principle of legality not only requires that the accused be aware that his act amounts to a criminal offence, but also that he knows the range of penalties attached to it, as provided by the maxim *nullum crimen, nulla poena sine lege*. The great disparity among states in sentencing policies and legislation could therefore impose in the state exercising pure universal jurisdiction a penalty that is excessive in comparison to the maximum penalty applicable in the territorial or the national state. For instance, for a war crime, the territorial state could provide for a penalty of, say, a maximum twenty years' imprisonment, while in the state exercising pure universal jurisdiction the same crime could receive the penalty of life imprisonment.

In order to bring the exercise of absolute universal jurisdiction into conformity with the principle of legality, one could envisage the obligation for the *forum* state to make the presence of the suspect in the territory of the state a requirement for the exercise of adjudicatory/enforcement jurisdiction. In other words, while the ambit of criminal law would extend to extraterritorial acts without a link with the forum state at the moment of their commission, this link would be required to trigger the adjudicatory/enforcement jurisdiction. The police and the prosecutor could therefore carry out investigations over the alleged commission of a crime abroad, if they wish, but the actual exercise of criminal jurisdiction would require the 'voluntary' presence of the suspect in the territory of the state after the alleged commission of the crime. His voluntary presence would imply that he subjects himself to the criminal jurisdiction of that state, knowing in advance that universal jurisdiction could be exercised in accordance with the criminal legislation of that state, which includes the range of penalties attached to the crime.

In this sense, the purpose of the presence requirement will not be confused with the one traditionally assigned to it under the *forum deprehensionis* principle. In the latter case, the presence of the suspect in the territory of the state is a condition for determining the ambit of application of criminal law (and therefore of legislative jurisdiction), and as a consequence it amounts to a requirement for the act to be considered a crime under the legislation of the state. This means that, until the suspect is present in the territory, investigation (let alone prosecution) cannot be initiated because the criminal law of the forum state is not applicable at all. Interestingly, it is this form of *legislative universal jurisdiction* that is mandatory for contracting states under some treaties concerning international crimes, although they make it conditional to the decision not to extradite the alleged culprit found in the territory of the state.[11] From the point of view of respect for the principle of legality, conditional universal jurisdiction would be even less problematical than in the scenario outlined above, since the criminal legislation of a state would regulate extraterritorial conduct only if the alleged wrongdoer has voluntarily entered the territory of the state.

B. Some Other Concerns About Absolute Universal Jurisdiction

In addition to the concerns about respect for the principle of legality, there are various reasons that militate against absolute universal jurisdiction, at least if resorted to with regard to political or military leaders.[12]

First of all, the existence in some states of national laws granting absolute universal jurisdiction may prompt victims of atrocities to engage in so-called forum-shopping. In other words, it may attract such victims and induce them to file complaints against alleged perpetrators.[13]

Second, if the accused never enters the country where the court is located, or is not extradited to that country, a situation that appears most likely, the judge will end up investigating hundreds of complaints about which he can do nothing.

Third, a judge who decides to go ahead with the trial regardless of the absence of the accused, conducting proceedings in absentia (if allowed), is likely to be criticized for violating the fundamental rights of the accused. Moreover, the absence of the accused, normally linked to the fact that the state of nationality refuses to extradite, could worsen the problem of establishing the facts because neither the accused nor the state in question will cooperate in the search for evidence.

Fourth, the power of national judges to issue arrest warrants against foreign former or incumbent state officials may lend itself to abuse if the power is not exercised with caution and is not predicated on two basic conditions: that *i*) compelling evidence is available against the accused; and *ii*) the person charged with international crimes does not enjoy, or no longer enjoys immunities (this holds true for heads of state, prime ministers, some senior members of cabinet, and diplomatic agents; see 13.2 and 17.4). Whenever the necessary prudence is not used, the exercise of universal jurisdiction may easily lead to international disputes. For instance, this happened in the aforementioned case of the Congolese former foreign minister, *Yerodia*, against whom a Belgian investigating judge had issued an arrest warrant (see 17.4). Thus, a case pertaining to the criminal

---

[11] A typical example is Art. 5(2) of the UN Convention Against Torture and Other Cruel, Inhuman and Degrading Treatment, which obliges a contracting state to establish their criminal jurisdiction 'in cases where the alleged offender is present in any territory under its jurisdiction and it does not extradite'. A similar provision is contained in almost all the treaties for the repression of so-called 'terrorist crimes' (an exception is the 1963 Tokyo Convention). On the face of it, these treaty provisions seem to provide that universal jurisdiction can be acquired only on condition that the alleged offender *is* in the territory of the state (provided that extradition is considered but not carried out), meaning that there is no possibility to launch a criminal investigation or to exercise any form of *adjudicatory jurisdiction* before he is found there. However, this would be an incorrect conclusion. Since the aim of these treaties is to create a jurisdictional web for the repression of given crimes the relevant treaties also contain another provision which clarifies that any criminal jurisdiction exercised by contracting states in accordance with their internal law is not excluded (see e.g. Art. 5(3) of the UN Convention Against Torture). These provisions could therefore be interpreted as permitting unconditional universal jurisdiction, among contracting states, if this head of jurisdiction is provided for by national legislation.

[12] See also the critical remarks by J. Verhoeven, 'Vers un ordre répressif universel? Quelques observations', in 55 AFDI (1999), at 62–3.

[13] On this issue see in particular J. F. Flauss, 'Droit des immunités et protection internationale des droits de l'homme', in *Revue suisse de droit international et de droit européen* (2000), at 304.

responsibility of individuals became the subject of an interstate dispute. In other words, the case was moved from an inter-individual level to that of state-to-state relations. This is contrary to the very logic of international criminal justice.

Finally, given the number of diplomatically and politically high-profile cases that would be brought before the courts, the judge would eventually become entangled in roles normally played by the political authorities,[14] with the consequent danger of infringing the sound principle of separation of powers. [15]

15.3 INTERNATIONAL RULES ON STATES' CRIMINAL JURISDICTION OVER INTERNATIONAL CRIMES

One may classify the international rules on criminal jurisdiction of states over international crimes into three categories. First, there are rules that confine themselves to *authorizing* states to establish or to exercise their criminal jurisdiction on the basis of specific grounds or with respect to a specific class of crimes. Second, there are rules that impose upon states the *obligation to enact the necessary national legislation* to provide for criminal jurisdiction on the basis of specific grounds. Finally, there are rules that *oblige states to exercise their criminal jurisdiction* over persons charged with international crimes on the basis of specific grounds.

The distinction between these categories is not merely formal, or dictated by purely technical requirements; it has important practical consequences. Clearly, rules that belong to the first category, being of a permissive nature, do not impose upon states any international obligation. Nonetheless, they might have other legal effects; in particular, they may preclude states from objecting that the assertion of foreign criminal jurisdiction upon a specific legal ground contradicts the principle of non-interference on domestic affairs.

By contrast, rules belonging to the second and third categories do impose international obligations, with the third more burdensome than the second. The obligation to exercise jurisdiction over persons charged with international crimes is an obligation to bring them

[14] Take the *Pinochet* case: it would seem difficult to prove that Pinochet committed *genocide* in Chile, whereas it would seem that he can be accused of gross violations of human rights, including torture; the fact that he was accused of genocide in Spain shows the sort of charges that can be put together, primarily for the purpose of taking into account the Spanish legislation (which provides for universal jurisdiction in the absence of a treaty only for genocide and terrorism). Arguably these political matters should be left to politicians, legislatures, etc., and not brought before judges.

[15] It is, however, a fact that US courts have for many years asserted universal jurisdiction by default, admittedly in *civil* proceedings, over serious violations of international law perpetrated by foreigners abroad (see the Alien Tort Claims Statute and the *Filartiga-Peña Irala* case; see e.g. L. F. Damrosch, 'Enforcing International Law through Non-Forcible Measures', in 269 HR (1997), at 161–7). Although civil jurisdiction is less intrusive than criminal jurisdiction, when it is exercised over foreigners who possess official status (for instance, high-ranking state officials), it nevertheless amounts to interference with the internal organization of foreign states. Whether or not this trend of US courts is objectionable as a matter of policy, or on legal grounds, it is a fact that it has not been challenged, or in other words has been acquiesced in, by other states. This implicit acceptance through non-contestation would seem to evidence the generally shared legal conviction that, where there are serious and blatant breaches of universal values, national courts are authorized to take action, subject to fulfilment of some fundamental requirements, such as ensuring a fair trial. (Admittedly there is a conspicuous difference between civil and criminal suits: in civil suits only money is at stake whereas in a criminal trial, the accused may be deprived of his liberty for a long time. So states may be prepared to tolerate civil suits of this nature, but shrink from allowing criminal trials.)

to trial if there exist serious allegations of wrongful conduct. By contrast, the obligation to pass the necessary domestic legislation on jurisdiction requires states merely to put in place the legislative *preconditions* for such punishment.

15.3.1 TREATY PROVISIONS AUTHORIZING STATES TO ADOPT SPECIFIC JURISDICTIONAL GROUNDS

The UN Convention on Torture as well as some conventions on terrorism include provisions authorizing contracting states to assert their criminal jurisdiction on the basis of the *passive nationality* principle, or other specific extraterritorial grounds.[16]

The object and scope of these provisions are not very clear on their face in that they seem merely to restate a power that, in accordance to the *Lotus* paradigm, is already in existence pursuant to customary international law. However, as the PCIJ emphasized, the freedom of states to adopt any ground of criminal jurisdiction, and to exercise it accordingly, is not unfettered. Existing international obligations constrain such freedom, in accordance with the notion that, in international law, 'all that is not specifically prohibited is allowed'. One could argue that the principle of non-interference in other states' international affairs constitutes a possible limit to the establishment and exercise of criminal jurisdiction. At the same time, one may contend that the principle of non-interference does not apply to cases of international crimes whose prohibition is rooted in customary international law, since prohibition of these crimes is intended to safeguard values regarded as fundamental by the whole international community. Arguably, with regard to such crimes, the assertion of criminal jurisdiction on the basis of extraterritorial principles (such as the passive nationality principle) can be regarded as fully authorized by customary international law.

The same may not be true, however, of crimes that are prohibited, or at the time of the adoption of the treaty were prohibited, *only* at the *treaty* level. In these circumstances, it cannot be safely assumed that the assertion of criminal jurisdiction by a state on the basis of extraterritorial grounds does not amount to a breach of the principle of non-interference in other states' internal affairs. Therefore, with regard to such offences, the inclusion in the relevant convention of a provision expressly granting contracting states the power to establish their jurisdiction in accordance with the passive nationality principle, or other specific extraterritorial grounds, is of considerable value. On the strength of this provision, contracting states recognize that, in their reciprocal relationships, the assertion of jurisdiction on the basis of those grounds is legitimate and does not run counter to the principle of non-interference in their internal affairs.

Similar considerations may apply with regard to those treaty provisions stipulating that the relevant convention does not exclude the exercise of any criminal jurisdiction in accordance with internal law.[17] Plainly, these provisions allow contracting states to

---

[16] See Art. 5(1) of the 1984 Torture Convention; Art. 5(1)(d) of the 1979 Convention against the Taking of Hostages; Art. 6(2) of the 1988 Rome Convention for the Suppression of Unlawful Acts against Safety of Maritime Navigation; Art. 6(2) of the 1998 Convention for the Suppression of Terrorist Bombings; and Art. 7(2) of the 1999 Convention for the Suppression of the Financing of Terrorism.

[17] Art. 3(3) of the 1963 Tokyo Convention on Offences and Certain Other acts Committed on Board Aircraft; Art. 4(3) of the 1970 Hague Convention for the Suppression of Unlawful Seizure of Aircraft; Art. 5(3) of the 1971 Montreal Convention for the Suppression of Unlawful Acts against the Safety of Civil Aviation; Art. 3(3) of the 1973 UN Convention on the Prevention and Punishment of Crimes against Internationally Protected Persons, including Diplomatic Agents; Art. 5(3) of the 1979 UN Convention against the Taking of Hostages; Art. 6(5) of the 1988 Rome Convention for the Suppression of Unlawful Acts against the Safety of Maritime Navigation; Art. 7(6) of the 1999 UN Convention for the Suppression of the Financing of Terrorism.

prosecute and punish alleged offenders under *any legal ground* provided for in national law other than those already envisaged in the convention itself. Hence, a contracting state, if it asserts its jurisdiction over the prohibited offence on the basis of a legal ground not mentioned in the convention, may not be deemed to have interfered into the internal affairs of another contracting state.

With regard to this class of provisions, however, the problem arises of ascertaining whether these provisions allow criminal jurisdiction upon *any possible legal* ground, or instead only are intended to refer to those grounds *generally recognized* by states in their criminal jurisdiction. A case in point is the 1963 Tokyo Convention. This Convention obliges contracting states to take all the necessary measures to include, in their criminal jurisdiction, the principle of the flag state. Article 3(3) of the Convention, however, expressly recognizes that contracting states retain the right to exercise their criminal jurisdiction on the strength of their national legislation. According to some commentators, this provision does not go so far as to allow state parties to exercise their criminal jurisdiction on the basis of *universality* (in both its variants), since this legal ground is not generally contemplated in national criminal systems. Others argue that the object and purpose of the Convention is to make sure that there is always a state having jurisdiction over the prohibited offences. Therefore, Art. 3(3) should be interpreted as allowing contracting states to include any legal grounds, including universality in its broadest terms.[18]

The uncertainties of Article 3(3) of the 1963 Tokyo Convention do not arise with regard to other treaties, and the 1984 UN Torture Convention is a particularly clear example. Article 5(1) and (2) of the Torture Convention obliges contracting states to include in their criminal jurisdiction the principles of territoriality, active nationality, as well as that of universality (on the basis of the *forum deprehensionis*); in addition, it expressly allows them to adopt the principle of passive nationality. Thus, the Convention already covers all of the traditional jurisdictional grounds, plus *universality*, although, in the latter case, it makes the establishment of jurisdiction contingent upon the presence of the accused on the state's territory. Nonetheless, Article 5(3) of the Convention stipulates that contracting states can also exercise criminal jurisdiction on the strength of their national legislation. It follows that Article 5(3) primarily applies to those contracting states whose criminal legislation provides for other jurisdictional grounds, including universality in its broadest terms, i.e., without any requirement that the accused should be present on the territory. Those states are therefore allowed to pursue alleged tortures on the basis of this broad notion of universality, and the other contracting states (in particular the territorial and national state) cannot object that such action would run counter to the principle of non-interference in internal affairs.[19]

---

[18] See the authors quoted by M. Henzelin, *Le principe de l'universalité en droit pénal international*, (Basel: Helbing and Lichtenhahn, 2000) at 297, nn. 1308 and 1309, who, on the basis of the preparatory works of the Convention, takes the view that Article 3(3) should be construed restrictively (at 298).

[19] A similar conclusion follows for the crime of apartheid. Art. 5 of the 1973 UN Convention on the Suppression and Punishment of the Crime of Apartheid provides: 'Persons charged with the acts enumerated in Article II of the present Convention *may be tried by a competent tribunal of any State Party to the Convention which may acquire jurisdiction over the person of the accused* or by an international tribunal having jurisdiction with respect to those State Parties which shall have accepted its jurisdiction' (emphasis added).

There is only one convention that, in providing that contracting states are allowed to exercise criminal jurisdiction in accordance with their internal law, expressly stipulates that such assertion of jurisdiction shall not run counter to the norms of general international law. Art. 7(6) of the 1999 Convention for the Suppression of the Financing of Terrorism provides as follows: '*Without prejudice to the norms of general international law*, this Convention does not exclude the exercise of any criminal jurisdiction established by a

15.3.2 TREATY PROVISIONS OBLIGING STATES TO ESTABLISH CRIMINAL JURISDICTION ON THE BASIS OF SPECIFIC GROUNDS

Some multilateral treaties on international crimes require contracting states to pass legislation *to establish* criminal jurisdiction (i.e. to provide for the applicability of the relevant criminal prohibition) on certain specific grounds.

The best illustration of this category of treaties may be found in the 1984 UN Torture Convention, whose Article 5(1) obliges each contracting state to 'take such measures as may be necessary to establish [their] jurisdiction' over acts of torture (or over participation or complicity in torture) on the basis of the principles of territoriality, active nationality, and conditional universality (but subject to the principle *aut dedere aut iudicare*).[20] Other multilateral treaties on international crimes, in particular those prohibiting terrorist acts, adopt the same pattern as the 1984 UN Torture Convention and oblige contracting states to adopt specific jurisdictional grounds.[21]

State Party in accordance with its domestic law' (emphasis added). Arguably, on the strength of the *incipit* of this provision, contracting states are not allowed to establish their criminal jurisdiction if, by doing so, they contravene the general principle of international law banning interferences in other states' internal affairs. This interpretation is bolstered by the fact that Art. 20 of the Convention expressly provides that 'The State Parties shall carry out their obligations under this Convention in a manner consistent with the principles of sovereign equality and territorial integrity of States and that of non-intervention in the domestic affairs of other States'.

[20] Art. 5 (1) provides that: 'Each State Party shall take such measures as may be necessary to establish its jurisdiction over the offences referred to in article 4 in the following cases: (1) When the offences are committed in any territory under its jurisdiction or on board a ship or aircraft registered in that State; (2) When the alleged offender is a national of that State [...]'; Article 5 (2) stipulates that 'Each State Party shall likewise take such measures as may be necessary to establish its jurisdiction over such offences in cases where the alleged offender is present in any territory under its jurisdiction and it does not extradite him pursuant to Article 8 to any of the States mentioned in paragraph 1 of this Article.'

[21] See the 1963 Tokyo Convention on Offences and Certain Other Acts Committed on Board Aircraft, whose Art. 3(2) obliges the state of registration of an aircraft to take the necessary measures to establish its jurisdiction over offences committed on board aircraft registered in such state; Art. 4(1) and (2) of the 1970 Hague Convention for the Suppression of Unlawful Seizure of Aircraft, which imposes upon each contracting state the obligation to establish its jurisdiction over the offence and any other act of violence against passengers or crew committed by the alleged offender in connection with the offence, in the following cases: *i*) when the offence is committed on board an aircraft registered in that state; *ii*) when the aircraft on board which the offence is committed lands in its territory with the alleged offender still on board; *iii*) when the offence is committed on board an aircraft leased without crew to a lessee who has his principal place of business or, if the lessee has no such place of business, his permanent residence, in that state; and *iv*) when the alleged offender is present in its territory and it does not extradite him pursuant to Article 8 to any of the states having jurisdiction according to the three aforementioned grounds; Art. 5(1) and (2) of the 1971 Montreal Convention for the Suppression of Unlawful Acts against the Safety of Civil Aviation, which, in addition to the legal grounds already envisaged in the 1970 Hague Convention, oblige each contracting state to establish its jurisdiction when the offence is committed in its territory, and when the aircraft on board which the offence is committed lands in its territory with the alleged offender still on board.

Similar provisions may be found in the 1973 Convention on the Prevention and Punishment of Crimes against Internationally Protected Persons, including Diplomatic Agents (Art. 3(1) and (2)); the 1979 Convention against the Taking of Hostages (Art. 5(1) and (2)); the 1988 Rome Convention for the Suppression of Unlawful Acts against the Safety of Maritime Navigation (Art. 6(1) and (4)); the 1998 Convention for the Suppression of Terrorist Bombings (Art. 6(1) and (4)). See also the 1977 European Convention on the Suppression of Terrorism, whose Art. 6(1) provides: 'Each Contracting State shall take such measures as may be necessary to establish its jurisdiction over an offence mentioned in Article 1 in the case where the suspected offender is present in its territory and it does not extradite him after receiving a request for extradition from a Contracting State whose jurisdiction is based on a rule of jurisdiction existing equally in the law of the requested State.'

Clearly, these conventions aim to prevent impunity and deter specific offences by guaranteeing that there is always a state that has jurisdiction over such offences. Nonetheless, to ensure the most effective repression of international crimes, it may be not sufficient merely to oblige contracting states to provide for the applicability of the relevant criminal prohibition on the basis of specific grounds of jurisdiction. This is particularly so if one considers that, in some states, prosecutors are not always obliged to institute criminal proceedings if faced with a *notitia criminis*; that is, if they become cognizant of the perpetration of a crime, but rather enjoy discretionary powers. A state may, then, fully comply with its international obligation by adopting the required criminal legislation, but nonetheless fail to bring to justice alleged perpetrators of international crimes.

15.3.3 TREATY PROVISIONS OBLIGING STATES TO EXERCISE CRIMINAL JURISDICTION ON THE BASIS OF SPECIFIC GROUNDS

The most effective means of preventing international crimes and avoiding impunity is the imposition of an international obligation to prosecute alleged perpetrators. This fact is all the more true if one takes into account the practical consequences stemming from such an international obligation. First, if a state is internationally duty-bound to prosecute and punish the alleged authors of international crimes, it may not enact national laws or conclude international agreements granting amnesty for such crimes without breaching international commitments and incurring international responsibility. Indeed, it would be appropriate for other states having jurisdiction over those crimes to refuse to recognize the validity of the state's national legislation and transactions, and to initiate their own proceedings against the alleged perpetrators. Second, the existence of an international obligation to exercise criminal jurisdiction has a considerable impact on those states where prosecutors enjoy discretionary powers as to the initiation of investigations and prosecution. In such states, the aforementioned international obligation would make judicial penal action by prosecutors mandatory. It follows that a state under such an obligation will incur international responsibility if a complaint about an international crime is lodged with one of its prosecutors, or the prosecutor in any way is made cognizant of the commission of any such crime, and on account of his/her general discretionary powers, the prosecutor fails to commence investigation or institute proceedings. Third, there may be rules of international law establishing an international obligation to prosecute on the basis of legal grounds not already envisaged by national systems; for instance, universality. If this is the case, such rules may have a self-executing character as far as jurisdictional grounds for penal action are concerned: this occurs where national legislation does contain a provision expressly referring back to international law; that is, providing that national courts may exercise jurisdiction on any legal ground (e.g. universality) provided for in an international treaty.[22]

Several multilateral treaties addressing international crimes impose an obligation to exercise criminal jurisdiction. The scope and purpose of such obligations, however, vary according to the relevant treaty.

---

[22] See e.g. Art. 7 (5) of the Italian Criminal Code, providing: 'Foreigners who commit abroad [crimes] with regard to which international conventions provide for the applicability of Italian criminal law, are punished under Italian law' ('E' punito secondo la legge italiana [...] lo straniero che commette in territorio estero [un reato] per il quale le convenzioni internazionali stabiliscono l'applicabilità della legge penale italiana').

A. Genocide Convention

It is common knowledge that the Genocide Convention obliges only the territorial state to prosecute the alleged perpetrators of acts of genocide.[23] Clearly, such an obligation is unlikely to be fulfilled whenever the alleged perpetrators are nationals of the territorial state. Genocide is normally perpetrated at the instigation, or at least with the acquiescence, of the authorities of the territorial state. It follows that this obligation is likely to be fulfilled only in cases of a change of regime (see, for instance, Rwanda).[24] However, if nationals of third states (especially of neighbouring countries) perpetrate genocide on the territory of a given state, the territorial state would be more inclined to exercise its criminal jurisdiction.

B. The 1949 Geneva Conventions and First Additional Protocol

Unlike the Genocide Convention, the 1949 Geneva Conventions and the First Additional Protocol contain a very broad obligation to punish the alleged perpetrators of a specific category of war crimes, the so-called 'grave breaches' of the Conventions. Indeed, they oblige contracting states to bring to justice alleged perpetrators of grave breaches on the basis of all possible grounds of criminal jurisdiction, *including* the *universality principle*.[25] In the alternative, contracting states may decide to hand over the alleged offender to another state party, to the extent to which such party has made out a prima facie case.[26]

Admittedly, the Geneva Conventions do not define the universality principle in clear-cut terms. The wording of those provisions, however, set out the obligation to bring alleged perpetrators to justice on *every* contracting party ('*Each High Contracting Party shall be under the obligation to search for persons alleged to have committed, or to have ordered to be committed, such grave breaches* [...]'), i.e. including states not parties to the international armed conflict where grave breaches appears to have been committed. It could therefore be contended that the mandatory system of criminal repression is *universal* in scope, and must be implemented by every state party; but it can also be contended

---

[23] See Art. VI of the Genocide Convention, according to which: 'Persons charged with genocide or any of the other acts enumerated in article III *shall be tried by a competent tribunal of the State in the territory of which the act was committed*, or by such international penal tribunal as may have jurisdiction with respect to those Contracting Parties which shall have accepted its jurisdiction' (emphasis added).

Obviously, the existence of a treaty obligation to exercise territorial jurisdiction over genocide does not rule out the possibility for the contracting states to establish their criminal jurisdiction on the basis of other legal grounds (in accordance with the permissive principle of customary international law).

[24] In this regard, see P. Benvenuti, 'Complementarity of the International Criminal Court to National Criminal Jurisdictions', in F. Lattanzi and W. Schabas (eds), *Essays on the Rome Statute of the International Criminal Court*, vol. I (Fagnano Alto: Il Sirente, 1999), at 27, where the author also stresses: 'The mandatory territorial jurisdiction of the State where the crime has been committed, although sometimes ineffective, has nevertheless a great importance from a general point of view, because it is a strong recognition of the heavy responsibilities that States have in guaranteeing, within their sovereignty, the fundamental values of humanity, which, if violated, constitute crimes.'

[25] The same obligation applies in the case of grave breaches of the First Additional Protocol.

[26] A commentator has rightly pointed out that the Geneva Conventions establish 'une obligation de poursuivre les personnes prévenues d'infractions graves aux Conventions de Genève *et non pas une compétence alternative aut dedere aut prosequi*, ni même une compétence alternative *aut prosequi aut dedere*. L'exercice de la compétence n'est pas subsidiaire à une extradition mais absolu [...] En ce sens, l'obligation prévue par [les Conventions] est une obligation de rechercher et de poursuivre en premier lieu, avec la possibilité facultative pour l'Etat où se trouve le prévenu de le remettre à un autre Etat, pour autant que celui-ci retienne également des charges suffisantes contre ce prévenu. On se trouve ainsi en présence [...] [du] modèle *primo prosequi, secundo dedere*'. See Henzelin, cit. n. 18, at 353 (emphasis in the original).

that the obligation to prosecute and try the alleged authors of grave breaches (regardless of their nationality) must be performed on the basis of the principles of criminal jurisdiction generally adopted by states in their domestic jurisdiction (and universal jurisdiction is not among them). Under that interpretation, the Geneva Conventions would confine themselves to obliging the contracting state to exercise criminal jurisdiction on one of the more 'classical' grounds of criminal jurisdiction.

Be that as it may, if one opts for the broader interpretation, the question arises whether a state can exercise universal jurisdiction over grave breaches only if the accused is present on the state's territory. The better view is that, under the 1949 Geneva Conventions, the universality principle requires the presence of the accused on the territory.[27] Three reasons support this proposition. First, the wording of the aforementioned *incipit*: it is only within the territories under its jurisdiction that a contracting party may fulfil the obligation to search for persons suspected or accused of grave breaches. Second, the relevant provisions of the Geneva Conventions, while obliging contracting states to bring those persons before their own courts, 'regardless of their nationality', at the same time allow states parties alternatively to hand such persons over for trial to another contracting party concerned. Hence, it is logical to infer that the obligation of contracting states also to exercise their criminal jurisdiction on the basis of extraterritorial grounds is made contingent upon the presence of the accused in their own territories. In other words, if an accused was not on the state's territory, the state would not be able to exercise its right to choose between commencing national proceedings, 'regardless of the nationality' of the alleged perpetrator of a grave breach, and surrendering him to another contracting state.

To bolster this interpretation, one may add that it is no coincidence that all subsequent treaties explicitly laying down the universality principle make the exercise of universal jurisdiction conditional on the presence of the accused on the territory of the contracting state (see Article (3) of the 1984 UN Torture Convention, and all the relevant conventions on terrorism) (see 15.3.2).

C. The UN Torture Convention

The normative framework for the penal repression of torture established by the 1984 UN Torture Convention is more intricate than the Geneva Conventions because the Torture Convention imposes different obligations upon contracting states depending on their jurisdictional link to the offence. First, each state party on whose territory an alleged torturer is found shall, if it does not extradite him, 'submit the case to its competent authorities for the purpose of prosecution' (Art. 7(1)). As is clear from the wording of the provision, this is not an obligation to prosecute, let alone to punish, but only to submit the case to the prosecuting authorities. Moreover, it seems that these authorities—although mandated '[to] take their decision in the same manner as in the case of any ordinary offence of a serious nature under the law of [the contracting] State'—may apply their discretionary powers if vested with such powers under their national criminal system. It is worth noting, however, that the obligation at stake is not intended to be conditional

---

[27] In this regard, see G. I. Drapper, 'The Geneva Conventions of 1949', in HR (1965), I, at 157. In addition, see the Pictet Commentary to the Geneva Conventions, where—with regard to the relevant provisions on penal repression of grave breaches—it is stressed that: 'The obligation on the High Contracting Parties to search for persons accused to have committed grave breaches imposes an active duty on them. As soon as a Contracting Party realizes *that there is on its territory a person who has committed such a breach*, its duty is to ensure that the person concerned is arrested and prosecuted with all speed.' For a contrary view, see R. Maison, 'Les Premiers Cas d'application des dispositions pénales des Conventions de Gèneve par le juridictions internes', in 5 EJIL (1995), at 260ff.; Henzelin, cit. n. 18, at 354.

upon a request for extradition by a third State.[28] Second, whenever an act of torture has allegedly been committed 'in any territory under the jurisdiction' of a contracting state,[29] the relevant state is obliged to proceed *ex officio* to a prompt and impartial investigation.[30] In addition, if seized with a complaint by an alleged victim, it must ensure that the competent state authorities examine the case promptly and impartially.[31] Hence, the obligations incumbent upon the territorial state are stricter than those imposed on the other contracting parties, in that the former, but not the latter, is mandated to start an investigation and to ensure that the prosecuting authorities duly examine an allegation of torture. Arguably, such obligations do not allow the prosecuting authorities to exercise any discretionary powers whenever there is sufficient evidence for instituting proceedings.

D. Conventions on Terrorism

While the 1963 Tokyo Convention merely obliges each contracting state to include in its criminal jurisdiction a specific legal ground (that is, to establish jurisdiction over the prohibited offences committed on board the aircraft registered in the relevant state), the 1970 Hague Convention and the 1971 Montreal Convention (as well as all the subsequent conventions addressing terrorist crimes) go somewhat further in that they also oblige the contracting states to at least submit cases relating to the relevant offences to their prosecuting authorities. As in the UN Torture Convention, such an obligation is subject to the condition that the alleged offender is found on the territory of the state party and that such state party does not extradite him.[32] In addition, the obligation allows the prosecutor

---

[28] See in this regard the stand taken by the ICJ in the case *Questions Relating to the Obligations to Prosecute or Extradite* (*Belgium* v. *Senegal*), where the Court states, '[t]he obligation to submit the case to the competent authorities, under Article 7, paragraph 1, may or may not result in the institution of proceedings, in the light of the evidence before them, relating to the charges against the suspect' (§ 94). However, the Court continues by noting: '[...] if the State in whose territory the suspect is present has received a request for extradition in any of the cases envisaged in the provisions of the Convention, it can relieve itself of its obligation to prosecute by acceding to that request. It follows that the choice between extradition or submission for prosecution, pursuant to the Convention, does not mean that the two alternatives are to be given the same weight. Extradition is an option offered to the State by the Convention, whereas prosecution is an international obligation under the Convention, the violation of which is a wrongful act engaging the responsibility of the State' (§ 95).

[29] Some commentators have rightly pointed out that this language is meant to broaden the notion of 'territorial State', in that it makes reference not only to 'a State's land territory, its territorial sea and the airspace over its land and sea territory' but also 'to territories under military occupation, to colonial territories and to territories over which a State has factual control'. In addition, this language would also cover 'certain maritime areas outside the territorial sea over which a State has a limited jurisdiction'. See J. H. Burges and H. Danielus, *The United Nations Convention against Torture* (Dordrecht/ Boston/London: Nijhoff, 1988), at 131.

[30] According to Art. 12: 'Each State party shall ensure that its competent authorities proceed to a prompt and impartial investigation, wherever there is a reasonable ground to believe that an act of torture has been committed *in any of the territory under its jurisdiction*' (emphasis added).

[31] The following Art. 13 provides: 'Each State party shall ensure that any individual who alleges he has been subjected to *torture in any territory under its jurisdiction* has the right to complain to and to have his case promptly and impartially examined by its competent authorities. Steps shall be taken to ensure that the complainant and witnesses are protected against ill-treatment or intimidation as a consequence of his complaint or any evidence given.' (Emphasis in both articles is added.)

[32] Art. 7 of the 1970 Hague Convention for the Suppression of Unlawful Seizure of Aircraft; Art. 7 of the 1971 Montreal Convention for the Suppression of Unlawful Acts against the Safety of Civil Aviation; Art. 7 of the 1973 Convention on the Prevention and Punishment of Crimes against Internationally Protected Persons, including Diplomatic Agents; Art. 8 of the 1979 Convention against the Taking of Hostages; Art. 10(1) of the 1988 Rome Convention for the Suppression of Unlawful Acts against the Safety of Maritime

to exercise discretionary powers, if he possesses any.[33] However, unlike the UN Torture Convention, states parties—including the territorial state—are not obliged to institute proceedings even if serious allegations are made or evidence is offered that offences prohibited by the Conventions were committed.

15.4 AN UNSATISFACTORY REGULATION

A general assessment of the relevant international rules on states' criminal jurisdiction over international crimes seems to lead to fairly pessimistic conclusions.

If one adopts the *Lotus* approach, the best one can state is that customary international law confines itself to authorizing states to exercise criminal jurisdiction, provided such exercise does not collide with existing rules and principles of international law. Clearly, this legal regulation is rather vague; in particular, it does not clarify which impediments under general international law may prevent the exercise of criminal jurisdiction by individual states, and it does not clarify to what extent, absent a treaty on the matter, states may exercise extraterritorial jurisdiction without breaching international principles or rules.

As for treaties, the normative system they establish in the field of national repression of international crimes is utterly unsatisfactory. First, existing treaties on the matter are few. In particular, treaties regulating the penal repression of some international crimes already prohibited by customary international law are lacking (this holds true for aggression crimes against humanity, and war crimes other than grave breaches of the 1949 Geneva Conventions). Hence, states are under no international obligation to establish criminal jurisdiction over these crimes, let alone to exercise it, even if they have a territorial link with them. Second, at least some of the treaties that contain provisions on criminal jurisdiction are badly in need of revision. Indeed, they have turned out to be unsuitable for achieving a truly effective repression of the international crimes over which they envisage national jurisdiction. This applies in particular to the Genocide Convention, which does not contain any provision on jurisdictional grounds and merely confines itself to imposing the obligation to exercise territorial jurisdiction. As far as the other treaties

---

Navigation; Art. 8(1) of the 1998 Convention for the Suppression of Terrorist Bombings; Art. 10(1) of the 1999 Convention for the Suppression of the Financing of Terrorism.

[33] With regard to the Hague Convention, see G. Guillaume, 'La Convention de la Haye du 16 décembre 1970 pour la répression de la capture illicite d'aéronefs', in AFDI (1970), at 50 ('L'obligation ainsi posée est quant à elle parfaitement claire: la décision de classement du dossier ne peut être prise par l'autorité de police. Celle-ci doit soumettre l'affaire au Parquet. Ce dernier prend sa décision dans les conditions fixées par le lois de l'Etat intéressé. Si cet Etat connaît le principe de l'opportunité des poursuites, le Parquet est donc libre d'engager de telles poursuites ou d'y renoncer'). With specific reference to all the relevant conventions on terrorism, see G. Guillaume, 'Terrorisme et droit international', in HR (1989), III, at 370, where the author stresses: '[L]es conventions fournissent un certain nombre d'indications utiles sur les conditions dans lesquelles les autorités compétentes pour l'exercice de l'action pénale doivent prendre leur décision. Ces autorités procèdent en premier lieu "conformément aux lois" de l'Etat de refuge [...] ou "selon une procédure conforme à la législation dudit Etat" [...] Par voie de conséquence, elles s'inspirent du principe de la légalité ou de celui de l'opportunité des poursuites, selon le droit interne applicable.' In addition, the author points out that the obligation to submit the case to the State's prosecuting authorities 'pèse sur tout Etat, partie aux conventions, sur le territoire duquel se trouve le délinquant. Elle joue dès lors que l'intéressé est découvert et qu'il n'est pas procédé à son extradition. En ce sens elle est absolue.' However, as he correctly underlines, 'il ne s'agit là que d'une obligation de soumettre l'affaire aux autorités qui ont compétence pour déclencher l'action pénale. Encore que ces autorités soient tenues les plus souvent de poursuivre, elles peuvent parfois ne pas le faire' (at 370).

are concerned, while they require (or at least expressly authorize) states to establish some specific grounds of jurisdiction, surprisingly they do not obligate the contracting states to exercise their jurisdiction, not even when there exists a territorial link with the crime (in that the crime has been perpetrated in their territory). This is the case for all conventions on terrorism. They confine themselves to requiring the custodial state to submit the case to its prosecuting authorities, unless it decides to extradite the accused; in addition, in the event the custodial state refrains from extraditing the accused, those conventions leave unaffected the discretionary nature of prosecution, whenever such discretion is provided for in national legislation. Furthermore, those conventions do not oblige the contracting state on whose territory the accused finds himself to detain him. Indeed, the obligation to arrest the accused applies only if the relevant contracting state considers that it should detain the accused. To put it differently, the conventions on terrorism do not impose a strict obligation, but simply provide for a discretionary power of the state to detain an accused who happens to be in its territory.

Things are different as far as the 1949 Geneva Conventions and the Convention on Torture are concerned. The latter, besides imposing (or authorizing) the adoption of the most common grounds of jurisdiction, at least obliges the territorial state to initiate investigations over acts of torture purportedly perpetrated on a territory subject to its jurisdiction, as well as to ensure that allegations of torture are brought before the competent courts. The Geneva Conventions go even further. They oblige all contracting states to exercise their criminal jurisdiction over grave breaches, and specify that jurisdiction should be exercised whatever the nationality of the alleged author of the grave breach. Arguably, the obligation to prosecute and punish, provided for in the Geneva Conventions, must be fulfilled in any case, regardless of the nature of the jurisdictional link between the grave breach and the state. However, the Geneva Conventions use broad language, and do not set out the universality principle in a clear and appropriate manner.

In sum, as far as the criminal repression of international crimes is concerned, the international community has opted for an approach that is both 'sectorial' (as opposed to a global approach intended to deal with all international crimes) and minimalist (in that it only settles some problems, eschews all the major issues, and in addition does not take a forward-looking attitude).

16

INTERNATIONAL VERSUS NATIONAL JURISDICTION

The establishment of international criminal courts has posed the tricky problem of how to coordinate their action with that of national courts: when both classes of courts are empowered to pronounce on the same crimes, which should take precedence, and under what conditions? Obviously, the problem does not arise in the area where those courts do not have *concurrent jurisdiction*; that is, with regard to crimes that fall under the exclusive jurisdiction of national courts (which is usually the case for domestic offences).

The problem only arises when one or more states may assert their criminal jurisdiction over a specific crime on the basis of one of the accepted heads of jurisdiction, as described above (see 15.2), and at the same time an international criminal court is empowered to adjudicate the same crime by virtue of its constitutive instrument. There are no rules of customary international law determinative of this matter, just as there are no customary international rules designed to resolve the question of concurrent jurisdiction of two or more states by giving pride of place to one legal ground of national jurisdiction (say, territoriality) over another such ground (say, active nationality). Though no treaty rules directly address the possible conflict of jurisdiction between states, conflicts between national and international criminal courts are addressed by the constitutive instruments of the relevant international criminal court.

These instruments also address the relationship between states and the relevant international criminal court in the matter of judicial cooperation. In particular, they lay down the powers of the relevant international criminal court to issue requests of cooperation to states as far as investigation, arrest and surrender of suspect, etc., are concerned, and lay down the corresponding obligations of states in this respect.

This chapter discusses the main models that have been established to regulate issues of concurrent jurisdiction of international and national criminal courts over certain international crimes. It also discusses the main models of states' judicial cooperation with international criminal courts adopted so far.

16.1 THE NUREMBERG SCHEME VERSUS THE ICC SCHEME

It may be useful to discuss the proper role to assign to an international criminal court vis-à-vis national courts. It would seem that two major models have so far been worked out.

One is that adopted in Nuremberg.[1] Under this scheme, an international criminal court is entrusted with the task of dealing with the major leaders accused of international

---

[1] This scheme was first drawn up in 1944 by an American officer (Lieutenant Colonel Murray C. Bernays, chief of the Special Projects Office of the Personnel Branch at the US War Department), was then refined by

crimes, whereas national courts are called upon to handle the criminal offences of minor culprits (after the Second World War, German criminal courts were requested to adjudicate upon crimes committed by Germans against other Germans, while national courts of the Allies pronounced on crimes perpetrated by Germans against foreign nationals).

Interestingly, the two ad hoc International Criminal Tribunals set up for the former Yugoslavia and Rwanda are based, on the principle of their primacy over national courts, as will be further discussed (16.2.1). In fact, at least initially, they were intended as a substitute for the national criminal courts of states deemed unable or unwilling to dispense justice. Nonetheless, from the outset the ICTR concentrated on military and civilian leaders, leaving to Rwandan courts the task of trying minor offenders. The ICTY, whose first prosecutor chose to focus on both major and minor offenders (perhaps because he did not distinguish from a prosecutorial perspective or for tactical reasons), gradually moved towards the Nuremberg scheme, in that *i*) it subsequently firmly decided to concentrate on major cases, concerning political and military leaders or other major defendants;[2] and *ii*) it has increasingly asked national courts of the states concerned to try lesser accused.[3]

A different division of labour is provided for in the Statute of the ICC. As emphasized in 16.3, all cases may be brought before national courts, whatever the magnitude of the crime or the status, rank, or importance of the accused. The ICC steps in only when such courts do not act, or prove unable or unwilling to do justice.

It would seem that the Nuremberg model still has much merit. It is logical and consistent for very serious international crimes allegedly perpetrated by leaders to be adjudicated by an international criminal court offering all the advantages outlined in 14.6. Trials held in the country where the crime has been committed or where the victims or their relatives live may arouse animosity and conflict; by the same token, it may turn out to be difficult for judges to remain impartial. In particular, when crimes are very serious and large scale (think, for example, of grave instances of genocide or crimes against humanity) and have been committed either by the central authorities or with their (tacit or explicit) approval

---

other staff, subsequently upheld by the US Secretary of War Henry L. Stimson, and finally accepted by the other three Great Powers in London in 1945.

[2] With respect to the last indictments of the ICTY, the Tribunals' Bureau (consisting of the President, the Vice-President, and the presiding judges), exercised a screening so as to exclude those that dealt with minor defendants. Under Rule 28(A), 'On receipt of an indictment for review from the Prosecutor, the Registrar shall consult with the President. The President shall refer the matter to the Bureau which shall determine whether the indictment, prima facie, concentrates on one or more of the most senior leaders suspected of being most responsible for crimes within the jurisdiction of the Tribunal. If the Bureau determines that the indictment meets this standard, the President shall designate one of the permanent Trial Chamber Judges for the review under Rule 47. If the Bureau determines that the indictment does not meet this standard, the President shall return the indictment to the Registrar to communicate this finding to the Prosecutor.'

In resolution 1329 (2000) the UN Security Council had taken 'note of the position expressed by the International Tribunals that civilian, military and paramilitary leaders should be tried before them in preference to minor actors'.

[3] See among other things the amended Rule 11 *bis* of the RPE. Under this provision, concerning 'Referral of the Indictment to Another Court':

(A) If an indictment has been confirmed, irrespective of whether or not the accused is in the custody of the Tribunal, the President may appoint a Trial Chamber for the purpose of referring a case to the authorities of a state (i) in whose territory the crime was committed; or (ii) in which the accused was arrested, so that those authorities should forthwith refer the case to the appropriate court for trial within that state.

(B) The Trial Chamber may order such referral *proprio motu* or at the request of the prosecutor, after having given to the prosecutor and, where applicable, the accused, the opportunity to be heard.

(C) In determining whether to refer the case in accordance with paragraph (A), the Trial Chamber shall, in accordance with Security Council Presidential Statement S/PRST/2002/21, consider the gravity of the crimes charged and the level of responsibility of the accused.

or acquiescence, it will be difficult for a national court to prosecute the alleged planner or perpetrators, unless there is a change in government. However, even if this is the case, there may be a risk of 'witch hunting' or of using the criminal courts for settling political accounts, a situation which cannot contribute to the fair and impartial administration of justice.[4] Hence, international criminal courts will often be better suited to pronounce upon large-scale and grave crimes allegedly perpetrated by political or military leaders. For such cases, the rule of complementarity laid down in the ICC Statute may appear to be questionable. However, since the draftsmen of the Statute have opted for that model, one can only hope that the Court will interpret and apply the relevant rules of the Statute in such a way as to assert the Court's jurisdiction whenever cases in that category are brought before the Court.[5]

16.2 THE PRIMACY OF INTERNATIONAL CRIMINAL COURTS WITH RESPECT TO NATIONAL JURISDICTIONS

16.2.1 ICTY AND ICTR

The Statutes of the ICTY and ICTR, at Articles 9 and 8 respectively, provide that each Tribunal shall have concurrent jurisdiction with national courts to prosecute persons for serious violations of IHL, but add in paragraph 2 that the Tribunal 'shall have primacy over national courts':

> At any stage of the procedure, the International Tribunal may formally request national courts to defer to the competence of the International Tribunal in accordance with the present Statute and the Rules of Procedure and Evidence [RPE] of the International Tribunal.

The reasons for proclaiming the Tribunals' primacy are clear. In the case of the former Yugoslavia, at the time of the establishment of the Tribunal, the still ongoing armed conflict among the successor states and the deep-seated animosity between the various ethnic and religious groups made national courts unlikely to be willing or able to conduct fair trials. It was considered that the authorities would have hesitated to bring their own people (Muslims, Croats, or Serbs) to book, whereas, had they initiated proceedings against their adversaries, probably such proceedings would have been highly biased, or at least perceived that way. As for other states, the experience built up until that time showed that they shied away from bringing to trial alleged perpetrators of crimes committed elsewhere. Hence the need was felt to affirm the overriding authority of the International Tribunal. Similar considerations held true for Rwanda, where in addition the national judicial system had collapsed and consequently seemed unable to render justice.

However, the Statutes do not specify under what conditions or how primacy is to be exercised. In his Report to the Security Council elaborating upon the draft Statute of the ICTY, the UN Secretary General simply stated that 'The details of how the primacy will be asserted shall be set out in the rules of procedure and evidence of the International

---

[4] At the same time, if the circumstances permit, there can be considerable merit to national systems bringing to justice their own leaders for international crimes.

[5] The first prosecutor of the ICC has adopted a policy of investigating and prosecuting only those most responsible when the court has jurisdiction, encouraging national jurisdictions to prosecute those having lesser responsibility in due course.

Tribunal' (§ 65). The judges of the ICTY skilfully drew up a set of rules on primacy in the RPE, which were subsequently taken up by the judges of the ICTR. These rules do not lay down the absolute primacy of the Tribunal; rather, they provide that the concurrent jurisdiction of the Tribunal and national courts may lead to the prevalence of national courts.

The RPE provides that at the request of the prosecutor the Tribunal may assert its primacy in three cases:

i) when a national prosecutor investigates an international crime or a national court conducts proceedings with regard to the criminal offence not as an international crime, but as an 'ordinary criminal offence' (for instance, genocide is being investigated or tried as 'multiple murder', or serious ill-treatment of prisoners of war is handled as 'assault', and not as a war crime). In this case, the classification of the offence as an ordinary crime presupposes a deliberate (or unconscious) proclivity to *misrepresent* the very nature, hence to *belittle the seriousness*, of international crimes. In other words, the national court shows that, either intentionally or unwittingly, it is not cognizant of both the international dimension and the gravity of the criminal offence;

ii) when a national court proves to be *unreliable*: this happens where it is proved, under Rule 9(ii) of the ICTY Rules, that there is 'a lack of impartiality or independence', or 'the investigations or proceedings are designed to shield the accused from international criminal responsibility', or else 'the case is not diligently prosecuted'. Clearly, in all these instances national authorities may not be trusted because they are intent on 'protecting' the accused or else take a patently persecutory attitude to him;

iii) when, although the relevant national court appears to be reliable and able to conduct a fair trial, nonetheless the case is *closely related, or may be relevant, to other cases* being tried by the International Tribunal. Under Rule 9(iii), 'what is in issue is closely related to, or otherwise involves, significant factual or legal questions which may have implications for investigations or prosecutions before the Tribunal'. Plainly, these cases are of such overriding significance, or general import or wide ramifications, that it appears appropriate for them to be brought before an international court.[6]

By and large, the scheme adopted by the judges of the ICTY and of the ICTR seems wisely to reconcile the need not to overload international institutions with relatively minor cases, leaving them to national courts, with the demands of state sovereignty in criminal matters. In addition, the approach takes into account the requirement that international criminal courts and tribunals should replace national institutions when these prove unreliable or unfair, and should as a general matter deal with major international crimes of relevance to the international community as a whole.

So far the two Tribunals have occasionally relied upon their primacy.[7]

---

[6] Interestingly the first two exceptions are also exceptions for *non bis in idem* (or in other words, prohibition of double jeopardy), and therefore can be justified by reference to the Statute's provisions on *non bis in idem*. (There is a clear parallel between conditions for exercising primacy and *non bis in* the sense that what justifies the court retrying an accused are surely also grounds for taking over the proceedings before they have reached their conclusion.) Exception (3) reflects a pragmatic approach and was designed to protect the integrity of cases selected by the ICTY. If an international criminal court and a national jurisdiction simultaneously prosecute cases with overlapping evidence and witnesses, both cases are likely to suffer, even if both jurisdictions are well intentioned. This provision insures, then, that ICTY cases will not be unintentionally undermined by prosecutors pursuing closely related cases.

[7] See e.g. the *Tadić* case, as far as the ICTY is concerned: on 8 November 1994 the ICTY made a request for deferral to the Federal Republic of Germany, whose authorities were investigating Tadić's alleged crimes; Germany immediately complied with the request and surrendered the accused to the Tribunal: see *Tadić*

The Rules also provide that the Tribunals may divest themselves of a case when they consider that the case may more appropriately be tried by a national court (Rule 11 *bis* of the ICTY and ICTR). Thus, judges worked out a mechanism whereby a case could be referred back to national courts whenever they deemed it appropriate. The two ad hoc Tribunals have emphasized the importance of national courts dealing with the crimes falling under their jurisdiction. There seem to be three grounds behind this new trend. First, national courts of the states concerned (those of the successors to the former Yugoslavia, and Rwanda) are now better structured, more efficient, and less prone to bias. Second, the workload of the two international Tribunals has increased and it therefore proves appropriate for national courts gradually to share the burden and even start to take over the job from the Tribunals, the more so in light of the so-called 'completion strategy' adopted by the UN Security Council for the two ad hoc Tribunals and aimed at closing down their activity in a few years. A number of cases have indeed been passed on by the ICTY to the War Crimes Chamber of the High Court in Bosnia and Herzegovina, as well as to courts in Croatia and Serbia[8] and by the ICTR to France and Rwanda.[9] Third, there is a normative argument in favour of national prosecutions. There is a growing recognition that the goals of prosecuting international crimes can sometimes be better served when the prosecutions occur in the states where the crimes happened or when national leaders responsible for crimes are called to account by their own people.

16.2.2 SCSL AND STL

While the ICTY and the ICTR enjoy primacy over any national court, the SCSL and the STL have been granted primacy only over the courts of Sierra Leone and Lebanon, respectively.[10]

It follows that these two Tribunals do not enjoy any primacy over national courts of *other* states, for which the Tribunal's Statute is a *res inter alios acta* (a legal instrument

---

(*Deferral to the competence of Tribunal*). See also the order of 4 October 2002 in *Republic of Macedonia* (*Prosecutor's Request for Deferral and Motion for Order to the Former Yugoslav Republic of Macedonia*), §§ 6–53.

[8] In his statement to the UN Security Council of 18 June 2007, in dealing with the referral of cases involving intermediate and lower-ranking accused to competent national jurisdictions by the International Tribunal (as authorized by Security Council resolution 1534 of 2004 and stipulated under Rule 11 *bis* of the Rules), the ICTY President pointed out that the impact of the referrals already processed on the overall workload of the International Tribunal had been substantial: 'Ten accused have been transferred to the Special War Crimes Chamber of Bosnia and Herzegovina, two accused have been transferred for trial before the domestic courts of Croatia, and one accused has been transferred to Serbia for trial. Only two accused remain to have their transfer finalized. Of the cases referred by the International Tribunal, two trial proceedings have been completed by the Sarajevo Special War Crimes Chamber. The International Tribunal is satisfied that the trials of both of these accused respected international norms of due process. Unfortunately, one of the accused convicted and sentenced to 20 years' imprisonment, Radovan Stanković, escaped from the custody of the Bosnia and Herzegovina authorities on 25 May 2007. The International Tribunal is extremely concerned about this escape and has requested a full report from the Bosnia and Herzegovina authorities. The International Tribunal is hopeful that those authorities, and other states, will do all in their power to return Stanković to custody. A failure to do so may impact upon the future integrity of the 11 *bis* referral process. With respect to the *Ademi and Norac* case referred to Croatia on 14 September 2005, the trial which has suffered some delays is expected to commence today, 18 June and I hope that it will proceed expeditiously.'

[9] For many years, the ICTR refused to refer any cases to Rwanda, finding that its courts were not yet adequately established and could not guarantee adequate fairness to the accused. On 28 June 2011, a Trial Chamber of the ICTR decided that the prosecution of Jean Uwinkindi could be transferred to Rwanda.

[10] Under Art. 8(2) of the SCSL Statute, 'The Special Court shall have primacy over the national courts of Sierra Leone. At any stage of the procedure, the SCSL may formally request a national court to defer to its

made by others and only binding upon others), with the consequence that: *i)* in principle those national courts may bring to trial persons who stand accused before one of the International Tribunals without breaching the Statute; *ii)* the International Tribunal may not oblige the relevant national court to defer to its jurisdiction; *iii)* the International Tribunal may not issue to state officials of third states or to third states as such, binding requests for judicial cooperation (for instance, for the carrying out of searches or seizures to gather evidence, for allowing or enabling a witness to be questioned, for the apprehension of a suspect).

These drawbacks would seem to be less serious in the case of the STL, because the provisions contained in its Statute have entered into force by virtue of a legally binding Security Council (resolution 1757 of 2007) passed on the strength of Chapter VII of the UN Charter. It would follow that, in principle, no member state of the UN may refuse to acknowledge the existence and functioning of the STL and should cooperate with it, by virtue of the general duty of cooperation with UN organs (or bodies set up by the UN or upon its authorization) underlying UN membership.

On the other hand, when a trial against one of the persons falling under one of the two International Tribunals' jurisdiction is held in a 'third' country, the ban on *ne bis in idem* (or double jeopardy) does not apply, for the SCSL and the STL may again try that person if the national trial did not prove to be fair and effective.[11]

16.3 THE COMPLEMENTARITY OF THE ICC

In contrast, the coordination of concurrent jurisdiction between the ICC and national courts over a specific case is based on the principle of complementarity.

competence in accordance with the [...]Statute and the Rules of Procedure and Evidence.' Under Art. 4 of its Statute the STL has primacy over Lebanese courts. Art. 4 provides as follows:

> '1. The Special Tribunal and the national courts of Lebanon shall have concurrent jurisdiction. Within its jurisdiction, the Tribunal shall have primacy over the national courts of Lebanon.
>
> 2. Upon the assumption of office of the Prosecutor, as determined by the Secretary-General, and no later than two months thereafter, the Special Tribunal shall request the national judicial authority seized with the case of the attack against Prime Minister Rafiq Hariri and others to defer to its competence. The Lebanese judicial authority shall refer to the Tribunal the results of the investigation and a copy of the court's records, if any. Persons detained in connection with the investigation shall be transferred to the custody of the Tribunal.
>
> 3. (a) At the request of the Special Tribunal, the national judicial authority seized with any of the other crimes committed between 1 October 2004 and 12 December 2005, or a later date decided pursuant to Article 1, shall refer to the Tribunal the results of the investigation and a copy of the court's records, if any, for review by the Prosecutor;
>
> (b) At the further request of the Tribunal, the national authority in question shall defer to the competence of the Tribunal. It shall refer to the Tribunal the results of the investigation and a copy of the court's records, if any, and persons detained in connection with any such case shall be transferred to the custody of the Tribunal;
>
> (c) The national judicial authorities shall regularly inform the Tribunal of the progress of their investigation. At any stage of the proceedings, the Tribunal may formally request a national judicial authority to defer to its competence.'

[11] Under Art. 9(2) of the SCSL Statute, 'A person who has been tried by a national court for the acts referred to in articles 2 to 4 of the present Statute may be subsequently tried by the Special Court if: (a) The act for which he or she was tried was characterized as an ordinary crime; or (b) The national court proceedings were not impartial or independent, were designed to shield the accused from international criminal responsibility or the case was not diligently prosecuted.'

Under Art. 5(2) of the STL Statute, 'A person who has been tried by a national court may be subsequently tried by the Special Tribunal if the national court proceedings were not impartial or independent, were designed to shield the accused from criminal responsibility for crimes within the jurisdiction of the Tribunal or the case was not diligently prosecuted.'

This principle is laid down in paragraph 10 of the Preamble, as well as in Article 1 of the ICC Statute (whereby the ICC 'shall be complementary to national criminal jurisdictions') and is spelled out in Articles 15, 17, 18, and 19. In short, the Court is *barred from exercising its jurisdiction over a case*, and must declare it inadmissible whenever a national court asserts its jurisdiction over the same person(s) for the same crime and *i*) under its national law the state has jurisdiction; and *ii*) the case is being duly investigated or prosecuted by its authorities or these authorities have decided, in a proper manner, not to prosecute the person concerned (see Article 17). In addition, the Court *iii*) may not prosecute and try a person who has already been convicted of or acquitted by another court with respect to the same conduct, if the trial was fair and proper (Article 20(3)).[12]

The Court is nonetheless authorized to exercise its jurisdiction over a case, even if it is pending before national authorities, and thus to override national criminal jurisdiction, whenever the state is unable or unwilling genuinely to carry out the investigation or prosecution, or its decision not to prosecute the person concerned has resulted from its unwillingness or inability genuinely to prosecute that person.

The question, of course, arises as to what is meant by 'unwillingness' or 'inability' of a state to prosecute or try a person accused or suspected of international crimes. It is important to note that this question arises *only* if the state undertakes an investigation or prosecution. If the state chooses not to investigate or prosecute, for whatever reason, then the case is admissible before the ICC.[13]

These two notions of 'unwillingness' or 'inability' are spelled out in Article 17(2) and (3). A state may be considered as '*unwilling*' when: *i*) in fact the national authorities have undertaken proceedings for the purpose of shielding the person concerned from criminal responsibility; or *ii*) there has been an 'unjustified delay' in the proceedings showing that in fact the authorities do not intend to bring the person concerned to justice; or *iii*) the proceedings are not being conducted independently or impartially or in any case in a manner showing the intent to bring the person to justice. A state is '*unable*' when, chiefly on account of a total or partial collapse of its judicial system, it is not in a position: *i*) to detain the accused or to have him surrendered by the authorities or bodies that hold him in custody; or *ii*) to collect the necessary evidence; or *iii*) to carry out criminal proceedings. One should also add cases where the national court is unable to try a person not because of a collapse or malfunctioning of the judicial system, but on account of legislative impediments, such as an amnesty law, or a statute of limitations, making it impossible for the national judge to commence proceedings against the suspect or the accused.

Complementarity applies not only with regard to the states parties to the ICC Statute but also with respect to states not parties (see Article 18(1)). Thus, for instance, if the national of a state not party (A) has committed an international crime on the territory of a state party (B) and then escapes to another state not party (C), and this state asserts its jurisdiction on the ground that the crime is provided for in an international treaty and the suspect is present on its territory (the *forum deprehensionis* principle) or on the ground of universality, the ICC may not exercise jurisdiction if it is proved that state C is willing and able to conduct a proper and fair trial.

Complementarity applies whatever the trigger mechanism of the Court's proceedings; that is, both when the case *i*) has been brought to the Court by a state party (Articles 13(a) and 14); or *ii*) has been initiated by the prosecutor *motu proprio*, and the prosecutor has been authorized by the Pre-Trial Chamber to commence a criminal investigation

---

[12] Art. 17 also contains a requirement that cases brought before the ICC be 'of sufficient gravity' to be admissible.

[13] *Katanga and Ngudjolo (Admissibility Appeal).*

(Articles 13(c) and 15), and when *iii*) it is the UN Security Council that has referred to the Court a 'situation in which one or more of [...the] crimes [falling under the Court's jurisdiction] appears to have been committed' (Articles 13(b) and 52(c)).

The complementarity of the ICC with respect to national courts has its own merits.

First, it avoids the Court being flooded with cases from all over the world. The Court, having a limited number of judges and limited financial resources and infrastructure, would be unable to cope with a broad range of cases. It is healthy to leave the vast majority of cases concerning international crimes to national courts, which may properly exercise their jurisdiction based on a link with the case (territoriality, nationality), or even on universality. Among other things, these national courts may be in a better position to collect the necessary evidence and to lay their hands on the accused. Second, complementarity is a principle more attuned to state sovereignty. Finally, if national courts are able to prosecute themselves, such an approach could better achieve the goals of accountability.

16.4 JUDICIAL COOPERATION OF STATES WITH INTERNATIONAL CRIMINAL COURTS

For international criminal courts, state cooperation is crucial to the effectiveness of judicial process. Only other bodies or entities, that is, national authorities or international organizations, can enforce the decisions, orders, and requests of such courts. International, unlike domestic criminal courts, have *no enforcement agencies* at their disposal: without the assistance of other authorities, they cannot seize evidentiary material, compel witnesses to give testimony, search the scenes where crimes have allegedly been committed, or execute arrest warrants. For all these purposes, international criminal courts must turn primarily to state authorities and request them to take action to assist the courts' officers and investigators. Without the help of these authorities, international criminal courts cannot operate.

Admittedly, this holds true for all international institutions, which need the support of states to be able to operate. However, international criminal courts are much more in need of such support, and more urgently, because their action has a direct impact on individuals living on the territory of sovereign states and subject to their jurisdiction. Trials must be expeditious; evidence must be collected before it becomes stale; international criminal courts must be able to summon witnesses to testify at short notice. The greatest challenge of the international criminal justice system is to establish, sometimes in unfriendly or chaotic environments, modalities in which both the prosecution and the defence have a reasonable opportunity to collect evidence and to obtain the arrest and surrender of persons accused. This was a not a major problem for the post-Second World War International Military Tribunals, whose investigations were conducted by authorities possessing, by way of military occupation of Germany and Japan, full enforcement powers.

16.4.1 MODELS OF STATE COOPERATION

In deciding upon how to regulate the cooperation of states with an international criminal court, one may choose between two possible models: the 'horizontal' and the 'vertical' model, as the ICTY Appeals Chamber put it in *Blaškić* (*Subpoena*) (§§ 47 and 54).

Under the former model the relations between states and the international criminal court are shaped on the pattern of interstate judicial cooperation in criminal matters.

As aptly stated by a distinguished commentator,[14] *interstate judicial cooperation and assistance* shows the following hallmarks: *i*) it has a consensual basis, being grounded on treaty relations; *ii*) treaties normally require that the offence for which extradition is requested be considered such in both the requesting and the requested state; *iii*) often treaties provide for exceptions to extradition, relating to certain offences (for example, political or fiscal offences) or to some categories of persons (for instance, nationals of the requested state), or for some sentences (for instance, extradition is often excluded when the requesting state may impose the death penalty); *iv*) extradition may be refused also when the requested state can assert its jurisdiction over the offence; *v*) judicial assistance or cooperation may normally be refused on grounds of security, public order, overriding national interests, etc.; *vi*) as a rule the collection of evidence, search, and other investigatory actions requested by a state may not be undertaken by the authorities of that state, but only by those of the requested state, through the system of 'letters rogatory'; normally a foreign country may not enter into direct contact with individuals subject to the sovereignty of the requested state.

If this model is applied to international criminal courts, it follows that the court has no superior authority over states except for the legal power to adjudicate crimes perpetrated by individuals subject to state sovereignty. Otherwise, the international court cannot in any way force states to lend their cooperation, let alone exercise coercive powers within the territory of sovereign states.

The second model could be termed 'vertical' or 'supra-state'. It departs from the traditional setting of state-to-state judicial cooperation, where by definition all cooperating states are on an equal footing. This more progressive scheme presupposes that the international judicial body is vested with sweeping powers not only vis-à-vis individuals subject to the sovereign authority of states, but also towards states themselves. The international criminal court is now empowered to issue binding orders to states and, in case of non-compliance, may set in motion enforcement mechanisms. What is no less important, the international criminal court is given the final say on evidentiary matters: states are not allowed to withhold evidence on grounds of self-defined national interests or to refuse to execute arrest warrants or other courts' orders. In short, the international court is endowed with an authority over states that markedly differentiates it from other international institutions.

16.4.2 JUDICIAL COOPERATION OF STATES WITH THE ICTY AND ICTR

A. Rules and Practice

The ICTY was charged with investigating ongoing crimes in territories still in the throes of a bitter armed conflict. The Security Council conferred powers appropriate to the situation, imposing a broad, open-ended obligation on States to 'cooperate fully with the International Tribunal and its organs in accordance with the present resolution [i.e. the one establishing the ICTY] and the Statute', and to 'take any measures necessary under their domestic law to implement the provisions of the [...] resolution and the Statute'.[15] Article 29(1) of the ICTY Statute reiterates that states 'shall cooperate with the International

---

[14] See the excellent paper by B. Swart, 'International Cooperation and Judicial Assistance—General Problems', in Cassese, Gaeta, and Jones, *ICC Commentary*, II (1592–1805), at 1590–2, on which the present discussion heavily relies.

[15] S/RES/827, § 4. According to one questionable decision, this obligation could not bind non-member states of the United Nations, such as the Vatican: *Bagosora and others* (*Decision on Defence Motion to Obtain*

Tribunal in the investigation and prosecution of persons accused of committing serious violations of international humanitarian law'. Trial Chambers are expressly endowed with authority under Article 29(2) to issue orders pursuant to this obligation, 'including, but not limited to' locating, arresting, or transferring persons; taking testimony; producing evidence; and serving documents. The ICTY's mandate, as the Appeals Chamber later affirmed, would be frustrated if it could not require states 'to investigate crimes, collect evidence, summon witnesses and have indictees arrested and surrendered to the International Tribunal'.[16] Precisely the same language was adopted for the ICTR.[17]

The powers of the ICTY and ICTR, and the corresponding obligations of states, fall well within the range of incursions on state sovereignty that had previously been deemed appropriate by the Security Council 'to maintain or restore international peace and security'.[18] The 'novel and unique'[19] feature of this arrangement, however, was that the two Tribunals were endowed with a relatively broad authority that would normally be exercised by the Security Council itself. The most commonly requested measures at the investigation stage are the disclosure of documents presumed to be in a state's possession,[20] and assistance to compel or authorize a reluctant potential witness to meet with the requesting party.[21] An ICTY Chamber has even gone so far as to issue a 'temporary restraining order' to a state, requiring it to 'cease and desist' actions against a member of a defence team, and to 'stop all searches of records and computers' already seized from that person.[22] A party seeking such orders from a Trial Chamber must normally first address a request for assistance to the state concerned, make all reasonable attempts to secure voluntary cooperation, and only then seek an order from a Chamber under Article 29.

What happens if a state refuses to cooperate? Though ICTY Trial Chamber decisions can prescribe obligations, sanctions for state non-compliance are a matter purely for the Security Council, to which the Tribunal's President may make a report of non-compliance (*Blaškić (Subpoena)*, § 36). The Security Council itself has never gone beyond publicly condemning the states concerned, but compulsive measures were sometimes taken by other international organizations. International forces stationed in Bosnia and Croatia pursuant to the Dayton Peace Agreement, for example, actively assisted ICTY investigators, including making arrests and conducting raids to secure documents.[23] These forces

---

Cooperation from the Vatican). See also *Milošević Slobodan and others (Decision on Review of Indictment and Application for Consequential Orders)* § 23.

[16] *Blaškić (Subpoena)* § 26.

[17] S/RES/955 (1994), § 4; ICTR Statute, Art. 28.

[18] UN Charter, Art. 39. See *Tadić (Interlocutory Appeal)*, AC, § 38 ('Its binding force derives from the provisions of Chapter VII and Article 25 of the United Nations Charter and from the Security Council resolution adopted pursuant to these provisions.')

[19] *Blaskić (Subpoena)* § 26.

[20] *Karadžić (Decision on the Accused's Application for Binding Order Pursuant to Rule 54 bis (Federal Republic of Germany)); Gotovina and others (Decision on the Prosecution's Application for an Order Pursuant to Rule 54 bis Directing the Government of the Republic of Croatia to Produce Documents or Information); Karemera and others (Decision on Joseph Nzirorera's Motion for Cooperation of the Government of Rwanda: RPF Archives).* The modalities for seeking documents are now codified in Rule 54 *bis* of the ICTY Rules.

[21] *Bizimungu and others (Decision on Mr. Bicamumpaka's Request for an Order for the Cooperation of the Republic of France); Bagosora and others (Decision on Bagosora's Request to Obtain the Cooperation of the Republic of Ghana).*

[22] *Gotovina and others (Requests for Temporary Restraining Orders Directed to the Public of Croatia and Reasons for the Chamber's Order of 11 December 2009)*, §1.

[23] *Kordić and Čerkez (Decision Stating Reasons for Trial Chamber's Ruling of 1 June 1999 Rejecting Defence Motion to Suppress Evidence)* describing a search of VRS military archives by ICTY investigators backed by SFOR in Bosnia on 23 September 1998; *Mrkšić and others (Decision on the Motion for Release by the Accused Slavko Dokmanović)*, § 10, describing the arrest of the accused by UN soldiers, but being given his advice of rights by an OTP investigator.

were not acting as agents of, or pursuant to, any direct obligation imposed by the ICTY itself; they acted voluntarily in territory where they exercised authority pursuant to the relevant Security Council resolutions and the Dayton Peace Agreement.[24] These measures demonstrated concretely, if there was any doubt, that the ICTY was not required to obtain the consent of the states of the former Yugoslavia in order to conduct its activities.

That same principle applies in respect of activities that do not require the exercise of any police power, such as voluntary interviews with witnesses, inspecting locations, video-link testimony, or even serving documents. The ICTY Appeals Chamber has drawn a distinction between the states of the former Yugoslavia, whose authorization is not required for such activities, and other states, who are permitted by legislation to require that such activities be conducted only with permission. These states are nevertheless prohibited from 'shielding behind their national law in order to evade international obligations'.[25]

Another remarkable principle established by the Chambers of the ICTY and ICTR is that orders and subpoenas can be directed to, and create legal obligations for, individuals. A subpoena is an order requiring a person to do something, or face punishment. Such orders have been obtained at the ICTY to compel a person to submit to an interview, or to appear in person before the Tribunal as a witness. The capacity to issue such orders has been found to arise from an 'incidental and ancillary jurisdiction over individuals [...] who may be of assistance in the task of dispensing criminal justice'.[26] Subpoenas have even been sought for sitting ministers of state, although an attempt to compel an interview with, and the appearance of, Tony Blair while he was still Prime Minister failed on the merits.[27] As a practical matter, state cooperation will often be a precondition for enforcement of any penalties arising from non-compliance with the order. France recently set back the principle of state cooperation by refusing to execute an arrest warrant for a former employee of the Office of the Prosecutor of the ICTY who had been convicted of contempt for the improper disclosure of confidential information.

Despite these various avenues of direct action, there is often no substitute for active state assistance. Any investigative act that cannot safely be performed without the assistance of police officers, or in relation to documents, things, or people under direct state control (such as government archives, prisoners, or officials who have been instructed not to answer questions because of an asserted duty of confidentiality towards the state), requires active state cooperation. The execution of search and arrest warrants, leaving

---

[24] *Simić and others (Decision on Motion for Judicial Assistance to be Provided by SFOR and others)*, §§ 39–45 (describing relationship between ICTY and SFOR in respect of arrests); P. Gaeta, 'Is NATO Authorized or Obliged to Arrest Persons Indicted by the International Criminal Tribunal for the Former Yugoslavia?', in 9 EJIL (1998), 174–81. The argument that SFOR was not bound by an obligation to arrest accused or otherwise assist the Tribunal under Art. 29 rests on lack of exclusive territorial control in Bosnia. That reasoning would not apply in respect of the temporary international administrations in Eastern Slavonia and Kosovo, for example.

[25] *Blaškić (Subpoena)* §§ 52–7. C. del Ponte, *Madame Prosecutor* (New York: Other Press, 2009), at 146–7 ('The senior trial attorneys and I dispatched lawyers and investigators to Serbia and Montenegro to knock on doors of military, police and political figures who, our research showed, would have had knowledge about key events: a surprising number agreed to provide information').

[26] *Blaškić (Subpoena)* § 47; *Bagosora and others (Decision on Request for Subpoena of Major General Yaache and Cooperation of the Republic of Ghana)*, § 4 ('the Chamber has incidental and ancillary jurisdiction over persons, other than an accused, that may assist the Tribunal in its pursuit of criminal justice').

[27] *Bagosora and others (Decision on Request for a Subpoena)*, compelling the appearance of Marcel Gatsinzi, then the Minister of Defence for Rwanda; *Milošević Slobodan (Decision on Assigned Counsel Application for Interview and Testimony of Tony Blair and Gerhard Schröder)*, TC; *Krstić (Decision on Application for Subpoenas)*, ICTY, AC, § 27.

aside the exceptional involvement of international forces in Croatia and Bosnia, can usually only be performed with state assistance. The political dimension of securing state cooperation cannot be overstated. Substantial financial aid and the prospect of membership in the EU for the states of the former Yugoslavia were important catalysts towards fuller cooperation with the ICTY.[28] A former prosecutor has written that the Tribunal's lack of direct enforcement authority 'ineluctably forces the tribunal into the realm of politics […] During my eight years in The Hague, I dedicated the bulk of my time to mustering political pressure upon States like Serbia and Croatia to comply with their international obligations.'[29] These efforts, combined with domestic developments, eventually did lead to very substantial, if not always enthusiastic, cooperation in the former Yugoslavia. All 161 persons indicted by the ICTY were ultimately arrested.

B. Main Feature of the Judicial Cooperation Model Under the ICTY and ICTR Scheme

The ICTY and the ICTR incarnate the coercive 'supra-state' model, both because they act under the authority of the mandate conferred to them by the Security Council under Chapter VII of the UN Charter, and on account of the practice developed by judges.

It is apparent from the provisions of the ICTY Statute as developed and spelled out by the Appeals Chamber in *Blaškić* (*Subpoena*) that the relations between the ICTY (and the ICTR) and states are shaped as follows.

First, the Statutes of the Tribunals impose upon states an obligation to cooperate. This obligation is at the same time sweeping (for it embraces any matter where the Tribunal may need the cooperation of a state), and strict (for it is assisted by the sanctioning powers of the SC in case of non-compliance by a state). Second, it follows from that obligation that states are not allowed to rely upon such traditional clauses for refusing cooperation or extradition as 'double criminality', political offence, nationality of the person requested for surrender, etc. Third, the Tribunal is endowed with broad and binding powers, for it can issue binding orders to states (for the handing over of evidence, arrest of suspects, etc.), or *subpoenas* to individuals acting in a private capacity. Fourth, although states may invoke national security concerns as a ground for refusing the transmission of documents and other evidence, this is subject to strict limitations, and the Tribunal may have the final say on the matter (see *Blaškić* (*Subpoena*), §§ 61–9). Fifth, the collection of evidence may be carried out by the authorities of the relevant state, but the Tribunal's prosecutor is authorized to undertake investigations and gather evidence directly (that is, without going through the official channels) on the territory of the states of the former Yugoslavia, as well as on the territory of those states which have passed implementing legislation authorizing such Tribunal's activity (see *Blaškić* (*Subpoena*), §§ 53–4). Sixth, in case of non-compliance by a state with the obligation to cooperate stemming from the Statutes, the Tribunals may make a judicial finding of failure to cooperate, and the President is then authorized to submit it to the UN Security Council. This body, according to *Blaškić* (*Subpoena*), §§ 36–7, is then legally bound by that finding; that is, it may not contest that that particular state has indeed failed to cooperate, as found by the Tribunal (the Security Council is, however, free to take, or not to take, sanctions); if it is an individual who fails to cooperate, the Tribunal may hold him in contempt and initiate contempt proceedings, even in absentia (*Blaškić* (*Subpoena*), §§ 57–60).

---

[28] See C. Gosnell, 'The Changing Context of Evidential Rules', in K. Khan, C. Buisman, and C. Gosnell (eds), *Principles of Evidence in International Criminal Justice* (Oxford: Oxford University Press, 2010), at 220–1 (describing the 'autonomous dynamic of cooperation' that emerged in the states of the former Yugoslavia and the steep increase in documentary and other evidence being generated between 1996 and 2006).

[29] Del Ponte, cit. n. 25, at 41–2.

The mechanisms the Appeals Chamber set out in *Blaškić* (*Subpoena*) have subsequently been codified in ICTY Rule 54(D–I).

16.4.3 JUDICIAL COOPERATION OF STATES WITH THE ICC

A. Rules and Practice

The ICC Statute, despite superficial similarities with the ICTY and ICTR Statutes, reflects a somewhat weaker model of state cooperation. Article 86 states that 'State Parties shall, in accordance with the provisions of this Statute, cooperate fully with the Court in the investigation and prosecution of crimes' within its jurisdiction. However, the obligation to cooperate arises only from 'requests' that fall within a form of cooperation specifically enumerated in Part IX of the ICC Statute. Although the forms of cooperation enumerated in Article 93 are broad and cover the needs of most investigations, states are theoretically permitted to prohibit any non-enumerated form of cooperation.[30] In other words, the ICC would have no ground for complaint if a state passed a law prohibiting any form of cooperation not expressly enumerated in Article 93, as long as that was a rule of general application in its legal system. There is no residual obligation to cooperate and no scope for judicial expansion based upon unforeseen circumstances: unless it is enumerated, it may be prohibited.

The ICC prosecutor may take direct action (that is, bypass the usual obligation of making 'requests') in only two circumstances. First, where a state party is 'clearly unable to execute a request for cooperation due to the unavailability of any authority or any component of its judicial system competent to execute the request'. This provision is not addressed to the case of a non-cooperative state, but rather to a situation where the apparatus of the state has broken down or been displaced by rebel force.[31] This provision requires inability and unavailability, not *unwillingness*. The Pre-Trial Chamber is even required, if possible, to have regard to the views of the state concerned. Second, under Article 99(4) (which itself falls within Part IX and is therefore predicated on a 'request' being made to the state party) the prosecutor, without judicial authorization, may execute a request that does not require 'compulsory measures' under three conditions: *i*) the act is 'necessary for the successful execution' of the request; *ii*) the act does not 'prejudice [...] other Articles in this Part"'; and *iii*) 'all possible consultations' have been made with the state. An interview with a willing witness in the absence of state authorities is cited as an example of the type of measure envisioned. The provision is ambiguous to the extent that 'requests' are supposed to provide '[a]s much detailed information as possible',[32] whereas Article 99(4) requires only 'possible' consultations.[33] Although the prosecutor need not

---

[30] ICC Statute, Art. 93(1)(l): 'States Parties shall [...] comply with requests by the Court to provide the following assistance in relation to investigations or prosecutions: [...] (l) Any other type of assistance which is not prohibited by the law of the requested State'.

[31] ICC Statute, Art. 57(3)(d). ICC Statute, Art. 87(6) also authorizes the court to ask intergovernmental organizations for 'forms of cooperation and assistance which may be agreed upon [...] and which are in accordance with its competence and mandate'.

[32] ICC Statute, Art. 96(2)(b) (requests 'shall, as applicable, contain or be supported by [...] [a]s much detailed information as possible about the location or identification of any person [...] that must be found or identified in order for the assistance sought to be provided').

[33] Art. 99(4) also requires that the request be to a state party where the alleged crime was committed. One potential answer is that the 'request' can be stated vaguely enough so as to conceal the identity of the person to be interviewed. The collision of statutory language—insisting on a request, but restricting consultations to those that are 'possible'—may ultimately need to be resolved by judicial decision. See C. Kress and K. Prost, 'Article 99', in Triffterer (*ICC Commentary*, 2008), at 1627–8.

seek prior judicial approval, states parties are expressly authorized under Regulation 108 of the ICC Regulations to challenge the action, either before or after its execution, before a Pre-Trial Chamber.[34] The mere existence of this provision suggests that the action may need to be disclosed to the state first, at least with enough particularity to permit a challenge pursuant to Regulation 108. None of these constraints binds the prosecutors of the ICTY, ICTR, and STL, who are authorized under their Statutes to 'conduct on-site investigations' and who 'may, as appropriate, seek the assistance of the State authorities concerned'.[35] Furthermore, employees of the ad hoc tribunal benefit from the full set of immunities accorded to United Nations employees, whereas the immunity of ICC staff depends either on the state agreeing to the separate ICC convention on immunities, or upon a grant of immunity by the Security Council.[36]

The ICC's request-based cooperation model, and the rather narrow exceptions thereto, epitomize a broader tension within the ICC Statute between the 'vertical' and 'horizontal' models of judicial cooperation. The ICC Statute was a product of inter-state negotiations and reflects a far greater solicitude for the prerogatives of states. States, for example, have the right to reject requests for the production of information relating to their national security, whereas at the ICTY and the ICTR this consideration is, at least formally, a matter for the Chambers to assess.[37] A further shortcoming is the absence of any express obligation of states to transfer a witness to appear before the ICC, although they are required to comply with requests for the 'taking of evidence, including testimony under oath' (ICC Statute, Art. 93(1)(b)). The more likely view, which would accord with the dominant practice in the inter-state context, is that states may be obliged to compel the appearance of a witness on its own territory (for example, for a video-link appearance or deposition), but need not compel a transfer outside of its territory.[38]

The prosecutors and investigators of the ICC, to say nothing of their colleagues on the defence, find themselves operating within weaker, and therefore sometimes more challenging, legal frameworks than their counterparts at the ICTY and ICTR. On the other hand, a referral by the state itself normally implies that it wishes to cooperate fully, and a Security Council referral usually imposes obligations of cooperation independent of the ICC Statute, such as in the case of the parties to the conflict in Darfur and of Libya. These Security Council resolutions have required the addressees to 'cooperate fully and provide any necessary assistance'—language that is virtually identical to that used in Security Council Resolution 827 establishing the ICTY.[39] However, the precise extent of these additional obligations remains unclear, and it may be hoped that future SC resolutions

[34] ICC Regulations of the Court, Regulation 108(1)–(2): 'In case of a dispute regarding the legality of a request for cooperation under article 93, a requested State may apply for a ruling from the competent Chamber […] In case of request under article 99, paragraph 4, and should no further consultations be possible, the requested State may seek a ruling within 15 days from the day on which the requests State is informed or became aware of the direct execution.'

[35] ICTY Statute, Art. 18(2); ICTR Statute, Art. 17(2). The wording of the STL Statute, Art. 11(5), is slightly different: 'the Prosecutor shall, as appropriate, be assisted by the Lebanese authorities'.

[36] ICTY Statute, Art. 30; ICC Statute, Art. 48(3). Seventy of the 121 states parties had, as of the date of publication, ratified the Agreement on the Privileges and Immunities of the International Criminal Court. The ICTY Appeals Chamber has insisted that defence counsel also enjoy a robust 'functional immunity' under Art. 30 of the ICTY Statute. *Gotovina and others (Decision on Gotovina Defence Appeal against 12 March 2012 Requests for Permanent Restraining Orders Directed to the Republic of Croatia)*, § 31.

[37] ICC Statute, Art. 93(4); *Blaškić (Subpoena)*, §§ 61–9.

[38] A. Alamuddin, 'Collection of Evidence', in Khan, Buisman, and Gosnell, cit. n. 28, at 250.

[39] S/RES/1593 (2005); S/RES/1970 (2011).

will be more precise in enumerating such obligations. Commentators disagree, for example, whether an arrest warrant arising from a Security Council referral prevails over any diplomatic immunity enjoyed under international law by a non-state party national wanted by the Court while visiting the territory of a state party. ICC Pre-Trial Chambers apparently are in no such doubt and, notwithstanding the language of Article 98, have reported to the SC on the non-execution by states parties of the warrants of arrest against Mr Bashir while on official visit to those states.[40]

B. Main Features of the State Cooperation Model Under the ICC Scheme

In contrast to the ICTY and ICTR, which are creatures of the Security Council moulded into their present shape in large part by the judges, the treaty-making process that led to the adoption of the ICC produced a more state-orientated approach. The final outcome, as has been rightly been pointed out, may be held to be 'a mixture of the "horizontal" and the "vertical" [model]'.[41]

A few points are relevant in this regard. First, the ICC Statute does lay down in Article 86 a general obligation to cooperate. However, this obligation essentially serves as a general statement that is specified and spelled out in a number of specific provisions. As has been stated, in the ICC Statute 'the choice has been made to list the specific obligations of the states parties exhaustively and to indicate their scope and contents as precisely as possible'.[42] Plainly, this specific enumeration is intended to restrict as much as possible the judicial power of interpretation of the duty to cooperate, and by the same token to lay down extensive 'legislative' safeguards for states. In addition, as noted above, under Article 93(1) state parties can refuse to comply with any other type of assistance which is prohibited by their law.

Second, the ICC Statute does not specify whether the taking of evidence, execution of summonses and warrants, etc. is to be undertaken by officials of the ICC prosecutor with the assistance, when needed, of state authorities, or whether instead it will be for state enforcement or judicial authorities to execute those acts at the request of the prosecutor. Judging from the insistence in the Statute on the need to comply with the requirements of *national* legislation, however, the conclusion seems warranted that the framers of the Statute intended the latter. It would seem that this conclusion is borne out by the implementing legislation so far adopted by some of the states parties.[43] In practice, however, much of the evidence gathered by the ICC has been collected directly by ICC investigators with the assistance of state authorities. The principal exception to this practice has been requests for coercive or invasive law enforcement measures, e.g. search warrants or wiretaps, which are executed by state law enforcement authorities on behalf of the ICC.

Third, both the principle of complementarity (with the ensuing power of the states concerned to decide whether they intend to exercise their jurisdiction over a crime) and the

---

[40] *Al-Bashir* (*Decision informing the United Nations Security Council and the Assembly of States Parties to the Rome Statute about Omar Al-Bashir's presence in the territory of the Republic of Kenya*); *Al-Bashir* (*Decision informing the United Nations Security Council and the Assembly of States Parties about Omar Al-Bashir's recent visit to the Republic of Chad*).

[41] Swart, cit. n. 14, at 1594.

[42] Swart, cit. n. 14, at 1595.

[43] See e.g. the Canadian Crimes Against Humanity and War Crimes Act 2000, the Norwegian Act on Implementation of the ICC Statute of 15 June 2001, the Swiss Federal Law on Cooperation with the ICC of 22 June 2001, and the French Law on the same matter of 26 February 2002. See, however, Art. 2(1) of Part II of the United Kingdom International Criminal Court Act 2001 (C.17) whereby the British Secretary of State transmits any ICC request for arrest or surrender to 'the appropriate judicial officer', without exercising any scrutiny (see also Art. 5(5) and (8)).

general right of states to challenge the Court's jurisdiction and the admissibility of a case may create obstacles to, or slow down or even hamper, states' cooperation and the exercise of the Court's jurisdiction (Article 19(7)).

Fourth, the possible surrender of persons to the Court is subject to a condition typical of interstate judicial cooperation: the principle of speciality, laid down in Article 101(1), whereby:

> A person surrendered to the Court under this Statute shall not be proceeded against, punished or detained for any conduct committed prior to surrender, other than the conduct or course of conduct which forms the basis of the crimes for which that person has been surrendered.

The impact of this provision, which is not found in the instruments of any of the ad hoc Tribunals, is likely to be limited for two reasons. First, the rule of speciality in the context of extradition ordinarily limits the requesting state to proceed only on the specific *crimes* for which the person has been surrendered, but here the provision is broader and allows the ICC to prosecute for the 'conduct or course of conduct' which formed the basis for surrender. Second, since the ICC is highly dependent on state cooperation, it can be expected that states that surrender suspects would be willing subsequently to expand the basis for surrender should the prosecutor seek to prosecute the suspect for a broader range of crimes.

Fifthly, in case of competing requests for surrender or extradition, i.e. a request for arrest and surrender of a person, emanating from the Court, and a request for extradition from a state not party, the request from the Court does not automatically prevail. Under Article 90(6) and (7), a state party may decide between compliance with the request from the Court and compliance with the request from a non-party state with which the state party is bound by an extradition treaty. This seems odd, for one would have thought that the obligations stemming from the ICC Statute should have taken precedence over those flowing from other treaties. Arguably, this priority would follow both from the 'inherent' primacy of a Statute establishing a *universal* criminal court over bilateral treaties (or multilateral treaties binding on a group of states) and from the very purpose of the Statute, to administer international criminal justice in the interest of peace. It seems instead that the Statute, faced with the dilemma of international versus national justice, has left the option to the relevant states.

Furthermore, as regards the protection of national security information, the Statute substantially caters to state concerns by creating a national security exception to requests for assistance. Article 93(4) provides that 'a state party may deny a request for assistance, in whole or in part, only if the request concerns the production of any documents or disclosure of evidence which relates to its national security'. Admittedly, Article 72, to which this provision refers, does envisage a complex mechanism designed to induce a state invoking national security concerns to disclose as much as possible of the information it wishes to withhold. This mechanism is largely based on the *Blaškić* (*Subpoena*) decision of the ICTY Appeals Chamber. However, the various stages of this mechanism are turned in the Statute into formal modalities that will be cumbersome and time-consuming.[44] In

---

[44] Indeed, Art. 72 ('Protection of national security information') establishes a three-step procedure when a state—or individual—invokes national security. Art. 72 is triggered when a state is of the opinion that 'disclosure of information [requested by the court or prosecutor] would prejudice its national security interests'. First, cooperative means are employed to reach an amicable settlement, e.g. modification of the request, a determination by the court of the relevance of the information sought or agreement of conditions under which the assistance could be provided. Second, if cooperative means fail, and the state decides against disclosure, it must notify the court or Prosecutor of the specific reasons for its decision, unless a specific

addition, in *Blaškić* (*Subpoena*) the emphasis was on the obligation of states to disclose information; only in exceptional circumstances were states allowed to resort to special steps for the purpose of shielding that information from undue disclosure to entities other than the Court. In Article 72, emphasis is instead on the right of states to deny the Court's request for assistance.

Finally, in the event of failure of states to cooperate, Article 87(7) provides for the means substantially enunciated by the ICTY in the Appeals Chamber's decision in *Blaškić* (*Subpoena*), namely, 'the Court may make a finding to that effect and refer the matter to the Assembly of states Parties or, where the Security Council referred the matter to the Court, to the Security Council'. However, the ICC could arguably have gone further and articulated the consequences of a Court's finding of non-cooperation by a state. The Statute could have specified that the Assembly of States Parties might agree upon countermeasures, or authorize contracting states to adopt such countermeasures, or, in the event of disagreement, that each contracting state might take such countermeasures. In addition, it would have been appropriate to provide for the possibility of the Security Council stepping in and adopting sanctions even in cases where the matter had not been previously referred by this body to the Court: one fails to see why the Security Council should not act upon Chapter VII if a state refuses to cooperate and such refusal amounts to a threat to the peace, even in cases previously referred to the Court by a state or initiated by the prosecutor *proprio motu*. Of course, the ICC Statute does not *exclude* this possibility, but it would also have been a good idea expressly to include it.

16.4.4 THE QUESTION OF SURRENDER OF NATIONALS

The constitution or the laws of many civil law countries lay down the principle that nationals may not be extradited for prosecution abroad.[45] This principle is clearly the remnant of a bygone era when states intended to protect their nationals as much as possible against any foreign interference. It is a typical expression of the Westphalian international community of sovereign states that distrust one another and lack any common values of universal scope and purport. In today's international community, where respect for human rights counts among the universal values that all states are required to abide by, this rule has become a relic of the past. Provided that the rights of the accused are safeguarded and the trial is fair and expeditious, why should a state have the right to refuse the extradition of one of its nationals to another state on the territory of which the individual has committed a crime? This legal tradition is not only outdated, but also risks leading to effective impunity if applied with respect to the requests by an international prosecutor to hand over a national accused of international crimes.

To avoid such a result, since the beginning of its judicial activity the ICTY held that, by virtue of a well-established principle of international law, states may not invoke their

---

description of the reasons would itself necessarily result in a prejudice to the state's national security interests. The court may then hold further consultations on the matter, if need be *ex parte* and/or in camera. The third step, in the event that the state is found not to be complying with its obligations, is for the court to refer the matter to the Assembly of States Parties or, if the Security Council originally referred the matter to the court, to the Security Council.

[45] The principle can be found, for example, in the Constitutions of Brazil (1988, revised in 1996; Art. 50), the German Federal Republic (1949, Art. 18(2), now amended to allow the handing over of Germans to the ICC and other members of the European Union), the Federal Republic of Yugoslavia (1992, Art. 17-3), Poland (1997, Art. 55-1) and Slovenia (1991, revised in 2000, Article 47). The principle finds legislative recognition in France, in Article 3 of the Law of 10 March 1927, as well as in most bilateral treaties concerning mutual judicial assistance.

national legislation, even of constitutional rank, to evade to comply with an international obligation (i.e. that of complying with a request for cooperation by the international Tribunal).[46] Second, and more importantly, it pointed out that the constitutional rules on the ban on extradition of nationals only apply to relations between sovereign states, and not to relations between a state and an international criminal court. The former relations are based on the principle of formal equality, whereas the latter are hierarchical in nature. Thus, while one may speak of *extradition* of the accused from one state to another, it is more appropriate to speak of *transfer* or *surrender* of the accused from a state to an international criminal court.[47] Furthermore, given that the rights of the accused are fully respected before international criminal courts, the concerns of the national state no longer make any sense. International criminal judges have thus introduced a new legal concept, dissociated from obsolete principles, where the vision of the international community propounded by Immanuel Kant prevails over that extolled by Hobbes. Consequently, the Rules of the ICTY and ICTR provide that the limitations to extradition stemming from national or international law do not apply in the matter of transfer of an accused person to the International Tribunals (Rule 58 of the ICTY/ICTR Rules).

This terminological distinction, which carries substantive consequences, has been accepted in the ICC Statute, which expressly distinguishes between surrender and extradition (Article 102).[48]

---

[46] For this argument see, although on different matters, the Order of the ICTY President in *Blaškić* (3 April 1996, § 7) and the annual report for 1996 of the ICTY President to the General Assembly (A/51/292, 18 August 1996).

[47] The argument is, for example, set forth in the ICTY President's report to the UN General Assembly on the activities of the Tribunal during 1977 (UN Doc. A/RES/52/375, 18 September 1997, §§ 186–9; also in *ICTY Yearbook 1997*, at 145).

[48] 'For the purpose of this Statute:

(a) "surrender" means the delivering up of a person by a State to the Court, pursuant to this Statute.

(b) "extradition" means the delivering up of a person by one State to another as provided by treaty, convention or national legislation.'

17

LEGAL IMPEDIMENTS TO THE EXERCISE OF CRIMINAL JURISDICTION

Many obstacles may hamper or put in jeopardy the institution of criminal proceedings for international crimes. The principal hurdles are: *i*) rules granting amnesty for broad categories of crimes; *ii*) statutes of limitation; *iii*) the prohibition of double jeopardy (the principle of *ne bis idem*), whereby a person may not be brought to trial twice for the same offence; *iv*) international rules on personal immunities.

17.1 AMNESTY

Many states have passed legislation granting amnesty, with regard to specific episodes in the states' histories, for war crimes or crimes against humanity, or for broad categories of crimes that include the two classes just referred to. They have thus cancelled the crimes. After the enactment of such laws, conduct that was previously criminal is no longer such, with the consequence that: *i*) prosecutors forfeit the right or power to initiate investigations or criminal proceedings; and *ii*) any sentence passed for the crime is obliterated.

After the Second World War, states such as France and Italy granted amnesty to those nationals who had fought against the Germans. (Later on the Italian authorities passed an amnesty law for fascists and collaborators as well.) On 18 June 1966, when the Algerian war was over, the French Parliament passed a law granting amnesty for all crimes committed in that conflict, as well as in Indochina. Chile and Argentina enacted laws providing for amnesty for all crimes committed during the post-Allende period, in the former case, and the military dictatorship, in the latter. Other countries such as Peru and Uruguay also enacted similar laws covering gross violations of human rights comprising torture or crimes against humanity.

The rationale behind amnesty is that in the aftermath of periods of turmoil and deep rift, such as those following armed conflict, civil strife, or revolution, it is best to heal social wounds by forgetting past misdeeds, hence by obliterating all the criminal offences that may have been perpetrated by any side. It is believed that in this way one may more expeditiously bring about cessation of hatred and animosity and attain national reconciliation. However, in some recent instances the incumbent military and political leaders themselves passed amnesty laws, in view of an expected change in government and for the clear purpose of exempting themselves from future prosecution (these are the so-called *self-amnesties*).

On the practical side, it is doubtful that amnesty laws may heal open wounds. Particularly when very serious crimes have been committed involving members of ethnic, religious, or political groups and eventually pitting one group against another, moral and psychological wounds may fester if attempts are made to sweep past horrors under the carpet. Resentment and hate are temporarily suppressed; sooner or later, however, they resurface and spawn even greater violence and crimes.

The choice between forgetting and justice must in any event be left to policy-makers and legislators. From a legal viewpoint, one can nevertheless note that international rules often oblige states to refrain from granting amnesty for international crimes. Here we should distinguish between treaty rules and customary rules.

In many instances international bodies or national courts have considered amnesty laws incompatible with treaty provisions on human rights, in particular with those provisions which require the granting of a right to judicial remedies for any violations of human rights. This is the opinion that the UN Human Rights Committee set out in 1994 in its General Comment no. 20, as well as its 'views' in *Laureano Atachahua v. Peru*, and in its comments on the reports of Peru and Haiti. The Committee took the same position in *Rodríguez v. Uruguay* with regard to torture.[1] The Inter-American Commission shared this view in its reports on El Salvador,[2] Uruguay,[3] Argentina,[4] Chile,[5] and Colombia.[6]

One can also recall that the Inter-American Court of Human Rights held in *Barrios Altos* (*Chumbipuma Aguirre and others v. Peru*) that the granting of amnesty to the alleged authors of such gross violations of human rights as torture, summary executions, and forced disappearances was contrary to the non-derogable rights laid down in the body of international law on human rights and in particular to some provisions of the American Convention on Human Rights. It consequently held that two laws passed by Peru to grant such amnesty were 'devoid of legal effects' and the Peruvian authorities were obliged to initiate criminal proceedings against the alleged authors of those crimes (§§ 41–4, and 51(3–5)).

Finally, a Spanish judge refused to take into account an amnesty law as being contrary to international law in *Fortunato Galtieri* (Order of 25 March 1997, at 7–9).[7]

It should be added that, as noted above (see 15.3.3), some treaties impose upon state parties the obligation to prosecute and punish the alleged authors of crimes prohibited by such treaties. To pass and apply amnesty laws to alleged authors of any such crime would run counter to those treaty obligations.

Let us now ask ourselves whether a rule of customary international law has evolved prohibiting amnesty for international crimes.

Against the existence of such a rule one could note that states have made agreements explicitly providing for amnesty for a set of offences, including such offences as war crimes, torture, or crimes against humanity. It may suffice to cite here the Evian Agreements of

---

[1] In its 'views' in that case, the UN Human Rights Committee stated that amnesties for gross violations of human rights 'are incompatible with the obligations of the State Party under the Covenant'. The Committee noted 'with deep concern that the adoption of this Law [a Uruguayan law of 1986, called the Limitations Act or Law of Expiry] effectively excludes in a number of cases the possibility of investigation into past human rights abuses and thereby prevents the State Party from discharging its responsibility to provide effective remedies to the victims of those abuses. Moreover, the Committee is concerned that, in adopting this law, the State Party has contributed to an atmosphere of impunity which may undermine the democratic order and give rise to further grave human rights violations' (§ 12).

[2] Report no. 26/92, IACHR Annual Report, 1992–3 (at www.oas.org).

[3] Report no. 29/92, IACHR Annual Report, 1992–3 (at www.oas.org).

[4] Report no. 24/92, IACHR, Annual Report, 1992–3 (at www.oas.org).

[5] Report no. 25/98, IACHR Annual Report, 1997 (at www.oas.org).

[6] Third Report on Colombia, Chapter IV, § 345, IACHR 1999 (at www.oas.org).

[7] The Chilean Supreme Court first held that amnesty laws were admissible and applicable (see *Osvaldo Romo Mena*, decision of 26 October 1995, at 3–5), then, in a decision of 9 September in the same case, held the contrary view (at 2–6).

1962 between France and Algeria.[8] Mention should also be made of a legally binding Community act, the Framework decision of the Council of the European Union of 10 December 2001 (Article 5 of which envisages amnesty as one of the legal grounds on which a state may refuse the execution of arrest warrants, without making any exception for the international crimes referred to in the enumeration of Article 2). All these treaties and other acts have as their underpinning the principle of respect for state sovereignty, and its implication that the power to decide who may be exempted from criminal punishment belongs to the sovereign prerogatives of each state.

To support instead the gradual evolution of a customary prohibition of amnesty for the crimes under discussion, other elements of state practice can be mentioned. On 7 July 1999 the Special Representative of the UN Secretary-General attached a disclaimer to the Peace Agreement between the Government of Sierra Leone and the Revolutionary United Front of Sierra Leone,[9] which provided for amnesty in Article 9. Under this disclaimer:

> The United Nations interprets that the amnesty and pardon in Article 9 of the Agreement shall not apply to international crimes of genocide, crimes against humanity, war crimes, and other serious violations of international humanitarian law.

In its turn, Article 10 of the Statute of the Special Court for Sierra Leone provides that an amnesty granted for the crimes falling under the Court's jurisdiction 'shall not be a bar to prosecution'.[10] Interestingly, the same language can be found in Article 40 of the Cambodian Bill of 2000 on the Establishment of Extraordinary Chambers in the Courts of Cambodia for the Prosecution of Crimes Committed during the Period of Democratic Kampuchea, as well as Article 6 of the 2007 Statute of the Special Tribunal for Lebanon. Furthermore, in 2000, France revised its Constitution to implement the Statute of the ICC, after the Constitutional Council had held in 1999, in *Constitutionality of the ICC Statute* (§ 34), that the principle of complementarity laid down in the ICC Statute entailed that France might have to arrest and hand over to the Court for trial a person benefiting from amnesty in France, and this consequence was contrary to the French Constitution, in particular to the principle laid down in Article 34 whereby it is the prerogative of the French Parliament to decide on amnesty. Thus, in the event France bowed to the principle that French laws on amnesty do not apply in the event of crimes falling under the Court's jurisdiction.

These innovative manifestations of international practice find their rationale in the notion that, as international crimes constitute attacks on universal values, no single state should arrogate to itself the right to decide to cancel such crimes or to set aside their legal consequences. These manifestations therefore reflect the concept that the requirement to dispense justice should trump the need to respect state sovereignty. However, they are not yet so widespread as to warrant the contention that a customary rule concerning all

---

[8] See also the 1977 Second Protocol Additional to the Geneva Conventions of 1949. In Art. 6(5) it provides that at the end of hostilities the authorities in power must endeavour to grant amnesty 'to persons who have participated in the armed conflict'. The idea is that those who have simply fought, *and not necessarily committed any crimes*, against the government—or for the government in a conflict where the government lost—should not be prosecuted for murder, treason, etc. or any of the offences under national law with which a person who fought against the government, and perhaps killed government soldiers in combat, could be charged. Art. 6(5) exists to promote national reconciliation by having those 'offences' forgiven. It must also be noted that, when the Protocol was drafted (between 1974 and 1977), the idea that serious violations of international rules on internal armed conflict could be classified as war crimes, had not yet been adopted.

[9] See UN Doc. S/1999/777.

[10] On this provisions, see the decisions by the Appeals Chamber of the SCSL in *Kallon, Norman and Kamara*, 13 March 2004, and in *Kondewa*, 25 May 2004.

international crimes (the so-called 'core crimes') has crystallized, the more so because no customary rule having a general purport has yet emerged imposing upon states the obligation to prosecute and punish the alleged authors of any international crime. Indeed, if such a rule could be held to have taken shape, one could infer from it that granting amnesty would conflict with such a rule. There are, however, exceptions: grave breaches of the four Geneva Conventions and the First Additional Protocol, arguably by now turned into customary law, prescribe that states on whose territory an alleged offender is found are bound to either prosecute or extradite them. Arguably another exception is the international crime of terrorism, as upheld by the STL (*Interlocutory Decision on the Applicable Law*, AC, at § 102). If this view is accepted, it would follow that states are enjoined to refrain from passing amnesty laws relating to terrorist acts, since such laws would be inconsistent with the international obligation just mentioned.

The current status of international practice, in particular its inconsistency combined with the more and more widespread *opinio juris* in the international community that international crimes should be punished, could be conceptualized as follows. Subject to what has been said above with regard to terrorism and what is stated below with regard to genocide and crimes against humanity, there is not yet any general obligation for states to refrain from enacting amnesty laws on these crimes. Consequently, if a state passes any such law, it does not breach a customary rule. Nonetheless, if the courts of another state having in custody persons accused of international crimes decide to prosecute them, although in their national state they would benefit from an amnesty law, such courts would not act contrary to general international law, in particular to the principle of respect for the sovereign prerogatives of other states. One might add that, in light of the current trends of the international community, one can find much merit in the distinction suggested, at least for minor defendants, by a distinguished judge and commentator,[11] between amnesties granted as a result of a process of national reconciliation and blanket amnesties. The legal entitlement of foreign states not to take into account an amnesty passed by the national state of the alleged perpetrator should apply to the second category. Instead, if the amnesty results from a specific individual decision of a court or a Truth and Reconciliation Commission, the exigencies of justice could be held to be fulfilled, and foreign courts should refrain from adjudicating those crimes.

It should be added that whenever general rules prohibiting specific international crimes come to acquire the nature of peremptory norms (*jus cogens*), they may be construed as imposing among other things the obligation not to cancel by legislative or executive fiat the crimes they proscribe. At any rate, this is the view an ICTY Trial Chamber spelled out in *Furundžija*, with regard to torture as a war crime (§ 155). An Argentinean judge took a similar view in *Simon Julio, Del Cerro Juan Antonio* (at 43–64, 103–4). Also the Spanish *Audiencia nacional* held amnesty laws concerning international crimes to be contrary to *jus cogens* in *Scilingo* (at 7, Legal Ground 8) and *Pinochet* (at 7–8, Legal Ground 8). The same argument should hold true for genocide and crimes against humanity, since there seems to be conclusive evidence that conduct amounting to such crimes is prohibited by peremptory norms of international law. It would follow that amnesty passed for such crimes would not be applicable as contrary to international law.

---

[11] D. Vandermeersch, 'Droit belge', in A. Cassese and M. Delmas-Marty (eds), *Juridictions nationales et crimes internationaux* (Paris: PUF, 2002), at 108. See also J. Dugard, 'Possible Conflicts of Jurisdiction with Truth Commissions', in Cassese, Gaeta, and Johns, *ICC Commentary*, at 695–8.

17.2 STATUTE OF LIMITATIONS

Many states lay down rules providing that after the elapse of a certain number of years (normally, ten or twenty) no prosecution may any longer be initiated with regard to some major categories of crimes such as murder, robbery, etc. Some states also add provisions whereby, if a final sentence pronounced for a crime has not been served after a certain number of years, it is no longer applicable. (For instance, in France, under Article 7 of the Code of Criminal Procedure, the right to prosecute a crime is forfeited within ten years of the perpetration of the crime, similar provisions can be found in the codes of such European countries as Austria, Germany, Switzerland, Portugal, and Denmark.)

The rationale behind this legislation is that the passage of time renders the collection of evidence very difficult (in that witnesses are no longer available, material evidence may have disappeared or got lost, etc.). In addition, it is felt that it is better for society to forget, the more so because, once many years have gone by, the victims or their relatives may feel less inclined to demand the prosecution and punishment of the authors of crimes. Another ground warranting statutes of limitation is often found in the fact that as a result of the failure of prosecuting officers to search for evidence or find the alleged culprit, the deterrent effect of criminalization dwindles and eventually comes to naught; consequently, leaving open the possibility for prosecution no longer proves appropriate.

In many states the general provisions on the statute of limitation also apply to at least some classes of international crimes. For instance, in Spain, pursuant to Article 113 of the Criminal Code, after twenty years no prosecution is admissible for crimes involving *reclusion mayor* (imprisonment of 26–30 years), whereas the statutory period is of fifteen years for crimes entailing *reclusion menor* (imprisonment of 12–20 years). In Italy, the twenty-year statute of limitation also applies to such international crimes as war crimes, crimes against humanity, and genocide as long as they do not entail a sentence of life imprisonment. (When such sentence is applicable, no statute of limitation applies.) A similar rule applies in Germany, where murder is not considered subject to statutes of limitation. In Japan, under the general rule laid down in Article 250 of the Code of Criminal Procedure, if a crime involves the death penalty, the period of statutory limitation is fifty years, whereas it runs to ten years if the crime involves life imprisonment, or to seven years if the penalty is imprisonment for more than ten years.

In other countries there are instead special rules for international crimes. For instance, in Colombia the statute of limitation for torture, genocide, and forced disappearances is thirty years; in Spain, twenty years for torture and terrorism. In France, the statute of limitation for terrorism is twenty years (if the offence amounts to a misdemeanour or *délit*) and thirty years if it amounts to a serious offence (*crime*). Furthermore, a distinction is made between war crimes and crimes against humanity: for the former, the statute of limitation is that provided for in general criminal rules (twenty years); for the latter, a law of 26 December 1964 provides that there may be no statute of limitation. In common law countries, where there is no general rule on statutory limitation but there may be specific rules concerning certain crimes, no statutory limitation is provided for such serious offences as international crimes.

To date a few international treaties have been concluded on this matter: for instance, the UN Convention on the Non-Applicability of Statutory Limitations to War Crimes and Crimes against Humanity, of 26 November 1968, and the European Convention of 25 January 1974, on the same subject. Only a relatively small number of states have, however, ratified such treaties. The ICC Statute provides in Article 29 that '[t]he crimes within the jurisdiction of the Court shall not be subject to any statute of limitation'.

Could one contend that the aforementioned treaty rules either reflect, or have gradually turned into, customary rules? Much depends on the legal weight one attributes to various elements of international practice.

In this regard, one should first of all recall a few regulations of the matter. Interestingly, the Cambodian Bill of 2000 on the Establishment of Extraordinary Chambers in the Courts of Cambodia for the Prosecution of the Crimes committed During the Period of Democratic Kampuchea provides in Articles 4 and 5 that there shall be no statute of limitation for genocide and crimes against humanity, whereas in Article 3 it extends for an additional period of twenty years the statute of limitation set forth in the 1956 Penal Code for homicide, torture, and religious persecution. Similarly, section 16 of Regulation no. 2000/15 adopted by the UN Transitional Administration in East Timor, on the Establishment of Panels with Exclusive Jurisdiction over Serious Criminal Offences, provides that genocide, war crimes, crimes against humanity, and torture 'shall not be subject to any statute of limitation' whereas the other crimes under the panels' jurisdiction (murder and sexual offences) 'shall be subject to applicable law'.

In addition, some national and international courts have ruled out the applicability of statutes of limitation for international crimes. It is worth noting that, in the aforementioned *Barrios Altos* case, the Inter-American Court of Human Rights held that the establishment of a statute of limitations for egregious violations of fundamental human rights was contrary to the non-derogable norms making up the international rules on human rights (*Barrios Altos*, § 41). An Argentinean federal judge took the same view on 6 March 2001 in *Simon, Julio, Del Cerro, Juan Antonio* (at 78–84). A Mexican federal judge shared this view in a decision on the extradition of an Argentinean officer to Spain (*Ricardo Miguel Cavallo* case).[12] In France the Court of Cassation held in 1985 that the inapplicability of statutes of limitation to crimes against humanity, laid down in French law, derives from principles recognized by all civilized nations.[13] In Italy, in 1997, the Rome Military Tribunal noted in *Hass and Priebke* that the inapplicability of statutes of limitation to war crimes was asserted to derive from a general principle of international law (at 49). In a significant *obiter*, a Trial Chamber of the ICTY held in *Furundžija* that, as a result of international rules on torture being of a peremptory nature, no statute of limitation may apply to that crime (*Furundžija*, TC, § 157).

Apart from referring to practice, the following arguments also support the existence of an international customary rule. The application of statutes of limitation to the most serious international crimes proves contrary to the very nature of international rules prohibiting such crimes. These are so abhorrent that their authors must be punished, even after the lapse of much time. Such punishment not only has a retributive effect, but also serves to deter potential perpetrators as far as possible from engaging in similar actions. Furthermore, the universal dimension of those crimes (that is, the fact that they affect the whole international community and not only the community of the state on whose territory they have been perpetrated) entails that it would be incongruous to take into account the statute of limitation of one particular state (for instance, the territorial state or the national state of the victim or of the perpetrator). In addition, as rightly pointed out by a

---

[12] It is notable that in this case the judge had held that the accused could only be extradited for the charges of genocide and terrorism, as that of torture was covered by the statute of limitation in Argentinean law. However, the Argentinean Minister of Foreign Affairs, to whom it fell to take the final decision, subsequently held that Cavallo could also be extradited for torture, because this crime could not be covered by any statute of limitation (at 58–9).

[13] 20 Dec. 1985, *Bulletin criminel* 1985 no. 407.

distinguished criminal lawyer,[14] in the case of international crimes the reasons militating for, or underpinning resort to, statutes of limitation no longer hold good. In particular: if the victims or their relatives do not set in motion criminal proceedings, normally this failure is not due to negligence or lack of interest; initiating such proceedings may indeed prove 'psychologically painful, or politically dangerous, or legally impossible'; as for the national authorities' failure to prosecute, it may be due to political motivations which the passage of time may sooner or later efface.

Nevertheless, the proposition that a customary rule has evolved on this matter could be objected to by noting that in some states only some categories of international crimes may fall under statutes of limitations. For instance, in France, as noted above, a law of 26 December 1964, restated in Article 213–5 of the Criminal Code in 1994, removes any statutory limitation for crimes against humanity alone (with the consequence that in *Barbie* and *Touvier*, French courts went to great lengths to prove that the crimes with which the defendants were charged were crimes against humanity and not war crimes, hence not subject to normal statutory limitations). It would seem that no state has ever protested against that law, nor has it been assailed in international fora as being contrary to internationally accepted legal standards.

It would therefore seem that the better view is that no customary rule endowed with a far-reaching content has yet evolved on this matter. In other words, no rule has come into being prohibiting the application of statutes of limitations to *all* international crimes. It appears to be a sounder view that customary rules render statutes of limitation inapplicable only with regard to some categories of crimes: genocide, crimes against humanity, torture.[15]

Whether or not the above arguments about the customary rule on the matter are held sound, in any case state parties to the ICC Statute are barred from invoking any statute of limitations in proceedings before the Court (see Article 29).

17.3 THE PROHIBITION OF DOUBLE JEOPARDY

Under the principle of double jeopardy a court may not institute proceedings against a person for a crime that has already been the object of criminal proceedings in the same state (internal *ne bis in idem* principle) or in another state, or in an international court (international *ne bis in idem*), and for which the person has already been convicted or acquitted.

The internal *ne bis in idem* principle may be held to be prescribed by a customary rule of international law grounded in an elementary principle of justice (and restated in treaty provisions).[16] In contrast, the legal status of the international equivalent principle is still

---

[14] M. Delmas-Marty, 'La Responsabilité pénale en échec (prescription, amnistie, immunités)', in Cassese and Delmas-Marty (eds), cit. n. 11, at 616–18.

[15] This view is to some extent consonant with the pronouncement of the French Court of Cassation in the *Barbie* case (judgment of 26 January 1984). There the Court held that 'This rule [on the absence of any statute of limitations for crimes against humanity] was applicable to such crimes by virtue of the principles of law recognised by the community of nations' (78 ILR (1988), at 126). The same Court, in another decision in the same *Barbie* case (judgment of 20 December 1985, at 136) held that the statute of limitations did not apply to war crimes.

See also the judgment of an Italian Military Tribunal in *Priebke and Haas*.

[16] See e.g. Art. 86 of the 1949 Geneva Convention on Prisoners of War ('No prisoner of war may be punished more than once for the same act, or on the same charge') and Art. 117(3) of the 1949 Geneva

controversial It is not clear whether this principle has turned into customary international law. Italian courts have held the view that it has not (see, for instance, the *Zennaro*
case (at 301–2), where the Italian Constitutional Court took this view in 1976). Similarly,
in 1987 the Italian delegate to the UN maintained in the discussion on the Draft Code
of Offences against Peace and Security of Mankind that it was difficult to consider the
principle as 'a full-fledged principle of customary international law applicable to criminal
judgments of foreign states' and found the reasons for this conclusion in

> that, outside some bilateral or limited multilateral circles of states, there is not sufficient
> trust in the administration of justice by other states, especially when offences with politi-
> cal aspects are concerned. States are concerned that a person having committed a heinous
> crime against peace and security of mankind might find protection from prosecution in
> the rest of the world in an acquittal or mild sentence given in a given State for reasons of
> political sympathy.[17]

The contention can be made that a customary rule, concerning all crimes generally, has
not yet crystallized. Even in Europe, where, due to the multiplicity of treaties on the execution of foreign judgments, there is an increasing tendency to apply the international *ne
bis in idem* principle in the relations between national courts of different countries, quite a
few states tend to hold the view that they are not bound to consider themselves foreclosed
from again trying crimes on which foreign courts have already pronounced, when these
crimes have been committed *on their own territory*. It is significant that Article 55 of the
Schengen Convention of 19 June 1990 authorizes a contracting state to declare that it is
not bound by Article 54 (on *ne bis in idem*) when the facts envisaged in the foreign judgment have taken place in whole or in part on its territory, except if, in the latter case, the
facts have occurred in part on the territory of the state where the judgment has been rendered. Plainly, this claim to the exercise of territorial jurisdiction is based on the notion
of sovereignty and, more specifically, on the claim of states that they are entitled to prosecute and punish crimes committed on their territory, because such crimes have troubled
the social order and infringed values upheld in the local community.

However, a customary rule should arguably evolve, *at least with regard to international
crimes*. Indeed, the rationale behind the claim of states to exercise territorial jurisdiction,
referred to above, does not hold true for international crimes. Such crimes breach values
that transcend individual countries and their communities; they affect and involve all
states. Hence, any state is entitled to prosecute and punish them. It follows that, as long
as the court of the state where those crimes are tried conforms to some fundamental
principles on fair trial and acts independently, impartially, and with all due diligence,
other states, including the state where the crime has been committed, as well as international courts, must refrain from sitting in judgment on the same offence. As exceptions,
however, the customary rule should provide that this principle does not apply when in
the first trial: *i*) the person was prosecuted and punished for the same fact or conduct, but
the crime was characterized as an 'ordinary crime' (e.g. murder) instead of an international crime (e.g. genocide) with a view to deliberately avoiding the stigma and implications of international crimes; or *ii*) the court did not fully comply with the fundamental
safeguards of a fair trial, or did not act independently or impartially; or *iii*) the court in

Convention on the Protection of Civilians ('No internee may be punished more than once for the same
act, or on the same count'). See also Art. 14(7) of the UN Covenant on Civil and Political Rights; Art. 8(4)
of the American Convention on Human Rights; Art. 4(1) of Protocol 7 of the European Convention on
Human Rights.

[17] See IYIL (1988–92), at 196–7.

fact conducted a sham trial, for the purpose of shielding the accused from international criminal responsibility; or *iv*) the prosecution or the court did not act with the diligence required by international standards; or *v*) the trial was conducted in the absence of the accused, and the accused after termination of trial and conviction turns himself in and requests a new trial in his presence (on this matter, see Article 22(3) of the Statute of the STL, providing that 'In case of conviction in absentia, the accused, if he or she had not designated a defence counsel of his or her choosing, shall have the right to be retried in his or her presence before the Special Tribunal, unless he or she accepts the judgment').

One must note, however, that the purport of the *ne bis in idem* principle might vary considerably, depending on the different meaning placed on the object of the prohibition (the *idem* in the Latin tag). The prohibition can cover the same historical facts or set of events that formed the basis of a prosecution for a criminal offence. Under this interpretation, the word *idem* means 'circumstances', and the principle of *ne bis in idem* prohibits trying again someone for the same historical facts, whatever their legal qualification. By contrast, the prohibition can cover the legal qualification of a historical episode, and not the historical episode per se. This means that if a person has been prosecuted for a specific offence arising from a given historical event (let's say, I enter a bank to commit robbery and kill someone, and I am prosecuted and tried and acquitted for robbery), he cannot be tried again for the same offence but for another offence that took place as part of that historical event (in our example, I can be prosecuted and tried for manslaughter). States that follow the first approach, and apply the *ne bis in idem* principle to the historical events, tend to confine it to the domestic dimension, and to apply the second approach with respect to prosecution and trials occurred abroad (i.e. when it comes to the external dimension of the *ne bis in idem*, they look at the legal qualification of the historical event in the foreign jurisdiction).

Interestingly, Article 20 of the ICC Statute, dealing with the prohibition of *ne bis in idem*, is not uniform on the meaning of *idem*, which varies depending on which court the prohibition applies to. If it is the ICC itself, the *ne bis in idem* prohibition concerns the historical facts that were at the basis of the first prosecution. Article 20(1) indeed provides that 'no person shall be tried before the Court with respect to *conduct which formed the basis of crimes* for which the person has been convicted or acquitted by the Court' (emphasis added). By contrast, if the prohibition applies to any other court (a domestic court, but also another international criminal court possessing jurisdiction), the *idem* refers to the legal qualification of the historical facts of the first prosecution, with the consequence that the person can be tried again for part of the same facts, but under a different legal qualification. According to Article 20(2), 'No person shall be tried by another court for *a crime referred to in article 5* for which that person has already been convicted or acquitted by the Court' (emphasis added). Finally, Article 20(3) prohibits the ICC from prosecuting a person for *conduct proscribed under Article 6, 7 and 8* when the person has been already tried for such conduct by another court (but subject to some exceptions).[18]

---

[18] 'No person who has been tried by another court for conduct also proscribed under Article 6, 7, or 8 shall be tried by the court with respect to the same conduct unless the proceedings in the other court:

(a) Were for the purpose of shielding the person concerned from criminal responsibility for crimes within the jurisdiction of the court; or

(b) Otherwise were not conducted independently or impartially in accordance with the norms of due process recognized by international law and were conducted in a manner which, in the circumstances, was inconsistent with an intent to bring the person concerned to justice.'

17.4 INTERNATIONAL RULES ON IMMUNITIES

17.4.1 THE DISTINCTION BETWEEN FUNCTIONAL AND PERSONAL IMMUNITIES

One of the possible obstacles to prosecution for international crimes may be constituted by rules intended to protect the person accused by granting him immunity from prosecution.

In international law there exist two categories of immunities that may in principle come into play and be relied upon. They may relate either to conduct of state agents acting in their official capacity, and therefore protecting the public nature of the act accomplished by the state agent in his official capacity (so-called *functional immunities*); or protect the person and property of the individual exercising a specific function abroad, for until such time as he holds the post (*personal immunities*). The former immunities, as explained above (see 13.2) apply to all state agents discharging their official duties. In principle, an individual performing acts on behalf of a sovereign state may not be called to account for any violations of international law he may have committed while acting in an official function. Only the state may be held responsible at the international level. By contrast, the latter category of immunities (personal immunities) are granted by international customary or treaty rules to some categories of individuals on account of their functions and are intended to protect both their private and their public life, or in other words to render them inviolable while in office (they cannot be arrested or be subject to any kind of enforcement measures against their person or property, nor brought to trial). Such individuals comprise heads of state, prime ministers or foreign ministers, diplomatic agents, and high-ranking agents of international organizations. They enjoy these immunities so as to be able to discharge their official mission free from any impairment or interference. These immunities end with the cessation of the agent's official duties.

This distinction, based on state practice [19] as well as some recent judicial decisions,[20] is important. *Functional immunities: i*) relate to substantive law—that is, amount to a substantive defence (although the state agent is not exonerated from compliance with either international law or the substantive law of the foreign country—if he breaches national or international law, this violation is not legally imputable to him but to his state);[21]

---

[19] With regard to the first class of immunities, suffice it to refer to the famous *McLeod* incident and the *Rainbow Warrior* case. For the *McLeod* case, see *British and Foreign Papers*, vol. XXIX, at 1139, as well as Jennings, 'The *Caroline* and *McLeod* Cases', 32 AJIL (1938), 92–9; see also the decision of 1841 of the New York Supreme Court in *People* v. *McLeod*, at 270–99. For the *Rainbow Warrior* case, see *UN Reports of International Arbitral Awards*, XIX, at 213. See also the *Governor Collot* case, in J. B. Moore, *A Digest of International Law*, vol. II (Washington: Government Printing House, 1906), at 23.

[20] One can mention the judgment rendered by the Supreme Court of Israel in *Eichmann* (at 308–9), that handed down by the German Supreme Court (*Bundesgerichtshof*) in *Scotland Yard*, at 1101–2 (the Director of Scotland Yard was not amenable to German civil jurisdiction for he had acted as a state agent). See also the judgment delivered by the ICTY in *Blaškić* (*Subpoena*), AC, at §§ 38 and 41). For other cases see in particular M. Bothe, 'Die strafrechtliche Immunität fremder Staatsorgane', in 31 *Zeit. Ausl. Öff. Recht Völk* (1971), at 248–53.

[21] Nevertheless, it would seem that if the state official acting abroad has breached criminal rules of the foreign state, he may incur criminal liability and be liable under foreign criminal jurisdiction if he exercises his function without the consent of the territorial state (at least, this is what happened both in *McLeod* and in the *Rainbow Warrior* case). Be that as it may, it seems certain, however, that the state official in question will not in any case be asked to pay for any damage his act may have caused. The state for which he acted remains internationally responsible for that act and will have to bear all the legal consequences of such responsibility.

ii) cover official acts of any *de jure* or *de facto* state agent; *iii*) do not cease at the end of the discharge of official functions by the state agent (the reason being that the act is legally attributed to the state, hence any legal liability for it may only be incurred by the state); *iv*) are *erga omnes*; that is, may be invoked towards any other state.

In contrast, *personal immunities*: *i*) relate to procedural law—that is, they render the state official immune from civil or criminal jurisdiction (a procedural defence); *ii*) cover official or private acts carried out by the state agent while in office, as well as private or official acts performed prior to taking office—in other words, they assure total inviolability; *iii*) are intended to protect only *some categories* of state officials, namely diplomatic agents, heads of state, heads of government, foreign ministers (under the doctrine set out by the ICJ in its judgment in the *Arrest Warrant* case §§ 51–5); *iv*) come to an end after cessation of the official functions of the state agent; *v*) may not be *erga omnes* (in the case of diplomatic agents they are only applicable with regard to acts performed as between the receiving and the sending state, plus third states through whose territory the diplomat may pass while proceeding to take up, or to return to, his post, or when returning to his own country: so-called *jus transitus innoxii*, i.e. the right to move from one place to another without hindrance).

The above distinction permits us to realize that the two classes of immunity might in some cases coexist and somewhat overlap as long as a state official who may also invoke personal or diplomatic immunities is in office. While he is discharging his official functions, he always enjoys personal immunity.[22] In addition, he enjoys functional immunity (except if his acts amount to an international crime; see 13.2).

All these immunities may be invoked by a state official before *foreign* courts or other foreign organs (for example, enforcement agencies).[23]

17.4.2 PERSONAL IMMUNITIES AND INTERNATIONAL CRIMES

Personal immunities normally apply to ordinary crimes. Do they also apply to international crimes?

---

[22] For a recent departure from this rule, see the 2002 decisions of the European Union concerning the freezing of the private assets of Mugabe (head of state in Zimbabwe): see Council Common Position of 18 February 2002 concerning restrictive measures against Zimbabwe (2002/145/CFSP), in *Official Journal of the European Communities*, 21.32.2002, L50/1; Council Regulation (EC) No. 310/2002 of 18 February 2002 on the same matter, *Official Journal of the European Communities*, 21.32.2002, L50/4; Council Common Position of 22 July 2002 amending Common Position 2002/145/CFSP, *Official Journal of the European Communities*, 21.32.2002, L195/1; Commission Regulation no. 1643/2002 of 13 September 2002, *Official Journal of the European Communities*, 21.32.2002, L247/22; and Council decision of 14 September 2002 implementing Common Position 2002/145/CFSP, *Official Journal of the European Communities*, 21.32.2002, L247/56.

[23] The immunities provided for in *national* legislation and normally granted to the head of state, members of cabinet, and members of parliament. They normally cover the acts of the individuals concerned and involve exemption from *national* jurisdiction. In addition, they also often include immunity from national prosecution for ordinary crimes having no link with the function and committed either before or during the exercise of the functions. However, such immunity terminates as soon as the functions come to an end, although normally the individual remains immune from jurisdiction for any official act performed during the discharge of his functions.

The rationale behind these national immunities is grounded in the principle of separation of powers and in particular the need to protect state officials (say, the head of state) from interference by other state organs (say, courts) that could jeopardize their independence or political action.

As stated, international law obliges national and international jurisdiction to set aside any functional immunity the accused may invoke as a defence, any time he is charged with an international crime (13.2). Consequently, the exercise of criminal jurisdiction cannot be hampered by the claim that an individual has acted qua state official, in the exercise of his function. *Quid iuris* with respect to personal immunities?

The issue was authoritatively decided by the ICJ in its judgment in the *Arrest Warrant* case (§§ 51–7). The Court logically inferred from the rationale behind the rules on personal immunities of such senior state officials as incumbent ministers of foreign affairs (but the reasoning of the Court can be applied equally to heads of state or government, and—to a limited extent—to diplomatic agents), that these immunities must perforce prevent any prejudice to the 'effective performance' of their functions. They therefore bar any possible interference with the official activity of such officials. It follows that an incumbent senior state agent (belonging to one of the categories mentioned above) is immune from foreign jurisdiction, even when he is on a private visit or acts in a private capacity while holding office. Clearly, not only the arrest and prosecution of such a state agent while on a private visit abroad, but also the mere issuing and international circulation of an arrest warrant, may seriously hamper or jeopardize the conduct of *international* affairs of the state for which that person acts.

In summary, even when accused of international crimes, the state agent entitled to personal immunities is inviolable and immune from prosecution on the strength of the international rules on such *personal* immunities. This proposition is supported by some case law (for instance, *Fidel Castro*[24] in Spain). If the allegations about international crimes committed by foreign state officials are known before they enter a foreign territory, the territorial state may ask the foreign state official to refrain from setting foot in the territory; if that official is already on the territory, the state may declare him *persona non grata* and request him to leave forthwith.

All this applies to *incumbent* senior state officials. As soon as the state agent leaves office, he may no longer enjoy personal immunities and, in addition, becomes liable to prosecution for any international crime he may have perpetrated while in office (or before taking office), pursuant to the aforementioned customary rule lifting functional immunities in the case of international crimes.

However, the situation is different for international criminal courts. First, the judgment of the ICJ in *Arrest warrant* implicitly seems to take the view that the customary international rule on personal immunities does not apply with regard to international criminal courts and to the arrest warrants they eventually issue. It held that 'the immunities enjoyed under international law by an incumbent (or former) Minister for Foreign Affairs do not represent a bar to criminal prosecution in certain circumstances' (§ 61). It then enumerated among such instances the case where 'an incumbent or former Minister for Foreign Affairs may be subject to criminal proceedings before certain international

---

[24] See Order (*auto*) of 4 March 1999 (no. 1999/2723). The Audiencia Nacional held that the Spanish court could not exercise its criminal jurisdiction, as provided for in Art. 23 of the Law on the Judicial Power, for the crimes attributed to Fidel Castro. He was an incumbent head of state, and therefore the provisions of Art. 23 could not be applied to him because they were not applicable to heads of state, ambassadors, etc. in office, who thus enjoyed immunity from prosecution on the strength of international rules to which Art. 21(2) of the same Law referred (this provision envisages an exception to the exercise of Spanish jurisdiction in the case of 'immunity from jurisdiction or execution provided for in rules of public international law'); see Legal Grounds nos 1–4. The Court also stated that its legal finding was not inconsistent with its ruling in *Pinochet*, because Pinochet was a former head of state, and hence no longer enjoyed immunity from jurisdiction (see Legal Ground no. 5). For the (Spanish) text of the order, see the CD-Rom, EL DERECHO, 2002, Criminal case law.

criminal courts, *where they have jurisdiction*' (§ 61, emphasis added). The Court then mentioned the ICTY, the ICTR, and the ICC, noting that the ICC Statute 'expressly provides, in Article 27(2), that "[i]mmunities or special procedural rules which may attach to the official capacity of a person, whether under national or international law, shall not bar the Court from exercising its jurisdiction over such a person"' (§ 61). It is thus clear that the ICJ did not make the lifting of personal immunities before international criminal courts contingent upon the express or implicit contemplation of such lifting in the relevant court's statute. It instead held that the non-invocability of personal immunity before international courts was admissible to the extent that the relevant court or tribunal *had jurisdiction* over the international crime with which the state official at stake was charged.[25]

Second, the rationale for *foreign* state officials being entitled to urge personal immunities before national courts does not apply to international criminal courts. That rationale resides in the need for foreign state officials not to be exposed to the prosecution by national authorities that might use this means as a way of interfering with the foreign state officials' activity, thereby unduly impeding or limiting their international action. In many states judicial authorities are not independent of the political power; they could therefore decide to prosecute foreign state officials on grounds that have little to do with their legal or illegal conduct and indeed amount to a way of unduly interfering with the action of those state officials. This danger of abuse does not arise instead with regard to international criminal courts and tribunals, which are totally independent of states and subject to strict rules of impartiality. In addition, these courts and tribunals are much better equipped than national courts to deal with international crimes, because they are 'specialized' in this area and their judges are selected on account of their particular competence or experience in the matter.

Thirdly, the unavailability of personal immunities before international criminal courts finds some support in international practice. In the *Taylor* case, the SCSL relied upon its *international* nature to reject the claim of the defence that the issuance of the arrest warrant against the then incumbent head of state of Liberia violated the rules on personal immunities. In particular, the SCSL insisted on the fact that the rules of international law on personal and state immunity have no bearing whatsoever in respect to the exercise

---

[25] The ICJ did not analyse the issue further (and was not required to do so for the purpose of the case *sub judice*); it therefore left a few questions unanswered. First, it did not specify what is an international criminal court and on what grounds personal immunities would not apply before competent international criminal courts and tribunals. Is it because these bodies are international in nature? Or rather because the statutes of these courts and tribunals contain a provision which derogates from the rules of customary international law on immunities? And what are the features that distinguish an international criminal court from a domestic one?

In addition, the ICJ did not specify the exact scope of the asserted non-application of personal immunities before international criminal courts. In particular, it did not distinguish between the power of an international criminal court *to issue an arrest warrant*, i.e. a coercive act against a person that constitutes the legal basis upon which a formal request for arrest and surrender can be addressed to a given authority, and *the obligations* (if any) *of states* to disregard the customary rules of international law on immunities, in order to comply with a request for arrest and surrender issued by such a court or tribunal. In addition, by asserting that personal immunities do not bar the exercise of jurisdiction of competent international criminal courts such as the ICTY, the ICTR, and the ICC, the ICJ did not take into account the profound differences between the two ad hoc international criminal tribunals (the ICTY and the ICTR) and the ICC. The ad hoc Tribunals were created by virtue of a decision of the UN Security Council and are vested with the authority of a Chapter VII 'measure'; the ICC is a treaty-based court and its existence and establishment rests upon the direct consent of contracting states. This distinguishing feature has a bearing on the scope of the obligation of states to execute the requests for arrest and surrender issued by those courts against persons entitled to personal immunities under customary international law. See P. Gaeta, 'Does President Al Bashire Enjoy Immunity from Arrest?', 7 JICJ (2009), 315–32.

of jurisdiction by international criminal courts. In this regard, it noted that those rules aim at protecting the sovereign equality of states; therefore they have no bearing on the functioning of international criminal courts, which do not act as organs of a particular state but exercise their mandate on behalf of the international community (*Taylor*, § 51). In addition, one can make reference to the fact that no one has ever claimed that the ICTY violated the immunities of the then President of the FRY, Slobodan Milošević, by issuing and circulating an arrest warrant against him. Arguably, the absence of any challenge to the issuance by the ICTY of an arrest warrant against a serving head of state in respect to his immunities, absent any derogation from personal immunities in the resolution of the Security Council establishing the ICTY or in the Statute of the ICTY itself, shows that states considered that such a derogating provision was unnecessary with regard to the exercise of jurisdiction by an international criminal court.[26]

Finally, the current thrust of international law is to broaden as much as possible the protection of human rights and, by the same token, to make those who engage in heinous breaches of such rights criminally accountable. The very logic of the present trends of international law therefore fully warrants the subjection of state officials to the judicial scrutiny of international independent bodies, whenever such officials *i*) are accused of serious criminal offences against basic values of the world community; and *ii*) there is no risk that such judicial scrutiny be surreptitiously used as a means of unduly restraining the official activity of the state agent concerned.

In summary, it seems justified to hold that under international law personal immunities of state officials may not bar international criminal courts from prosecuting and trying persons suspected or accused of having committed international crimes, or at any rate the criminal offences over which the relevant international court or tribunal has jurisdiction.

17.4.3 THE DISTINCTION BETWEEN ADJUDICATORY JURISDICTION OF INTERNATIONAL CRIMINAL COURTS AND ENFORCEMENT JURISDICTION OF STATES

That personal immunities do not hamper a competent international criminal court to exercise jurisdiction over persons accused of international crimes does not mean necessarily that, if an arrest warrant is issued by such an international criminal court and a request to execute it is made to a particular state, that state can lawfully disregard the personal immunities eventually accruing to the concerned individual under international law in executing the arrest warrant. One thing is the jurisdiction of an international

---

[26] In this respect one commentator has contended that those immunities have been removed by the Security Council (see e.g. D. Akande, 'International Law Immunities and the International Criminal Court', 98 AJIL (2004), at 415). The ICTY has been created by a Chapter VII decision of the Security Council, and therefore—so the argument runs—the ICTY Statute is capable of removing the immunities accruing to the officials and representatives of all member states: it could do so by virtue of the acceptance by member states of the authority of Security Council decisions under Arts 25 and 103 of the UN Charter. However, it is not trivial to note that neither the Security Council resolution adopting the ICTY Statute nor the ICTY Statute itself contains a provision removing personal immunities, let alone the immunities of serving heads of state. Therefore, one fails to understand how the Security Council or the ICTY Statute can have derogated from the customary rules on personal immunities by simply remaining silent on the matter. Clearly, it would not be sufficient to counter that this derogation is 'implicit' because the Security Council has created an international tribunal vested with jurisdiction over persons responsible for given crimes. As the ICJ aptly noted in the *Arrest Warrant* case, the existence of jurisdiction does not imply the absence of immunities and this statement of course also applies to international criminal courts established by the Security Council to prosecute international crimes.

criminal court to sit in judgment over a particular individual accused of an international crime (so-called adjudicatory jurisdiction), and another thing is the powers and obligations of states concerning the exercise of their enforcement jurisdiction over foreign states or foreign state officials.[27]

One could be tempted to contend that since international criminal courts do not have enforcement power it would be logical to require that if those courts can exercise their jurisdiction against persons protected by personal immunities in a foreign national jurisdiction, states are necessarily allowed to lawfully disregard those immunities to comply with a request for surrender by an international criminal court. However, at present, the logic of international criminal justice does not work this way: the fact that an international criminal court is endowed with jurisdiction over a particular case but is deprived of enforcement powers does not imply that national judicial authorities are permitted to do whatever an international court asked them to do; and more so if that court has been established by virtue of a treaty, like the ICC, and therefore its authority derives from an instrument based upon consent.

Clearly, the constitutive instrument of an international court can derogate from the rules of customary international law on immunities with the respect to the exercise of jurisdiction by national authorities, including the execution of an arrest warrant issues by an international criminal court.[28] This is what the ICC Statute does, although only with respect to the relationship among contracting states. Indeed, Article 98(1) of the ICC Statute provides that the Court *may not proceed* with a request for surrender and assistance if compliance with it would require the requested state to act inconsistently with its

---

[27] See in this regard Gaeta, cit. n. 25, on which the revision of this section is partially based.

[28] In the case of the ICTY and the ICTR, the contention can be made that, since the obligation for UN member states to cooperate with those tribunals is laid down in a binding resolution of the Security Council, any order or request for judicial assistance emanating from the two ad hoc Tribunals has the authority of a decision of the Security Council. Therefore, UN member states are obliged to comply with any such orders and requests, which prevail over other international obligations incumbent upon them by virtue of Article 103 of the UN Charter. With regard to personal immunities, therefore, if the ad hoc Tribunals order a UN member state to arrest and surrender a serving head of state, or any other person entitled to claim personal inviolability under international law, the requested state has no other choice than to comply with the order.

This argument, however, on its face does not dispose of the issue of the 'lawfulness' of the arrest and surrender vis-à-vis the state that the arrested person represents qua head of state. As a matter of fact, Art. 103 mainly serves to solve issues of conflicting obligations incumbent upon member states in favour of those stemming from the UN Charter. Nevertheless, one could argue that Art. 103 produces a sort of 'legality effect' in the reciprocal relationship among UN member states, whenever one of them complies with an obligation deriving from the UN Charter. It would be preposterous for a UN member state to violate an international obligation vis-à-vis another member state for the purpose of complying with Article 103 and then bear international responsibility for having acted in accordance with the overarching obligations following from Art. 103. The prevalence, under Art. 103, of Charter obligations over other bilateral or multilateral obligations must logically entail that observance of Art. 103 involves the absence of any responsibility for the breach of bilateral or multilateral obligations existing outside the Charter. Therefore, concerning orders of arrest and surrender, a member state of the United Nations would not be responsible for a breach of the rules on personal immunities if the person arrested and surrendered to the ad hoc Tribunals is a state official of another UN member state. The state proceeding with the arrest and surrender can invoke Art. 103 of the UN Charter and its obligation to comply with the binding decision of a UN body to avoid incurring international responsibility. Clearly, the same would not be true when the person sheltered by immunities is a representative of a non-member state of the United Nations: in this instance, the state proceeding with the arrest and surrender would violate the customary international rule on immunities towards the non-member state, and would therefore commit a wrongful act vis-à-vis that state (think, for instance, of the hypothetical arrest and surrender to the ICTY of Slobodan Milošević by a UN member state, when Milošević was still serving as head of state of the FRY and at a time when the question of the FRY's membership of the United Nations was still questionable).

obligations under international law with respect to immunities of a person or property of a *third* state, unless the Court can first obtain a waiver of the immunity from the third state. As a commentator has noted, under Article 98(1) the Court is obliged 'not to put a state in the position of having to violate its international obligations with respect to immunities'.[29] Therefore, before issuing the request, the Court must first seek the cooperation of the third state concerned, and obtain a waiver of immunity.

'Third state' in this context clearly means 'non-contracting state'. A waiver of immunity would be therefore a necessary condition to the execution of a request for surrender only in those cases where the requested (contracting) state is internationally obliged to respect the immunities of states *not party* to the Statute. By contrast, in the relationship between the requested (contracting) state and other contracting states, such a waiver is not necessary, since contracting states have accepted the provision embodied in Article 27(2), according to which no international immunity can bar the exercise of the jurisdiction of the ICC (including the issuance of warrants of arrest against persons enjoying international immunities). In other words, the ICC Statute contains a derogation from the international system of personal immunities for charges of international crimes, but only among states parties to the Statute and in the 'vertical' relationship with the Court.[30]

One could argue that to recognize that the ICC may exercise its jurisdiction over individuals who are entitled to personal immunities before foreign national courts is illogical if domestic authorities continue to be bound by the rules of customary international law on personal immunities when it comes to the need to surrender those individuals to said international court. However, this is not so. Once issued, the arrest warrant produces its autonomous legal effects and constitutes the legal basis upon which a state can surrender a person subject to the jurisdiction of the ICC. Therefore the possibility remains that a state, on the basis of such an arrest warrant, can surrender a person to the ICC once this person is no longer entitled to immunities because he or she has relinquished his or her post, or because the requesting state has managed to obtain a waiver of immunities from the foreign state that the person represents. On the other hand, a state could freely decide to disregard the personal immunities of this same foreign state official and surrender him or her to the Court. However, in this latter case, the state will commit an international wrongful act, even though this wrongful act will not infringe upon the jurisdiction of the ICC over the person concerned.

In the light of the above, the contention can therefore be made that the request by the ICC to arrest and surrender President Al Bashir[31] is not in conformity with Article 98(1) of the ICC Statute.[32] Sudan is not party to the ICC Statute, nor was it at the moment of the issuance of the request to the member states to execute the arrest warrant against Al Bashir. The incumbent head of state of Sudan, President Al Bashir, enjoys personal immunities under international law vis-à-vis other states, including states parties to the

---

[29] C. Kress and K. Prost, 'Article 98', in Triffterer, *ICC Commentary*, at 1603.

[30] Art. 27(2) and Art. 98(1) only deal with cases related to the exercise of jurisdiction *by the court*. Therefore, the contention is warranted that the ICC Statute derogates from the customary international rules on personal immunities, among contracting states, only on condition that the requested state needs to arrest a person for surrender to the ICC. The derogation from the regime on personal immunities set up by the ICC Statute does not encompass a request for arrest and extradition issued by domestic authorities, for proceedings *before national courts*. Therefore the derogation applies only at the 'vertical' level (i.e. when compliance with a request by the ICC is at stake) and not at the 'horizontal' level (i.e. at the level of the relations between state parties to the ICC Statute). For a contrary view see J. Kleffner, 'The Impact of Complementarity on National Implementation of Substantive Criminal Law', in 1 JICJ (2003), 86–113.

[31] *Al Bashir (Prosecution's Application for a Warrant of Arrest)*.

[32] For a different view, according to which personal immunities accruing to state officials of third state do not apply when the ICC jurisdiction has been triggered by the Security Council, as has been the case for Sudan, see Akande, ci. n. 26,

ICC Statute, and will continue to enjoy them as long as he holds his position. The ICC has not obtained from the government of Sudan any waiver of the immunities of President Al Bashir; hence, it is not empowered by the Statute to proceed with a request for surrender. The steps taken by the ICC in this respect are *ultra vires* and at odds with Article 98(1). Therefore, states parties to the Statute are not obliged to execute the ICC request for surrender of President Al Bashir, and can lawfully decide not to comply with it. Clearly, however, the fact that states parties to the ICC Statute are not obliged under the Statute to execute the request for arrest and surrender of Omar Al Bashir does not mean that they cannot freely decide to do so. In such a case, the state will commit a wrongful act against Sudan. The ICC—being not bound to respect international immunities of incumbent heads of state from any state, could dispose of the illegality of the arrest by applying the principle *male captus bene detentus*. Admittedly, however, this scenario is highly implausible. Before travelling abroad, President Al Bashir will be very careful and will certainly be sure that the state he wishes to visit gives appropriate and sufficient guarantees that he will not be arrested and surrendered to the ICC.

There is no doubt that justice for the horrendous crimes committed in Sudan must be done, and that even those in power should be brought to justice. However, the rules enshrined and agreed upon in the ICC Statute must be respected, even if this leads to unpleasant results, such as that of protecting some officials of states not parties to the ICC Statute from arrest and surrender in foreign states. To hold otherwise would undermine the credibility of the entire system set up by the ICC Statute, and the ability of the ICC and its member states to generate the perception that this legal system is not susceptible to being 'manipulated' in order to attain specific political goals.

SECTION II

INTERNATIONAL CRIMINAL TRIALS

18

THE ADOPTION OF THE ESSENTIAL FEATURES OF THE ADVERSARIAL SYSTEM

Systems of criminal procedure have traditionally been categorized as *inquisitorial* or *adversarial*. Such analyses often walk a fine line between generalization and stereotype, especially given the cross-fertilization that has now lessened many of the traditional distinctions and the wide variation of practice within these categories. These traditional generalizations, treated with caution and with the understanding that they are not comprehensive paradigms, can nevertheless provide a useful framework within which to design and analyse a brand new criminal justice system facing unprecedented practical challenges. They serve as 'abstract intellectual constructs' of 'ideal types' of legal system, to borrow the language of Max Weber.[1]

Precursors of the *adversarial system* are said to have emerged as the earliest substitute for private vengeance, according to anthropologists. 'Arbiters' or 'judges', often drawn from the community, heard complaints between aggrieved parties. Individuals or their relatives or clan members, but not a public official, would accuse the alleged wrongdoer; find evidence or bring witnesses; and present their case against an accused who could respond. The Greek *polis*[2] and Republican Rome offer two early examples. Proceedings tended to be public and oral, as many participants were illiterate and paper costly. Trial

---

[1] See e.g. M. Weber, 'Religious Rejections of the World and Their Directions' (1915), in H. H. Gerth and C. Wright Mills (eds), *From Max Weber: Essays in Sociology* (London: Routledge & Kegan Paul, 1970), 323ff. ('Such constructions make it possible to determine the typological locus of a historical phenomenon. They enable us to see if, in particular traits or in their total character, the phenomena approximate one of our constructions: to determine the degree of approximation of the historical phenomenon to the theoretically constructed type. To this extent, the construction is merely a technical aid which facilitates a more lucid arrangement and terminology' (at 324).)

[2] The trial of Socrates, in 399 BC is indicative of the system prevailing in the Greek polis. He was accused by three Athenian citizens (Meletus, Anytus, and Lycon) of three crimes (not recognizing the gods worshipped in Athens, introducing new deities, and corrupting the young). The prosecution was conducted by the three accusers, whereas the defence was made by Socrates himself: there was no professional prosecutor nor defence counsel. Socrates was tried by 501 citizens (chosen by lot out of the roughly 25,000 citizens) who acted as jurors, no separate judge presiding over the proceedings. The proceedings were divided up into two parts: the establishment of whether Socrates was guilty or innocent, and the penalty. After the first round of speeches by the accusers and the defendant, the jury took a vote on the issue of guilt or innocence and decided by 280 votes to 221 that Socrates was guilty of the crimes with which he had been charged. Then Meletos requested the death penalty, whereas Socrates suggested as 'an appropriate penalty which is strictly in accordance with justice' that he be given 'free maintenance at the state's expense'. After the jury decided to uphold Meletos' request and sentenced him to death, Socrates made a third speech, where he explained

would normally take place before a popular assembly of sorts, or at any rate in a public place.

The modern adversarial system emerged gradually in the Middle Ages as part of a much broader movement, particularly in England, to limit the power of royal officials. Instead of royal judges determining guilt based on charges investigated and brought by other royal officials, an accused was entitled to be tried by a jury of lay persons from the local community. Though most adversarial systems now reserve jury trials for only the most serious crimes, many elements of that procedure have remained, including: *i*) a bifurcation of issues of law (to be decided by the judge) and issues of fact (to be decided by the jury), where the judge remains neutral in respect of the facts but, conversely, applies robust rules of evidence and procedure to ensure the fairness of the proceedings and prevent the jury from being exposed to improper or prejudicial information; and, *ii*), the presentation of all evidence, including of witnesses, at trial (i.e. directly to the jury). The institution of the jury was a vital catalyst in the creation of the adversarial system, which shows its attributes most prominently in respect of jury trials; but that mould has been retained even in trials determined by a judge sitting alone, known as a 'bench trial'. This system remains dominant in most former British colonies and, over the past three decades, has been transplanted to, or at least had a major influence on reforms in, Chile, Italy, Russia, and elsewhere.

The *inquisitorial model* originated in ancient Rome, at the time of the Empire; was developed in the ecclesiastical courts of the Catholic Church through the Middle Ages, including for such crimes as heresy and offences against the clergy; and was in full bloom by the thirteenth century, when it had been adopted by kings and princes throughout Europe. Investigations under this model were conducted in secret by officials who questioned the suspect, the victim, and any witnesses; recorded their statements in writing; and then decided on guilt or innocence. One and the same person therefore was responsible, without any public hearing whatsoever, for both investigation and adjudication. The inquisitorial model, despite opening the door to notorious abuses, did at least aspire to the view that justice should be administered according to professional learning and, presumably, for the general good. Legal representation of the suspect during the investigative phase, access by the suspect to the results of the investigative stage, and the rigorous separation of investigating and adjudicating judges, were later innovations. The inquisitorial model remains dominant on the European continent in such countries as France, Belgium, The Netherlands, and Spain, and most of their former colonies, as well as in China and Japan.

that death was not an evil. Whereas normally sentences were carried out at once, that of Socrates could not be executed forthwith, for the day before Socrates' trial was the first day of an important ceremony (the Annual Mission of the state galley to Delos to commemorate the deliverance of the Cretan Minotaur by Theseus). As the absence of the galley lasted a month, Socrates awaited his execution in prison, which was then carried out by having him drink hemlock. See Plato, *Apology*, in Plato, *The Last Days of Socrates*, ed. H. Tredennick (Harmondsworth: Penguin,1969), 45–76; Xenophon, 'Socrates' Defence', in R. Waterfield (ed.), *Conversations of Socrates* (Harmondsworth: Penguin, 1990), at 41–67. See also C. Mossé, *Le Procès de Socrate* (Brussels: Éditions Complexe, 1987), at 89–114.

18.1 A COMPARISON OF THE TWO MODELS IN OPERATION

The significance of individual rules in any given legal system cannot be viewed in isolation from the broader system. Juxtaposing individual rules from different criminal justice systems is therefore fraught with 'the danger of comparing apples and pears'.[3] Identical rules often serve very different purposes; and identical purposes are often served by very different rules. This section offers a brief overview of the relatively constant features of most inquisitorial and adversarial systems which must, of necessity, understate the exceptions and variations. The compatibility of individual rules with effectiveness and fairness can best be evaluated once the broader mechanisms are in view; at the same time, the great diversity of practices suggests that variation is possible without destroying the coherence of the system as a whole. The discussion that follows offers a comparative overview of the adversarial and inquisitorial systems based primarily on the procedures in respect of the most serious national crimes, rather than the abbreviated practices that often apply for lesser offences.

18.1.1 INITIATION OF INVESTIGATION, PROSECUTION, AND TRIAL PROCEEDINGS

Modern inquisitorial and adversarial systems alike confer primary, if not exclusive, responsibility for initiating criminal investigations and prosecutions on a public official. They also both confer initial responsibility for investigating on the police, under the general supervision of a prosecutor's office. From there, the systems diverge.

Adversarial prosecutors are then responsible for deciding whether to bring charges before a judicial authority against a suspect, which may lead to the person's arrest and preparation for trial. The decision is somewhat discretionary: even where there is sufficient evidence to believe that a crime has been committed, a prosecutor may choose not to bring a charge where it is not in the public interest.[4] This discretion, though usually exercised only in respect of relatively minor offences, allows prosecutors to avoid 'plea bargaining' (see 18.1.3). A decision not to prosecute is not subject to challenge by victims or other private citizens, although a very limited number of criminal statutes (such as antitrust and fraud statutes in the United States) do permit a private individual to seek punitive damages for violation of criminal prohibitions,[5] as well as pursuing any civil claims against the alleged culprit as may be available.

---

[3] J. Nijboer, 'The American Adversarial System in Criminal Cases: Between Ideology and Reality', 5 *Cardozo J. Int'l & Comp. L.* (1997), 79, at 84.

[4] The 'Code for Crown Prosecutors' of the Crown Prosecution Service (CPS) of England and Wales (www.cps.gov.uk/publications/docs/code2010english.pdf, February 2010) expressly sets out, in s. 4.17, the public interest factors that might outweigh the public interest in a prosecution, including, for example, the fact that only a nominal penalty is likely to be imposed, the availability of some other penalty or 'out-of-court disposal' of the matter, the fact that the offence was committed 'as a result of genuine mistake', or that prosecution would require 'details to be made public that could harm sources of information, international relations or national security'. The United States Attorneys' Manual offers a slightly different list of public interest factors, including the suspect's 'willingness to cooperate in the investigation or prosecution of others' (s. 9-27.320).

[5] Private parties in the United States may commence proceedings under certain federal criminal statutes, such as the Racketeer Influenced and Corrupt Organizations Act, 18 USC §§ 1961–8, but the remedy is limited to punitive monetary awards against the defendant.

The prosecutor in an inquisitorial system is usually duty-bound, once there is some basis to believe a crime has been committed, to hand over a case to an investigating judge (*juge d'instruction*), who then becomes the central protagonist of the investigative stage.[6] The investigating judge, depending on the system, either takes primary control over the investigation, or at least closely supervises the work of the prosecutor. The decision to charge a suspect, which is also supposed to be non-discretionary, then rests with the investigating judge. In some inquisitorial systems a victim or even private organizations (trade unions, associations, etc.) may, in respect of some offences, commence a criminal prosecution or seek review of any decision not to proceed.[7] In almost all systems, they may join the criminal proceedings as 'civil parties' (*constitution de partie civile*) even at the investigative stage. The degree to which a civil party has the right to be informed and to actively participate in the proceedings, for example by introducing evidence or questioning witnesses, varies from system to system, but the overall purpose is the same: 'to obtain a ruling on the guilt of the person and to obtain compensation for the damage suffered'.[8]

18.1.2 INVESTIGATION

A hallmark of the adversarial system is that both parties conduct their investigations without contemporaneous judicial supervision, except for intrusive techniques such as property searches or telephone surveillance. The consequence of the unsupervised nature of investigations is that the fruits of those investigations are not 'evidence' until admitted at trial. This imposes a powerful, albeit retrospective, incentive for the parties to conduct proper and non-abusive investigations. The parties are also bound by ethical and legal constraints, including the prosecution's obligation to investigate fully before deciding whether to charge an accused. The results of these prosecution investigations must be disclosed to the accused at some point before trial, but unlike an inquisitorial system, need not be disclosed contemporaneously with the investigation. The accused usually bears no reciprocal disclosure obligation, an asymmetry that arises from the accused's right against self-incrimination, which would be infringed by forcing the accused to produce any and all information generated during an investigation.

Inquisitorial systems, by contrast, rely on the investigating judge to supervise and/or directly conduct investigations. The parties are not eliminated from the process. Many inquisitorial systems permit the prosecutor and any legal representative of the suspect to continuously consult the 'case file' (or 'dossier') which records the results of any investigative steps. Parties usually have the right to propose specific investigative steps, including questioning of specific witnesses or accepting certain documents into the case file.[9]

---

[6] Many inquisitorial systems do, however, confer discretion similar to that generally prevailing in adversarial systems. German prosecutors, under some circumstances even without leave of the competent court, may dispense with prosecutions under circumstances similar to those mentioned in the English and American codes mentioned above: see German Code of Criminal Procedure, § 153.

[7] See C. Buisman, 'Principles of Civil Law', in K. Khan, C. Buisman, and C. Gosnell (eds), *Principles of Evidence in International Criminal Justice* (Oxford: Oxford University Press, 2010), at 28 (noting that German procedure permits private prosecutions for trespass, libel, slander, violation of mail secrecy, destruction of property, patent and trademark violations, unfair competition, assault and battery, and negligent wounding).

[8] See V. Dervieux, 'The French System', in M. Delmas-Marty and J. R. Spencer (eds), *European Criminal Procedures* (Cambridge: Cambridge University Press, 2002), at 227.

[9] J. Pradel, *Droit pénal comparé* (Dalloz: Paris, 2008), 287–90; M. Damaška, 'Evidentiary Barriers to Conviction and Two Models of Criminal Procedure: A Comparative Study', 121 U. Pa. L. Rev. (1973), 506, at 533–4.

Nevertheless, the investigating judge usually dominates the investigative process, deciding what steps should be taken; what information should be accepted into the case file; and presiding over interviews of witnesses, including deciding what questions are asked and whether both parties may be present and how they may participate. Transcripts of those proceedings may, often be admitted at trial, depending on the circumstances. The European Court of Human Rights has affirmed that an accused must, 'as a general rule', be permitted to participate in the taking of such statements if they are later admitted at trial without any opportunity to examine the witness, and if they are of decisive importance to the finding of guilt.[10] The purpose of the investigative phase in an inquisitorial system is not only to discover information, but to facilitate its admission as 'evidence' at a future trial. The rigorous procedure, disclosure rules, and participation of the parties during the investigative stage perform largely the same function as the rules of evidence applied in an adversarial trial: to ensure a minimum standard of reliability.[11]

The investigating judge is a powerful figure. He or she decides the course of the investigation in most respects and, therefore, the scope of the information that will determine guilt or innocence; determines whether and when the dossier should be handed over for trial; and whether there are justifications for special procedures, such as excluding the defence from the hearing of a witness. The investigating judge is therefore expected to act with rigorous impartiality and pursue incriminating and exonerating information equally to reach the truth. The existence of an investigating judge ostensibly favours poor defendants who may not have sufficient resources to pay a legal team to conduct investigations. This benefit is counter-balanced by a number of drawbacks. Proceedings before an investigating judge are usually discontinuous and therefore can stretch over a long period. The quality of investigations depends very much on the skill, disposition, and motivation of a single official. The concentration of authority can sometimes lead to abuse, as when an investigating judge who wishes information from a suspect pressures him by ordering his pre-trial detention. Finally, the supposed equalization of position of impoverished defendants is questionable, given that those with money can still retain private counsel to appear before the investigating judge.

Systems adopting the adversarial model tend to distrust the potential for abuse or unfairness in the exercise of governmental power, no matter how well intentioned may be the official. The antidote is to place the prosecutor and defence in a position of parity with one another in a fully public trial, during which the propriety and reliability of any information tendered during trial may be openly tested. Inquisitorial systems, also recognizing the potential for abuse of authority, have also sought in various ways to limit the power of the investigating judge (as in the case of France, which has separated the power to investigate from the power to order the detention of the accused, the latter now vested in an independent judge, called *juge des libertés et de la détention*). Other systems, as in Germany, have abolished the position of investigating judge entirely; or, as in Italy and Chile, have adopted the adversarial model wholesale.

---

[10] See e.g. *Lucà* v. *Italy*, §§ 39–40 ('where a conviction is based solely or to a decisive degree on depositions that have been made by a person whom the accused has had no opportunity to examine or to have examined, whether during the investigation or at the trial, the rights of the defence are restricted to an extent that is incompatible with the guarantees provided by Article 6').

[11] Pradel, cit. n. 9, at 248 ('Alors qu'en common law, la preuve se fait essentiellement à l'audience (devant le juge qui sera amené à rendre un jugement sur la poursuite), dans la famille romano-germanique au contraire, la preuve est rassemblé surtout lors de la phase préparatoire, notamment là ou il y a une instruction préparatoire'); M. Damaška, 'Evidentiary Barriers', 535 ('evidence contained in the dossier is in a sense 'canned' for subsequent use at trial'); Buisman, 'Principles of Civil Law', at 25 ('In many aspects, the pre-trial investigation is akin to a trial').

18.1.3 GUILTY PLEA

Guilty pleas by an accused before trial are, as a practical matter, a common feature of adversarial systems. A variety of procedures, often applied in combination, may be used to encourage guilty pleas. The traditional 'plea bargain' involves the prosecution dropping a charge in return for a guilty plea in respect of a lesser charge, sometimes with a specific recommendation from the prosecution to the judge as to sentence. Plea agreements in many systems, however, are judicially or statutorily regulated in some way. A plea may be given specified weight in sentencing, as in the United Kingdom, where the reduction is a diminishing percentage depending on the timeliness of the accused's plea. Judges may in some systems, at their discretion, indicate in advance of the plea the sentence that would be imposed, taking into account aggravating and mitigating circumstances, if a guilty plea were to be entered.[12]

The main merit of the procedure is to arrive at a sentence acceptable to both parties, following well-established precedent, while avoiding a time-consuming trial. The vast majority of criminal cases are resolved through plea bargaining, thus significantly reducing the workload of courts.[13] In England only some 1 or 2 per cent of all cases are finally disposed of by jury trial, the routine method being summary trial in the magistrates' courts (which normally simply record the guilty plea entered by the accused and the sentence inflicted).[14]

Plea bargaining of sorts has also started to be introduced in inquisitorial systems for medium- or low-level offences.[15] Even in respect of those offences where a trial is mandatory, an admission of guilt means, in effect, that the trial focuses directly on factors relevant to sentencing.

18.2 TRIAL PROCEEDINGS

The adversarial trial commences from a clean slate: none of the evidence disclosed between the parties or notified to the trial court constitutes evidence until it has been accepted as such during the trial itself. The general principle is that witnesses must give their testimony before the court, and that any statements previously given to the police or prosecution are not admissible as evidence.[16]

An inquisitorial trial does not commence from a clean slate. The case file transmitted to the trial court by the investigating judge is, in most investigative systems, presumptively admitted as evidence. In other words, any piece of information, document, or exhibit in the case file constitutes 'evidence' before being submitted to the court in oral proceedings. Testimony or statements recorded in the case file can, subject to certain conditions, be admitted without the witness's appearance during the trial itself, or if they do appear,

---

[12] See e.g. Illinois Supreme Court Rules, Rule 402(d); *R. v. Goodyear* (Practice Note) [2005] 1 WLR 2532 (English CA).

[13] See, for the United Kingdom, the details provided by A. Ashworth, *The Criminal Process: An Evaluative Study*, 2nd edn (Oxford: Oxford University Press, 1998), 268–84. According to Ashworth, 'in the magistrates' courts the rate of guilty pleas is well over 90 per cent' (at 268).

[14] See J. R. Spencer, 'Introduction', in Delmas-Marty and Spencer (eds), cit. n. 8, at 18.

[15] Pradel, cit. n. 9, at 450–4.

[16] Proof of uncontroversial or peripheral matters may, however, be adduced in English courts by written statements. See sections 9 and 10 of the British Criminal Justice Act 1967.

may be simply asked whether they confirm the testimony they gave to the investigating judge.

18.2.1 THE COMPOSITION AND ROLE OF THE TRIAL COURT

Adversarial trials for serious offences are normally presided over by a judge, with the verdict being decided by a jury selected from the general public.[17] The modern jury system relies on a bifurcation of the role of judge and jury. The judge decides issues of law, which include *i*) the admissibility of information as evidence; *ii*) defining the legal elements of crimes for the jury; and *iii*) advising the jury as to the proper legal parameters for assessing the evidence, including the standard of proof required for a finding of guilt. The presence of the lay jury explains the vitality of the rules of procedure and evidence, and the judge's role in screening prejudicial or improper information from the jury's knowledge.[18] An additional role for the judge in some systems is a final charge to the jury which can include a summary of the evidence. The jury then deliberates in private and renders a simple verdict of 'guilty' or 'not guilty' without any further explanation. The privacy, inscrutability, and almost sanctity of the reasoning process may explain the need for rigorously fair proceedings in which the jury is not exposed to improper elements.

The judge in an adversarial system, though not prohibited from posing questions to witnesses or asking the parties to present evidence on particular issues, is expected to play a rather passive role. This passivity arises from the tripartite logic of the adversarial system, which relies on the parties presenting their cases, the jury deciding the case, and the judges preserving the fairness of the proceedings. An overactive bench could, for example, unduly influence the jury or interfere with the methodical presentation of a case. The principle continues to apply, albeit with lesser force, in the case of bench trials.

Jury trials are not mandatory, and may be waived by the accused. The same rules of trial fairness, including the standards of admissibility, continue to apply even in the absence of the lay jury. Further, judge verdicts tend to be accompanied by at least an oral explanation of the judge's reasoning. Regardless of whether the verdict is made by judge or jury, sentencing is almost always in the hands of the judge. The sentencing hearing follows very loose rules of evidence, permitting the accused to present evidence in mitigation, and the victim and families to present their views. Guidelines on sentencing have become increasingly strict in England and many American jurisdictions in recent decades, thus reducing judicial discretion.[19]

---

[17] The role of a popular jury, going back to ancient Greece, re-emerged in England in the late Middle Ages when people living in the place where the alleged offence had been committed would be asked to answer under oath whether the person was guilty or innocent. The practice was codified in Art. 39 of the *Magna Charta* (1215), which proclaimed a set of fundamental rights for 'freemen' (that is, for members of the aristocracy and the middle classes and for them only, as opposed to the monarch and members of the lower classes), including the right to trial for criminal offences 'by the lawful judgment of [their] *peers* and by the law of the land'. Interestingly, the medieval jury was expected to know something about the crime and the accused, whereas such knowledge would disqualify participation in a modern jury.

[18] A. Orie, 'Adversarial v. Inquisitorial Approach in International Criminal Proceedings Prior to the Establishment of the ICC and in the Proceedings before the ICC', in Cassese, Gaeta, and Jones, *ICC Commentary*, at 1427 ('It is logical in a common-law system, where the jury is entirely dependent on the evidence presented to it at trial, that the trial judge be called by the parties to intervene whenever necessary in order to prevent the information on which the jury will base its verdict being polluted by improper elements').

[19] Felonies are sentenced by juries in six American states, and in respect of capital punishment in all American jurisdictions where it remains available. M. Hoffman, 'The Case for Jury Sentencing', 52 Duke LJ

The jury system is not unknown to inquisitorial systems. Thinkers of the Age of Reason and the French Revolution, admiring the English jury system, imported it into France and bolstered the notion by appealing to 'people's justice'. The appalling abuses of the French revolutionary courts substantially discredited the involvement of juries and let to its abandonment in most of continental Europe. Modern inquisitorial systems now often rely on mixed panels of professional judges and lay persons. French Assize Courts, for example, which have jurisdiction over serious criminal offences, consist of a panel of three professional judges, one of whom presides over the trial hearings, and a lay 'jury' of up to nine persons, chosen by lot. They deliberate together, and then pronounce upon both the facts and the law, on guilt or innocence and, in case of conviction, on the sentence. Any decision against the accused must be taken by a minimum of eight votes to four. Assize Courts in Italy are similarly comprised of a mixed panel of professional judges and a lay panel members.

In many civil law systems, decisions taken by mixed panels in inquisitorial systems are reasoned (they are drafted by the presiding judge or any of the professional judges serving on the court along with the lay judges). Unlike adversarial systems, guilt and sentencing are assessed concurrently by the adjudicators, whether judges alone or comprised of professional and lay judges.

Judges in an inquisitorial system play a much more active role in the production of evidence at trial. The judges are already informed of both the facts of the case and the main legal issues through the case file. The presiding judge is a dominating figure in the conduct of proceedings. He or she may determine the order in which evidence is discussed or witnesses are called; question the witnesses before the parties; and periodically question the accused (who does not, however, take an oath) as evidence is heard. A witness's testimony before the judges is often treated as supplementary to the record of their testimony before the investigating judge. The court may also call evidence *proprio motu*.

The different philosophy behind the two systems can perhaps be summed up as follows: in the inquisitorial system the court (and the investigating judge before it) aims to discover the truth through an analytical procedure and comprehensive information; in an adversarial system, the truth is conceived as emerging only from a dialectic of opposing views and information presented in accordance with a structured procedure designed to guarantee maximum fairness.

18.2.2 ADMISSION OF EVIDENCE AND DETERMINATION OF GUILT

The admissibility of information is decided in the adversarial system at the trial itself on the basis of strict and detailed rules. Some of these rules have tended to become more flexible in recent decades, such as the traditional rule excluding 'hearsay' evidence—i.e. proving that a fact is true because the witness heard someone else say that it was true. The problem with this evidence is that the truth-value (i.e. reliability) of the statement reported by the witness is notoriously difficult to ascertain if the person who made it cannot be questioned. The traditional rule on inadmissibility of hearsay was justified by the concern that this evidence was likely to be given undue weight by a lay jury which, it must be recalled, deliberates without the supervision of a judge. Such information is nevertheless often of some value, and became subject to a host of judicial or statutory exceptions

(2003), 951; N. King and R. Noble, 'Felony Jury Sentencing in Practice: A Three-State Study', 57 Vand. L. Rev. (2004), 885; Pradel, cit. n. 9, at 535–8.

over the years. This culminated in the UK with the Criminal Justice Act, which dispensed with the general rule and affirms that hearsay is admissible 'if it is in the interests of justice'.[20]

The rules of evidence and procedure continue to be vital to the fairness of adversarial trials in a variety of respects. Testimonial evidence must still, in general, be heard orally before the court so that it can be properly tested. The party calling the witness must adduce the testimony using non-suggestive questions, whereas the party testing the witness is entitled to challenge the testimony through leading questions. The differing modes of questioning arise from the premise that the calling party is seeking to adduce evidence that should be told by the witness in his or her own words, not the words of the lawyer; the cross-examining party, in contrast, is seeking to challenge rather than adduce evidence, and is therefore entitled to suggest contrary propositions.

Adversarial systems have a strong attachment to live testimony of witnesses. Previous statements made out of court by a witness are not admissible as evidence, but they may be used: *i*) on cross-examination to impeach the witness's credibility by showing that he or she said something contradictory on a previous occasion; and *ii*) on direct examination to refresh the witness's recollection or to rebut an allegation of recent fabrication.

The order of the presentation of evidence is important to the fairness of an adversarial proceeding. In principle, the accused is entitled to know and test the entirety of the prosecution case before being obliged to determine whether to call evidence. The prosecution is not thereafter permitted to adduce additional evidence to fill gaps or repair damage to its case, but is only permitted to call rebuttal evidence in relation to highly specific or unforeseeable defence evidence. The defence may thereafter present evidence in rejoinder. Closing statements by the prosecution and then the defence bring the trial proceedings to an end.

Inquisitorial systems are flexible both as to trial procedure and information that may be relied on to determine guilt. The notion of 'admissibility' of evidence has much less significance in most inquisitorial systems, where the investigating judge has already determined the threshold of reliability of information, and where professional judges participate in deliberations and can guard against undue weight being placed on presumptively dubious information (for example, hearsay). In other words, in the inquisitorial system the principle of freedom of evidence employed (*liberté des preuves*) is upheld.[21] Procedure also tends to be less strict, since the judges determine the order of calling witnesses and the presentation of evidence, without regard to any sequence of incriminating or exculpatory evidence.

Inquisitorial systems often describe the standard of proof for establishing the guilt of the accused as relying on the judge's 'inner conviction', whereas adversarial systems usually rely on the standard of 'beyond a reasonable doubt'.

18.2.3 THE POSITION OF THE ACCUSED

Trials *in absentia* are generally impermissible under the adversarial model which, after all, depends on a contest between the prosecution and the defence. If the defendant is absent, the trial cannot start, but it may continue if he absconds after the trial starts, or is

---

[20]   Criminal Justice Act, 2003, Part 11, s. 114(1)(d).

[21]   On the limitations of the principle in, for instance, the French system, see, however, G. Stefani, G. Levasseur, and B. Bouloc, *Procédure pénale*, 16th edn (Paris: Dalloz, 1996), at 34–8.

removed from the courtroom for disruptive behaviour; in either case, the defence would be obliged to continue to represent the interests of the accused as effectively as possible.

Many systems of inquisitorial tradition do permit trials *in absentia*—that is, even when the accused never appeared in court and is on the run or in hiding. France, Belgium, Italy, Greece, the Netherlands, most Latin American countries, and China permit such trials, although Spain and Germany do not. In most civil law systems (including those such as Italy where the adversarial model has been adopted) the public interest of the community in adjudicating alleged criminal offences generally outweighs the right of the accused to be present in court, at least whenever the accused voluntarily tries to evade justice. (Nonetheless, we will see below, that trials in absentia are only admissible if a set of safeguards are respected, as repeatedly stated by the European Court of Human Rights.)

In most adversarial systems, the accused may refuse to give any statements at any time, and no adverse inferences may be drawn from such a refusal.[22] If an accused chooses to testify at trial, however, he or she is obliged to take an oath or make a solemn declaration to tell the truth, and must answer all permissible questions put to him or her. The inquisitorial system does not accord an unequivocal right to remain silent during trial proceedings, and questions may be posed to the accused intermittently by the trial judges. The accused is not obliged, however, to take an oath—implicitly permitting the accused to lie without any danger of penal sanction for having done so.

18.2.4 THE ROLE OF VICTIMS

Victims in adversarial systems may pursue civil claims in respect of the actions that form the basis of a criminal charge, although such proceedings are normally pursued separately and subsequent to any criminal trial. Though victims have no formal role during the determination of guilt or innocence of the accused, many adversarial systems do permit victims to make submissions during sentencing hearings.

In contrast, as pointed out above, in the inquisitorial system victims may in some cases institute proceedings or take part in the criminal proceedings initiated by the prosecution, through the so-called *constitution de partie civile* (application to join criminal proceedings as a 'civil petitioner') aimed at claiming compensation. 'Civil petitioners' participate in the proceedings: they have access, through their lawyers, to the case file (*dossier*) during the investigation by the investigating judge (*instruction préparatoire*) and may call for certain investigations; at trial, they can call evidence, question witnesses, and set out their legal views as to the guilt of the accused. Thus, in contrast with the adversarial system, criminal and civil proceedings are not separate but may be merged.

18.3 APPELLATE PROCEEDINGS

Resort to appeal proceedings is relatively restricted in most adversarial systems. Prosecutors are sometimes barred from appealing at all, and appeals judges often accord substantial discretion to factual findings of a judge or jury below. Appellate judges normally restrict themselves to issues of law (for instance, on whether the trial judge gave

---

[22] However, in 1964 a law passed in the UK, the Criminal Justice and Public Order Act, authorized trial courts to draw adverse inferences against defendants who, in some well-defined conditions, fail to give evidence. Furthermore, in *John Murray v. UK* the European Court of Human Rights held that the drawing of inferences from the refusal of a suspect or accused, when arrested, to give an account of his presence in a certain place could not be regarded as 'unfair or unreasonable in the circumstances' (§ 54).

wrong instructions to the jury), and will not intervene unless there is a gross misrepresentation by the judge in jury instructions that resulted in a miscarriage of justice.

The rationale behind this restrictive approach is twofold. First, there is a fundamentally ideological reason. As explained by J. Spencer, 'In England, the jury was introduced as a substitute for the judgment of God pronounced through the ordeal, and like the judgment of God it was not open to challenge on the ground that it had given an answer that was wrong.'[23] It was thought that it would be improper and illogical to ask an 'appellate' jury to pass judgment again on guilt or innocence (unless, on account of gross errors of law the appeal court remits a case to the trial court for a new trial). In other words, the verdict of the jury at the trial level is final, unless it is invalidated by serious mistakes made by the judge in his instructions to the jury. Hence, there is no jury in the appeal court. The second reason is economic: reducing the number of cases appealed alleviates the burden of appeal courts.

In the inquisitorial system both parties may lodge an appeal against conviction or sentence, but the prosecutor may also appeal against an acquittal. Furthermore, appellate proceedings may entail a sort of retrial, in that the same evidence may be scrutinized a second time and legal arguments reheard. In short, appellate proceedings consist of a full rehearing of the case. According to a leading authority, M. R. Damaška, the reason behind this civil law approach is twofold. First, prosecution is conceived of as an ongoing process, while in common law countries there is a tendency to see it as a one-off event. Second, members of the judiciary (often both prosecutors and judges) are professionals working in a hierarchical system; it is therefore taken for granted that higher courts should normally redo what has allegedly been done badly by inferior courts.[24]

18.4 A SUMMARY OF THE MAIN DISTINGUISHING FEATURES

The adversarial model rests on two fundamental features: *i*) investigations are conducted autonomously by the parties without any ongoing judicial supervision or control; *ii*) the establishment of truth is a contest through a public, oral trial between the parties, adjudicated in the most serious cases by a jury, as supervised by a judge (or by a judge acting as a trier or fact). The virtues commonly ascribed to this system include: *i*) a vigorous, independent and public administration of justice; *ii*) the separation of the establishment of facts (reserved to the jury) from the settlement of legal issues (entrusted to the judge); and *iii*) greater protection of the rights of the accused by ensuring that judges do not become enmeshed too deeply in the practicalities of the case, thus preserving their exclusive role as guardian of the procedural fairness of the system itself. The weakness of this system, however, is that it relies heavily on the competence of the lawyers to ensure substantive fairness and equality. This may pressure an impecunious defendant into accepting a plea agreement even if he is innocent or, perhaps more common, not as guilty as the charges suggest.[25] Further, the generally passive role that is expected of most trial judges in a jury

---

[23] Spencer, cit. n. 14, at 28. See also at 7.

[24] M. R. Damaška, *The Faces of Justice and State Authority: A Comparative Approach to the Legal Process* (New Haven: Yale University Press, 1986), 48–50; M. R. Damaška, 'Models of Criminal Procedure', 51 *Zbornik, Collected Papers of Zagreb Law School* (2001), at 495–6.

[25] See S. Bogira, *Courtroom 302* (New York: Vintage, 2005), 37–48.

trial does not necessarily fit naturally with the need to manage and control the parties' presentation in respect of extremely complex matters.

The inquisitorial model is conceived as a controlled process in which both the investigation and the trial is, in large measure, within the control of judicial officials purportedly acting in the *public interest*. The main merit of this system is that, in principle, the judicial institution is bent on the impartial and efficacious administration of justice, without regard to the strength of the prosecution or defendant's attorneys and without the hindrance of procedural obstacles that may, in a particular case, interfere with discovering the truth. Though the investigation phase may tend to be lengthy, the trial proceedings may proceed quickly and relatively informally, and permit questions to be posed to the accused throughout the proceedings.

Notable weaknesses of this system include: *i*) undue reliance on the impartiality, competence, and goodwill of judicial officials in the exercise of their powers, sometimes without adequate checks and balances; *ii*) the duration of the investigative phase, arising from the heavy burdens imposed on investigating judges; *iii*) the lack of plea bargaining which could generate efficiencies; and *iv*) a procedural model that may be less protective of the rights of the accused, and which depends heavily on the competence, ability, and thoroughness of judges before, during, and after trial, often exercised behind closed doors.

Despite these differences, however, it must be emphasized that these characteristics are merely trends. General observations may too easily become stereotypes that ignore the substantial variations that exist within the inquisitorial and adversarial families. Some inquisitorial systems do possess a more robust conception of admissibility of evidence; some adversarial judges, particularly in bench trials, question witnesses vigorously and guide the parties in the presentation of their case; and some adversarial systems apply relatively flexible standards for the admission of evidence.

18.5 THE ADOPTION OF THE ADVERSARIAL MODEL AT THE INTERNATIONAL LEGAL LEVEL

18.5.1 THE NUREMBERG AND TOKYO TRIBUNALS

The adversarial model, albeit without a jury, predominated in the design of the International Military Tribunal sitting in Nuremberg. American and British delegates, with the general if not wholehearted support of their French colleagues, generally succeeded in imposing their views over the reluctant Soviet delegation.[26] The choice, in retrospect, was sensible. The French and Soviet delegations were not united in presenting a comprehensive inquisitorial alternative and, indeed, their proposals would not likely have satisfied the requirements of a fair trial with basic protections for the rights of the accused. Inquisitorial notions did find their way into the Statute and practice of the Nuremberg Tribunal in four important respects: *i*) the power of the judges to play an active role, in particular by calling and questioning witnesses and the accused;[27] *ii*) the right of the

---

[26] For the history of the London negotiations leading to the acceptance of the adversarial model, see the first edition of this book (2003), at 376–81.

[27] The Soviet and French delegates insisted that the Tribunal have the power to ask questions of the accused and the witnesses, in spite of Justice Jackson's misgivings of (*International Conference on Military Trials*, at 257, 262–4). The British delegate, however, did not object who noted that the Tribunal was 'a complete master of the situation' (263).

accused to make an unsworn statement at the end of trial; *iii*) the possibility of trying the accused *in absentia*;[28] and *iv*) very flexible rules of evidence.[29]

These inquisitorial elements were more the result of consensus than compromise, reflecting a strong common desire for rules that would simplify proceedings and expedite trials to the greatest extent possible.

The Charter of the Tokyo Tribunal was drafted mainly by the Americans under the direction of the future Chief Prosecutor, J. B. Keenan, and propounded as an executive decree of General MacArthur. The Charter largely reproduced the substance of the Statute of the Nuremberg Tribunal. The dangers of a loosely defined procedure appear to have emerged more tangibly than in the Nuremberg trial. Judge Pal and Bernard, the Indian and French judges, respectively, issued dissenting opinions criticizing the inconsistency of procedural decisions taken by the majority (at 629–56) and the failure to safeguard the rights of the defendants.[30] A major issue was the failure to give the defence access to the

---

[28] The initial US draft, departing from domestic practice, left open the possibility of such proceedings: 'The Tribunal shall determine to what extent proceedings against defendants may be taken without their presence' (*International Conference on Military Trials*, 25). The provision was restated in the subsequent drafts (58, 123 (with a slight change), 179, 183), until the Soviet delegation proposed a more express amendment: 'The Tribunal shall have the right to take proceedings against persons charged with the crimes, set out in Article 2 of this Agreement, in the absence of the defendant, if the defendant should be hiding or if the Tribunal should for other reasons find it necessary to conduct the hearing in the absence of the defendant' (183). Subsequently modifications were made by the British delegation (at 206 and 353) before being codified as Art. 12 of the Statute. The American prosecutor Justice Jackson was then called upon to defend the provision in proceedings against Krupp von Bohlen und Halbach (because of his incapacity to stand trial): 'Of course, trial *in absentia* has great disadvantages. It would not comply with the constitutional standard for citizens of the United States in prosecutions conducted in our country. It presents grave difficulties to counsel under the circumstances of this case. Yet, in framing the Charter, we had to take into account that all manner of avoidances of trial would be in the interests of the defendants, and therefore, the Charter authorized trial *in absentia* when in the interests of justice, leaving this broad generality as the only guide to the Court's discretion [...] the Court should not overlook the fact that of all the defendants at this Bar, Krupp is unquestionably in the best position, from the point of view of resources and assistance, to be defended. The sources of evidence are not secret. The great Krupp organization is the source of most of the evidence that we have against him and would be the source of any justification. When all has been said that can be said, trial *in absentia* still remains a difficult and an unsatisfactory method of trial, but the question is whether it is so unsatisfactory that the interests of these nations in arraigning before your Bar the armament and munitions industry through its most eminent and persistent representative should be defeated' (*Trial of the Major War Criminals*, vol. II, at 5–6.) Jackson lost his argument on the facts but not in principle, with the Tribunal's President, Lord Justice Lawrence, declaring: 'upon the facts presented the interests of justice do not require that Gustav Krupp von Bohlen be tried *in absentia*. The Charter of the Tribunal envisages a fair trial, in which the Chief Prosecutors may present the evidence in support of an indictment and the defendants may present such defense as they may believe themselves to have. Where nature rather than flight or contumacy has rendered such a trial impossible, it is not in accordance with justice that the case should proceed in the absence of a defendant' (*Trial of the Major War Criminals*, vol. II, 21).

[29] The Tribunal was enjoined, pursuant to Art. 19 of the Nuremberg Statute, to 'adopt and apply to the greatest possible extent expeditious and nontechnical procedure' and to admit any evidence which it 'deems to be of probative value'. The American and British delegates easily accepted a very flexible standard for the dispensation of the rules of evidence that would apply in their domestic practice. Justice Jackson described those rules of evidence as 'a complex and artificial science to the minds of Continental lawyers, whose trials usually are conducted before judges and do not accord the jury the high place it occupies in our system' (*Trial of the Major War Criminals*, vol. II, xi).

[30] The French judge, Bernard, in his Dissenting Opinion, stated: 'The Defendants, in spite of the fact that the charges concerned crimes of the most serious nature, proof of which [involved] the greatest difficulties, were directly indicted before the Tribunal and without being given an opportunity to endeavour to obtain and assemble elements for the defense by means of a preliminary inquest conducted equally in favour of the Prosecution as of the Defence by a magistrate independent of them both and in the course of which they would have been [*sic*] benefited by the assistance of the defence counsel. The actual consequences of this

archives of the Japanese government, then in the possession of the United States, which would have been vital for the presentation of exculpatory evidence concerning chain of command. The appearance of unfairness was compounded by the authoritarian conduct of business by the President, the Australian Judge Webb who, in addition to sometimes treating witnesses in a derogatory manner, did not allow his fellow judges to question the witnesses directly. Another member of the panel, Judge Röling, later criticized the conduct of proceedings in scholarly writings.[31]

18.5.2 THE ICTY AND ICTR

The Statutes of the ICTY and ICTR, adopted by the Security Council as part of its resolutions setting up the two Tribunals, do not specify a form of criminal procedure to be followed. That was left mainly to the judges who were given responsibility to 'adopt [...] the rules of procedure and evidence for the conduct of the pre-trial phase of the proceedings, trials and appeals'. (ICTY Statute, Article 15; ICTR Statute, Article 14). The form of proceedings was decidedly adversarial in one important respect: the prosecutor was charged with acting 'independently as a separate organ' of the two Tribunals, and to prepare 'an indictment' against an accused, subject to confirmation or dismissal by a judge. Thus, the ICTY prosecutor (who until 2003 also served as the prosecutor of the ICTR) was accorded robust authority and latitude to conduct investigations commensurate with the unpredictability of the situation on the ground. That necessarily left the judges with the responsibility to construct a counter-balancing mechanism without specifying its form, shifting the difficulty from the drafters to the judges. The decision is, in a sense, logical: the judges responsible for applying the system should also be the ones to determine its form and amend it according to actual experience.

The first edition of the Rules of Procedure and Evidence of the ICTY, adopted collectively by its judges on 11 February 1994, followed through on this adversarial premise in a number of respects: non-supervision of investigations by the judiciary; disclosure to (and hence, participation of) the defence only after the issuance of an indictment; a prescribed order for the presentation, starting with the prosecution; the 'principle' that testimony should be heard 'directly by the Chambers', implying the rejection of pre-recorded written evidence; specific acknowledgement of the modes of questioning as 'examination-in-chief, cross-examination and re-examination'; and a general standard for the admissibility of evidence in Rule 89—albeit very flexible—which implied that the judges would learn the facts of the case only through evidence admitted during trial, and not by way of any written dossier handed by the prosecutor to the judges.

A number of rules provided a foundation for practices more commonly associated with an inquisitorial system, while other practices have emerged and were subsequently codified in the Rules. Rule 98, reserving a judicial authority to 'order either party to produce additional evidence' and to 'itself summon witnesses', signalled that the judges would not

---

violation of principle have been, in my opinion, particularly serious at the present case' (*Araki and others*, at 494). The French judge also criticized the fact that, the Tribunal having no power of review of the action taken by the prosecutors, the prosecution had not been exercised 'in an equal and sufficiently justified manner regarding all justiciable' (*sic*). In particular, the judge regretted that the Emperor of Japan had not been indicted. In his view, the Emperor's 'absence from the trial, while making one wonder whether, if his case is measured by a different standard, international justice would merit to be exercised, was certainly detrimental to the defense of the Accused' (494).

[31] See e.g. B. V. A. Röling and A. Cassese, *The Tokyo Trial and Beyond* (Cambridge: Polity Press, 1993), at 50–5.

necessarily be passive audiences. Trial judges have in some instances summoned critical witnesses and questioned them, usually after both parties have closed the presentation of their evidence.[32]

Judges have also become more active in case management, increasingly aware of the potential need to supervise the parties in complex cases. Rule 65 *ter* codifies the practice of judicial supervision of pre-trial meetings between the prosecution and defence to discuss issues such as disclosure, possible agreements as to facts that could reduce the scope of the trial, and the time anticipated for presentation of a case. The parties are also required to file pre-trial briefs describing the evidence they intend to call, including a summary of each prospective witness's testimony. Early ICTY Trial Chambers flirted with the practice of requiring the parties to provide, in advance of trial, all previous statements of witnesses expected to testify; the ICTR (but not the ICTY) Rules expressly permit such an order. The practice, which might look very similar to the transfer of an investigative case file or dossier, is not now followed, perhaps in recognition that this would give the appearance, if not the reality, of undermining the trial as the crucible for the presentation (and testing) of evidence. In any event, the parties may tender written statements under circumstances in lieu of oral testimony—a mainly inquisitorial innovation introduced in the form of Rule 92 *bis*.

The managerial role of judges has been strengthened by the addition of Rules 73 *bis* and 73 *ter*, which confer on the Chamber broad powers to determine the number of witnesses to be called by the parties; the time available for its presentation; and even to 'fix a number of crime sites or incidents comprised in one or more of the charges' which 'are reasonably representative of the crimes charged'. Most Trial Chambers use these powers as a sword of Damocles to encourage the parties to voluntarily reduce their cases, as when the Trial Chamber in *Karadžić* warned the prosecution that it was 'gravely concerned about the scope of the Prosecution's case and the potential effect that this will have on the fair and expeditious conduct of the trial [...] [K]eeping the trial manageable is simply necessary to ensure that justice is done in a fair and expeditious manner, which is in the interests of all the parties'.[33] In *Gotovina*, the Trial Chamber, having apparently felt that the case was not being reduced sufficiently, followed through on its admonitions by limiting the number of crime events that could be presented by the prosecution.[34] The effect of these rules, as one judge recently explained, is 'to exert considerable influence over the course of proceedings with a view to resolving the problems that are presented by the use of a pure and undiluted form of adversarial process'.[35] The result is a heavily managed adversarial proceeding.

The evolution of the practice of the ICTY and ICTR reveals that, ironically, proceedings have become more inquisitorial through the common law method. Mixed benches of common law judges have gradually modified their practices in light of daily courtroom experience, incrementally amending the RPE to reflect these experiences more than forty-five times since their first edition was adopted in 1994.

---

[32] *Krajišnik* (*Reasons for Decision Denying Defence Motion Regarding Chamber Witnesses Biljana Plavšić and Branko Đerić and Decision on Admission into Evidence of Biljana Plavšić's Statement and Book Extracts*), TC; *Popović and others* (*Order to Summon Momir Nikolić*), TC; *Stakić* (*Decision summonsing Mr Baltić proprio motu to appear as a witness*), at 2–3.

[33] *Karadžić* (*Decision on the Application of Rule 73 bis*), § 5.

[34] *Gotovina and others* (*Order Pursuant to Rule 73 bis (D) to Reduce the Indictment*), § 2.

[35] I. Bonomy, 'The Reality of Conducting a War Crimes Trial', 5 JICJ (2007), 348, at 351. See also O-Kwon, 'The Challenge of an International Criminal Trial as Seen from the Bench', 5 JICJ (2007), at 363–75.

18.5.3 THE ICC

The ICC Statute and Rules adopted by the Assembly of State Parties in 1998 and 2002, respectively, also reflect a primarily adversarial structure. The prosecutor is again free to conduct investigations without judicial supervision, subject to jurisdiction and satisfaction of the conditions for opening an investigation. The Statute of the ICC does contain a number of inquisitorial elements, including Article 56, permitting the parties to seek special investigative measures from a pre-trial judge to preserve evidence for trial; a relatively extensive hearing, to determine whether charges should be confirmed; and Article 68, concerning the participation of victims in proceedings, albeit not as fully-fledged parties. On the other hand, the ICC (whose Statute and Rules have not been significantly amended since their adoption) has not kept pace with some of the more important and practical inquisitorial innovations put in place at the ICTY and ICTR. No counterpart is to be found, for example, of Rule 92 *bis* and there is, accordingly, no mechanism is defined by which an out-of-court written statement may be admitted without the appearance of the witness. The prosecutor is also, in a major symbolic shift, required under Article 54(1)(a) of the ICC Statute to investigate 'incriminating' and 'exonerating' circumstances 'equally'. The prosecutor is therefore an 'organ of justice' pursuing the truth impartially.[36] The early practice of the ICC shows, however, that the prosecutor is every bit as partisan as his counterparts at the ICTY and ICTR, and the Statute and Rules provide few, if any, mechanisms by which the judges could contemporaneously instruct the prosecutor to perform specific tasks under this obligation.[37]

18.5.4 THE ECCC AND THE STL

The criminal procedure of the ECCC and the STL accord a much greater, if not predominant, influence to inquisitorial procedures. Expectations arising from domestic legal systems undoubtedly played a substantial role in this choice, but may also have reflected the particular priorities of these tribunals: a strong role for victims and domestic lawyers in Cambodia; and the possible need for *in absentia* proceedings (STL Statute, Art. 22) and for summary procedures to obtain highly sensitive evidence in the case of the STL.

The 2004 Cambodian Law on the Establishment of the ECCC provides that the investigating judge exercises supervision and control over the prosecutor, who is charged with primary responsibility to collect evidence and prepare the case for trial. Under Article 23 of the Law, the two investigating judges (one Cambodian and one foreign) have the power to conduct investigations, question suspects and victims, hear witnesses, and to generally collect evidence. Under Rule 55(5) they must 'ascertain the truth' and for that purpose

---

[36] See S. Zappalà, *Human Rights in International Criminal Proceedings* (Oxford: Oxford University Press, 2003), at 29–45.

[37] The one area where ICC judges have moved towards instructing specific investigative steps concerns information contained in victim application forms. Victims have no obligation to disclose exculpatory information to the defence, but their application forms are often disclosed to the prosecution in unredacted form. The prosecution, despite its obligation to disclose exculpatory information to the accused, is not permitted to disclose the unredacted versions of the application forms. ICC decisions have reconciled this contradiction by holding that where a victim's applications 'indicate that victims may possess potentially exculpatory information', then the prosecution should extend its investigation to discovering any information in the victim's possession. Such information, independently generated by the prosecutor, must then be disclosed to the defence. This onerous obligation, articulated so far only in very general terms, has not yet translated into specific orders or instructions. *Katanga and Chui* (*Appeal of Mr. Katanga against the Decision of Trial Chamber II of 22 January 2010 Entitled 'Decision on the Modalities of Vitim Participation at Trial'*), § 81; *Muthaura and others* (*Decision on the Defence Requests in Relation to the Victims' Applications for Participation in the Present Case*), §§ 10, 12.

'they shall conduct their investigation impartially, whether the evidence is inculpatory or exculpatory'. They may also 'order the provisional detention of a charged person after an adversarial hearing' (Rule 63(1)). They are responsible for issuing a closing order at the end of the investigation that either indicts a person charged and commits him or her for trial, or dismisses the case (Rule 67). The investigating judges then hand over a case file both to the judges and the parties, as well as to the victims who, in theory, are given wide participatory rights at both the investigative and trial stage.

Trial proceedings are conducted by the presiding judge who, together with the other judges, may start the proceedings by asking the accused 'any questions which they consider to be conducive to ascertaining the truth' (Rule 90(1)). After the questioning by the judges, the accused may be questioned by the co-prosecutors 'and all the other parties' (Rule 90(2)). Witnesses are then questioned by the judges and the various parties (Rule 91). The judges have wide latitude to adopt procedures that they consider expeditious and fair.

The STL does not rely on an investigating judge, but does confer a significant role on a dedicated Pre-Trial judge. This judge, who is prohibited from subsequently sitting at trial, not only confirms or dismisses the indictment, but is given certain conditional investigative powers. The most direct of these is the Pre-Trial judge's obligation, upon a party's request, to question a witness in the party's absence if it is believed that disclosure of the person's identity would seriously endanger them or seriously risk 'that imperative national security interests might be revealed should the witness's identity or affiliation be revealed' (SCSL Rule 93). The parties are then expected to convey a list of questions for the witness (even though one of the two parties will not know that witness's identity); the Pre-Trial judge will conduct the questioning; and the transcript, duly redacted, may then be amenable to admission during the trial. Though resembling Article 56 of the ICC Statute, the measure is far more specific both as to the procedure to be followed and in accepting the principle that anonymous evidence could be admitted into the proceedings (SCSL Rules 149(F), and 159). Further, upon confirming the charges the Pre-Trial judge is to hand over a 'complete file' of proceedings before him or her, including 'any evidentiary material received by him' (SCSL Rule 95(A). This material is presumably not evidence (and may not, therefore, be taken into account by the judges in determining the merits of the case) unless and until admitted pursuant to the applicable provision on the admission of evidence (which is similar to that of the ICTY and ICTR);[38] nevertheless, the transfer of the information has the appearance of the transfer of a case file typical of an inquisitorial system.

The STL Rules prescribe a sequence for the presentation of evidence that is characteristic of an adversarial trial, but also expressly permit the judges to commence the questioning of any witness, and to direct questions to the accused at any time throughout the proceedings.[39] Indeed, the accused himself is permitted to make statements at any time throughout the proceedings, provided the intervention is relevant. One of the incongruous mixtures of adversarial and inquisitorial elements is the apparent rule that no 'adverse inference' is to be drawn when an accused person remains silent in respect of any particular 'specific question'. This means, in effect, that the accused can offer exculpatory observations when he thinks of them, but then may simply decline to answer the inconvenient questions. This is an outcome that would be permissible in neither an adversarial

---

[38] SCSL Rules 149, 150, 155, 156, 158.
[39] SCSL Statute, Art. 20(2); SCSL Rules 145(A), 146(B).

system (where the accused is obliged to assert or waive the right in its entirety) nor an inquisitorial system (where such adverse inferences would be permitted).

18.6 TOWARDS A FELICITOUS AMALGAMATION OF PROCEDURAL ELEMENTS

The evolution of a criminal procedure based primarily on the adversarial model, but with substantial inquisitorial elements, is ongoing. The path forward lies through practical experience in addressing the unique challenges of international crimes, including the complexity and duration of proceedings; standards of evidence that properly balance reliability and efficacy; access all available information; and enough predictability to the rules to engender confidence that the process is fair and transparent. Merging rules from different habitats is a challenge, and yet those rules are gradually adjusting to the particular habitat of international criminal justice.

19

GENERAL PRINCIPLES GOVERNING INTERNATIONAL CRIMINAL TRIALS

Human rights instruments, whether international or constitutional, have had a pervasive impact on domestic criminal procedure. The standards for making an arrest, the information to be provided to an accused upon arrest, the entitlement to remain silent and to counsel, the rules of evidence at trial, the nature of searches that can be carried out during an investigation and the ability to increase sentence on appeal are just a few of the areas in which legislation or court practice has been significantly altered by judicial interpretation of generally worded individual rights.

The Statutes of the ICC and of the ICTY and ICTR enumerate a list of rights that mirrors many of the same rights as are found in international human rights instruments and domestic constitutions. The ICC Statute goes even further, declaring that the '*application and interpretation* of [applicable] law [. . .] must be consistent with internationally recognized human rights'.[1] These various rights may be distilled into six minimum principles: *i*) no implicit or explicit measure requiring self-incrimination; *ii*) adjudication by impartial judges; *iii*) a presumption of innocence and corresponding burden of proof on the prosecutor; *iv*) prompt and detailed communication of the charges and sufficient time, opportunity, and resources to challenge those charges; *v*) trial without undue delay; and *vi*) a public hearing.

These principles are subsidiary to, but do not necessarily exhaust the requirements of, an even broader principle: fairness. Fairness, as stated in *Tadić*, 'is central to the rule of law: it upholds the due process of law' (*Tadić*, AC, § 43). The ICC Statute similarly declares a general obligation of trial chambers to 'ensure that a trial is fair and expeditious and is conducted with full respect for the rights of the accused and due regard for the protection of victims and witnesses'.[2] Fairness pertains not only to the accused, but is an attribute of

---

[1] ICC Statute, Art. 21(3). The term 'internationally recognized' does not appear to have been intended to have a technical or narrow meaning. The ICTR (and ICTY) Appeals Chamber has, in the interpretation of its own enumerated rights, relied on a breadth of sources of international human rights law, including, *inter alia*, the texts and decisions made under the 1950 European Convention on Human Rights, the 1969 American Convention on Human Rights, the 1981 African Convention on Human and Peoples' Rights and, in particular, the 1966 UN Covenant on Civil and Political Rights.

[2] ICC Statute, Art. 64(2), 64(8) (allowing the presiding judge to give directions to 'ensure that they are conducted in a fair and impartial manner'); (ICTY Statute, Art. 20(1) ('The Trial Chambers shall ensure that a trial is fair and expeditious and that proceedings are conducted in accordance with the rules of procedure and evidence, with full respect for the rights of the accused and due regard for the protection of victims and witnesses'; ICTR Art. 19(1); STL Statute, Art. 18(2).

proceedings that may be demanded by any participant in the proceeding, including the prosecution and victim participants.[3]

This chapter discusses the interpretation of these rights and principles before international criminal courts, and their application to selected practical issues.

19.1 THE PROTECTION FROM SELF-INCRIMINATION

The ICC Statute prohibits anyone, as of their first contact with an investigative authority, from being 'compelled to incriminate himself or herself or to confess guilt', and prohibits an accused from being 'compelled to testify or to confess guilt and to remain silent'.[4] The ICC Statute states expressly that the invocation of this right may not be used as a 'consideration in the determination of guilt or innocence', following a standard set out in the case law of the ICTY and ICTR.[5] The ICTY jurisprudence has held that this principle extends to, and prohibits the admission as evidence of, questioning by national authorities.[6] The ICC Statute takes the same stand, at least to the extent that the questioning was pursuant to a request made to the state authorities.[7]

Suspects—i.e. those whom the investigator has 'reasonable grounds' to believe committed a crime—have an immediate right at the ICC and at the ICTY/ICTR to the assistance of counsel upon being questioned, primarily to protect the right to silence.[8] The need for immediate legal assistance 'is rooted in the concern that an individual, when detained by officials for interrogation, is often fearful, ignorant and vulnerable; that fear and ignorance can lead to false confessions by the innocent; and that vulnerability can lead to abuse of the innocent and guilty alike, particularly when a suspect is held incommunicado and in isolation'.[9] The rights to the assistance of counsel and to remain silent may be waived, but any waiver must be fully informed and unequivocal. A signed waiver form was deemed ineffective in one case where the suspect was confused as to the rights available to him, and where he had even, before signing the waiver, tried to invoke them.[10] The prosecution bears the burden of showing the existence of a waiver 'convincingly and beyond reasonable doubt', a standard that is underpinned by the procedural requirement

---

[3] *Haradinaj and others (Corrigendum to Judgment of 19 July 2010)*, (where the Appeals Chamber altered the basis for reversing a trial decision from 'the Prosecution's right to a fair trial' to 'the Trial Chamber's duty to safeguard the fairness of the proceedings'); *Prlić and others (Decision on Prosecution Appeal Concerning the Trial Chamber's Ruling Reducing the Time for the Prosecution Case)*, § 14 ('the requirement of the fairness of a trial in not uniquely predicated on the fairness accorded to any one party').

[4] ICC Statute, Arts 55(1)(a) (in respect of any 'person'); 15(2)(b) (in respect of a person for whom there are 'grounds to believe that [the] person has committed a crime'); and 67(1)(g) (an accused).

[5] ICTY Statute, Art. 21(4)(g); ICTR Statute, Art. 20(4)(g). *Delalić and others*, AC, § 783 ('an absolute prohibition *against* consideration of silence in the determination of guilt or innocence is guaranteed within the Statute and the Rules, reflecting what is now expressly stated in the ICC Statute. Similarly, this absolute prohibition must extend to an inference being drawn in the determination of sentence'); *Orić*, TC, § 16 ('silence may not be used as evidence to prove guilt and may not be interpreted as an admission'); *Martić*, TC § 22. See also *Niyitegeka*, TC, § 46 (refraining from drawing any adverse inferences from silence, but asserting that this was not obliged by international human rights law).

[6] *Delalić and others (Decision on Zdravko Mucic's Motion for the Exclusion of Evidence)*, § 43.

[7] ICC Statute, Art. 55(2) 'or by national authorities pursuant to a request made under Part 9'.

[8] ICC Statute, Art. 55(2)(c); ICTY Rule 42(A)(i); ICTR Rule 42(A)(i); STL Rule 65(A)(i) (notably supplementing the provisions of the other tribunals by specifying that this right applies whether the suspect is 'free or in detention').

[9] *Bagosora and others (Decision on Prosecutor's Motion for the Admission of Certain Materials Under Rule 89(C))*, § 16.

[10] *Bagosora and others*, §§ 18–21. A written waiver is expressly required by the ICC RPE, Rule 112(1)(b).

that such interviews must be audio-recorded, permitting the Chamber to carefully examine the information given to a suspect about the nature of his rights, and any responses. The ICC Statute and STL Rules do permit exceptions to recording 'where the circumstances prevent' it, or it is 'absolutely impractical', respectively.[11]

19.2 THE PRINCIPLE THAT JUDGES MUST BE INDEPENDENT AND IMPARTIAL

This principle of judicial impartiality is embedded in all legal systems, giving effect to one of the most fundamental human rights.[12] Indeed, it is difficult to see how other principles or rights could be safeguarded in its absence. The principle encompasses both independence and freedom from bias, which pertains to both the manner of their appointment terms of service (structural bias), as well as more specific sources of bias that may arise (specific bias).

Judicial independence and impartiality can be protected structurally by: *i*) adopting selection mechanisms that facilitate the selection of persons who are not only competent, of moral integrity, and unbiased, but also independent of any political or governmental authority; *ii*) prohibiting judges from seeking or receiving instructions from outside authorities or being in any way involved in the interests or concerns of the parties; and *iii*) setting up monitoring procedures that prevent judges from practising or showing bias and, if they are found to be partial or slanted, removing judges from a case or even from the court.

In international criminal proceedings the authorities that might in some way interfere with the judges' impartiality are most likely to be the appointing authority or States (in particular, the judge's national state). Hence, election by a 'parliamentary' body, as is the case for both the ICTY and the ICTR (the UN General Assembly, upon proposal by the UN Security Council) and the ICC (the Assembly of States Parties), is the best mechanism for selecting judges. The independence of ICC judges is further strengthened by Article 36(9)(a) of the ICC Statute, whereby judges are not eligible for re-election after the expiry of their mandate.

Once judges have been elected, various means exist for ensuring that they remain independent. First, they must refrain from engaging in activity that might jeopardize their independence or affect confidence in their independence (see, for instance, Article 40(1) of the ICC Statute). Second, they enjoy privileges and immunities including immunity from states' jurisdiction. Third, judges who do feel that their independence may be compromised may recuse themselves, or the parties may seek their disqualification or recusal.

Disqualification at the request of the parties has been extremely rare.[13] Impartiality requires not only that judges be free of actual bias, but that there 'be nothing in the

---

[11] ICC Rule 112(2); STL Rule 65(B).

[12] See *Furundžija*, AC, §§ 177, 189, and 191.

[13] To date the issue of disqualification has been raised in a number of cases: *Delalić and others* (*Decisions of the Bureau of 4 September 1998 and 1 October 1999*); *Kordić and Čerkez* (*Decision of the Bureau of 4 May 1998*); *Brđanin and Talić* (*Decision of 18 May 2000*), *Furundžija*, AC. In *Delalić and others* (*Decision of the Bureau of 4 September 1998*), the Bureau held that the fact of having been elected second Vice-President of Costa Rica did not disqualify Judge Odio Benito because she had pledged not to assume any function in the Costa Rican government before the completion of her mandate as a judge, and the commitment had been confirmed by the President of Costa Rica. Subsequently, some of the defendants filed with the Appeals Chamber a motion for disqualification of three judges sitting on that Chamber on their appeal against conviction; they claimed that these judges, by participating in the plenary session of the ICTY judges which

surrounding circumstances which objectively gives rise to an appearance of bias' as 'would lead a reasonable observer, properly informed, to reasonably apprehend bias' (*Furundžija*, AC, § 189). Allegations of bias on the basis of decisions in the trial itself are almost never sufficient; usually some external indication of partiality to one side or the other is required.[14] The ICC Rules expressly mention as potential grounds for bias: a personal interest in the case, as by some close 'family, personal or professional relationship';[15] previous involvement in a case in which the accused was 'an opposing party'; or the performance of functions prior to becoming a judge, or expression of opinions, that could objectively indicate bias.[16] The judge may excuse himself or herself from the case (at the ICC, with the permission of the President) upon an allegation of bias; otherwise, the initial ruling at the ICTY and ICTR, if deemed necessary by the presiding judge of that bench, is made by judges who are not sitting on the case.[17] In contrast, at the ICC the initial ruling is to be made by 'an absolute majority' of the remaining judges on the bench, which means unanimity on a three-judge panel, from which an appeal could be sought in accordance with the usual rules (ICC Statute, Art. 41(2)(c)).

19.3 THE PRESUMPTION OF INNOCENCE

All statutes of international criminal courts proclaim that an accused is presumed innocent until proved guilty.[18] The presumption of innocence specifically entails that an

---

found that Judge Odio Benito was not disqualified from sitting on the case at the trial level, were disqualified from sitting on the appeal. The Tribunal's Bureau, by a decision of 25 October 1999, dismissed the motion. It found that the three judges had participated in an administrative decision concerning the general question of whether Judge Odio Benito was entitled to continue to exercise her functions as a judge; they had not participated in any judicial decision on the specific question of whether Judge Odio Benito should be disqualified from sitting in *Delalić and others* (§ 14). In *Furundžija* the appellant had recused Judge Mumba because, before being elected judge of the ICTY, she had been a delegate of her government in the UN Commission on the Status of Women, where the definition of rape (the offence submitted to the Trial Chamber in the case at issue) had been discussed; in addition, she had met persons who were later involved in the trial, namely three authors of the *amicus curiae* briefs submitted in the case, as well as one of the prosecutors. The Appeals Chamber found that the link of the judge with these persons had been 'tenuous' (*Furundžija*, AC, § 194) and in addition her membership in the UN body, her sharing the goals of that body, and her concern for the protection of the rights of women had not created any bias in her (§§ 195–215).

[14] See e.g. *Karemera and others* (*Motion by Karemera for Disqualification of Trial Judges*) (rejecting allegation of reasonable apprehension of bias based on the content and timing of certain decision, and an allegation of an 'adversarial stance' in some proceedings); *Blagojevic and others* (*Blagojevic's Application Pursuant to Rule 15 (B)*), § 14; *Karemera* (*Reasons for Decision on Interlocutory Appeals Regarding the Continuation of Proceedings with a Substitute Judge and on Nzirorera's Motion for Leave to Consider New Material*), § 69 ('*Karemera* (*Disqualification Decision*)') (finding a reasonable apprehension of bias in respect of two judges who 'though aware of the circumstances' requiring the recusal of the third judge, 'acquiesced in rejecting [the] motion and, therefore, continuing the trial').

[15] See e.g. *Karemera* (*Disqualification Decision*), §§ 65, 67 (referring to withdrawal of a judge on the basis of a period of cohabitation between a judge and senior prosecution counsel while the case was ongoing).

[16] ICC Rule 34(1). *Sesay* (*Decision on the Defence Motion Seeking the Disqualification of Justice Robertson from the Appeals Chamber*), disqualifying a judge from one case on the basis of extrajudicial writing prior to his involvement with the Court referring to the superior of the accused as a 'butcher' and other statements attributing responsibility for crimes to the armed force of which they were a part).

[17] The issue at the ICTR is referred to the Bureau, consisting of the President and Vice-President of the Tribunal and the presiding judges of the other Trial Chambers. At the ICTY and STL, the decision is made by a panel appointed by the President. ICTR Rule 15; ICTY Rule 15(B); STL Rule 25(D).

[18] ICTY Statute, Art. 21(3); ICTR Statute, Art. 20(3); ICC Statute, Art. 66 ('everyone shall be presumed innocent until proved guilty').

accused: *i*) may only be detained in accordance with the possibility that he or she is not guilty; *ii*) is not subject to any reversal of the burden of proof in respect of any element that must be proven to establish guilt;[19] and *iii*) may not be convicted except on the basis that a finding of guilt can be entered unless the evidence satisfies a standard of some certainty, not mere suspicion or possibility. The presumption extends, not surprisingly, to suspects as well as accused,[20] and includes a duty on the prosecutor not to make public statements that prematurely give the impression that an accused facing charges should already be considered guilty.[21]

The prohibition on reversing the burden of proof can have a potentially pervasive influence on the conduct of trial and interpretation of rules. An accused's failure to enter a plea, based on the presumption of innocence, requires that a plea of not guilty be entered on his behalf. The 'defence' of alibi must not impose a burden of proof on the defence, but requires only the creation of a reasonable doubt as to whether the accused was present as alleged.[22] Evidence that was deemed '*prima facie* admitted', without having first been scrutinized according to the relevant standard, was found by the ICC Appeals Chamber to have imposed on the defence an impermissible 'burden of disproving the admissibility of items'.[23] Charges may be summarily dismissed at the close of the prosecution case, either at the request of the defence or by the court acting *proprio motu*, where no evidence has been presented on a particular charge.[24]

A trier of fact is also expected to give reasons that explain how the burden was met, and to do so with sufficient particularity as to permit meaningful appellate review.[25] The

[19] ICC Statute, Art. 67(1)(i) ('the accused shall be entitled [...] [n]ot to have imposed on him or her any reversal of the burden of proof or any onus of rebuttal'). See *Delalić and others*, TC, §§ 599, 601. In *Wolfgang Zeuss and others* (the *Natzweiler* trial) in his summing up the Judge Advocate insisted on the point that 'the onus of proving the charge which is made against these accused rests upon the Prosecution, and they have to satisfy you beyond reasonable doubt of the guilt of any of the accused before such accused can be convicted' (at 199). It follows that Rule 92 of the ICTY Rules ('a confession by the accused given during questioning by the Prosecutor shall [...] be presumed to have been free and voluntary unless the contrary is proved') is perhaps of doubtful legality. See S. Zappalà, *Human Rights in International Criminal Proceedings* (Oxford: Oxford University Press, 2003), at 94.

[20] See C. J. M. Safferling, *Towards an International Criminal Procedure* (Oxford: Oxford University Press, 2001), at 67–75; Zappalà, cit. n. 19, at 84–5.

[21] *The Situation in the Republic of Kenya* (*Decision on Application for Leave to Participate in the Proceedings before the Pre-Trial Chamber Relating to the Prosecutor's Application under Article 58(7)*), § 22 (expressing its 'deprecation' of the prosecutor's decision to name publicly those for whom he had sought summonses to appear, and concern that 'his actions have the potential to affect the administration of justice and the integrity of the present proceedings'); *Mbarushimana* (*Decision on the Defence Request for an Order to Preserve the Impartiality of the Proceedings*), § 17 ('it would have been preferable if the Press Release had made it clear that there are reasonable grounds to believe that acts of rape were committed [...] And that [the accused] is alleged to bear individual criminal responsibility'); *Lubanga* (*Decision on the Press Interview with Ms. Le Fraper du Helen*), §§ 38, 52 (indicating that comments made by a representative of the prosecutor, in the context of a trial that had been largely held in private session due to witness protection concerns, had been 'prejudicial to the ongoing proceedings (in the sense that they tend to prejudice the public's understanding of the trial' and had improperly expressed 'views on matters that are awaiting resolution by the Chamber, thereby intruding on the latter's role').

[22] *Zigiranyirazo*, AC, §§ 17, 43; *Karera*, AC, § 330.

[23] *Bemba* (Admissibility Decision), § 73.

[24] In *Jelisić* an ICTY Trial Chamber, based on Rule 98 *bis*, at the end of the prosecutor's case acquitted the accused of some of the charges, namely those concerning genocide (*Jelisić*, TC, §§ 16–17), although this decision was much criticized on appeal. See *Jelisić*, AC, §§ 30–77.

[25] In *Kupreškić and others*, the ICTY found that the appraisal of the evidence by the Trial Chamber had been so fallacious as to generate a miscarriage of justice (*Kupreškić and others*, AC, §§ 21–76).

accused is also entitled to a finding of guilt or innocence on *all* the charges preferred against him by the prosecution, unless they are cumulative. Even alternative charges, according to a British Court of Appeal ruling in a post-Second World War case, should be determined by a trial court if it has sufficient evidence to enter a finding.[26]

19.4 COMMUNICATION OF THE CHARGES AND OPPORTUNITY TO CHALLENGE THEM

The right of the accused to be informed promptly and in detail of the charges against him is listed as the first right in the litany of rights that are said to apply 'in the determination of any charge'.[27] In a very real sense, it is a precondition for all the other principles governing the conduct of proceedings. The crimes and modes of responsibility alleged against a person must be set out in the charging instrument, along with 'all material facts underpinning the charges' (*Kvocka*, AC, § 29). This principle is so fundamental that an accused may even raise this defect for the first time on appeal, even though its untimeliness will be a factor in deciding whether the objection should be granted.

The Statutes of the ICC and of the ICTY and ICTR require the accused to have 'adequate time and facilities for the preparation of his defence', which includes the ability to 'communicate with counsel of his own choosing' and to have the assistance of an interpreter as necessary.[28] In addition, the accused must be able to confront witnesses and call his or her own witnesses 'on the same conditions as witnesses against him or her', and to present other evidence. In other words, the accused must have the opportunity—both in terms of material resources and legal opportunity—to mount an effective defence. The principle is often stated as requiring an 'equality of arms' between the prosecution and the defence.

Equality is a precondition of fairness in adversarial proceedings between two contesting parties. The concept implies, according to the case law of the European Court of Human Rights, that the accused may not be put at a serious procedural disadvantage with respect to the prosecutor. Equality cannot, however, be applied mechanically and must take into consideration the numerous asymmetries between the prosecution and defence.[29] The

---

[26] *Schwittkowski*, decided in 1950. The appellant had stabbed a Norwegian officer in a café in Flensburg. He had been charged with assaulting a member of the Allied Forces in Germany contrary to a Military Government Ordinance, and on an alternative charge with causing dangerous bodily injury, contrary to the German Criminal Code. The trial judge found that the accused did not know that the man he had stabbed was a Norwegian officer, and convicted him on the second charge, adding, 'We do not think that if charges are framed as alternatives there should be conviction under both'; he consequently pointed out that there would be no verdict on the first charge, 'but it will of course remain on the Record' (at 20–2). The Court of Appeal held instead that, 'In a case where there are alternative charges, if a Court finds the necessary facts proved which would justify a conviction on each of the alternative charge (*sic*), we consider that it is a proper course to convict on one charge, but to record no formal finding in respect of the other; should an Appellate Court subsequently find it necessary to quash the conviction on the one charge, it would then be open to that Court, in a case where all the necessary elements constituting the alternative offence have been clearly stated by the Trial Court to have been proved, to substitute a conviction on that alternative charge. If, however, as in the present case, the Court finds that a material element constituting the offence has not been proved, we consider that the accused is entitled to a formal finding of not guilty in respect of the charge which has not been proved' (at 22).

[27] ICC Statute, Art. 67(1)(a); ICTY Statute, Art. 21(4)(a); ICTR Statute, Art. 20(4)(a); STL Statute, Art. 16(4)(a).

[28] ICC Statute, Art. 67(1)(b); ICTY Statute, Art. 21(4)(b).

[29] The principle has been more aptly described by the ICTY Appeals Chamber as 'reasonable proportionality' or 'basic proportionality': *Prlić and others* (*Decision on Defendant's Appeal against 'Décision*

prosecution knows nothing about the facts, whereas the accused may know a great deal; the prosecution must prove its case beyond a reasonable doubt, whereas the defence need prove nothing; the defence knows the prosecution case when presenting its case, whereas the prosecution does not; the defence enjoys a battery of rights, some of which will have no application or relevance to the prosecution; one party may have liberal access to the crime scenes, the other may not. These differences do not excuse unequal treatment at the expense of the defence or vice versa; on the contrary, there may be circumstances where the defence must be put in a 'better' or more advantageous position to compensate for some other disadvantage to preserve an overall balance in the proceedings.[30] For example, there may be cases where the prosecutor is in a better position to collect the important evidence in a particular case. Either party may claim inequality,[31] although such assertions by the prosecution are founded not on an individual right to equality, but the public interest in an intrinsically fair proceeding.[32]

Establishing equality of arms in the context of international crimes can be especially challenging given their complexity, breadth, and, often, asymmetrical relationship of the parties with the state where investigations must mainly take place. An accused therefore has the right to be assisted by competent counsel[33] backed up by an adequately funded

---

Portant Attribution du Temps à la Défense Pour La Présentation des Moyens à Décharge'), § 32. See also *Prlić and others (Decision on Prosecution's Further Appeal Following Trial Chamber's Decision on Remand and Further Certification)*, § 38.

[30] Lack of access to Darfur provoked the defence in an ICC case (*Banda and Jerbo*) to claim a violation of several of these rights, including to have 'adequate facilities for the preparation of the defence' and to 'obtain the attendance and examination of witnesses', as well as the impact on overall trial fairness. In the submission of the defence, the prosecution case was not impacted equally, since it was still able, despite also being barred from entering Darfur, to call its witnesses, former UN peacekeepers, who were mainly Nigerian. The witnesses for the defence, on the other hand, were mainly rebels still fighting inside Sudan who could not easily pass across the border into Chad for interviews with the defence. The request for a stay of proceedings had not yet been determined as of the date of going to press; *Banda and Jerbo (Defence Request for a Temporary Stay of Proceedings)*.

[31] *Prlić and others (Decision on Prosecution Appeal Concerning the Trial Chamber's Ruling Reducing Time for the Prosecution Case)*, §§ 14, 24 (quashing a Trial Chamber decision on the time accorded to the prosecution to present its case and remanding for a 'renewed assessment and consideration of whether the reduction of time would allow the Prosecution a fair opportunity to present its case in light of the complexity and number of issues that remain'); *Tadić*, AC, § 48 ('equality of arms obligates a judicial body to ensure that neither party is put at a disadvantage when presenting its case'). On the notion that the excessively succinct and summary nature of many defence witness statements violated the principle of equality of arms, see the ICTY decision in *Kupreškić and others, Decision*, of 11 January 1999, TC at 2. In *Aleksovsi (Decision on Prosecutor's Appeal on Admissibility of Evidence)* (§§ 22–8), the ICTY Appeals Chamber refused to apply more lenient standards of admissibility to (hearsay) evidence presented by the defence, stating that the prosecution is also entitled to a fair trial within the meaning of human rights conventions.

[32] *Haradinaj (Corrigendum to Judgment of 19 July 2010)*, § 2.

[33] *Blagojevic and Jokić*, AC, § 23. *Kottsiepen*, a post-Second World War case before a British Court of Appeal sitting in Germany, describes an alarming scenario: 'Counsel who appeared on behalf of the Appellant stated that he had only been instructed on the previous day, owing to the illness of Counsel who drew the Notice of Appeal. He was offered an adjournment by the Court, but he stated that he had read the papers, interviewed his client, and was ready to proceed. It soon became apparent, however, that Counsel had not read the Record of trial which had been supplied to the Appellant, and he did not appear to appreciate the nature of the proceedings before the Court of Appeal. In spite of repeated invitations to argue the questions of law raised in the Notice of Appeal, he persisted in irrelevancies' (at 110). 'In such circumstances it was obviously unfair to the Appellant to proceed with the case, and it was adjourned to enable him to be adequately represented. [...] We cannot but deplore that a lawyer should be so lacking in respect for the Court or for his client's interests as to appear to argue a case without familiarizing himself with the issues involved, or with the procedure of the Court' (at 108–12).

legal team.[34] The choice of counsel rests mainly with the accused, subject to certain conditions, paid from a legal aid fund if the accused is indigent.[35] One or more investigators, legal assistants, and experts are often an indispensable part of any proper defence, and are also funded by legal aid.

Disclosure of prosecution evidence, discussed in 19.5, is an important component of the right to be informed of the case.[36] Disclosure of exculpatory material is deemed so important in the ICC Statute that it has been moved out of the provisions on disclosure and is listed as a separate right of the accused.[37]

The defendant has the right to call witnesses and to cross-examine any witness called by the prosecution. He also has the right to request depositions. In addition, he has the right to *obtain the attendance* of witnesses (for instance, by asking the court for subpoenas, or to call as court witnesses persons who would be reluctant to testify on behalf of the defence).[38] Furthermore, the accused may request the granting of safe-conducts to witnesses who might fear for their liberty, as well as the taking of testimony by videoconference, whenever witnesses refuse to attend court proceedings at the court's seat. Whereas the prosecution has a battery of powers to request the assistance of states, the defence often has no choice but to seek orders from the Chambers to compel the assistance of a reluctant state. Indeed, Part IX of the ICC Statute on 'International cooperation and assistance' specifically refers to requests from 'the Court'—a term that includes the office of the prosecutor, but presumably not the defence, which is not institutionally part of the Court.

19.5 TRIAL WITHOUT UNDUE DELAY

One of the obvious requirements of a fair trial is that trial proceedings be as speedy as possible. A variety of factors may be considered in determining whether a delay was

[34] The exceptional challenges of investigation and trial of international crimes is amply reflected in the cost of domestic prosecution of such crimes, which has been recognized as requiring exceptional levels of legal aid funding. In *van Anraat*, the Hague Court of Appeal rejected a defence claim that equality of arms had been violated by underfunding, but recognized the principle that exceptional levels of funding were justified: 'the present criminal case has exceptional proportions, partly because of its international dimensions and the fact that the offences (serious international crimes) would have taken place decades ago and mainly in a non-European country. In hearing such a case, especially when the police and the Public Prosecution Service apparently have ample (extra) financial means available for the execution of their tasks, one should make sure that the defence does not end up in a relatively disadvantageous position. This could be true if the present rules for financed legal aid should not acknowledge the special nature of this case. According to the Court, from this special nature arises the need for a defence carried out by two counsels working closely together, which indeed they did, also during the hearings' (§ 6.1).

[35] *Prlić and others* (*Decision on Appeal by Bruno Stojic against Trial Chamber's Decision on Request for Appointment of Counsel*), § 19 ('In principle the choice of any accused regarding his Defence counsel in proceedings before the International Tribunals should be respected unless there are sufficient grounds to override the accused preference in the interests of justice'); *Karadžić* (*Decision on the Request for Review of Registrar Decision and for Summary Dismissal*), § 12 ('I would ask that the Registrar exercise particular caution before attempting to determine the inner functioning of individual defence teams').

[36] *Banda and Jerbo* (*Decision on Issues Relating to Disclosure*), § 9.

[37] ICC Statute, Art. 67 (2): 'In addition to any other disclosure provided for in this Statute, the Prosecutor shall, as soon as practicable, disclose to the defence evidence in the Prosecutor's possession or control which he or she believes shows or tends to show the innocence of the accused, or to mitigate the guilt of the accused, or which may affect the credibility of prosecution evidence.'

[38] This was repeatedly done, for instance, in *Kupreškić and others* (*Decision on Defence Motion to Summon Witnesses*), at 2–3.

undue, including the length of the delay, the complexity of proceedings, the conduct of the parties, the conduct of the authorities involved, and the nature of any prejudice to the accused.[39] The right has not yet been found to have been violated at the international level, although the dissent of a judge at the ICTR did find undue delay in respect of the time taken to issue a judgment following the close of trial, and would have ordered therefore a five-year reduction in sentence.[40]

The proper length of an international criminal trial is difficult to generalize. A great number of witnesses may be called from a variety of different countries, and masses of information may need to be disclosed, digested, and potentially presented and reviewed in court. International criminal courts must usually rely on state cooperation to complete their investigations and for the appearance of witnesses, and typically operate in multiple languages, which require translation. Nevertheless, under the right conditions and with good judicial management, some complex international criminal trials have proceeded with impressive expedition. *Popović and others*, an ICTY trial involving seven accused, 315 witnesses, 34,915 transcript pages, and 87,392 pages of evidence was completed from the first day of trial until judgment, in less than four years. The fastest ICTR single-accused trials have taken, from opening statements until judgment, about nine months.[41] The need to proceed without undue delay is made more urgent where, as is most often the case, the accused is in pre-conviction detention.

Guilty pleas are not nearly as common in international criminal proceedings as in domestic adversarial systems. A guilty plea is undoubtedly a mitigating factor that should be taken into account in sentencing,[42] but there may simply be little room for any reduction in sentence in respect of extremely serious allegations.[43] Further, the inducement of such agreements is weakened insofar as the judges, who are not involved in the plea agreement process, may choose to ignore any sentencing range recommended by the parties.[44] The ICTY has had somewhat greater success with guilty pleas than has the ICTR, possibly on the basis that there was more room to reduce sentence.[45]

---

[39] *Nahimana*, AC, § 1074; *Nyiramasuhuko and others (Judgment and Sentence)*, TC, §§ 137–43; *Bizimungu and others (Judgment and Sentence)*, TC, § 73. In *Nyiramasuhuko*, the Chamber mentions an additional factor, i.e. the 'gravity of the charges'. It is hard to see why gravity, in addition to complexity, would justify longer proceedings.

[40] *Bizimungu and others (Judgment and Sentence)*, TC, partially Dissenting Opinion of Judge Emile Francis Short, § 7.

[41] By comparison, a verdict in the first ICC trial, in *Lubanga*, which involved a single count, came three years and two months after the opening of trial.

[42] *Erdemović (Sentencing Judgment)*, TC, ('An admission of guilt demonstrates honesty and it is important for the International Tribunal to encourage people to come forth, whether already indicted or as unknown perpetrators. Furthermore, this voluntary admission of guilt which has saved the International Tribunal the time and effort of a lengthy investigation and trial is to be commended'); *Todorović (Sentencing Judgment)* § 80 (a plea 'relieves victims and witnesses of the necessity of giving evidence with the attendant stress which this may incur').

[43] A guilty plea of Jean Kambanda, Prime Minister of Rwanda from April through July 1994, was followed by a sentence of life imprisonment. *Kambanda (Judgment and Sentence)*, § 48; *Kambanda*, AC, § 62.

[44] *Nikolić (Sentencing Judgment)* (imposing a sentence of 27 years upon a recommendation by the prosecution of 15 to 20 years, following the accused's agreement to cooperate fully as a prosecution witness in other cases and to plead guilty only to the crime of persecution, in return for dropping a range of other charges against the accused, including participating in a JCE to commit genocide, extermination, and murder).

[45] *Obrenović (Sentencing Judgment)* (imposing a sentence of 17 years upon a recommendation by the prosecution of 15 to 20 years, following the accused's agreement to cooperate fully as a prosecution witness in other cases and to plead guilty only to the crime of persecution, in return for dropping a range of other charges against the accused, including complicity in genocide, extermination, and murder). *Todorović*

19.6 A PUBLIC HEARING

That the proceedings must be public, subject to some exceptions, is a general principle of modern criminal law. Publicity of the hearings is a means of better ensuring that the trial, being under public scrutiny, is fair, in particular that the rights of the accused are not infringed and that the court conducts the proceedings impartially.[46]

Nevertheless, the conduct of *in camera* hearings is provided for whenever this is required by the need to protect the victims and witnesses.[47] The decision to hold hearings behind closed doors is taken by the court, at the request of one of the parties or *proprio motu*.

19.7 FAIRNESS

All the foregoing principles and rights, and their interaction, give effect to this singular and universal principle: criminal proceedings must be fair.[48] The principle is enshrined in all major international human rights conventions (for instance, the UN Covenant on Civil and Political Rights (Articles 14(1) and (26) and in the European Convention on Human Rights (Article 6) and the American Convention on Human Rights (Article 8)), and has been elaborated in the jurisprudence developed thereunder.[49] The principle has a fundamental and practical value in international criminal proceedings whose modalities, given the context in which they operate, are flexible and in their infancy. A rule that seems invariably fair in a highly developed system with a level playing field for investigations may not be in the unique context of international criminal justice. Proceedings before international criminal tribunals are expressly subject to this overarching principle,[50] and its independent significance has been upheld by case law.[51] The principle was given very

(*Sentencing Judgment*) (imposing a sentence of ten years after a joint recommendation of 5 to 12 years made by the parties).

[46] This requirement was not set out in the Charters of the Nuremberg and Tokyo Tribunals. It is, however, laid down in the Statutes of the ICTY (Art. 21(2)), the ICTR (Art. 20(2)), and the ICC (Art. 67(1)), as a fundamental right of the accused. It is also proclaimed with regard to national trials, in the European Convention on Human Rights (Art. 6(1)), the UN Covenant on Civil and Political Rights (Art. 14(1)), and the American Convention on Human Rights (Art. 8(5)).

[47] ICTY Statute, Art. 22; ICTR Statute, Art. 21; ICC Statute, Art. 68.

[48] *Tadić*, AC, § 47 ('the relationship between Art. 20(1) [fairness] and Art. 21(4)(b) [adequate time and facilities] is of the general to the particular. It also agrees that, as a minimum, a fair trial must entitle the accused to adequate time and facilities for his defence'); *Nahimana and others*, AC, § 181 ('the concept of a fair trial includes equal opportunity to present one's case').

[49] See, in particular, such cases as *Artico* (§ 32); *Barberà, Messegué and Jabardo* (§ 67); *Edwards* (§ 36); *Raffineries grecques* (§ 49); *Birutis and others* (§§ 26–35); and *Beckles* (§§ 48–66). The requisites of a fair trial in international law were discussed, with regard to war crimes, by the Supreme Court of Norway in *Latza and others* (at 52–85).The principle is set forth in the Charter of the Nuremberg Tribunal (Art. 16) and that of the Tokyo Tribunal (Art. 9); in the Statutes of the ICTY (Art. 21(2)); the ICTR (Art. 20(2)); and the ICC (Art. 67, also on the rights of the accused).

[50] See e.g. Art. 21 of the ICTY Statute; Art. 20 of the ICTR Statute; and Arts 64, 66, and 67 of the ICC Statute; Art. 17 of the SCSL Statute; and Section 2.1 of the Rules on Criminal Procedure issued by the UNTAET Regulation 2000/30 as amended by Regulation 2001/25.

[51] *Tadić* (*Decision on the Prosecution's Motion Requesting Protective Measures for Witness R*), 4; *Brđanin* (*Third Motion by Prosecution for Protective Measures*), § 13; *Jelisić*, AC, at § 27; *Kraijsnik* (*Decision on the Prosecutions' Motion for Judicial Notice of Adjudicated Facts and Admission of Written Statements Pursuant to Rule 92 bis*), § 20; SCSL, *Brima and others* (*Decision on the Prosecution's Motion for Concurrent Hearing of Evidence Common to Cases*), §§ 35, 47.

practical and robust application before the ICC in *Lubanga*, causing proceedings to be stayed because of the unfairness of not disclosing substantial amounts of information, even though this non-disclosure was lawful under another provision of this Statute.[52]

The principle of fairness seems now to undoubtedly be a customary norm of international law. Arguably the principle is even endowed with the force of a peremptory norm (*jus cogens*), i.e. may not be derogated from by treaty; this proposition, absent state practice and case law on this specific issue, seems nevertheless warranted by the insistence of all states on the importance of fair and expeditious trials.

19.8 THE PRINCIPLE THAT THE ACCUSED SHOULD BE PRESENT AT HIS TRIAL

Systems predominantly influenced by the adversarial model generally require the presence of the accused at trial. The rationale for this rule, as for example arising from the constitutional guarantees recognized by the United States Supreme Court in *Gagnon* (at 1484), derives from the right of an accused to 'be confronted with the witnesses against him' and the consequential impact on the state's obligation not to 'deprive any person of life, liberty, or property, without due process of law'.[53] These rights are not violated, however, if, after appearing in court, the defendant deliberately absconds to avoid trial.[54] The ICTY and ICTR have followed this tendency, emphasizing in particular the role of the accused in participating effectively in his or her own defence.[55]

In absentia trials are more common in inquisitorial than adversarial systems, but are neither intrinsic to the former, nor categorically excluded by the latter. Thus, *in absentia* trials are permitted in the predominantly adversarial system in Italy, but not in the predominantly inquisitorial systems in Germany and Spain. [56] The tendency nevertheless does exist and reflects a diverging conceptions of justice. As Judge Riachy recently pointed out:

the fact that the Anglo-American system does not admit trial *in absentia*, by contrast to the civil law, reflects a crucial difference between the two systems: in the latter, especially in France and Lebanon, the notion of public order is an important legal concept that constitutes a mainstay of criminal justice. This is a distinguishing feature of the criminal

---

[52] *Lubanga* (*Judgment on the Appeal of Mr. Thomas Lubanga Dyilo against the Decision on the Defence Challenge to the Jurisdiction of the Court Pursuant to Article 19(2)(a) of the Statute of 3 October 2006*), § 37 ('Human rights underpin the Statute; every aspect of it, including the exercise of jurisdiction by the Court. Its provisions must be interpreted and more importantly applied in accordance with internationally recognized human rights; first and foremost, in the context of the Statute, the right to a fair trial, a concept broadly perceived and applied, embracing the judicial process in its entirety').

[53] See also *Poitrimol* v. *France*, § 35 and *Krombach* v. *France*, § 86.

[54] US Supreme Court (see *Taylor*, at 20–9) and *Crosby* (at 748–53).

[55] *Zigiranyirazo* (*Decision on Interlocutory Appeal*); *Milosević Slobodan* (*Decision on Interlocutory Appeal of the Trial Chamber's Decision on the Assignment of Defence Counsel*), §§ 11, 13.

[56] Probably this is so because they regard the right of the accused to be present as an overriding human right, or because they consider it 'uneconomic' to hold trials that are not directed at attaining the ultimate purpose of any criminal trial, namely, to do justice, and therefore put the accused in jail, if convicted. However, in Germany another ground is advanced: as C. Roxin (*Strafverfahrensrecht* (Munich: Beck, 1991), at 405) put it, 'the trial judge must personally see the accused in front of him, in order to arrive at the right picture of his personality'. See also B. Swart, 'La Place des critères traditionnels de compétence dans la poursuite des crimes internationaux', in A. Cassese and M. Delmas-Marty (eds), *Juridictions nationales et crimes internationaux* (Paris: PUF, 2002), at 581–3.

justice systems in these countries, inasmuch as the notion of a criminal offence strikes not only at personal interests, but also at stability of society. Consequently, public prosecution does not belong exclusively to the parties to the case (i.e. the Office of the Public Prosecutor and the accused), as is the case in common law systems, where each of the parties pursues its own interests; rather, it belongs to society, and its aim is to arrive at truth and justice. It follows that the defendant's absence from the trial cannot of itself halt the course of justice, which must continue to move forward regardless of his absence in order to achieve its result (the restoration of the 'social peace' that was disturbed by the criminal offence).[57]

The rationale behind trials *in absentia* is that one should not allow justice to be thwarted by the accused, when he chooses to escape instead of standing trial. In these systems, the defendant has a legal entitlement to be present at his trial; if he absconds and flees the jurisdiction even before commencement of trial, he implicitly waives that entitlement. Were judges to be barred from proceeding by the defendant's absconding, this would mean that ultimately criminal justice could be kept at bay by the accused. In addition, as the European Court of Human Rights put it, 'the impossibility of holding a trial by default may paralyse the conduct of criminal proceedings, in that it may lead, for example, to dispersal of the evidence, expiry of the time-limit for prosecution or a miscarriage of justice' (*Colozza* v. *Italy*, § 29).

The disadvantage to an accused is, at least in theory, mitigated where the investigating judge has primary responsibility to gather exculpatory evidence. A defence counsel appointed to represent the absent accused may then use this impartially collected information to defend his client's interests. Though the accused is undoubtedly in a less advantageous position than if he or she was present, the European Court of Human Rights has held that overall balance of the community's interest in administering justice outweighs the interests of the accused where certain conditions are satisfied: *i*) the accused has been formally notified of the charges against him; *ii*) there is evidence that he is deliberately absconding or at any rate absenting himself from the proceedings; *iii*) the accused is represented in court by counsel; and *iv*) the accused has the right at any time during the proceedings, or even after conviction, to appear and request 'a fresh determination of the merits of the charge' in his presence[58] (provided that he had not waived his right to be present, for instance by appointing and instructing a defence lawyer of his choice).[59]

As national legal systems differ on this matter, can one find an international rule prohibiting or allowing such trials? Indisputably, there is no international treaty provision prohibiting them. In addition, the existing treaty rules on trial proceedings, contained in such treaties as the UN Covenant on Civil and Political Rights (Article 14(3)) and the European Convention on Human Rights (Article 6(1)) have been interpreted by the relevant international bodies as not ruling out trials *in absentia*.[60]

---

[57] R. Riachy, 'Trials *in Absentia* in the Lebanese Judicial System and at the Special Tribunal for Lebanon: Challenge or Evolution?', 8 JICJ (2010), at 1297.

[58] *Lala and Pelladoah* v. *The Netherlands*, §§ 33–4, 40–1; *Colozza* v. *Italy*, § 29; *Krombach* v. *France*, §§ 85–91.

[59] See *Battisti* v. *France* (*Decision on admissibility*).

[60] Thus, the UN Human Rights Committee held in *Daniel Mbenge* v. *Zaire* (1983) (§§ 13–14.2), in *Hiber Conteris* v. *Uruguay* (1985) (§§ 9.2–10), and in *Dieter Wolf* v. *Panama* (1992) (§ 6.5) that the relevant state had breached Art. 14(3)(d), but only because trial proceedings had commenced without the accused having knowledge of the proceedings against him. In *Raphael Henry* v. *Jamaica* (1991) (§ 8.3) the Committee held that the state had not breached that provision because the accused had opted for representation by counsel and therefore could not claim that his absence during the appeal hearing constituted a violation of the Covenant. Furthermore, in *Daniel Mbenge* v. *Zaire* the Committee stated that Article 14(3)(d) 'and other

What should then be the condition of international criminal proceedings? Article 12 of the Charter of the Nuremberg Tribunal explicitly allowed trials *in absentia* 'in the interests of justice'.[61] In contrast, SCSL Rule 60, allows for trial *in absentia* when, after having made his or her initial appearance, the accused refuses to be present at his or her trial, or is at large and does not appear in Court (in accordance with the principle *semel praesens semper praesens*, to be present at trial once entails being present always). In contrast, Article 63(1) of the ICC Statute makes the presence of the accused a basic requirement for the commencement of trials (with the exception, normally provided for in common law countries, that the defendant's presence is not required if he disrupts the trial: see Article 63(2) and Rule 124 of the ICC Rules;[62] Article 5 of the Special Panels for East Timor Regulations 2000/30 (as amended by Regulation 2001/25) and Rule 80 of the ECCC Rules exclude trials *in absentia*. More recently, however, Article 22 of the Statute of the STL takes a contrary stand: it allows trials *in absentia*, subject to a set of conditions.[63] Similarly, trials in the absence of the accused are provided for in Rule 56 of the

requirements of due process enshrined in Article 14 cannot be construed as invariably rendering proceedings *in absentia* inadmissible irrespective of the reasons for the accused person's absence. Indeed, proceedings *in absentia* are in some circumstances (for instance, when the accused person, although informed of the proceedings sufficiently in advance, declines to exercise his right to be present) permissible in the interest of the proper administration of justice' (§ 14.1).

The European Court of Human Rights held that the right of the accused to participate in the trial, although not expressly laid down in Article 6 of the European Convention on Human Rights, is a right 'whose existence is shown by the object and purpose of the Article taken as a whole' (*Colozza* v. *Italy*, § 27, *Brozicek* v. *Italy*, § 45). Nonetheless, the Court did not rule that trials *in absentia* were as such incompatible with Art. 6: see e.g. *Colozza* v. *Italy* (§§ 27–30); *Poitrimol* v. *France* (1993, §§ 30–9); and *Krombach* v. *France* (§§ 82–91).

[61] Indeed, one of the accused, Martin Borman, was tried and sentenced in his absence (vol. I, at 338–41). The fact that trials *in absentia* were contemplated in the Charter of the Nuremberg Tribunal (Art. 12), and that such a trial was conducted against the absent Martin Bormann, indicate that, at the international level, trials *in absentia* were, at least in the post-Second World War period, held to be acceptable. However, this precedent gives rise to mixed feelings. Two of the states behind that Charter, namely the US and the UK, both common law countries, only grudgingly accepted the upholding of trials *in absentia* (see B. F. Smith, *Reaching Judgment at Nuremberg* (New York: Basic Books Inc., 1977), at 229–32). Furthermore, one cannot ignore the fact that the proceedings against Bormann proved difficult for defence counsel, who was unable to find witnesses for the defence (see *Trial of the Major War Criminals*, vol. III, at 547–9; vol. XIV, p. 420; vol. XVII, at 244–9). Only the existence of numerous documents that were deemed authentic and incontrovertibly bore the signature of the accused made it possible for the Tribunal to convict and sentence him to death. In its judgment, the Nuremberg Tribunal noted that Bormann's counsel had 'laboured under difficulties', adding that he 'was unable to refute this evidence [presented by the prosecution]. In the face of these documents, which bear Bormann's signature, it is difficult to see how he could do so even were the defendant present' (vol. I, at 340).

[62] On this matter see, among other things, *Milošević Slobodan* (*Decision on Interlocutory Appeal of the Trial Chamber Decision on the Assignment of Defence Counsel*), AC, § 20; *Barayagwiza* (*Decision on Defence Counsel Motion to Withdraw*), TC, §§ 5–7; *Gbao* (*Ruling on the Refusal of the Third Accused, Augustine Gbao, to Attend Hearing of the Special Court for Sierra Leone*), § 8; *Sesay* (*Refusal of the Accused Sesay and Kallon to Appear for their Trial*), § 15. See also *Naletilić and Martinović* (*Decision on the Prosecutor's Motion to Take Depositions for Use at Trial*), TC, at 1–2.

[63] '1. The Special Tribunal shall conduct trial proceedings in the absence of the accused, if he or she:

    a. has expressly and in writing waived his or her right to be present;

    b. has not been handed over to the Tribunal by the State authorities concerned;

    c. absconded, or otherwise cannot be found and all reasonable steps have been taken to secure his or her appearance before the Tribunal and to inform him or her of the charges confirmed by the Pre-Trial Judge.

2. When hearings are conducted in the absence of the accused, the Special Tribunal shall ensure that:

    a. the accused has been notified, or served with the indictment, or notice has otherwise been given of the indictment through publication in the media or communication to the State of residence or nationality;

Iraqi High Court's Rules, which refers to Iraqi law (pursuant to which defendants can be tried in their absence if they may not have been arrested, or escape after being taken into custody).[64]

The relevant provisions of the Statutes of the ICTY, the ICTR, and the SCSL do not enshrine any specific provision on the matter. They provide that the accused has the right 'to be tried in his presence' (Articles 21(4)(d), 20(4)(d), respectively). However, nothing is said about the case where the accused implicitly waives this right by absconding before trial proceedings commence. The question therefore arises of how international criminal courts should behave when their statutory or other applicable provisions are silent on the matter.

A convincing solution may be found by both drawing upon general principles and looking at the specificities of international criminal proceedings. In favour of trials *in absentia* one can argue that it would be contrary to law and justice to authorize the alleged perpetrator of gruesome crimes to make a mockery of international criminal justice by preventing trials through his deliberate absence. In addition, the contention is warranted that the rights of the accused are not jeopardized if provision is made for his right to a fresh trial, should he decide to surrender after being tried and convicted in his absence. Furthermore, if the procedure before the relevant court is shaped in such a manner as to ensure that the judges are in a position fully to consider and appraise the evidence, in particular exculpatory evidence, the absence of the accused does not necessarily taint the proceedings as unfair.

However, whenever international criminal proceedings are substantially based on the adversarial system, in case of doubt the specificities of international criminal trials may warrant the view that the accused must be present at trial, before trial proceedings are commenced. The combination of the demands and implications of the adversarial system with the unique features of international criminal proceedings may make this requirement indispensable. In international criminal trials the *search for and collection of evidence* may prove extremely difficult, because: *i*) as a rule the court is headquartered in a country far away from the place of the crime; *ii*) witnesses may be scattered over many countries; *iii*) there is no investigating judge charged with collecting evidence on behalf of both the prosecution and defence; under the accusatorial system each party must search for and find the necessary evidence; *iv*) the lack of an international body of investigators under the control of the prosecutor endowed with the power of freely going wherever the evidence may happen to be, to question witnesses and collect material evidence, makes investigations undertaken for the purpose of supporting or dismissing charges extremely complex. This task is all the more difficult for the defence, given that, in addition to the problems facing the prosecution, the defence encounters a further hurdle: it may not count on the considerable number of investigators normally available to the prosecution, nor on the court's power to order investigators to collect evidence on the defence's behalf; *v*) in most cases matters are further complicated by the fact that the crimes with which the accused is charged have been perpetrated years before the court proceedings start.

> b. the accused has designated a defence counsel of his or her own choosing, to be remunerated either by the accused, or if proven to be indigent, by the Tribunal;
>
> c. whenever the accused refuses or fails to appoint a defence counsel, such counsel has been assigned by the Tribunal's Defence Office with a view to ensuring full representation of the interests and rights of the accused.
>
> 3. In case of conviction *in absentia*, the accused, if he or she had not designated a defence counsel of his or her choosing, shall be retried in his or her presence before the Special Tribunal, unless he or she accepts the judgement.'

[64] § 135 of the Iraqi Criminal Proceedings Law, with Amendments no. 23 of 1971.

As a result of these features of international criminal trials, it proves crucial for the fair conduct of proceedings that the accused be present when the fundamentals of the adversarial model are upheld. If present, the defendant may, first, issue instructions to his defence counsel, or consult with them, on the evidence that could be collected to support his case, so as to make counsel able to muster all the necessary probative materials in rebuttal of the prosecution's case. Second, the presence of the accused is important for the cross-examination of prosecution witnesses, for he can suggest to his defence counsel points or issues on which to conduct cross-examination. Thirdly, the accused may prove of great importance for the court in its findings, because he may decide to testify in court, and in any case his behaviour and appearance might be of some relevance to the court in establishing whether he may be found guilty or innocent.

It is doubtful whether one should infer from the above that, if the defendant escapes after the commencement of trial, one should opt for the extreme solution of staying proceedings until he is arrested and brought to trial again, or voluntarily surrenders. Arguably the characteristics of international criminal proceedings emphasized above should rule out the solution normally adopted at the national level by countries that ban trials *in absentia*; that is, continuation of trial if the accused absconds after the initiation of proceedings (see, for instance, Rule 43 of the US Federal Court Rules of Procedure). It could be argued that at the national level this solution is justified by the need both to safeguard the public interest in dispensation of justice and to prevent individuals from evading adjudication. At the international level—so it could be held—the need to ensure a fair trial and to avoid any miscarriage of justice should instead prevail.[65] In addition, there would be no problem with regard to statutes of limitations (another rationale for holding trials *in absentia* in civil law countries), since international crimes do not fall under any statute of limitations.

However, it seems to me that this extreme legal solution should be avoided, because otherwise a defendant absconding after commencement of trial would be in a position to stultify international justice outright. Moreover, as most international criminal courts are not permanent, a possible stay of proceedings might result in the defendant evading justice for good, once the court is terminated.

It should be added, nevertheless, that even courts which in principle rule out *in absentia* trials have held that under certain circumstances *in absentia* proceedings may

---

[65] When it seemed that states were intent on refusing to cooperate with the Tribunal and therefore no trial could be held for lack of indictees at The Hague, the ICTY adopted an imaginative measure designed to respect the principle whereby the accused must be present for a proper trial to be conducted, while at the same time taking some action to react to the lack of cooperation of states and their consequent refusal to detain persons accused of appalling crimes. This measure was Rule 61 of the Rules of Procedure and Evidence ('Procedure in Case of Failure to Execute a Warrant'). Under this Rule, if an arrest warrant has not been executed, the confirmation judge may order that the prosecutor submit the indictment to the Trial Chamber of which the judge is a member. The prosecutor then submits the indictment in open court, together with the evidence available, and may call and examine witnesses. The Trial Chamber may conclude that 'there are reasonable grounds for believing that the accused has committed all or any of the crimes charged in the indictment', whereupon it: *i*) issues an international arrest warrant to be transmitted to all states; and *ii*) may freeze the assets of the accused; if the absence of the accused is due to lack of cooperation of a state, it *iii*) may request the Tribunal's President to notify the Security Council of the failure of the relevant state to comply with Art. 29 of the ICTY Statute (on the obligation of states to cooperate). Clearly, this procedure is not a trial proper. It is a sort of fall-back, designed to stimulate states to arrest indictees, by making public and exposing the charges preferred by the prosecutor against some persons.

The procedure was resorted to on five occasions between 1995 and 1996 (*Nicolić*; *Martić*; *Mrskić, Radić, and Šlijvančanin*; *Raijć*; *Karadžić and Mladić*). Since then it has not been relied upon, on account of the increasing number of arrests made either by states or by the NATO forces in Bosnia and Herzegovina, which enabled the Tribunal's Chambers to conduct trials proper.

exceptionally be warranted. The ICTY Appeals Chamber envisaged such a case in *Blaškić* (*Subpoena*). It held that if an individual does not comply with a subpoena or order issued by the Tribunal, he can be held in contempt of the Tribunal and the specific contempt procedure can therefore be set in motion. Should the individual also fail to attend contempt proceedings, '*in absentia* proceedings should not be ruled out'.[66]

[66] The Appeals Chamber held that, although it was not appropriate to hold such proceedings against persons falling under the primary jurisdiction of the Tribunal (that is, accused of one of the international crimes over which the Tribunal had jurisdiction under its Statute), 'By contrast, *in absentia* proceedings may be exceptionally warranted in cases involving contempt of the International Tribunal, where the person charged fails to appear in court, thus obstructing the administration of justice. These cases fall within the ancillary or incidental jurisdiction of the International Tribunal' (*Blaškić* (*Subpoena*), § 59). The Appeals Chamber added, however, that all the necessary judicial safeguards should be offered to the absent defendant (§ 59).

It should be noted that the Chamber's judgment was unanimous; this means that the three judges from common law countries sitting on the Appeals Chamber concurred with the Chamber's ruling on the question of *in absentia* proceedings as well.

20

INVESTIGATION AND TRIAL BEFORE INTERNATIONAL CRIMINAL COURTS

International criminal courts have been established to investigate and punish crimes on such a scale as to trigger international concern and involvement. Paradoxically, since they are not endowed with a police force that can operate freely on the territory of the affected states, international investigators are often forced to rely on, or even overcome the obstruction of, the very officials whose inactivity, whether because of inability or unwillingness, necessitated international involvement in the first place. The challenge, particularly in respect of states which are overtly or tacitly hostile to such investigations, is to find the right combination of legal compulsion and, to the extent possible, direct action to permit proper investigations. International criminal courts have found ways over time, more or less successfully depending on the strength of the political will behind them and the legal tools with which they are endowed, to overcome these difficulties through a combination of legal constraints on states, persuasion, and, where possible, direct action on national territory.

The party-driven investigative model offers flexibility to overcome these challenges, but also increases the importance of testing the reliability of evidence at trial. International criminal courts have developed a number of principles, rules, and practices to deal with this investigative context. Many of the jurisprudential and statutory developments arising from the experience of the ICTY and ICTR have been incorporated into the Statute and Rules of the ICC. Some important differences are nevertheless to be found in the practices of different international criminal courts, often reflecting different circumstances on the ground.

The present chapter highlights the most significant features of investigation and trial procedure before international criminal courts; and assesses how fairness has been balanced with effectiveness in the unique and challenging context of conflict or post-conflict environments.

20.1 INTERNATION CRIMINAL INVESTIGATION

20.1.1 THE CHOICE TO OPEN AN INVESTIGATION

The prosecutors of the ad hoc international criminal courts have unfettered discretion, within their jurisdiction, as to whom or what they may investigate.[1] Since that discretion

---

[1] ICTY Statute, Art. 18(1) ('The Prosecutor shall initiate investigations *ex officio* or on the basis of information obtained from any source, particularly from Government, United Nations organs, intergovernmental

is exercised within a limited jurisdiction, as in any domestic jurisdiction, no additional mechanism was put in place to supervise the Prosecutor's discretion.

The ICC, on the other hand, has potentially unlimited geographic jurisdiction over international crimes. Conferring such broad discretion on the prosecutor a *proprio motu* power to start investigations aroused reasonable concern at the Rome Conference.[2]

The compromise adopted in the ICC Statute was to allow the prosecutor to open an investigation only if: *i)* a state party or the Security Council refers a 'situation' to the prosecution for investigation (Articles 13(a) and (b), 14); or *ii)* at the request of the prosecutor, a Pre-Trial Chamber has authorized an 'investigation' once satisfied that 'there is a reasonable basis to proceed with the investigation' (Articles 13, 15(4)). Every investigation can therefore be initiated only at the request of 'political authorities' (the Security Council or a state party); or, alternatively, initiated *proprio motu* by the prosecutor, but subject to judicial scrutiny (a Pre-Trial Chamber of the ICC). A referral by the Security Council or a state party does not oblige the prosecutor to open an investigation, although a decision not to open it following referral is subject to judicial review.[3] The standards are set forth in Article 53 of the ICC Statute, which requires the prosecutor to open an investigation 'unless he or she determines that there is no reasonable basis to proceed' according to three criteria: *i)* the availability of information providing a 'reasonable basis to believe' that a crime within the Court's jurisdiction had been, or was being, committed; *ii)* the admissibility of the case; and *iii)* whether, 'given the gravity and the interests of victims, there are nonetheless substantial reasons to believe that an investigation would not serve the interests of justice' (Article 53(1)). 'Gravity' does double-duty as it is also a factor in determining admissibility.[4] Of the

and non-governmental organizations. The Prosecutor shall assess the information received or obtained and decide whether there is sufficient basis to proceed'); ICTR Statute, Art. 17(1); SCSL Statute, Art. 15(1); STL Statute, Art. 11(1).

[2] Report of the Preparatory Committee on the Establishment of an International Criminal Court, UN GAOR, 51st Sess., vol. I, Supp. No. 22, UN Doc. A/51/22 (1996), § 151; *Situation in the Republic of Kenya (Decision on the Authorization of an Investigation)*, § 18.

[3] ICC Statute, Arts 53(3)(a) ('At the request of the State [...] or the Security Council [...] the Pre-Trial Chamber may review a decision [...] not to proceed and may request the Prosecutor to reconsider that decision').

[4] ICC Statute, Art. 17(1)(d). The first judicial decision interpreting this standard divided gravity according to the identity of the likely targets of the investigation (whether they 'bear the greatest responsibility of the alleged crimes'), and the qualitative nature of the crime (which encompasses their geographic and temporal scale, their nature, the means used and their impact on victims and their families. The post-election violence in Kenya, alleged to involve some 1,200 murders, 900 rapes and other acts of sexual violence, 350,000 displaced persons, and 3,500 acts of serious injury in six of Kenya's eight provinces, was considered sufficiently grave to justify the opening of an investigation. *Situation in the Republic of Kenya (Decision on the Authorization of an Investigation)*, § 190.

seven formal investigations opened or pending to date, five were opened on the basis of referrals (three from state parties[5] and two from the Security Council[6]), and two were initiated by the prosecutor.[7]

---

[5] The three state referrals all concerned situations within the referring states themselves: the Democratic Republic of Congo, the Central African Republic, and Uganda. Investigations were opened two, four, and six months, respectively, following these referrals, reflecting a sensible deference to the states that would otherwise exercise jurisdiction over the crimes. The same could not be said if, as is permitted under the ICC Statute, one state party were to refer a situation in another state party. An unresolved but potentially significant issue is whether and how a state may limit the scope of a referral. Uganda purported to refer the 'situation concerning the Lord's Resistance Army', but the prosecutor determined that this should be broadened to 'the situation of northern Uganda by whomsoever committed'. The President expanded, at least nominally, the situation further still to 'the situation in Uganda' (*Situation in Uganda* (*Assigning the Situation in Uganda to Pre-Trial Chamber II*), Annex). The arrest warrants ultimately issued only concerned members of the Lords Resistance Army, leaving untested the potential disagreement over the scope of the referral.

[6] In the case of Darfur (Sudan): SC Res. 1593 (2005), adopted with 11 votes in favour and 4 abstentions (Algeria, Brazil, China, United States); and in the case of Libya, SC Res. 1970 (2011), also deciding sanctions against Libya, adopted unanimously.

Arguably, the prosecutor is not likely to decline to open an investigation following a Security Council referral made pursuant to Chapter VII of the UN Charter, which requires the Security Council to determine the existence of a breach of, or a threat to peace, or an act of aggression. The existence of a 'reasonable basis to proceed' with an investigation, which shall guide the prosecutor in his decision to open an investigation (ICC Statute, Art. 53(1)), would be easily satisfied in light of the determination under Chapter VII by the Security Council. In the unlikely event that a prosecutor refused to initiate an investigation upon a referral, the Security Council or a state party may request a Pre-Trial Chamber to 'review' that decision and to 'request the Prosecutor to reconsider that decision' (ICC Statute, Art. 53(3)). Neither the ICC President nor the prosecutor has attempted, unlike in the case of Uganda, to broaden the Darfur referral to the territory of Sudan as a whole. The Darfur and Libya referrals exempt from the ICC's jurisdiction personnel or nationals from non-state parties taking part in authorized peacekeeping or enforcement actions (see SC Res. 1593(2005), §6, on the situation in Darfur, whereby 'nationals, current or former officials or personnel from a contributing State outside Sudan which is not a party to the Rome Statute of the International Criminal Court shall be subject to the exclusive jurisdiction of that contributing State for all alleged acts or omissions arising out of or related to operations in Sudan established or authorized by the Council or the African Union, unless such exclusive jurisdiction has been expressly waived by that contributing State'). See also § 6 of the SC Res. 1970 (2011) on the situation in Libya. One could express doubts whether these exemptions are consistent with international law and the ICC Statute (see S. Williams and W. Schabas, 'Article 13', in Triffterer, *ICC Commentary*, at 572).

[7] At the time of writing, the prosecutor has initiated formal investigations twice, in Kenya and Côte d'Ivoire. The latter may be described as a quasi-referral, the elected President of the country having made a declaration accepting the exercise of the ICC's jurisdiction (*Situation Côte d'Ivoire* (*Request for Authorization of an Investigation*), § 17). The Kenya investigation was authorized by the ICC Pre-Trial Chamber by a majority, and a dissent exposed differences about the Pre-Trial Chamber's gate-keeping function. Nominally, the issue separating the dissent from the majority was whether, as required in the ICC definition of crimes against humanity, the crimes had been committed as part of a 'state organizational policy'. The majority's finding was predicated on the view that 'reasonable basis to believe' was a low threshold, and that the Pre-Trial Chamber's function was simply to prevent 'unwarranted, frivolous, or politically motivated investigations that could have a negative effect on [the Court's] credibility' (*Situation in the Republic of Kenya* (*Decision on the Authorization of an Investigation*), §§ 20, 32). The dissent espoused a more robust approach, insisting that the 'decision whether or not the Prosecutor may commence an investigation rests ultimately with the Pre-Trial Chamber'. Its function was not only to conduct an 'administrative or procedural' review, but to engage in a 'substantial and genuine examination' of the request. The majority also suggested that the Chamber should not raise *proprio motu* the 'interests of justice' criterion as a basis for denying the opening of an investigation. The majority implicitly reflects a more party-driven, adversarial orientation in which the prosecutor has broadly unfettered discretion; the dissent espouses a more inquisitorial perspective, with the Pre-Trial Chamber acting in a more inquisitorial role. The only other counter-weight to the prosecutor's discretion is the SC's authority to defer any open investigation for periods of twelve months at a time (ICC Statute, Art. 16).

The ICC prosecutor, prior to being authorized to open a formal investigation, may make a 'preliminary examination' to establish whether the conditions for opening an investigation are satisfied.[8] The parameters of such a 'preliminary examination' are vaguely defined. The prosecutor may, according to the ICC Statute, 'receive written or oral testimony at the seat of the Court',[9] and even elsewhere according to some commentators.[10] Field missions have apparently been undertaken within the context of preliminary investigations,[11] and requests for information can be made to states, the United Nations and 'other reliable sources that [the prosecutor] deems appropriate'. The extent of information that may need to be proactively gathered in a preliminary examination will depend on the information provided from the outside sources. Some cases may arrive on the prosecutor's doorstep having already been thoroughly documented by a credible investigative authority.[12] Preliminary examinations can thus reflect a very active investigative effort, whether by the Office of the Prosecutor itself, or as reflected in the fruits of outside agencies.

20.1.2 THE IMPACT OF THE INTERNATIONAL INVESTIGATIVE MODEL ON TRIAL PROCEEDINGS

International prosecutors enjoy wide latitude within the scope of their powers as to how they should conduct their investigations. The Office of the Prosecutor of the ICTY, ICTR, SCSL, and STL are the sole organs in each institution 'responsible for the investigation and prosecution of persons'.[13] They have the 'power to question suspects, victims and witnesses, to collect evidence and to conduct on-site investigations', and to request the assistance of states in these investigations as appropriate.[14] The extent to which the ICTY and ICTR prosecutors can actually do so has been discussed in 16.4.2. From the point of view of the internal law of these international criminal courts, however, no prior judicial authorization or contemporaneous oversight is imposed on the

---

[8] The expression 'preliminary examination' does not appear in Art. 15(2) of the ICC Statute, but is used in Art. 15(6) to describe the function the prosecutor must perform under Arts 15(1) and 15(2).

[9] ICC Statute, Art. 15(2); ICC Rule 47.

[10] According to M. Bergsmo and J. Pejić, ('Article 15', in Triffterer, *ICC Commentary*, at 588) the 'seat of the Court' should be deemed to include 'field offices and temporary arrangements which the Office [...] may establish and which may prove to be more accessible to witnesses'.

[11] Such missions have apparently been conducted, albeit within the rubric of 'positive complementarity' whereby the state is encouraged to pursue its own investigations and prosecutions. See 'Policy Paper on Preliminary Examinations (Draft)', 4 October 2010.

[12] One of the 10,000 communications received by the ICC prosecutor was a 300-page report, along with the investigative files, of a Commission of Inquiry presided over by three judges set up with the assistance of the United Nations into post-election violence in Kenya (*Situation in the Republic of Kenya* (*Request for Authorization of an Investigation*). The Commission even identified a list of suspects that was ultimately handed over to the prosecutor by the former Secretary-General of the United Nations, Kofi Annan, following a prescribed period of inactivity by the Kenyan government. The preliminary examination of alleged crimes in Côte d'Ivoire relied heavily on reports from the UN mission there, interviews by NGO's with alleged victims, and media sources (*Situation in Côte d'Ivoire* (*Request for Authorization of an Investigation*), § 31).

[13] Art. 16(1) ICTY Statute; Art. 15(1) ICTR Statute; Art. 11(1) STL Statute; Art. 15(1) SCSL Statute.

[14] Art. 18(1) ICTY Statute; Art. 17(1) ICTR Statute; Art. 11(5) STL Statute; Art. 15(2) SCSL Statute. Rules 92 and 93 of the STL RPE do accord the Pre-Trial judge two investigative functions: *i*) 'exceptionally' gather or request, either *proprio motu* or at the request of a party, evidence that the party is not in a position to obtain, or that is necessary 'to ensure a fair and expeditious trial'; or *ii*) question witnesses whose identity, if revealed to the other party, would pose a 'serious risk' that the witness or a person close to the witness 'would lose his life or suffer grave physical or mental harm'. STL RPE, Rules 92, 93.

prosecutor. The hybrid ECCC is the exception, relying primarily on the investigating judge to conduct investigations with the formalized participation of the prosecution and defence.

The ICC prosecutor is similarly charged with the exclusive mandate to 'ensure the effective investigation and prosecution of crimes', which includes to 'collect and examine evidence', 'request the presence of and question persons, being investigated, victims and witnesses', and 'seek the cooperation' of states and other entities (ICC Statute, Arts 54(1) and (3); for the state cooperation scheme with the ICC, see 16.4.3). The Pre-Trial Chamber's role is largely confined to issuing orders during the investigation 'at the request of the Prosecutor' (ICC Statute, Art. 57(3)).

The prosecutor is subject to judicial regulation in two relatively minor ways, however. First, the ICC Statute requires the prosecutor to 'investigate incriminating and exonerating circumstances equally'.[15] The obligation is, however, not supported by any procedural mechanisms to ensure that it is actually respected, and there appears to be no tangible remedy for non-compliance. Suspects have no right, for example, to review the investigative dossier or propose investigative acts, nor do they have any access to a judicial remedy should they believe that exonerating information is not being pursued with equal zeal. Further, no prosecutor could meaningfully discharge this obligation without first consulting with the suspect to find out what exonerating circumstances should be investigated. Practice to date does not suggest that the ICC prosecutor, with extremely limited resources, has acted much differently than his adversarial counterparts at other courts. A second potential judicial regulation of the prosecutor's discretion is provided by way of Court Regulation 108, which—as mentioned already—permits states parties to challenge the legality of investigative acts carried out under Part IX of the Statute.[16] The purpose of Rule 108 is to ensure that the prerogatives of states are respected, and judicial review on the basis of this provision, therefore, does little to ensure the fairness or reliability of investigations.

These regulations do not resemble the procedural protections afforded to a suspect in an inquisitorial system (see 18.1.2). The ICC investigative model, despite the vague obligation to investigate exonerating circumstances, is therefore fundamentally adversarial. Ensuring reliability, and retroactive sanctioning of investigative impropriety, can only be accomplished by judicial scrutiny of the information at trial. Indeed, the weakness of the investigative authority of the ICC suggests an even greater need to carefully scrutinize the reliability of information brought to court.

---

[15] ICC Statute, Art. 54(1)(a). The prosecutor is also required to 'respect the interests and personal circumstances of victims and witnesses' and to 'fully respect the rights of persons arising under this Statute'. One can hardly imagine, however, that the prosecutors of the other international criminal tribunals would take a different view of their own obligations and responsibilities in the absence of any explicit provision.

[16] Regulation 108 of the Regulations of the Court authorizes states to seek rulings from a Chamber as to the legality of 'requests' for cooperation. Every investigative step by the ICC prosecutor, even those that can be carried out 'without any compulsory measures' under Art. 99(4) of the ICC Statute, must be carried out on the basis of a 'request' to the state. See C. Kress and K. Prost, 'Article 99' in Triffterer, *ICC Commentary*, at 1628. The prosecutor may, apparently, delay informing the state until after direct execution. Regulation 108 seems to accommodate just this scenario, indicating that 'the request State may seek a ruling within 15 days from the day on which the requested state *is informed of or became aware* of the direct execution'. Kress and Prost comment that 'the State Party will be aware of the matter, generally, as a result of the request presented to initiate the process [...] But the request need not specify the details which might defeat the intent of the process such as the time and place of any proposed interviews.'

20.2 THE INITIATION OF PROCEEDINGS AND PREPARATION FOR TRIAL

20.2.1 THE CHARGES AND ARREST

Proceedings against an accused at the ICTY, ICTR, SCSL, and STL commence with the indictment. The reason is that the confirmation of charges against a person before these courts is a one-step process conducted in judges' chambers without the involvement of the suspect; only when the indictment is confirmed (because the judges find that the prosecutor has made 'a *prima facie* case')[17] may an arrest warrant be issued. The procedure is inverted at the ICC, where the initiating document is a request for an arrest warrant or a summons: the prosecution first seeks an arrest or a summons, upon which the person has no right to make submissions, and only once the warrant is executed or the person appears before the Court may the confirmation process proceed.[18] The standard for the issuance of a warrant or summons at the ICC is the broadly similar 'reasonable grounds to believe', but then rises to 'substantial grounds to believe' for the confirmation of charges.[19]

At the ICTY, a single judge designated by the President of the Tribunal reviews the indictment, which must set out 'a concise statement of the facts of the case and of the crime with which the suspect is charged', and may be supported by 'accompanying material' to reach the requisite threshold for confirmation (ICTY Rule 47(C) and (D)). The judge, applying the prima facie standard, may: *i*) confirm the indictment; *ii*) dismiss it; *iii*) request the prosecutor to present additional material; or *iv*) adjourn the review so as to give the prosecutor the opportunity to modify the indictment. The procedure is, accordingly, informal and based primarily, if not exclusively, on written material such as witness statements or documents. If the indictment is confirmed, the person becomes an accused, and an arrest warrant may be issued. The indictment and warrant for arrest may be kept under seal so as to facilitate the person's arrest.

A request for an ICC arrest warrant or summons must similarly contain a 'concise statement of the facts which are alleged' to constitute crimes under the Court's jurisdiction and a 'summary of the evidence and any other information' to establish those crimes (ICC Statute, Article 58(2)). The application, which can be kept under seal along with any arrest warrant subsequently issued, is submitted to a full Pre-Trial Chamber and is typically supported by documentation such as witness statements or documentary evidence.[20]

---

[17] ICTY Statute, Art. 19(1); ICTR Statute, Art. 18(1); STL Statute, Art. 18(1). The SCSL Statute and Rules contain no standard as such, saying only that the reviewing judge should approve the indictment if the crimes charged are within the Court's jurisdiction, and if the allegations alleged, if proven, would amount to those crimes. For a detailed discussion of the prima facie threshold, see D. Hunt, 'The Meaning of Prima Facie Case', in R. May et al. (eds), *Essays on ICTY Procedure and Evidence* (The Hague: Kluwer, 2001), at 137–9.

[18] See e.g. *Situation in the Libyan Arab Jamahiriya (Prosecutor's Application Pursuant to Article 58 as the Muammar Mohammed Abu Minyar Gaddafi, Saif Al-Islam Gaddafi and Abdullah Al-Senussi)*.

[19] ICC Statute, Arts 58(1)(a) (warrant), Art. 58(7) (summons), Art. 61(5) (confirmation).

[20] Of the fourteen arrest warrants known to have been issued so far, six were issued and kept under seal for some time or until the person was arrested (Lubanga, Katanga, Ngudjolo, Ntaganda, Bemba, Mbarushimana). Five of these were successfully executed. Three summonses have also been issued, followed by the voluntary appearance of the named persons. The remaining eight public warrants remain, as of the moment of publication, unexecuted.

The person named, even if the application is made public, has no right to participate or otherwise make submissions.[21]

The ICC's functional equivalent of an indictment is called a 'document containing the charges', which must be disclosed no later than thirty days prior to the confirmation hearing itself. ICC Pre-Trial Chambers have insisted that confirmation 'is neither a trial before the trial nor a mini-trial',[22] and yet confirmation hearings do exhibit certain trial-like aspects. For example, the suspect is not only entitled but customarily required to be present at the hearing, unless that right has been waived or the person has absconded. Substantial pre-hearing disclosure, albeit short of what is required before the start of trial, is customarily ordered to assist the suspect in knowing the grounds for the case against him or her. The evidence presented during the confirmation hearing may be confined to 'documentary or summary' evidence, but both parties are also entitled to call live witnesses.[23] The hearings themselves can take days or weeks, involving opening and closing statements, the calling of evidence, and the submission of post-hearing briefs (*Katanga and Chui* (*Confirmation of Charges*), § 59). One important difference from trial proceedings, however, is that a much lower evidential standard applies.[24] The thorough review of evidence reflected in the confirmation decisions demonstrate, however, that the 'substantial grounds to believe' standard is anything but a trifle: charges against four persons (out of twelve total) have not been confirmed at the ICC, and one of these decisions was 226 pages long.[25]

The prosecutors of all the international criminal courts have a wide discretion as to who should be charged. The ICTR and ICTY prosecutor, according to the Statutes, 'shall prepare an indictment' upon 'a determination that a *prima facie* case exists', which then 'shall be transmitted' for confirmation.[26] The apparent strictness of this provision is not followed in practice, however. Indeed, prosecutors must have discretion in a world of limited resources to focus only on 'those most responsible for crime within the jurisdiction of the Tribunal' (ICTY Rule 28). The ICC prosecutor is not even nominally subject to such an obligation, but his decision not to prosecute can be judicially reviewed if he does not at least pursue prosecution within a situation. In such a case, the prosecutor must inform the referring body (i.e. the state party or the Security Council) of the reasons for such a decision, which may seek a review thereof before a Pre-Trial Chamber (ICC Statute, Article 53(2)–(3)).

Indictments at the ICTY and ICTR may be withdrawn or amended without leave of the reviewing judge up until the moment of confirmation. The ICC prosecutor is similarly

---

[21] *Situation in the Republic of Kenya* (*Decision on the Application for Leave to Participate in the Proceedings before the Pre-Trial Chamber Relation to the Prosecutor's Application under Article 58(7)*), § 18 ('No role, actual or potential, is provided or anticipated for the person named in the Prosecutor's application under Article 58 of the Statute').

[22] *Katanga and Chui* (*Decision on the Confirmation of Charges*), § 64; *Abu Garda* (*Decision on the Confirmation of Charges*), § 39.

[23] ICC Statute, Art. 61(1)–(6); ICC Rule 121.

[24] *Bemba* (*Admissibility Decision*), § 80 (the applicable rules are 'more relaxed than at trial'); *Banda and Jerbo* (*Corrigendum of the 'Decision on the Confirmation of Charges'*), § 40 ('given the limited purpose of the confirmation hearing, the evidentiary threshold at the pre-trial stage is lower than that applicable at the trial stage').

[25] *Abu Garda* (*Decision on the Confirmation of Charges*), §§ 217–36 (in which the Pre-Trial Chamber decided that propositions in witness statements could not be accepted as reliable in light of internal contradictions, and contradictions with other evidence submitted during the confirmation hearing).

[26] ICTY Statute, Art. 18(4); ICTR Statute Art. 17(4) (italics added). Rule 47 of the ICTY and ICTR Rules similarly provide: 'The Prosecutor, if satisfied in the course of an investigation that there is sufficient evidence to provide reasonable grounds for believing that a suspect has committed a crime within the jurisdiction of the Tribunal, shall prepare and forward to the Registrar an indictment for confirmation by a Judge, together with supporting material.'

not limited by the allegations in the application for an arrest warrant, and only becomes bound and limited once the 'document containing the charges' is filed.[27]

A related question is the extent to which an indictment may charge cumulatively. The prevailing view at the ICTY and ICTR, despite some dissonant chords, is that cumulative charging is permissible even where the two offences are identical or very similar, or the same acts are the foundation for both characterizations. The justification for this approach, again reflecting the extraordinary complexity and difficulty of investigation that is so often typical of such cases, is that it is 'not possible to determine to a certainty which of the charges against the accused will be proven' and that the Chamber is 'better poised, after the parties' presentation of the evidence, to evaluate which of the charges may be retained'.[28] This broad approach has been disapproved before ICC Chambers which have remarked that cumulative charging imposes 'an undue burden on the Defence' and is 'detrimental to the rights' of the accused.[29] Paradoxically, Trial Chambers have endowed themselves with the authority to 'change the legal characterization of facts to accord with the crimes under articles 6, 7 or 8, or to accord with the form of participation of the accused' (ICC Regulation 55). It is difficult to see how cumulative charging could be viewed as impermissibly detrimental to the rights of the accused, whereas an ex post facto recharacterization of the crimes or charges would not.

Most accused arrested in the early ICTY cases were held in custody through the period leading up to and during their trials, in part because of problems concerning the residency status of such persons in the Netherlands and Tanzania. The ICTY, but not the ICTR, has in recent years tended to grant periods of provisional release to accused persons, in particular those who surrendered voluntarily, provided that the state to which they are released provides guarantees that they will be monitored. Further, the ICC prosecutor has the discretion, which he has recently exercised in the *Banda and Jerbo* case and

---

[27] An issue that has proven particularly vexing is the level of detail that must be provided in an indictment in order to properly inform the accused or suspect of the charges. This problem is intrinsic to international criminal cases where difficulty of access to the crime scenes and witnesses, and the sheer breadth of events can make it difficult to give exact dates and locations, which may later turn out to be wrong. Standards of specificity to which domestic criminal lawyers may be accustomed are not necessarily appropriate in the international context. ICTY and ICTR jurisprudence requires the indictment not only to set out the crimes and modes of responsibility, but also the 'material facts underpinning the charges in the indictment, but not the evidence by which the material facts are to be proven' (*Naletilic and Martinovic*, AC, § 23). A fact-specific jurisprudence has developed around this issue, which can emerge at many different stages of the proceedings and with different potential consequences. Suffice to say for present purposes that the defective or vague nature of an indictment may not be apparent at the time it is confirmed.

[28] *Delalić and others*, AC, § 400. See also *Brđanin and Talić (Decision on the Amended Indictment)*, §§ 29–43. More limited approaches have been suggested by other Chambers: *Akayesu*, TC, at 461–70 (cumulative charges could be made in three instances: where the offences charged had different legal ingredients; where the relevant provisions protected different interests; and where it proved necessary to record a conviction for multiple offences in order fully to describe what the accused had done; *Kupreškić and others*, TC, §§ 720–7 (expressing the need to reconcile 'the requirement that the rights of the accused be fully safeguarded' and the requirement that 'the Prosecutor be granted all the powers consistent with the [ICTY] Statute to enable her to fulfill her mission efficiently and in the interests of justice'; the Chamber went on to conclude that the prosecutor should charge *cumulatively* if the facts charged violated simultaneously two or more provisions of the Statute, and charge *in the alternative* when an offence appeared to be in breach of more provisions, one of them being special to the other (for instance, a murder could be charged as a crime against humanity and in the alternative, for the event of the widespread or systematic practice not being proved, as a war crime).

[29] *Bemba (Decision Pursuant to Article 61(7)(a) and (b) of the Rome Statute)*, § 202. The Chamber went on, at § 204, to strike the allegation of torture where cumulated with rape, finding that the latter, which contained 'the additional specific material element of penetration', was 'the most appropriate legal characterization' of the facts alleged.

the Kenya cases, to seek only a summons for the appearance of the suspects or accused, rather than seeking their arrest. Once arrested, however, accused persons before the ICC and ICTR are much less likely to be provisionally released than their ICTY counterparts, mainly because there appears to be greater difficulty finding states who are willing to offer the necessary guarantees to monitor the person. Whether the person has surrendered voluntarily is often of great significance in determining whether a person should be provisionally released.

20.2.2 PREPARATION FOR TRIAL

At the ICTY and ICTR, a defendant's participation in the case begins only once the indictment has been confirmed, a process which is held in camera and without the defendant's participation or input. The pre-trial phase therefore occurs in one step, following the issuance of the indictment.

The pre-trial phase at the ICC consists of two steps: the confirmation phase, in which the 'suspect' participates; and the post-confirmation phase, when the person becomes, if the charges are confirmed, an 'accused'. Many of the procedural steps and disclosure that are required for the confirmation hearing carry over to the post-confirmation phase, and assist in trial preparation. Thus, although these are two distinct steps, the confirmation process (if the charges are confirmed) fits into the overall process of preparing for trial.

The initial appearance of an accused before the ICTY and ICTR, or of a 'suspect' before the ICC is a unique event in that the judges hear from the accused directly that he or she is informed of his or her rights and the charges. An accused before the ICTY and ICTR is also required, after the charges have been read, to enter a plea at this initial appearance, or within thirty days thereafter.[30] A suspect need make no plea at his initial appearance at the ICC; indeed, he or she need only be given 'an opportunity' to plead guilty or not guilty at 'the commencement of trial'. The initial appearance is of special procedural significance if the person has been arrested, requiring his prompt appearance before a judge to review and approve the detention.

A guilty plea may be accepted on generally similar conditions at the ICC and the ICTY and ICTR, essentially that the plea is voluntary and informed.[31] A sentencing hearing is then held to determine an appropriate sentence, which may include hearing witnesses and receiving other evidence. The ICTY and ICTR prosecutors are permitted to amend the indictment as part of a plea agreement, for example by withdrawing charges; but the reduction in the charges, assuming leave is granted to do so, in no way precludes the Chamber from imposing any sentence that it considers appropriate in light of any remaining charges. The ICC Statute expressly codifies this practice.[32] Sentencing following a plea is an area where the presence of victims' representatives could have a particular impact, potentially permitting the presentation of information in opposition to the plea, or favouring a sentence above the range agreed upon by the parties.

---

[30] ICTY Statute, Art. 20(3); ICTY RPE, Rule 62(A); STL Statute, Art. 20. The accused is permitted to defer entering a plea for thirty days, and if no plea is then forthcoming the judge enters a plea of not guilty (ICTY RPE, Rule 62(A)(iii); ICC Statute, Art. 64(8)).

[31] ICTY RPE, Rule 62 *bis*, codifying the judicial standards set out in *Erdemović*, AC; ICC Statute, Art. 65(1).

[32] ICTY Rules 62 *ter* (B) and 62 *bis* (B); ICC Statute, Art. 65(5). Plea agreements by the prosecution, in practice, do carry significant, but by no means determinative, weight: *M. Nikolić* (*Judgment on Sentencing Appeal*), lowering trial sentence from 27 to 20 years, in response to a prosecution recommendation of 15–20 years; *Rutaganira* (*Sentencing Judgment*), § 167 ('The Chamber reiterates that it has an unfettered discretion in determining the appropriate sentence [...] and that it is not bound by the parties' agreement').

The quantity of disclosure is a key determinant of the time needed to prepare for a trial and of the duration of trial itself. Disclosure is the process by which information in the prosecution's possession is handed over to the defence, so that it is properly informed of the case against the accused and can provide a proper defence. The same four categories of information must be disclosed at ICC and other international criminal tribunals: *i*) material submitted to confirm the charges (or, at the ICC, for the issuance of the arrest warrant);[33] *ii*) statements of prospective trial or confirmation hearing witnesses;[34] *iii*) information that is material to the preparation of the defence;[35] and *iv*) exculpatory information—i.e. that which 'shows or tends to show the innocence of the accused, or to mitigate the guilt of the accused, or which may affect the credibility of prosecution evidence'.[36] In a simple investigation of a simple event, disclosure does not usually pose major difficulties. In the international context, however, it is one of the most intractable challenges for a variety of reasons, including: the sheer volume of the information;[37] the precarious position of many witnesses and the consequent imposition of protective measures that permit delayed disclosure of certain identifying material,[38] or segregation of confidential information available in different cases; the existence of parallel investigations in which relevant information from one team of investigators may not be known to another; insistence on non-disclosure agreements by certain information providers; and non-cooperation by state authorities leading to late discovery of critical information. Non-disclosure on one or more of these grounds has sometimes required substantial adjournments so that newly disclosed material, whether improperly withheld or not, can be adequately reviewed.[39] Avoiding these problems starts at the pre-trial phase by putting in place an effective system of information management that permits disclosure of large volumes of information while segregating that which should not be. Achieving that balance involves not only efficient and flexible technology, but also rules that can demarcate disclosure according to conditions that are as simple as possible.

The statutory instruments provide for close judicial supervision of the pre-trial phase to ensure, to the extent possible, that matters vital for the preparation of trial are dealt with reasonably and expeditiously. The STL Pre-Trial judge is empowered to put in place and oversee a 'working plan' in the lead-up to trial.[40] Status conferences to oversee disclosure, any potential agreed facts that could narrow the scope of trial, translation

---

[33] ICC Statute, Art. 61(3); ICTY Rule 66(a)(i); STL Rule 110(A)(i).

[34] ICC Rule 76(1); ICTY Rule 66(a)(ii); STL Rule 110(A)(ii).

[35] ICC Rule 77; ICTY Rule 66(B); STL Rule 110(B).

[36] ICC Statute, Art. 67(2); ICTY Rule 68; STL Rule 113.

[37] An ICTY judge has written that there were more than 500,000 pages of disclosure in his multi-accused case—which was probably not the most document intensive in the ICTY's history. I. Bonomy, 'The Reality of Conducting a War Crimes Trial', 5 JICJ (2007), at 356.

[38] Pre-Trial Chambers at the ICC are apparently systematically reviewing proposed redactions of disclosure by the OTP—an astonishingly labour-intensive endeavour. See e.g. *Muthaura and others* (*Decision on the Prosecution's application requesting disclosure after a final resolution of the Government of Kenya's admissibility challenge and Establishing a Calendar for Disclosure between the Parties*), § 17.

[39] *Karadžić*, T. 8908 (ordering a trial adjournment of one month, and insisting that 'the size and complexity of this case is not an excuse for its failure to properly organize itself to ensure that disclosure is carried out in accordance with the Rules'); *Lubanga* (*Decision on the Consequences of Non-disclosure, etc.*), ordering a stay of proceedings, subsequently overturned on appear after the material was disclosed, because of excessive reliance on non-disclosure agreements under ICC Statute, Art. 54(3)(e).

[40] STL RPE, Rule 91(A). Periodic pre-trial status conferences are a common feature at the ICTY and ICTR as well in order to ensure that disclosure and other matters are proceedings, and encouraging agreements such as agreed facts.

issues, representation by counsel, and any other issues affecting the timetable for the commencement of trial are a common feature of the ICC, ICTY, and ICTR alike.[41]

The prosecution is often reluctant to narrow its case unless it feels absolutely sure of a conviction. The judges of the ICTY have, however, conferred upon themselves a robust power to limit the counts and crime-sites encompassed by the charges.[42] They are also permitted to set a time limit for the presentation of a case, allotting a specific number of hours for case presentation which is then closely monitored by the Registry. These procedural levers can induce the parties to voluntarily narrow the scope of their cases, focusing on their best evidence.

Other important matters that must be, or typically are, resolved during the pre-trial phase include challenges to the court's jurisdiction; defects in the form of the indictment or charges; severance or joinder of trials; objections concerning the assignment of counsel; provisional release of the accused; and recusal of judges.

Prosecutors are required to submit a pre-trial brief before the start of trial which, in effect, serves as the blueprint for the presentation of evidence.[43] The pre-trial brief presents the prosecution's case theory in more detail than the indictment, and the testimonial and documentary evidence to be relied upon to prove the charges. A list of witnesses and documents to be relied upon must be included in this document, although those lists may be amended with leave of the Chamber as the trial proceeds. When the volume of disclosure is massive, as is commonly the case, the pre-trial brief provides the critical link for giving notice to the defence (and in the other direction for the defence case) of what evidence will be relied upon in respect of which charges. Though no mention is made of a pre-trial brief in the statutory instruments of the ICC, the judges have recognized in practice that the prosecutor must notify the defence of the evidence it plans to present at confirmation and trial, and to offer a 'sufficiently detailed legal analysis relating the alleged facts with the constituent elements corresponding to each crime charged'. Hence, the prosecution has been required in each case to prepare an 'in depth analysis chart', which shows 'page by page or, where required, paragraph by paragraph' how its proposed evidence is relevant 'to the constituent elements of the crimes with which the person is charged'.[44]

20.3 TRIAL PROCEEDINGS

20.3.1 TRIAL PROCEDURE IN OUTLINE

Trial proceedings start on a clean slate. Guilt must be assessed exclusively on the basis of evidence admitted at trial, and may not be based 'on items that have come to the Chamber's knowledge but that have not been submitted and discussed at trial'.[45] The ICC Appeals Chamber has insisted that the admissibility of evidence must be tested 'on an

---

[41] ICC Statute, Art. 121(2); ICTY RPE, Rule 65 *bis*; ICTR RPE, Rule 65 *bis*.

[42] The judges have usually used this power to oblige the prosecutor to make the difficult choices as to how the indictment should be reduced: *Gotovina and others* (*Order Pursuant to Rule 73 bis (D) to Reduce the Indictment*); *Karadžić* (*Decision on the Application of Rule 73 bis*).

[43] ICTY RPE, Rule 65 *ter* (E); ICTR RPE, Rule 73 *bis* (B); STL RPE, Rule 91 (G); SCSL RPE, Rule 73 *bis* (B).

[44] *Bemba* (*Decision on the Evidence Disclosure System and Setting a Timetable for Disclosure between the Parties*), § 70; *Muthaura and others* (*Decision Setting the Regime for Evidence Disclosure and Other Related Matters*), § 23.

[45] *Bemba* (*Admissibility Decision*), § 45; ICC Statute, Art. 74(2) ('The Court may base its decision only on evidence submitted and discussed before it at the trial').

item-by-item basis' in accordance with the relevant admissibility standards.[46] The trial is therefore the exclusive crucible through which information is presented to the judges, and on which they may make their decision about the guilt of the accused.

Procedure is important in this context, and amongst the most important aspects of procedure is the sequence in which evidence is presented. The ICTY, ICTR, and SCSL Rules expressly require the prosecution to present its evidence first,[47] reflecting the principle that the accused ought to know the entire case against him before having to present evidence.[48] The narrowness of the exceptions to this sequence, rebuttal and reopening, underscore the importance of the rule. Rebuttal is restricted to material that responds to some aspect of the defence case that could not have been foreseen; it is not appropriate to fill 'some gap in the proof of guilt', nor can it be called 'merely because [the prosecution] case has been met by certain evidence to contradict it'.[49] Reopening, which has been described as 'exceptional',[50] only permits the prosecution to introduce information that is newly discovered, and that could not have been discovered even with the exercise of due diligence.[51]

The ICC Statute does not expressly set out a sequence for the presentation of evidence, generally empowering the presiding judge to 'give directions for the conduct of proceedings, including to ensure that they are conducted in a fair and impartial manner'.[52] ICC trials have so far proceeded according to the same sequence as at the ICTY and ICTR, and have recognized that the same standard in respect of rebuttal evidence ought to also apply, describing it as 'likely to be an exceptional event'.[53]

Courtroom hearings during an international trial are devoted mainly to the sometimes time-consuming process of hearing witnesses, bracketed by opening and closing statements, and punctuated by not infrequent disputes over procedure and evidence. The prosecution's case is presented within the framework of the indictment, the pre-trial

---

[46] *Bemba*, § 53.

[47] ICTY RPE, Rule 85; ICTR RPE, Rule 85; SCSL RPE, Rule 85. The STL Rules prescribe the same sequence, '[u]nless otherwise directed by the Trial Chamber in the interests of justice'.

[48] *R. v. P. (M.B.)*, [1994] 1 SCR 555 (Supreme Court of Canada): 'What is so objectionable about allowing the Crown's case to be reopened after the defence has started to meet that case is that it jeopardizes, indirectly, the principle that an accused not be conscripted against him or herself [...] there is a real risk that the Crown will, based on what it has heard from the defence, once it is compelled to "meet the case" against it, seek to fill in gaps or correct mistakes in the case of which it had on closing and to which the defence has started to respond.'

[49] *Mucic and others*, AC, § 275; ICTY RPE, Rule 85 (A)(iii).

[50] *Milošević Slobodan (Decision on Application for a Limited Re-opening of the Bosnia and Kosovo Components of the Prosecution Case)*, § 37.

[51] *Tadić (Decision on Appellant's Motion for the Extention of the Time-Limit and Admission of Additional Evidence)*, § 60; *Ntagerura and others (Decision on Prosecution Motion for Admission of Additional Evidence)*, § 9 ('Counsel is expected to apprise the Trial Chamber of all the difficulties he or she encounters in obtaining the evidence in question, including any problems of intimidation, and his or her inability to locate certain witnesses. The obligation to apprise the Trial Chamber constitutes not only a first step in exercising due diligence but also a means of self-protection in that non-cooperation of the prospective witness is recorded contemporaneously'); *Popović and others (Decision on Vujadin Popovic's Interlocutory Appeal Against the Decision on the Prosecution's Motion to Reopen Its Case-in-Chief)*, § 19 ('The issue to be determined by the Trial Chamber was whether despite the exercise of due diligence in its investigation, the Prosecution would have failed to discover the evidence prior to the close of its case [...] The Appeals Chamber is thus satisfied that it was within the discretion of the Trial Chamber to find that the Prosecution had established that, despite the exercise of due diligence, it could not have discovered the new evidence during its case-in-chief [...]').

[52] ICC Statute, Art. 64(8)(b); ICC RPE, Rule 140(1).

[53] *Lubanga (Decision on the Prosecution's Application to Admit Rebuttal Evidence from Witness DRC-OTP-WWWW-0005)*, § 43.

brief, and the opening statement, which offers the most up-to-date and concise roadmap of the evidence to be heard. The defence usually waits until the beginning of its own case to make an opening statement, allowing it to hear the prosecution case in its totality before taking a detailed position in response.[54]

The defence case is subject to roughly the same forms of judicial management as the prosecution case. The defence is required, in advance of its case but after the close of the prosecution case, to disclose a list of witnesses to be called, statements they may have given, and the documents it intends to use.[55] As during the prosecution case, these lists can be amended with leave of the judges. While new documents can be relatively easily added, the addition of new witnesses tends to be subject to greater judicial scrutiny. The defence then presents its evidence subject largely to the same rules and procedures as the prosecution.

The prosecutor and defence summarize the evidence presented and their legal arguments in written closing briefs and final arguments before the Court.[56] ICTY accused are also permitted, 'under the control of the Trial Chamber', to make an unsworn statement during the trial and recent experience seems to favour doing so immediately after closing arguments.[57] The statement is not testimony and, hence, the accused is not examined or cross-examined, but the Chamber may accord it probative value. Interestingly, the IMT Charter, in Article 24(j) specifically permitted an accused to make a statement after the closing statements. (Thus defendants effectively spoke *after* the case was closed—that is, after the trial had finished and all the evidence had been produced—so the IMT could probably tolerate this departure because in effect it was happening 'outside the trial proper'.) The reason behind this departure from most common law systems is that this is the only opportunity for defendants freely—that is, without being cross-examined—to set out their general views and explain their motivations or why they consider they are innocent.

The ICC and SCSL, but not ICTY or ICTR, hold a separate hearing after the verdict to determine sentence,[58] which permits an accused person to express contrition for their acts before being sentenced. Another unique feature of ICC proceedings is the potential for reparations being awarded to victims, whether from the convicted person or the independent trust fund set up for that purpose.

---

[54] The practice of the defence of refraining from making an opening statement at the beginning of trial highlights two major differences between a typical international criminal trial and a typical domestic criminal trial. First, the hearings are conducted before professional judges who may be presumed to be better able to methodically analyse the totality of evidence without being unduly swayed by the emotion of an opening statement. Second, the duration of a typical international trial ensures that the effect of the opening statement has largely worn off by the time the judges deliberate. The effectiveness of the legal and factual response to the evidence presented is, therefore, of much greater importance than any emotional response that may be engendered by an opening statement.

[55] ICC RPE, Rules 78, 79(4); *Katanga and Chui (Decision on the Prosecution's Application Concerning Disclosure by the Defence Pursuant to Rules 78 and 79(4))*; ICTY RPE, Rule 65 *ter* (G); ICTY RPE, Rule 73 *ter*.

[56] ICTY RPE, Rule 86(C). The lack of a separate sentencing hearing has been much attacked by the defence, who say: how can we address sentencing matters when (a) our position at that point is that the accused is completely innocent ('Your Honours, my client is completely innocent, but if you find him guilty, please bear in mind that he only beat the victims with his fists and not with a stick'!); and (b) we do not know what factual findings the Chamber will make. It is like the old schoolboy plea, when charged with breaking the window in the headmaster's study: (i) first, there is no witness in the headmaster's study; (ii) if there is a window, it is not broken; (iii) if it is broken, I did not do it; (iv) if I did it, it was an accident. This does not sound very convincing as a closing speech—the protestation of innocence is undercut by what sounds like admissions by the accused.

[57] ICTY RPE, Rule 84 *bis*.

[58] ICC Statute, Art. 76(3); ICC RPE, Rule 143.

20.3.2 ORAL TESTIMONY, EXAMINATION, AND CROSS-EXAMINATION

All of the international courts recognize that, in principle, witness evidence is to be given by way of oral testimony before the judges. Article 69(2) of the ICC Statute, echoing the rules of the ICTY and ICTR, prescribes that '[t]he testimony of a witness at trial shall be given in person' subject to the exceptions set out in the Statute. The value of this mode of evidence, as the ICC Appeals Chamber has explained, derives from the fact that the witness gives his or her narrative 'under the observation and general oversight of the Chamber,' which is then 'able to observe his or her demeanour and composure, and is able to seek clarification on aspects of the witness' testimony that may be unclear so that it may be accurately recorded'.[59]

Testimony at all the international criminal courts is elicited through questioning. The dominant procedure is for the party calling the witness 'to examine' the witness through 'non-leading' or non-suggestive questions; followed by cross-examination by the adverse party using, if it wishes, 'leading questions' and propositions; followed again by the party calling the witness, which may re-examine the witness on matters raised for the first time during the cross-examination, again using only non-suggestive questions.[60] The prohibition on leading questions by the party presenting the witness is inherent in the Appeals Chamber's passage quoted above explaining the importance of such evidence. The 'directness' of the witness's testimony will be weakened if the lawyer suggests the answers through his or her questions. Thus, asking 'Was the car yellow?' is a much less useful question that 'What was the colour of the car?' A witness may answer the latter question confidently, may be unable to recall, or fall somewhere between these two reactions; whatever the case may be, a leading question would conceal this range of potential reactions and interfere with the Chamber's opportunity to observe the witness's 'demeanour and composure'.[61]

---

[59] *Bemba (Admissibility Decision)*, § 76.

[60] ICTY RPE, Rule 85(B); ICTR RPE, Rule 85(B); ICC RPE, Rule 140(2)(a)–(b); *Lubanga*, T. 16 January 2009, at 37; *Katanga and Chui (Directions for the Conduct of Proceedings and Testimony in accordance with Rule 140)*, §§ 61, 66, 68, 74, 77. As happens in the practice of some common law countries (but not in England, where it is strictly forbidden), also in international criminal tribunals before examining witnesses in court, each party is entitled to undertake 'witness preparation', also called '*witness proofing*'; that is, to rehearse the examination-in-chief, by asking the witness all the necessary questions. In this way, the whole testimony is rehearsed. It is commonly stated that, as a rule of thumb, a prosecutor or defence counsel should never ask a question in examination-in-chief or cross-examination without previously knowing the answer. This practice, which could sound odd or unfair to lawyers of civil law countries, is among other things aimed at: *i)* focusing, in the questions and answers, on the key issues of testimony; *ii)* reducing the witness's anxiety about his testimony in court and at the same time building in him a feeling of security and confidence; and *iii)* putting the witness in a proper frame of mind to be effective in his testimony or with a view to avoiding receiving a surprising answer which could be damaging to one's client (especially in cross-examination, although in examination-in-chief it could also be partly a way of making the witness comfortable). It is also important to 'control' the witness, for instance asking short, specific questions, so that the witness does not go ranting off on other subjects. Often, prosecutors and defence counsel also simulate cross-examination, so as to better prepare the witness to questions from the other side.

In *Kupreškić and others (Decision on communications between the parties and their witnesses)*, the Trial Chamber ruled that, once a witness had made the 'solemn declaration' provided for in Rule 90(1) he could no longer communicate with the party that had called him, except with the leave of the Chamber (at 3).

[61] Leading questions by the calling party to elicit undisputed or peripheral information are, in appropriate circumstances, harmless and may expedite proceedings. Such questions are therefore sometimes permitted where appropriate, particularly when there is no significant objection or ground for objection.

The main function of the non-calling party, on the other hand, is to confront the person with contrary information (i.e. to 'put its case' to the witness) or to challenge his or her credibility. The rules of the ICTY and ICTR affirmatively require: 'In the cross-examination of a witness who is able to give evidence relevant to the case for the cross-examining party, counsel shall put to that witness the nature of the case of the party for whom that counsel appears which is in contradiction of the evidence given by the witness.'[62] This requirement promotes the Chamber's truth-finding function by bringing the issues into sharper relief. For example, a prosecution witness testifies that he saw the accused commit a killing and the defence does not put to the witness in cross-examination that his identification of the accused is mistaken. The defence during its own case elicits information that the killing occurred on a moonless night, making identification difficult. The failure to put the proposition to the witness deprives the Chamber to hear the witness's potential response, which might be as simple as 'Nonsense, it was broad daylight' or 'But I was standing only a metre away'. Requiring the direct postulation of such issues through leading questions sharpens and clarifies issues of this sort, where neutral questions could not do so. The ICC Rules contain no requirement that the case of the opposing party be put to a witness. Indeed, in one case the Trial Chamber even prohibited the use of leading questions on cross-examination.[63]

Cross-examination at the ICTY and ICTR may address not only those issues raised during the witness's direct examination, but also 'the subject-matter' of the cross-examining party's case—i.e. any information that might be relevant to that party's case can be elicited from the other party's witness.[64] The prosecution can thus elicit incriminating testimony notwithstanding the fact that its case has closed, which may generally be viewed as a fair consequence of the defence's own choice to call the witness. Problems arise, however, when documents are put to a witness not because of any genuine connection with the witness's knowledge, but simply as a vehicle to introduce documentary evidence. The danger of surprise is particularly great, since documents used in cross-examination need not be listed as evidence and, indeed, notification of its use is given only shortly before, or even after, the witness's direct examination begins.[65] Chambers have recognized the potential for prejudice arising from this situation and have attempted to control or limit this practice, in particular, by disallowing the introduction of information on matters that had not been addressed during the prosecution case,[66] or by insisting on at least some meaningful connection between the document and the witness's knowledge.[67]

---

[62] ICTY RPE, Rule 90(H)(i); ICTR RPE, Rule 90(G)(i).

[63] *Bemba* (*Decision on Directions for the Conduct of Proceedings*), § 15 ('With regard to the mode of questioning, the Chamber expects all parties and participants to ask neutral questions to the witnesses'). The *Lubanga* and *Katanga* Trial Chambers did permit leading questions on cross-examination.

[64] Many common law jurisdictions do permit questioning to this extent, but some others limit the questions to the scope of the direct examination and credibility only.

[65] *Tolimir* (*Revised Order Concerning the Guidelines on the Presentation of Evidence and Conduct of the Parties During Trial*), Annex A, § 5 ('24 hours before the witness is called to give evidence').

[66] *Bagosora and others* (*Decision on Request for Severance of Three Accused*), 27 March 2006, § 7. ('Accordingly, the "case for the cross-examining party" must now be understood as defined and limited by the evidence presented during the Prosecution case. The Prosecution may adduce evidence during its cross-examination which corroborates or reinforces evidence presented during the presentation of its case, but may not, at this stage, venture into new areas.') See generally *Delić R.* (*Decision on Rasim Delić's Interlocutory Appeal against Trial Chamber's Oral Decisions on Admission of Exhibits 1316 and 1317*; *Prlić* (*Decision on Interlocutory Appeal against the Trial Chamber's Decision on Presentation of Documents by the Prosecution in Cross-Examination of Defence Witnesses*).

[67] *Karadžić* (*Decision on Guidelines for the Admission of Evidence through Witnesses*), recognizing that certain documents might be independently admissible by way of a bar table motion, but rejecting their

Victims at the ICC are considered to be 'participants', not parties, to the proceedings, and the extent of their participation is largely a matter of judicial discretion. When permitted to ask questions of a witness at trial, they are normally required to do so after the calling party and only after having given a written list of questions in advance of the witness's appearance—a requirement that significantly limits their capacity to adjust questioning depending on the direct examination. Although they are 'less likely' to need to resort to the 'combative technique' of cross-examination, circumstances may arise in which it may be 'fully consistent with the role of the victims' legal representatives to seek to press, challenge or discredit a witness'.[68] The same approach, incidentally, governs questioning by defence teams who wish to cross-examine a co-accused's witness: when eliciting favourable evidence they should in principle 'avoid asking leading questions to the witness as this will undermine the credibility of such testimony',[69] but may ask leading questions when the witness is, or is potentially, adverse to their position.

20.3.3 THE ROLE OF JUDGES

Judges may potentially play a significant role in the presentation of testimonial evidence. They have broad powers in directing the questioning of witnesses, ordering protective measures for vulnerable witnesses, determining the appropriate line between proper confrontation and harassment, and deciding on written or oral motions submitted by the parties with respect to the questioning of witnesses.[70] They are also entitled to put questions to witnesses at any stage and may order the appearance of witnesses or the presentation of other evidence.[71] Some ICTY judges, albeit rarely, have engaged in sustained questioning of witnesses; more commonly they intervene at propitious moments to clarify testimony. An often overlooked but extremely important role has been played in some trials when the judges, as they are entitled to do at the ICC and other international criminal tribunals, have decided to call witnesses after the cases have closed.[72] The defence is normally permitted to cross-examine these witnesses after the Chamber and the prosecution, ensuring that they have the last opportunity to respond to any incriminating material that may have been elicited.

An even broader judicial role is envisaged in the STL Statute, which provides: 'Unless otherwise decided by the Trial Chamber in the interests of justice, examination of witnesses shall commence with questions posed by the presiding judge, followed by questions posed by other members of the Trial Chamber, the Prosecutor and the Defence.'[73] Here the Statute—it would seem—adopts a mixture of the inquisitorial system (where

---

admission through a particular witness on the basis of 'no apparent connection between the documents tendered', and requiring that 'the witness to whom it is shown is able to confirm its content or make some other positive comment about it' and the witness on the stand. *Stanisic and Zulpjanin (Order on Guidelines on the Admission and Presentation of Evidence)*, Annex A, §3.

[68] *Lubanga (Decision on the Manner of Questioning Witnesses by the Legal Representatives of Victims)*, § 28.

[69] *Bagosora and others (Decision on Modalities for Examination of Defence Witnesses)*, § 6.

[70] ICC Statute, Art. 64(3)(a); ICC RPE, Rule 134(1); ICTY RPE, Rule 90(F): 'The Trial Chamber shall exercise control over the mode and order of interrogating witnesses and presenting evidence so as to *i)* make the interrogation and presentation effective for the ascertainment of the truth; and *ii)* avoid needless consumption of time.'

[71] ICC Statute, Art. 64(6)(d) (authorizing the Chamber to 'order the production of evidence'); ICTY RPE, Rule 98 ('A Trial Chamber may order either party to produce additional evidence. It may proprio motu summon witnesses and order their attendance'). ICC RPE, Rule 140(2)(c).

[72] *Popović and others (Order to Summon Momir Nikolić)*; *Krajisnik*, TC, §§ 1255–7.

[73] STL Statute, Art. 20(2).

witnesses are first questioned by the judges and then, if need be, by the parties, but cross-examination proper is absent), and the adversarial system (where witnesses are always examined and cross-examined by the parties, and the judges tend to play a passive role). The advantage of the former system's approach is that the judges, in their search for judicial truth, tend to go to the heart of the case and refrain from putting questions that may lead to a distortion of the evidence; in addition, they prove to be fairer than the contending parties to vulnerable witnesses. However, if the accused feels that the questions put by the judges to a witness are not fair and tend to damage him, he or she has no means of putting things right (unless his defence counsel then asks the witness questions that aim at supporting the defendant's case). As for the adversarial system's approach, it no doubt ensures a more thorough and in-depth questioning of witnesses. However, as has been rightly noted, it 'can easily distort the evidence, because the people who ask the questions do so in the hope of obtaining answers that fit the case they are putting forward'.[74]

20.3.4 RULES ON EVIDENCE

Evidence is information that has been received in a particular proceeding to prove or disprove factual claims. The threshold at which information becomes evidence varies from legal system to legal system. In an adversarial system, the threshold is crossed at trial; in an inquisitorial system, the threshold is crossed earlier, through the work and procedures adopted by the investigating judge, who then transfers the information to the deciders of fact. Whatever system is chosen, no rational system of legal procedure can do without some means of identifying the information upon which the deciders of fact, whether judge or jury, are to make their decision.

The evidential threshold for the determination of charges before international criminal courts is crossed at the trial, which is a logical corollary of the absence of judicial control over investigations. The rules of evidence applied at trial are a means of controlling, albeit retroactively, the manner of these investigations, and of ensuring at least a basic standard of reliability and relevance. Their primary purpose is not, as when a case is heard before a lay jury, to prevent the presentation of inflammatory or improperly prejudicial material; the dominant purpose, instead, is to ensure the focus and efficiency of the proceedings. This is a concern of growing importance as international investigations have become progressively more successful, generating increasing volumes of information. The rules of evidence, particularly in respect of documentary evidence that may be admitted by written procedure alone, may assist in keeping a trial within proper bounds and precluding information of little or no value.[75]

The evidential standards from the IMT to the ICC have developed around general principles, rather than a detailed code of technical rules that would be ill-suited to the difficult and varied circumstances in which international investigations may take place. Article 19 of the IMT Statute provided: 'The Tribunal shall not be bound by technical

---

[74] J. R. Spencer, 'Evidence', in Delmas-Marty and Spencer, *European Criminal Procedures*, at 629.

[75] *Karadžić* (*Decision on Guidelines for the Admission of Evidence through Witnesses*), § 22 ('The Chamber here reiterates its concern that the case record does not become overburdened with an enormous volume of documents that have no apparent relationship to the case or where it is not clear how they fit into the cases of either party'); *Prlic and others* (*Revised Version of the Decision Adopting Guidelines on Conduct of Trial Proceedings*) § 8 ('it would not facilitate the completion of the trial without a reasonable amount of time to set limits on the amount of time available for in-court testimony and then to flood the Chamber with documentary evidence'). See generally C. Gosnell, 'The Changing Context of Evidential Rules', in K. Khan, C. Buisman, and C. Gosnell (eds), *Principles of Evidence in International Criminal Justice* (Oxford: Oxford University Press, 2010), at 221–7.

rules of evidence. It shall adopt and apply to the greatest possible extent expeditious and non-technical] procedure, and shall admit any evidence which it deems to be of probative value.'[76]

The ICC has followed the same approach:

[T]he Chamber has concluded that it enjoys a significant degree of discretion in considering all types of evidence. This is particularly necessary given the nature of the cases that will come before the ICC: there will be infinitely variable circumstances in which the Court will be asked to consider evidence, which will not infrequently have come into existence, or have been compiled or retrieved, in difficult circumstances, such as during particularly egregious instances of armed conflict, when those involved will have been killed or wounded, and the survivors or those affected may be untraceable or unwilling— for credible reasons—to give evidence.[77]

Three broad principles govern the general admissibility of evidence before the modern international criminal courts: relevance, probative value, and any prejudicial effect on trial fairness.[78] These principles apply to all evidence, but subsidiary principles or rules can be found in the courts' Statutes or RPE, or have been developed in the jurisprudence in respect of specific types of information. For example, a category of enormous practical and theoretical interest is witness statements (for example, notes of interviews with potential witnesses or affidavits) or transcripts of previous testimony. The ICC Statute requires that witness testimony 'shall be given in person', echoing the original ICTY and ICTR rule that 'witnesses shall, in principle, be heard directly by the Chambers'. This 'principle of orality' requires that, subject to any exceptions in the Statute, 'witnesses must appear before the Trial Chamber in person to give their evidence orally'.[79] By implication, witness statements cannot be admitted in lieu of testimony that must be heard live before the Court.[80] The same principle applies at the ICTY, but Chambers in their early proceedings occasionally admitted witness statements for limited purposes essentially by invoking the broad discretion accorded under the three main principles of admissibility. A divergence of practice ensued that was evidently considered unsound by the judges of the ICTY who, in December 2000, codified the conditions for admitting such statements in Rule 92 *bis*. This provision, subsequently adopted at the ICTR and STL, permits written statements or transcripts to be admitted if they comply with certain formalities and avoid describing the 'acts and conduct of the accused'.[81] The Rule also enumerates a

---

[76] Justice Robert H. Jackson, the American delegate at the conference negotiating the IMT Statute, explained: 'We do not want technical rules of evidence designed for jury trials to be used in this case to cut down what is really and fairly of probative value, and so we propose to lay down as a part of the statute [of the future IMT] that utmost liberality shall be used [...] The idea may have more significance to British and American lawyers than it does to Continental lawyers' (*International Conference on Military Trials*, at 83).

[77] *Lubanga* (*Corrigendum to Decision on the admissibility of four documents*), § 24.

[78] ICC Statute, Art. 69(4) ('The Court may rule on the relevance or admissibility of any evidence, taking into account, inter alia, the probative value of the evidence and any prejudice that such evidence may cause to a fair trial or to a fair evaluation of the testimony of any witness'); ICTY, Rule 89(C) ('A Chamber may admit any relevant evidence which it deems to have probative value'); ICTR Rule 89(C); STL Rule 149(C) and (D). The standards adopted at the ECCC are radically different, in light of the investigative procedure followed there, and the SCSL statute adopted ICTR Rule 89(C), but only after removing the 'probative value' element. *Katanga* (*Decision on the Prosecutor's Bar Table Motions*), ('the Chamber will first assess the relevance of the material, then determine whether it has probative value and finally weight its probative value against its potentially prejudicial effect').

[79] *Bemba* (*Admissibility Decision*), § 76.

[80] ICC Statute, Art. 68(1) offers a potential exception in respect of vulnerable witnesses.

[81] The ICTY Rules now even allow the admission of statements that do concern the acts and conduct of the accused if the person who made the statement is deceased or otherwise unavailable. ICTY RPE, Rule 92

series of factors in favour and against admission, and Chambers have a wide discretion to require the person to attend for cross-examination on the statement.[82] Rule 92 *bis* came five months too late for consideration by the Committee preparing the ICC Rules, and neither it nor the Statute make any allowance for the admission of written statements as evidence unless the person is available to be, or has been, questioned by both parties.[83]

The foregoing example illustrates how subsidiary rules and practices have developed within the discretion afforded under the three general principles of admissibility. The routine work of trial practice has tended to encourage readily applicable rules so that the parties will, for the most part, know in advance how to prepare information so that it will be admissible.

The admissibility of witness evidence is governed mainly by procedural rules governing the proper form of questioning; the admissibility of documentary evidence is assessed according to its inherent attributes or any surrounding information that shows its relevance and probative value. No technical procedural rules govern the admission of documentary evidence, which can even be tendered by way of written motion without having ever been mentioned in court.[84] The tendering party need show only enough 'indicia of reliability' to suggest that it could be accorded probative value in light of all the other evidence to be heard.[85] ICTY Trial Chambers have disapproved the practice of the bulk introduction of thousands of documents presented, often demanding particularized submissions on relevance and probative value of each and every document, and encouraging the parties, where possible, to contextualize documents through witnesses.[86] The mass introduction of evidence may not only undermine the Chamber's obligation to make a document-by-document assessment of reliability, but also the relevance of the

quater; STL RPE, Rules 155 (equivalent of Rule 92 *bis*); 158 (equivalent of Rule 92 *quater*). The ICTR, though adopting Rule 92 *bis*, has not adopted Rule 92 *quater*.

[82] Cumulativeness with other evidence and its contextual or peripheral connection to the key issues of guilt are factors favouring admission; factors against admission include indications of unreliability or the existence of an 'over-riding interest' in hearing the testimony orally.

[83] ICC RPE, Rule 68 permits the admission of 'previously recorded audio or video testimony of a witness, or the transcript or other documented evidence of such testimony' if *i*) both 'the Prosecutor and the defence had the opportunity to examine the witness during the recording'; or *ii*) the person is 'present before the Trial Chamber' and available to be questioned, and does not object to its submission. This does not seem to encompass any statement taken by one party alone, nor is it likely that 'the defence' could be interpreted as including the defence of another accused in a different trial. Art. 56, concerning a unique investigative opportunity, may arguably be a method of providing some relief from the strictness of this rule,

[84] *Katanga* (Decision on the Prosecutor's Bar Table Motions), § 12; *Stanišić and Zulpjanin* (Order on Guidelines on the Admission and Presentation of Evidence), Annex A, §4 ('There is no rule which prohibits the admission into evidence of documents merely because their alleged source was not called to testify').

[85] *Lubanga* (Corrigendum to Decision on the Admissibility of Four Documents), §§ 29, 31 (finding documents to have 'sufficient apparent indicia of reliability' and underlining that there is 'no finite list of possible criteria that are to be applied' to make a determination of probative value); *Kordić and Cerkez* (Decision on the Appeal Regarding Statement of a Deceased Witness), § 20 ('A piece of evidence may be so lacking in terms of the indicia of reliability that [it] is not probative'); *Bagosora and others* (Admission of Tab 19 of Binder Produced in Connection with Appearance of Witness Maxwell Nkole), § 8 ('Indicia of reliability which have justified admission of documents in the jurisprudence of the UN Tribunals include: the place in which the document was seized, in conjunction with testimony describing the chain of custody since the seizure of the document; corroboration of the contents of the document with other evidence; and the nature of the document itself, such as signatures, stamps, or even the form of the handwriting').

[86] *Boskoski and Tarculovski* (Decision on Tarculovksi Second Motion for Admission of Exhibits from the Bar Table with Annex A), ('It is desirable that documents are tendered for admission through witnesses who are able to comment on them').

information to the case as a whole.[87] The admissibility of a document, particularly one that has evident importance, may be endangered if the tendering party appears to have avoided putting it to a witness obviously competent to discuss it.[88]

Video-conference testimony is considered at the ICC to be 'live testimony' before the court and, hence, is considered 'testimony [,.,] given in person'.[89] This view has never been expressly adopted at the ICTY and ICTR, although frequent resort has been had to video-conference testimony 'if consistent with the interests of justice'.[90] More than mere inconvenience to the witness is required; there must be at least some objectively justified basis for the witness's unwillingness or inability to appear in person.[91] Whether the more permissive standard adopted by the ICC will translate into more frequent reliance on video-conferencing may well depend on the preferences of the parties and the availability of adequate technology to ensure clear, effective, and speedy testimony and translation.

Otherwise admissible evidence may be excluded if obtained in breach of fundamental principles of law, for instance in violation of fundamental human rights safeguards.[92] Violations of the law where the investigation occurred do not necessarily lead to the exclusion of evidence, although it may be a relevant factor for assessing prejudice or probative value. Whether violations of the provisions contained in Part IX of the ICC Statute will be considered as a basis for exclusion of evidence remains to be decided.

The protection of vulnerable witnesses is one of special significance in the international context. Measures may often need to be taken both inside and outside the courtroom to ensure that the security and dignity of those persons are protected, while at the same time not prejudicing the rights of the accused to a fair trial. Specific rules, as in many domestic jurisdictions, apply to evidence to be given concerning sexual assault, including that no evidence may be adduced of the complainant's sexual history, and no consent can be inferred from words or conduct where force, threat of force, or other coercive factors were present.[93] Video-link testimony is permitted as a method of witness protection, although that is not the only basis for allowing it.

Alternatives to proof by evidence include *judicial notice* of facts of common knowledge or of public documents, accepting 'adjudicated facts' from previous cases and thus creating a rebuttable presumption that those facts, or accepting as true facts that have been agree by the parties.

The usual rule that witnesses must answer all relevant questions is subject to a number of exceptions. Witnesses, if they legitimately fear that their answers may incriminate themselves, may ask not to answer. Trial Chambers nonetheless have the discretion to compel an answer on the basis of a 'guarantee' that the information will be kept confidential

---

[87] *Bemba (Admissibility Decision)*, § 53 ('article 69(4) and (7) of the Statute and rule 71 of the Rules of Procedure and Evidence thus anticipates that a Chamber's determination of the relevance or admissibility of evidence be made on an item-by-item basis').

[88] *Mrksić (Decision on Mile Mrksic's Motion for Admission of Documents)*, § 2 ('a number of witnesses [...] who came to testify before the Tribunal apparently could have provided information as to the circumstances in which these documents were issued but there was no attempt [...] to put these documents to any of those witnesses').

[89] ICC RPE, Rule 67.

[90] ICTY RPE, Rule 81 *bis*.

[91] *Haradinaj (Decision on Prosecution's Motion for Testimony Via Video-link for Witness 54)*, § 5; *Aloys Simba (Decision Authorizing the Taking of the Evidence of Witnesses IMG, ISG, and BJK1 by Video-Link)*, TC. Video-testimony has also been justified at the ICTR as a witness protection measure.

[92] ICTY RPE, Rule 95 ('No evidence shall be admissible if obtained by methods which cast substantial doubt on its reliability or if its admission is antithetical to, and would seriously damage, the integrity of the proceedings'). See also Article 69(7), ICC Statute.

[93] ICC RPE, Rules 70–1; ICTY RPE, Rule 96.

and will not be used in subsequent prosecutions. That guarantee extends only to future proceedings 'by the Court' at the ICC, whereas at the ICTY they may extend to national proceedings as well.[94] A witness may assert certain other privileges, including communications between lawyer and client; national security information; information supplied to the prosecution pursuant to a non-disclosure agreement; and special categories such as information obtained in confidence by ICRC officials.[95]

20.3.5 CONTROL OF PROCEEDINGS

International criminal courts, like any court, have an inherent power to control their proceedings. A Trial Chamber may close the hearings to the public when necessary to protect victims or witnesses, public order or morality, security, or the interests of justice. Persons, including the accused, may be removed from the courtroom to maintain the dignity and decorum of the proceedings.

Resort to contempt proceedings has become increasingly common at the ICTY, ICTR, and SCSL, particularly in respect of perjury, violations of confidentiality orders, interference with witnesses, and refusal to appear as a witness in accordance with a subpoena. Three contempt proceedings have been initiated against a self-represented accused at the ICTY for publishing the identities of protected witnesses in books and on his website; the first resulted in a sentence of fifteen months' imprisonment.[96] The maximum penalty for contempt at the ICTY is seven years' imprisonment, or a fine not exceeding 100,000 Euros, whereas the maximum sentence foreseen under the ICC Statute is five years. A thorny issue is whether the ICC could validly assert contempt jurisdiction against someone who would not be subject to its jurisdiction for a substantive crime. This problem does not arise at the ICTY or ICTR, whose jurisdiction presumptively encompasses all states; a significant problem could arise were the ICC to purport to place someone in custody who neither committed a crime on the territory, nor is a national, of a state party.

20.3.6 DELIBERATIONS

When both parties have completed their presentation of the case, the court declares the hearings closed and retires to deliberate in private on the basis of the trial record. The standard of proof to be applied is proof of all necessary elements of the crime *beyond a reasonable doubt*.[97] Many formulations have been attempted to help further clarify these words, but the words themselves are the best expression of the standard. As the European Court of Human Rights put it in *Barberà, Messegué and Jabardo*, 'any doubt should benefit the accused' (§ 77). In 1947 Lord Denning set out a clear definition of the standard of proof under discussion in *Miller v. Minister of Pensions*. He pointed out that:

> the degree of cogency as is required in a criminal case before an accused person is found guilty [...] is well settled. It need not reach certainty, but it must carry a high degree of

[94] ICC RPE, Rule 74; *Popović and others*, T.3789–91 (8 November 2006); T. 4074–5 (16 November 2006); T. 11591 (16 May 2007).

[95] ICTY RPE, Rule 97; *Tadić (Decision on Prosecution Motion for Production of Defence Witness Statements)*, at 2, and Separate Opinion of Judge Stephen, at 3–7. *Simić (Prosecution motion under Rule 73 for a ruling concerning the Testimony of a Witness)*, §§ 34–80; ICC RPE, Rule 73(4–6).

[96] *Šešelj*, AC, which confirmed the Trial Chamber's conviction of the accused for contempt for knowingly disclosing confidential information regarding protected witnesses.

[97] ICC Statute, Art. 66(3); ICTY RPE, Rule 87(A); *Jelisić* (§ 108), *Kunarac (Decision on Motion for Acquittal)* (§ 3); *Kvočka (Decision on Defence Motions for Acquittal)* (§ 12); *Delalić and others*, AC, § 434); *Jelisić*, AC, §§ 34–7). For a case where the Appeal Chamber found that the standard had not been correctly applied, see ICTR, *Akayesu*, AC, §§ 171–2.

probability. Proof beyond reasonable doubt does not mean proof beyond the shadow of a doubt. The law would fail to protect the community if it admitted fanciful possibilities to deflect the course of justice. If the evidence is so strong against a man as to leave only a remote possibility in his favour which can be dismissed with the sentence 'of course it is possible, but not in the least probable', the case is proved beyond reasonable doubt, but nothing short of that will suffice (3).[98]

The reasonable doubt standard can be illuminated by contrast with the less stringent standard for civil actions in common law countries. Different civil cases, for example, require proof on the 'balance of probabilities', or 'by a preponderance of the evidence' (that is, evidence showing, as a whole, that the fact sought to be proved is more probable than not, evidence that is more convincing than that offered in opposition to it), or, under a test requiring a higher degree of proof, 'by clear and convincing evidence' (that is, by evidence that is clear and explicit and is sufficient to make out a prima facie case). The upholding of different standards of proof for criminal and civil proceedings accounts for the possibility that trial proceedings may be terminated with the acquittal of the defendant and be followed by proceedings for damages in tort law (as, for instance, in the famous *O. J. Simpson* case). It should, however, be noted that in some instances a rule different from that prevailing is applied even in criminal proceedings: for instance, under Rule 850(a)(b) of the US Uniform Code of Military Justice, 'The accused has the burden of proving the defense of lack of mental responsibility by clear and convincing evidence.'[99]

Criminal convictions in civil law countries require the '*intime conviction*' of the judge. The standard differs from that of 'beyond a reasonable doubt', but commentators disagree on how different they really are, and whether one is lower or higher than the other.[100] A

[98] In *Heinz Heck and others* (the *Peleus* trial) the Judge Advocate in his summing up explained: 'A reasonable doubt does not mean some fanciful or imaginary doubt such as a weak mind may grasp if it is struggling to avoid an honest conclusion on evidence that is plain. It means the kind of doubt that might affect you in the conduct of some important affair of your own. If, having considered this case as I know you will, most anxiously, you are left with a reasonable doubt such as I have described, then it is your duty to give to any accused person as to whom you entertain such a doubt the benefit of it and to acquit him. If, on the other hand, the evidence that you have heard drives your minds to the conclusion that he is guilty, it is equally your duty to say so without regard to the consequences of this finding' (at 123). In *Wolfgang Zeuss and others* (the *Natzweiler* trial) the Judge Advocate, in his summing up, stated that 'Probably there are few things in the world about which we can be utterly and completely certain. In most things there is some doubt—some little doubt—in one's mind, but you are not obliged to take into account any sensitive doubt—anything which would not affect your judgment in your own affairs. What you have to do is to be satisfied beyond reasonable doubt. That means you must not be left, having decided that a person is guilty, feeling that perhaps you were wrong about that' (at 199).

[99] The standard of proof, even under Rule 850, is still 'beyond a reasonable doubt', e.g. if the accused is charged with murder under the US Uniform Code, the prosecution will have to prove that he committed the murder beyond a reasonable doubt. The question is—what happens if the accused then turns around and says, yes I killed intentionally, but I was insane or otherwise deranged at the time? It would be very hard for the prosecution to prove '*beyond a reasonable doubt*' that the person is not insane. So what the law does instead is to put a burden on the defence to prove that he was insane. But it would equally be too harsh on a defendant to require him to prove '*beyond a reasonable doubt*' that he was insane. Insanity is a tricky question and no certainties exist. Therefore the law imposes on the defendant this intermediate standard of 'clear and convincing evidence'. This is known as a reversible burden of proof and is often imposed for 'special defences'. Interestingly, the ICC Statute forbids any reversing of burdens of proof. See ICC Statute, Art. 67(1)(i).

[100] For, instance, Pradel (at 474). According to J. R. Spencer, cit. n. 74, 'It is questionable whether the actual level of certainty the two tests require is really different' (at 601). Indeed, the question arises of whether one can really have an '(*intime*) *conviction*' if one is not convinced beyond reasonable doubt that the accused is guilty.

useful insight into the difference between the two standards is the distinction between civil and criminal cases within a typical civil law jurisdiction. In the former, the probative weight of particular classes of evidence is defined, whereas the latter is based on the free evaluation of evidence without any such categorization. What matters is that the judge reaches the 'conviction' that the accused is guilty or innocent.[101]

The modern international criminal courts and tribunals are required to state their reasons for judgment, and often do so over hundreds of pages in meticulous detail. This contrasts with some post-Second World War judgments that were under a single page. Judges who do not concur with the majority may append their separate or dissenting opinions to the judgment.

20.3.7 SENTENCING

International crimes are not subject to any sentencing guidelines or tariff. The determination is instead fact-specific and can 'take into account such factors as the gravity of the crime and the individual circumstances of the convicted person'.[102] The crimes for which a person is convicted or the forms of participation, though having an impact on sentencing, are not determinative for assessing gravity. There is no necessary hierarchy of penalties, for example, between commission and aiding and abetting, or between persecution and murder. Any and all circumstances may be taken into account in reaching a determination of the appropriate sentence in view of the accused's contribution to, and gravity of, the crime. Sentences may range from a suspended sentence to life in prison; the only penalty that is categorically excluded is capital punishment.[103]

Usually, international criminal courts are to refer to the relevant sentencing practice in the countries that would have jurisdiction but for the existence of the international criminal court. Thus, the ICTY Statute stipulates that 'in determining the terms of imprisonment, the Trial Chambers shall have recourse to the general practice regarding prison sentences in the courts of the former Yugoslavia' (Article 24(1)). The ICTR Statute provides similarly in Article 23(1), referring, of course, to the courts of Rwanda. By the same token, Article 19 (1) of the SCSL refers to the practice of the ICTR and the national courts of Sierra Leone; Rule 10.1 of the Regulation no. 2000/15, s. 10 of the ETSP provides that the Special Panels 'shall have recourse to the general practice regarding prison sentences in the courts in East Timor' (it is, however, specified that imprisonment 'may not exceed a maximum of 25 years'); Article 24(1) of the Statute of the STL enjoins the Tribunal to take the sentencing practice of Lebanese courts into account.

---

[101] For instance, in French law Arts 1315ff. and 1341–8 of the Civil Code set out the modes of evidence and the probative force of each class of admissible evidence in civil proceedings, whereas Arts 353, 427, and 536 of the Code of Criminal Procedure lay down the standards of the *intime conviction* of the judges and provide that the court need not explain why they have attached value to one piece of evidence rather than to another. Art. 192(1) of the Italian Code of Criminal Procedure is stricter: 'The judge appraises evidence and gives account in the judgment's legal grounds of the conclusions reached and the criteria adopted.'

Arguably the provisions in French law on standards of proof in criminal trials do not force the jury or the court to convict a person whenever a certain amount of evidence is available (hence the word *intime*); on the other hand, as a matter of principle, they may, in reaching a decision of guilty, use all evidence available, unless otherwise provided by law, and attach to it the value it deserves in their eyes (this is called in German legal literature *freie Beweiswürdiging*).

In the Netherlands and Germany the courts must be convinced beyond reasonable doubt.

[102] ICC Statute, Art. 78(1).

[103] *Bulatović (Sentencing)*, ICTY, § 19.

The gravity of the crime and the individual circumstances of the convicted person must be considered against certain 'purposive considerations' of punishment.[104] Retribution and deterrence have been identified as two of the main guiding principles in sentencing for international crimes,[105] followed in importance by the need for reprobation and stigmatization of the criminal conduct.[106] Some Chambers have also mentioned the rehabilitation of the accused, particularly when he was of a young age.[107] Reconciliation is sometimes indicated as one of the objectives pursued in punishing the perpetrators of serious crimes (see, for instance, SPSC, *Consta Nunes*, § 85; *Cloe*, § 22). The ICC, SCSL, and East Timor statutory instruments expressly permit the imposition of fines, forfeitures, and reparation orders.[108]

20.4 THE ROLE OF VICTIMS AND REPARATIONS

Victims, who have no autonomous role in proceedings before the ICTY, ICTR, or SCSL may be recognized as 'participants' in proceedings before the ICC and the STL. The extent of participation at the ICC, in the absence of any significant guidance in the Statute or Rules, is largely a matter of judicial discretion and has, in consequence, varied widely from

---

[104] *Todorović*, (*Sentencing Judgment*) § 28. The Chamber went on to say that the principle of retribution 'must be understood as reflecting a fair and balanced approach to the exaction of punishment for wrongdoing. This means that the penalty imposed must be proportionate to the wrongdoing: in other words that the punishment be made to fit the crime' (§ 29). As for deterrence, it held that it meant that 'the penalties imposed by the International Tribunal must, in general, have sufficient deterrent value to ensure that those who would consider committing similar crimes will be dissuaded from doing so'. The Chamber went on to say that, 'Accordingly, while the Chamber recognises the importance of deterrence as a general consideration in sentencing, it will not treat deterrence as a distinct factor in determining sentence in this case' (§ 30).

[105] See e.g. *Delalić and others*, AC, § 806; *Aleksovski*, AC, § 185); *Akayesu* (*Sentencing*), § 19; *Kayishema and Ruzindana* (*Sentencing*), § 2; *Kambanda* (*Sentencing*), § 28; SPSC, *Joni Marques and others* (*Los Palos* case), at § 310; *Manuel Gonçalves Leto Bere*, at 12.

[106] See e.g. *Erdemović* (*Sentencing*) (§ 65); *Furundžija* (§289); and *Blaškić* (§§ 763–4).

In *Erdemović* (*Sentencing*) the ICTY Trial Chamber held that: 'The International Tribunal sees public reprobation and stigmatisation by the international community, which would thereby express its indignation over heinous crimes and denounce the perpetrators, as one of the essential functions for a prison sentence for a crime against humanity' (§65).

[107] For instance, in *Furundžija* (§ 291) an ICTY Trial Chamber stated that none of the various purposes of punishment such as retribution, deterrence, and stigmatization was to detract 'from the TC's support for rehabilitative programmes in which the accused may participate while serving his sentence; the Trial Chamber is especially mindful of the age of the accused in this case'. In the same case, the TC also stated that it was to be guided in its determination of the sentence by the principle proclaimed as early as 1764 by Cesare Beccaria (*An Essay on Crimes and Punishment*, 1775, reprinted (Brookline Village, Mass.: Brandon Press Inc., 1983)), namely that 'punishment should not be harsh, but must be inevitable'. It went on to state that 'It is the infallibility of punishment, rather than the severity of the sanction, which is the tool for retribution, stigmatisation and deterrence. This is particularly the case for the international tribunal; penalties are made more onerous by its international stature, moral authority and impact upon world public opinion, and this punitive effect must be borne in mind when assessing the suitable length of sentence' (§ 290). This proposition, while it seems correct in that it stresses the particular stigma attaching to punishment by an international tribunal, as well as the need for the penalties not to be excessively harsh, could appear questionable in another respect: it does not seem that inevitability of punishment is a major feature of international courts; these courts must of necessity concentrate on major instances of gross violations of international criminal law and therefore cannot but be selective; it follows that in many instances perpetrators will not be punished, unless they are brought before national courts.

See also *Delalić and others* (AC, § 806); *Obrenović* (*Sentencing*), § 53; ICTR, *Kayishema and Ruzindana* (*Sentencing*) § 26.

[108] ICC Statute, Art. 77(2); SCSL Statute, Art. 19(3); ETSP Regulation no. 2000/15, s. 10, Rule 10(1).

case to case. The judges are required to assess how the 'personal interests' of the victims are affected by the particular stage of proceedings.[109] Participation is undoubtedly narrower than is accorded to civil parties (*parties civiles*) in most inquisitorial systems, especially in terms of the capacity to adduce or present evidence.[110] This approach, particularly in cases with large numbers of victims, appears to arise from a concern for efficiency and the potential that victim participation could substantially lengthen the proceedings.

Proving the damage caused by the perpetration of the crimes alleged is one of the purposes of allowing victims to participate at the trial stage of proceedings.[111] The ICC Statute permits orders for 'reparations' to be paid to victims, either individually or a collective basis, by a convicted person or the Court's trust fund.[112] Most victims file a single form seeking permission to both participate in the proceedings and to receive reparations, reflecting the interrelationship between the purpose of participation and the ultimate remedy. No reparations hearings have yet been held and the principles of proof, nature of proceedings, quantification, types of awards, and any other practicalities remain, as yet, undeveloped. Nowhere does the ICC Statute or Rules exclude the possibility that a conviction is a prerequisite to reparations. Indeed, one could imagine a Trial Chamber, having heard substantial evidence of horrific crimes wishing to validate that evidence by way of an award of some sort, even though the evidence is insufficient to establish the guilt of the accused.

One of the major issues will be the standard of proof. Detailed evidential hearings into the claims of each victim will, given the sheer numbers of victims, in many cases be impossible. The *Bemba* case already has more than 1,000 participating victims; many more than that may be recognized in the Kenya cases. Expert testimony, as specifically contemplated for a reparations hearing, is most likely to address the optimal form of reparations in these circumstances. The potential for direct compensation to certain subclasses of victims who have suffered particular harm should not, however, be too easily dismissed on the grounds of impracticality. Even a relatively modest award could have a profound impact on the life of a rape victim in eastern Congo, for example. At the same time, the Court needs to be mindful of the potential arbitrariness arising from case-defined reparations which could well exclude a rape victim who happens to fall just outside of the scope of the charges, even though he or she was a victim of the same crime committed by the same perpetrators and suffered the same harm. This potential for arbitrariness arises, in part, precisely because victims may not make applications to enlarge the charges.

The ICTY and ICTR Statutes do not provide for reparations but do provide for restitution. Articles 24(3) of the ICTY Statute and 23(3) of the ICTR Statute stipulate that

---

[109] ICC Statute, Art. 68(3); *Lubanga* (*Decision on Victims' Participation*) (trial stage participation); *Ruto and others* (*Decision on Victims' Participation at the Confirmation of Charges Hearing and in the Related Proceedings*), §§ 84–101.

[110] Victims have so far not been permitted to seek an expansion of the charges during the confirmation stage, a prohibition which could have drastic consequences if, for example, the harm they have suffered happens not to fall within the geographic scope of the charges. Hence, if the prosecution charges the accused only with crimes in village A, but a victim suffered from the same crime by the same perpetrators in village B, he or she will be excluded from the proceedings and has no avenue by which to join the proceedings or seek the extension of the charges. Indeed, the ICC judges have interpreted the ICC Statute and Rules as not permitting victim-applicants to make any legal submissions as to whether their application properly fall within the scope of the charges, even though the prosecution and defence are permitted to do so. *Muthaura and others* (Decision on the OPCV's Request for Leave to Respond to 'Defence Observations on 4 Applications for Victim Participation in the Proceedings'), 1 July 2011.

[111] *Lubanga* (*Decision on Victims' Participation*), § 97.

[112] ICC Statute, Art. 75(1); ICC RPE, Rule 97(1). The trust fund is an entity independent of the Court, set up by the Assembly of States Parties. ICC Statute, Art. 79.

in addition to imprisonment, a TC 'may order the return of any property and proceeds acquired by criminal conduct, including by means of duress, to their rightful owners'.[113] The latter provision was presumably inserted to specifically remedy widespread forcible transfer that had occurred in the former Yugoslavia.

---

[113] Rule 105 of the ICTY RPE regulates restitution in detail. It stipulates that after a judgment of conviction containing a specific finding of unlawful taking of property, at the request of the prosecutor or *proprio motu* the Trial Chamber may hold a special hearing on the question of restitution. If such property or its proceeds are in the hands of third parties not otherwise connected with the crime, they will be summoned before the Trial Chamber and given the opportunity to justify their claim to the property or its proceeds. The Trial Chamber, if it is able to determine the rightful owner 'on the balance of probabilities', orders its restitution or the restitution of its proceeds. If instead it is unable to determine ownership, it requests the competent national authorities to do so, and orders thereafter the restitution of the property or of its proceeds.

Rule 106, on compensation to victims cannot, of course, grant victims a right to compensation, absent any provision on the matter in the Statute. Nonetheless it provides that the Registrar shall transmit to the relevant national authorities the judgment finding the accused guilty of a crime that has caused injury to a victim. It will be for the victim to claim compensation before the competent national court. For this purpose, 'the judgment of the Tribunal shall be final and binding as to the criminal responsibility of the convicted person for such injury'. (The final and binding nature of the Tribunal's findings seems to be an aspect of the ICTY's primacy).

21

APPEALS AND ENFORCEMENT

The right to appeal a conviction is a fundamental human right. Article 14 of the ICCPR provides: 'Everyone convicted of a crime shall have the right to his conviction and sentence being reviewed by a higher tribunal according to law.' The Statutes of each of the modern international criminal courts implement this right by providing for an appeals chamber, to which the parties can appeal the decisions of the Pre-Trial and Trial Chambers. In contrast, the Statutes of the Nuremberg and the Tokyo Tribunals, which pre-date the human rights developments of the mid-twentieth century, did not contemplate appeals.

Many legal systems, including the modern international criminal courts, also allow the prosecutor to appeal against acquittals and sentence. The rationale is not to affirm a fundamental human right, but rather to ensure the proper administration of justice by enabling the prosecutor to appeal to a higher court when an acquittal is based on an error of law or is a miscarriage of justice.

The purposes of appellate proceedings vary in national systems. In general terms, appeals proceedings in civil law countries of the Romano-Germanic legal tradition involve a retrial by a higher court. Very often both law and fact are argued on appeal. An appellate court, which hears the case anew, may call the same or new witnesses. The right of appeal is granted to both the convicted person and the prosecutor, who may appeal both an acquittal and sentence. However, appeal courts may be subject to strict limits in their ability to increase sentence on appeal. An appellate court in a civil law jurisdiction can confirm, reverse, or quash the trial court's judgment or sentence (see also 18.3).

In contrast, in most common law countries appellate proceedings are corrective and do not amount to a retrial (see also 18.3). Historically, this approach was adopted because the professional judges of an appellate court could not substitute for a jury, the only body entitled to make findings of fact. Hence appeals courts decide on the basis of the trial record. Only exceptionally do common law courts of appeal receive evidence. Usually evidence on appeal is limited to that which would have been admissible at trial but was not adduced because, for instance, it was not then available. The appellate court may allow or dismiss the appeal, quash the trial judgment, order a retrial by the trial court or even substitute a new verdict under certain conditions.

Common law countries generally limit prosecution appeals from acquittals and sentence. This limitation implements the double jeopardy principle, which protects a person from being tried twice for the same offence. In a few common law jurisdictions, the prosecutor has no ability to appeal against a verdict of acquittal under any circumstances. In many others, however, prosecution appeals are permitted, but are limited to questions of law. Depending on the jurisdiction, prosecution appeals on questions of law may be without prejudice to the accused, meaning that the decision would serve only as an advisory opinion applicable to future cases. Common law jurisdictions may also limit a defendant's access to an appeals court by requiring a convicted person to seek leave to appeal. This procedure serves a gate-keeping function, with the aim of minimizing frivolous, vexatious, or unmeritorious appeals. However, leave to appeal is not required when the appellant challenges the conviction or sentence on legal grounds. When appealing a purely legal ground, the appellant may bring the case before the court of appeal as of right.

International criminal appellate proceedings do not strictly follow either the civil law model or the common law model. Rather, a mixed system has been applied, as we shall see below.

21.1 APPEALS

All of the modern international criminal tribunals have an appellate chamber. In order to promote consistency, the ICTY and ICTR Appeals Chambers are composed of the same judges, who are drawn from both Tribunals. Although none of the Statutes prescribe a system of precedence, where appeal decisions are formally binding on Trial Chambers, this hierarchy has been adhered to in practice. In *Aleksovski*, the ICTY Appeals Chamber concluded that in order to ensure consistency and fairness, appeals decisions are binding on Trial Chambers (*Aleksovski*, AC, § 113; see also 1.2.6). Although appellate rulings should also be followed by the Appeals Chamber in subsequent cases, it is 'free to depart from them for cogent reasons in the interests of justice' (*Aleksovski*, AC, § 107; see also 1.2.6).

21.1.1 APPEALS AGAINST INTERLOCUTORY DECISIONS

Appeals chambers of international criminal courts may issue interlocutory appeal decisions on matters that arise before the trial judgment has been handed down. Interlocutory decisions are appealed much more frequently in international criminal cases than in domestic cases for two key reasons. First, the rules of procedure and evidence, and even the substantive law, are less established in ICL and thus it is more likely that novel or unexpected situations arise that require appellate oversight. Second, since international criminal trials are often complex and lengthy, it is crucial that the parties are able to challenge the trial chamber on important issues during the proceedings, rather than waiting to raise them after the completion of the proceedings, thus risking a retrial.

The evolution of interlocutory appeal procedures at the various international criminal courts reflects an attempt to ensure appellate oversight of trial decisions while limiting interlocutory appeals to the most important issues.[1]

Some categories of trial decisions are appealable as of right, meaning that the appellant can always lodge an appeal from the decision without seeking any prior authorization. The ICTY and ICTR rules provide for appeals as of right from Trial Chamber's decisions on: preliminary motions concerning jurisdiction,[2] provisional release,[3] referral of a case to a national jurisdiction,[4] continuation of proceedings with a substitute judge;[5] certain

---

[1] The first version of the ICTY Rules made no mention of interlocutory appeals, but the concept was added in the third revision of the Rules in early 1995 (Rule 72(b)). Gradually, the judges expanded the scope of interlocutory appeals, first to other preliminary decisions in 1996 and then to other decisions without categorical restriction in 1997. These changes were introduced more slowly at the ICTR, which only allowed interlocutory appeals from ordinary decisions in 2003.

[2] ICTY Rule 72 (B)(i); ICTR Rule 72 (B)(i).

[3] ICTY Rule 65 (D); ICTR Rule 65 (D).

[4] ICTY Rule 11 *bis* (I); ICTR Rule 11 *bis* (H).

[5] ICTY Rule 15 *bis* (D); ICTR Rule 15 *bis* (D).

issues arising during contempt proceedings;[6] and requests that a state be ordered to produce documents or other information.[7]

At the ICC, interlocutory appeals as of right are restricted to: decisions on jurisdiction or admissibility;[8] decisions on provisional release;[9] decisions of the Pre-Trial Chamber to act on its own initiative pursuant to Article 56(3) to take testimony or a statement by a witness or to examine, collect, or test evidence which may not be available subsequently for the purpose of trial;[10] and decisions ordering reparations.[11] According to Article 82(4) of the ICC Statute, a legal representative of the victims or an adversely affected owner of property is also accorded the right to appeal against an order for reparations.

The SCSL does not permit any interlocutory appeals as of right. Instead, the Appeals Chamber has a special 'original' jurisdiction to hear preliminary motions challenging jurisdiction filed prior to the prosecution's opening statement.[12] Instead of being decided by the Trial Chamber and then possibly appealed, these motions are instead referred directly to the Appeals Chamber for decision.

Interlocutory appeals from other trial decisions require 'certification' by the Trial Chamber. This procedure serves to limit the scope of interlocutory appeals. At the ICC, ICTY, and ICTR the party seeking certification to appeal must satisfy the Trial Chamber that the decision 'involves an issue that would significantly affect the fair and expeditious conduct of the proceedings or the outcome of the trial' and that 'an immediate resolution of the Appeals Chamber may materially advance the proceedings'.[13]

21.1.2 APPEALS AGAINST JUDGMENT OR SENTENCE

All of the modern international criminal courts confer the right of appeal on both the defendant and the prosecutor.[14] According to the Statutes of the ICTY and ICTR, either party may appeal a judgment or sentence based on: *i)* an error of law invalidating the judgment; or *ii)* an error of fact occasioning a miscarriage of justice. The ICC and SCSL Statutes explicitly provide that appeals may also allege 'procedural errors',[15] a ground implicitly covered by the ICTY and ICTR provisions. Article 81 of the ICC Statute provides the convicted person (or the prosecutor on that person's behalf) with an additional basis for an appeal, namely 'any other ground that affects the fairness or reliability of the proceedings or decision'.

As typically seen in common law systems, international appellate proceedings are corrective, party driven, and do not involve a retrial. On many occasions the ICTY Appeals Chamber has emphasized that an appeal is not an opportunity for the parties to re-argue their cases.[16] Instead, the parties are required to focus their appeals on specific errors of fact or law.

---

[6] ICTY Rule 77 (J); ICTR Rule 77 (J).

[7] ICTY Rule 54 *bis* (C).

[8] ICC Statute, Art. 82(1)(a).

[9] ICC Statute, Art. 82(1)(b).

[10] ICC Statute, Arts 82(1)(c), 56(3).

[11] ICC Statute, Art. 82(4).

[12] SCSL Rule 72(E).

[13] ICC Statute, Art. 82(1)(d); ICTY Rules 72(B)(ii); 73(B); ICTR Rules 72(B)(ii); 73(B).

[14] ICC Statute, Art. 81; ICTY Statute, Art. 25; ICTR Statute, Art. 24.

[15] ICC Statute, Art. 81(1)(a)(i); 81(1)(b)(i); SCSL Statute Art. 20(1)(a).

[16] See e.g. *Furundžija*, AC, §40; *Kupreškić and others*, AC, §22; *Kordić and Čerkez*, AC, § 21; *Kvočka and others*, AC, § 14.

The Appeals Chambers employ a 'reasonableness' standard when evaluating alleged errors of fact.[17] As the ICTY Appeals Chamber explained in *Krstić*:

[T]he Appeals Chamber must give deference to the Trial Chamber that received the evidence at trial, and it will only interfere in those findings where no reasonable trier of fact could have reached the same finding or where the finding is wholly erroneous. Furthermore, the erroneous finding will be revoked or revised only if the error occasioned a miscarriage of justice (§ 40).

This deferential standard is appropriate because the Trial Chamber that heard the evidence is best placed to make findings of fact.[18] In contrast, the standard of review for errors of law is one of 'correctness'. The Appeals Chamber, as the final arbiter of the law, does not show any deference to the Trial Chamber's reasoning. Alleged errors of fact or law that are not sufficiently pleaded or which have no possibility of success may be summarily dismissed.[19]

Although an appeal is not a new trial, the Appeals Chamber has a broad power to hear fresh evidence. Under Rule 115 of the ICTY and ICTR Rules a party to the appellate proceedings may file a motion asking to present additional evidence. The party must show that the evidence was not available at trial and its admission *could* affect the verdict. In order to avoid a miscarriage of justice, the Appeals Chamber will also admit additional evidence that was available at trial if its admission *would* affect the verdict. When authorization is granted, the Appeals Chamber admits the new evidence or calls the relevant witnesses to testify. The same rules governing the presentation of evidence before Trial Chambers also apply before the Appeals Chamber.

The ICTY and ICTR Statutes provide that the Appeals Chambers may 'affirm, reverse or revise' the trial judgment and sentence. When a defendant's ground of appeal is successful, the Appeals Chamber may enter an acquittal on one or more counts of the indictment. When a prosecution appeal succeeds, the Appeals Chamber can enter a conviction. The Appeals Chamber may also modify the sentence, either as a result of a successful appeal against sentence or in order to adjust the sentence to reflect a change in the conviction.

In a very limited number of cases, the ICTY and ICTR Appeals Chambers have remitted an issue back to the Trial Chamber for determination. For example, in the *Muvunyi*

---

[17] *Haradinaj and others*, AC, § 12; *Muvunyi*, AC, 2011, § 10. In *Bagilishema*, the Appeals Chamber specified that '[b]ecause the Prosecution bears the burden at trial of proving the guilt of the accused beyond a reasonable doubt, the significance of an error of fact occasioning a miscarriage of justice is somewhat different for a prosecution appeal against acquittal than for a defence appeal against conviction. An accused must show that the Trial Chamber's factual errors create a reasonable doubt as to his guilt. The Prosecution faces a more difficult task. It must show that, when account is taken of the errors of fact committed by the Trial Chamber, all reasonable doubt of the accused's guilt has been eliminated' (*Bagilishema*, AC, § 14).

[18] As the ICTY Appeals Chamber put it in *Kupreškić and others*, AC, § 32: 'The Trial Chamber has the advantage of observing witnesses in person and so is better positioned than the Appeals Chamber to assess the reliability and credibility of the evidence. Accordingly, it is primarily for the Trial Chamber to determine whether a witness is credible and to decide which witness' testimony to prefer, without necessarily articulating every step of the reasoning in reaching a decision on these points.'

[19] The *Brdanin* Appeals Chamber held that it could summarily dismiss alleged errors which: *i)* challenge factual findings that do not constitute the basis of a conviction; *ii)* misrepresent the Trial Chamber's factual findings or ignore other relevant factual findings; *iii)* constitute mere assertions that the Trial Chamber failed to consider relevant evidence; *iv)* constitute mere assertions that the Trial Chamber could not have reasonably inferred a particular conclusion from circumstantial evidence; *v)* are clearly irrelevant or lend support to the challenged finding; *vi)* challenge the Trial Chamber's reliance or lack of reliance on one piece of evidence without explaining why the finding should not stand on the basis of the remaining evidence; *vii)* are contrary to common sense; *viii)* relate to factual findings whose relevance is unclear (*Brdanin*, AC, §§ 17–31). For additional categories of summary dismissal, see also *Strugar*, AC, § 20–4; *Martić*, AC, § 18–21.

case, the ICTR Appeals Chamber quashed the conviction, finding that the Trial Chamber had failed to give sufficient reasons. The case was remitted to the Trial Chamber for retrial pursuant to Rule 118(C) of the ICTR Rules on the single count of direct and public incitement to commit genocide during a speech given by Muvunyi. The 'exceptional measure' of remittal was used in this case because, although the accused had already spent eight years in custody, the seriousness of the offence and the interests of justice demanded a retrial (*Muvunyi*, AC, 2008, §§ 147–8). The Appeals Chamber ruled that in accordance with the 'principle of fairness' (*reformatio in peius*) the sentence after a retrial cannot exceed the original sentence, in this case twenty-five years imposed by the original Trial Chamber (§ 170). In *Haradinaj*, the Appeals Chamber found that the Trial Chamber failed to safeguard the fairness of the proceedings by denying the prosecution adequate time to secure the testimony of two important witnesses. The Appeals Chamber accordingly ordered a limited retrial concerning two crime sites (*Haradinaj and others*, AC, §§ 40, 48–50).

In other cases the Appeals Chambers have declined to exercise their discretion to order a retrial in accordance with ICTY Rule 117(C). For example, the *Krajišnik* Appeals Chamber found that although the majority of Krajišnik's convictions had been quashed on appeal, it was 'not in the interests of justice to remit the case for further proceedings' (*Krajišnik*, AC, § 799). In reaching this conclusion the Appeals Chamber took into account that Krajišnik's remaining convictions for persecution, deportation, and forcible transfer warranted a 'severe and proportionate sentence'.

Judge Pocar has systematically dissented from appeals judgments that enter convictions or increase sentences on appeal.[20] Since there is no further appeal to a higher court from a judgment of the Appeals Chamber, he argues that this practice violates the convicted person's fundamental human right to have his conviction and sentence reviewed by a higher tribunal in accordance with Article 14(5) of the ICCPR. In Judge Pocar's view 'no reasons exist to permit the International Tribunal to subtract itself from applying the principles enshrined in the ICCPR, in accordance with the meaning given to them by the Human Rights Committee'.[21] The proper course, in his view, is to remit the case for limited retrial by the Trial Chamber.

21.1.3 ADVISORY APPEALS

The ICTY and ICTR Statutes establish a corrective jurisdiction for the Appeals Chambers, allowing for appeals on 'errors of law invaliding the decision' and 'errors of fact occasioning a miscarriage of justice.' Nevertheless, in practice the ICTY and ICTR Appeals Chambers have expanded the scope of appeals to include legal issues of general significance to the jurisprudence.[22] This is an important additional power, limited only by the caveat that there should be some connection with the case at hand. Used relatively rarely, and exclusively by the prosecution, this additional power has been a potent tool for correcting and clarifying legal standards in a timely fashion. The Appeals Chamber has explained that this is a 'necessary means of moving forward this *ad hoc* International Tribunal's jurisprudence within the limited time in which it operates and contributing meaningfully to the overall development of international criminal law'.[23] In order to compensate for the

---

[20] See e.g. *Mrkšić and Šljivančanin*, AC, Partially Dissenting Opinion of Judge Pocar; *Galić*, AC, Partially Dissenting Opinion of Judge Pocar; *Semanza*, AC, Dissenting Opinion of Judge Pocar; *Rutaganda*, AC, Dissenting Opinion of Judge Pocar.

[21] *Mrkšić and Šljivančanin*, AC, Partially Dissenting Opinion of Judge Pocar, § 3.

[22] See e.g. *Tadić*, AC 1999, §§ 247, 281; *Akeyesu*, AC, § 19; *Mucić and others*, AC §§ 218, 221.

[23] *Brđanin* (*Decision on Motion to Dismiss Ground 1 of the Prosecutor's Appeal*).

fact that the defendant may have no incentive to respond to issues that do not directly affect the case, the Appeals Chamber has invited *Amicus Curiae* submissions to ensure an adversarial hearing.[24]

The STL Rules have introduced another innovative form of appellate advisory opinion. According to STL Rule 68 (G), 'The Pre-Trial Judge may submit to the Appeals Chamber any preliminary question, on the interpretation of the Agreement, Statute and Rules regarding the applicable law, that he deems necessary in order to examine and rule on the indictment.' Pursuant to Rule 176 *bis*, an accused has the opportunity to challenge the outcome of such 'preliminary decisions'. The first decision of this type dealt with a number of legal issues of fundamental importance to the cases at the STL, including the elements of terrorism, conspiracy, homicide, perpetration, and the issue of cumulative charging.[25]

21.2 REVISION AND REVIEW

Although a judgment or sentence may be endowed with the legal force of *res judicata* (that is, the force of a binding and final judicial decision), it would be contrary to elementary principles of justice not to revise it in light of a newly discovered fact that would have led to a different decision. National jurisdictions rely on a variety of mechanisms to address potential miscarriages of justice that often include judicial as well as political or administrative procedures. Modern international criminal courts allow for the possibility to 'review' or 'revise' a final decision in light of a newly discovered fact that would change the verdict. However, review proceedings are exceptional and, as the ICTY and ICTR Appeals Chambers have repeatedly emphasized, they are 'not an additional opportunity for a party to re-litigate arguments that failed at trial or on appeal'.[26]

Under Article 26 of the ICTY Statute and Article 25 of the ICTR Statute, when a new fact is discovered which *i*) was not known to the party concerned at the time of trial or appellate proceedings; and *ii*) could have been 'a decisive factor in reaching the decision', the convicted person or the prosecutor may apply for review of the judgment. Rule 119 ICTY and Rule 120 ICTR add a further condition: the new fact 'could not have been discovered through the exercise of due diligence'.[27] At the ICTY and ICTR, the convicted person may file an application for review at any time, while the prosecutor has a time limit of 'one year after the final judgment has been pronounced'. If the reviewing Chamber finds that the new fact, if proved, could have been a decisive factor in reaching the impugned decision, then it will hear the parties and pronounce a further judgment (Rule 120 ICTY, Rule 121 ICTR). Review is not limited to judgments: it also encompasses other decisions that put an end to proceedings.[28]

As the ICTR Appeals Chamber summarized in *Barayagwiza (Prosecutor's Request for Review or Reconsideration)*:

[I]t is clear from the Statute and the Rules that, in order for a Chamber to carry out a review, it must be satisfied that four criteria have been met. There must be a new fact; this

[24] *Brdanin (Decision on Motion to Dismiss Ground 1 of the Prosecutor's Appeal)*.

[25] STL, AC (*Interlocutory Decision on the Applicable Law*).

[26] See e.g. *Barayawiza (Decision on Jean-Bosco Barayagwiza's Motion for Review and/or Reconsideration of the Appeal Judgement of 28 November 2007)*, § 22; *Niyitegeka (Fourth Request for Review)* (public redacted version), § 21; *Tadić (Decision on Request for Review)*, § 24.

[27] See *Barayagwiza (Decision on Prosecutor's Request for Review or Reconsideration)*, § 65; and *Tadić (Request for Review)*, § 27.

[28] See *Barayagwiza (Decision on Prosecutor's Request for Review or Reconsideration)* 49.

new fact must not have been known by the moving party at the time of the original proceedings; the lack of discovery of the new fact must not have been through the lack of due
diligence on the part of the moving party; and it must be shown that the new fact could
have been a decisive factor in reaching the original decision.[29]

The case law draws a formalistic distinction between new *evidence* of a fact at issue
during the proceedings and a new *fact*. As the ICTY Appeal Chamber held, '[t]he mere
subsequent discovery of evidence of a fact which was known at trial is not itself a new fact
within the meaning of Rule 119 of the Rules'.[30] The 'newness' of the fact does not rest solely
on whether it existed before or during the original proceedings, but rather '"whether the
deciding body and the moving party knew about the fact or not" in arriving at its decision'.[31] For example, both the ICTY and ICTR Appeal Chambers have rejected requests
to review judgments on the basis that the accused had discovered new evidence showing
that trial witnesses lacked credibility, reasoning that witness credibility had already been
litigated at trial and was not a new fact.[32]

In cases involving potential miscarriages of justice, however, these technicalities should
not stand in the way of a review application. The ICTR and ICTY Appeals Chambers have
allowed that in 'wholly exceptional circumstances' in order to prevent a miscarriage of
justice, review may still be permitted, although the new fact may have been discoverable
or even known to the moving party. The Appeals Chambers have limited this exceptional
category to situations where the applicant can present the Chamber with 'a new fact that is
of such strength that it *would* affect the verdict'.[33] In my view, this exceptional jurisdiction
to rectify a miscarriage of justice must also extend to fresh evidence of a fact litigated at
trial, an opinion also voiced by Judges Shahabuddeen and Meron.[34]

To date, the only two successful review proceedings at the ICTY or ICTR involved
review of ICTR Appeals Chamber decisions. In *Barayagwiza*, the prosecutor successfully
sought review of a final decision of the ICTR Appeals Chamber dismissing the indictment against the appellant and terminating the proceedings.[35] In *Šljivančanin*, the ICTY

---

[29] *Barayagwiza (Decision on Prosecutor's Request for Review or Reconsideration)*, § 41.

[30] *Tadić (Appeal on Admission of Additional Evidence)*, § 32.

[31] *Mrkšić and Šljivančanin (Decision with Respect to Veselin Šljivančanin's Application for Review*, 14 July
2010).

[32] *Niyetigeka (Decision on Fourth Request for Review)*, § 47; *Naletilić and Martinović (Decision on Mladen
Naletilić's Request for Review)*, § 25.

[33] See e.g. *Mrkšić and Šljivančanin (Decision with Respect to Veselin Šljivančanin's Application for
Review)* at 3; *Blaškić (Decision on Prosecutor's Request for Review or Reconsideration*, 23 November 2006
(public redacted version), § 8); *Naletilić (Decision on Mladen Naletilić's Request for Review)*, § 10; *Rutaganda
(Decision on Requests for Reconsideration, Review, Assignment of Counsel, Disclosure, and Clarification)*,
§ 8).

[34] *Niyitegeka (Decision on Request for Review)* Declaration of Judge Shahabuddeen, § 14 and Separate
Opinion of Judge Meron, § 3–5; *Niyitegeka (Request for Reconsideration of the Decision Request for Review)*
Declaration of Judge Shahabuddeen and Separate Opinion of Judge Meron. In contrast, the ICTY Appeals
Chamber has held that the remedy of 'reconsideration', which could potentially address the problem of the
discovery of new evidence, is not available for judgments: see *Žigić (Zoran Žigić's Motion for Reconsideration
of Appeals Chamber Judgment)* § 9, departing from *Mucić (Judgment on Sentence Appeal)*, §§ 49–53.

[35] *See Barayagwiza (Decision (Prosecutor's Request for Review or Reconsideration))*. The Appeals Chamber
reviewed its Decision of 3 November 1999, finding that the violations of the accused's rights were not as serious as had been found in its previous decision. In the 3 November 1999 Decision, the Appeals Chamber
had dismissed the indictment against the accused 'with prejudice' on the basis that the Appellant had been
detained for a total period of eleven months before being notified of the charges against him. It stressed that
the prosecutor had thus breached her duty of prosecutorial due diligence, and applied the 'abuse of process
doctrine'. The abuse of process doctrine is well known in common law countries, but is generally unknown
to countries of the Romano-Germanic tradition.

Appeals Chamber had convicted Veselin Šljivančanin of aiding and abetting the murder of 194 prisoners as a violation of the laws or customs of war. The Appeals Chamber had inferred from circumstantial evidence that Šljivančanin learned in a particular conversation that prisoners were unprotected and that he therefore had the mens rea for their murders. After the appeal, Šljivančanin initiated review proceedings, proposing a witness who heard the conversation and contradicted the finding. After hearing the witness in a 'Pre-Review Hearing', as well as further evidence from the prosecutor, the Appeals Chamber granted the request for review and vacated the additional conviction.

Under Article 84 of the ICC Statute, only the convicted person or those acting on behalf of the convicted person have standing to apply for revision. Unlike the ICTY and ICTR, the prosecutor can only seek revision on the convicted person's behalf. After the convicted person's death, the ICC Statute provides that 'spouses, children, parents or one person alive at the time of the accused's death who has been given express written instructions from the accused to bring such a claim' may make an application for revision.

The ICC Statute does not limit revision to the discovery of new 'facts'. Instead it contemplates revision based on the discovery *i*) of new evidence that was previously unavailable and that 'would have been likely to have resulted in a different verdict'; *ii*) that decisive evidence was false, forged, or falsified; or *iii*) of serious misconduct of a trial judge. If the ICC Appeals Chamber finds that an application for revision has merit, it may reconvene the original Trial Chamber, constitute a new Trial Chamber, or retain jurisdiction over the matter.

21.3 ENFORCEMENT OF SENTENCES

International criminal courts do not maintain a prison in which to detain convicted persons and, as with so many aspects of their functioning, they must consequently turn to states to assist in the execution of sentences. International criminal courts must equally count on states to address the problems faced by persons who have been acquitted. Particularly in cases involving non-international conflicts, the acquitted person may not have a state to which he can safely return. In the ICTR experience, finding states willing to accept those who have been acquitted or who have served their sentences has proved to be difficult.

21.3.1 PLACE OF IMPRISONMENT

Article 27 of the ICTY Statute provides that 'imprisonment shall be served in a state designated by the International Tribunal from a list of states which have indicated to the Security Council their willingness to accept convicted persons'. Thus far the ICTY and the ICTR have entered into agreements with a number of states, which have agreed to hold persons convicted by the Tribunals in their national prisons.[36] Article 29(1) of the Statute of the STL is almost identical. Articles 26 of the ICTR Statute has a fairly similar tenor, providing that imprisonment shall be served in Rwanda or in any other

---

[36] The UN has made agreements for the ICTY with seventeen European states, including ad hoc arrangements with Germany. The agreement with Spain differs in many respects from the other agreements. Among other things, it provides that Spain will only consider the enforcement of sentences pronounced by the ICTY where the duration of the sentence imposed does not exceed the highest maximum sentence for any crime under Spanish law (currently thirty years). The UN has entered into agreements for the ICTR with Benin, France, Italy, Mali, Swaziland, Sweden, Rwanda, and Senegal.

state that has concluded an agreement on the matter. In similar terms, Article 103(1) (a) of the ICC Statute provides that 'a sentence of imprisonment shall be served in a state designated by the Court from a list of states which have indicated to the Court their willingness to accept sentenced persons'. Article 22 of the SCSL Statute indicates a preference for imprisonment in Sierra Leone.

21.3.2 CONDITIONS OF DETENTION

Imprisonment of persons convicted by international criminal courts must be in conformity with the general laws and regulations applicable in the relevant state. However, the conditions of detention must also accord with international standards. This requirement, although not explicitly laid down by statute, is implicit in the international legal system: these judicial bodies are bound to respect international standards on human rights and in particular those on the rights of the accused, victims, and witnesses. It follows that international courts and tribunals may hand over convicted persons to states for their detention only on condition that the states abide by those standards. It is therefore quite natural for the bilateral agreements concluded by these tribunals with states to require full respect for international standards,[37] and in addition for the tribunals to envisage and make provision for, in agreement with states, international oversight of conditions of detention (see 21.3.4). The ICC Statute makes these requirements explicit: Article 106(2) provides that 'the conditions of imprisonment [...] shall be consistent with widely accepted international treaty standards governing treatment of prisoners'.

21.3.3 REDUCTION OR COMMUTATION OF SENTENCE AND PARDON

The statutes of modern international criminal courts stipulate that the state where the convicted person serves his sentence is not allowed to reduce or change the penalty, or release the person, before expiry of the sentence pronounced by the relevant international criminal tribunal (see, for instance, Article 110(1) and (2) of the ICC Statute). Only the latter may decide upon any change in the sentence.

However, conflicts may arise with the legislation of the state enforcing the penalty. For instance, it may be that according to national rules detainees are entitled to a reduction of sentence, or to early release, or to special treatment (for instance, parole) after serving a certain number of years, or in case of good behaviour. In order to retain control over internationally convicted persons, the bilateral agreements generally provide that if the convicted person becomes eligible for national release programmes, then the President of the sentencing Tribunal should be consulted. If the President disagrees with the proposed national measure, then the convicted person should be transferred back to the custody of the Tribunal.[38]

---

[37] In the various Agreements concluded by International Tribunals with states for the enforcement of sentences it is provided that 'conditions of detention shall be compatible with the Standard Minimum Rules for the Treatment of Prisoners, the Body of Principles for the Protection of All Persons under Any Form of Detention or Imprisonment and the Basic Principles of the Treatment of Prisoners' (Art. 3 of various Agreements).

[38] For instance, in the first such agreement with the ICTY, which also served as a model for subsequent agreements, as that with Italy of 6 February 1997, it is provided that 'if pursuant to the applicable national law of the requested state, the convicted person is eligible for non-custodial measures or working activities outside the prison, or is entitled to benefit from conditional release, the Minister of Justice shall notify the President of the Tribunal' (Art. 3(3)). The provision then stipulates that, if the President of the Tribunal, in

The question of *pardon* is particularly difficult. In most states only the head of state may grant pardon. States are extremely jealous of this prerogative. Article 28 of the ICTY Statute (similarly to the corresponding Article 27 of the ICTR Statute, as well as Article 23 of the SCSL's Statute and Article 30 of the STL Statute) provides:

> If, pursuant to the applicable law of the State in which the convicted person is imprisoned, he or she is eligible for pardon or commutation of sentence, the State concerned shall notify the International Tribunal accordingly. The President of the Tribunal, in consultation with the judges, shall decide the matter on the basis of the interests of justice and the general principles of law.

On the face of it, the matter is 'decided' by the President of the Tribunal in consultation with judges. The power of pardon thus ultimately belongs to the international body, in contrast to the regulation of most national constitutions.

The judges of the ICTY skilfully smoothed out the problem in the Rules. Under Rule 123, if the person is eligible for pardon or commutation of sentence under national legislation, the state concerned shall notify the Tribunal, and then the Tribunal's President, in consultation with the judges shall determine 'whether pardon or commutation is appropriate' (Rule 124), on the basis of a set of criteria laid down in Rule 125. Thus, the international judicial body only decides on the *appropriateness* of pardon (or commutation), and the final decision is left to the relevant national authority (Rules 124–6 ICTR are identical in content).

There is a marked difference between the ICTY and ICTR practice on commutation of sentences. At the ICTY, convicted persons are generally considered eligible for early release once they have served two-thirds of their sentence. While early release is not guaranteed, this practice was so ingrained that one Trial Chamber even took this fact into account in calculating the appropriate sentence.[39] In contrast, the ICTR first granted early release to a convicted person in late 2011.[40] The ICTR President justified this difference in practice on the basis of the gravity of the crimes tried at the ICTR, particularly of genocide.[41] Decisions on commutation of sentence are at the discretion of the President and cannot be appealed.[42]

The ICC Statute does not make any provision for the granting of pardon. Article 110 requires review of the sentence once the convicted person has served two-thirds of the sentence, or twenty-five years of a life term. It is for the Court alone to make any decision on the reduction of sentences, whereas Rule 211(2) makes provision for a convicted person to participate in national prison programmes or benefits entailing 'some activity outside the prison facility', and simply provides that the Court must be notified and shall exercise

---

consultation with the judges, does not consider those national measures appropriate, the convicted person shall be transferred to the international tribunal, presumably for the purpose of being transferred to another state willing to have him serve the remainder of his sentence. A similar provision (Art. 8) covers the issue of pardon or commutation of sentence.

[39] See *D. Nikolić*, AC, § 97 (finding, by majority, that the Trial Chamber erred in attaching too much weight to the possibility of an early release in calculating the sentence).

[40] *Bagaragaza* (*Decision on the Early Release of Michel Bagaragaza*). See also *Rugambarara* (*Decision on the Early Release Request of Juvenal Rugambarara*); *Muvunyi* (*Decision on Tharcisse Muvunyi's Application for Early Release*).

[41] See e.g. *Serushago* (*Decision of the President on the Application for Early Release of Omar Serushago*); *Ruggiu* (*Decision of the President on the Application for Early Release of Georges Ruggiu*). In a later decision, not involving a genocide conviction, the ICTR President explained the difference with the ICTY on the basis that the ICTY convicts who were released early had 'not been convicted for the same combination of crimes': see *Imanishimwe* (*Decision on Samuel Imanishimwe's Application for Early Release*).

[42] *Rutaganira* (*Appeal of a Decision of the President on Early Release*) § 3.

its supervisory function. It is therefore probable that a solution similar to that set out by the ICTY and ICTR Rules will be adopted, the more so because Article 104 of the ICC Statute provides that the Court 'may, at any time, decide to transfer a sentenced person to a prison of another state'.

21.3.4 SUPERVISION OF IMPRISONMENT

The Statutes of the ICTY and the ICTR provide that imprisonment served in a state designated by the Tribunal shall be 'subject to the supervision of the International Tribunal' (Articles 27 and 26, respectively). The ICTY entered into an agreement with the International Committee of the Red Cross (ICRC), authorizing the Committee to make inspections not only in the Detention Unit in The Hague (where accused are held pending trial or appeal) but also, subject to the consent of the relevant state, in the countries where the sentences are enforced. Indeed, almost all bilateral agreements on the enforcement of sentences provide for inspection by the ICRC.[43]

Under Rule 211 of the ICC RPE the Court's Presidency 'may [...] request any information, report or expert opinion from the State of enforcement or from any reliable sources'. The Presidency may also delegate a judge or a staff member of the Court to supervise the conditions of detention.[44]

---

[43] For instance, the Agreement with Italy of 6 February 1997 stipulates in Article 6 that the ICRC may carry out inspections 'at any time and on a periodic basis', 'the frequency of visits to be determined by the ICRC'. The ICRC submits a 'confidential report based on the findings of these inspections' to the Italian Minister of Justice and the President of the ICTY, who will consult each other on those findings. The Tribunal's President may then request the Italian Minister of Justice 'to report to him any changes in the conditions of detention suggested by the ICRC'. The Agreement with Spain differs from the other Agreements on the enforcement of sentences in that it provides for inspections of the conditions of detention and treatment of the convicted persons by a Parity Commission instead of by the ICRC.

[44] Under Rule 211(1)(c) the judge or the staff member 'will be responsible, after notifying the State of enforcement, for meeting the sentenced person and hearing his or her views, without the presence of national authorities'.

INDEX